TEXTS AND STUDIES

CONTRIBUTIONS TO

BIBLICAL AND PATRISTIC LITERATURE

EDITED BY

J. ARMITAGE ROBINSON B.D.

HON. PH.D. GÖTTINGEN HON. D.D. HALLE

NORRISIAN PROFESSOR OF DIVINITY

VOL. IV.

No. 2. COPTIC APOCRYPHAL GOSPELS

COPTIC
APOCRYPHAL GOSPELS

TRANSLATIONS
TOGETHER WITH THE TEXTS
OF SOME OF THEM

BY

FORBES ROBINSON M.A.

LECTURER IN THEOLOGY AT
CHRIST'S COLLEGE CAMBRIDGE

Wipf & Stock
PUBLISHERS
Eugene, Oregon

Wipf and Stock Publishers
199 W 8th Ave, Suite 3
Eugene, OR 97401

Coptic Apocryphal Gospels
Translations together with the Texts of some of them
By Robinson, Forbes
ISBN: 1-59244-895-X
Publication date 9/29/2004
Previously published by Cambridge, 1896

TO MY FRIEND

ARTHUR BROWNLOW FFORDE

PREFACE.

THE editor of Apocryphal literature has in some measure to work in the dark. He often collects fragments in the hope that sooner or later he may discover the larger work to which they belong. As this book is going to press, my attention has been called by Dr James to a fresh volume of M. Basset's *Les Apocryphes Éthiopiens* (vol. V), in the appendix to which he has given a translation from an Arabic MS (Bibliothèque Nationale, suppl. 73) of the *Prière de la Vierge à Bartos.* This apocryphon proves to be closely connected with the third fragment of the Life of the Virgin, which I have published on pp. 20—25. It narrates how the Virgin delivered S. Matthias, when he was confined in prison in Bart'os, i.e. among the Parthians. The Christians apprehended with him were being given one by one to the governor's mad son to eat. This, we may note, is the only allusion in the piece to the *anthropophagi*; as the incidental mention of them contained in our fragment (p. 23 *v.* 9) does not appear in the Arabic. The Virgin releases the prisoners by means of a prayer taught her by Christ, when He was on the cross. The words of the prayer are not given; but it forms the substance of an Ethiopic apocryphon, also translated by M. Basset (pp. 11—30), when it is again connected by a prefatory note with the release of S. Matthias. The effect of the prayer is to melt iron, and make it become as water. The gates of the prison and the fetters of the prisoners are suddenly melted. Tools of labourers, chains of savage dogs become as water. A barber's razor is melted when he has only half shaved his customer. The governor's son is healed, and the governor himself is converted. The name of the governor is variously given as Makrinous, Makrouinous, Makdouinous and Malarouinous (see note on p. 50, and cf. *v.* 23 of our fragment). On the morrow the governor brings the Virgin in state through the town. She is carried in a litter, and trumpets sound in her honour. Certain cooks, who had been preparing a banquet for the Virgin, meet the litter, and explain that at the sound of the trumpets the animals which they had cooked had come to life again. This introduces our fragment. In the light of the Arabic *v.* 1 is seen to contain words spoken by the animals; and the first part of *v.* 3 may be translated thus: 'and we have come and have told thee,' etc. For the text I must refer my readers to M. Basset's translation (pp. 66—69). Here I would only notice that where our fragment speaks of 'standards' or 'signa,' the Arabic has 'idols of gold' (p. 68), and that in Arabic there is an allusion to S. Matthias, which is not found in the corresponding Coptic (*v.* 25). The Arabic concludes by telling how the Virgin was carried away from Bart'os on a cloud, and joined the virgins who were at Jerusalem. The Arabic appears to give a later form of the story, and to omit passages which presented difficulties.

I desire to express my gratitude to Professors Guidi and Lanzone for valuable suggestions in the editing and translating of the Coptic texts, and to Dr E. A. Wallis Budge for help in Egyptological matters. My thanks are further due to the Earl of Crawford and Balcarres, who placed at my disposal in the University Library one of his volumes of Coptic fragments. The index of Biblical quotations has been made for me by my eldest sister: the index of subjects is the work of Mr J. Lupton, of St John's College. From Mr W. E. Crum and other friends I have received help in various forms: but I am especially indebted to Dr M. R. James and to my brother, the editor of this series, without whose aid I could not have dealt with the relations of these narratives to other Apocryphal Literature.

F. R.

CHRIST'S COLLEGE,
Mar. 14, 1896.

TABLE OF CONTENTS.

PAGE

INTRODUCTION.

Importance of this Literature xi
Parallel Literature xv
Method of this Edition xvii
Description of Manuscripts xx

COPTIC TEXTS AND TRANSLATIONS.

Sahidic Fragments of the Life of the Virgin . . . 2
Bohairic Accounts of the Falling Asleep of Mary, with Sahidic Fragments 44
Bohairic Account of the Death of Joseph, with Sahidic Fragments 130
Various Sahidic Fragments 162

NOTES ON THE TEXT 186

INDICES.

Index of Scripture Passages 247
Index of Coptic Words 257
Index of Greek Words 258
Index of Subjects 259

"But some one will say to me, Art thou then adding a supplement to the Gospels? Let that beloved one listen attentively, and . . . . ."

p. 165 *vv.* 15, 16.

INTRODUCTION.

Importance of Coptic Gospel Apocryphal Literature.

THE fragments of Gospel Apocryphal literature which are here collected together have not before been translated into English. Indeed only a small portion has been translated into any European language. Two great scholars, Lagarde and Guidi, have printed some of the texts; but they have published them without a commentary and without a translation. Yet the importance of this literature is considerable. For even when the Coptic narratives resemble those already known to us, yet they have strongly marked features of their own. And in some instances we have no knowledge of any similar accounts. The Gospel Apocrypha which we possess in other languages deal almost exclusively with the history of our Lord's Infancy and Passion, or with the lives of Mary and Joseph. We have practically nothing which relates to the period of the Ministry. Any fragments connected with that period have a peculiar interest; for they may throw light upon the composition of early Apocryphal Gospels which we have lost, such as the Gospel according to the Hebrews and the Gospel according to the Egyptians. Three such fragments are collected in the present work. The first is an account of the miracle of turning water into wine; the other two describe the feeding of the multitudes, the raising of Lazarus and the fishing of the devil (see pp. 164—179).

The form in which these narratives have come down to us seems to be peculiar to Egypt. In almost every case—

the account of the Death of Joseph, written in the northern or Bohairic dialect, is the one certain exception—the stories are used as the material of sermons. This fact points to a developed ecclesiastical system, and makes us hesitate to ascribe a very early date to the documents in their present form. The discourses resemble in their general features those of a modern preacher. They are expositions of Christian faith and duty. But suddenly the preacher stops his exhortation, and introduces some Gospel narrative. It is at this point that the MS becomes of interest to the student of Apocryphal literature. Again and again he is disappointed: the story frequently proves to be nothing but an elaboration of an incident in our Canonical Gospels, and contains no definite Apocryphal matter. But occasionally he finds an indication that the writer is 'adding a supplement to the Gospels[1].' He detects him either introducing some statement not recorded in our Bible, or else using the first person plural and narrating the incident from the point of view of an eyewitness. The eyewitness is usually a follower of the Apostles.

The most interesting of these sermons are written in southern or Sahidic dialect. This presents greater difficulty to the translator than the northern dialect; and some of the discourses are preserved only in small fragments. These fragments, though clearly written, are occasionally so torn, crumpled and soiled, that it is no easy matter to decipher them with accuracy. Frequently moreover at the interesting point the MS comes to an end. Yet our knowledge of the origin of Gospel Apocryphal literature will not be complete until all the fragments in the different libraries of Europe have been catalogued and transcribed. When this is done, we shall be able to piece together different leaves of the same MS, and to study the narrative as a more complete whole. Excellent work in describing and cataloguing such fragments has already been done for the Bodleian Library by M. Hyvernat, and is now being done for the British

[1] See p. 165, c. 15.

Museum by Mr W. E. Crum. When I first examined the fragments in the Museum, they were not arranged at all: but now they are gradually being catalogued and reduced to order.

While these narratives are primarily of importance for the study of Apocryphal literature, they have also a wider interest. If, as there is reason to believe, they were moulded into their present shape on Egyptian soil, they throw light on the popular religion of Coptic Christians. They shew us more clearly than formal history or merely didactic discourses the way in which the ordinary man was being influenced by his religion. Even if the groundwork of tradition upon which they are built originated elsewhere, yet there was considerable scope left to the imagination of the writer. Thus if he had—and he almost always had—to give a description of the approach of death or the misery of the lost, that description would be coloured by conceptions current in his own country regarding death and hell. An examination of such passages shews us that popular Coptic Christianity, like the Gnostic systems preserved to us in Coptic books, borrowed from the ancient religion of the Egyptians. I have in my notes given some illustrations of this point derived from the Book of the Dead. The influence of the old Egyptian religion was not confined to Coptic Christianity. It had already influenced the Orphic religion of Greece; and this in its turn affected Greek Christianity. In this connection I need only refer to the work done by Dieterich in his *Abraxas* (1891) and his *Nekyia* (1893).

Besides the Gospel Apocrypha here published, there is among the papyri preserved at Turin a Sahidic version of the Acta Pilati. A Latin translation of this by Peyron is used by Tischendorf in his notes on the first Greek form of the Acta Pilati (*Evangelia Apocrypha,* ed. 2, pp. 210—286). The text has recently been published by F. Rossi, *I Papiri Copti del Museo Egizio di Torino* (Turin, 1883), vol. I fasc. I pp. 10—64. These papyri as a whole deserve even more careful study than has yet been bestowed upon them: for we find amongst them sermons containing Apocryphal matter. The Sahidic fragments of a sermon ascribed to Evodius, to which I have alluded in my notes, are specially interesting in this respect. It has been published and translated into Italian by Rossi, *op. cit.* vol. II fasc. IV. I have not given a translation of it, as I have only had opportunity to collate a very small portion of his published text with the original papyrus.

Dr Schmidt has recently called attention[1] to a Coptic papyrus fragment containing Gospel Apocryphal matter of importance: and he has promised a further study of the work. The account which this fragment gives of the resurrection is an interesting example of the way in which Scripture narratives were expanded and embellished, and put into the lips of eyewitnesses. 'Maria, Martha und Maria Magdalena gehen zum Grabe, um den Leichnam zu salben. Da sie das Grab leer finden, sind sie betrübt und weinen. Der Herr erscheint ihnen und spricht: "Was weinet ihr? höret auf zu weinen, ich bin, den ihr suchet. Aber möge eine von euch zu euren Brüdern gehen und sagen: Kommet, der Meister ist von den Todten auferstanden. Martha ging und sagte es uns. Wir sprachen zu ihr: Was hast du mit uns zu schaffen, o Weib? Der, welcher starb, ist begraben und nicht ist die Möglichkeit, dass er lebe. Nicht glaubten wir ihr, dass der Erlöser von den Todten auferstanden wäre. Da ging sie zum Herrn und sprach zu ihm: Niemand unter ihnen hat mir geglaubt, dass du lebst. Er sprach: Möge eine andere von euch zu ihnen gehen und es ihnen wiederum sagen. Maria ging und sagte es uns wiederum, und nicht haben wir ihr geglaubt. Sie kehrte zurück zum Herrn, und auch sie sagte es ihm. Da sprach der Herr zur Maria und ihren anderen Schwestern: Lasst uns zu ihnen gehen. Und er ging und fand uns drinnen und rief uns heraus. Wir aber dachten, dass es ein Gespenst (φαντασία) sei, und glaubten nicht, dass er der Herr sei. Da sprach er zu uns: Kommet und.......Du, o Petrus, der du ihn dreimal ver-

[1] See Schmidt, *Eine bisher unbekannte altchristliche Schrift in koptischer Sprache* in the *Sitzungsberichte der Akademie der Wissenschaften zu Berlin* for June 20, 1895 (XXXI), pp. 705—711.

leugnet hast, und auch jetzt leugnest du? Wir traten zu ihm heran, indem wir im Herzen zweifelten, dass er vielleicht es nicht wäre. Da sprach er zu uns: Warum zweifelt ihr noch und seid ungläubig? Ich bin der, welcher euch gesagt hat wegen meines Fleisches und meines Todes und meiner Auferstehung, damit ihr wisset, dass ich es bin. Petrus, lege deine Finger in die Nägelmale meiner Hände, und du Thomas lege deine Finger in die Lanzenstiche meiner Seite, du aber Andreas, berühre meine Füsse, so siehst du, dass sie......denen der Erde. Denn es stehet im Propheten geschrieben: Phantasieen von Träumen........auf Erden. Wir antworteten ihm: Wir haben in Wahrheit erkannt, dass......im Fleisch. Und wir stürzten uns auf unser Angesicht und bekannten unsere Sünden, dass wir ungläubig gewesen waren."'

Parallel Literature.

The Fragments of the Life of the Virgin resemble in many of their details the Greek account contained in the *Protevangelium Jacobi.* The text of this is published by Tischendorf, *Evangelia Apocrypha,* ed. 2, pp. 1—50. There is a fragment of a shortened form of it extant in Syriac, the text of which has been published from a Syriac MS in the British Museum by W. Wright, *Contributions to the Apocryphal Literature of the New Testament* (1865): he has also given an English translation of it (pp. 1—5). Besides the *Protevangelium* there are two less important accounts in Latin, *Pseudo-Matthaei Evangelium* and *De Nativitate Mariae,* published by Tischendorf, *op. cit.* pp. 51—121.

There is a large literature relating to the Assumption of the Virgin in Greek, Latin, Syriac and Arabic. One Greek and two Latin accounts have been edited by Tischendorf, *Apocalypses Apocryphae,* pp. 95—136. One complete Syriac narrative and three other fragments have been published and translated into English by Wright in the work previously mentioned, and in the *Journal of Sacred Literature and Biblical Record* for January and April, 1865 (vols. VI, VII, new series). The Arabic version, which is almost certainly derived from the Syriac, had been previously edited and translated into Latin by Enger, *Iohannis Apostoli de Transitu beatae Mariae Virginis liber* (Elberfeld, 1854). The publication of the Coptic accounts is of importance, because it may serve to throw light upon the difficult problem of the origin of the story and the relations of the documents in which it is narrated. I have noticed in the course of my notes the most remarkable features peculiar to the Coptic narratives. I will here only draw attention to the episode of the virgins in the Temple, found in both the northern and southern dialects (see pp. 57 f.; 70 ff.). The incident appears to be due to a desire to find parallels in Jewish history to later ecclesiastical institutions.

There are two Coptic recensions of the Death of Joseph, written in the Sahidic and Bohairic dialects. The Sahidic appears to represent an older form of the story. Stern (*Z. f. wiss. Theol.* 1883, p. 269) regards them as independent versions. I am unable to adopt his view. Some of the differences between the two can best be explained by supposing that in places the Bohairic is a translation of the Sahidic. I have referred to such passages in my notes. The only other extant account of Joseph's death is in Arabic. The Arabic text was first printed with a Latin translation and notes by Wallin, *Historia Josephi fabri lignarii* (Leipzig, 1722). His translation was reprinted by Fabricius, *Codices Pseudepigraphi Veteris Testamenti* (Hamburg, 1723, 1741), vol. II, pp. 313—336. Thilo published a corrected text of the Arabic together with a translation in his *Codex Apocryphus Novi Testamenti* (Leipzig, 1832), tom. I, pp. 3—61. His translation is substantially the same as that of Wallin. Since then Lagarde has printed the Arabic text in his *Aegyptiaca* (Göttingen, 1883), pp. 1—37; and Tischendorf has given Thilo's translation in his *Evangelia Apocrypha*, ed. 2, pp. 122—139, comparing in the footnotes the Sahidic text as far as it was known to him. The Arabic version cannot be regarded as original: it is more closely connected with the Bohairic than the Sahidic recension. I have little doubt that the narrative, whether first written in Coptic or Greek, originated in Egypt. It has some striking points of resemblance with the account of Abraham's death published by James, *The Testament of Abraham* (*Texts and Studies*, vol. II, no. 2).

Portions of the Sahidic fragments published on pp. 162—185 have no parallels in other languages. I have noticed in my notes the connection of the last three with the literature relating to Pilate, as represented by such works as the *Acta Pilati* and the *Anaphora Pilati*, published by Tischendorf, *Evangelia Apocrypha*, ed. 2, pp. 210 ff, pp. 435 ff. The third and fourth fragments (pp. 168—179) are part of one or more sermons dealing with several events connected with our Lord's life (see note at the foot of p. xxxi). The last fragment of all has an account of the figure of the cross coming forth from the tomb (see p. 185), which reminds us of the recently discovered *Gospel of Peter*.

Method of this Edition.

The editor of Coptic texts is confronted by two main problems. In the first place he has to decide upon what principle the words of his MS are to be divided. In many MSS there is no indication of the end of a word; and it is not easy to say how far a particular group of letters was regarded as a single whole. Some editors have gone far in the attempt to split up these groups into their most primitive components. But the process is uncertain in itself; a text so divided is difficult to read; and indeed it may well be doubted whether such fragments can really be regarded as separable words. Erman has recently advocated[1] a practice the very opposite of this. He would write letters

[1] See *Zeitschrift für Aegyptische Sprache*, 1883, pp. 37—40.

in still larger groups than has hitherto been customary. After carefully considering his arguments, I have been unable to adopt his conclusions. Nor have I been willing, with Steindorff in his *Koptische Grammatik*, to join groups of letters by means of hyphens; because to use these is to introduce signs not found in the MSS. On the whole I have adhered to the rules laid down by Stern, who divides words according to principles adopted by many scholars in the past[1].

The next and more serious problem is that presented by the signs which occur above certain letters. These are not represented at all by Zoega. Other editors usually place them, not as they occur in the particular MS they transcribe, but in accordance with a conventional rule. Sometimes an attempt is made to reproduce them wholly or in part, as they are found in the original. I have taken special pains to adhere as closely as possible to my MSS, in the hope that the materials thus collected may serve to throw light on the meaning of such signs. The authorities of the University Press have kindly acceded to my wishes, and enabled me to reproduce them with approximate exactness. It is impossible to give their exact size; and it would have added to the expense of the work to represent all the curves of the lines or accents. I have been content with placing the symbol which on the whole most nearly represented the original. In this edition a line of uniform length is used above a single letter, and another line of almost uniform length above two letters. But in the MSS the length of such lines is continually changing, and is sometimes so minute that it is hard to say whether a line or a point is intended.

An attempt is also made to reproduce the stops and large initial letters found in the MSS. When a single point is used as a stop, its position often varies. I have placed it uniformly in the centre. When a line is employed, it is usually

[1] See *Z. f. Aeg. Spr.* 1886, pp. 56—73. In a few instances I find to my regret that in the course of printing I have not been quite consistent in my practice.

curved in various ways. I have not attempted to represent such curves. All marks in red—most of them are merely decorative—I have omitted, except in the case of the one Bohairic MS which I publish, where the stops are written in red. When the large initial letters have been postponed in the MS in order to come at the beginning of a line, I have transferred them to the beginning of the sentences which they are intended to mark. Where two occur together, I have only indicated the first[1]. Signs occur in the margin of MSS indicating Biblical quotations. These I have not thought it necessary to reproduce.

As regards the text, I have almost always printed it as it stands in the MS. I have seldom ventured to introduce corrections, as our knowledge of the language is still so incomplete. Every alteration is mentioned in the notes. When earlier editors have divided the text into chapters and verses, I have reproduced their arrangement. In other cases I have myself made similar divisions for convenience of reference.

In translating I have tried to reproduce faithfully the Coptic idioms. Occasionally, however, I have had to introduce some changes. Thus in Coptic the passive is often expressed by the third person plural of the active voice. In such cases I have generally used the passive voice in English. In my rendering of Biblical quotations or allusions, I have used as far as possible the language of the Revised English Version (1881—4), whenever the Coptic appeared to be based upon and to have interpreted in the same way a similar Greek original. Hence readers who have not studied Coptic will in some measure be enabled to judge the type of text underlying the Biblical citations. A study of such passages shews us that as a general rule the citations in either dialect agree with the Version of the Bible—as far as it is known to us—current in that dialect.

[1] When I have had occasion in my notes to refer to MS readings or to quote printed texts, I have as a rule not indicated initials, stops, or signs above the letters.

F. R.

Description of Manuscripts.

In the account of MSS given below, fragments in either dialect have been described in detail. My object in this has been to enable scholars to determine the relation of fragments which they may discover to those here published.

With two exceptions I have transcribed or fully collated all the texts translated in this edition. These exceptions are Cod. Vat. LXII 5 and Cod. Vat. LXVI 11. Lagarde has published the text of these MSS, and I have relied upon his edition; only occasionally comparing his copy of the latter MS with the original, and making the necessary corrections.

The measurements which I have given of the columns, unless I have stated the contrary, represent the *average* length and breadth. As many of the lines vary greatly in size, it is not always easy to give the breadth with certainty. The Sahidic MSS have two columns, the Bohairic MSS one column, on the page. I have not attempted to date the fragments.

Previous editions of the text to which I refer are the following: Revillout, *Apocryphes Coptes du Nouveau Testament*, fasc. I (Paris, 1876); Lagarde, *Aegyptiaca* (Göttingen, 1883); Guidi, *Frammenti Copti, Rendiconti della R. Accademia dei Lincei* (Classe di scienze morali, storiche e filologiche), 1887, ser. IV vol. III sem. 2. Selections from the text of some of the MSS are given by Zoega in his Catalogue. The most important piece of translation hitherto done is Stern's translation into German of the *Death of Joseph* in the *Zeitschrift für wissenschaftliche Theologie*, 1883, pp. 270—294.

Reference is made to the following catalogues: Zoega, *Catalogus Codicum Copticorum qui in Museo Borgiano Velitris adservantur* (Rome, 1810); Mai, *Codices Coptici Bibliothecae Vaticanae* (see *Scriptorum veterum nova collectio*, tom. V, Rome, 1831); Hyvernat, *Catalogue of the Clarendon Press MSS*, preserved in manuscript in the Bodleian Library.

MSS of Sahidic Fragments of the Life of the Virgin.

CLAREND. B 3 14, a Sahidic fragment in the Bodleian Library, Oxford. It consists of two leaves: the numbering of the first leaf is gone; the second is numbered ιΓ, ιΔ. The first page is indistinct. The greatest length of a page is now 13½ in., the greatest breadth 10⅛ in. The columns (9¾ to 10 × 3 in.) contain from 30 to 32 lines. The stops are black and decorated with vermilion. The writing is plain, rarely protracted into the margin. The ο of Φ is large, and decorated with two vermilion points. Initial letters are rather large, are quite in the margin, and are decorated with vermilion. They are ornamented with ⊳ or ÷ written in black, and decorated with red. Hyvernat in his *Catalogue of the Clarendon Press MSS* dates this MS 'about the eleventh or twelfth century.' It is printed and translated in the present edition, pp. 2—5, 12—15. It is part of the same MS as the following:

BORG. CXVII, a Sahidic fragment in the Borgian Museum at the Propaganda, Rome. It consists of four leaves: the numbers of the first and third are lost; the second and fourth are numbered ζ, Η and ιΑ, ιΒ. The condition of these leaves is good; and the writing is never so torn as to be illegible. The greatest length of a page is now 12 in., the greatest breadth 9⅛ in. The columns (9⅞ to 10¼ × 3 in.) contain from 29 to 32 lines. Ϯ is once, and ϭ is twice decorated with vermilion. The first of the Oxford leaves immediately precedes this fragment, and the second immediately follows. Zoega in his Catalogue (p. 223) places it in class VI. Written and lithographed by Revillout, *Apoc. Copt.* pp. 1—6; printed and translated in this edition, pp. 4—13.

BORG. CXVIII, a Sahidic fragment at the Propaganda. It consists of three leaves. On the *verso* of the first leaf is the number ιΗ. The rest of the early numbering is gone. On the *recto* of the second leaf the number ΚΓ is written in a modern hand. This may represent an old number, now torn away: see further in the note on p. 195. The condition of the MS is fairly good. Part of the bottom of the first leaf, and part of the margin of the second leaf are lost. The greatest length of a page is 11½ in., the greatest breadth 9¼ in. The columns (breadth 2¾ to 3¼ in.) contain from 28 to 30 lines. The stops are often decorated with red. Initial letters are either wholly or partly in the margin, and are sometimes not much larger than ordinary letters. They are decorated with red. ⊳ is found below one of them, and ⊥ below two. There is very little ornamentation. Zoega (*Catal.* p. 223) places it in class VIII. Written and lithographed by Revillout, *Apoc. Copt.* pp. 7—11; printed and translated in this edition, pp. 14—21.

Borg. cxix, a Sahidic fragment at the Propaganda. It consists o two leaves, numbered ⲗⲑ, ⲙ, ⲙⲁ, ⲙⲃ. The first leaf is slightly torn on the left: the second leaf is badly torn on the right. The greatest length of a page is 11⅛ in., the greatest breadth 8. The columns (9¼ × 2¾ to 3¼ in.) contain from 27 to 29 lines. The stops are never decorated with red. Initial letters are in the margin; they are not large, and are decorated with red, which is now of a dull colour. Almost the only ornamentation is > written in the margin before ⲧⲱⲟⲩⲛ in *v.* 16. Zoega (*Catal.* p. 223) places it in the same class (vi) as cxvii. But it is much less adorned, and apparently older than cxvii. Written and lithographed by Revillout, *Apoc. Copt.* pp. 12—14; printed and translated in this edition, pp. 20—25.

Borg. cxx, a Sahidic fragment at the Propaganda. It consists of six leaves. The numbering of the first leaf is gone. The second leaf is numbered ⲝ⌜ⲑ⌝ (the ⲑ being lost), ⌜ⲟ⌝. The numbers of the other four leaves (ⲟⲁ to ⲟⲏ) are all preserved. The MS is torn on the left side. The greatest length of a page is 12¾ in., the greatest breadth 9¼ in. The columns (11⅛ × 3¼ in.) contain about 34 lines. Initial letters are either wholly or partly in the margin; they are not very large, and are generally decorated with red. The ornamentation is somewhat profuse. The signs ÷ and ⯈ and ⲍ are found in the margin, and are decorated with red. The writing is small, and the margin irregular. Zoega (*Catal.* p. 223) places it in class viii. It is more ornamented than cxviii. Zoega in his Catalogue (p. 224 f.) has printed *vv.* 26—28, 103—127. These selections have been translated into French by Dulaurier, *Fragment des Révélations Apoc. de S. Barthélemy*, p. 20 ff. It is written and lithographed by Revillout, *Apoc. Copt.* pp. 15—27; printed and translated in this edition, pp. 24—41.

In addition to these MSS of *The Life of the Virgin* there is a Sahidic fragment in the possession of Lord Crawford, Coptic MS 36, which contains an account of our Lord's birth and of the massacre of the Innocents. This and the other two MSS belonging to Lord Crawford came into my hands after the main body of the work was printed. I have translated two selections from it in notes on pp. 196 f., 235 f. This fragment consists of six leaves, numbered continuously from ⲧⲙⲑ to ⌜ⲧⲝ⌝. It is in good condition, and plainly written on clean vellum. The average length of a page is 12¾ in., the average breadth 9¾ in.: but the margins have been considerably cut away in binding. 20 out of 24 columns (10⅜ × 3½ in.) contain 36 lines apiece: each of the remaining four columns containing 34 or 35 lines. A simple point is used as a stop. The marks above the letters are lines (—), and only occasionally points. Two points are sometimes written above the letter ⲓ. Another sign (‿) is often placed above a word, to mark its ending. This sign varies in size, and is sometimes very small, in fact scarcely more than a point. Initial letters are usually somewhat small and completely in the margin. On p. ⲧⲛⲉ a long initial ⲫ occurs. Many of the capitals have green or green and purple ornamentation either above or beside them. The letter ⲩ has in one instance (at the end of a line) its stem prolonged below the line of writing. The fragment forms part of a sermon, and begins in the middle of an account of certain communications made by the angel to Joseph in the night. The preacher then gives comments of his own, and tells how because of his purity Joseph was allowed to take Mary to his house. At the end of the fourth page (ⲧⲛⲏ) comes the account of our Lord's birth, which I have translated on p. 196 f. This is followed by a reference to the wonders which were manifested at Bethlehem, including the message of the angels to the shepherds, and (on p. ⲧⲛⲥ) the visit of the Magi and the slaughter of the Innocents. I have translated the latter part of this on p. 235 f. The preacher then explains the meaning of Rachel's weeping for her children. Rachel was the wife of a man of the tribe of Levi named Eleazar, who lived at the time when the children of Israel were in Egypt. He was diseased in his feet, and unable to work at making bricks. The taskmasters struck his wife, and compelled her to work. She was in a state of pregnancy, and the work was beyond her strength. Her child was prematurely born. The next night God smote the firstborn, and the Egyptians in fear sent the Israelites forth. The Israelites were joyful; but Rachel was weeping for her child in the midst of the children of Israel, and no one could comfort her. As God smote Pharaoh and his multitude, so He smote Herod and all his servants. The fragment concludes with a reference to the phoenix in connection with the death of Abel (cf. Clem. Rom. *Ep.* c. xxv). 'There is a bird called (reading ⲉϣⲁⲩⲙⲟⲩⲧⲉ for ⲉϣⲁⲩⲙⲟⲩⲉ) phoenix. *As for* this *bird*, when the fire came from heaven and consumed (ⲟⲩⲱⲙ) the sacrifice of Abel the righteous—now *as for* that bird, the fire of that sacrifice burnt (reading ⲁϥⲣⲟⲕϩϥ for ⲁⲩϩⲟⲕϩϥ) it, and made it ashes. On the third day a little worm came forth from the ashes of the bird, and advanced little by little; until it put forth wings, and again became even as it was. Every five hundred years the phoenix, the bird, comes flying in the height, and goes into the temple to the altar *where* (?) they offer.' (Here the fragment ends).

Mr Crum has also found and transcribed for me a Papyrus fragment in the British Museum, Pap. xi Sams, which contains allusions to Joseph and to the pregnancy of the Virgin. I have not published it, as it is very fragmentary.

MSS of the Falling Asleep of Mary.

VAT. LXII 5, a Bohairic MS in the Vatican Library, Rome. It consists of thirty leaves; and begins on p. 90 *a* of the volume, and ends on p. 119 *b*. It is catalogued thus in Mai, *Codices Coptici Bibliothecae Vaticanae* p. 158, 'S. P. N. Euchodii magnae urbis Romae archiepiscopi (imo Evodii antiocheni archiepiscopi primi) homilia de domina omnium nostrorum sancta Maria' (Mai, *Script. Vet.* tom. v). I have not seen this MS. There is a copy of it made by Tuki in the Borgian Museum at the Propaganda. This copy (Borg. XLIX Boh.) is briefly described by Zoega (*Catalogue* p. 93 f.). The text of the original MS is written and lithographed by Revillout, *Apocryphes Coptes*, pp. 75—112. It is printed by Lagarde, *Aegyptiaca*, pp. 38—63; and a translation from his text is made in this edition, pp. 44—67.

BORG. CCLXXIII, a Sahidic fragment in the National Library of the Museum, Naples. It consists of one leaf, numbered ⲕⲁ, ⲕⲃ. It is part of the same MS as BORG. CCLVIII, FRAGMENT I, also at Naples, which consists of two leaves, numbered ⲗⲁ, ⲗⲃ (these numbers are in an imperfect condition) and ⲙⲁ, ⲙⲃ. The first leaf of the MS is badly torn. The second leaf is also torn, and is occasionally difficult to read. The greatest length of a page is 14 in., the greatest breadth $11\frac{3}{4}$ in.: but the pages were originally larger. The columns ($10\frac{7}{8} \times 3\frac{1}{4}$ to $3\frac{5}{8}$ in.) contain from 32 to 36 lines. The stops are usually decorated with red. There is but little ornamentation. The sign ÷ occurs three times. The letter ⲉ is sometimes difficult to distinguish from ⲓ, and ⲟ is narrow, and thick at the bottom. The writing is regular. Initial letters are often small, but vary in size; are always adorned with red; and are either wholly or partly in the margin. Zoega (*Catal.* pp. 615, 621) places it in class VI. The third leaf—written by the same hand—is part of a eulogy on the Virgin. The last two leaves have been bound together by means of a fragment from an earlier part of the same MS. Here the remains of two columns of one page can still be seen. The first column contains a few letters of c. IV *v.* 9 ⲉⲓⲃⲧ ⲉⲛⲉϥϭⲓϫ and ⲧⲉ ⲉⲧⲟⲩⲁⲁⲃ and ⲧⲁⲩⲛ 'nails His hands,' 'holy,' 'which.' The second column contains part of c. IV *v.* 11 f. ⲛⲓⲙ ⲉⲧϫⲱ ⲙⲛ⸢ϭⲟ⸣ⲗ ⲉⲧⲃⲉ ⲟⲩ ⲁⲕϫⲟⲟⲥ ⲉⲡⲉⲓⲗⲁⲧⲟⲥ ⲉⲕⲕⲁⲧⲏⲅⲟⲣⲉⲓ ⲛⲓⲥ ⲉⲕⲟⲩⲱϣ ⲉⲧⲣⲉϥϭⲱⲛⲧ ⲛϥϯⲁⲡⲟⲫⲁ 'all that speak falsehood. Wherefore didst thou speak to Pilate, accusing Jesus, wishing that he should be angry and that he should give sentence?' About three letters of another leaf can also be deciphered. The first leaf of the MS is written and lithographed by Revillout, *Apoc. Copt.* pp. 72—74: it is printed and translated in this edition, pp. 66—69. The second leaf is referred to by Revillout, *op. cit.* p. X; it is printed and variants in translation noted on pp. 80—87.

BORG. CCLIX*, a Sahidic fragment in the National Library of the Museum, Naples. It consists of two leaves, still united, numbered ⲗⲉ, ⲗⲋ and ⲙⲉ, ⲙⲋ. The condition of the leaves is fairly good. The top of the left side has been torn, but scarcely any letters lost. The greatest length of a page is $10\frac{3}{4}$ in., the greatest breadth $9\frac{5}{8}$ in. The columns ($7\frac{7}{8}$ to $8\frac{1}{8} \times 2\frac{3}{4}$ to $3\frac{1}{4}$ in.) contain about 26 lines. Stops are almost entirely absent. Spaces are sometimes left between words, and at the end of lines. From the condition of the MS it is not always easy to determine whether or not the scribe intended to place a point above a letter. Initial letters are usually completely in the margin. For the most part they are rather small; but in one instance an initial ⲉ is large. Sometimes also initial ⲁ is large, and written almost above the letter which follows. There is no ornamentation in red. The sign ⊳ once occurs on the last page; and two figures which resemble a 8 are found in the margin, apparently for ornamentation. On the third page the sign 2 is once found above an initial ⲁ. With these exceptions, there is no ornamentation. The writing is unlike any of the other Sahidic fragments. The hand is later and more cursive. The spelling is bad. The stem of the letter ⲩ is sometimes prolonged. Zoega (*Catal.* p. 616) places it between class VIII and IX. Referred to by Revillout, *Apoc. Copt.* p. x; printed and either translated or variants in translation noted in this edition, pp. 70—73, 82—89.

CLAREND. B 3 15, a Sahidic fragment in the Bodleian Library at Oxford. It consists of five leaves. The numbers have perished owing to the bad condition of the upper margin. The MS begins with the word ϩⲓⲟⲩⲥⲟⲡ ('together'), which probably goes with the previous sentence. The columns contain from 27 to 30 lines. Mr A. C. Headlam has given me the following description of the MS. The greatest length of a page is $11\frac{1}{4}$ in., the greatest breadth $8\frac{5}{8}$ in. The columns are from $9\frac{1}{2}$ to $9\frac{5}{8}$ in. $\times 2\frac{1}{2}$ to 3 in. The stops are decorated with vermilion. The writing is long and upright. Initial letters are rather small. In some cases they are of a larger size and more elaborate. They are almost completely in the margin. The sign 7 occurs. Vermilion is used to ornament this sign as well as the points above letters.

Hyvernat dates this MS about the tenth century. Printed and translated in this edition, pp. 70—87.

VAT. LXI 5, a Bohairic MS in the Vatican Library. It begins on p. 122 *a* of the volume, and ends on p. 147 *b*. The end of the MS is missing. The page is $13\frac{5}{8} \times 10\frac{7}{8}$ in., the column $10\frac{1}{4}$ to $10\frac{3}{4} \times 6\frac{3}{4}$ to $7\frac{1}{8}$ in. The writing is in one column. The stops are in red. The marks above the letters are lines (—), and single or double points. It is not always easy to distinguish between these marks. Initial letters are in the margin: they are fairly large, and are sometimes decorated with red. The MS is ornamented with red. There is also ornamentation at the top of some of the pages; and the words ιηс ('Jesus'), ιηс πχ̅с ('Jesus Christ'), ναι ναν ('have mercy on us') are found. At the top of the first page these words occur, ϕαι μμεθμηι ⲛⲥⲟⲩ ⲓⲋ̅ ⲙⲙⲉⲥⲱⲣⲏ ϧⲉⲛ ϯⲡⲁⲣⲑⲉⲛⲟⲥ. The writing is rather large, and is in a round uncial hand. The fragment breaks off on p. 147 *b* of the present vol. (ⲛⲃ̅ of the old numbering): on p. 148 *a* is a colophon, which perhaps refers to this work on the *Falling asleep of Mary*. But as colophons are written in a cursive style, it is not clear whether this refers to the preceding or following MS. The date given in the colophon is 678 of the martyrs. I have transcribed the main part of the MS. The fifteen pages which I have omitted at the beginning, and the three pages at the end, are didactic. On p. 14 of the MS the preacher says: 'Let us turn to the theme (ⲡⲣⲟⲕⲩⲙⲉⲛⲟⲛ) which is laid down for us of this great festival, which is spread out for us (ⲉⲧϥⲟⲣϣ ⲛⲁⲛ ⲉⲃⲟⲗ) to-day; that we may bring into the midst her who is worthy of all honour: beginning from the dispensation (ⲟⲓⲕⲟⲛⲟⲙⲓⲁ) of Christ unto the death (*or* consummation) of this holy Virgin and her holy assumption: even as I found it in detail (ⲓⲥⲧⲟⲣⲓⲕⲱⲥ) in ancient records in Jerusalem, which came into my hand in the Library of the holy Mark at Alexandria.' There is a copy of it made by Tuki in the Borgian Museum. This copy (Borg. L Boh.) is briefly described in Zoega's Catalogue (p. 94). The original MS is catalogued in Mai, *Script. Vet.* tom. v (*Cod. Cop. Bibl. Vat.* p. 156), where by a misprint it is called LXI 4. Printed and translated in this edition, pp. 90—127.

In addition to this MS of the *Falling asleep of Mary*, there is a fragment of a Bohairic MS in the possession of Lord Crawford, COPTIC MS 46; the various readings of which I have given on p. 219. This fragment consists of two leaves, and is numbered on alternate pages ⲛⲃ̅ and ⲛⲏ. The first and last pages are hard to decipher: the other two are in good condition. The vellum is stained and soiled. The greatest length of a page is 11¼ in., the greatest breadth 7⅝ in.: but the margins have been cut away. The writing is in a single column. The greatest length of a column is 8¼ in., the average breadth about 5 in. Three of the four pages contain 28 lines: the remaining page contains 27. There are no stops. The marks above the letters are lines (—) or points. Initial letters are not large, and are quite in the margin. The writing is rather small; and there is no ornamentation.

I have also noticed a short fragment of an Assumption of the Virgin among the Coptic fragments in the Cambridge University Library, ADD. 1876 8. It is very imperfect, but, as far as I can read it, presents a different recension to the other accounts. The following are selections from it, where the sense is fairly certain. ⌈ϯ⌉ⲡⲁⲕⲱ ⲛⲥⲱⲓ ⲙⲡⲉⲓⲕⲟⲥⲙⲟⲥ ⲉⲧϣⲧⲣⲧⲱⲣ ⲁⲩⲱ ⲉⲧⲙⲉϩ ⲛϩⲓⲥⲉ ⲛⲓⲙ ⲛⲁⲡⲟⲥⲧⲟⲗⲟⲥ ⲇⲉ ⲁⲩⲣ ⲧⲉⲩϣⲏ ⲧⲏⲣⲥ ⲉⲩϣ'ⲗⲏ'ⲗ ⲁⲩⲱ ⲉⲩⲯⲁⲗⲗ'ⲉⲓ ..ⲝ' ⲡⲙⲏⲧⲉ ⲇⲉ ⲛ⸢ⲧⲉ⸣ⲩϣⲏ ⸢ⲁ⸣ⲥⲧⲱⲟⲩⲛ 'I will leave this world which is distressed and full of all trouble. And the apostles spent all the night praying and singing. Now in (?) the middle of the night she arose.' On the same page, and in the next column come these words: ⲁ ⲡ⸢ⲉⲭ︦ⲥ︦⸣ ⲉⲓ ϣⲁⲣⲟⲥ ⲙⲛ ⲟⲩ⸢ⲙⲏ⸣ⲏϣⲉ ⲛⲁⲅ⸢ⲅⲉⲗⲟⲥ⸣ ⲁⲩⲱ ⲡⲉϫ⸢ⲁϥ ⲛⲁⲥ⸣ ϫⲉ ϯⲣⲏ⸢ⲛⲏ ⲛⲉ⸣ ⲭⲁⲓⲣⲉ ⲱ ⸢ⲙ⸣ⲁⲣⲓⲁ ⸢ⲧⲁ⸣ⲙⲁⲁⲩ ϯⲣⲏ⸢ⲛⲏ⸣ ⲛⲧⲟⲩϭⲓⲛ-ⲡⲱⲱ⸢ⲛⲉ ⲉ⸣ⲃⲟⲗ ⸢ϩ⸣ⲙ ⲡⲉⲓⲁⲓ⸢ⲱⲛ⸣ 'Christ came unto her with a multitude of angels and said unto her, Peace be unto thee. Hail, O Mary My mother. Peace be unto thy departure from this world.' The column breaks off with the words ϯⲣⲏⲛⲏ ⲛⲏⲧⲛ ⸢ⲛⲁⲁ⸣ⲡⲟⲥⲧⲟⲗⲟⲥ ⲉⲧⲥⲙ⸢ⲁ⸣ⲁⲧ ⲙⲛⲛ⸢ⲥⲱⲥ⸣ ⲁϥⲕⲟⲧϥ ⲉⲙⲁⲣⲓⲁ ⸢ⲧⲉϥ⸣ⲙⲁⲁⲩ ⲡⲉϫⲁϥ ⸢ⲛⲁⲥ⸣ ϫⲉ ⲙⲡⲣⲣϩⲟⲧ⸢ⲉ ⲱ⸣ ⲙ⸢ⲁⲣ⸣ⲓ⸢ⲁ ⲧⲁⲙⲁⲁⲩ⸣ 'Peace be unto you, My blessed apostles. Afterwards He turned to Mary His mother, and said to her, Be not afraid, O Mary My mother.' On the other side of the leaf there is a reference to Gabriel and to the crucifixion. ⲡⲓⲗⲁ⸢ⲧⲟⲥ ⲡⲏ⸣ⲅⲉⲙⲱⲛ ⸢ⲁ ⲡⲁ⸣ⲥⲱⲙⲁ ⲧⲣⲧⲱⲣ ⸢ϩⲛ⸣ ϩⲉⲛⲉⲓϥⲧ ϩⲛ ⲧ⸢ⲙⲏ⸣ⲧⲉ ⲙⲡⲁⲏⲣ ⲙⲡⲛⲁⲩ ⲙⲡⲛⲟϭ ⸢ⲛ⸣ⲕⲁⲩⲥⲱⲛ ⲭⲱⲣⲓⲥ ⲧⲣⲁϫ⸢ⲟ⸣ⲟⲩ ⲧⲏⲣⲟⲩ ⲧⲉⲥⲟⲟⲩⲛ ⲙⲙⲟⲟⲩ ϩⲱⲱⲧⲉ ⲱ ⲧⲁⲙⲁⲁⲩ ⲙⲛ ⲡⲉⲧⲟ ⲛⲛⲟϭ ⸢ⲉ⸣ⲛⲁⲓ ⲁϥϫⲟⲟⲩ ⲛⲁⲥ ⲛϭⲓ ⲡⲉⲭ︦ⲥ︦ 'Pilate the governor. My body was fastened with nails in the midst of the air at the hour of the great heat (*or* scorching wind). Without My saying them all, thou also knowest them, O My mother, and greater things than these. Christ said them to her.' The fragment consists of the remains of a single page, the numbering of which is lost. The greatest length of the page is now $7\frac{5}{8}$ in., but it was once about twice as great. The greatest breadth is now $9\frac{3}{8}$ in. The columns (breadth irregular; sometimes about $3\frac{1}{2}$ in.) contain portions of 17 or 18 lines. Stops are occasionally indicated by single or double points; but generally a space is left instead. The writing is bold and irregular. The marks above letters are single or double points and lines. Initial letters are partly in the margin. They vary greatly in size: sometimes they are fairly large. There is one long initial ϯ. There is no ornamentation.

MSS of the Death of Joseph.

VAT. LXVI 11, a Bohairic MS in the Vatican Library. It begins on p. 269 *a* of the volume, and ends on p. 287 *a*. The numbering is from ⲃ︦ to ⲗ︦ⲋ︦. The page is $13\frac{1}{2} \times 10\frac{1}{4}$ in., the column $10\frac{3}{4} \times 6\frac{3}{4}$ in. The writing is in one column. There are no stops, but spaces are left. The marks above the letters are lines (—) and points. Initial letters are in the margin, and are not much ornamented. There is some illumination on the first page: but after this there is no ornamentation in red. The writing is rather large, and is in a round uncial hand. The date given in the colophon is 783 of the martyrs. Hyvernat (*Album de Paléographie Copte* XXXIV) has given a facsimile of the first page). There is a copy of it made by Tuki in the Borgian Museum. This copy (Borg. XXV Boh.) is briefly described in Zoega's Catalogue (p. 33). The original MS is catalogued in Mai, *Script. Vet.* tom. V (*Cod. Cop. Bibl. Vat.* p. 162). The text of it is written out and lithographed by Revillout (*Apoc. Copt.* pp. 43—71). It is printed by Lagarde, *Aegyptiaca* pp. 1—37; and a translation from his text is made in this edition, pp. 130—147.

In addition to this MS of the *Death of Joseph*, there is a fragment of a Bohairic MS in the possession of Lord Crawford, COPTIC MS 39, the various readings of which I have given on p. 221 ff. This fragment consists of two leaves, the numbering of which is lost. The first and last pages are hard to decipher: the last being sometimes quite illegible. The page is now $12\frac{3}{4} \times 9\frac{7}{8}$ in.: but the margins have been cut away. The writing is in a single column. The average length of a column is $11\frac{1}{4}$ to $11\frac{1}{2}$ in.; the breadth is irregular, being sometimes about 8 in. The first and last pages contain 30 lines, the second 29, the third 31. There are no stops. The marks above the letters are lines (—). Initial letters are very large, and are quite in the margin. The writing is thick and dark. It is written in a large and bold hand. The letters ⲫ and ϫ are especially large. There is no ornamentation.

BORG. CXVI, a Sahidic fragment at the Propaganda. It consists of one leaf, numbered ⲡⲍ, ⲡⲏ. The leaf is torn on the right and left sides, but little of the writing is gone. Its greatest length is 12 in., its greatest breadth $9\frac{3}{8}$ in. The columns ($10\frac{1}{2} \times 2\frac{3}{4}$ to 3 in.) contain from 29 to 32 lines. The stops are sometimes decorated with red. Initial letters are in the margin. They are large, and are decorated with red. The signs ÷ and ⳩ are found in the margin. The letter ⲣ is once written with a large flourish at the top. Zoega (*Cat.* p. 223) places it in class VIII. The writing is rougher and more adorned than CXVIII, which he places in the same class. Written and lithographed by Revillout, *Apoc. Copt.* p. 28 f.; printed and translated in this edition, pp. 146—149.

BR. MUS. OR. 3581 B, a Sahidic fragment in the British Museum. It consists of one leaf, the numbering of which is gone. The right side is badly torn, and many letters are completely lost. The greatest length of the leaf is about $13\frac{1}{4}$ in.; the greatest breadth about $7\frac{7}{8}$ in. But it is torn and crumpled. The columns ($9\frac{1}{4}$ in. × 3 in.) contain about 25 lines. Initial letters are rather small, and are wholly or partly in the margin. They contain a space for ornamentation in red, which has never been filled in. The only trace of ornamentation is a sign (∸) in black over initial ⲙ. The writing is plain and regular. The tail of ϥ is very small. Printed and translated in this edition, pp. 148—151.

Borg. cxxi, a Sahidic fragment at the Propaganda. It consists of eight leaves. It is numbered continuously from p. ⲝ⌜ⲉ⌝ (the ⲉ is now gone) to ⲡ. The condition is generally good : p. ⲟⲉ is stained with a yellow substance. The page measurements are 12⅜ in. × 9¾ in. The columns (9½ to 10¼ × 3¼ in.) contain from 24 to 30 lines. A simple point, a line (—), two points (:), • : — and • — are used as stops, and sometimes they are decorated with red. The points and lines above the letters are often similarly decorated. Initial letters vary in size. Initial ⲋ and ϯ, and sometimes ⲁ, ⲡ, ⲧ are written long and thin. Thus in one place the length of initial ⲁ is 2⅝ in., and in another place the length of initial ϯ is even more. These initial letters are specially prominent : they are for the most part highly decorated with red, and are usually quite in the margin. On the top line of one page ϭ is twice written with a flourish. The ornamentation is elaborate. At the bottom of four of the pages are rude pictures of animals in black, ornamented with red. There are a large number of erasures in the MS. The writing is fairly regular, and not unlike that of cxx. Zoega in his Catalogue (p. 225) places it in class viii. He gives (p. 225 ff.) selections from it (cc. xiv 3—xv 2 ; xxi—xxiii), which have been translated into French by Dulaurier (see note on p. 220). Written and lithographed by Revillout, *Apoc. Copt.* pp. 30—42 ; printed by Lagarde (from a transcript made by Guidi), *Aegyptiaca* pp. 9—29 ; translated in this edition, pp. 152—159.

MSS of various Sahidic Fragments.

Br. Mus. Or. 3581 b, a Sahidic fragment in the British Museum It consists of one leaf, numbered—as it seems—ⲋ, ⲍ. The right side is torn, but only one letter completely lost. The greatest length of the leaf is 12⅞ in. ; the greatest breadth 10⅛ in. The columns (9½ to 10 × 3 in.) contain 31 lines. The stops are adorned with red. Initial letters are large, and completely in the margin. Red is used for purposes of ornamentation. Thus the marks indicating a quotation (ϧ), some of the letters on the top lines, and the ⲗ at the beginning or end of a line, are ornamented with it. The sign ⊳ occurs ; part of it being in green, the rest in red ; and ÷ is also found. The handwriting is large and bold. There is also half of another leaf, numbered ⲉ, ⲋ, the first and third columns of which are completely gone. Another fragment, numbered ⲙⲉ, ⲙⲋ is in the same handwriting, and is perhaps part of the same MS. The most interesting leaf is printed and translated in this edition, pp. 162—165.

Br. Mus. Or. 3581 b, a Sahidic fragment in the British Museum. It consists of one leaf, of which the numbering is gone. The top is torn away, and it is not easy (see note on p. 237) to say how much is lost. The MS is occasionally hard to decipher. The greatest length of the page is now 9⅞ in., the greatest breadth 8⅞ in. The columns (greatest length 8⅜ in., the greatest breadth about 3 in.) now consist of 27 lines on the first page, 26 lines on the second. The lines placed above letters are long and adorned with red. Initial letters are small, and are wholly or partly in the margin, and are adorned with red. In one case there are the remains of a somewhat larger initial ⲡ, ornamented with red and yellow. The sign 7 is placed below, above or by the side of initial letters. The writing is rather small, regular and thin. Printed and translated in this edition, pp. 164—167.

Borg. cxi, a Sahidic fragment at the Propaganda. It consists of four separate leaves. The numbers of the first, second, third, and fifth pages are lost. The fourth page is numbered ⲕⲇ, the sixth ⌜ⲕ⌝ϛ (ⲕ is gone), the seventh ⲕ⌜ⲍ⌝ (ⲍ is gone), the eighth ⲕⲏ. The first two leaves are badly torn at the bottom on the right side. The writing of the two following leaves is cramped in places, and sometimes difficult to read. Parts of the MS are stained by a dark red stain. The greatest length of a page is rather more than 11½ in.: the greatest breadth 9⅛ in. The columns (10 × 2¾ to 3¼ in.) contain 30 or 31 lines. The stops are points or :— or •:— or •:•— and are decorated with red. The marks above the letters are a line (—), a point, and over ⲓ two points. Initial letters are as a rule large, and quite in the margin. They are decorated with red. The signs ÷ and ᐅ are found. Red is freely used for ornamentation. Sometimes a round red dot is placed in the letter ⲟ. The letters ⲫ, ⲩ, ⲗ and ⲧ are occasionally adorned with red. The upper part of ⲩ when it occurs at the top of a column is sometimes enlarged. Zoega (*Catal.* p. 222) places the MS in class vi. The handwriting resembles that of cxvii, which he places in the same class. But it is also strikingly like that of cxiii (see p. xxxii). The last letters of the fragment are ⲡⲉⲙ not ⲡⲉⲙϩ (Guidi). Written and lithographed by Revillout, *Apoc. Copt.* pp. 113—117; printed by Guidi, *Rendiconti della R. Accademia dei Lincei* (1887) vol. iii sem. 2 pp. 373—376; translated from his text in this edition, pp. 168—171.

Clarend. B 3 16, a Sahidic fragment in the Bodleian Library. It consists of two leaves. The numbering of the first page is lost: the second is numbered ⲓⲏ (the numbers given in Guidi's edition are wrong). The third and fourth pages are ⲕⲍ, ⲕⲏ. It is part of the same MS as a fragment at the Propaganda, numbered Borg. cxii, which consists of three leaves: the first leaf being numbered ⲓⲑ, ⲕ, whilst the numbering of the other two leaves is gone. Part of the MS is badly torn, and is stained with some yellow substance. The greatest length of a page is about 12½ in., the greatest breadth about 9¾ in. The columns (9½ × 3 in.) contain about 29 lines. A simple point is used for a stop, or else a space is left. The marks above the letters are usually points, but sometimes lines. Initial letters are completely in the margin, and are decorated with red. They vary in size, but are often small. There is not much ornamentation: sometimes the sign ÷ is found. The scribe occasionally shews a tendency to omit words. Hyvernat dates the Oxford fragment 'about the ninth century.' I have not translated the last leaf of the Oxford Fragment, which contains an account of the confession of Simon Peter on the Mount, and of his ordination as archbishop. It concludes with these words, 'Straightway He placed His hand on his head: and all the ranks of the heavens said the Trisagion; so that the stones that *were* in the mount cried out with them, *saying*, Holy, holy, holy, Apa Peter, archbishop. Now when he had received this...' (here the fragment ends). The following corrections should be made in Guidi's edition which is taken from a transcript by Hyvernat. In line 1 read **ⲛⲥϯⲛⲟⲩϥⲉ** for **ⲛϯⲥⲛⲟⲩϥⲉ**: line 7, read **ⲛⲉⲥⲟⲩⲱϩ** for **ⲛⲥⲟⲩⲱϩ**, and **ⲧⲧⲁⲡⲣⲟ** for **ⲧⲁⲡⲣⲟ**: line 26, read **ⲁⲩⲱ** before **ⲛⲧⲉⲣⲉϥⲑⲉⲱⲣⲉⲓ**. Page **ⲕⲏ** begins at the words **ϩⲓϫⲙ ⲛⲧⲟⲟⲩ** in line 19. The Borgian fragment is written and lithographed by Revillout, *Apoc. Copt.* pp. 118—123: both fragments are given by Guidi, *Rendiconti della R. Ac. dei Linc.* (1887) vol. III sem. 2 p. 34 f.; pp. 376—380 (the first part of the Oxford fragment is from a transcript made by Budge). The whole of the Borgian and the first leaf of the Oxford fragment is translated or variants in translation noted in this edition pp. 171—176.

BORG. CXIII[1], a Sahidic fragment at the Propaganda. It consists of four leaves, the first and last of which are still united. The numbering of the first two leaves is gone. The third leaf is numbered **ⲛⲍ**, **ⲛⲏ** (the **ⲏ** is almost gone). The remains of the nos. **ⲛⲑ**, **ⲝ** are legible on the fourth leaf. The MS is in fairly good condition; and the first and last pages are well preserved. The greatest length of a page is $12\frac{7}{8}$ in.: the greatest breadth $10\frac{3}{8}$ in. The columns ($10\frac{3}{4}$ in. × $2\frac{3}{4}$ to $3\frac{1}{4}$ in.) contain from 28 to 32 lines. The stops are points or :— or •:— or ⁛— and are decorated with red. The

[1] Codd. Borg. CXI, CXII, CXIII belong to the same cycle of narratives as those contained in Codd. Borg. CXIV, CXV. These are briefly described by Zoega (*Catal.* p. 222 f.), who places them in class V. The text of them is published by Guidi, *Rendic. della R. Acc. dei Linc.* (1887) vol. IV sem. 1 pp. 60—70. They contain allusions to the gift of the keys of the kingdom of heaven to Peter, the Last Supper, the Crucifixion, the conversations of our Lord with Thomas and Peter after the resurrection, and His appearance by the lake. I have not published a translation, as they contain but little definite apocryphal matter. They are generally didactic or rhetorical expansions of canonical narratives. They are interesting as showing that *Various Sahidic Fragments* III and IV (see pp. 168—179) are but a portion of one or more sermons upon several events connected with the life of our Lord.

marks above the letters are a line (—), a point, and over ɪ two points. Initial letters are as a rule large, and quite in the margin. They are decorated with red. The signs ÷ and ᐅ are found. Red is freely used for ornamentation. Sometimes a round red dot is placed in the letter ⲟ. The letters ⲫ, ⲩ, ⲗ, ⲧ and ⲡ are occasionally adorned with red. The upper part of ⲩ, when it occurs at the top of a column, is sometimes enlarged. Zoega (*Catal.* p. 222) places the MS in class VI. This may be part of the same MS as Borg. CXI. Both appear to have been written by one scribe. He usually wrote a large hand, and put few letters in a column. But in CXI the writing is cramped at the bottom of the page. In both fragments he shews a tendency to repeat himself (cf. *Various Sah. Frag.* III *v.* 12 and IV *v.* 25). In both he has a marked preference for forms in ⲁ. Written and lithographed by Revillout, *Apoc. Copt.* pp. 124—128; printed by Guidi, *Rendic. della R. Acc. dei Linc.* (1887) vol. III sem. 2 pp. 381—384; translated in this edition, pp. 176—179.

Borg. CCLVII, a Sahidic fragment in the National Library of the Museum, Naples. It consists of four leaves, numbered continuously from ⲗⲉ to ⲗⲏ and from ⲙⲅ to ⲙⲋ. They are in fair condition. It is part of the same MS as Borg. CCLXVII, also at Naples, which consists of six leaves. The first two are numbered from ⲗⲑ to ⲙⲃ: the third ⲙⲍ, ⲙⲏ: the last three from ⲣⲁ to ⲣⲋ. The second of these leaves is in a bad, crumpled state: the third is incomplete: more than half of the sixth is gone. The greatest length of a page is 13⅝ in.: the greatest breadth 10¾ in. The columns ($10 \times 2\frac{3}{4}$ to $3\frac{1}{4}$ in.) always seem to contain 31 lines. The stops are decorated with red. Initial letters are large, and are usually entirely or almost entirely in the margin. They are copiously adorned with red. The ornaments ÷ and ᐅ are found. I have only published the part of the sermon which contains interesting Apocryphal matter. On the first leaf occurs the name of 'Apa Cyril,' to whom the sermon is apparently ascribed. Zoega who gives short selections from both fragments in his Catalogue (pp. 614 f.; 620 f.) wrongly places them in separate classes. Printed and translated in this edition, pp. 178—185.

EXPLANATION OF SIGNS AND ABBREVIATIONS EMPLOYED IN THIS EDITION.

Letters in half brackets (⌜ ⌝) in the Coptic text are wholly or in part illegible in the MS. When letters are entirely lost and I am unable to replace them, I have represented their number by dots. When the number is uncertain, I have placed half brackets above the dots. Letters in full brackets ([ ]) indicate conjectural insertions. Words italicised in the translation are not represented in the Coptic. I have in almost all cases indicated the end of a column or a page in the MS by a vertical line.

For the sake of convenience I have used an asterisk to mark such Sahidic Biblical quotations as are not found in the editions of Old Testament fragments published by Ciasca, or of New Testament fragments published by Amélineau (*Z. f. Aeg. Sprache*, 1886—1888) and by Woide.

The following abbreviations are used:

A.Z. = *Zeitschrift für Aegyptische Sprache und Alterthumskunde.*
PS. = *Pistis Sophia* (ed. Petermann, Berlin, 1851).
Z. = Zoega's *Catalogue.*

SAHIDIC FRAGMENTS
OF THE LIFE OF THE VIRGIN.

SAHIDIC FRAGMENTS OF THE LIFE OF THE VIRGIN.

FRAGMENT I.

Cod. Clarend. b 8 14 p. 3

1 ⲁⲥϣⲧⲟ ⲙⲡⲉⲥϣⲏⲣⲉ ⲛϩⲏⲧϥ̄ · ⲛ̄ⲧⲉⲣⲉⲥϫⲡⲟϥ ϩⲛ̄ ⲟⲩⲕⲁϩ ⲛ̇ϣⲙ̄ⲙⲟ ·
2 Ⲁⲛ⌈ⲟ⌉ⲛ ⲇⲉ ⲛⲧⲁⲛϣⲓⲛⲉ ⲛⲧⲟⲟ̇ⲧⲟⲩ ⲛ̄ⲛⲉⲛⲉⲓ̄ⲟ̇ⲧⲉ ⲛⲁⲡⲟⲥⲧⲟⲗⲟⲥ · ⲛⲁⲓ
ⲛ̇ⲧⲁ ⲡⲉⲩϩⲣⲟⲟⲩ ⲉⲓ̄ ⲉ̄ⲃⲟⲗ ⲉϫⲙ̄ ⲛ̇ⲕⲁϩ ⲧⲏⲣⲉϥ · Ⲁⲩⲱ ⲁ̇ ⲡⲉⲩϣⲁϫⲉ
ⲡⲱϩ ϣⲁ ⲛⲉⲕⲣⲱⲟⲩ ⲛⲧⲓ̈ⲕⲟⲩⲙⲉⲛⲏ · ⲉⲩϯⲥ̇ⲃⲱ ⲛⲁⲛ ⲉⲡⲉⲛⲟⲩϫⲁⲓ̈ ⳾
3 Ⲁⲩⲧⲁⲙⲟⲛ̄ ⲉⲡⲃⲓ̈ⲟⲥ ⲛⲧⲉⲓ̈ⲡⲁⲣⲑⲉⲛⲟⲥ · ⲕⲁⲧⲁ ⲑⲉ ⲛ̄ⲧⲁⲩⲛⲁⲩ ϩⲛ
ⲛⲉⲩⲃⲁⲗ · ⲁⲩⲱ̄ ⲁⲩϣⲱⲡⲉ ⲛϩⲩⲡⲉⲣⲉⲧⲏⲥ ⲙ̇ⲡϣⲁϫⲉ ⳾ 4 Ⲉⲡⲉⲓ̄ⲇⲏ :
ⲛ̇ⲧⲁⲛϫⲓ̄ⲥⲃⲱ ⲉⲃ⌈ⲟ⌉ⲗ ϩⲓⲧⲟⲟⲧⲟⲩ · ⲁⲩⲱ̄ ϣⲁⲩⲧⲁⲛϩⲉⲧ̄ ⲛ̄ⲛⲁⲩ ϩⲛ ⲛⲉⲃⲁⲗ
ϩⲟⲧⲉ̇ ⲛⲥⲱⲧⲙ̄ | ϩⲛ ⲛⲉⲙⲁⲁϫⲉ · 5 Ⲗⲓ̄ⲡⲱⲛ · ⲙⲡⲉⲣⲧⲣⲉ ⲗⲁⲁⲩ ⲙ̄ⲙⲉⲉⲩⲉ
ⲉϥϩⲟⲟⲩ · ⲁⲗⲉ ⲉϩⲣⲁⲓ̈ ⲉ̄ϫⲙ̄ ⲡⲉⲛϩⲏⲧ ⲉ̇ϩⲟⲩⲛ ⲉⲧⲉⲣⲱ[a] ⲛⲁⲗⲏⲑⲓⲛⲱⲛ ·
6 Ⲏⲑⲉ ⲛⲛⲓ̄ⲟⲩⲇⲁⲓ ⲛⲁⲧⲛⲟⲩⲧⲉ · ⲛⲁⲓ ⲛⲧⲁⲩϫⲓ̄ⲟⲩⲁ ⲉ̄ⲣⲟⲥ[b] ϩⲙ̇ ⲡⲉⲩⲗⲁⲥ
ⲛ̇ϣⲟⲩⲥ⌈ⲟ⌉ⲗⲉⲡϥ · ⲙⲛ ⲧⲉⲩⲧⲁⲡ̇ⲣⲟ ⲛϣⲟⲩⲧⲟⲙⲥ ⳾ Ⲏϫⲓⲛ ⲉⲥⲟⲛϩ ·
7 ⲙⲛⲛⲥⲁ ⲡⲉⲥⲙⲟⲩ · ⲁⲩⲟⲩⲱϣ ⲉⲣⲱ⌈ⲕϩ⌉ ⲙⲡⲉⲥⲥⲱⲙ⌈ⲁ⌉ ⲉⲧⲟⲩⲁⲁⲃ · ⲉⲧⲃⲉ
ⲡⲉⲩⲙⲟⲥⲧ ⲉϩⲟⲩⲛ ⲉ̇ⲣⲟ⌈ⲥ⌉ · 8 Ⲁⲗⲗⲁ · ⲙⲡⲉ⌈ⲣ⌉ϫⲟⲟⲥ ⲛ̄ⲑⲉ ⲛⲛ⌈ⲉ⌉ⲣⲉⲧⲓ-
ⲕⲟⲥ · ϫ⌈ⲉ⌉ ⲟⲩ⌈ⲇ⌉ⲩⲛⲁⲙⲓⲥ ⌈ⲧⲉ⌉ⲧ⌈ⲧ⌉ⲁⲣ⌈ⲡⲥ⌉ ⌈Ⲏ⌉ ⲛ⌈ⲧ⌉ⲉⲧⲛ⌈ϫⲟⲟ⌉ⲥ · ⌈ⲛ⌉ⲑⲉ

p. 4

⌈....ⲉ⌉..ⲧ⌈ⲁ⌉ⲛ⌈..⌉ | ϫⲉ ⲛⲧⲁⲩⲁ̇ⲛⲁⲗⲁⲙⲃⲁⲛⲉ ⲙ̄ⲙⲟⲥ ϩ̄ⲙ ⲡⲉⲥⲥⲱⲙⲁ
ⲉϩⲣⲁⲓ̈ ⲉⲧⲡⲉ ⳾ 9 Ϥⲥ̇ϩⲟⲩⲟⲣⲧ ⲛ̄ϭⲓ̄ ⲡⲉⲧⲛⲁϫⲟⲟⲥ · ϫⲉ ⲛⲟⲩϫⲡⲟ ⲁⲛ ⲧⲉ
ⲧⲡⲁⲣⲑⲉⲛⲟⲥ ⲛ̄ⲧⲉⲛϩⲏ ⳾ 10 Ϥⲥ̇ϩⲟⲩⲟⲣⲧ̇ · ⲛ̄ϭⲓ̄ ⲡⲉⲧⲛⲁϫⲟⲟⲥ · ϫⲉ ⲁ
ⲓ̄ⲱⲥⲏⲫ ⲕⲟⲓ̄ⲛⲱⲛⲉⲓ̈ ⲙⲛ̄ ⲧ̄ⲡⲁⲣⲑⲉⲛⲟⲥ · ⲙ̄ⲡⲁⲧⲉⲥⲱ ⲙ̇ⲡⲉⲭ̅ⲥ̅ ⳾ 11 Ⲉⲓ̄ⲧⲁ

[a] ⲉϩⲟⲩ⌈ⲛ⌉⌈ⲉ⌉ⲧⲉⲣⲱ   [b] ⲉ̄ⲣⲟϥ

SAHIDIC FRAGMENTS
OF THE LIFE OF THE VIRGIN.

FRAGMENT I.

......she laid her Son in it, when she had brought Him cf. Lc ii 7
forth in a strange land. 2 But we enquired of our fathers the
apostles, whose sound went out into all the earth and their Ps xviii 5
words reached unto the ends of the world, whilst they were cf. Ro x 18
teaching us our salvation; 3 and they told us the life of this
Virgin, even as they saw with their eyes and became ministers Lc i 2
of the word: 4 since we were taught by them, and seeing with
the eyes is believed more than hearing with the ears[a].

5 But let no evil thought come up into our heart against
the true Queen, 6 as the godless Jews who blasphemed her
with their tongue that ought to be cut off and their mouth
that ought to be closed, whilst she was still living; 7 and
after her death they wished to burn her holy body, because
of their hatred against her. 8 But do not say as the heretics
that a power caught her away, or say as......that she was
taken up in her body into heaven. 9 Cursed is he who shall
say that the Virgin was not born as we are. 10 Cursed is he
who shall say that Joseph had intercourse with the Virgin
before she conceived Christ. 11 Then again after she bare

[a] The words *and seeing with the eyes is believed more than hearing with the ears* are marked in the margin of the MS as a quotation. A similar quotation is found in Evodius' On the Falling asleep of the Virgin (iv 25), translated below [b] The MS has *him*

ⲟⲛ · ⲙ̅ⲛ̅ⲛ̅ⲥⲁ ⲧⲣⲉⲥϫ̅ⲡⲟϥ ϥ̓ⲥ̓ϩⲟⲩⲟⲣⲧ̓ ⲛ̄ϭⲓ ⲡⲉⲧⲛⲁϫⲟⲟⲥ · ϫⲉ ⲛⲧⲁⲩⲁ-
ⲡⲁⲗⲁⲙⲃⲁⲛⲉ ⲛ̄ⲧⲡⲁⲣ⌜ⲑ⌝ⲉⲛⲟⲥ ⲉ̓ⲛ̄ⲙ̄ⲡⲏⲩⲉ̓ ϩⲙ̄ ⲡⲉⲥⲥⲱⲙⲁ · 12ⲁⲗⲗⲁ ·
ⲁⲥⲙⲟⲩ ⲛ̄ⲑⲉ ⲛ̄ⲣⲱⲙⲉ ⲛⲓⲙ · ⲁⲩⲱ̄ ⌜Ⲛ̄⌝ⲧⲁⲩⲱ ⲙ̄ⲙⲟⲥ[a] · ⌜ϩ⌝ⲛ̄ ⲟⲩⲥⲡⲉⲣⲙⲁ
ⲛ̄ⲣⲱⲙⲉ ⲛ̄ⲧⲛ̄ϩⲏ · 13Ⲡ̄ⲗⲏⲛ | ⲥⲱⲧⲙ̄ ⲉ̄ⲣⲟⲓ̈ · ⲧⲁϯⲕ̄ⲡⲉⲧⲉ̓ ⲛⲏⲧⲛ̄ ⲙ̄ⲡϣⲁϫⲉ ·
ⲕⲁⲧⲁ ⲑⲉ ⲉ̓ⲧⲉⲛⲱϣ ϩⲛ̄ ⲛ̄ⲥⲩⲛⲧⲁⲅⲙⲁ ⲛ̄ⲛⲉⲛⲉⲓ̈ⲟⲧⲉ ⲛⲁⲡⲟⲥⲧⲟⲗⲟⲥ ⁘
Ⲥⲱⲧⲙ̄ ⲧⲉⲛⲟⲩ ⲧⲁⲧⲁⲙⲱⲧⲛ̄ : 14Ⲛⲉⲩⲛ ⲟⲩⲣⲱⲙⲉ ⲉⲃⲟⲗ ϩⲛ̄ ⲧⲉϥⲩⲗⲏ
ⲛ̄ⲓⲟⲩⲇⲁ · ⲛ̄ⲙⲉϩϣⲟⲙⲛ̄ⲧ ⲛ̄ϫⲡⲟ ⲉ̄ⲃⲟⲗ ϩⲛ̄ ⲓ̈ⲁⲕⲱⲃ ⲡⲓ̈ⲏ̄ⲗ̄ · Ⲁⲩⲱ̄ ⲉ̓ⲃⲟⲗ
ϩⲙ̄ ⲡ̄ⲅⲉⲛⲟⲥ ⲛ̄ⲇⲁⲩⲉⲓ̈ⲇ ⲡⲣ̄ⲣⲟ · ⲛ̄ϣⲏⲣⲉ ⲛ̄ⲓⲥⲥⲁⲓ̈ · ⲛ̄ⲣⲙ̄ ⲧ̄ⲡⲟⲗⲓ̈ⲥ ⲃⲉⲑ-
ⲗⲉⲉⲙ ⁘ 15Ⲁ ⲡϩⲱⲃ ⲟⲩⲱ̄ⲛ̄ϩ ⲉ̄ⲃⲟⲗ ⲧⲉⲱⲥ ⲙ̄ⲡⲉⲓ̈ⲙⲁ · ϫⲉ ⲛ̄ⲧⲁ ⲧⲡⲁⲣ-
ⲑⲉⲛⲟⲥ ϫⲡⲟ ⲙ̄ⲡⲉⲥ̄ϣⲏⲣ⌜ⲉ⌝ ϩ⌜ⲙ̄⌝ ⲡ̄ⲕⲁϩ ⲛ̄ⲛⲉⲥⲉⲓⲟⲧⲉ · ⲕⲁⲧⲁ ⲑⲉ ⲛ̄ⲧⲁ
Cod. Borg. cxvii p. 5 ⲡϣⲁϫⲉ ⲧⲁⲙⲟⲛ ϫⲉ ⲇⲁⲩⲉⲓ̈ⲇ · ⲟⲩⲉ|ⲃⲟⲗ ϩⲛ̄ ⲃⲉⲑⲗⲉⲉⲙ ⲡⲉ ⁘ 16Ⲛⲉⲩⲛ
ⲟⲩⲣⲱⲙⲉ ⲇⲉ ⲉ̓ⲃⲟⲗ ϩⲙ̄ ⲡ̄ⲅⲉⲛⲟⲥ · ⲁⲩⲱ ⲧ̄ⲛⲟⲩⲛⲉ ⲛ̄ⲇⲁⲩⲉⲓ̈ⲇ · ⲉ̓ⲡⲉϥⲣⲁⲛ
ⲡⲉ ⲓ̈ⲱ̄ⲁ̄ⲕⲓ̈ⲙ ⁘ 17Ⲡⲉⲓⲣⲱⲙⲉ ⲛ̄ⲧⲉⲓ̈ⲙⲓ̈ⲛⲉ · ⲡⲉϥⲣⲁⲛ ⲛ̄ϣⲟⲣⲡ ⲡⲉ ⲕ̓ⲗⲉⲱ-
ⲡⲁⲥ · 18Ⲁ ⲡⲉϥⲉⲓ̈ⲟⲧⲉ ϫⲓ̈ ⲛⲁϥ ⲛⲟⲩⲥϩⲓ̈ⲙⲉ ⲛ̄ⲥⲉⲙⲛⲏ · ⲉⲡⲉⲥⲣⲁⲛ ⲡⲉ
ⲁⲛⲛⲁ · ⲉ̓ⲃⲟⲗ ⲟⲛ ϩⲛ̄ ⲧ̄ⲛⲟⲩⲛⲉ ⲛ̄ⲓⲥⲥⲁⲓ̈ ⲡⲉⲓ̈ⲱⲧ ⲛ̄ⲇⲁ̅ⲇ̅ ⲡ̄ⲣ̄ⲣⲟ ⁘
19Ⲁⲛⲛⲁ ⲇⲉ · ⲛⲉ ⲟⲩⲁϭⲣⲏⲛ ⲧⲉ ⲙ̄ⲡⲉⲥϫ̄ⲡⲉ ϣⲏⲣⲉ ⲉ̓ⲛⲉϩ · ⲟⲩⲇⲉ
ϩⲟⲟⲩⲧ · ⲟⲩⲇⲉ ⲥϩⲓ̈ⲙⲉ ⁘ 20Ⲁⲩⲱ ⲛⲉⲩⲙⲟⲕ̄ϩ̄ ⲛ̄ϩⲏⲧ ⲉ̓ⲙⲁⲧⲉ ⲉⲧⲃⲉ
ⲡⲉⲓ̈ϩⲱⲃ ⲛⲁⲓ̈ · ϫⲉ ϩⲛ̄ⲣⲙ̄ⲙⲁⲟ ⲅⲁⲣ ⲛⲉ · ϩⲙ̄ ⲛ̄ⲛⲟⲩⲃ ⲙⲛ̄ ⲛ̄ϩⲁⲧ ⲙⲛ̄
ⲛ̄ⲧⲃ̄ⲛⲏ · ⲉⲙⲉⲛ ⲡⲉⲧⲛⲁⲕⲗⲏⲣⲟⲛⲟⲙⲉⲓ̈ ⲙ̄ⲙⲟⲟⲩ ⁘ 21Ⲡⲗⲏⲛ · ⲁ ⲡⲉⲩⲟ̄ⲉⲓϣ
ϣⲱⲡⲉ · ⲉⲧⲣⲉⲩⲡⲱⲧ ⲉϩⲣⲁⲓ̈ ⲉ̓ⲃⲉⲑⲗⲉⲉⲙ · ⲉⲛⲧⲟⲩϯ ⲛ̄ⲛⲉⲩⲣⲉⲙⲛⲧ ·
ⲙ̄ⲡϫⲟⲉⲓⲥ · ⲕⲁⲧⲁ ⲡⲛⲟⲙⲟⲥ ⲙ̄ⲙⲱⲩⲥⲏⲥ ⁘ 22Ⲁⲩⲱ̄ ⲡⲉϥϩⲏⲛ ⲉϩⲟⲩⲛ ·
ⲛ̄ϭⲓ ⲡⲡⲁⲥⲭⲁ[b] ⲛ̄ⲛⲓ̈ⲟⲩⲇⲁⲓ̈ · ⲧⲉⲥⲕⲩⲛⲏⲛⲡⲏⲅⲓ̈ⲁ ⁘ 23Ⲛⲧⲉⲣⲉ ⲡⲗⲁⲟⲥ ⲇⲉ
ⲥⲱⲟⲩϩ ⲉⲛ̄ⲣ̄ⲡⲉ · ⲉ̓ϣⲱⲱⲧ ⲙ̄ⲡⲡⲁⲥⲭⲁ ⁘ Ⲁⲛⲛⲁ ϩⲱⲱⲥ · ⲙⲛ̄ ⲓ̈ⲱ̄ⲁ̄ⲕⲓ̈ⲙ ·
ⲁⲩⲡⲱⲧ ⲉϩⲣⲁⲓ ⲉⲃⲉⲑⲗⲉⲉⲙ̓[c] · 24ϫⲉ ⲧⲥⲩⲛⲏⲑⲓ̈ⲁ ⲇⲉ ⲛ̄ⲛⲉⲧϩⲙ̄ ⲡⲕⲱⲧⲉ
p. 6 ⲛ̄ⲑⲓ̈ⲗⲏ̄ⲙ̄ ⲉⲥⲱⲟⲩϩ ⲉⲟⲩⲱⲙ ⲙ̓ⲡⲡⲁⲥ⌜ⲭⲁ ⁘⌝[d] | 25Ⲁ ⲓ̈ⲱ̄ⲁ̄ⲕⲓ̈ⲙ · ⲁϥϫⲓ̈
ⲛⲁⲛⲛⲁ · ⲁⲩⲡⲱⲧ · ⲉϩⲣⲁⲓ̈ ⲉⲛ̄ⲣ̄ⲡⲉ ⁘ Ⲛⲉϩⲓ̈ⲟⲙⲉ ⲙⲛ̄ ⲛⲉⲩⲉ̓ⲣⲏⲩ · ⲛⲉϩⲟⲟⲩⲧ
ⲙⲛ̄ ⲛⲉⲩⲉ̓ⲣⲏⲩ ⁘ 26Ⲉⲣϣⲁⲛ ⲁⲛⲛⲁ ϩⲱⲛ ⲉ̓ϩⲟⲩⲛ ⲉⲩⲥ̓ϩⲓ̈ⲙⲉ · ϣⲁⲥϩ̄ⲃⲁⲣⲃⲉⲣ
ⲙ̄ⲙⲟⲥ ⲉ̓ⲛⲟⲩⲏ̓ · 27ϫⲉ ⲙⲡⲉⲣϫⲱϩ ⲉ̄ⲣⲟⲓ̈ ϫⲉ ⲛ̄ⲧⲉ ⲟⲩⲁϭⲣⲏⲛ · ϫⲉ ⲛ̄ⲛⲉ
ⲛⲟⲩϣⲱⲡⲉ ⲛ̄ϣⲱ̓ⲛⲉ ⲉ̓ⲣⲟⲛ · ⲛ̄ⲧⲉ ⲛⲉⲛϩⲟⲟⲩⲧ ⲙⲉⲥⲧⲱⲛ · ϫⲉ ⲁ̓ⲛⲉⲣⲁ-

[a] ⌜Ⲛ̄⌝ⲧⲁⲩⲱ̄ⲙ̄ⲙⲟⲥ [b] ⲡⲁⲥⲭⲁ [c] Punctum sup ⲙ ut vid
[d] ⲙ̓ⲡⲉⲥ⌜ⲭⲁ ⁘⌝

Him, cursed is he who shall say that the Virgin was taken
up into the heavens in her body. 12 But she died like all
men, and was conceived by man's seed as we are. 13 But
hear me and I will shew you the word, even as we read in
the works of our fathers the apostles. Hear now and I will
tell you.

14 There was a man from the tribe of Judah, the third
born[a] from Jacob *who is* Israel; and from the offspring of David
the king, the son of Jesse the citizen of Bethlehem. 15 The
matter is manifest thus far that the Virgin bare her son in
the land of her fathers, even as the word told us that David
was[b] from Bethlehem. 16 Now there was a man from the Ap xxii
offspring and the root of David, whose name was[b] Joakim. 16*
17 *As for* such a man, his name formerly was Cleopas[c]. 18 His
parents took for him an honourable wife, whose name was[b]
Anna, also of the root of Jesse the father of David the king. cf. Is xi
19 And Anna was barren, she never bare a child, neither male 10*; Mt i 6
nor female. 20 And they were very sad of heart because of cf. 1 Sa i
this thing; for they were[d] rich in gold and silver and cattle, 6* cf. Ge xiii
with no one to inherit them. 2; xv 3

21 But the time came for them to go up[e] to Bethlehem,
to give their tithes to the Lord according to the law of cf. Lc ii 22
Moses. 22 And the passover of the Jews was at hand, *even* Jn ii 13*
the feast of tabernacles. 23 Now when the people was cf. vi 4*; vii 2*
gathered together to the temple to sacrifice the passover,
Anna also and Joakim went up[f] to Bethlehem. 24 For it was[b]
the custom of those round about Jerusalem to gather together cf. Ro xv
to eat the passover. 25 Joakim took Anna, and they went up[f] 19*
into the temple, the women by themselves and the men by
themselves.

26 When Anna drew nigh unto a woman, she would thrust
her far away, *saying*, 27 Touch me not, for thou art barren,
lest thy sickness pass over to us, and our husbands hate

[a] According to the narrative in Genesis Judah is the fourth son of Jacob: cf. Ge xxix 32—35 [b] Lit. *is* [c] Or *his first name was* (lit. *is*) *Cleopas* [d] Lit. *are* [e] Or *to go* [f] Or *went*

ⲧϣⲏⲣⲉ ⲛ̇ⲧⲉϩⲏ ⁘ 28 Ϩⲱⲙⲉⲟⲥ ⲟⲛ ⲛⲉϩⲟⲟⲩⲧ · ⲛⲉⲩϫⲱ ⲙ̄ⲡⲉⲓ̈ϣⲁϫⲉ
ⲛⲟⲩⲱⲧ ⲉ̄ϩⲟⲩⲛ ⲉϩⲣⲁϥ ⲛ̄ⲓ̈ⲱ̇ⲁ̇ⲕⲓⲙ ⁘ 29 ⲁⲩⲱ ⲉⲣϣⲁⲛ ⲓ̈ⲱⲁⲕⲓⲙ · ⲥⲱⲧⲙ̄
⸢ⲉ̇⸣ⲛⲉⲓ̈ϫⲡⲓⲟ̄ ⲛ̇ⲧⲉⲓ̈ⲙⲓ̈ⲛⲉ · ϣⲁϥϯ ⲙ̇ⲡⲉϥϩⲟ ⲉ̄ⲡⲉⲥⲏⲧ ⲉⲧⲉϥϣ̄ⲧⲏⲛ ⲛ̄ϩⲣ̄ⲓ̈ⲙⲉ ·
ⲛ̄ϥⲱϣ ⲉ̇ⲃⲟⲗ ⲉϥϫⲱ ⲙ̄ⲙⲟⲥ · 30 ϫⲉ ⲡⲛⲟⲩⲧⲉ ⲡⲉⲕⲃⲁⲗ ⲛⲁⲩ · ⲁⲩⲱ
ⲡⲉⲕⲙⲁⲁϫⲉ ⲥⲱⲧⲙ̄ ⲉ̄ⲡⲉⲓ̈ϫⲡⲓⲟ ⲛ̄ⲧⲉⲓ̈ⲙⲓ̈ⲛⲉ · ⲉ̇ⲧⲟⲩϯ ⲙ̄ⲙⲟⲟⲩ ⲛⲁⲓ̈ · ⲙⲛ̄
ⲧⲁⲉ̄ⲃ̄ⲓⲏⲛ ⲛ̄ⲥ̄ϩⲓ̈ⲙⲉ · 31 ⲁⲗⲗⲁ ⲡⲁⲛⲧⲱⲥ ⲡⲉⲛⲛⲟⲃⲉ ⲡⲉ · ⲉⲛϣⲟⲟⲡ ϩⲙ̄
ⲡⲓ̈ⲙ̄ⲕⲁϩ · ⲡⲁⲣⲁ ⲡⲉⲧⲉ ⲛⲱⲛ ⲧⲏⲣⲟⲩ ⲡⲉ ⁘ 32 Ⲟⲩⲟⲓ̈ ⲛⲁⲛ · ⲟⲩⲛⲟϭ ⲡⲉ
ⲡⲉⲛϩⲛ̇ⲃ̇ⲉ · ⲡⲁⲣⲁ ⲡⲉⲓ̈ⲗⲁⲟⲥ ⲧⲏⲣϥ̄ ⲉⲩⲛⲟϭⲛⲉϭ ⲙ̄ⲙⲟⲛ ⲛ̄ⲧⲉⲓ̈ϩⲉ
p. ζ ⲧⲏⲣⲥ̇ ⁘ 33 Ⲡⲛⲟⲩⲧⲉ ⲙ̄ⲡⲉⲣⲟⲃϣⲉⲕ ⲉⲡⲉⲛⲥⲟⲡⲥ · ⲙⲛ̄ ⲡⲉⲛ|ⲛⲟϭⲛⲉϭ ⁘
34 Ⲛⲁⲓ̈ ⲙⲉⲛ ⲛⲉϯⲡⲉ ⲙ̇ⲙⲟⲟⲩ · ⲡⲉⲣⲉ ⲡⲉⲓ̈ⲙⲁⲕⲁⲣⲓ̈ⲟⲥ ϫⲱ ⲙⲙⲟⲟⲩ ·
ϣⲁⲛⲧⲟⲩϫⲉⲕ ⲛ̇ⲡⲁⲥⲭⲁ ⲉ̇ⲃⲟⲗ ϩⲉⲛ ϩⲛ̄ⲗⲩⲡⲏ · ⲙⲛ̄ ϩⲛ̄ⲁϣⲁϩⲟⲙ ·
ⲉⲩⲛⲟϭⲛⲉϭ ⲙ̄ⲙⲟⲟⲩ ⁘ 35 Ⲁⲩⲱ̇ ⲁⲩⲡⲱⲧ ⲉ̇ⲡⲉⲩⲏ̇ⲓ ϩⲙ̄ ⲟⲩⲛⲟϭ ⲛ̄ⲗⲩⲡⲏ
ⲙⲛ̄ ⲟⲩⲱⲗⲥ̄ ⲛ̄ϩⲏⲧ · ⲉⲣⲉ ⲡϫⲟⲉⲓ̈ⲥ ⲟ ⲛⲛⲁϣⲧⲉ ⲛⲁⲩ ⁘ 36 Ⲁⲩⲱ̇ ⲁⲩⲡⲱⲧ
ⲉⲧⲥⲩⲛⲁⲅⲱⲅⲏ · ⲛ̄ⲥⲟⲩⲁ ⲙ̄ⲡⲉⲃⲟⲧ ⲡⲁⲣⲙⲟⲩⲧⲉ · ⲁⲩⲱ ⲁⲩⲡⲱⲧ ⲉⲡⲉⲩⲏⲓ̈
ⲛ̇ⲥⲟⲩⲙⲛ̄ⲧⲏ ⲙ̄ⲡⲁⲣⲙⲟⲩⲧⲉ ⁘ 37 Ϩⲣⲁⲓ̈ ⲇⲉ ϩⲙ̄ ⲧ̄ⲕⲉⲣⲟⲙⲡⲉ ⲉⲧⲛⲛⲏⲩ ·
ⲁϥⲛⲁⲩ ⲛ̄ϭⲓ ⲓ̈ⲱⲁⲕⲓ̈ⲙ ⲉⲩϩⲟⲣⲟⲙⲁ ⲛ̄ⲧⲉⲩϣⲏ · ϩⲁⲑⲏ ⲛ̄ⲣ̄ⲙⲉ ⲛ̄ϩⲟⲟⲩ ·
ⲉⲧⲣⲉ ⲁⲛⲛⲁ ⲱ̇ · ⲛⲧ̇ⲡⲁⲣⲑⲉⲛⲟⲥ ⁘ 38 Ⲛ̄ⲑⲉ ⲉϣϫⲉ ϥ̄ϩⲓ̈ϫⲛ̄ ⲟⲩⲡⲏⲅⲏ
ⲙ̇ⲙⲟⲟⲩ · ⲉⲓ̈ⲥ ⲟⲩϭⲣⲟⲟⲙⲡⲉ ⲛⲟⲩⲱ̇ⲃϣ · ⲉⲥⲟⲩⲏϩ ϩⲓ̈ϫⲛ̄ ⲟⲩⲡⲩⲅⲏ ⲙ̄ⲙⲟⲟⲩ ·
ⲉⲥⲥⲁⲙⲟⲟⲩ ⲉ̇ⲃⲟⲗ ⲛ̄ϩⲏⲧⲥ̄ ⁘ 39 Ⲁⲥϩⲱⲗ ⲛ̇ⲧⲉⲩⲛⲟⲩ · ⲁⲥⲟⲩⲱϩ ϩⲓ̈ϫⲛ̄
ⲧ̄ⲁⲡⲏ[a] ⲛ̄ⲓ̈ⲱ̇ⲁⲕⲓ̈ⲙ · ⲁⲥϭⲱ ⲉⲥⲕⲱⲧⲉ ϩⲓ̈ϫⲱϥ ⁘ 40 Ⲁⲩⲱ̄ ⲁϥⲧⲱⲟⲩⲛ ⲛ̄ϭⲓ̈
ⲓⲱ̄ⲁⲕⲓ̈ⲙ · ⲁϥϫⲱ ⲙⲛ̄ϩⲟⲣⲟⲙⲁ · ⲉⲁⲛⲛⲁ ⲧⲉϥⲥ̇ϩⲓ̈ⲙⲉ · ⲁⲥⲉⲣϣ̄ⲡⲏⲣⲉ
p. η ⲉ̄ⲙⲁⲧⲉ · 41 Ⲛⲧⲉⲣⲉⲥⲥⲱⲕ ϩⲱⲱⲥ ϩⲁ ⲛ̄ϩⲓ̈ⲡⲛⲏϥ ⲛ̄ⲧⲉⲓ̈ⲟⲩϣⲏ | ⲛⲟⲩⲱⲧ ·
Ⲁⲩⲧ̄ⲥⲁⲃⲟⲥ ⲟⲛ ⲉⲩϩⲱⲣⲟⲙⲁ · 42 Ⲛ̄ⲑⲉ ⲉϣϫⲉ ⲛⲉⲩⲛⲁⲩ ⲉⲩϣⲏⲛ ⲉϥⲣⲏⲧ
ϩⲓ̈ϫⲛ̄ ⲛⲉⲥⲡⲟⲧⲟⲩ ⲛⲟⲩⲡⲩⲅⲏ ⲙ̄ⲙⲟⲟⲩ · ⲉ̇ⲣⲉ ⲟⲩϭⲣⲟⲟⲙⲡⲉ ⲛⲟⲩⲱ̄ⲃⲉϣ
ϩⲙ̄ ⲛ̇ϩⲏⲧ ⲙ̄ⲡϣⲏⲛ ⁘ 43 Ⲁⲥϩⲱⲗ ϩⲙ̄ ⲡ̄ϣⲏⲛ · ⲁⲥⲟⲩⲱϩ ϩⲓ̈ϫⲛ̄[b] ⲛⲉϭⲓϫ
ⲛⲁⲛⲛⲁ · Ⲁⲩⲱ̄ ⲁⲥⲟⲩⲱϩ ϩⲓ̈ϫⲉⲛ ⲕⲟⲩⲛⲥ̄ · ⲁⲥϭⲱ ⲉⲥϯⲡⲉⲓ̈ ⲉ̇ⲣⲱⲥ
ⲛⲁⲛⲛⲁ ⲛⲟⲩⲛⲟϭ ⲛ̄ⲛⲁⲩ ⁘ 44 Ⲁⲥⲧⲱⲟⲩⲛ ⲁⲥϫⲱ ⲙ̄ⲡⲉⲥϩⲟⲣⲟⲙⲁ ⲉⲓ̈ⲱ̇-
ⲁⲕⲓ̈ⲙ ⁘ 45 Ϩⲣⲁⲓ̈ ⲇⲉ ϩⲙ̄ ⲥⲟⲩⲁ ⲙ̄ⲡⲉⲃⲟⲧ ⲡⲁⲣⲙⲟⲩⲧⲉ · ⲁⲥⲱ ⲛ̇ϭⲓ
ⲁⲛⲛⲁ · ⲉ̇ⲃⲟⲗ ϩⲙ̄ ⲡⲉⲥⲡⲉⲣⲙⲁ ⲛ̄ⲓ̈ⲱⲁⲕⲓ̈ⲙ ⁘ 46 ⲙⲁⲣⲟⲩϫⲓ̈ϣⲓ̈ⲡⲉ ⲧⲉⲛⲟⲩ ·

[a] ϩⲓ̈ϫⲛ̄ⲧⲁⲡⲏ   [b] ϩⲓ̈ϫ̄·ⲛ

us, because we have become childless as thou. 28 In the
same manner also the men were saying the like words
against Joakim. 29 And when Joakim heard such taunts
as these, he would cover his face with[a] his raiment and
weep and cry out, saying, 30 God, Thine eyes see and Thine
ears hear such taunts as these, which they bring against me
and my unhappy wife. 31 But altogether our sins, as we are
in these griefs, are more than *those of* all that belong to us.
32 Woe to us! Our mourning is greater than *that of* all this
people, as we are reproached in all this manner. 33 God,
forget not our supplication and our reproach. 34 These and
the like things these blessed ones were saying, until they
completed the passover in sorrow[b] and groanings, being re-
proached. 35 And they went to their house in great sorrow
and distress of heart, the Lord being their protector[c]. 36 And
they went to the synagogue on the first of the month
Parmoute, and they went to their house on the fifteenth
of Parmoute.

37 Now in the coming year also[d] Joakim saw a vision in
the night, forty days before Anna conceived the Virgin.
38 As though he were[e] by a spring of water, and behold a
white dove sitting by a spring of water, drinking water from
it. 39 It flew straightway and sat on the head of Joakim and
kept going round about him. 40 And Joakim arose and told
the vision to Anna his wife, and she wondered greatly.
41 When she herself fell asleep[f] on this same night, she also
was shewn a vision. 42 As though a tree were seen[g] planted
by the banks of a spring of water, a white dove being in the
midst[h] of the tree. 43 It flew from the tree and sat on the
hands of Anna; and it sat on her bosom, and kept kissing
the mouth of Anna a great while. 44 She arose and told her
vision to Joakim.

45 And on the first of the month Parmoute Anna con-
ceived from the seed of Joakim. 46 Let now the godless and

[a] Lit. *would put his face down into* [b] Lit. *sorrows* [c] Or *protection*
[d] Or *in the next year that came* [e] Lit. *is* [f] Lit. *came* (or *was borne*) *under sleep* [g] Lit. *they were seeing a tree* [h] Lit. *heart*

ⲛ̄ϭⲓ ⲛⲓⲟⲩⲇⲁⲓ̈ ⲛⲁⲧⲛⲟⲩⲧⲉ · ⲁⲩⲱ̀ ⲛⲁⲑⲏⲧ · ⲛⲁⲓ̈ ⲉⲧϯ ⲛⲟⲩⲧⲱⲗⲙ̄
ⲉⲧⲡⲁⲣⲑⲉⲛⲟⲥ ⲉⲧⲟⲩⲁⲁⲃ ⲙⲁⲣⲓ̈ⲁ ⁘ [47]Ⲗⲓ̄ⲡⲱⲛ · ⲡⲉϥϩⲏⲛ ⲉϩⲟⲩⲛ ⲛ̄ϭⲓ
ⲡⲡⲁⲥⲭⲁ ⲛ̄ⲛⲓ̈ⲟⲩⲇⲁⲓ̈ ⁘ Ⲁⲩⲡⲱⲧ ⲟⲛ ⲉ̀ⲑⲓ̈ⲗⲏⲙ̄ · [48]ⲁⲩⲛⲁⲩ ⲛ̄ϭⲓ
ⲛⲉϩⲓ̈ⲟⲙⲉ ⲛⲁⲣⲭⲉⲱⲛ · ϫⲉ ⲁⲥⲱ · ⲁⲩⲣⲁϣⲉ ⲙ̄ⲙⲁⲥ ⁘ [49]Ⲁⲥⲛⲁⲩ ⲟⲛ
ⲉⲩϩⲟⲣⲟⲙⲁ ⲛ̄ⲧⲉⲩϣⲏ · ϩⲱⲥ ⲛ̄ⲧⲁⲥϯ ⲙ̄ⲡⲉⲥϩⲙ̄ⲙⲏⲧ ⲉϩⲟⲩⲛ ⲉ̀ⲡⲣ̄ⲡⲉ
ⲙ̄ⲡⲉⲟⲩⲏⲏⲃ ⲙ̄ⲡⲛⲟⲩⲧⲉ ⁘ Ϩⲱⲥⲇⲉ · ⲛⲉⲣⲉ ⲛⲉⲟⲩⲏⲏⲃ ⲙⲟⲩⲧⲉ ⲉ̄ⲣⲟⲥ ⁘
p. 9 [50]Ⲉⲓ̈ⲥ ⲟⲩⲁⲅⲅⲉⲗⲟⲥ ⲁϥϫⲓ̈ ⲙ̄ⲡⲓⲛⲉ ⲛ̄ⲟⲩⲣⲱⲙⲉ · ⲁϥ|ϣⲁϫⲉ ⲙⲛ̄ ⲁⲛⲛⲁ
ⲉϥϫⲱ ⲙ̄ⲙⲟⲥ · [51]ϫⲉ ϫⲡⲟ ⲙ̄ⲙⲟ ⲛ̄ⲧⲉϭⲙ̄ϭⲟⲙ ⁘ Ⲉⲓ̈ⲥ ϩⲏⲏⲧⲉ · ⲧⲉⲣⲛⲁⲱ̀
ⲛ̄ⲧⲉϫⲡⲟ ⲛⲟⲩϣⲉⲉ̀ⲣⲉ · ⲙⲟⲩⲧⲉ ⲉ̀ⲛⲉⲥⲣⲁⲛ ϫⲉ ⲙⲁⲣⲓ̈ⲁ ⁘ [52]Ⲥⲁϩⲱⲱⲓ̄
ⲉⲃⲟⲗ ⲙ̄ⲡⲙⲁ ⲛⲉⲛⲕⲟⲧⲕ ⲛ̄ⲓ̈ⲱ̄ⲁⲕⲓ̈ⲙ · ⲟⲩⲇⲉ ⲙ̄ⲡⲉⲣⲟⲩⲉⲙ ⲗⲁⲁⲩ ⲛ̄ⲧⲱⲗⲙ̄ ·
ϣⲁⲛⲧⲉⲧⲥⲉⲛⲕⲟ ⲛ̄ⲧϣ̄ⲉⲉⲣⲉϣⲏⲙ ϩⲛ̄ ⲟⲩⲧⲃ̄ⲃⲟ · [53]Ⲁⲩⲱ̀ ⲁ ⲡⲁⲅⲅⲉⲗⲟⲥ
ⲥ̀ⲙⲟⲩ ⲉⲁⲛⲛⲁ · ⲉ̀ⲣⲉ ⲛⲉⲟⲩⲏⲏⲃ ⲟⲩⲱ̀ϩⲙ̄ ⲛ̄ⲥⲱϥ · ϫⲉ ϩⲁⲙⲏⲛ ⁘ [54]Ⲁⲛⲛⲁ
ⲇⲉ · ⲛ̄ⲧⲉⲣⲉⲥⲧⲱⲟⲩⲛ ⲉ̀ⲃⲟⲗ ϩⲙ̄ ⲡ̄ϩⲟⲣⲟⲙⲁ · ⲁⲥϫⲟⲟⲥ ⲉ̀ⲓ̈ⲱ̀ⲁⲕⲓ̈ⲙ
ⲡⲉⲥϩⲁⲓ̈ ⁘ Ⲁⲩⲱ̀ ⲁⲩϯⲉ̀ⲟⲟⲩ ⲙ̄ⲡⲛⲟⲩⲧⲉ ⲙ̄ⲡⲓ̈ⲏ̄ⲗ ⁘ [55]Ⲛⲧⲉⲣⲟⲩϫⲱⲕ ⲇⲉ
ⲉ̀ⲃⲟⲗ ⲛ̀ϭⲓ ⲛⲉϩⲟⲟⲩ ⲙ̀ⲡϣⲙ̄ϣⲉ · ⲁⲩⲕⲟⲧⲟⲩ ⲉⲡⲉⲩⲏⲓ̈ · ⲉⲩϣⲟⲟⲡ ϩⲛ̄
ⲟⲩⲛⲟϭ ⲛ̄ⲣⲁϣⲉ ⲉ̄ϫⲙ̄ ⲡⲉϩⲙⲟⲧ ⲛ̄ⲧⲁϥϣⲱⲡⲉ ⲛⲁⲩ ⁘ [56]Ⲛ̄ⲧⲉⲣⲟⲩϫⲱⲕ
ⲇⲉ ⲉ̀ⲃⲟⲗ ⲛ̄ϭⲓ ⲛⲉϩⲟⲟⲩ ⲉⲧⲣⲉⲥⲙⲓ̈ⲥⲉ · ⲁⲥϫ̄ⲡⲟ ⲛⲟⲩϣⲉⲉ̀ⲣⲉ ⲛ̀ⲥϩⲓ̈ⲙⲉ ·
ⲁⲥⲙⲟⲩⲧⲉ ⲉ̄ⲛⲉⲥⲣⲁⲛ ϫⲉ ⲙⲁⲣⲓ̈ⲁ · ⲕⲁⲧⲁ ⲑⲉ ⲛ̄ⲧⲁⲩⲧⲟⲩⲛⲓ̈ⲁⲧⲥ̄ ⲉ̀ⲃⲟⲗ
ϩⲙ̄ ⲡ̄ϩⲟⲣⲟⲙⲁ · ⲉⲧⲣⲉⲥⲙⲟⲩⲧⲉ ⲉ̄ⲣⲟⲥ ⲙ̄ⲡⲉⲓ̈ⲣⲁⲛ ϫⲉ ⲙⲁⲣⲓ̈ⲁ ⁘ [57]Ⲡⲉϩⲟⲟⲩ
ⲛ̄ⲧⲁⲩϫⲡⲟ ⲛ̄ⲧⲡⲁⲣⲑⲉⲛⲟⲥ ⲛ̄ϩⲏⲧϥ̄ ⲡⲉ ⲥⲟⲩⲙⲛ̄ⲧⲏ ⲙ̄ⲡⲉⲃⲟⲧ ϩⲁⲑⲱⲣ ·
ⲕⲁⲧⲁ ⲡⲉⲣⲉⲙⲛ̄ⲕⲏⲙⲉ ⁘ [58]Ⲁⲗⲗⲁ ⲙⲡⲉⲣⲧ̀ⲣⲉ ⲡⲉϩⲓ̈ⲇⲓ̈ⲱⲧⲏⲥ · ⲱⲛ|
p. 10 ⲛ̀ⲡⲉⲃⲟⲧ · ⲛ̄ⲥⲉϫⲟⲟⲥ · ϫⲉ ⲙⲡⲉ ⲯⲓ̄ⲥ ⲛⲉⲃⲟⲧ ϫⲱⲕ ⲉ̄ⲃⲟⲗ · ⲙⲛ̄ ⲕⲉⲙⲛ̄-
ⲧⲁϥⲧⲉ ⲛ̄ϩⲟⲟⲩ · ⲙ̄ⲡⲏ ⁘ [59]Ⲁⲗⲗⲁ · ⲉⲛϣⲁⲛⲱⲡ ⲛⲧⲉⲓ̈ϩⲉ · ⲉ̀ϭⲉⲛ ⲥⲟⲩⲁ
ⲙⲡⲁⲣⲙ̄ϩⲁⲧ . ϣⲁ ⲥⲟⲩⲁ ⲙ̄ⲡⲁⲣⲙⲟⲩⲧⲉ · ⲟⲩⲉ̀ⲃⲟⲧ ⲡⲉ · Ⲁⲩⲱ̀ ⲉϭⲉⲛ
ⲥⲟⲩⲁ ⲙ̄ⲡⲁⲣⲙⲟⲩⲧⲉ · ϣⲁ ⲥⲟⲩⲁ ⲙ̄ⲡⲁϣⲟⲛⲥ̄ · ⲥ̀ⲛⲁⲩ ⲛⲉⲃⲟⲧ ⲡⲉ ·
[60]ϩⲁⲡⲗⲱⲥ ϫⲉ ⲛⲛⲉⲛⲧⲁϣⲉ ⲛ̀ϣⲁϫⲉ ⲉ̀ⲛⲉϩⲟⲩⲟ̀ · ϫⲓ̈ⲛ ⲥⲟⲩⲁ ⲙⲡⲁⲣⲙ̄ϩⲁⲧ
ϣⲁ ⲥⲟⲩⲁ ⲛ̄ϩⲁⲑⲱⲣ · ϣⲙⲟⲩⲛ ⲛⲉⲃⲟⲧ ⁘ Ⲁⲩⲱ̀ ⲛ̀ⲕⲉⲙⲛ̄ⲧⲁϥⲧⲉ ⲛ̄ϩⲟⲟⲩ
ⲁⲥϭⲁⲛⲟⲩ ϩⲙ̄ ⲡⲙⲁϩⲯⲓ̄ⲥ ⲛⲉⲃⲟⲧ · [61]Ⲁ ⲁ̄ⲛⲛⲁ · ⲧ̄ⲥⲉⲙⲛⲏ · ϫ̄ⲡⲟ
ⲙ̄ⲙⲁⲣⲓ̈ⲁ ⲧⲉⲣⲱ · ⲧⲉϭⲣⲟⲟⲙⲡⲉ ⲛ̄ⲁⲧⲧⲱⲗⲙ̄ ⁘ [62]Ⲱⲛⲧⲱⲥ · ⲧⲉⲛⲙ̄ⲡϣⲁ
ⲛ̀ⲥⲱⲟⲩϩ ⲉ̀ϩⲟⲩⲛ · ϩⲙ̄ ⲡⲉⲓϩⲟⲟⲩ ⲧⲉⲣⲟⲙⲡⲉ · ⲉ̀ⲧⲉ ⲡ̄ϩⲟⲩⲙⲓ̈ⲥⲉ ⲡⲉ ·
ⲛ̄ⲧⲉⲣⲱ ⲛ̄ⲛⲉϩⲓ̈ⲟⲙⲉ ⲧⲏⲣⲟⲩ · ⲙⲁⲣⲓ̈ⲁ ⲧ̄ⲡⲁⲣⲑⲉⲛⲟⲥ · ⲧⲛ̄ⲧⲁⲥϩⲱⲃⲥ̄

foolish Jews be ashamed, who cast a stain on the holy Virgin
Mary. [47]But the passover of the Jews was at hand, and Jn II 13*
they went again to Jerusalem. [48]The old women saw that cf. XI 55
she had[a] conceived, and they rejoiced with her. [49]She saw
again a vision in the night; as though she had brought[b] her
tithes into the temple of the priests of God, so that the
priests were calling her. [50]Behold, an angel took the likeness
of a man and spake with Anna, saying, [51]Take courage and
be strong. Behold thou shalt conceive and bring forth a cf. Lc I 31
daughter. Call her name Mary. [52]Depart from the bed of
Joakim and eat not anything unclean[c], until thou wean the cf. Jud XIII
child in purity. [53]And the angel blessed Anna, the priests 4*, 7*
answering him, Amen. [54]And when Anna had arisen from the
vision, she spake to Joakim her husband, and they glorified Mt XV 31*
the God of Israel. [55]Now when the days of the ministration cf. Lc I 23
were fulfilled, they returned to their house, being in great
joy for the grace which was *shewn* to them. [56]And when the cf. Lc II 6,
days were fulfilled that she should be delivered, she brought 7
forth a daughter; and she called her name Mary, even as
she was warned by the vision to call her by this name cf. Mt II
Mary. 22

[57]The day whereon the Virgin was brought forth was[d]
the fifteenth of the month Hathor according to the Egyptians.
[58]But let not the unskilful reckon the months and
say that nine months were not fulfilled and other fourteen
days of that *month*[e]. [59]But if we reckon in this wise: from
the first of Paremhat to the first of Parmoute, there is a
month; and from the first of Parmoute to the first of
Pashons, there are two months. [60]In a word, that we may
not prolong the discourse[f] too much, from the first of
Paremhat to the first of Hathor, *there are* eight months;
and the fourteen days also she received in the ninth
month. [61]*So* Anna the honourable brought forth Mary the
Queen, the stainless Dove. [62]Truly we are worthily[g]
gathered together every year on this day, which is the
birthday of the Queen of all women, of Mary the Virgin

[a] Lit. *has* [b] Lit. *as having brought* [c] Lit. *any stain* [d] Lit. *is* [e] See note [f] Lit. *the word* [g] Lit. *we are worthy to be*

ⲉⲛϣⲓ̈ⲛⲉ ⲛ̄ⲛⲉⲩϩⲁ[a] · ⲁⲥϯ ⲛ̄ⲣⲁϣⲉ ⲛ̄ⲛⲉϩⲓ̈ⲟ̈ⲙⲉ ⲧⲏⲣⲟⲩ ⳾ 63ⲙ̄ⲛ̄ⲛ̄ⲥⲱⲥ · ⲁ ⲇⲁ̅ⲇ̅ ⲉⲓ̈ ⲉⲧⲙⲏⲧⲉ · ⲙⲛ̄ ⲧⲉϥⲕⲓ̈ⲑⲁⲣⲁ · ⲁϥϩⲱⲥ ⲉⲁⲛⲛⲁ · ⲙⲛ̄ ⲓ̈ⲱⲁⲕⲓ̈ⲙ ⲉϥϫⲱ ⲙ̄ⲙⲟⲥ · 64ϫⲉ ⲁⲛⲧⲉⲗⲏⲗ · ⲁⲛⲟⲩⲛⲟϥ · ⲉⲛⲙⲁ ⲛ̄ⲛⲉϩⲟⲟⲩ ⲛ̄ⲧⲁⲕⲟⲑⲃ̄ⲃ̄ⲓ̈ⲟⲛ · 65ϩⲙ̄ ⲛ̄ⲧⲣⲉ ⲡⲁ|(p. ια)ϩⲏⲧ ⲙ̄ⲕⲁϩ · ⲁⲕϫⲁⲥⲧ[b] ϩⲓ̈ϫⲉⲛ ⲟⲩⲡⲉⲧⲣⲁ · ⲁⲕϫⲓ̈ⲙⲟⲓ̈ⲧ ϩⲏⲧ · ⲁⲕⲉⲛⲧ ⲉⲡⲟⲩⲱϣⲥ̄ ⲉ̀ⲃⲟⲗ ⳾ 66ⲁⲕⲧⲁⲗⲟ ⲛ̄ϩⲛ̄ⲣⲱⲙⲉ ϩⲓ̈ϫⲉⲛ ⲛⲉⲛⲁ̀ⲛⲏⲩⲉ̀ ⳾ ⲁⲕⲉⲛⲧⲉⲛ ⲉⲃⲟⲗ ϩⲓⲧⲛ̄ ⲟⲩⲕⲱϩⲧ̄ ⲙⲛ̄ ⲟⲩⲙⲟⲟⲩ ⳾ 67ⲛⲁⲓ̈ ⲙⲛ̄ ⲛⲉⲓ̈ⲕⲉⲕⲟⲟⲩⲉ · ⲁ ⲇⲁ̅ⲇ̅ ϫⲟⲟⲩ · ⲙ̄ⲡⲉϩⲟⲟⲩ ⲛ̄ⲧⲁⲩϫⲡⲟ ⲛ̄ⲧⲡⲁⲣⲑⲉⲛⲟⲥ ⲛ̄ϩⲏⲧϥ̄ ⳾ 68ⲁⲩⲥⲱⲧⲙ̄ ⲛ̄ϭⲓ ⲛⲉⲥⲣⲙ̄ⲣⲁⲩⲏ · ⲁⲩⲉⲓ̈ⲛⲉ ⲛⲁⲥ ⲛ̄ⲛⲉⲩⲧⲁⲓ̈ⲟ ⳾ ⲛⲉϩⲟⲟⲩⲧ ϩⲱⲟⲩ ⲁⲩⲉⲓ̈ⲛⲉ ⲛ̄ⲛⲉⲩⲧⲁⲓ̈ⲟ ⲛ̄ⲓ̈ⲱⲁⲕⲓ̈ⲙ ⳾ 69ⲁⲩⲉⲣ ⲥⲁϣϥ̄ ⲛ̄ϩⲟⲟⲩ · ⲉⲩⲟⲩⲱⲙ ⲉⲩⲥⲱ · ⲉⲩⲉⲩⲫⲣⲁⲛⲉ · ⲉϫⲙ̄ ⲛ̄ϩⲱⲃ̄ ⲛ̄ⲧⲁ ⲡⲛⲟⲩⲧⲉ ⲁⲁϥ ⲙ̄ⲙⲁⲩ · ⲉⲧⲃⲉ ⲓ̈ⲱⲁⲕⲓ̈ⲙ · ⲙⲛ̄ ⲁⲛⲛⲁ ⲧⲉϥⲥ̄ϩⲓ̈ⲙⲉ ⳾ 70ⲛⲧⲉⲣⲟⲩϫⲟⲕⲙⲉⲥ ϩⲙ̄ ⲡ̄ⲙⲟⲟⲩ · ⲁⲩϣⲓ̈ⲛⲉ ϫⲉ ⲉⲛⲛⲁⲙⲟⲩⲧⲉ ⲉⲡⲣⲁⲛ ⲛ̄ⲧϣⲉⲉ̄ⲣⲉϣⲏⲙ ϫⲉ ⲛⲓ̈ⲙ ⳾ 71ⲡⲉϫⲁⲥ · ϫⲉ ⲙⲟⲩⲧⲉ ⲉ̀ⲡⲉⲥⲣⲁⲛ · ϫⲉ ⲙⲁⲣⲓ̈ⲁ · ⲕⲁⲧⲁ ⲑⲉ ⲛ̄ⲧⲁⲩϩⲱⲛ ⲉ̀ⲧⲟⲟⲧ ⲙ̄ⲙⲟⲥ ⳾ 72ⲁⲩⲱ̀ ⲛ̄ⲧⲉⲓ̈ϩⲉ · ⲁⲩⲙⲟⲩⲧⲉ ⲉⲡⲣⲁⲛ ⲛ̄ⲧϣⲉⲉ̀ⲣⲉϣⲏⲙ ϫⲉ ⲙⲁⲣⲓ̈ⲁ · ⲁⲩⲛⲟϭ ⲛ̄ⲣⲁϣⲉ ϣⲱⲡⲉ ⲛⲁⲩ ⲙⲛ̄ ⲡⲉⲩⲏⲓ ⲧⲏⲣϥ ⳾ 73ⲛⲉⲩⲛ ⲟⲩⲟⲩⲏⲏⲃ[c] ⲇⲉ ϩⲙ̄ ⲡⲉⲣⲡⲉ ⲙ̄ⲡⲉⲟⲩⲟ̄ⲉⲓ̈ϣ ⲉ̀ⲧⲙ̄ⲙⲁⲩ |(p. ιβ) ⲉϥϣⲙ̄ϣⲉ ϩⲁⲣⲁⲧϥ̄ ⲙ̄ⲡϫⲟⲉⲓ̈ⲥ ⲉϥⲟ ⲛ̄ⲛⲟϭ ⳾ ⲛ̄ⲧⲟϥ ⲡⲉ ⲡⲉⲓ̈ⲱⲧ ⲙ̄ⲡⲗⲁⲟⲥ ⲧⲏⲣϥ̄ ⲙ̄ⲡⲉⲩⲟ̄ⲉⲓ̈ϣ ⲉ̀ⲧⲙ̄ⲙⲁⲩ ⳾ 74ⲡⲁⲓ̈ ⲇⲉ ⲁϥⲛⲁⲩ ⲉⲩϩⲟⲣⲟⲙⲁ ⲛ̄ⲧⲉⲩϣⲏ · [ⲁϥⲟⲩⲱⲛϩ ⲛⲁϥ ⲉⲃⲟⲗ] ⲛ̄ϭⲓ̈[d] ⲟⲩⲁⲅⲅⲉⲗⲟⲥ ⲛ̄ⲧⲉ ⲡϫⲟⲉⲓ̈ⲥ · ⲡⲉϫⲁϥ ⲛⲁϥ · 75ϫⲉ ⲡϣⲏⲣⲉ ⲙ̄ⲡϩ̄ⲗ̄ⲗⲟ ⲙⲁⲗⲁⲭⲓ̈ⲁⲥ ⳾ ⲛⲁⲓ̈ ⲛⲉⲧⲉⲕϫⲟⲟⲩ ⲛⲁⲛⲛⲁ · ⲙⲛ̄ ⲓ̈ⲱⲁⲕⲓ̈ⲙ · ϫⲉ ϩⲁⲣⲉϩ ⲉ̀ⲧⲉⲧⲉⲛϣⲉⲉ̀ⲣⲉ ⲛⲟⲩⲡⲁⲣⲑⲉⲛⲟⲥ ⲉⲥⲟⲩⲁⲁⲃ · ⲛⲟⲩϩⲁⲓ̈ ⲛⲟⲩⲱⲧ ⲡⲉⲭ̅ⲥ̅ ⳾ 76ⲁⲩⲱ̀ ⲙ̄ⲛ̄ⲛ̄ⲥⲁ ϣⲟⲙⲧⲉ ⲛ̄ⲣⲟⲙⲡⲉ · ⲥⲉⲛⲁⲉⲛⲧⲥ̄ ϣⲁⲣⲟⲕ ⳾ 77ⲁϫⲓ̈ⲥ ⲛⲁⲥ · ϫⲉ ⲙⲡⲉⲣⲧ̄ⲣⲉ ⲗⲁⲁⲩ ⲛⲁⲕⲁⲑⲁⲣⲧⲟⲛ ⲛⲱⲧ ⲉ̄ϩⲟⲩⲛ ⲉ̄ⲧⲟⲩⲧⲁⲡⲣⲟ · ϣⲁⲛⲧⲉⲥⲱⲙ̄ϫ̄ ⲛ̄ⲧ|ϣⲉⲉ̄ⲣⲉϣⲏⲙ · ϩⲛ̄ ⲧⲟⲩⲉ̀ⲣⲱⲧⲉ ⳾ 78ϯϩⲧⲏⲕ ⲉ̀ⲣⲟⲕ ϫⲉ ⲙ̄ⲛ̄ⲛ̄ⲥⲁ ϣⲟⲙⲧⲉ ⲛ̄ⲣⲟⲙⲡⲉ · ⲥⲉⲛⲁⲧⲁⲁⲥ ⲛⲁⲕ · ⲛ̄ⲑⲉ ⲛⲟⲩⲡⲁⲣⲁⲑⲏⲕⲏ · ϣⲁ ⲡⲉϩⲟⲟⲩ ⲉ̀ⲧⲉⲣⲉ ⲡⲛⲟⲩⲧⲉ ⲛⲁⲉⲣϩ̄ⲛⲁϥ · ϫⲉ ⲟⲩⲉ̀ⲣⲏⲧ ⲛ̄ⲧⲉ ⲧⲡⲉ ⲧⲉ · 79ⲍⲁⲭⲁⲣⲓ̈ⲁⲥ ⲇⲉ ⲛ̄ⲧⲉⲣⲉϥⲥⲱⲧⲙ̄ ⲉ̄ⲛⲁⲓ̈ ϩⲙ̄ ⲡ̄ϩⲟⲣⲟⲙⲁ · ⲁϥⲛⲏϩⲥⲉ · ⲁⲩⲱ̀ ⲁϥⲑⲁⲩⲙⲁⲍⲉ ⲉ̄ϫⲛ̄ ⲛⲉⲛⲧⲁϥⲥⲟⲧⲙⲟⲩ · ⲁⲩⲱ̀ ⲁϥϯⲉ̀ⲟⲟⲩ ⲙ̄ⲡⲛⲟⲩ-

[a] ⲡⲉⲧⲣⲁ [b] ⲁϥϫⲁⲥⲧ [c] ⲟⲩⲏⲏⲃ [d] ⲛ̄ⲧⲉⲩϣⲏ · ⲛ̄ϭⲓ̈

who covered the shame of their faces and gave joy to all
women.

[63]Afterwards David came into the midst with his harp
and sang the praise of Anna and Joakim, saying, [64]We exulted Ps LXXXIX
and were glad, instead of the days that Thou didst afflict us. 14, 15
[65]When my heart was sad, Thou didst set[a] me up on a rock. Ps LX 3
Thou didst guide me, Thou didst bring me into the broad cf. Ps XVII
way[b]. [66]Thou didst cause men to ride over our heads, Thou 20
broughtest us through fire and water. [67]These and other[c] Ps LXV 12
things also David spake on the day whereon the Virgin was
brought forth.

[68]Her neighbours heard and brought her their gifts. Lc I 58
The men also brought their gifts to Joakim. [69]They spent
seven days eating and drinking, and rejoicing over the thing
which God had[d] wrought with them concerning[e] Joakim
and Anna his wife. [70]When she had been washed with
water, they asked, What shall we call the name of the
child? [71]She said, Call her name Mary, even as it was
commanded me. [72]And so they called the name of the
child Mary; and there was great joy to them and to all their
house.

[73]Now there was a priest in the temple at that time cf. Lc I 5,
ministering under the Lord, and he was old[f]. He was[g] the 7, 8
father of all the people at that time. [74]Now this man saw a
vision in the night. An angel of the Lord [appeared to him cf. Lc I 11
and[h]] said to him, [75]Thou son of the old man Malachias,
these things shalt thou say[i] to Anna and Joakim, Keep your
daughter a holy Virgin for one Husband Christ. [76]And after cf. 2 Co
three years she will be brought unto thee. [77]Say to her, Let XI 2
nothing unclean enter thy mouth, until thou wean the child cf. Jud XIII 4*, 7*
from thy milk. [78]Take heed that after three years she be
given to thee as a deposit until the day that God shall see
fit, for she is a votive offering of heaven. [79]Now Zacharias,
when he had heard these things in the vision, awoke and
wondered at those things that he heard, and glorified God.

[a] The MS has *He set* [b] Lit. *the breadth* [c] Lit. *these and these other* [d] Lit. *has* [e] Or *for the sake of* [f] Lit. *being old* [g] Lit. *is*
[h] These words are not in the MS, but see note [i] Lit. *thou sayest*

ⲧⲉ⁘ 80Ϩⲧⲟⲟⲩⲉ ⲇⲉ ⲛ̇ⲧⲉⲣⲉϥϣⲱⲡⲉ· ⲙ̄ⲡⲉϥⲉⲣⲁⲙⲉⲗⲏⲥ ϩⲱⲗⲟⲥ· ⲁⲗⲗⲁ
ⲁϥϫⲱ[a] ⲛⲛⲓ̈ϣⲁϫⲉ ⲧⲏⲣⲟⲩ· ⲉⲉⲗⲓ̄ⲥⲁⲃⲉⲧ· ⲁⲥⲣⲁϣⲉ ⲉ̄ⲙⲁⲧⲉ· ⲁⲩⲧⲱⲟⲩⲛ
Cod. Clarend. b 3 14 p. ιⲅ ⲁⲩⲡⲱⲧ ϣⲁ ⲓ̈ⲱⲁⲕⲓ̄ⲙ⁘ 81Ⲉⲡⲉⲓ̈ⲇⲏ· ⲁⲛⲛⲁ ⲙⲛ̄ ⲉⲗⲓ̄ⲥⲁⲃⲉⲧ | ⲛⲉϣⲉⲉⲣⲉ
ⲛ̇ⲥⲱⲛⲉ ⲥⲉⲛⲧⲉ ⲛⲉ⁘ Ⲁⲩⲱ̇ ⲟⲛ· ⲍⲁⲭⲁⲣⲓ̄ⲁⲥ ⲙⲛ̄ ⲓ̈ⲱⲁ̄ⲕⲓ̄ⲙ· ⲥⲟⲛ ⲥ̄ⲛⲁⲩ
ⲛⲉ· Ⲡ̇ⲗⲏⲛ ⲛ̄ⲛϣⲙ̄ⲙⲟ ⲁⲛ ⲛⲉ ϩⲛ̄ ⲛⲉⲩⲉ̄ⲣⲏⲩ[b]⁘ 82Ⲛ̄ⲧⲉⲣⲟⲩⲛⲱⲧ ⲇⲉ
ⲉ̄ϩⲟⲩⲛ ⲉ̄ⲛⲏⲓ̈ ⲛ̄ⲓ̈ⲱⲁⲕⲓ̄ⲙ· ⲁⲩⲁⲛⲁⲅⲅⲓ̄ⲗⲉ[c] ⲉ̇ⲣⲟⲟⲩ ⲛ̇ϩⲱⲃ ⲛⲓⲙ· ⲛ̇ⲧⲁ
ⲡⲁⲅⲅⲉⲗⲟⲥ ϫⲟⲟⲩ ⲛ̄ⲍⲁⲭⲁⲣⲓ̈ⲁⲥ· 83Ⲡⲉϫⲉ ⲁⲛⲛⲁ· ϫⲉ ϩⲱⲃ ⲛⲓⲙ
ⲉ̇ⲧⲉⲕⲛⲁϫⲟⲟⲩ ⲛⲁⲓ̈ ⲡⲁϫⲟⲉⲓ̄ⲥ ⲡⲉⲓ̄ⲱⲧ· ⲁⲩϭⲟⲗⲡⲟⲩ ⲛⲁⲓ̈ ⲉ̇ⲃⲟⲗ· ϩⲁⲑⲏ
ⲙ̄ⲡⲁⲧⲟⲩⲱ̇ ⲙ̄ⲙⲟⲥ⁘ 84Ⲁⲩⲱ̇ ⲟⲛ ⲁⲓ̈ⲉ̇ⲣⲏⲧ ⲙ̄ⲙⲟⲥ· ϫⲉ ⲕⲁⲛ ⲟⲩϩⲟⲟⲩⲧ
ⲡⲉ· ⲕⲁⲛ ⲟⲩⲥϩⲓ̄ⲙⲉ ⲧⲉ· ϯⲛⲁⲧⲁⲁϥ ⲙ̄ⲡϫⲟⲉⲓ̄ⲥ ⲉ̄ⲡⲉϥⲉⲣⲡⲉ⁘ 85Ⲡⲗⲏⲛ
ⲁ̄ ⲍⲁⲭⲁⲣⲓ̄ⲁⲥ· ⲥ̇ⲙⲟⲩ ⲉⲧϣⲉⲉ̇ⲣⲉϣⲏⲙ· ϩⲉⲛ | ⲑⲟⲣⲙⲏ ⲙ̄ⲡⲉϥⲡ̄ⲛ̄ⲁ̄
ⲁϥⲉⲓ̄ ⲉ̄ⲃⲟⲗ· ⲁϥⲡⲱⲧ ⲉⲧⲱⲣⲓ̈ⲛⲏ ⲧⲉϥⲡⲟⲗⲓ̄ⲥ· ⲉ̇ⲃⲟⲗ ϫⲉ ⲛⲉⲣⲉ ⲓ̄ⲱⲁ̄ⲕⲓ̄ⲙ·
ⲟⲩⲏϩ ϩⲛ̄ ⲛⲁⲍⲁⲣⲉⲑ ⲛ̄ⲛⲉϩⲟⲟⲩ ⲉ̇ⲧⲙ̄ⲙⲁⲩ⁘ 86Ⲁⲛⲛⲁ ⲇⲉ· ⲁⲥϫⲓ̈
ⲛ̇ⲧϣ̄ⲉⲉⲣⲉϣⲏⲙ ⲉ̇ⲡⲉⲥϩⲁⲙⲏⲣ· ϫⲉ ⲉⲥⲛⲁϫⲟⲕⲙⲉⲥ⁘ Ⲁⲥϭⲱϣⲧ ⲉ̄ⲡⲉⲥⲏⲧ
ⲉϫⲙ̄ ⲡⲉⲥϩⲟ· ⲁⲥⲛⲁⲩ ⲉⲣⲟϥ ⲉϥⲙⲉϩ ⲛ̄ⲭⲁⲣⲓ̇ⲥ ⲛ̇ⲧⲉ ⲡⲛⲟⲩⲧⲉ· 87ⲁⲥϫⲱ
ⲛ̄ⲧⲉⲓ̄ⲱ̇ⲇⲏ ⲉⲡϫⲟⲉⲓ̄ⲥ· ⲉⲣⲉ ⲇⲁ̄ⲇ̄ ⲫⲓ̈ⲉ̇ⲣⲱⲯⲁⲗⲧⲏⲥ ⲟⲩⲱϩⲙ ⲛ̄ⲥⲱⲥ[d]·
88ϫⲉ Ⲛ̇ⲧⲟⲕ ⲡⲉ ⲡϫⲟⲉ̇ⲓ̈ⲥ ⲕ̇ⲛⲁϫⲓ̄ⲥⲉ ⲙ̄ⲡⲗⲁⲟⲥ ⲉ̄ⲧⲑⲃ̄ⲃⲓ̄ⲏⲩ[e]⁘ ⲁⲩⲱ̇
ⲕ̇ⲛⲁⲑⲃ̇ⲃⲓ̇ⲟ ⲡⲉⲛⲃⲁⲗ ⲡⲉⲛϫⲁⲥⲓ̈ϩⲏⲧ· 89Ⲡⲉ̇ϫⲉ ⲁⲛⲛⲁ ϩⲱⲱⲥ· ϫⲉ ⲁ
p. ιⲇ ⲡϫⲟⲉⲓ̄ⲥ ϭⲱϣⲧ ⲉ̄ⲃⲟⲗ ϩⲛ̄ ⲧ̄ⲡⲉ· ⲉϫⲛ̇ | ⲛⲏⲓ̈[f] ⲡⲉⲛϩⲏⲕⲉ· ⲁϥⲁⲁⲩ
ⲛ̇ⲣⲙ̄ⲙⲁⲟ ϩⲁⲙⲏⲛ⁘ 90Ⲛⲉⲁⲣⲭⲁⲅⲅⲉⲗⲟⲥ ⲙ̇ⲡϫⲟⲉⲓ̈ⲥ· ⲁⲙⲱⲓ̈ⲛⲉ ⲣⲁϣⲉ
ⲛ̇ⲙⲙⲁⲓ̄· ϫⲉ ⲁⲓ̈ⲥⲟⲩⲧⲉⲛ ⲡⲉϫⲡⲟ· ϩⲁⲙⲏⲛ· 91Ⲛⲉⲭⲉⲣⲟⲩⲃⲓ̄ⲛ· ⲛⲉⲧⲟ
ⲛ̇ⲑⲣⲟⲛⲟⲥ ⲉ̇ⲡⲉⲓ̄ⲱⲧ· ⲣⲁϣⲉ ⲛ̄ⲙⲙⲁⲓ̄ ϩⲱⲱⲧ· ϫⲉ ⲁ ⲛⲁⲛⲁⲩ ⲧⲱⲟⲩⲛ
ϩⲁ ⲡⲕⲁⲣⲡⲟⲥ ⲙ̄ϣⲏⲣⲉ· ϩⲁⲙⲏⲛ⁘ 92Ⲛⲉⲭⲉⲣⲟⲩⲃⲓ̈ⲛ ⲙ̄ⲡⲉⲓ̈ⲱⲧ· ⲛⲁ
ⲡ̇ⲓ̈ⲥⲟⲟⲩ ⲛ̄ⲧⲉⲛϩ̄· ⲛⲁ ⲡⲓ̈ϥⲧⲟⲟⲩ ⲙ̄ⲡⲣⲟⲥⲟⲡⲟⲛ⁘ Ⲛⲁ ⲡⲓ̈ϣⲁ ⲛ̄ⲃⲁⲗ
ⲉⲧⲙⲉϩ ⲛⲟⲩⲟⲉⲓ̄ⲛ· ⲁⲙⲱⲓ̄ⲛⲉ ⲣⲁϣⲉ ⲛ̄ⲙⲙⲁⲓ̄· ϫⲉ ⲁⲓ̈ⲧⲥⲁⲃⲟ· ⲉ̇ⲥⲉⲕⲟⲩ-
ⲉⲗⲗⲓ̄ ⲉ̇ⲧⲁϣⲉⲉ̇ⲣⲉⲕⲟⲩⲓ̄ ⲛ̇ⲥⲁⲃⲏ· ϩⲁⲙⲏⲛ⁘ | 93Ⲡⲉϫⲟⲩⲧⲁϥⲧⲉ ⲙ̄ⲡⲣⲉⲥ-
ⲃⲩⲧⲉⲣⲟⲥ ⲛⲁⲥⲱⲙⲁⲧⲟⲥ· ⲁⲙⲱⲓ̄ⲛⲉ ⲣⲁϣⲉ ⲛ̄ⲙⲙⲁⲓ̄· ϫⲉ ⲁⲩⲙⲏⲧⲣⲁ
ⲉⲥⲟ ⲛⲉⲣⲏⲙⲟⲥ· ϫⲟ ⲛⲟⲩϭⲣⲟϭ· ϩⲁⲙⲏⲛ⁘ 94Ⲛⲉⲁⲣⲭⲱⲛ ⲙ̄ⲡⲟⲩⲟ̇ⲉⲓ̈ⲛ·

[a] ⲁⲩϫⲱ [b] ϩⲛ̄ⲛⲉⲩⲉ̄ⲣⲏⲩ [c] ⲁⲩⲁ·ⲛⲁⲅⲅⲓ̄ⲗⲉ
[d] ⲟⲩⲱϩⲛ̄ⲥⲱϥ· [e] ⲉ̄ⲑⲃ̄ⲃⲓ̄ⲏⲩ [f] ⲛⲏⲓ̈

80 And when morning was come, he was not at all careless,
but he told[a] all these words to Elisabeth, and she rejoiced
greatly; and they arose and went unto Joakim, 81 since Anna
and Elisabeth were[b] the daughters of two sisters, and also
Zacharias and Joakim were[b] two brothers. Moreover they
were not strangers one with the other.

82 Now when they had gone into the house of Joakim,
they announced to them all things that the angel spake to
Zacharias. 83 And Anna said, All things that thou wouldst
say to me, my lord *and* father, have been revealed to me
before she was conceived. 84 And also I promised, *saying*,
Whether it be a male or a female, I will give it to the Lord
for His temple. 85 Moreover Zacharias blessed the child in the cf. Ez III 14*
impulse of his spirit and departed and went to Torine[c] his
city; because that Joakim was dwelling at Nazareth in those
days. 86 Now Anna took the child into her arms that she
might wash her; and she looked down on her face, and saw
it full of *the* grace of God. 87 And she spake this song to
the Lord; whilst David the holy singer answered her[d],
saying, 88 Thou art the Lord, Thou wilt exalt my people that Ps XVII 28
is humble and wilt humble the eyes of the haughty ones.
89 Anna also said, The Lord hath looked from heaven on the cf. Ps XIII 2; XXXII 13
houses of the poor, He hath made them rich. Amen. 90 Ye
archangels of the Lord, come and rejoice with me, for I have
known birth. Amen. 91 Ye Cherubin, that are thrones for cf. Ps XVII 11; LXXIX 2
the Father, rejoice with me also, for my knees have carried
the fruit of child. Amen. 92 Ye Cherubin of the Father
with the six wings, with the four faces, with the thousand cf. Is VI 2*; Ap IV 8
eyes full of light, come and rejoice with me, for I have cf. Ez I 6*; X 12*, 21*
learned to make melody to[e] my wise child. Amen. 93 Ye four cf. Ap IV 4
and twenty elders without body, come and rejoice with me,
for a deserted womb hath sown[f] a seed. Amen. 94 Ye rulers

[a] The MS has *they told* [b] Lit. *are* [c] Or *the hill country*: see note [d] The MS has *followed him* [e] Or *to sing of* [f] Or, reading ϫⲓ for ϫⲟ, *received*

ⲁⲙⲱⲓ̈ⲛⲉ ⲣⲁϣⲉ ⲛ̄ⲙⲙⲁⲓ̈ ϫⲉ ⲁⲓ̈ϫⲡⲟ ⲛⲟⲩⲕⲁⲣⲡⲟⲥ ⲛ̀ⲣⲱⲙⲉ· ϩⲁⲙⲏⲛ⁘
95 Ⲛⲉⲉⲓ̈ⲕⲟⲛⲟⲙⲟⲥ ⲙ̀ⲡⲣⲁϣⲉ· ⲁⲙⲱⲓ̈ⲛⲉ ⲣⲁϣⲉ ⲛ̄ⲙⲙⲁⲓ̈· ϩ̄ⲙ ⲡⲁⲣⲁϣⲉ
ⲙ̀ⲡⲟⲟⲩ· ϩⲁⲙⲏⲛ⁘ 96 Ⲛⲉⲕⲓ̈ⲑⲁⲣⲧⲟⲥ· ⲙⲛ̄ ⲛⲉϩⲩⲙⲛⲉⲩⲧⲏⲣⲓ̈ⲟⲛ ⲙ̄ⲡⲉⲓ̈ⲱⲧ·
ⲁⲙⲱⲓ̈ⲛⲉ ⲣⲁϣⲉ ⲛ̄ⲙⲙⲁⲓ̈ ϩⲁ ⲡⲁⲣⲁϣⲉ ⲙ̄ⲡⲟⲟⲩ· ϩⲁⲙⲏⲛ⁘ 97 Ⲛⲉ-
ⲑⲣⲟⲛⲟⲥ· ⲙⲛ̄ ⲛⲉⲙⲛ̄ⲧϫⲟⲉⲓ̈ⲥ· ⲙⲛ̄ ⲛⲉϭⲟⲙ ⲙ̄ⲛ̄ |

FRAGMENT II. A.

Cod. Borg. cxviii p.17

1 Ⲁⲩⲱ ⲛ̄ⲧⲉⲓϩⲉ· ⲁ ⲁⲡⲡⲁ ⲧⲉⲥⲙⲁⲁⲩ· ⲕⲁⲁⲥ ⲉⲡⲉⲥⲏⲧ· ⲁⲥⲙⲟⲟϣⲉ
ⲙⲁⲩⲁⲁⲥ· ⲁⲥⲃⲱⲕ ⲉϩⲟⲩⲛ ⲉⲡⲉⲑⲩⲥⲓⲁⲥⲧⲏⲣⲓⲟⲛ ⲉⲧⲟⲩⲁⲁⲃ· ⲁⲥⲁϩⲉ-
ⲣⲁⲧ̄ⲥ· 2 Ⲁⲩⲱ ⲁ ⲡⲗⲁⲟⲥ ⲧⲏⲣϥ· ⲙ̄ⲡⲓⲏ̄ⲗ̄ ϭⲱϣⲧ· ⲁⲩⲛⲁⲩ ⲉⲧⲉⲭⲁⲣⲓⲥ·
ⲉⲁⲥϣⲁ· ⲉϩⲣⲁⲓ ⲉ̀ϫⲱⲥ· 3 ⲁⲩⲱ ⲁ ⲡⲉⲥϩⲟ· ⲣ̄ⲟⲩⲟⲉⲓⲛ ⲛ̄ⲧⲉⲩⲛⲟⲩ ⲁⲥ-
ⲃⲟⲩⲃⲟⲩ ⲛ̀ⲑⲉ ⲛ̀ⲛⲉϥⲱⲥⲧⲏⲣ ⲛ̀ⲧⲡⲉ· ϩⲱⲥⲇⲉ ⲛ̄ⲧⲉ ⲟⲩⲟⲛ ⲛⲓ̈ⲙ ⲣ̄ϣⲡⲏⲣⲉ·
4 Ⲁⲩⲱ ⲙⲡⲉⲥⲟⲩⲱϩ ⲉⲧⲟⲟⲧ̄ⲥ ⲉ̀ⲃⲱⲕ ⲙⲛ̄ ⲛⲉⲥⲉⲓⲟ̈ⲧⲉ ⲉⲡⲉⲥⲏⲓ̈· ⲁⲗⲗⲁ
ⲁⲥϭⲱ· ⲉⲥⲙⲟⲟⲛⲉ ⲛ̄ⲑⲉ ⲛ̄ⲛⲉⲓ̈ϭⲣⲟⲟⲙⲡⲉ· ⲉⲥⲇⲓⲁⲕⲟⲛⲉⲓ̈ ⲉⲡϣⲙ̄ϣⲉ·
ⲙ̄ⲡⲛⲟⲩⲧⲉ· 5 ⲉ⸢ⲁ ⲁⲛ⸣ⲛⲁ ⲧⲉⲡⲣⲟ⸢ⲫⲏⲧⲏⲥ⸣ | ⲙⲛ̄ ⲙ̄ⲡⲁⲣⲑⲉⲛⲟⲥ ⲉⲧϩⲙ
ⲡⲣⲡⲉ ⲧⲥⲁⲃⲟ ⲙ̀ⲙⲟⲥ· ⲉⲣ ϩⲱⲃ ⲛ̄ϭⲓϫ· 6 Ⲁⲩⲱ ⲛⲉⲣⲉ ⲛⲉⲥⲉⲓ̈ⲟⲧⲉ ⲛⲏⲩ
ϣⲁⲣⲟⲥ· ⲕⲁⲧⲁ ϩⲟⲟⲩ· ⲥⲛⲁⲩ· ⲏ ϣⲟⲙⲛⲧ· ⲉⲩϭⲓⲛⲉ ⲙ̄ⲡⲉⲥϣⲓⲛⲉ·
7 Ⲛⲉⲥⲡ̄ⲣⲟⲕⲟⲡⲧⲉⲓ̈ ⲇⲉ ⲁⲩⲱ ⲛⲉⲥϯ ⲉ̀ⲡⲁⲛⲁⲓ ϩⲛ̄ ⲑⲟⲧⲉ ⲙ̄ⲡϫⲟⲉⲓⲥ·
8 Ⲛⲧⲉⲣⲉⲥⲣ̄ⲛⲟϭ ⲇⲉ ⲛⲟⲩⲕⲟⲩⲓ· ⲁⲥϥⲓ̈ ⲉⲃⲟⲗ· ⲙⲙⲟⲥ ⲛϩⲟⲙⲉⲗⲓ̈ⲁ ⲛⲓ̈ⲙ
ⲉⲧϣⲟⲩⲉⲓ̈ⲧ· ⲁⲩⲱ ⲡⲉⲥϩⲏⲧ ⲁⲥϥⲓⲧϥ̄ ⲉⲃⲟⲗ· ⲙ̀ⲡⲥⲁ ⲧⲏⲣϥ ⲙ̀ⲡⲉⲓ̈ⲁⲓ̈ⲱⲛ·
9 Ⲁⲩⲱ ⲙⲡⲉ ⲡⲙⲉⲉⲩⲉ ⲛ̄ⲛⲉⲥⲉⲓ̈ⲟⲧⲉ· ⲁⲗⲉ ⲉϩⲣⲁⲓ ⲉϫ̄ⲙ̄ ⲡⲉⲥϩⲏⲧ· ⲟⲩⲇⲉ
ⲗⲁⲁⲩ ⲙⲙⲉⲉⲩⲉ ⲛ̄ⲧⲉ ⲡⲉⲓ̈ⲕⲟⲥⲙⲟⲥ· 10 ⲁⲗⲗⲁ ⲛⲉⲥⲙⲟⲟ̄ⲛⲉ ϩⲙ̄ ⸢ⲡⲣⲡⲉ

p. ιη ⲛ̄ⲑ⸣ⲉ ⲛⲛ̄⸢ⲉ⸣ | ϭⲣⲟⲟⲙⲡⲉ· ⲉⲩⲉⲓⲛⲉ ⲛⲁⲥ ⲛ̄ⲧⲉⲥⲧⲣⲟⲫⲏ ⲉⲃⲟⲗ ϩⲛ̄ ⲙ̄ⲡⲏⲧⲉ·
ϩⲓⲧⲛ ⲛⲁⲅⲅⲉⲗⲟⲥ ⲛⲧⲉ ⲡⲛⲟⲩⲧⲉ· 11 Ⲁⲩⲱ ⲉⲛⲉⲥⲗⲓⲧⲟⲩⲣⲅⲉⲓ ϩⲙ̄ ⲡⲣⲡⲉ·
ⲉⲣⲉ ⲛⲁⲅⲅⲉⲗⲟⲥ ⲙ̄ⲡⲛⲟⲩⲧⲉ ⲇⲓⲁⲕⲟⲛⲉⲓ ⲛⲁⲥ· 12 Ϩⲁϩ ⲇⲉ ⲟⲛ ⲛ̄ⲥⲟⲡ·
ⲉ̀ϣⲁⲩⲉⲓ̈ⲛⲉ ⲛⲁⲥ ⲛ̀ⲛ̀ⲕⲁⲣⲡⲟⲥ· ⲉⲃⲟⲗ ϩⲙ̄ ⲡϣⲏⲛ ⲙ̄ⲡⲱⲛϩ ⲛⲥⲟⲩⲱⲙ
ⲉⲃⲟⲗ ⲛ̄ϩⲏⲧⲟⲩ ϩⲛ ⲟⲩⲟⲩⲣⲟⲧ· 13 Ⲙ̄ⲡⲉ ⲧⲉⲥϣⲧⲏⲛ ⲗⲱⲱⲙⲉ ⲉⲛⲉϩ·
ⲟⲩⲇⲉ ⲙ̀ⲡⲉⲥϩⲓⲧⲉ· ⲟⲩⲇⲉ ⲙ̀ⲡⲉⲥⲡⲱϩ· ⲁⲗⲗⲁ ⲧⲉϣⲧⲏⲛ ⲛⲧⲁ ⲧⲉⲥⲙⲁⲁⲩ·

of light, come and rejoice with me, for I have brought forth
fruit of man. Amen. 95 Ye stewards of joy, come and rejoice
with me in my joy to-day. Amen. 96 Ye harpers and praisers
of the Father, come and rejoice with me by reason of my
joy to-day. Amen. 97 Ye thrones and dominions and powers cf. Col I 16
of the [Father].........

FRAGMENT II. A.

And so Anna her mother put her down, and she walked
by herself, and she went in unto the holy altar and stood.
2 And all the people of Israel looked, and they saw the grace
shine upon her. 3 And her face became[a] bright straight-
way, and[b] she was dazzling as the luminaries of heaven,
so that every one wondered. 4 And she went no more with her
parents to her house; but she kept feeding as the doves,
ministering to the service of the priests; 5 Anna the pro-
phetess and the virgins that were in the temple having
taught her to do handiwork. 6 And her parents used to come
to her every two or three days and visit her[c]. 7 And she cf. Lc II 52*
was advancing and was pleasing[d] in the fear of the Lord.
8 And when she grew a little, she put away from her all vain
intercourse, and her heart she turned from all the beauty of
this life[e]; 9 and the thought of her parents did not come up
into her heart, nor any thought of this world; 10 but she was
feeding in the temple as the doves, whilst her nourishment
was brought her from the heavens by the angels of God.
11 And she was serving in the temple, whilst the angels of cf. Mt IV 11; Mc I 13*
God ministered to her. 12 And oftentimes also they would
bring her the fruits from the tree of life, that she might cf. Ap XXII 2*
eat of them with cheerfulness[f]. 13 Her raiment never became
foul nor wore out nor tore, but the raiment which her mother

[a] Or *was* [b] Or *bright, and straightway* [c] Lit. *visiting her*
[d] See note [e] Lit. *age* [f] Or *and she ate of them readily*

ⲧⲁⲁⲥ ϩⲓⲱⲱⲥ · ⲙ̅ⲡⲉϩⲟⲟⲩ ⲛ̅ⲧⲁⲥⲧⲁⲁⲥ ⲉⲛⲣⲡⲉ ⲛⲧⲟⲥ ⲧⲉⲧϩⲓϫⲱⲥ ϣⲁ
ⲡⲉϩⲟⲟⲩ · ⲙⲡⲉⲥϫⲱⲕ ⲉⲃⲟⲗ · [14]Ⲡⲉⲧⲉⲣⲉ ⲧⲡⲁⲣⲑⲉⲛⲟⲥ ⲙⲁ⸢ⲣⲓⲁ . . .
. . .⸣ | ⲙⲙⲟϥ ⲙ̅ⲙⲏⲛⲉ ϣⲁⲣⲉ ⲧⲉϣⲧⲏⲛ ⲣⲛⲟϭ ⲙⲙⲟϥ ⲛⲙⲙⲁⲥ ·
[15]Ⲙⲡⲉⲥⲕⲟⲥⲙⲉⲓ̈ ⲙ̅ⲙⲟⲥ ⲉⲛⲉϩ ⲛϭⲓ̈ ⲙⲁⲣⲓⲁ · ⲟⲩⲇⲉ ⲙⲡⲉⲥϣⲓⲛⲉ ⲛⲥⲁ
ϩⲉⲛⲥⲁⲕ · ⲛ̅ⲑⲉ ⲛⲛⲉϩⲓ̈ⲟⲙⲉ · [16]ⲙⲡⲉⲥϯⲥⲧⲏⲙ ⲉⲛⲉⲥⲃⲁⲗ ⲉⲛⲉϩ · ⲙⲡⲉⲥϯ
ⲛⲟⲩⲕⲣⲟⲕⲟⲥ ⲉⲛⲉⲥⲟⲩⲟⲟϭⲉ · ⲙⲡⲉⲥϩⲱⲗⲕ̅ ⲙⲡⲉⲥϥⲱ · ⲉⲛⲉϩ [17]Ⲙⲡⲉⲥϫⲱ-
ⲕⲙ̅ ϩⲛ̅ ⲟⲩⲥⲓⲟⲟⲩⲛ · ⲉⲛⲉϩ · Ⲙⲡⲉⲥϯ ⲛⲟⲩⲥϯⲛⲟⲩϥⲉ ⲉϥⲥⲟⲧⲛ̅ ⲉⲣⲟⲥ
Ⲟⲩⲇⲉ ⲙⲡⲉⲥⲧⲱϩⲥ̅ ⲙⲡⲉⲥⲥⲱⲙⲁ ϩⲛ ⲟⲩⲥⲟϭ̅ⲛ · · ⲙ̅ⲡⲉⲥϫⲱⲕⲙ̅ ϩⲛ̅
ⲟⲩⲙⲟⲟⲩ · [18]Ⲙ̅ⲡⲉⲥϯ ⲙ̅ⲡⲉⲥϩⲟ · ⲉⲛⲥⲁⲛⲃⲟⲗ ⲙⲡ̅ⲣⲡⲉ · ϫⲉ ⲛⲛⲉⲥⲛⲁⲩ
ⲉϩⲟⲟⲩⲧ · ⲛϣⲙ̅ⲙⲟ · [19]Ⲟⲩⲇⲉ ⲙ⸢ⲡⲉⲥⲁ⸣ⲡⲉϫⲉ ⲉ . . . . . ⲣⲉ ⲟⲩϩⲣ . . . .
ⲱⲣⲉⲓ |

B.

p. [ⲕⲅ] [1]ⲉⲛⲥⲁ · ⲛⲧⲁⲛⲁⲧⲟⲗⲏ ⲛⲟⲩⲟⲉⲓϣ ⲛⲓⲙ · ⲉⲥϯ ⲛⲛⲉⲥϣⲗⲏⲗ ⲙⲛ
ⲛⲉⲥⲡⲣⲟⲥⲉⲩⲭⲏ ⲙⲡⲉⲥⲛⲁⲩϣⲉⲗⲗⲉⲉⲧ ⲁⲩⲱ ⲛⲉⲥⲛⲩⲙⲫⲓⲟⲥ ⲡⲉⲭ̅ⲥ̅ ·
[2]Ⲛⲉⲣⲉ ⲛⲁⲅⲅⲉⲗⲟⲥ ⲙⲡϫⲟⲉⲓⲥ ⲕⲱⲧⲉ ⲉⲣⲟⲥ ⲙⲡⲉϩⲟⲟⲩ · ⲙⲛ̅ ⲧⲉⲩϣⲏ ·
[3]Ⲁⲥⲣ̅ ⲥ̅ⲛⲧⲉ ⲇⲉ ⲣ̅ⲣⲟⲙⲡⲉ ϩⲙ̅ ⲡⲏⲓ̈ ⲛⲓⲱⲥⲏⲫ ⲙⲡⲁⲧⲉ ⲡⲁⲣⲭⲁⲅⲅⲉⲗⲟⲥ
ⲉⲩⲁⲅⲅⲉⲗⲓ̈ⲍⲉ ⲛⲁⲥ · [4]Ⲙⲛⲛⲥⲁ ⲛⲁⲓ̈ ⲇⲉ ⲁ ⲡⲉⲩⲟⲉⲓϣ ϣⲱⲡⲉ ⲉⲧⲣⲉ
ⲡⲛⲟⲩⲧⲉ ϣⲛϩⲧⲏϥ · ϩⲁ ⲡⲉϥⲡⲗⲁⲥⲙⲁ · [5]ⲁ ⲡⲕⲁⲓⲣⲟⲥ ϣⲱⲡⲉ ⲉⲧⲣⲉⲩ-
ⲁⲛⲁⲕⲁⲗⲉⲓ̈ · ⲛ̅ⲧⲁⲓⲭⲙⲁⲗⲱⲥⲓ̈ⲁ · ⲛⲧⲁⲩⲁⲓⲭⲙⲁⲗⲱⲧⲓⲍⲉ ⲛ̅ⲧⲙⲛ̅ⲧⲣⲱⲙⲉ
ⲛ̅ϩⲏⲧⲥ̅ · [6]Ⲁ ⲧⲉⲩⲛⲟⲩ ⲉⲓ̈ · ⲉⲧⲣⲉ ⲡⲣⲣⲟ ⲡⲣⲟⲉⲗⲑⲉ ⲛ⸢ⲧⲉ⸣ ⲛⲃⲁⲣⲃⲁⲣⲟⲥ
⸢ϭⲟ⸣ⲧⲡ̅ ϩⲁⲧⲉϥϩⲏ [7]Ⲗⲟⲓⲡⲟⲛ · ⲁⲩϫⲟⲟⲩ ⲛⲅⲁⲃⲣⲓⲏⲗ · ⲉⲧⲣⲉϥϯ ⲡϣⲙ-
ⲛⲟⲩϥⲉ · ⲛ̅ⲧⲡⲁⲣⲑⲉⲛⲟⲥ · [8]Ⲁⲩϫⲟⲟⲩ ⲙⲡⲁⲅⲅⲉⲗⲟⲥ ϣⲁ ⲧⲙⲁⲁⲩ
ⲙⲡⲛⲟⲩⲧⲉ · ⲉⲧⲣⲉϥⲕⲏⲣⲩⲥⲥⲉ ⲛⲁⲥ ⲙⲡⲛⲟϭ ⲛϣⲙ̅ⲛⲟⲩϥⲉ · [9]Ⲁⲩⲱ
ⲁϥⲃⲱⲕ ⲉϩⲟⲩⲛ ϣⲁ ⲧⲡⲁⲣⲑⲉⲛⲟⲥ · ⲉⲣⲉ ⲣⲟ · ⲙⲡⲉⲥⲕⲟⲓ̈ⲧⲱⲛ ϣⲟⲧⲙ ·
[10]ⲁϥⲱϣ ⲉⲃⲟⲗ ϫⲉ ⲭⲁⲓⲣⲉ ⲧⲉⲛⲧⲁⲥϭⲛϩⲙⲟⲧ · ⲡϫⲟⲉⲓ̈ⲥ ⲛⲙⲙ⸢ⲉ⸣ · ⲉⲓⲥ
ϩⲏⲏⲧⲉ ⲧⲉⲛⲁⲱ̈ⲱ ⲛⲧⲉϫⲡⲟ ⲛⲟⲩϣⲏⲣⲉ · ⲛⲧⲉⲙⲟⲩⲧⲉ ⲉⲡⲉϥⲣⲁⲛ · ϫⲉ
ⲉⲙⲙⲁⲛⲟⲩⲏⲗ · [11]Ⲧⲡⲁⲣⲑⲉⲛⲟⲥ ⲇⲉ ⲛⲧⲉⲣⲉⲥⲥⲱⲧⲙ̅ ⲉⲛⲁⲓ · ⲁ̅ⲥⲣ̅ϩⲃⲁ |
p. [24] ⲡⲉϫⲁⲥ ⲙ̅ⲡⲁⲅⲅⲉⲗⲟⲥ ϫⲉ ⲛⲁϣ ⲛϩⲉ ⲛⲁⲓ ⲛⲁϣⲱⲡⲉ ⲙ̅ⲙⲟⲓ̈ · ⲙⲡⲉⲓⲥⲟⲩⲛ
ϩⲟⲟⲩⲧ · [12]ⲁⲛⲟⲕ ⲅⲁⲣ ⲁⲛⲅ ⲟⲩⲡⲁⲣⲑⲉⲛⲟⲥ ⲉⲥⲧⲃⲃⲏⲩ ϩⲛ ⲧⲁⲯⲩⲭⲏ ·
ⲙⲛ ⲡⲁⲥⲱⲙⲁ · ⲛⲑⲉ ⲛ̅ⲧⲁⲩϫⲡⲟⲓ̈ ⲙⲙⲟⲥ · [13]Ⲡⲉϫⲉ ⲡⲁⲣⲭⲁⲅⲅⲉⲗⲟⲥ

put upon her on the day that she gave her to the temple, it
was[a] upon her until the day of her death[b]. 14 That which
the Virgin Mary......daily, the raiment became greater with
her[c]. 15 Mary did not ever adorn herself, nor did she seek
after outward shows[d] as women do. 16 She never painted her cf. 2 Ki
eyes, nor put saffron on her cheeks, nor ever plaited her hair. ix 30*
17 She never washed in a bath. She did not put choice per-
fume upon her, nor did she anoint her body with ointment.
She did not wash with water. 18 She did not put her face
outside the temple, lest she should see a strange man. 19 Nor
did she allow............................

B.

eastwards always, offering her petitions and her prayers
to her Spouse and her Bridegroom Christ. 2 The angels of
the Lord were surrounding her day and night. 3 And she
spent two years in the house of Joseph before the archangel
brought her good tidings.

4 Now after these things the time was *come* for God to
have compassion on that which He had formed. 5 The season
was *come* for the captivity wherein mankind was led captive
to be recalled. 6 The hour came for the King to go forth and
the barbarians to be defeated before Him. 7 But Gabriel cf. Lc i 19,
was sent to give the good tidings to the Virgin. 8 The angel 26
was sent to the mother of God to proclaim to her the great
good tidings. 9 And he went in unto the Virgin, the doors of cf. Jn xx 19
her bedchamber being shut; 10 and he cried out, *saying*, Hail, Lc i 28
thou that hast found[e] favour, the Lord *is* with thee. Behold Lc i 31
thou shalt conceive and shalt bring forth a Son, and shalt cf. Mt i 23
call His name Emmanuel. 11 Now the Virgin when she cf. Lc i 29
heard these things was disquieted, and said to the angel, How Lc i 34
shall this be to me? I have not known *a* man. 12 For I am
a virgin pure in my soul and my body, even as I[f] was born.

[a] Lit. *is* [b] Or *consummation* [c] See note [d] Or *adornments*
[e] Lit. *she that has found* [f] Lit. *she*

ϫⲉ ⲟⲩⲡ̅ⲛ̅ⲁ̅ ⲉϥⲟⲩⲁⲁⲃ ⲡⲉⲧⲛⲏⲩ ⲉϩⲣⲁⲓ ⲉϫⲱ[a]· ⲁⲩⲱ̅ ⲧϭⲟⲙ ⲙⲡⲡⲉⲧϫⲟⲥⲉ
ⲧⲉⲧⲛⲁⲣ̅ϩⲁⲓⲃⲉⲥ ⲉⲣⲟ·· ⲉⲧⲃⲉ ⲡⲁ̈ⲓ ⲡⲉⲧⲉⲣⲛⲁϫⲡⲟϥ ϥⲟⲩⲁⲁⲃ· ⲥⲉⲛⲁ-
ⲙⲟⲩⲧⲉ ⲉⲣⲟϥ ϫⲉ ⲡϣⲏⲣⲉ ⲙⲡⲛⲟⲩⲧⲉ· 14ⲛⲧⲉⲣⲉ ⲧⲡⲁⲣⲑⲉⲛⲟⲥ ⲇⲉ
ⲉⲧⲟⲩⲁⲁⲃ ⲥⲱⲧⲙ̅ ⲉⲛⲁ̈ⲓ· ⲡⲉϫⲁⲥ ϫⲉ ⲁⲛⲅ̅ ⲧϩⲙ̅ϩⲁⲗ ⲙⲡϫⲟⲉⲓⲥ· ⲙⲁⲣⲉⲥ-
ϣⲱⲡⲉ ⲛⲁⲓ· ⲕⲁⲧⲁ ⲡⲉⲕϣⲁϫⲉ· ⲁⲩⲱ̇ ⲁ ⲡⲁⲅⲅⲉⲗⲟⲥ ⲃⲱⲕ ⲉⲃⲟⲗ ϩⲓ-
ⲧⲟⲟⲧⲥ̅· 15ⲁⲥⲱⲱ̇ ⲗⲟⲓ̈ⲡⲟⲛ ϩⲓⲧⲙ̅ ⲡⲥⲱⲧⲙ ⲛⲛⲉⲥⲙⲁⲁϫⲉ· ⲁⲥⲣ ⲕⲉϣⲟⲙⲛⲧ
ⲛⲉⲃⲟⲧ· ⲛϩⲟⲩⲛ ⲙⲡⲏⲓ̈ ⲛⲓⲱⲥⲏⲫ· ⲉ̇ⲥⲉⲉⲧ ⲙⲡϣⲏⲣⲉ ⲙ̅ⲡⲛⲟⲩⲧⲉ ⲉⲧⲟⲛϩ̅·
16ⲗⲟⲓⲡⲟⲛ ⲛⲧⲉⲣⲉ ⲡϩ̅ⲗ̅ⲗⲟ ⲛ̇ⲇⲓⲕⲁⲓⲟⲥ ⲛⲁⲩ ⲉⲣⲟⲥ· ⲉ̇ⲥⲉⲉⲧ· ⲉⲣⲉ ϩⲏⲧⲥ̅·
ⲃⲟⲟⲣⲉ ⲉ̇ⲃⲟⲗ ⲙⲡⲉϥⲟⲩⲱϣ· ⲉϯ ⲙⲡⲉⲥⲥⲟⲉⲓⲧ· ⲁⲗⲗⲁ ⲁϥⲟⲩⲱϣ ⲉⲛⲟϫⲥ
ⲉⲃⲟⲗ ⲛ̅ϫⲓⲟⲩⲉ· ⲉϥϫⲱ ⲙⲙⲟⲥ ϫⲉ 17ⲁⲗⲏⲑⲱⲥ̇ ⲡⲁϣⲏⲣⲉ ⲙⲛ ⲡⲁ-
ⲥⲩⲅⲅⲉⲛⲏⲥ· ⲛⲁⲥⲱⲃⲉ ⲛⲥⲁ ⲧⲁⲙⲛⲧϩⲗⲗⲟ ⲛⲥⲉϫⲟⲟⲥ ϫⲉ ⲁϥϫⲓ ⲛ̅ⲟⲩ-
ⲥϩⲓⲙⲉ· ϩⲛ̅ ⲧⲉϥⲙⲛⲧϩⲗⲗⲟ ⲁϥϩⲉ ⲉⲣⲟⲥ ⲉⲥⲉⲉⲧ· 18ⲛϩⲟⲩⲟ ⲇⲉ ⲛⲟⲩⲏⲏⲃ
ⲙⲡⲣⲡⲉ ⲛⲁϭⲛⲁⲣⲓⲕⲉ ⲉⲣⲟⲓ̈· ϫⲉ ⲁⲓⲁⲡⲉϫⲉ ⲁⲩϩⲱⲃ[b] ⲛ̇ϯⲙⲓ̈ⲛⲉ
p. [25] ϣⲱⲡⲉ· ⲛ|ϯⲡⲁⲣⲑⲉⲛⲟⲥ· ⲛ̇ϩⲟⲩⲛ ⲙ̅ⲡⲁⲏⲓ̈ ⲙⲁⲗⲓⲥⲧⲁ ϫⲉ ⲁ̅ⲩϩⲱⲛ
ⲉⲧⲟⲟⲧ ⲉⲧⲃⲏⲏⲧⲥ̅· 19ⲁⲗⲗⲁ ϯⲣ̅ϣⲡⲏⲣⲉ ϫⲉ ⲙⲡⲉⲓ̈ⲛⲁⲩ ⲉⲣⲟⲥ ⲉⲥϣⲁϫⲉ
ⲙⲛ ϩⲟⲟⲩⲧ ⲉⲛⲉϩ ⲛⲧⲁⲥⲱ̇ⲱ̇· ϭⲉ· ⲉⲃⲟⲗ ⲧⲱⲛ· ⲛ̇ϯⲥⲟⲟⲩⲛ ⲁⲛ· 20ϩⲛ
ⲧⲉⲩϣⲏ ⲇⲉ ⲉⲧⲙⲙⲁⲩ· ⲁ ⲡⲁⲣⲭⲁⲅⲅⲉⲗⲟⲥ ⲉⲧⲟⲩⲁⲁⲃ ⲅⲁⲃⲣⲓⲏⲗ· ⲉⲓ
ϣⲁⲣⲟϥ· ⲡⲉϫⲁϥ ⲛⲁϥ ϫⲉ ⲱ̅ ⲓⲱⲥⲏⲫ ⲡϣⲏⲣⲉ ⲛ̅ⲇⲁⲩⲉⲓⲇ ⲙ̅ⲡⲣⲣϩⲟⲧⲉ·
ⲉϫⲓ̈ ⲙ̅ⲙⲁⲣⲓⲁ ⲧⲉⲕⲥϩⲓ̈ⲙⲉ· ⲡⲉⲧⲟⲩⲛⲁϫⲡⲟϥ ⲅⲁⲣ ⲉⲃⲟⲗ ⲛϩⲏⲧⲥ̅·
ⲟⲩⲉⲃⲟⲗ ⲡⲉ ϩⲙ̅ ⲟⲩⲡ̅ⲛ̅ⲁ̅ ⲉϥⲟⲩⲁⲁⲃ· 21ⲥⲛⲁϫⲡⲟ ⲇⲉ ⲛⲟⲩϣⲏⲣⲉ
ⲛ̅ⲅ̅ⲙⲟⲩⲧⲉ· ⲉⲡⲉϥⲣⲁⲛ ϫⲉ ⲓ̅ⲥ̅· ⲛⲧⲟϥ ⲅⲁⲣ ⲡⲉⲧⲛⲁⲧⲟⲩ|ϫⲟ ⲙ̅ⲡⲉϥⲗⲁⲟⲥ
ⲉⲃⲟⲗ ϩⲛ ⲛⲉⲩⲛⲟⲃⲉ·· 22ⲡϩⲗⲗⲟ ⲇⲉ ⲛ̇ⲇⲓⲕⲁⲓⲟⲥ· ⲁϥⲥⲱⲧⲙ· ⲛⲥⲁ
ⲡϣⲁϫⲉ ⲛ̇ⲧⲁ ⲅⲁⲃⲣⲓⲏⲗ ϫⲟⲟϥ ⲛⲁϥ· ⲁⲩⲱ ϫⲓⲛ ⲙⲡⲉϩⲟⲟⲩ· ⲉⲧ̅ⲙ̅ⲙⲁⲩ
ⲁϥϭⲱ· ⲉϥϩⲩⲡⲉⲣⲏⲧⲉⲓ ⲛ̇ⲧⲡⲁⲣⲑⲉⲛⲟⲥ ⲉϥϭⲱϣ̅ⲧ̅ ⲉⲃⲟⲗ ϩⲏⲧϥ̅ ⲙⲡⲉⲧ-
ⲛⲏⲩ ⲉⲃⲟⲗ ⲛϩⲏⲧⲥ̅· 23ⲉⲓⲧⲁ ⲙ̅ⲛ̅ⲛ̅ⲥⲁ ⲛⲁ̈ⲓ ⲁⲩⲇⲟⲅⲙⲁ· ⲉⲓ ⲉⲃⲟⲗ ϩⲓⲧⲙ
ⲡⲣⲣⲟ· ⲁⲩⲅⲟⲩⲥⲧⲟⲥ· ⲉⲧⲣⲉ ⲧⲟⲓⲕⲟⲩⲙⲉⲛⲏ ⲧⲏⲣⲥ̅ ⲥϩⲁⲓⲥ· ⲛⲥⲁ ⲛⲉⲥⲧⲙⲉ[c]·
24ⲧⲁ̈ⲓ ⲧⲉ ⲧϣⲟⲣⲡⲉ ⲛⲁⲡⲟⲅⲣⲁⲫⲏ ⲛⲧⲁⲥϣⲱⲡⲉ ⲁⲩⲱ ⲛⲉⲩⲃⲏⲕ
ⲧⲏⲣⲟⲩ· ⲡⲟⲩⲁ ⲡⲟⲩⲁ· ⲉⲥϩⲁⲓϥ· ⲛ̇ⲥⲁ ⲧⲉϥⲡⲟⲗⲓⲥ 25ⲁ ⲓⲱⲥⲏⲫ ϩⲱⲱϥ
p. [26] ⲧⲱⲟⲩⲛ· ⲁϥϫⲓ̈ | ⲛⲧⲡⲁⲣⲑⲉⲛⲟⲥ ⲙⲁⲣⲓⲁ ⲉⲧⲣⲉⲩⲃⲱⲕ ⲉⲧⲁⲡⲟⲅⲣⲁⲫⲏ·

[a] ⲉϫⲱⲓ̈ [b] ⲁ ϩⲱⲃ
[c] ⲉ 2° supra lin., sed pr. man. ut vid.

13 The archangel said, The[a] Holy Ghost shall come upon Lc I 35
thee, and the power of the Most High shall overshadow
thee: wherefore that which thou shalt bring forth is holy;
it[b] shall be called the Son of God. 14 Now when the holy
Virgin heard these things, she said, I am the handmaid of Lc I 38
the Lord: be it unto me according to thy word. And the
angel departed from her. 15 She conceived moreover by the
hearing of her ears, and she spent three other months in the
house of Joseph, being pregnant with the Son of the living cf. Mt XVI 16*
God. 16 But when the righteous old man saw her pregnant, cf. Mt I 19
her womb being swollen out, he did not wish to make her a
public example[c], but he wished to put her away privily,
saying, 17 Truly my children[d] and my kinsmen will mock my
old age and say, He took a wife in his old age and found
her pregnant. 18 But most of all the priests of the temple
will blame me, because I have allowed such a thing
to happen[e] to the virgin in my house; especially as they
charged me concerning her. 19 But I wonder that I never
saw her speaking with *a* man. Whence then she has
conceived I know not. 20 Now in that night the holy arch-
angel Gabriel came unto him, and said to him, O Joseph, thou Mt I 20, 21
son of David, fear not to take Mary thy wife: for that which
shall be brought forth from her is from the[f] Holy Ghost. 21 And
she shall bring forth a Son; and thou shalt call His name
Jesus, for it is He that shall save His people from their sins.
22 And the righteous old man obeyed the word that Gabriel
spake to him, and from that day he kept attending upon
the Virgin, waiting for that which should come forth from
her[g].

23 Then after these things there went out a decree from cf. Lc II 1 ff
the king Augustus that all the world should enrol[h] itself after
its villages. 24 This is the first enrolment that was made. And
they were all going, each one to enrol[h] himself after his city.
25 Joseph also arose, and took the Virgin Mary, that they
might go to the enrolment. 26 Now as they were going in cf. Ac VIII 36

[a] Lit. *A* [b] Or *He* [c] Lit. *to spread her report* [d] Or *sons*
[e] See note [f] Lit. *a* [g] Or *from her womb* [h] Lit. *write*

26Ⲉⲩⲙⲟⲟϣⲉ ⲇⲉ ϩⲓ ⲧⲉϩⲓⲏ ϩⲛ ⲛⲧⲟϣ ⲛ̄ⲃⲉⲑⲗⲉⲉⲙ · ⲁ ⲡϩⲗⲗⲟ
ⲛ̄ⲃⲁⲗϩⲏⲧ · ϭⲱϣⲧ̄ ⲉ̄ϩⲟⲩⲛ ϩⲙ̄ ⲡϩⲟ ⲛⲧⲡⲁⲣⲑⲉⲛⲟⲥ ⲁϥϩⲉ ⲉⲣⲟϥ ·
ⲉϥⲣ̄ⲟⲩⲟⲉⲓⲛ ⲛ̄ⲑⲉ ⲙⲡⲣⲏ ⲁⲩⲱ ⲡⲉⲥϣⲧⲣⲧⲱⲣ ⲡⲉ · 27ⲛⲧⲟϥ ⲇⲉ ⲡⲉϫⲁϥ
ⲛⲁⲥ ϫⲉ ⲁϩⲣⲟϥ ⲛⲟⲩϩⲟ · ⲉϥⲟⲕⲙ̄ ⲙ̄ⲡⲟⲟⲩ · 28Ⲛⲧⲟⲥ ⲇⲉ ⲡⲉϫⲁⲥ ⲛⲁϥ
ϫⲉ ⲡⲉⲧϩⲛ̄ ⲧⲁⲕⲁⲗⲁϩⲏ · ϣⲧⲟⲣⲧⲣ ⲙⲙⲟⲓ · ⲉⲧⲣⲁϫⲡⲟϥ · 29Ⲓⲱⲥⲏⲫ ⲇⲉ
ⲡⲇⲓⲕⲁⲓⲟⲥ ⲡⲉϫⲁϥ ⲛⲧⲡⲁⲣⲑⲉⲛⲟⲥ ϫⲉ ⲱ ⲙⲁⲣⲓⲁ ⲙⲡⲣⲣ̄ϩⲟⲧⲉ · ⲡⲉⲧⲛⲏⲩ
ⲉⲃⲟⲗ ⲛ̄ϩⲏⲧⲉ ⲛ̄ⲧⲟϥ ⲡⲉⲧⲛⲁⲃⲟⲏ̄ⲑⲉⲓ ⲉ̄ⲣⲟ · 30ⲁⲩⲱ ⲁϥ|ϫⲓⲧⲥ̄ ⲉϩⲟⲩⲛ
ⲉⲩⲡⲁⲛⲧⲟⲕⲓ̈ⲟⲛ · ⲉϥϩⲛ̄ ⲧⲉϩⲓⲏ · ⲙ̄ⲛ ⲡⲉⲩⲁⲛϩⲟⲗⲱⲙⲁ ⲉⲧⲛⲧⲟⲟⲧⲟⲩ ·
31Ⲉⲓⲧⲁ ⲡⲉϫⲁⲥ ⲛⲁϥ ϫⲉ ⲁⲣⲓ ⲧⲁⲅⲁⲡⲏ ⲛⲅⲃⲱⲕ ⲉϩⲟⲩⲛ ⲉⲧⲉⲓⲡⲟⲗⲓ̈ⲥ ·
ⲛⲅϣⲓⲛⲉ ⲛⲥⲁ ⲟⲩⲥϩⲓ̈ⲙⲉ ⲙⲙⲉⲥⲉⲓ̈ⲱ̄ ⲛⲉⲥⲉⲓ · ⲛ̄ⲥϩⲙⲟⲟⲥ ϩⲁϩⲧⲏⲓ̈ ·
ϣⲁⲛⲧⲉ ⲡⲛⲟⲩⲧⲉ ⲃⲱϣ ⲛⲁⲓ̈ · ⲧⲁϫⲡⲟ · ⲙⲡⲉⲧϩⲛ̄ ⲧⲁⲕⲁⲗⲁϩⲏ ·
32Ⲡϩⲗⲗⲟ ⲇⲉ ⲉⲧⲥⲙⲁⲙⲁⲁⲧ · ⲁϥⲉⲓ ⲉⲃⲟⲗ ϩⲛ ⲡⲉⲭⲱⲣⲓⲟⲛ ⲉⲧⲙⲙⲁⲩ
ⲉϥⲕⲱⲧⲉ ⲛ̄ⲥⲁ ⲟⲩⲥϩⲓⲙⲉ · ⲙ̄ⲙⲉⲥⲉⲓ̈ⲱ̄ · 33Ϩⲟⲥⲟⲛ ⲉϥⲛⲃⲟⲗ ⲉϥⲕⲱⲧⲉ · ⲁ
ⲧⲡⲁⲣⲑⲉⲛⲟⲥ ⲉⲧⲟⲩⲁⲁⲃ ϫⲡⲟ ⲙⲡⲉⲥϣⲏⲣⲉ · ϩⲛ ⲟⲩⲙⲛⲧⲁⲧⲉⲓⲙⲉ ⲉⲣⲟⲥ ·
ⲁⲥϭⲟⲟⲗⲉϥ |

FRAGMENT III.

Cod. Borg. cxix p. ⲗⲑ

1... ⲁⲩⲱϣ ⲅ̄ⲉ̄ⲃⲟⲗ ϫⲉ ⲁ ⲧⲙⲁⲁⲩ ⲙⲡⲣⲣⲟ ⲛ̄ⲁ ⲛⲁⲛ · ⲁⲥϯ ⲛ̄ⲱⲛ̄ϩ
ⲛⲁⲛ · 2Ⲁⲩⲱ ⲁⲛϣⲱⲱⲧ̄ ⲛ̄ϩⲉⲛⲕⲉⲁⲗⲉⲕⲧⲱⲣ ⲙⲛ ϩⲉⲛⲕⲉⲥⲧⲣⲟⲩⲑⲟⲥ ·
ⲁⲩϫⲓⲧⲛ̄ϩ ⲁⲩϩⲱⲗ ⲉⲃⲟⲗ ⲙⲡⲉⲥⲏⲧ̄ ⲙ̄ⲡⲉⲭⲁⲗⲭⲓ̈ⲟⲛ · 3ⲁⲛⲉⲓ̈ ⲁⲛϫⲱ
ⲉⲣⲟ ⲙⲡⲉⲛⲧⲁϥϣⲱⲡⲉ · Ⲙⲏⲡⲱⲥ ⲛⲧⲉ ⲛ̄ϩⲏⲅⲉⲙⲱⲛ ϭⲱⲛ̄ⲧ ⲉⲣⲟⲛ
ⲛ̄ϥϩⲱⲧⲃ̄ ⲙⲙⲟⲛ · 4Ⲧⲟⲧⲉ ⲙⲁⲣⲓ̈ⲁ ⲁⲥⲱϣ ⲉⲃⲟⲗ ⲉⲥϫⲱ ⲙⲙⲟⲥ ϫⲉ
ⲡⲛⲁ ⲧⲏⲣϥ̄ ⲛ̄ⲱⲕ ⲡⲉ ⲡ̄ⲁϫⲟⲉⲓⲥ · 5Ⲁⲥⲕⲟⲧⲥ̄ ⲉⲙⲙⲁⲅⲉⲓⲣⲟⲥ ⲉⲥϫⲱ
ⲙ̄ⲙⲟⲥ · ϫⲉ ⲙ̄ⲡⲣ̄ⲣ̄ϩⲟⲧⲉ ⲉⲃⲟⲗ ϫⲉ ⲛⲧⲁ ⲡⲁⲓ̈ ϣⲱ|ⲡⲉ ⲉⲧⲃⲏⲏⲧ̄ · ⲉⲃⲟⲗ
ϫⲉ ⲙⲡⲉⲓ̈ϫⲓϯⲡⲉ ⲙⲡⲕⲟⲥⲙⲟⲥ ⲉⲡⲉϩ · 6Ⲧⲟⲧⲉ ⲡⲉϫⲁⲥ ⲙ̄ⲡⲙⲟⲩⲗⲗⲓ̈ⲁⲣⲏⲥ
ϫⲉ ϫⲱⲣⲙ̄ ⲟⲛ ⲉⲑⲏ ⲛ̄ⲕⲉⲕⲟⲩⲓ̈ · 7Ⲛ̄ⲧⲉⲣⲟⲩϫⲱⲣⲙ̄ ⲟⲛ ⲉⲑⲏ ⲛ̄ⲕⲉⲕⲟⲩⲓ ·
ⲁⲩⲧⲁϩⲉ ⲟⲩⲓ̈ⲟⲩⲱⲧ̄ ⲛⲁⲗⲁⲃⲁⲥⲧⲣⲟⲛ̄ ⲉϣⲁⲩⲙⲟⲩⲧⲉ ⲉⲣⲟϥ ϫⲉ ⲉⲗⲁ-
ⲭⲓⲥⲧⲏⲥ ⲁϥϩⲉ ⲉⲡⲉⲥⲏⲧ̄ 8ⲁⲩⲱ ⲛ̄ⲕⲉⲧⲟⲩⲱⲧ̄ ⲧ̄ⲏⲣⲟⲩ ⲛ̄ϩⲟⲙⲛⲧ · ⲙⲛ

the way at the borders of Bethlehem, the guileless old man cf. Mt II 16
looked into the face of the Virgin, and found it shining as
the sun; and she was troubled. 27 And he said to her, Where- cf. Ge XL
fore is thy face sad to-day? 28 And she said to him, That 6, 7
which is in my womb troubleth me, that I should bring it
forth. 29 And Joseph the righteous said to the Virgin, cf. Mt I 19
O Mary, fear not: that which cometh forth from thee[a]
shall succour thee. 30 And he took her into an inn in the
way[b] with their money which they had. 31 Then she said to
him: Do *me* the kindness to go into this city and seek
a midwife, to come and sit by me, till God relieve me and
I bring forth that which is in my womb. 32 And the blessed
old man went forth among those places searching for a mid-
wife. 33 Whilst he was without searching, the holy Virgin cf. Lc II 7
brought forth her Son in virginity[c]; and she wrapped
Him.........

FRAGMENT III.

They cried out, The mother of the King had mercy on
us and gave us life. 2 And we killed[d] other cocks and other
birds, and they took wings and flew from under the caldrons;
3 and we came and told thee what took place, lest perchance
the governor be angry with us and slay us. 4 Then Mary
cried out, saying, All the mercy is Thine, my Lord. 5 And
she turned to the cooks[e], saying, Fear not, because this hath
taken place on my account, because I have never tasted the
world.

6 Then she said to the muleteer, Drive again forward a
little more. 7 When they had again driven forward a little
more, they reached an image of alabaster called Elachistes;
and it fell down: 8 and all the images also[f] of bronze and

[a] Or *from thy womb* [b] Lit. *being in the way* [c] Lit. *ignorance*
[d] Or *sacrificed* [e] Or *butchers* [f] Or *all the other images*

ⲛϣⲉ · ⲙⲛ ⲛⲱⲛⲉ ⲉⲧⲙⲡⲉϥⲕⲱⲧⲉ · ⲁⲩϩⲉ ϩⲓⲑⲏ ⲙⲙⲁⲣⲓⲁ ⲧⲏⲣⲟⲩ ·
9 ⲡⲉϫⲉ ⲙⲁⲣⲓ̈ⲁ ⲛⲁⲩ ϫⲉ ⲟⲩ ⲡⲉ ⲡⲉⲧⲛϩⲱⲃ ⲉⲧⲉⲧⲛⲡⲗⲁⲛⲁ ⲛⲛⲣⲱⲙⲉ
p. ⲙ ⲛⲧⲉⲓⲡⲟⲗⲓⲥ ⲉⲩⲟⲩⲉⲙ ⲥⲁⲣⲝ | ⲛⲣⲱⲙⲉ · 10 ⲛⲧⲉⲩⲛⲟⲩ ⲁⲥⲕⲓⲙ ⲉⲣⲟⲟⲩ
ⲉⲧⲣⲉⲩϣⲁϫⲉ ϩⲛ ⲟⲩⲁⲥⲡⲉ ⲛⲣⲱⲙⲉ · ⲁⲩⲱ ⲁⲩϣⲁϫⲉ ⲉⲩⲛ̇ⲏϫ ⲉⲃⲟⲗ
ϩⲓϫⲙ ⲡⲕⲁϩ 11 ϫⲉ ⲧⲛϫⲟⲉⲓⲥ ⲧⲣⲣⲱ ⲙⲡⲣⲧⲁⲕⲟⲛ ϩⲁ ⲛ̇ⲉⲛⲡⲉⲑⲟⲟⲩ ϫⲉ
ⲉⲣⲉ ⲡⲁⲣⲓⲕⲉ ⲉⲣⲟⲛ ⲁⲛ · 12 ⲁⲥϣⲱⲡⲉ ⲛⲧⲉⲣⲉ ⲧⲉⲛϫⲟⲉⲓ̈ⲥ ⲉⲓ̈ ⲉϩⲟⲩⲛ
ⲉⲧⲉⲓⲡⲟⲗⲓ̈ⲥ ϩⲓ ⲣⲟⲩϩⲉ · ⲁ ⲡⲇⲓⲁⲃⲟⲗⲟⲥ ⲉⲓ̈ ⲁϥⲣⲓⲙⲉ ⲙⲡⲉⲛⲙⲧⲟ ⲉⲃⲟⲗ
13 ϫⲉ ⲟⲩⲟⲓ ⲛⲁⲛ ϫⲉ ⲉⲣⲉ ⲙⲁⲣⲓ̈ⲁ ⲛⲁⲧⲁⲕⲟ ⲛⲧⲁⲉⲣⲅⲁⲥⲓⲁ ⲛⲧⲟⲟⲧ
ⲛⲣⲁⲥⲧⲉ · 14 ⲁⲛⲟⲛ ⲇⲉ ⲁⲛϫⲛⲟⲩϥ ϫⲉ ⲉϣⲱⲡⲉ ⲟⲩⲛ ϭⲟⲙ ⲙⲙⲟⲕ ·
ⲙⲁⲕⲃⲟⲏⲑⲉⲓ ⲉⲣⲟⲛ̇ · 15 ⲁϥⲟⲩⲱϣⲃ ϫⲉ ⲁ ⲧⲁϭⲟⲙ ⲱϫⲛ ⲛ|ⲛⲁϩⲣⲛ
ⲧⲉⲧ⌜ⲙ⌝ⲙⲁⲩ · ⲁⲗⲗⲁ ϯⲥⲟⲟⲩⲛ ⲙⲡⲉϯⲛⲁⲁⲁϥ · 16 ϯⲛⲁⲧⲱⲟⲩⲛ ⲧⲁⲃⲱⲕ
ⲛⲁⲓ̈ ⲉⲛⲧⲟⲟⲩ ϣⲁⲛⲧⲉⲥⲃⲱⲕ ⲛⲁⲥ ϩⲛ ⲧⲡⲟⲗⲓⲥ ⲉⲃⲟⲗ ϫⲉ ⲛ̇ϯⲛⲁ-
ϣⲁϩⲉⲣⲁⲧ ⲁⲛ ϩⲁϩⲧⲏⲥ ⲁⲩⲱ ⲉⲓ̈ⲥ ϩⲏⲏⲧⲉ ⲉⲥⲛⲁⲧⲁⲕⲉⲧⲏⲩⲧⲛ ⲛⲣⲁⲥⲧⲉ ·
17 ⲁⲩⲱ ⲉⲥϣⲁⲛⲃⲱⲕ ⲛⲁⲥ ϯⲛⲁⲕⲧⲟⲓ̈ ⲡⲉϯⲛⲁⲉϣϭⲙϭⲟⲙ[a] ⲉⲡⲗⲁⲛⲁ
ⲙⲙⲟϥ ⲟⲛ · ϯⲛⲁⲥⲟⲕϥ ⲛⲁⲓ̈ ⲛⲕⲉⲥⲟⲛ · 18 ⲧⲟⲧⲉ ⲙⲁⲣⲓⲁ ⲡⲉϫⲁⲥ
ⲛⲛⲣⲱⲙⲉ ⲛⲧⲡⲟⲗⲓⲥ ⲙⲛ· ⲡϩⲏⲅⲉⲙⲱⲛ̇ ϫⲉ ⲁⲧⲉⲧⲛⲥⲱⲧⲙ ϫⲉ ⲉⲣⲉ
p. ⲙⲁ ⲡⲉⲓⲡⲗⲁⲛⲟⲥ ϫⲱ ⲙⲙⲟⲥ ϫⲉ ⲟⲩ · 19 ⲗⲟⲓⲡⲟⲛ ⲉⲓⲥϩⲏⲏ|⌜ⲧⲉ ⲁ⌝ⲧⲉⲧⲛⲉⲓ̈ⲙⲉ
⌜ϫ⌝ⲉ ⲙⲛⲧⲁϥ ⲗⲁⲁⲩ ⲛϭⲟⲙ ⲙⲙⲁⲩ · ⲙⲡⲣⲕⲁⲁϥ ⲉⲣϩⲁⲗ ⲛⲕⲉⲥⲟⲛ ·
20 ⲧⲟⲧⲉ ⲁⲥⲟⲩⲉϩⲥⲁϩⲛⲉ ⲉⲧⲣⲉ ⲛⲉⲧⲟⲩⲱⲧ ⲛⲧⲡⲟⲗⲓⲥ ⲧⲏⲣⲟⲩ ⲃⲱⲕ
ⲉⲡⲉϫⲁⲟⲥ ⲙⲡⲛⲟⲩⲛ ϣⲁ ⲡⲉϩⲟⲟⲩ ⲙⲡϩⲁⲡ ⲛⲥⲉⲣⲙⲛⲧⲣⲉ ⲉⲡⲉⲓ̇ⲧⲁⲩ-
ⲧⲁⲙⲓ̈ⲟⲟⲩ · 21 ⲁⲩⲱ ⲁ ⲛⲉⲧⲧⲱⲟⲩⲛ ϩⲁ ⲛⲥⲓ̈ⲅⲛⲟⲛ ϫⲓⲧⲟⲩ ⲉϫⲙ ⲡⲃⲏⲙⲁ
ⲛϣⲟⲣⲡ ⲁⲩⲕⲁⲁⲩ ⲉϫⲙ ⲡⲃⲏⲙⲁ ⲙⲙⲁ ⲛⲧⲁⲩⲡⲱⲣϣ ⲙⲡⲉⲑⲣⲟⲛⲟⲥ
ⲙⲙⲁⲣⲓ̈ⲁ · 22 ⲁⲩⲱ ⲁ ⲡⲥⲓⲅⲛⲟⲛ ⲕⲟⲗϫⲟⲩ ⲁⲧⲟⲩⲱϣⲧ ⲙⲡⲉⲑⲣⲟⲛⲟⲥ
ⲉⲩϫⲱ ⲙⲙⲟⲥ ϫⲉ ⲧⲛⲛⲁⲟⲩⲱϣⲧ ⲙⲡⲙⲁ ⲉⲧⲉⲣⲉ | ⲧⲣⲣⲱ ⲛⲁϩⲙⲟⲟⲥ
ϩⲓϫⲱϥ · 23 ⲡⲉϫⲉ ⲙⲁⲣⲓ̈ⲁ ⲙⲡϩⲏⲅⲉⲙⲱⲛ · ϫⲉ ⲙⲁⲅⲣⲓⲛⲟⲥ ⲁⲕⲧⲣⲉⲩϫⲓ
ⲛⲛⲥⲓ̈ⲅⲛⲟⲛ ⲉⲡⲃⲏⲙ̇ⲁ ⲛϣ⌜ⲟ⌝ⲣⲡ ⲉⲕϫⲱ ⲙⲙ⌜ⲟⲥ⌝ ϫⲉ ⲙⲙⲟⲣⲫⲏ ⌜ⲛⲉ⌝
ⲛⲛⲉⲣⲱⲟⲩ · 24 ⲛⲅⲥⲟⲟⲩⲛ ⲁⲛ ⌜ϫⲉ⌝ ⲁ ⲡϣⲟⲙⲛⲧ ⲛⲉⲣⲱⲟⲩ ⲣϣ⌜ⲟⲣⲡ⌝
ⲉⲡⲃⲏⲙⲁ ⲉ⌜ⲧⲉ⌝ ⲛⲁⲓ ⲡⲉ ⲡⲉⲩ⌜ⲣⲁⲛ⌝ ⲡⲉⲓⲱⲧ ⲙ⌜ⲛ⌝ ⲡϣⲏⲣⲉ ⲙ⌜ⲛ⌝ ⲡⲉⲡⲛⲁ
ⲉⲧ⌜ⲟⲩⲁⲁⲃ ·⌝ 25 ⲛⲧⲉⲩⲛⲟⲩ ⲛⲧ⌜ⲁ⌝ ⲙⲁⲣⲓⲁ ϩⲙⲟⲟ⌜ⲥ⌝ ⲉϫⲙ ⲡⲃⲏⲙ⌜ⲁ⌝

[a] ⲛ in marg.

of wood and of stone which were around it, they all fell
before Mary.

9 Mary said to them, What do ye deceiving the men of
this city, whilst they eat[a] men's flesh? 10 Straightway she
moved them so that they should speak in human language;
and they spake lying down on the ground, 11 Our lady *and*
queen, destroy us not for our evil deeds, for we are not to
blame. 12 It came to pass when our lady came into this city
at even, the devil came and wept before us, *saying*, 13 Woe to
us, for Mary is about to destroy my craft for[b] me to-morrow.
14 And we asked him, If thou canst, wilt thou not help us? cf. Mc ix
15 He answered, My power has failed before her[c]. But I know 22*
what I will do; 16 I will arise and go to the mount until she
go from the city, because I shall not be able to stand with
her, and behold she will destroy you to-morrow. 17 And when
she goeth, I will return, and him whom I shall have power
to deceive still, I will draw[d] to me again.

18 Then Mary said to the men of the city and to the
governor, Ye have heard what this deceiver saith. 19 But cf. Mt
behold ye knew that he had[e] not any power: do not suffer xxvii 63*
him to beguile *you* again. 20 Then she commanded all the
images of the city to go to the chasm of the abyss until cf. Job
the day of judgment, to bear witness against those that xli 23
made them.

21 And they that bare the standards took them to the
judgment seat first, and set them at the judgment seat,
where the throne of Mary was prepared[f]. 22 And the stand-
ards bowed themselves, and worshipped the throne, saying,
We will worship the place whereon the queen will sit.
23 Mary said to the governor, Magrinus, hast thou caused the
standards to be taken to the judgment seat first, saying,
They are the shapes of kings? 24 Knowest thou not that
the three Kings came first to the judgment seat, whose
names are the Father and the Son and the Holy Ghost?
25 Straightway when Mary sat on the judgment seat, the earth cf. Ps
xcviii 1*

Lit. *eating* [b] Or *from* [c] Or *before that* power [d] Or *drag*
[e] Lit. *has* [f] Lit. *was strewn* with coverings

ⲁϥⲕⲓ̈ⲙ ⲛ̄ϭⲓ ⲡ̄⸢ⲕⲁϩ⸣ ⲁⲩⲱϣ ⲉⲃⲟⲗ ⲛ̄ϭⲓ ⲛⲉϩⲣⲟⲩⲃⲃⲁ⸢ⲓ⸣ ⲁⲩⲃⲱϭⲉ ⲛ̄ϭⲓ
ⲛⲉⲃⲣⲏϭⲉ · [26]ⲁ ⲛⲉⲧⲙⲟⲟⲩⲧ̄ ⲧⲱⲟⲩⲛ ⲁⲩⲉⲓ ⲉⲃⲟⲗ ϩⲛ ⲛⲧⲁⲫⲟⲥ · ⲁⲩⲉⲓ |
p. ⲙⲃ ⲉϫⲙ̄ ⲡ̄ⲃⲏⲙ̄ⲁ ⲁⲩⲁϩⲉⲣⲁⲧⲟⲩ ⲛ̄ⲥⲉϣⲁϫⲉ ⲁⲛ̄ · [27]ⲁϥⲟⲩⲱⲛ̄ϩ ⲉⲃⲟⲗ
ⲛ̄ϭⲓ ⲡ̄ⲛⲟⲩⲛ̄ · ⲁⲩⲟⲩⲱⲛ̄ϩ ⲉⲃⲟⲗ ⲛ̄ϭⲓ ⲛⲧⲁⲙⲓ̈ⲟⲛ ⸢ⲙ⸣ⲛ ⲛⲧ̄ⲁⲣⲧⲁⲣⲟⲥ ·
ⲁⲩⲁϩⲉⲣⲁⲧⲟⲩ ⲛ̄⸢ϭⲓ⸣ ⲛ̄ⲁⲅⲅⲉⲗⲟⲥ ⲛ̄⸢ⲣⲉ⸣ϥϫⲓ̈ⲕⲃⲁ · ⲛ̄⸢ⲑⲉ⸣ ⲛ̄ϩⲉⲛ̄ϣⲁϩ
⸢ⲛ⸣ⲕⲱϩ̄ⲧ [28]ⲁⲩ⸢ⲟⲩ⸣ⲱⲛ̄ϩ ⲉⲃⲟⲗ ⸢ⲛϭ⸣ⲓ̈ ⲛ̄ⲧⲁⲙⲓⲟⲛ̄ ⸢ⲉⲧ⸣ⲙⲏϩ ⲛ̄ⲁⲙ⸢ⲣⲏ⸣ϩⲉ ·
ⲙ̄ⲛ ⲡ̄⸢ⲧⲟ⸣ⲡ̄ⲟⲥ ⲛ̄ⲑⲏⲛ̄ : [29]⸢Ⲁⲩ⸣ⲱ ⲁϥⲉⲓ ⲛ̄ϭⲓ ⲙⲓ̈⸢ⲭ⸣ⲁⲏ̄ⲗ ⲙ̄ⲛ ⲛⲉϥ-
⸢ⲁ⸣ⲅⲅⲉⲗⲟⲥ ⲉⲣⲉ ⸢ϩ⸣ⲉⲛ̄ⲕⲗⲟⲙ ⲛ̄ⲧⲟⲟⲧⲟⲩ ⲛ̄ϩⲟⲓ̈ⲛ̄ⲉ · ⲉⲣⲉ ϩⲉⲛⲛⲧ̄ⲏⲙⲁ
ⲛ̄ⲧ̄ⲛ ϩⲉⲛⲕⲟⲟⲩⲉ · [30]Ⲁⲩⲱ ⲁⲥϣⲁϫⲉ ⲙ̄ⲛ ⲡ̄| ⲣⲉϥⲙ̄ⲟⲟⲩⲧ̄ ϫⲉ ⲛ̄ⲉⲓⲙⲏⲥ-
ⲧ⸢ⲏ⸣ⲣⲓⲟⲛ ⲛⲁⲓ ⲙⲡ̄⸢ⲱⲓ⸣ ⲁⲛ ⲡ̄ⲉ ⲁⲗⲗⲁ ⲡ̄⸢ⲁ⸣ ⲡ̄ⲁϣⲏⲣⲉ ⲡ̄ⲉ ⲁⲩⲱ ⲡϣⲏⲣⲉ
ⲙⲡ̄ⲣ̄ⲣⲟ ⲙ̄ⲙⲉ ⲡ̄ⲣⲉϥϯϩⲁⲡ̄ · [31]Ⲃⲱⲕ ⲛⲏⲧⲛ̄ ⲉⲛ̄ⲉⲧⲛ̄ⲧⲁⲫⲟⲥ ⲛ̄ⲧⲉⲧⲛ̄ⲙⲧⲟⲛ
ⲙ̄ⲙⲱⲧⲛ̄ ϣⲁ ⲧ̄ⲡⲁⲣⲣⲟⲩⲥⲓⲁ ⲙ̄ⲡⲁϣⲏⲣⲉ · [32]ⲁⲥϩⲱⲛ̄ ⲅⲁⲣ ⲉϩⲟⲩⲛ̄ ⲡ̄ⲁⲣⲁ
ⲕⲉⲕⲟⲩⲓ ⲛ̄ⲧⲉ ⲡ̄ⲟⲩⲁ ⲡ̄ⲟⲩⲁ ϫⲓ ⲡ̄ⲣⲟⲥ ⲛ̇ⲉⲛ̇ⲧⲁϥⲁⲁⲩ ⲉⲓ̈ⲧ̄ⲉ ⲁⲅⲁⲑⲟⲛ̄
ⲉⲓ̈ⲧ̄ⲉ ⲡⲉⲑⲟⲟⲩ · [33]Ⲁⲥⲕⲟⲧⲥ̄ ⲟⲛ̄ ⲉⲡ̄ϩⲏⲅⲉⲙⲱⲛ̄ · ⲡ̄ⲉϫⲁⲥ ϫⲉ ⲁⲧⲉⲧⲛ̄ⲛ̄ⲁⲩ
ⲉⲧⲉⲓⲁϣⲏ ⲛ̄ⲃⲁⲥⲁⲛⲟⲥ · [34]ⲉⲓⲥ ⲡ̄ⲕⲱϩ̄ⲧ · |

FRAGMENT IV.

Cod. Borg. cxx p. 67 [1].ⲙⲡⲟⲩϩⲏⲧ ⲧⲏⲣϥ Ⲁⲩⲱ ⲛ̇ⲑⲉ ⲉϣϫⲉ ⲉⲣⲉ ⲡⲥⲱⲧⲉ ⲙⲡⲓ̄ⲏ̄ⲗ ⲛⲏⲩ
ⲉⲃⲟⲗ ϩⲛ ⲓⲟⲩⲇⲁ · [2]Ⲁⲥⲟⲩⲱϣⲃ ⲛ̄ϭⲓ ⲙⲁⲣⲓ̈ⲁ ⲡⲉϫⲁⲥ ϫⲉ Ϥⲥⲙⲁⲙⲁⲁⲧ
ⲛ̇ϭⲓ ⲡϫⲟⲉⲓⲥ ⲥⲁⲃⲁⲱⲑ ⲡⲉⲛⲧⲁϥⲧⲁϩⲙⲉⲧ ϫⲓ̈ⲛ̇ ⲉⲓ̈ⲛϩⲏⲧⲥ ⲛ̇ⲧⲁⲙⲁⲁⲩ
ⲉⲧⲣⲁϣⲙϣⲉ ⲛⲁϥ ⲛ̇ⲛⲉϩⲟⲟⲩ ⲧⲏⲣⲟⲩ ⲙ̇ⲡⲁⲱⲛϩ · [3]Ⲁⲩⲱ ⲛ̇ⲉⲩⲥⲟⲗⲥⲗ
ⲛ̇ⲛⲉⲩⲉⲣⲏⲩ ⲛ̇ⲧⲥⲛⲧⲉ ⲛ̇ⲟⲩⲙⲏⲏϣⲉ ⲛ̇ϩⲟⲟⲩ ⲉⲃⲟⲗ ϩⲛ ⲛⲉⲅⲣⲁⲫⲏ ⲛ̇ⲛⲓϥⲉ
ⲛ̇ⲧⲉ ⲡⲛⲟⲩⲧⲉ · [4]Ⲙⲛ̇ⲛ̇ⲥⲱⲥ ⲁ ⲉⲗⲓ̈ⲥⲁⲃⲉⲧ ⲕⲟⲧⲥ ⲉϩⲣⲁⲓ̈ ⲉⲛⲉⲥⲏⲓ̈ ⲁⲩⲱ
ⲉⲧⲉⲥⲡⲟⲗⲓ̈ⲥ ⲧⲟⲣⲓ̈ⲛⲏ [5]ⲛⲉ ϣⲁⲥϭⲓⲛⲉ[a] ⲅⲁⲣ ⲙ̇ⲡⲉⲥϣⲓⲛⲉ ⲛⲟⲩⲙ̄ⲏⲏϣⲉ
ⲛ̇ⲥⲟⲡ ⲧⲉⲣⲟⲙⲡⲉ · ⲉⲥⲇⲓ̈ⲁⲕⲟⲛⲉⲓ ⲉⲣⲟⲥ ϩⲛ ⲛⲉⲧⲥⲣⲭⲣⲓ̈ⲁ ⲙⲙⲟⲟⲩ
ⲧⲏⲣⲟⲩ̇ ϣⲁ[a] ⲡⲉϩⲟⲟⲩ ⲛ̇ⲧⲁ ⲅⲁⲃⲣⲓ̈ⲏⲗ ⲡⲁⲣⲭⲁⲅⲅⲉⲗⲟⲥ ϫⲟⲟⲥ

[a] ϣ in marg.

was moved, the thunders sounded, the lightnings flashed. cf. Ps xvii 8 ff; Mt
26 The dead arose and came forth from the tombs, and came xxvii 51 ff
to the judgment seat, and stood in silence[a]. 27 The abyss cf. Ps xvii 16
was manifested: the storehouses and the nether regions were
manifested: the avenging angels stood like flames of fire.
28 The storehouses full of pitch and the places of brimstone
were manifested. 29 And Michael came together with his
angels; some having garlands, and others garments. 30 And
she spake with the dead, *saying*, This mystery is not mine,
but it belongs to my Son and the Son of the true King,
the Judge. 31 Go to your tombs, and rest until the
coming of my Son; 32 for it is almost at hand, that each one 2 Co v 10*
may receive according to the things that he hath done,
whether good or evil. 33 She turned again to the governor,
and said, Ye have seen this multitude of torments. 34 Behold
the fire.........

FRAGMENT IV.

...all thy heart, and as if the redemption of Israel cometh
forth from Judah. 2 Mary answered and said, Blessed is the
Lord Sabaoth, who hath called me from my mother's womb, cf. Ga i 15
to serve Him all the days of my life. 3 And they twain were cf. Lc i 74, 75
comforting one another many days from the scriptures in- cf. 2 Ti
spired[b] of God. 4 Afterwards Elisabeth returned unto her iii 16*
house and to her city Torine. 5 For she used to visit her cf. Lc i 39, 56
many times each year, ministering to her in all those things
of which she had[c] need; until the day that Gabriel the

[a] Lit. *they speak not* [b] Lit. *the scriptures, the inspirations* [c] Lit. *has*

ⲙⲙⲁⲣⲓ̈ⲁ ϫⲉ ⲃⲱⲕ | ϣⲁ ⲉⲗⲓⲥⲁⲃⲉⲧ[a] ⲧⲟⲩⲥⲩⲅⲅⲉⲛⲏⲥ [6]ⲁ̄ ⲡϩⲱⲃ[b] ⲟⲩⲁϩϥ
ⲛ̄ⲥⲁ ⲡϣⲁϫⲉ ⲕⲁⲧⲁ ⲡⲉⲛⲁⲛⲧⲓ̈ⲟⲛ ϫⲉ ⲁⲩⲣ̄ϣⲃⲏⲣ ⲙ̄ⲛ ⲛⲉⲩⲉⲣⲏⲩ ⲉⲃⲟⲗ
ϫⲉ ⲁⲩϫⲟⲟⲥ[c] ⲛ̄ⲧⲡⲁⲣⲑⲉⲛⲟⲥ ϫⲉ ⲧⲟⲩⲥⲩⲅⲅⲉⲛⲏⲥ ⲧⲉ [7]ⲕⲁⲓ̈ ⲧⲟ̈ⲉⲛⲁⲛⲧⲓⲟⲛ
ⲧⲉⲥⲥⲩⲅⲅⲉⲛⲏⲥ ⲧⲉ ⲕⲁⲧⲁ ⲡϩⲱⲃ ⲥⲛⲁⲩ ⲛ̄ⲧⲁⲓ̈ϫⲟⲟⲩ ⲛⲁ ⲛⲉϥⲩⲗⲏ ⲙ̄ⲛ
ⲛⲁ ⲙⲛⲧϣⲃⲉⲉⲣⲉ[d]· ⁘ [8]ⲁⲩⲉⲓ̈ⲥ ϭⲉ ⲛ̄ⲧⲛⲕⲧⲟⲛ ⲉϫⲛ· ⲟⲩⲩⲡⲟⲑⲉⲥⲓ̈ⲥ ⲛ̄ⲧⲣ̄ⲣⲱ
ⲧⲙⲁⲁⲩ ⲙ̄ⲡⲣⲣⲟ [9]ⲛⲟⲩϩⲓ̈ⲥⲉ ⲁⲛ ⲡⲉ ⲉϣⲁϫⲉ ⲉⲣⲟⲥ[e] ⲟⲩⲇⲉ ⲛⲟⲩⲁ-
ⲧⲟⲡⲟⲛ ⲁⲛ ⲡⲉ ⲛⲛⲉⲧⲥⲱⲧⲙ ⲉⲣⲟⲥ[e] [10]ⲙ̄ⲡⲉⲥⲙⲟⲧ ⲅⲁⲣ ⲛ̄ⲟⲩⲁ ⲉϥⲟⲩⲱϣ
ⲉϣⲓⲕⲉ ⲛ̄ⲥⲁ ⲟⲩⲙⲟⲟⲩ ⲉϥⲟϣ ⸢ⲏ̄⸣ ⲉϥⲛⲟⲛⲧ̄ ⲛ̄ⲟⲩⲡⲓ̈ⲅⲏ· ⲕⲁⲓ̈ ⲙ̄ⲛⲛ ⲣⲱ
ϩⲙ ⲡⲧⲣⲉϥϩⲓ̈ⲧⲟⲟⲧϥ ⲉϣⲓ̈ⲕⲉ ϣⲁⲣⲉ ⲧⲡⲓ̈ⲅⲏ ⲃⲉⲉⲃⲉ ⲉ̀ϩⲣⲁⲓ̈ ⲉⲡⲉϩⲟⲩⲟ
p. 68 [11]ⲧⲁⲓ̈ ϭⲉ[f] ϩⲱ̈ ⲧⲉ ⲧⲁϩⲉ ϩⲙ ⲡ|ⲧⲣⲁϩⲓ̈ⲧⲟⲟⲧ ⲉⲁⲣⲭⲉⲓ̈ ⲛ̄ϣⲁϫⲉ
ⲛⲙⲙⲛⲧⲛ̄ ⲉⲧⲃⲉ ⲡⲉⲛⲕⲟⲧⲕ ⲛ̄ⲧⲡⲁⲣⲑⲉⲛⲟⲥ ⲉⲧⲧⲁⲉⲓ̈ⲏⲩ ⲧⲙⲁⲁⲩ ⲙⲡⲉⲛ-
ⲣⲣⲟ ⲧⲏⲣⲛ ⲡⲉⲭ͞ⲥ ⲁⲥⲃⲉⲉⲃⲉ ⲛⲁⲛ ⲉϩⲣⲁⲓ̈ ⲉⲡⲉϩⲟⲩⲟ ⲛ̄ϭⲓ̈ ⲧⲡⲏⲅⲏ
ⲙ̄ⲡⲗⲟ̀ⲅⲟ̀ⲥ· [12]ⲡⲕⲁⲓⲣⲟⲥ ⲅⲁⲣ ⲗⲟⲓⲡⲟⲛ ⲡⲉ ⲉⲧⲣⲉⲛⲱϣ ⲉⲃⲟⲗ ϩⲱⲱⲛ
ⲙ̄ⲛ ⲡⲉⲡⲣⲟⲫⲏⲧⲏⲥ ⲇⲁⲩⲉⲓⲇ ⲁⲩⲱ ⲛ̄ⲧⲛ̄ϫⲓⲥⲉ ⲛ̄ⲧⲛⲥⲙⲏ[g]· ⲙ̄ⲛ ⲡⲣⲉϥ-
ⲥⲉϩⲟⲩⲉⲗⲗⲉ ⲉⲧⲛⲟⲧⲙ ϩⲙ[h] ⲡⲉⲡⲛ͞ⲁ ⲉⲧⲟⲩⲁⲁⲃ ⲉⲛϫⲱ ⲙⲙⲟⲥ [13]ϫⲉ
ⲁⲕⲧⲥⲁⲃⲟⲛ ⲉϩⲟⲩⲉ ⲉⲛⲉⲧⲧⲥⲁⲃⲟ· ⲙⲙⲟⲛ ⲧⲏⲣⲟⲩ [14]ⲁⲩⲱ ⲟⲛ ϫⲉ
ⲡⲟⲩⲱⲛϩ ⲉⲃⲟⲗ ⲛ̄ⲛⲉⲕϣⲁϫⲉ ⲡⲉⲧⲣ̄ⲟⲩⲟⲉⲓⲛ ⲉ̀ⲣⲟⲓ̈· [15]ⲉ̄ⲓ̈ⲙⲟⲩϣⲧ ⲅⲁⲣ
ⲙ̄ⲙⲟⲓ̈ ϫⲉ ⲉⲓⲛⲁϯⲁⲣⲭⲏ ⲙ̄ⲡϣⲁϫⲉ ⲉⲃⲟⲗ ⲧⲱⲛ ⲁⲓ̈ⲣ̄ⲡⲙⲉⲉⲩⲉ ⲙ̄ⲡ-
ϣⲁϫⲉ ⲙ̄ⲡⲉⲛⲥⲱⲧⲏⲣ ⲡⲁⲓ̈ ⲛ̄ⲧⲁϥϫⲟⲟϥ ⲉⲧⲉϥⲙⲁⲁⲩ· ⲉⲧⲓ ⲉϥⲧⲁⲗⲏⲩ
ⲉϫⲙ ⲡⲉⲥ͞ⲧ͞ⲟ͞ⲥ ⲙ̄ⲛ ⲛⲕⲉ|ⲙⲁⲑⲏⲧⲏⲥ ⲉⲡⲉϥ⸢ⲙⲉ⸣ ⲙⲙⲟϥ ⲉϥϫⲱ̈ ⲙⲙⲟⲥ
ϫⲉ ⲧⲉⲥϩⲓ̈ⲙⲉ ⲉⲓ̈ⲥ ⲡⲟⲩϣⲏⲣⲉ [16]ⲁⲩⲱ ⲟⲛ ⲁϥⲕⲟⲧϥ ⲉⲓ̈ⲱϩⲁⲛⲛⲏⲥ ⲡⲉϫⲁϥ
ⲛⲁϥ ϫⲉ ⲡⲣⲱⲙⲉ ⲉⲓ̈ⲥ ⲧⲉⲕⲙⲁⲁⲩ· [17]ϫⲓⲛ ⲡⲉϩⲟⲟⲩ ⲉⲧⲙⲙⲁⲩ ⲡⲉϫⲉ
ⲡⲉⲥϩⲁⲓ̈ ⲉⲧⲟⲩⲁⲁⲃ ⲁϥϫⲓ̈ⲧⲥ ⲉϩⲟⲩⲛ ⲉⲡⲉϥⲏⲓ̈ ϣⲁ ⲡⲉϩⲟⲟⲩ ⲙ̄ⲡⲉⲥϫⲱⲕ
ⲉⲃⲟⲗ [18]ⲁⲩⲱ ⲡⲉϥⲇⲓ̈ⲁⲕⲟⲛⲉⲓ ⲛⲁⲥ ϩⲛ ⲇⲓ̈ⲁⲕⲟⲛⲓ̈ⲁ ⲛⲓⲙ ⲉⲧⲣ̄ⲭⲣⲓ̈ⲁ
ⲛⲁⲩ ⲁⲩⲱ ⲉⲛⲉϥⲥⲱⲧⲙ ⲛ̄ⲥⲱⲥ ⲛ̄ⲑⲉ ⲛ̄ⲟⲩϩⲙϩⲁⲗ ⲉϥⲥⲱⲧⲙ̄ ⲛ̄ⲥⲁ
ⲡⲉϥϫⲟⲉⲓ̈ⲥ [19]ⲛ̄ⲧⲟⲥ ⲇⲉ ϩⲱⲱⲥ ⲟⲛ ⲧⲡⲁⲣⲑⲉⲛⲟⲥ ⲉⲧⲟⲩⲁⲁⲃ ⲛⲉⲥⲙⲉ
ⲙ̄ⲙⲟϥ ⲛ̄ⲑⲉ ⲛ̄ⲟⲩⲙⲁⲁⲩ ⲛ̄ⲛⲉⲥϣⲏⲣⲉ [20]ⲁⲩⲱ ⲉⲛⲉⲥⲉⲓ̈ⲣⲉ ⲡⲉ ⲛ̄ϩⲉⲛ-
ⲙⲏⲏϣⲉ ⲛ̄ⲧⲁⲗϭⲟ ⲉⲃⲟⲗ ϩⲙ̄ ⲡⲗⲁ̀ⲟⲥ ⲉⲩⲧⲛⲧⲱⲛ ⲉⲛⲁ ⲛⲉⲥϣⲏⲣⲉ

[a] ⲉ 2° supra lin., sed pr. man. ut vid. [b] ⲛ in marg. [c] ϫ in marg. [d] ⲙ script. sup. ⲙ [e] ⲉⲣⲟϥ [f] ϭ in marg. [g] ⲛⲧⲛϫⲓⲥⲙⲏ [h] om. ϩⲙ

archangel said to Mary, Go to Elisabeth thy kinswoman. cf. Lc i 36
6 The matter followed the word contrariwise; for they became[a]
friends one with the other, because that it was told the
Virgin, She is thy kinswoman. 7 And contrariwise she was[b]
her kinswoman according to the two things which I have
said, that of the tribes and that of friendship.

8 Come then, let us turn to the subject of the Queen, the
mother of the King. 9 It is not a trouble to speak of it[c] nor
is it amiss for those who hear it[c]. 10 For as one wishing to
dig for much water or drawing forth *the water of* a fountain—
and indeed when he undertakes to dig, the fountain wells up
exceedingly—11 so then also with me, when I undertake to
begin to speak with you of the falling asleep of the glorious[d]
Virgin, the mother of the King of us all *even* Christ, the
fountain of the word has welled up for us exceedingly. 12 For
moreover the season is *come* for us also to cry out with the
prophet David, and to lift up our voice with the sweet
psalmist in[e] the holy Spirit, whilst we say, 13 Thou hast Ps cxviii 98*, 99*
taught us more than all those who teach us; 14 and again,
The manifestation of Thy words giveth light unto me. Ps cxviii 130*

15 For when I bethought me whence I should begin the
word, I remembered the word of our Saviour, which He Jn xix 26
spake to His mother, whilst still placed upon the cross, and cf. Jn xx 2
to the other disciple whom He loved, saying, Woman, behold,
thy son! 16 And again He turned to John, and said to him,
Man, behold, thy mother! 17 From that day, saith the holy Jn xix 27
scripture, he took her into his house till the day of her
death[f]; 18 and he was ministering to her in all ministrations
that she needed[g], and was obeying her as a servant obeying
his master. 19 And she also the holy Virgin was loving him
as a mother *loves* her children.

20 And she was working many cures from among the cf. Ac vi 8
people like those of her beloved Son Jesus Christ our Lord;

[a] Or *were* [b] Lit. *is* [c] The MS has *him* [d] Or *honourable*
[e] The MS omits *in* [f] Or *consummation* [g] Lit. *needs*

ⲙⲙⲉⲣⲓⲧ ⲓ̅ⲥ̅ ⲡⲉⲭ̅ⲥ̅ ⲡⲉⲛϫⲟⲉⲓ̈ⲥ [21]ⲁⲗⲗⲁ ⲉⲛⲉⲥⲕⲱⲗⲩ ⲛⲛⲁⲡⲟⲥⲧⲟⲗⲟⲥ
p. ⲝ⸢ⲑ⸣ ⲉⲧⲙ | ⸢ⲥ⸣ϩⲁⲓⲥⲟⲩ[a] · ⲉⲃⲟⲗ ϫⲉ ⲛⲉⲥⲛⲏⲧ ⲉⲃⲟⲗ ⲙⲡⲉⲟ̂ⲟⲩ ⲉⲧϣⲟⲩⲉⲓ̈ⲧ
ⲛ̄ⲛⲣⲱⲙⲉ [22]Ⲛⲉⲩⲟⲩⲏϩ ⲇⲉ ⲛ̄ⲥⲱⲥ ⲛ̄ϭⲓ̈ ⲛⲁⲡⲟⲥⲧⲟⲗⲟⲥ ⲛⲟⲩⲉⲓ̈ϣ ⲛⲓ̈ⲙ
ⲉⲩϫⲓ̈ⲥⲃⲱ ⲉⲛⲧⲁϣⲉⲟⲉⲓ̈ϣ ⲙ̄ⲡⲉⲩⲁⲅⲅⲉⲗⲓ̈ⲟⲛ ⲉⲃⲟⲗ ϩⲓ̈ⲧⲟⲟⲧⲥ [23]Ⲁⲩⲱ ⲛⲉ
ⲁⲥⲥⲉⲕ ⲟⲩⲙⲏⲛⲓϣⲉ ⲙ̄ⲡⲁⲣⲑⲉⲛⲟⲥ ϣⲁⲣⲟⲥ ⲉⲥⲡⲣⲟϩⲓ̈ⲥⲧⲁ ⲉϫⲱⲟⲩ
ⲉⲥϯⲟⲩⲣⲟⲧ ⲛⲁⲩ ⲉϩⲟⲩⲛ ⲉⲡⲁⲅⲱⲛ ⲛ̄ⲧⲡⲁⲣⲑⲉⲛⲓ̈ⲁ ⲉⲥϫⲱ ⲙⲙⲟⲥ [24]Ϫⲉ
ⲛⲁϣⲉⲉⲣⲉ ⲧⲡⲁⲣⲑⲉⲛⲓⲁ · ⲧⲉⲛⲧⲁⲥⲥⲉⲕ ⲡϫⲟⲉⲓ̈ⲥ ϣⲁⲣⲟⲓ̈ · ⲁϥⲉⲓ̈ ⲁϥⲟⲩⲱϩ
ϩⲛ ⲧⲁⲕⲁⲗⲁϩⲏ ⲙ̄ⲯⲓ̈ⲥ ⲛⲉⲃⲟⲧ [25]Ⲁⲩⲱ ⲛⲉⲥϫⲓⲙⲟⲉⲓⲧ ϩⲏⲧⲟⲩ ϩⲛ
ⲧⲉϩⲓⲏ ⲉⲧⲥⲟⲩⲧⲱⲛ ϣⲁⲛⲧⲟⲩⲃⲱⲕ ⲉϩⲣⲁⲓ̈ ϣⲁ ⲡⲉⲥⲙⲉ̂ⲣⲓⲧ ⲛ̄ϣⲏⲣⲉ
ⲁ̂ϫⲛ̄ ϫⲣⲟⲡ [26]Ⲁⲥϣⲱⲡⲉ ⲇⲉ ⲙ̄ⲛ̄ⲛⲥⲁ ⲙ̄ⲛⲧⲏ ⲛ̄ⲣⲟⲙⲡⲉ ⲙ̄ⲛ̄ⲛⲥⲁ ⲧⲣⲉ
ⲡϫⲟⲉⲓ̈ⲥ ⲧⲱⲟⲩⲛ ⲉⲃⲟⲗ ϩⲛ ⲛⲉⲧⲙⲟⲟⲩⲧ | ⲕⲁⲧⲁ ⲡⲁⲣⲭ̅ⲛⲟⲗⲟⲅⲓ̈ⲁ
ⲛ̄ⲓ̈ⲱⲥⲏⲡⲡⲟⲥ ⲙ̄ⲛ ⲓ̈ⲉⲣⲓ̈ⲛⲛⲁⲓ̈ⲟⲥ ⲛⲁⲛⲟ ϩⲉⲃⲣⲁⲓ̈ⲟⲥ [27]Ⲁⲩϫⲟⲟⲥ ⲅⲁⲣ ϫⲉ
ⲛⲉⲣⲉ ⲧⲡⲁⲣⲑⲉⲛⲟⲥ ⲉⲧⲟⲩⲁⲁⲃ · ⲁⲩⲱ ⲛⲁⲡⲟⲥⲧⲟ'ⲗⲟⲥ[b] ⲙⲛ ⲙⲁⲣⲓ̈ⲁ
ⲧⲙⲁⲁⲩ ⲙ̄ⲡϫⲟⲉⲓ̈ⲥ ⲛⲉⲩⲟⲩⲏϩ ϩⲛ ⲟⲩ ⲙⲁⲓ̈ⲛϣⲱⲡⲉ ⲛ̄ⲟⲩⲱⲧ ϩⲛ ⲑⲓⲗ̅ⲏ̅ⲙ̅
[28]Ⲁϥϣⲱⲡⲉ ⲛ̄ϭⲓ̅ ⲟⲩϩⲟⲟⲩ ⲛ̄ⲧⲓ̈ϩⲉ ⲡⲉϫⲁⲩ ⲁ̂ ⲧⲡⲁⲣⲑⲉⲛⲟⲥ ⲉⲧⲟⲩⲁⲁⲃ
ⲙⲁⲣⲓ̈ⲁ ⲙⲟⲩⲧⲉ ⲉ̂ⲓ̈ⲱϩⲁⲛⲛⲏⲥ Ⲡⲉϫⲁⲥ ⲛⲁϥ ϫⲉ ⲙⲟⲩⲧⲉ ⲛⲁⲓ̈ ⲉⲡⲉⲧⲣⲟⲥ
ⲙⲛ ⲓ̈ⲁⲕⲱⲃⲟⲥ ⲙⲁⲣⲟⲩⲉⲓ̈ ϣⲁⲣⲟⲓ̈ ⲉⲡⲓ̈ⲙⲁ [29]Ⲛ̄ⲧⲟϥ ⲇⲉ ⲁϥⲡⲱⲧ ϩⲛ
ⲟⲩϭⲉⲡⲏ ⲁϥⲙⲟⲩⲧⲉ ⲉⲣⲟⲟⲩ ⲛⲁⲥ [30]Ⲛ̄ⲧⲉⲣⲟⲩⲉⲓ ϭⲉ ϣⲁⲣⲟⲥ Ⲧⲟⲧⲉ
ⲁⲩϩⲙⲟⲟⲥ ϩⲁϩⲧⲏⲥ ⲙ̄ⲡϣⲟⲙⲛⲧ Ⲁⲥⲟⲩⲱⲛ ⲣⲱⲥ ⲛ̄ϭⲓ̈ ⲧⲡⲩⲅⲏ ⲙⲙⲟⲟⲩ
ⲛ̄ϣⲏϩ · ⲡⲉϫⲁⲥ ⲛⲁⲩ [31]Ϫⲉ ⲥⲱⲧⲙ ⲉ̂ⲣⲟⲓ̈ ⲱ ⲛⲉⲧⲁ ⲡϫⲟⲉⲓⲥ ⲥⲟⲧⲡⲟⲩ
p. ⸢ⲟ⸣ ⲛⲁϥ ⲉⲧⲣⲉⲩⲧⲁϣⲉⲟⲉⲓ̈ϣ ⲙ̄ⲡⲉⲩⲁⲅⲅⲉⲗⲓⲟⲛ ⲛ̄ⲧⲙ̄ⲛⲧⲉⲣⲟ | ⲛⲙ̄ⲡⲏⲩⲉ ϩⲙ̄
ⲡⲕⲟ̂ⲥⲙⲟⲥ ⲧⲏⲣϥ [32]Ⲛ̄ⲧⲱⲧⲛ ϭⲉ ⲁⲧⲉⲧⲛ̄ⲛⲁⲩ ϩⲛ ⲛⲉⲧⲛⲃⲁⲗ ⲉ̂ⲛⲉϭⲟⲙ
ⲙ̄ⲛ ⲡⲉϣⲡⲏⲣⲉ ⲛⲧⲁ ⲓ̅ⲥ̅ ⲡϣⲏⲣⲉ ⲙ̄ⲡⲛⲟⲩⲧⲉ ⲉⲧⲟⲛϩ ⲁⲁⲩ ⲙ̄ⲡⲉⲟⲩⲟⲉⲓ̈ϣ
ⲉϥⲡⲉⲙⲙⲁⲛ ϩⲛ ⲧⲥⲁⲣⲝ ϩⲓ̈ϫⲙ̄ ⲡⲕⲁϩ · [33]ⲛ̄ⲕⲉⲟⲩⲁ ⲁⲛ ⲡⲉⲧⲣ̄ⲙⲛ̄ⲧⲣⲉ
ⲙⲙⲟϥ ⲛⲏⲧⲛ̄ · ⲁⲗⲗⲁ ⲛ̄ⲧⲱⲧⲛ̄ ⲙⲡϣⲟⲙⲛⲧ ⲛⲉⲛⲧⲁϥϫⲓ̈ⲧⲟⲩ ⲉϫⲙ
ⲡⲧⲟⲟⲩ ⲁϥⲧⲥⲁⲃⲱⲧⲛ ⲉⲩⲙⲉⲣⲟⲥ ϩⲙ̄ ⲡⲉϥⲉⲟⲟⲩ [34]Ⲁⲩⲱ ⲁ ⲡⲉⲧⲛⲙⲁⲁϫⲉ
ⲥⲱⲧⲙ ⲉⲧⲉⲥⲙⲏ ⲙⲡⲓ̈ⲱⲧ ⲉⲥⲣ̄ⲙⲛ̄ⲧⲣⲉ ϩⲁⲣⲟϥ ϫⲉ ⲡⲁⲓ̈ ⲡⲉ ⲡⲁϣⲏⲣⲉ
ⲙⲙⲉⲣⲓⲧ ⲡⲉⲛⲧⲁ ⲡⲁⲟⲩⲱϣ ϣⲱⲡⲉ ϩⲣⲁⲓ̈ ⲛ̄ϩⲏⲧϥ [35]Ⲁⲧⲉⲧⲛⲛⲁⲩ ⲇⲉ
ⲟⲛ̄ ⲉⲛϩⲓⲥⲉ ⲛ̄ⲧⲁ ⲛⲓⲟⲩⲇⲁⲓ̈ ⲁⲁⲩ ⲛⲁϥ ⲉⲁⲩⲧⲁⲗⲟϥ ⲉϫⲙ̄ ⲡϣⲉ

[a] ⲧⲙ | ⸢ⲥ⸣ϩⲁⲓⲥⲟⲩ   [b] ⲛⲁⲡⲟⲥⲧⲟ'ⲗⲟⲥ

21 but she would not allow the apostles to write them, because
she was fleeing from the vain glory of men. 22 Now the
apostles were following her always, being taught by her the
preaching of the gospel. 23 And she had drawn many virgins
to her, ruling over them and making them eager for the
struggle of virginity, saying, 24 My daughters, it was virginity
that drew the Lord to me. He came and dwelt in my
womb nine months. 25 And she was leading them in the **cf. Ps**
straight way, until they went up to her beloved Son without **xxvi 11**
stumbling[a].

26 Now it came to pass after fifteen years after the Lord
rose from the dead according to the Antiquities of Josephus
and Irenaeus who *were* of *the* Hebrews—27 For they said
that the holy virgins and the apostles[b] and Mary the mother **cf. Ac i**
of the Lord were abiding in one dwelling place in Jerusalem. **12 ff**
28 Such a day came, say they, and the holy Virgin Mary
called John, and said to him, Call to me Peter and James,
and let them come hither unto me. 29 And he ran in haste,
and called them to her. 30 When therefore they were come
unto her, then they three sat by her; and the Fountain of **Ap xxi 6***
the water of life opened her mouth, and said to them, 31 Hear
me, O ye[c] whom the Lord hath chosen for Himself to preach **cf. Mt xxiv**
the gospel of the kingdom of the heavens in all the world. **14***
32 Ye therefore have seen with your eyes the mighty works[d]
and the wonders that Jesus the Son of the living God wrought **cf. Mt xvi**
aforetime[e] whilst He was with us in the flesh on the earth. **16***
33 It is not another that beareth witness of Him to you, but **cf. Jn v 32***
ye the three whom He took into the mountain, and He **cf. Mc ix 2;**
shewed you a portion of His glory. 34 And your ears heard **2 Pet i 17, 18**
the voice of the Father as it bare witness to Him, This is My **cf. Mt xvii**
beloved Son, in whom is My good pleasure. **5**

35 And also ye saw the sufferings that the Jews inflicted
on Him, when they placed Him upon the wood of the cross **cf. Ac ii 23, 24**

[a] Or *offence* [b] The MS has *apostle* [c] Lit. *those* [d] Lit. *the powers* [e] Or *then*

ⲙⲡⲉⲥ̄ⲧ̄ⲣ̄ⲟ̄ⲥ̄ ⲁⲩⲙⲟⲟⲩⲧϥ 36 Ⲡⲁⲓ ⲁ ⲡⲉϥⲉⲓ̈ⲱⲧ ⲧⲟⲩⲛⲟⲥϥ ⲉⲃⲟⲗ ϩⲛ
ⲛⲉⲧⲙⲟⲟⲩⲧ ϩⲙ̄ ⲡⲙⲉϩ|ϣⲟⲙⲛⲧ ⲛ̄ϩⲟⲟⲩ 37 ⸢Ⲁⲩⲱ⸣ ⲟⲛ ⲁⲓ̈ⲃⲱⲕ ⲉⲛ-
ⲧⲁⲫⲟⲥ ⲛ̄ⲙⲙⲏⲧⲛ ⲁⲛϩⲉ ⲉⲣⲟϥ ⲉⲁϥⲧⲱⲟⲩⲛ ⲉⲃⲟⲗ ϩⲛ ⲛⲉⲧⲙⲟⲟⲩⲧ
ⲁⲩⲱ ⲁⲓ̈ϣⲁϫⲉ ⲛⲙ̄ⲙⲁϥ ⲛ̄ⲧⲁⲡⲣⲟ ϩⲓ̈ ⲧⲁⲡⲣⲟ ϩⲓ̈ⲣⲙ̄ ⲡⲣⲟ ⲙⲛⲧⲁⲫⲟⲥ
38 ⲁϥϣⲁϫⲉ ⲛⲙ̄ⲙⲁⲓ̈ ϫⲉ ⲃⲱⲕ ⲧⲁⲙⲉ ⲛⲁⲥⲛⲏⲩ ⲙⲁⲣⲟⲩⲉⲓ̈ ⲉϩⲣⲁⲓ̈
ⲉⲧⲅⲁⲗⲓ̈ⲗⲁⲓ̈ⲁ ⲧⲁⲟⲩⲟⲛϩⲧ ⲉⲣⲟⲟⲩ ϩⲙ ⲡⲙⲁ ⲉⲧⲙⲙⲁⲩ · 39 Ⲁⲩⲱ
ⲁⲓ̈ⲧⲁⲙⲉⲧⲏⲩⲧⲛ ⲧⲏⲣⲧⲛ · ⲁ̇ⲧⲉⲧⲛ̄ⲥⲱⲟⲩϩ ⲉⲧⲅⲁⲗⲓ̈ⲗⲁⲓ̈ⲁ 40 ⲁϥⲉⲓ̈ ⲉϩⲟⲩⲛ
ϣⲁⲣⲱⲧⲛ̄ · ⲉⲣⲉ ⲡⲣⲟ ϣⲟⲧⲙ · Ⲁⲩⲱ ⲁⲧⲉⲧⲛⲛⲁⲩ ⲉⲣⲟϥ ⲁⲩⲱ ⲁϥϣⲁϫⲉ
ⲛⲙ̄ⲙⲏⲧⲛ 41 Ⲁⲩⲱ ⲁϥⲣ̄ ϩⲙⲉ ⲛ̄ϩⲟⲟⲩ ⲉϥⲟⲩⲱⲙ ⲁⲩⲱ ⲉϥⲥⲱ ⲛⲙ̄ⲙⲏⲧⲛ̄
ⲉϥϣⲁϫⲉ ⲛⲙ̄ⲙⲏⲧⲛ̄ ⲉⲧⲃⲉ ⲧⲙ̄ⲛⲧⲉⲣⲟ ⲙ̄ⲡⲛⲟⲩⲧⲉ · · · 42 Ⲡϫⲱⲕ ϭⲉ
p. οα ⲙ̄ⲡⲉϩⲙⲉ ⲛ̄ϩⲟⲟⲩ ⲉⲧⲉⲧⲛⲥⲟⲟⲩϩ ⲧⲏⲣⲧⲛ ⲉⲩⲙⲁ ⲛ̄|⸢ⲟⲩ⸣ⲱⲧ : ⲁⲩⲱ
ⲡⲉⲓ̈⸢ⲙ⸣ⲙⲁⲩ ϩⲱ̇ ⲛⲙ̄ⲙⲏⲧⲛ̄ · ϩⲓ̈ϫⲙ̄ ⲡⲧⲟⲟⲩ ⲛ̄ⲛ̄ϫⲟⲉⲓ̈ⲧ Ⲁϥⲉⲓ ϣⲁⲣⲟⲛ
ⲟⲛ ⲛ̄ϭⲓ ⲡϫⲟⲉⲓⲥ ⲡⲉϫⲁϥ ⲛⲁⲛ ϫⲉ ϯⲣⲏⲛⲏ ⲛⲏⲧⲛ[a] · 43 ⲁⲩⲱ ⲛ̄ⲧⲉ-
ⲣⲉϥϫⲉ ⲛⲁⲓ̈ ⲡⲉϫⲁϥ Ϫⲉ ⲁⲩϯ ⲛⲁⲓ̈ ⲛⲉⲝⲟⲩⲥⲓ̈ⲁ ⲛⲓ̈ⲙ ϩⲛ̄ ⲧⲡⲉ ⲁⲩⲱ
ϩⲓ̈ϫⲙ ⲡⲕⲁϩ · 44 Ⲡⲟⲟϣⲉ ⲉⲃⲟⲗ ϩⲙ̄ ⲡⲕⲟⲥⲙⲟⲥ ⲧⲏⲣϥ ⲛⲧⲉⲧⲛⲃⲁⲡⲧⲓⲍⲉ
ⲛ̄ⲛ̄ϩⲉⲑⲛⲟⲥ ⲧⲏⲣⲟⲩ ⲉⲡⲣⲁⲛ ⲙ̄ⲡⲉⲓⲱⲧ ⲙⲛ̄ ⲡϣⲏⲣⲉ ⲙⲛ̄ ⲡⲉⲡ̄ⲛ̄ⲁ̄
ⲉⲧⲟⲩⲁⲁⲃ 45 Ⲁⲩⲱ ⲡⲉϫⲁϥ ⲟⲛ ⲛⲁⲛ ϫⲉ ⲉⲓ̈ⲥ ϩⲏⲏⲧⲉ ⲁⲓϫⲉⲕ ⲧⲟⲓ̈ⲕⲟ-
ⲛⲟⲙⲓ̈ⲁ ⲧⲏⲣⲥ ⲉⲃⲟⲗ ⲧⲁⲓ̈ ⲉⲧⲕⲏ ⲛⲁⲓ̈ ⲉϩⲣⲁⲓ̈ ϩⲙ ⲡⲕⲟⲥⲙⲟⲥ · · :
Ⲧⲉⲛⲟⲩ ϭⲉ ⲉⲓ̈ⲛⲁⲃⲱⲕ ⲉϩⲣⲁⲓ̈ ϣⲁ ⲡⲁⲉⲓ̈ⲱⲧ ⲙ̄ⲡⲟⲟⲩ ⲛ̄ϩⲟⲟⲩ ·
46 Ⲛ̄ⲧⲱⲧⲛ ϭⲉ ϩⲱⲧⲧⲏⲩⲧⲛ ⲡⲉϫⲏⲧⲛ ⲛⲁϥ ϫⲉ ⲉⲕⲛⲁⲃⲱⲕ ⲛⲅⲕⲁⲁⲛ
ⲉⲛⲟ ⲛⲟⲣⲫⲁⲛⲟⲥ 47 Ⲁϥⲟⲩⲱϣⲃ ⲡⲉϫⲁϥ | ⲛⲏⲧⲛ ϫⲉ ⲛ̄ϯⲛⲁⲕⲁⲧⲏⲩⲧⲛ
ⲁⲛ ⲉⲧⲉⲧⲛⲟ̇ ⲛⲟⲣⲫⲁⲛⲟⲥ 48 ⲁⲗⲗⲁ ⲉⲓ̈ϣⲁⲛⲃⲱⲕ ϯⲛⲁϫⲉⲩ ⲡⲉⲡ̄ⲛ̄ⲁ̄
ⲙⲡⲁⲣⲁⲕⲗⲏⲧⲟⲥ ϣⲁⲣⲱⲧⲛ̄ ⲉⲡⲁⲙⲁ · Ⲛ̄ⲛ̄ⲥⲁ ϩⲁϩ ⲁⲛ ⲛ̄ϩⲟⲟⲩ · ⲁⲗⲗⲁ
ϣⲁ ⲧⲡⲉⲛⲧⲏⲕⲟⲥⲧⲏ · 49 Ⲁⲩⲱ ⲉⲓⲥ ⲧⲉⲛⲧⲁⲥϣⲱⲡⲉ ⲛⲁⲓ̈ ⲙⲙⲁⲛⲟⲩⲱϩ ·
ⲁⲓϣⲱⲡⲉ ⲛⲁⲥ ⲛ̄ϣⲏⲣⲉ · ϩⲛ ⲧⲥⲁⲣⲝ ⲙⲛ ⲧⲙⲛⲧⲛⲟⲩⲧⲉ ⲧⲁⲓ̈ ⲉⲧⲉⲣⲉ
ⲡⲉⲭⲁⲣⲁⲕⲧⲏⲣ ⲛ̄ⲧⲉⲥϩⲓ̈ⲕⲱⲛ ⲉⲓⲛⲉ ⲛⲧⲱⲓ̈ ⲕⲁⲧⲁ ⲥⲁⲣⲝ ⲉⲓ̈ⲥ ϩⲏⲏⲧⲉ
ⲥϩⲁϩⲧⲛⲧⲏⲩⲧⲛ ⲧⲉⲛⲟⲩ 50 Ⲁⲛⲟⲕ ⲇⲉ ϯϣⲟⲟⲡ ⲛⲙⲙⲏⲧⲛ ϣⲁ ⲧⲥⲩⲛ-
ⲧⲉⲗⲓ̈ⲁ ⲙ̄ⲡⲁⲓ̈ⲱⲛ 51 Ⲁⲩⲱ ⲛ̄ⲧⲉⲣⲉϥϫⲉ ⲛⲁⲓ̈ ⲁϥⲥⲟⲕϥ ⲛ̄ⲥⲁⲃⲟⲗ ⲙⲙⲟⲛ
ⲛⲟⲩⲕⲟⲩⲓ̈ · ⲁϥⲣⲁⲕⲧϥ ⲉϫⲙ ⲡⲧⲟⲟⲩ ⲙ̄ⲡⲓⲏⲃⲧ 52 ⲁⲩⲧⲁⲗⲟϥ ⲛ̄ϭⲓ̈

[a] ϯⲣⲏⲛⲏⲧⲛ

and killed Him. 36 Him did His Father raise from the dead
on the third day. 37 And also I went to the tomb with you,
and we found Him risen from the dead, and I spake with
Him mouth to mouth at the door of the tomb. 38 He spake
with me, *saying,* Go tell my brethren that they go into Mt XXVIII 10*
Galilee, and I will appear to them there. 39 And I told all of
you, and ye were gathered together to Galilee. 40 And He
came in unto you, the doors being shut, and ye saw Him, Jn XX 19, 26
and He spake with you; 41 and He spent forty days eating cf. Ac I 3, 4
and drinking with you, and speaking with you concerning
the kingdom of God. 42 At the end then of the forty days,
when ye were all gathered together to one place, and I also cf. Ac I 6, 12
was with you, on the mount of Olives, the Lord came unto
us again, and said to us, Peace *be* unto you. 43 And when cf. Jn XX 21, 22
He had said these things, He said, All authority hath been Mt XXVIII 18*, 19*
given unto Me in heaven and on earth; 44 go ye forth in all
the world, and baptize all the nations into the name of the cf. Mc XVI 15*
Father and of the Son and of the Holy Ghost. 45 And He
also said to us, Behold I have finished all the dispensation cf. Jn XVII 4
which is laid down for Me in the world. Now therefore I
will ascend unto My Father this very day. 46 Ye then said cf. Jn XX 17
to Him, Wilt thou go and leave us desolate? 47 He answered
and said to you, I will not leave you desolate; 48 but if I go, Jn XIV 18
I will send the Spirit, *the* Comforter, unto you in My place, Jn XVI 7 Ac I 5
after not many days, but when Pentecost cometh[a]. 49 And
behold she who was My dwelling place, and I was her Son in
the flesh and in the Godhead, *even* she the expression of
whose image is like Mine according to flesh, behold she is
with you now. 50 And I am with you unto the end of the Mt XXVIII 20*
age.

51 And when He had said these things, He drew Himself
away from us a little and turned[b] Himself on the mount to[c]
the east; 52 and was taken up by the ranks of the Cherubin

[a] Lit. *but until Pentecost* [b] Or *bowed* [c] Lit. *in*, or *of*

ⲛⲧⲁⲅⲙⲁ ⲛ̄ⲛⲉⲭⲉⲣⲟⲩⲃⲓⲛ ⲙⲛ̄ ⲛ̄ⲥⲉⲣⲁⲫⲓⲛ ⲁⲩϫⲓⲧϥ ⲉϩⲣⲁï ⲉⲧⲡⲉ ϩⲛ̄
p. ⲟⲃ ⲧⲥⲁⲣⲝ ⲛ̄ⲧⲁïϫⲡⲟϥ | ⲛ̄ϩⲏⲧⲥ 53ⲁⲩⲱ ⲉⲡⲉⲩⲉϣⲗⲟⲩⲗⲁï ⲉⲃⲟⲗ ϩⲁ-
ⲧⲉϥϩⲏ ⲛ̄ϭⲓ ϩⲉⲛϣⲟ ⲛ̄ϣⲟ ⲙⲛ̄ ϩⲉⲛⲧⲃⲁ ⲛⲧⲃⲁ ·· 54Ⲁⲛⲟⲛ ⲇⲉ
ⲡⲉⲛϭⲱϣⲧ ⲛ̄ⲥⲱϥ ⲉϥⲛⲁⲃⲱⲕ ⲉϩⲣⲁï ⲉⲧⲡⲉ Ⲁⲩⲱ ⲉⲓⲥ ϩⲏⲏⲧⲉ ⲉⲓⲥ
ⲥⲛⲁⲩ ⲛ̄ⲣⲱⲙⲉ ⲁⲛⲛⲁⲩ ⲉⲣⲟⲟⲩ ⲉⲩⲁϩⲉⲣⲁⲧⲟⲩ ϩⲁϩⲧⲏⲛ ⲉⲩⲫⲟⲣⲉï
ⲛ̄ϩⲉⲛϩⲃ̄ⲥⲱ ⲉⲩⲟⲩⲟⲃϣ 55Ⲁⲩⲱ ⲡⲉϫⲁⲩ ⲛⲁⲛ ϫⲉ ⲱ̄ ⲛ̄ⲣⲱⲙⲉ ⲉⲧⲃⲉ
ⲟⲩ ⲧⲉⲧⲛ̄ϭⲱϣⲧ ⲉϩⲣⲁï ⲉⲧⲡⲉ ⲉⲧⲉⲧⲛ̄ⲣ̄ϣⲡⲏⲣⲉ ⲛⲁⲓ ⲡⲉ ⲓ̅ⲥ̅ ⲡⲉⲛⲧ-
ⲁⲩϥⲓⲧϥ ⲛ̄ⲧⲉⲧⲛⲏⲩⲧⲛ ⲉϩⲣⲁï ⲉⲧⲡⲉ Ⲧⲁï ⲟⲛ ⲧⲉ ⲑⲉ ⲉⲧϥⲛⲏⲩ ⲙⲙⲟⲥ
ⲉⲕⲣⲓⲛⲉ ⲛ̄ⲛⲉⲧⲟⲛϩ ⲙⲛ̄ ⲛⲉⲧⲙⲟⲟⲩⲧ 56Ⲁⲩⲱ ⲙⲛ̄ⲛ̄ⲥⲁ ⲡϫⲱⲕ ⲙ̄ⲡⲧⲁïⲟⲩ
ⲛ̄ϩⲟⲟⲩ[a] ⲁϥⲧⲛ̄ⲛⲟⲟⲩ ⲉϫⲱⲧⲛ ⲙ̄ⲡⲉⲡ̅ⲛ̅ⲁ̅ ⲉⲧⲟⲩⲁⲁⲃ· 57ⲁⲩⲱ ⲉⲓⲥ ϩⲏⲏⲧⲉ·
ⲉϥⲉⲛⲉⲣⲅⲉï ⲛ̄ⲛⲓϭⲟⲙ ⲛ̄ⲙⲙⲏⲧⲛ ϣⲁ ⲧⲉⲛⲟⲩ ⲉϥϯ| ⲛⲏⲧⲛ[b] ⲛ̄ⲛⲉⲧ⌜ⲉⲧⲛ⌝-
ϣⲓⲛⲉ ⲛ̄ⲥⲱⲟⲩ · 58Ⲧⲉⲛⲟⲩ ϭⲉ ⲙ̄ⲡⲣ̄ⲕⲱ ⲛ̄ⲥⲱⲧⲛ ⲛ̄ⲛⲉⲛⲧⲁϥⲧⲥⲁⲃⲱⲧⲛ̄
ⲉⲣⲟⲟⲩ ⲛ̄ϭⲓ ⲡⲙⲉⲣⲓⲧ ⲙ̄ⲡⲛⲟⲩⲧⲉ ϩⲛ ⲟⲩⲙⲉ · 59Ⲙⲡⲣ̄ⲣ̄ϩⲟⲧⲉ ϩⲏⲧⲥ
ⲛ̄ⲧⲁⲡⲓⲗⲏ ⲛ̄ⲛⲉⲣⲱⲟⲩ ⲙ̄ⲡⲕⲁϩ ⲙⲛ̄ ⲛⲁⲣⲭⲱⲛ ⲛ̄ⲧⲉⲧⲛ̄ⲕⲱ ⲛ̄ⲥⲱⲧⲛ̄
ⲛ̄ⲛ̄ⲇⲓⲕⲁⲓⲱⲙⲁ ⲙⲛ̄ ⲛ̄ϩⲁⲡ ⲙ̄ⲡⲛⲟϭ ⲛ̄ⲥⲁϩ ⲁⲩⲱ ⲡϫⲟⲉⲓⲥ ϩⲛ ⲟⲩⲙⲉ·
60Ⲧⲉⲛⲟⲩ ϭⲉ ⲙ̄ⲡⲣ̄ⲗⲩⲡⲏ ϩⲙ ⲡⲉⲧⲛϩⲏⲧ ϩⲙ̄ ⲡⲉⲧϯⲛⲁϫⲟⲟϥ ⲉⲣⲱⲧⲛ̄
ⲧⲉⲛⲟⲩ 61Ⲉⲓⲥ ϩⲏⲏⲧⲉ ⲅⲁⲣ ⲁϥϩⲱⲛ ⲉϩⲟⲩⲛ ⲉⲣⲟï ⲛ̄ϭⲓ ⲡⲉⲩⲟⲉⲓϣ
ⲙ̄ⲡⲁⲃⲱⲗ ⲉⲃⲟⲗ ⲉⲧⲣⲁⲕⲱ ⲉϩⲣⲁï ⲙ̄ⲡⲁⲥⲱⲙⲁ ⲛⲧⲉ ⲧⲁⲯⲩⲭⲏ ⲙⲛ
ⲡⲁⲡ̅ⲛ̅ⲁ̅ ⲃⲱⲕ ϣⲁ ⲡϫⲟⲉⲓⲥ 62ϫⲉⲕⲁⲥ ⲉϥⲉϯ ⲛⲁⲓ ⲛ̄ⲛⲁⲅⲁⲑⲟⲛ ⲛⲧⲁϥ-
ⲉⲣⲏⲧ ⲙⲙⲟⲟⲩ ⲛⲁⲓ 63Ⲛⲁï ⲉⲧⲉ ⲙⲡⲉ ⲃⲁⲗ ⲛⲁⲩ ⲉⲣⲟⲟⲩ ⲙ̄ⲡⲉ
p. ⲟⲅ ⲙⲁⲁϫⲉ ⲥⲟⲧⲙⲟⲩ· | ⌜ⲟⲩⲇⲉ⌝ ⲙⲡⲟⲩⲁⲗⲉ ⲉϩⲣⲁï ⌜ⲉ⌝ϫⲙ̄ ⲡϩⲏⲧ ⲛ̄ⲣⲱⲙⲉ
ⲛⲁï ⲛ̄ⲧⲁ ⲡⲛⲟⲩⲧⲉ ⲥⲃⲧⲱⲧⲟⲩ ⲛ̄ⲛⲉⲧⲙⲉ ⲙⲙⲟϥ 64ⲕⲁï ⲅⲁⲣ ⲁϥⲉï
ϣⲁⲣⲟï ⲛ̄ϭⲓ ⲡϫⲟⲉⲓⲥ ⲛ̄ⲧⲉⲩϣⲏ ⲛ̄ⲥⲁϥ ⲉⲓⲁϩⲉⲣⲁⲧ ⲉⲓϣⲗⲏⲗ Ⲡⲉϫⲁϥ
ⲛⲁï 65ϫⲉ ⲁⲣⲥⲟⲩⲱⲛⲧ ϫⲉ ⲁⲛⲟⲕ ⲛⲓⲙ · Ⲁïⲟⲩⲱϣⲃ ⲛⲁϥ ϫⲉ ⲛ̄ⲧⲟⲕ
ⲡⲉ ⲡⲁϫⲟⲉⲓⲥ ⲁⲩⲱ ⲡⲁⲛⲟⲩⲧⲉ ⲁⲩⲱ ⲡⲁϣⲏⲣⲉ ⲙⲙⲉⲣⲓⲧ ⲟⲩ ⲡⲉⲧ-
ⲕⲟⲩⲉϩⲥⲁϩⲛⲉ ⲙⲙⲟϥ ⲛⲁï ⲧⲁⲁⲁϥ ⲱ̄ ⲡⲁϫⲟⲉⲓⲥ 66Ⲛ̄ⲧⲟϥ ⲇⲉ ⲡⲉϫⲁϥ
ⲛⲁï ϫⲉ ⲧⲁⲙⲉ ⲡⲉⲧⲣⲟⲥ ⲙⲛ̄ ⲓⲁⲕⲱⲃⲟⲥ ⲙⲛ̄ ⲓⲱϩⲁⲛⲛⲏⲥ ⲉⲛⲉïϣⲁϫⲉ·
ϫⲉ ⲛⲧⲟⲟⲩ ⲡⲉⲧⲛⲁⲕⲱ ⲛ̄ⲛⲉⲩϭⲓϫ ϩⲓϫⲛ ⲛⲟⲩⲃⲁⲗ · 67Ⲧⲉⲛⲟⲩ ϭⲉ
ⲕⲉϣⲟⲙⲛⲧ ⲛ̄ϩⲟⲟⲩ ⲡⲉⲧⲉ ⲟⲩⲛⲧⲏ · ϩⲙ̄ ⲡⲓⲕⲟⲥⲙⲟⲥ ⲧⲁⲉⲓ ⲛ̄ⲥⲱ · ⲧⲁϥï

[a] ⲛ̄ϩⲟⲟⲩ ⲛ̄ϩⲟⲟⲩ [b] ⲉϥϯ|ϯ ⲛⲏⲧⲛ

and the Seraphin, and received up into heaven in the flesh
wherein I brought Him forth; 53 and there were shouting
before Him thousand thousands and ten thousand ten thou- cf. Dan vii 10
sands. 54 And we were looking after Him as He went up cf. Ac i 10, 11
into heaven, and behold we saw two men[a] standing by us,
wearing white apparel; 55 and they said to us, Ye men, why
look ye into heaven wondering? This is Jesus who was
received up from you into heaven: this also is the manner
in which He shall come to judge the quick and the dead.
56 And after the end of the fifty days He sent upon you the
Holy Ghost, 57 and behold He worketh these mighty works[b]
with you until now, giving you those things for which ye
seek. 58 Now therefore forsake not those things which He
taught you, *even He* the beloved of God in truth. 59 Fear cf. Ac iv 26, 29
not the threat of the kings of the earth and of the rulers,
that ye forsake the ordinances and the judgments of the
great Teacher and of the Lord in truth.

60 Now therefore grieve not in your heart at that which I
will tell you now. 61 For behold the time of my departure is 2 Ti iv 6*
at hand, that I should lay down my body, that my soul and
my spirit may go to the Lord; 62 in order that He may give
us the good things which He hath promised us, 63 the things 1 Co ii 9
which eye saw not, and ear heard not, neither did they come
up into the heart of man, *even* the things which God prepared
for them that love Him. 64 For indeed the Lord came unto
me yesternight whilst I stood praying, and said to me, 65 Dost[c]
thou know Me who I *am*? I answered Him, Thou art my Lord cf. Jn xx 28
and my God and my beloved Son. What dost Thou bid me do,
O my Lord? 66 And He said to me, Tell Peter and James and
John these words, for they shall lay their hands on thine
eyes. 67 Now therefore yet three days hast thou in this
world, and I will come for thee, and take thy soul and thy

[a] Lit. *behold two men, we saw them* [b] Lit. *these powers* [c] Lit. *Didst*

ⲛ̄ⲧⲟⲩⲯⲩⲭⲏ ⲙⲛ̄ ⲛⲟⲩⲡ̄ⲛ̄ⲁ · ⲉϩⲟⲩⲛ̄ ⲉⲧⲁⲡⲟⲗⲓ̈ⲥ ⲙ̄ⲡⲛ̄ⲁⲧⲓ̈ⲕⲟⲛ ⲑⲓⲗⲏⲙ | ⲛ̄ⲧⲡⲉ · 68ⲛ̄ⲧⲉ ⲛⲁⲡⲉⲧⲟⲩⲁⲁⲃ ⲧⲏⲣⲟⲩ ⲣ̄ϣⲡⲏⲣⲉ ⲙ̄ⲡⲛⲟϭ ⲛⲉⲟⲟⲩ ⲉϯⲛⲁⲧⲁⲁϥ ⲛⲉ · ϩⲙ̄ ⲡⲙⲁ ⲉⲧⲙ̄ⲙⲁⲩ ⲉⲃⲟⲗ ϩⲓ̈ⲧⲙ̄ ⲡⲁⲉⲓ̈ⲱⲧ ⲛⲁⲅⲁⲑⲟⲥ 69ϫⲉ ⲛ̄ⲧⲟ̄ ⲁⲣϩⲱⲧⲛ̄ ⲉⲡⲉⲓ̈ⲱⲧ ⲙⲛ̄ ⲛⲉϥⲁⲅⲅⲉⲗⲟⲥ ⲛ̄ⲧⲙⲛ̄ⲧⲣⲱⲙⲉ ⲛ̄ⲕⲉⲥⲟⲡ 70ⲁⲩⲱ ⲛ̄ⲧⲉϣⲱⲡⲉ ⲉⲣϫⲟⲥⲉ̄ ⲉ̄ⲛⲉⲧⲟⲩⲁⲁⲃ ⲧⲏⲣⲟⲩ ϫⲉ ⲛ̄ⲧⲟ̄ ⲡⲉ ⲡϣⲟⲩϣⲟⲩ ⲛ̄ⲧⲉⲩϭⲟⲙ 71ϯⲛⲁⲧⲣⲉ ⲛⲁⲁⲅⲅⲉⲗⲟⲥ ϭⲱ ⲉⲩϩⲩⲙⲛⲉⲩⲉ ⲉⲣⲟ̄ ⲛ̄ⲟⲩⲟⲉⲓϣ ⲛⲓ̈ⲙ ϫⲉ ⲉⲣⲧⲛ̄ⲧⲱⲛ ⲉⲣⲟⲟⲩ ϩⲙ̄ ⲡⲟⲩⲧⲃ̄ⲃⲟ ⲙⲛ̄ ⲧⲟⲩⲙⲛ̄ⲧⲕⲁⲑⲁⲣⲟⲥ 72ⲥⲉⲛⲁⲣⲁϣⲉ ⲛ̄ϭⲓ ⲛ̄ⲧⲁⲅⲙⲁ ⲧⲏⲣⲟⲩ ⲛ̄ⲙ̄ⲡⲏⲩⲉ ⲉϫⲛ̄ ⲧⲟⲩϭⲓⲛⲉⲓ̈ ϣⲁⲣⲟⲟⲩ 73ⲛ̄ⲡⲁⲧⲣⲓ̈ⲁⲣⲭⲏⲥ ⲙⲛ̄ ⲛⲉⲡⲣⲟⲫⲏⲧⲏⲥ ⲥⲉⲛⲏⲩ ⲉⲃⲟⲗ ⲉⲧⲟⲩⲁⲡⲁⲛⲧⲏ ⲉⲩⲧⲉⲗⲏⲗ ⲙ̄ⲙⲟⲟⲩ ⲉⲩϫⲱ ⲙ̄ⲙⲟⲥ 74ϫⲉ p. ⲟⲁ ⲉⲓⲥ ⲧⲙⲁⲁⲩ ⲙ̄ⲡⲉⲡⲱⲛϩ ⲁⲥⲉⲓ̈ ϣⲁⲣⲟⲛ 75ⲕⲁⲛ ⲙ̄ⲡⲉⲛⲉⲙⲡ|ϣⲁ̄ ⲛ̄ⲛⲁⲩ ⲉⲣⲟⲥ ϩⲛ̄ ⲧⲥⲁⲣⲝ̄ ⲉⲓ̈ⲥ ϩⲏⲏⲧⲉ ⲁⲛⲛⲁⲩ ⲉⲣⲟⲥ ⲧⲉⲛⲟⲩ ⲉⲩϯⲉⲟⲟⲩ ⲛⲁⲥ ϩⲓⲧⲙ[a] ⲡⲛⲟⲩⲧⲉ ⲡⲓⲱⲧ 76ⲛ̄ⲡⲁⲣⲑⲉⲛⲟⲥ ⲛ̄ϩⲟⲟⲩⲧ ⲙⲛ̄ ⲙ̄ⲡⲁⲣⲑⲉⲛⲟⲥ ⲛ̄ⲥϩⲓ̈ⲙⲉ ⲛ̄ⲧⲁⲩϩⲁⲣⲉϩ ⲉⲧⲉⲩⲡⲁⲣⲑⲉⲛⲓ̈ⲁ ⲥⲉⲛⲏⲩ ⲉⲃⲟⲗ ϩⲁⲧⲟⲩϩⲏ ⲉⲩϯⲉⲟⲟⲩ ⲛⲉ ⲉⲩϫⲱ ⲙ̄ⲙⲟⲥ 77ϫⲉ ⲕⲁⲗⲱⲥ ⲁⲣⲉⲓ̈ ϣⲁⲣⲟⲛ ⲙ̄ⲡⲟⲟⲩ ⲧⲙⲁⲁⲩ ⲛ̄ⲙ̄ⲡⲁⲣⲑⲉⲛⲟⲥ ⲧⲏⲣⲟⲩ · 78ⲗⲟⲓⲡⲟⲛ ⲁ ⲡⲉⲟⲩⲟⲉⲓ̈ϣ ϣⲱⲡⲉ ⲁ ⲡⲕⲁⲓⲣⲟⲥ ϩⲱⲛ̄ ⲉϩⲟⲩⲛ̄ ⲉⲧⲣⲉϣⲱⲡⲉ ϩⲛ̄ ⲟⲩⲙⲁ ⲛ̄ⲟⲩⲱⲧ ⲛ̄ⲙⲙⲁⲓ̈: 79ⲛ̄ⲡⲣ̄ⲗⲩⲡⲏ ⲉⲧⲃⲉ ⲡⲟⲩⲥⲱⲙⲁ ⲉⲧⲟⲩⲁⲁⲃ ϫⲉ[b] ⲟⲩ ⲁⲣⲁ ⲡⲉⲧⲛⲁϣⲱⲡⲉ ⲙ̄ⲙⲟϥ · ⲏ̄[c] ⲉⲩⲛⲁⲕⲁⲁϥ ⲧⲱⲛ 80ⲛⲓⲙ ϭⲉ ⲛ̄ⲣⲱⲙⲉ ⲛ̄ϫⲡⲟ ⲛ̄ⲥϩⲓ̈ⲙⲉ ⲱ̄ ⲧⲁⲙⲁⲁⲩ ⲡⲉⲧⲙ̄ⲡⲉϥϫⲓ̈ϯⲡⲉ ⲙ̄ⲡⲙⲟⲩ ⲁⲩⲱ ⲛ̄ⲧⲉ ⲡⲉϥⲥⲱⲙⲁ ⲕⲟⲧϥ ⲉϩⲣⲁⲓ̈ ⲉ̄ⲡⲕⲁϩ ⲛ̄ⲧⲁⲩϫⲓⲧϥ ⲉⲃⲟⲗ | ⲛ̄ϩⲏⲧϥ · 81⌜ⲁⲓⲙⲟⲩ⌝ ϭⲉ[d] ϩⲱ̄ ⲉⲃⲟⲗ ϫⲉ ⲁ⌜ϥⲓ⌝ⲥⲁⲣⲝ̄ ⲛ̄ϩⲏⲧⲉ · ⲁⲗⲗⲁ[e] ⲁⲓ̈ⲧⲱⲟⲩⲛ̄ ϩⲙ̄ ⲡⲙⲉϩϣⲟⲙⲛ̄ⲧ ⲛ̄ϩⲟⲟⲩ ⲁⲓ̈ⲃⲱⲗ ⲉⲃⲟⲗ ⲙ̄ⲡⲉⲧⲉⲣⲉ ⲡⲁⲙⲁϩⲧⲉ ⲛ̄ⲁⲙⲛ̄ⲧⲉ ⲛ̄ⲧⲟⲟⲧϥ ⲉⲧⲉ ⲡⲙⲟⲩ ⲡⲉ 82ϯⲛⲁⲥⲕⲉⲡⲁⲍⲉ ⲙ̄ⲡⲟⲩⲥⲱⲙⲁ ϩⲙ̄ ⲡϩⲏⲧ ⲙ̄ⲡⲕⲁϩ ⲧⲁⲧⲣⲉ ⲛⲁⲁⲅⲅⲉⲗⲟⲥ ϭⲱ ⲉⲩϭⲓⲛⲉ ⲙ̄ⲡⲉϥϣⲓⲛⲉ · ⲛ̄ⲛⲁⲩ ⲛⲓⲙ 83ⲙⲛ̄ ⲗⲁⲁⲩ ⲛ̄ⲣⲱⲙⲉ ⲛⲁϭⲙ̄ ⲡⲙⲁ ⲉϯⲛⲁⲕⲁⲁϥ ⲛ̄ϩⲏⲧϥ ϣⲁ ⲡⲉϩⲟⲟⲩ ⲛ̄ⲧⲡⲁⲣⲣⲟⲩⲥⲓ̈ⲁ ⲧⲁⲧⲟⲩⲛⲟⲥϥ ⲉϥⲟ · ⲛⲁⲧⲧⲁⲕⲟ · 84ⲁⲗⲗⲁ ⲟⲩⲛ ⲟⲩⲥϯⲛⲟⲩϥⲉ ⲛⲁϣⲱⲡⲉ ⲉϥϣⲱϣ ⲉⲃⲟⲗ ϩⲙ̄ ⲡⲉϥⲕⲱⲧⲉ ϣⲁ ⲡⲉϩⲟⲟⲩ ⲉⲧϥⲛⲁⲧⲱⲟⲩⲛ̄ ⲛ̄ϩⲏⲧϥ 85ⲥⲉⲛⲁⲕⲱⲧ ⲛ̄ⲟⲩⲁⲩⲑⲉⲛⲧⲓⲕⲟⲛ ⲛ̄ⲧⲟⲡⲟⲥ ϩⲁϩⲧⲙ̄ ⲡⲟⲩⲥⲱⲙⲁ ⲉϥⲥⲟⲧⲡ

[a] ϩⲓ · ⲧⲙ [b] ϫ in marg. [c] ⲏ in marg. [d] ϭ in marg.
[e] ⲁ 1° in marg.

spirit into My spiritual city, the heavenly Jerusalem; [68]and cf. He XII 22
all My holy ones shall wonder at the great glory which I
will give thee there through My good Father—[69]for thou
didst reconcile mankind again to the Father and His angels—
[70]and thou shalt be exalted above all the holy ones, for thou
art the glory of their strength. [71]I will cause My angels to cf. Ps LXXXVIII 18
keep singing thy praises always, for thou art like them in
thy holiness and thy purity. [72]All the ranks of the heavens
shall rejoice over thy coming unto them. [73]The patriarchs
and the prophets shall come forth to meet thee, exulting and
saying, [74]Behold the mother of our Life is come unto us.
[75]If we have not been worthy to see her in the flesh, *yet*
behold we have seen her now glorified by God the Father.
[76]The virgins that are men and the virgins that are women, cf. Ap XIV 4
who have kept their virginity, shall come forth to meet thee,
glorifying thee, and saying, [77]Full well art thou come unto us
to-day, thou mother of all the virgins.

[78]But the time has come, the season is at hand that thou
shouldest dwell in the same place with Me. [79]Grieve not for
thy holy body, *saying*, What then shall befall it, or where
shall it be laid? [80]What man then born of woman is there,
My mother, who has not tasted death and his body returned cf. Ge III 19, 23
unto the ground from whence he[a] was taken? [81]I died then
because I took flesh in thy womb; but I rose on the third
day, and destroyed him that hath the power of Amente, cf. He II 14*
even death. [82]I will cover thy body in the heart of the cf. Mt XII 40*
earth, and will make My angels ever keep visiting it. [83]No cf. Deut
man shall find the place wherein I shall lay it until the day XXXIV 6*
of My coming, and I will raise it incorruptible. [84]But a cf. 1 Co XV 52*
sweet savour shall be given forth around it until the day
wherein it shall rise. [85]A lordly shrine[b] shall be built by

5 ★

[a] Or *it* [b] See note

p. ⲟⲉ ⲉϩⲟⲩ ⲉⲙ̇|⸢ⲡⲁⲗⲗ⸣ⲁⲧⲓ̈ⲟⲛ ⲛⲛⲉ⸢ⲣⲱⲟ⸣ⲩ. 86 ϭⲉⲡⲏ ⲟⲩⲛ ⸢ⲙ⸣ⲙ̄ⲟ̈ ⲟ̇ⲩⲉϩⲥⲁϩⲛⲉ
ⲛⲛⲁⲁⲡⲟⲥⲧⲟⲗⲟⲥ ϯ ⲛⲧⲱϣ ⲛⲙⲡⲁⲣⲑⲉⲛⲟⲥ 87 ⲁⲩⲱ ⲉⲓⲥ ϩⲏⲏⲧⲉ ϯⲛ̄ⲏⲩ
ϣⲁⲣⲟ ϩⲛ̄ ⲟⲩϭⲉⲡⲏ · ⲙⲛ̄ ⲛⲁⲁⲅⲅⲉⲗⲟⲥ̇ ⲧⲁⲱⲗ ⲙ̇ⲡⲟⲩⲗⲓ̈ⲯⲁⲛⲟⲛ
ⲉⲧⲟⲩⲁⲁⲃ ⲧⲁϩⲁⲣⲉϩ ⲉⲧⲟⲩⲯⲩⲭⲏ ⲧⲁⲧⲙⲕⲁⲁⲥ ⲉⲣϩⲟⲧⲉ ϩⲏⲧϥ ⲙ̇ⲡⲙⲟⲩ
88 Ⲛⲁⲓ̈ ϭⲉ ⲛⲧⲉⲣⲉϥϫⲟⲟⲩ ⲛⲁⲓ̈ ⲁⲓ̈ⲗⲟ ⲉⲓⲛⲁⲩ ⲉⲣⲟϥ 89 Ⲧⲉⲛⲟⲩ ϭⲉ
ⲧⲱⲟⲩⲛ̇ ⲙⲟⲩⲧⲉ ⲛⲁⲓ̈ ⲉⲙⲡⲁⲣⲑⲉⲛⲟⲥ ⲧⲁϯ ⲛⲧⲱϣ ⲛⲁⲩ 90 ⲁⲩⲱ
ⲛⲧⲉⲩⲛⲟⲩ ⲁⲩⲥⲱⲟⲩϩ · ⲉⲣⲟⲥ ⲛ̇ⲙ̇ⲡⲁⲣⲑⲉⲛⲟⲥ ⲧⲏⲣⲟⲩ ⲁⲩⲁⲥⲡⲁⲍⲉ
ⲙ̇ⲙⲟⲥ ⲁⲩⲱ ⲁⲩϩⲙⲟⲟⲥ 91 Ⲛ̇ⲧⲟⲥ ⲇⲉ ⲡⲉϫⲁⲥ ⲛⲁⲩ ϫⲉ ϯϣⲓ̈ⲛⲉ̇ ⲉ̇ⲣⲱⲧⲛ
ⲙⲙⲟⲛ ⲉⲓ̈ⲃⲏⲕ ⲉⲑⲓ̈ⲗ̅ⲏ̅ⲙ̅ ⲛⲁⲗⲏⲑⲓ̈ⲛⲟⲛ 92 Ⲛ̇ⲧⲟⲟⲩ ⲇⲉ ⲙ̇ⲡⲟⲩⲉⲓ̈ⲙⲉ ϫⲉ
ⲉⲥϫⲱ̇ ⲙ̇ⲙⲟⲥ ϫⲉ ⲟ̅ⲩ̅ 93 Ⲛⲧⲟⲥ ⲇⲉ ⲁⲥⲁⲙⲁϩⲧⲉ[a] · ⲛ̇ⲧϭⲓϫ ⲛ̇ⲟⲩⲉⲓ̈ |
ⲉⲃⲟⲗ ⲛ̈ϩⲏⲧⲟⲩ : Ⲉⲁⲥⲣ̄ϩⲗⲗⲱ ⲉⲙⲁⲧⲉ ⲧⲁⲓ ϭⲉ ⲧⲉ ⲙⲁⲣⲓ̈ⲁ ⲧⲙⲁⲅ-
ⲇⲁⲗⲓⲛⲏ ⲧⲉⲛⲧⲁϥⲛⲟⲩ̈ϫⲉ ⲉⲃⲟⲗ ⲛ̇ϩⲏⲧⲥ ⲛ̇ⲥⲁϣϥ ⲛⲇⲁⲓⲙⲱⲛⲓⲟⲛ
ⲛⲧⲉⲣⲉϥⲃⲱⲕ ⲉϩⲣⲁⲓ̈ ⲉⲧⲙⲁⲅⲇⲁⲗⲓ̈ⲁ 94 Ⲡⲉϫⲁⲥ ⲛⲁⲩ ⲧⲏⲣⲟⲩ ϫⲉ ⲉⲓⲥ
ⲧⲉⲧⲛⲙⲁⲁⲩ ϫⲓⲛ̇ ⲙⲡⲟⲟⲩ ⲉⲃⲟⲗ ϯⲙⲧⲟⲛ ⲙ̇ⲡⲉⲥⲡ̅ⲛ̅ⲁ̅ ⲛⲑⲉ ⲛ̇ⲧⲁⲥ-
ϯⲙⲧⲟⲛ̇ ⲙ̇ⲡⲱⲓ̈ 95 ϩⲁⲣⲉϩ ⲉⲛⲉⲥⲩⲛ̇ⲑⲏⲕⲏ ⲛⲧⲁⲧⲉⲧⲛ̇ⲥⲙⲛⲧⲟⲩ ⲙⲛ̇ ⲡⲉⲭ̅ⲥ̅
ϫⲉⲕⲁⲥ ⲉⲧⲉⲧⲛⲁⲕⲗⲏⲣⲟⲛⲟⲙⲉⲓ̈ ⲙ̇ⲡⲙⲁ ⲉⲧⲟⲩⲛⲁϫⲓ̈ⲧ ⲉⲣⲟϥ 96 Ⲛ̿ⲁⲓ ϭⲉ
ⲛ̇ⲧⲉⲣⲉⲥϫⲟⲟⲩ ⲙ̇ⲡⲥⲧⲁⲙⲟⲟⲩ ⲉⲧⲃⲉ ⲡⲉⲥⲛ̇ⲕⲟⲧⲕ · 97 Ⲧⲟⲧⲉ ⲁⲥⲕⲟⲧⲥ
ⲉⲛⲁⲡⲟⲥⲧⲟⲗⲟⲥ ⲡⲉϫⲁⲥ ⲙ̇ⲡⲉⲧⲣⲟⲥ ϫⲉ ⲥⲓ̈ⲙⲱⲛ̇ ⲡⲉⲧⲣⲟ̈ⲥ Ⲉⲡⲓⲇⲏ ⲁ
ⲡⲉⲛϫⲟⲉⲓ̈ⲥ ⲧⲁⲛϩⲟⲩⲧⲕ ⲉⲛϣⲟϣⲧ ⲛ̇ⲧⲙⲛⲧⲉⲣⲟ ⲛⲙⲡⲏⲩⲉ Ϣⲱⲡⲉ
p. ⲟⲋ ⲛ̇ϣⲛ̄ϩⲧⲏϥ | ϫⲉ ⲟⲩϣⲛ̇ϩⲧⲏϥ ⲡⲉ ⲡⲉⲧⲛⲉⲓ̈ⲱⲧ ⲉⲧϩⲛ ⲙⲡⲏⲩⲉ · 98 Ⲓ̈ⲁ-
ⲕⲱⲃⲟⲥ ⲙⲛ̇ ⲓ̈ⲱϩⲁⲛⲛⲏⲥ ⲛ̇ϣⲏⲣⲉ ⲙ̇ⲡⲉϩⲣⲟⲩⲃⲁⲓ ⲣⲟⲉⲓⲥ ⲉⲛⲉⲧⲛ[illegible]ⲟ-
ⲗⲓ̈ⲕⲟⲛ̇ ⲉϥⲟⲩⲁⲁⲃ · Ϣⲱⲡⲉ ⲛ̇ⲣⲙⲣⲁϣ · ⲉϩⲟⲩⲛ ⲉⲟⲩⲟⲛ ⲛⲓ̈ⲙ 99 Ⲛⲧⲟⲕ
ⲇⲉ ⲱ̇ ⲡⲉⲧⲣⲟⲥ̇ ⲧⲱⲟⲩⲛ ⲛⲅ̄ⲃⲱⲕ ⲉϩⲟⲩⲛ ⲉⲡⲏⲓ̈ ⲙ̇ⲃⲩⲣⲣⲟⲥ ⲡⲉⲕⲙⲁ-
ⲑⲏⲧⲏⲥ ϫⲓ̈ ⲛⲛⲥⲓ̈ⲇⲱⲛⲓⲟ̇ⲛ ⲛ̇ⲧⲁⲓ̈ϭⲁⲗⲱⲟⲩ ⲉ̇ⲣⲟϥ̇ ⲁⲛ̇ⲓ̈ⲥⲟⲩ ⲛⲁⲓ̈ ⲉⲡⲓ̈ⲙⲁ
100 Ⲛ̇ⲧⲟϥ̇ ⲇⲉ ⲁϥⲉⲓ̈ⲣⲉ ⲕⲁⲧⲁ ⲑⲉ ⲛ̇ⲧⲁⲥϫⲟⲟⲥ ⲛⲁϥ̇ ⲁϥⲃⲱⲕ ⲁϥⲉⲓ̈ⲛⲉ
ⲛⲁⲥ ⲛ̇ⲛ̇ⲥⲓ̈ⲛ̇ⲇⲟⲛⲓ̈ⲟⲛ̇ 101 Ⲁⲩⲱ̇ ⲟⲛ ⲡⲉϫⲁⲥ ⲛⲓⲁⲕⲱⲃⲟⲥ ϫⲉ ⲧⲱⲟⲩⲛ
ⲛⲅ̄ϫⲓ ⲛ̇ⲧⲓ̈ⲥⲁⲧⲉⲉⲣⲉ ⲛⲅ̄ⲃⲱⲕ ϣⲁ ⲡⲉⲧϯ ⲉⲃⲟⲗ ⲛⲅ̄ϫⲓ̈ ⲛⲟⲩⲥⲧⲟⲓ̈
ⲉⲛⲁⲛⲟⲩϥ ⲛⲅ̄ⲛⲧϥ ⲛⲁⲓ̈ ⲉⲡⲓ̈ⲙⲁ 102 Ⲛ̇ⲧⲟϥ ⲇⲉ ⲟⲛ ⲁϥⲉⲓ̈ⲣⲉ ⲕⲁⲧⲁ
ⲡⲉⲥϣⲁ̇ϫⲉ ⲁϥⲃⲱⲕ ⲁϥⲉⲓⲛⲉ ⲛⲁⲥ ⲛ̇ϩⲉⲛⲥϯⲛⲟⲩϥⲉ ⲉⲛⲁϣⲱⲟⲩ | 103 Ⲛ̇ⲧⲉⲣⲉ

[a] ⲁⲥⲁⲙⲁϩ · ⲧⲉ

thy body better than the palaces of kings. 86 Haste thee
then, command My apostles, give the order to the virgins;
87 and behold I come unto thee quickly with My angels, to cf. Ap II
take away thy holy remains, and to guard thy soul, and not 16*; XXII 7*, 12*
to suffer it to fear death. 88 When therefore He had said
these things to me, I saw Him no more. 89 Now therefore
arise and call me the virgins, that I may give the order to
them.

90 And straightway they gathered together to her all the
virgins, and they saluted her and sat down. 91 And she said
to them, I greet you, for I am going to the true Jerusalem.
92 But they knew not what she was saying. 93 And she took
hold of the hand of one of them who was very old—now she
was[a] Mary Magdalene, from whom He cast out seven devils, cf. Mc XVI
when He went into Magdalia—94 and she said to them all, 9*; Lc VIII 2*
Behold your mother from this day forth. Refresh her spirit cf. Jn XIX
as she refreshed mine. 95 Keep the covenants that ye made 27
with Christ, in order that ye may inherit the place whither
I shall be taken.

96 When therefore she said these things she did not tell
them of her falling asleep. 97 Then she turned to the apostles,
and said to Peter, Simon Peter, seeing that our Lord hath
intrusted to thee the keys of the kingdom of the heavens, cf. Mt XVI
be merciful, for your Father which is in the heavens is 19* Lc VI 36
merciful. 98 James and John, the sons of thunder, keep your cf. Mc III
Catholic *Church* (?) holy, and be meek towards everyone. 17*
99 And thou, Peter, arise and go into the house of Birrus thy
disciple, and get the linen cloths which I have committed to
him, and bring them hither to me. 100 And he did as she
said to him. He went and brought her the linen cloths.
101 And again she spake to James, Arise, take this shekel, go cf. Mt XXV
unto those that sell, and get a perfume and bring it hither 9*
to me. 102 And he also did according to her word. He went
and brought her many perfumes. 103 When the day of her

[a] Lit. *she therefore is*

ⲡⲉ⸢ϩⲟⲟⲩ⸣ ⲛ̄ⲧⲉⲥⲁⲡⲁ⸢ⲗⲩ⸣ⲥⲓⲥ ϣⲱⲡⲉ ⸢ⲁⲥ⸣ⲙⲟⲩⲧⲉ ⲉⲓ̈ⲱϩⲁⲛⲛⲏⲥ ⲛ̄ϭⲓ
ⲧⲉⲑⲉⲟⲇⲱⲕⲟⲥ ⲉⲧⲟⲩⲁⲁⲃ ⲡⲉϫⲁⲥ ⲛⲁϥ ϫⲉ ⲧⲱⲟⲩⲛ ⲡ̄ⲣ̄ϫⲉⲣⲟ ⲛ̄ϩⲉⲛ-
ⲫⲁⲛⲟⲥ · ⲙⲛ ϩⲉⲛⲗⲁⲙⲡⲁⲥ ⲉⲃⲟⲗ ϫⲉ ⲁ ⲣⲟⲩϩⲉ ϣⲱⲡⲉ [104]ⲛ̄ⲧⲟⲥ
ⲇⲉ ⲁⲥϫⲓ ⲛ̄ⲛⲥⲓⲛⲇⲱⲛⲓⲟⲛ ⲁⲥⲡⲟⲣϣⲟⲩ ⲉϫⲙ ⲡⲕⲁϩ · ⲙⲡⲉⲥⲙⲟⲧ
ⲛⲟⲩⲙⲁ ⲛ̄ⲛ̄ⲕⲟⲧⲕ ⲏ̄ ⲟⲩⲙⲁ ⲙ̄ⲡⲱⲣϣ ⲁⲥⲡⲱϩⲧ ⲛ̄ⲛⲉⲥϯⲛⲟⲩϥⲉ ⲉϩⲣⲁⲓ̈
ⲉϫⲱⲟⲩ [105]ⲁⲥⲕⲟⲧⲥ · ⲉⲛⲁⲡⲟⲥⲧⲟⲗⲟⲥ ⲡⲉϫⲁⲥ ⲛⲁⲩ ϫⲉ ⲙⲁⲣⲉⲛϣⲗⲏⲗ
ⲉϩⲣⲁⲓ̈ ⲉⲡⲛⲟⲩⲧⲉ ⲛ̄ⲛⲁⲛⲧ ⲉⲧⲣⲉϥⲛⲁ ⲛⲁⲛ̄ [106]ⲁⲩⲱ ⲛ̄ⲧⲓ̈ϩⲉ ⲁⲥⲕⲧⲉ
ⲡⲉⲥϩⲟ · ⲉⲛⲥⲁ ⲛ̄ⲧⲁⲛⲁⲧⲟⲗⲏ ⲁⲥϣⲗⲏⲗ ⲉⲥϫⲱ ⲙⲙⲟⲥ [107]ϫⲉ ϯϣⲡ̄ϩⲙⲟⲧ
p. ⲟⲍ ⲛ̄ⲧⲟⲟⲧⲕ ⲡⲛⲟⲩⲧⲉ ⲡⲡⲁⲛ̄ⲧⲱⲕⲣⲁⲧⲱⲣ ϯϣⲡ̄ϩⲙⲟⲧ ⲛ̄ⲧⲙ |⸢ⲡⲉⲕⲙⲟⲛⲟ⸣-
ⲅⲉⲛⲏⲥ ⸢ⲡϣⲏⲣⲉ⸣ ⲡⲁⲓ̈ ⲛ̄ⲧⲁϥ⸢ⲉⲓ ⲉⲡⲕ⸣ⲟⲥⲙⲟⲥ ⲉⲛ̄ⲟⲩ⸢ϩⲙ ⲙ⸣ⲯⲩⲭⲏ
ⲛⲓⲙ [108]⸢ⲡ⸣ϣⲏⲣⲉ ⲁⲩⲱ ⲡϣⲟϫⲛⲉ ⲙ̄ⲡⲉⲓ̈ⲱⲧ · ⲡⲁⲓ̈ ⲛ̄ⲧⲁϥⲉⲓ̈ ϣⲁⲣⲟⲛ̄ ·
ⲁⲛⲟⲛ ⲡⲉϥϩⲙϩⲁⲗ ⲁϥⲕⲱⲧ ⲛⲁϥ ⲛ̄ⲟⲩⲥⲱⲙⲁ ϩⲱⲥ ⲣⲱⲙⲉ ⲉϩⲣⲁⲓ̈
ⲛ̄ϩⲏⲧ[a] [109]ⲁⲓϫⲡⲟϥ ⲁϫⲛ ⲥⲩⲛⲟⲩⲥⲓ̈ⲁ ⲁⲩⲱ ⲁϫⲛ̄ ϫⲱϩⲙ · ⲁⲓ̈ⲥⲁⲛⲟⲩϣϥ
ⲁϫⲛ ⲣⲟⲟⲩϣ · ⲛ̄ⲧⲟϥ ⲡⲉⲧⲥⲁⲁⲛϣ ⲙⲙⲟⲛ̄ ⲧⲏⲣⲛ̄ [110]ϯϣⲡ̄ϩⲙⲟⲧ ⲛ̄ⲧⲙ̄[b]
ⲡⲉⲕⲡ̄ⲛ̄ⲁ̄ ⲉⲧⲟⲩⲁⲁⲃ ⲡⲁⲓ̈ ⲛ̄ⲧⲁϥⲉⲓ̈ ⲉϩⲣⲁⲓ̈ ⲉϫⲱⲓ̈ · ⲁⲩⲱ ⲧⲉⲕϭⲟⲙ
ⲉⲧⲟⲩⲁⲁⲃ ⲧⲁⲓ̈ ⲛⲧⲁⲥⲣ̄ϩⲁⲓⲃⲉⲥ ⲉⲣⲟⲓ̈ [111]ⲧⲉⲛⲟⲩ ϭⲉ ⲡⲁϫⲟⲉⲓ̈ⲥ ⲁⲩⲱ
ⲡⲁⲛⲟⲩⲧⲉ · ⲁ ⲡⲛⲁⲩ ϣⲱⲡⲉ ⲉⲧⲣⲉⲕⲉⲓ̈ ϣⲁⲣⲟⲓ̈ ⲛ̄ⲅ̄ⲛⲁ ⲛⲁⲓ̈ ⲛ̄ⲅ̄ⲛⲟⲩϫⲉ
ⲛ̄ⲥⲁⲛⲃⲟⲗ ⲙ̄ⲙⲟⲓ̈ ⲛ̄ⲛ̄ⲓ̈ⲱⲛⲉ ⲛ̄ϫⲣⲟⲡ ⲙⲛ̄ ⲛ̄ⲓ̈ϩⲟ ⲧⲏⲣⲟⲩ ⲉⲧϣⲟⲃⲉ
[112]ⲙⲁⲣⲟⲩϩⲉ ϩⲓ̈ⲑⲏ ⲙ̄ⲙⲟⲓ̈ ⲛ̄ϭⲓ ⲡⲉⲧⲥⲁϩⲃⲟⲩⲣ ⲙ̄ⲙⲟⲕ | ⲛ̄ⲧⲉ ⲡⲉⲧ-
ⲥⲁⲟⲩⲛⲁⲙ ⲉⲣⲉⲣⲁⲧⲟⲩ ϩⲛ ⲟⲩⲣⲁϣⲉ [113]ⲙⲁⲣⲉ ⲡⲉⲍⲟⲩⲥⲓⲁ ⲧⲏⲣⲟⲩ
ⲙ̄ⲡⲕⲁⲕⲉ ϫⲓϣⲓ̈ⲡⲉ ⲙ̄ⲡⲟⲟⲩ ϫⲉ ⲙ̄ⲡⲟⲩϭⲛ ⲗⲁⲁⲩ ⲛ̄ⲧⲁⲩ ϩⲓⲱⲱⲧ ·
[114]ⲁⲟⲩⲱⲛ ⲛⲁⲓ̈ ⲛ̄ⲙⲡⲩⲗⲏ ⲛ̄ⲧⲇⲓⲕⲁⲓ̈ⲟⲥⲩⲛⲏ ⲧⲁⲉⲓ ⲉϩⲟⲩⲛ̄ ⲛ̄ϩⲏⲧⲟⲩ
ⲉⲧⲣⲁⲟⲩⲱⲛϩ ⲉⲃⲟⲗ ⲙ̄ⲡϩⲟ ⲙ̄ⲡⲁⲛⲟⲩⲧⲉ [115]ⲙⲁⲣⲉ ⲡⲉⲇⲣⲁⲕⲱⲛ ϩⲟⲡϥ
ϩⲁⲧⲁϩⲏ ⲉϥⲛⲁⲩ ⲉⲣⲟⲓ̈ ⲉⲓⲡⲁⲣⲣⲏⲥⲓⲁⲍⲉ ⲙ̄ⲙⲟⲓ̈ ⲉⲓ̈ⲛⲏⲩ ⲉⲣⲁⲧⲕ ⲡⲛⲟⲩⲧⲉ
ⲙⲙⲉ ⲙⲁⲩⲁⲁϥ · [116]ⲙⲁⲣⲉ ⲡⲓ̈ⲉⲣⲟ ⲛ̄ⲕⲱϩⲧ ⲡⲁⲓ̈ ⲉⲧⲟⲩⲇⲟⲕⲓⲙⲁⲍⲉ
ⲙ̄ⲡⲙⲉⲣⲟⲥ ⲥⲛⲁⲩ ⲛ̄ϩⲏⲧϥ ⲛ̄ⲇⲓⲕⲁⲓⲟⲥ ⲙⲛ̄ ⲛ̄ⲣⲉϥⲣ̄ⲛⲟⲃⲉ ⲙⲁⲣⲉϥⲉⲥⲩⲭ-
ⲁⲍⲉ ⲙⲙⲟϥ ϣⲁⲛϯⲡⲁⲣⲁⲅⲉ ⲙⲙⲟϥ [117]ϫⲉ ⲛ̄ⲧⲟⲕ ⲡⲉ ⲡⲁⲛⲟⲩⲧⲉ[c] ⲁⲩⲱ
ⲡⲁϫⲟⲉⲓⲥ ⲁⲩⲱ ⲛⲧⲟⲕ ⲡⲉ ⲡⲓ̈ⲱⲧ ⲛⲟⲩⲟⲛ ⲛⲓⲙ ⲙⲛ̄ ⲡⲉⲕⲙⲟⲛⲟⲅⲉⲛⲏⲥ
ⲡϣⲏⲣⲉ ⲓ̄ⲥ̄ ⲡⲉⲭ̄ⲥ̄ [118]ⲉⲧⲟ̄ ⲛ̄ϩⲟⲙⲟⲟⲩⲥⲓ̈ⲟⲛ ⲛⲙⲙⲁⲕ ⲙⲛ̄ ⲡⲉⲕⲡ̄ⲛ̄ⲁ̄

[a] Littera erasa ut vid. post ⲧ [b] ⲛ̄ in marg. [c] ⲁ̇ supr. script. pr. man.

departure was come, the holy God-bearer called John and
said to him, Arise, light lamps and torches, for evening has[a] cf. Jn XVIII 3
come. 104 And she took the linen cloths and spread them on
the ground like a bed or a couch, and poured out the
perfumes upon them.

105 She turned to the apostles and said to them, Let us
pray to God the merciful to have mercy on us. 106 And so
she turned her face eastwards, and prayed, saying, 107 I thank
Thee God the Almighty, I thank Thine only begotten Son,
who came into the world to save all souls, 108 the Son and the
Counsel of the Father, who came unto us His servants and
built Himself a body as man in my womb. 109 I bare Him
without intercourse *with man* and without defilement, I
nourished Him without anxiety, even Him who nourisheth
us all. 110 I thank Thy Holy Ghost, that came upon me, and cf. Lc I 35
Thy holy power that overshadowed me. 111 Now therefore,
my Lord and my God, the hour has come for Thee to come
unto me and have mercy on me, and remove from me these
stones of stumbling and all these divers faces. 112 Let those
that are on Thy left hand fall before me, and those on *the*
right stand up with joy. 113 Let all the powers of darkness cf. Lc XXII 53; Col I 13; Jn XIV 30
be ashamed to-day, because they have found nothing of
theirs in[b] me. 114 Open to me the gates of righteousness, and Ps CXVII 19*; XLI 3
I will enter into them, and be manifested to the face of
my God. 115 Let the dragon hide himself before me, as he
seeth me coming boldly[c] to Thee the only true God. 116 Let Jn XVII 3
the river of fire, wherein are proved the two portions, the cf. Dan VII 10
righteous and the sinners[d], be still until I pass by it. 117 For
Thou art my God and my Lord, and Thou art the Father of
every one and of Thine only begotten Son Jesus Christ;
118 who is of one essence with Thee and with Thy Holy Ghost,

[a] Or *was* [b] Or *on* [c] Lit. *being bold and coming* [d] Or *righteous and sinners*

p. ⲟⲏ ⲉⲧⲟⲩ|ⲁⲁⲃ ⲡⲁⲓ̈ ⲉⲃⲟⲗ ϩⲓⲧⲟⲟⲧϥ[a] ⲡⲉⲟⲟⲩ ⲛⲁⲕ ⲛ̄ⲙⲙⲁϥ ϣⲁ ⲉⲛⲉϩ ⲛ̄ⲛⲉⲛⲉϩ ϩⲁⲙⲏⲛ̄ 119 Ⲁⲥϣⲱⲡⲉ ⲇⲉ ⲛ̄ⲧⲉⲣⲉⲥϯ ⲙ̄ⲡⲉϩⲁⲙⲏⲛ ⲛ̄ϭⲓ ⲧⲡⲁⲣⲑⲉⲛⲟⲥ ⲉⲧⲟⲩⲁⲁⲃ ⲁⲥⲁⲗⲉ̀ ⲉ̀ϩⲣⲁⲓ̈ ⲉϫⲛ̄ ⲛ̄ⲥⲓⲛⲇⲱⲛⲓ̄ⲟⲛ Ⲡⲛ̄ ⲛ̄ϣⲟⲩϩⲏⲛⲉ : ⲁⲥⲕⲧⲉ ⲡⲉⲥϩⲟ · ⲉ̀ⲡⲥⲁ̀ ⲛ̄ⲧⲁⲛ̄ⲁⲧⲟⲗⲏ 120 ⲁⲥⲥⲫⲣⲁⲅⲓⲍⲉ[b] ⲙ̄ⲙⲟⲥ ϩⲙ̄ ⲡⲣⲁⲛ̄ ⲙ̄ⲡⲓ̈ⲱⲧ ⲙ̄ⲛ̄ ⲡϣⲏⲣⲉ ⲙⲛ̄ ⲡⲉⲡⲛ̄ⲁ ⲉⲧⲟⲩⲁⲁⲃ ⲁⲥⲛ̄ⲕⲟⲧⲕ 121 Ⲁⲩⲱ ⲛ̄ⲧⲉⲩⲛⲟⲩ ⲉⲓⲥ̄ ⲡϫⲟⲉⲓⲥ̄ ⲁϥⲉⲓ̈ ϣⲁⲣⲟⲥ ⲉϥⲧⲁⲗⲏⲩ ⲉϫⲛ̄ ⲛ̄ϩⲁⲣⲙⲁ ⲛ̄ⲛⲉⲭⲉⲣⲟⲩⲃⲓ̈ⲛ̄ Ⲉⲣⲉ ⲛⲁⲅⲅⲉⲗⲟⲥ[c] ⲥⲱⲕ ϩⲁⲧⲉϥϩⲏ · 122 ⲁϥⲉⲓ̈ ⲁϥⲁϩⲉⲣⲁⲧϥ ϩⲓϫⲱⲥ Ⲡⲉϫⲁϥ ⲛⲁⲥ ϫⲉ ⲙ̄ⲡⲣ̄ⲣ̄ϩⲟⲧⲉ ϩⲏⲧϥ ⲙ̄ⲡⲙⲟⲩ ⲱ̀ ⲧⲁⲙⲁⲁⲩ Ⲉⲣⲉ ⲡⲱⲛ̄ϩ ⲧⲏⲣϥ ϩⲁϩⲧⲏ 123 ϩⲁⲡⲥ ⲡⲉ ⲉⲧⲣⲉⲛⲁⲩ ⲉⲣⲟϥ ϩⲛ̄ ⲛⲟⲩⲃⲁⲗ ⲙ̄ⲙⲁⲧⲉ ⲙ̀ⲟⲛⲟⲛ[d] ⲉⲓ̈ⲧⲙⲟⲩⲉϩⲥⲁϩⲛⲉ ⲛⲁϥ ⲛϥⲛ̄ⲁϣⲉⲓ̈ ⲁⲛ̄ ϣⲁⲣⲟ ⁘ 124 ⲁⲩⲱ ⲛ̄ⲧⲓϩⲉ | ⲁϥⲟⲩⲉ⸢ϩⲥⲁϩⲛⲉ ⲛⲁϥ⸣ ⲛ̄ϭⲓ ⲡⲣⲣ⸢ⲟ .....⸣ ⲉϥϫⲱ ⲙ̀ⲙ⸢ⲟⲥ ϫⲉ ⲁ⸣ⲙⲟⲩ ⲡⲉⲧⲛⲏ⸢ⲩ ⲉⲃⲟⲗ⸣ ϩⲛ̄ ⲡⲧⲁⲙⲓ̈ⲟⲛ̄ ⲙ⸢ⲡ⸣ⲣⲏⲥ ϩⲙ̀ ⲡⲙⲁ ⲉⲧϩⲏⲡ · — 125 Ⲁⲩⲱ̀ ⲛ̄ⲧⲉⲩⲛⲟⲩ ⲛ̄ⲧⲁ ⲧⲡⲁⲣⲑⲉⲛⲟⲥ[e] ⲛⲁⲩ ⲉⲣⲟϥ ⲁ ⲧⲉⲥⲯⲩⲭⲏ ϥⲟϭⲥ ⲉⲛ̄ϩⲁⲙ̀ⲏⲣ ⲙ̀ⲡⲉⲥϣⲏⲣⲉ ⲁϥⲥⲕⲉⲡⲁⲍⲉ ⲙ̄ⲙⲟⲥ ϩⲛ̄ ⲡⲉⲡ̄ⲧⲏⲙⲁ ⲛ̄ⲛⲉⲡⲟⲩⲣⲁⲛⲓⲟⲛ ⁘ 126 Ⲁⲥϣⲱⲡⲉ ⲇⲉ ⲛ̄ⲧⲉⲣⲉⲥϯ ⲙ̄ⲡⲉⲥⲡⲛ̄ⲁ ⲉⲛ̄ϭⲓϫ ⲙ̄ⲡⲛⲟⲩⲧⲉ · ⲁ ⲛⲁⲡⲟⲥⲧⲟⲗⲟⲥ ⲧⲁⲗⲟ · ⲛ̄ⲛⲉⲩϭⲓϫ ⲉϫⲛ̄ ⲛⲉⲥⲃⲁⲗ 127 ⲁⲥⲛ̄ⲕⲟⲧⲕ ϩⲛ̄ ⲟⲩⲉⲛⲕⲟⲧⲕ ⲉⲛⲁⲛⲟⲩϥ Ϩⲛ̄ ⲧⲉⲩϣⲏ̄ ⲛ̄ⲥⲟⲩ ϫⲟⲩⲱⲧ ⲙ̄ⲡⲉⲃⲟⲧ ⲓ̈ⲁⲛⲟⲩⲁⲣⲓ̈ⲟⲥ ⲉϩⲧⲟⲩⲉ · ⲛ̄ⲥⲟⲩ ϫⲟⲩⲧⲟⲩⲉ ⲙ̀ⲡⲉⲃⲟⲧ ⲧⲱⲃⲉ ϩⲛ̄ ⲟⲩⲉⲓⲣⲏⲛⲏ ⲛ̄ⲧⲉ ⲡⲛⲟⲩⲧⲉ ϩⲁⲙⲏⲛ
128 Ⲁⲩⲱ ⲡⲉϫⲉ ⲡϫⲟⲉⲓⲥ̄ ⲛ̄ⲛⲁⲡⲟⲥⲧⲟⲗⲟⲥ ϫⲉ ⲕⲱⲱⲥ ⲙ̄ⲡⲉⲥⲥⲱⲙⲁ ⲕⲁⲗⲱⲥ ϫⲓⲧⲥ ⲉϩⲣⲁⲓ̈ ⲉⲡⲓ̈ⲁ ⲛ̄ⲓ̈ⲱⲥⲁⲫⲁⲧ ⲓⲙ̄ |

[a] ϩⲓⲧⲟⲟⲧⲕ [b] punct. sup. ⲅ ut vid. [c] ⲛⲁⲅⲅⲉⲗⲟⲥ [d] punct. sup. ⲙ ut vid. [e] ⲟ sup.

through whom *be* the glory to Thee with Him unto *the* ages of the ages. Amen.

119 Now it came to pass when the holy Virgin had said[a] the Amen, she entered the linen cloths and the spices, and turned her face eastwards; 120 and signed herself in the name of the Father and of the Son and of the Holy Ghost, and lay down[b]. 121 And straightway behold the Lord came unto her riding on the chariots of the Cherubin, the angels going before Him. (cf. Ps xvii 11) 122 He came and stood by her, and said to her, Fear not death, O My mother, whilst all the Life is with thee. 123 Thou must needs see him with thine eyes alone. Only unless I command him, he will not be able to come unto thee.

124 And so the King...commanded him, saying, Come thou that comest from the storehouses of the south in the hidden place. 125 And straightway when the Virgin saw him, her soul leaped into the arms of her Son, and He covered it[c] with the garments of the heavenly *places*. 126 And it came to pass when she had given her spirit into the hands of God, the apostles put their hands on her eyes; 127 and she fell asleep in a goodly sleep on the night of the twentieth of the month January, early in the morning of the twenty-first of the month Tobe; in the[d] peace of God, Amen. 128 And the Lord said to the apostles, Prepare her body well for burial and take her into the valley of Jehoshaphat, and bury[e]...

[a] Lit. *given* [b] Or *and fell asleep* [c] Or *her* [d] Lit. *a*
[e] Reading ⲧⲙ̈|[ⲥ]

BOHAIRIC ACCOUNTS OF THE FALLING ASLEEP OF MARY

WITH SAHIDIC FRAGMENTS.

THE FALLING ASLEEP OF MARY.

INSTRUCTION BY EVODIUS[a].

An instruction which our holy and in every wise honourable[b] father Abba Evodius[c], the archbishop of the great city Rome, who was[d] the second after Peter the apostle, delivered. Now he delivered it concerning the Lady of us all, the holy God-bearer Mary; manifesting the matter to us, that she ended her holy life on the twenty-first of the month Tobi according to the Egyptians; in the[e] peace of God, Amen.

I. If a king of this world wishes to make a marriage feast for his son, a great multitude is gathered unto him, rejoicing with him, and wearing white garments, keeping festival at the marriage feast of the king's son. [2]And all the orders wear royal garments, and rejoice with his son on the day of his marriage. [3]The courtiers adorn their children[f]: [4]the tribunes stand adorned: [5]the counts are gathered together and all their order: [6]all the governors come and those who are governors over them: [7]the generals and the commanders wear purple, and they all come to the joy of the marriage of the king's son. [8]The standard-bearers adorn their standards, and stand and honour the king's son and his bride. [9]The trumpeters make ready their trumpets, in order that all may know perfectly that the king has made a mar-

[a] The Bohairic text is given by Lagarde: *Aegyptiaca*, pp. 38—63
[b] Or *glorious*
[c] The Coptic has *Euchodios*
[d] Lit. *is*
[e] Lit. *a*
[f] Or *sons*

riage feast for his son, and that they all may be gathered
together, each with his order. 10 Places[a] of beholding are pre-
pared in the midst of the city, and performers go up on ropes,
and stand, that those who see them may wonder. 11 The
actors stand acting: 12 the keepers prepare all their wild
beasts: 13 the harpers encompass the king and his palace[b],
and harp with their harps, bringing forth sweet strains,
befitting the marriage feast of the king's son: 14 the players
are gathered with their instruments, and many others are
gathered unto them, listening to the sweet sounds which they
pipe on their instruments of music. 15 The people of the
market cleanse the market places, and hang up veils and linen
cloths in the streets and torches giving light. 16 Every one
crowns the streets and the doors of his house with branches
of palm and branches of olive; and the sailors also of the
waters adorn their ships. 17 In short all crafts are zealous
to manifest more zeal, keeping festival at the festival of the
marriage of the king's son. 18 And these are not the only
ones who rejoice, but also the others, 19 the robbers who are in
the prisons, with the iron set on their hands and their feet,
intended to be put to death[c]; even they forget the troubles
which are upon them, and they also rejoice at the marriage
feast of the king's son, when they are shewn mercy for a little
while in the iron which is set upon them. 20 The poor and
the sick are gathered unto the king's palace[b], and eat and
drink, rejoicing and waiting for the king's charity. 21 All the
craftsmen according to *their* craft make their workshops idle,
and they are all gathered to the palace[b] of the king, and eat
and drink at the marriage feast of the king's son. 22 And the
king also when he sees all these rejoicing at the marriage
feast of his son, his heart is much enlarged, and he is com-
passionate[d] towards the poor and the orphans. 23 Then he
hastily commands to send forth orders by cities and by
villages, bidding *them* not to treat the poor with violence in
any matter henceforth.

[a] Lit. *Ways* [b] Lit. *house* [c] Lit. men *wishing to put them to death* [d] Lit. *and he is* (or *becomes*) *in compassion*

II. And if these things take place at a marriage feast of *a* king's son of this world which shall pass away, *and* its[a] joy must needs be turned into mourning after but a little while, by reason of that which is set against[a] all men, even death, whose name is bitter; how great joy is spread out for us to-day in heaven and on earth because of the true bride Mary the Virgin, more beautiful than any offspring of man that God hath made, who went away to-day unto her pure Bridegroom, her true Spouse, her Son and her God?
[2]All ye inhabitants of heaven rejoice to-day, because it is
her festival that we keep, Mary the Virgin, the mother of
the King of kings. [3]Again, ye inhabitants of the earth
rejoice exceedingly, because the freedom of our race be-
cf. Ro vi 17 f came ours by means of her: and we ceased being servants
of sin, and became servants of righteousness; and came forth
cf. Ga iii 13 from the curse of the law, by means of Him whom the Virgin
brought forth, Jesus Christ, the Word of the Father, who
was before the worlds[b].

III. Verily blessed art thou in truth, Mary the true
bride. [2]Blessed art thou many times, O thou holy Virgin,
because thy holy virgin womb was made worthy to be-
come *a* dwelling place of the Word of the Father. [3]Thou
art higher than heaven, O Mary thou Virgin, because He
cf. 2 Co xii 2 who sitteth on the right hand of His Father in the third
heaven on high—thy holy knees were worthy of Him, that
He should sit upon them. [4]Blessed art thou, O Mary thou
Virgin, thou Queen of all women, because thou wast made
worthy that thy two breasts should nourish Christ Jesus
our Lord, who nourisheth all the creation that His hands
have made. [5]What is the honour wherewith I shall honour
thee, O thou holy Virgin, O thou that shinest more than the
sun and art better than the moon, O thou that art higher
than the angels that have no body, [6]O thou that art more
beautiful than the Cherubim and the Seraphim and the
cf. Col i 16 thrones and the dominions?

[a] See note [b] Lit. *ages*

IV. Verily thou art more honourable[a] than all the ranks
of the heavens, O Mary thou Virgin. 2 But perchance a[b]
senseless wicked Jew may hear me ascribing such great
honours as these to[c] this holy Virgin, and be troubled by
his wicked jealousy, and be torn asunder in the midst, and
dare to speak with his mouth that ought to be closed and
his tongue that ought to be cut off in folly, *saying*, Cease
ascribing all these honours to[d] this Virgin born of a man and
a woman. 3 Now this indeed I fully confess[e], O thou lawless
one, that the holy Virgin Mary also was born of a father
and a mother even as all men. 4 For her father was[f] Joakim
and her mother was[f] Anna, the honourable[a] and blessed
root, the pure offspring, the nursling full of all gladness. 5 O
thou senseless Jew, wherefore didst thou say in truth that
the holy Virgin Mary was[f] born of intercourse *with man*, and
didst not confess this also without doubting, that the holy
Virgin brought forth Christ without intercourse with man?
6 O thou lawless Jew, wherefore didst thou cry out, saying, cf. Mt XII
This man casteth out devils by[g] Belzeboul; but didst not 24; Lc XI 15
remember him from whom the legion of devils came out, cf. Mc V 9,
and her from whom the seven devils came out at one time? 13; Lc VIII 2
7 Wherefore didst thou cry out to Pilate, Crucify[h] Him, crucify cf. Lc XXIII
Him, crucify Him; but didst not rather remember those of 21; Jn XIX 6
thine whom He raised from the dead, even Lazarus when he cf. Jn XI
had been four days in the tomb[i], and the son of the widow 17, 39 cf. Lc VII
that was in Nain, and the daughter of Jairus the ruler of 11, 12
the synagogue, and the rest that cannot be numbered? cf. Mc V 22, 23
8 Wherefore, O thou lawless Jew, didst thou dare to spit[k] cf. Mt XXVI
in His divine face, *when* it was[f] He who formed thee, but 67; XXVII 30
thou didst not rather remember that He[l] it was[f] who
caused the eyes of the man born blind to see, with the spittle cf. Jn IX 6
of His divine and blessed mouth? 9 Wherefore, O thou law-
less one, didst thou pierce[l] with nails His hands and His feet

[a] Or *glorious* [b] Lit. *the* [c] Lit. *speaking such...concerning* [d] Lit. *speaking all...concerning* [e] Lit. *with confession I confess* [f] Lit. *is* [g] Lit. *in* [h] Here a Greek word is used for *crucify*; in the next two cases a Coptic one [i] Lit. *on his fourth day, being in the tomb* [k] Lit. *didst thou dare, didst thou spit* [l] See note

which made thee, O thou wicked and foul man of impurity[a];
cf. Mt xii 10, 13 and didst not rather remember the withered hand which He
caused to be stretched forth? 10 And wherefore also didst
cf. Jn xix 28 f; Mt xxvii 34, 48 thou hear Him *say*, I thirst; and gavest Him to drink
vinegar mingled with gall; but didst not rather remember
that this is He who brought forth the water from the rock,
cf. 1 Co x 4, 5 and gave thy forefathers to drink in the wilderness, in
order that thou also mayest confess Him? 11 Wherefore
didst thou speak false words[b] against Him, O thou senseless
cf. 2 Th ii 8 *and* foul one, thou Jew whom the Lord shall destroy with
cf. Ps v 7 the breath of His mouth; even as it is written, The Lord
shall destroy all that speak falsehood. 12 Wherefore didst
thou speak to Pilate, accusing the Lord Jesus, wishing that
he should give sentence against Him and put Him to death,
cf. Lc xxiii 2 *saying*, This man forbiddeth us to give custom to Caesar[c]?
13 Wherefore didst thou not speak the truth, O thou that art
fouler than all men, and didst not remember the time that ye
cf. Lc xi 54; xx 20 ff came unto Him, laying wait, wishing to take hold of a word
at His mouth, when ye said to Him, Dost Thou wish that we
cf. Mt xxii 18 give[d] toll to Caesar[c]? But knowing your wicked device, He
cf. Mc xii 15 f said to you, Bring Me a penny; and ye brought it to Him.
And He took it, and blotted out the letters which were upon
cf. Mt xxii 21 it, and wrote on it thus, Give to God the things that are
God's, and give to Caesar[c] the things that are Caesar's[e]. But
cf. Jn viii 44 ye would not speak the truth, for ye are liars from *the* first.
14 Wherefore did ye have pity on a wicked slayer that was *a*
cf. Lc xxiii 18 murderer, who also was[f] one of you, and said, Release him
unto us? and Him who saved you and your sons, ye did to
Him many evils, *though* He raised your dead, and opened
the eyes of your blind, and made those who had been long
cf. Mt ix 6 sick[g] among you take up their bed and go to their house,
without medicine and herbs, and healed your women who
cf. Mt ix 20 had issues of blood twelve years. 15 But ye envied Him,
Mt xxvii 25 wishing to put Him to death, and cried out to Pilate, His
blood *be* on us, and on our children. 16 O ye lawless Jews,

[a] Lit. *impure one* [b] Lit. *words of falsehood* [c] Lit. *the king* [d] See note [e] Lit. *the king's* [f] Lit. *is* [g] Lit. *long in their sicknesses*

wherefore did ye not read in the first vision of Daniel the
prophet, and know the rebukes which the prophet gave to
your fathers of old, even the false prophets, called elders,
who plotted and bare false witness against Susanna the
daughter of Chelkias, the wife of Joakim, the honourable
and perfect, when the prophet said unto them, Behold now cf. Sus
there hath come upon you and upon your head the sin which 52 f
ye do, letting go those to whom the sins belong, and destroy-
ing the sinless, when the Lord saith, The sinless and the cf. Ex
righteous shalt thou not slay. [17]But ye have filled up the xxiii 7 cf. Mt
measure of your fathers, and also ye have put to death xxiii 32
Him that liveth for ever, the only sinless One, *even* Christ;
and have said, Release unto us the sinful one and him to cf. Lc
whom all sins belong, even Barabbas the murderer *that was* xxiii 18
a robber. [18]O woe to you and to your children many times,
O ye that are fouler than any race of man, and impurer than
any unclean woman. [19]Woe, woe to you on the day in the cf. Ac
which God will sit and judge all the world in righteousness xvii 31
and give to every man according to his works; [20]and ye are cf. Ro ii 6
on the side of those on the left, clothed with shame and dis- cf. Mt xxv
honour, condemned because ye knew not the Lord and His 41
holy law. [21]But this I say that ye must needs hear the
sentence which *is* bitter and sharper than any two-edged He iv 12
sword, Mine enemies, which would not that I should reign Lc xix 27
over them, bring them hither and slay them before me; and cf. Mt xxii
bind them hand and foot, and cast them into the outer dark- 13
ness, where shall be the weeping and the gnashing of teeth.
[22]Behold these things we have spoken unto you, O people
that love God, whilst I manifest to you the wicked purpose
of the Jews *that are* transgressors, and the unmercifulness
that they shewed towards the Lord of glory and the King of cf. 1 Co ii
heaven and of earth, our Lord Jesus Christ. [23]But come 8
now, let us leave the wicked sayings of those men, and let us
turn to the death[a] of the holy Virgin Mary, and manifest the
matter to you, on what day she died[b] and how she laid down
her body. [24]But think not, my beloved, that these words,

[a] Or *consummation* [b] Or *was perfected*

which I shall speak to you, are idle words, or that we have
heard them from others, and have spoken them to you. Nay,
cf. 1 Jn i 1 but those things which I have seen with mine eyes and have
handled with my hands, *even* I Evodius who speak with you
now in this instruction, they are *the things* which I speak to
you. 25 For it is written, Better is the seeing of the eyes than
the hearing of the ears: and these are those things that I
will now speak.

V. It came to pass at the time that God manifested in
the world His Son and the Son of the holy Virgin Mary in
cf. Jn xxi 1, 2 truth— 2 Now when He came walking by[a] the sea of
Tiberias, I Evodius and Alexander my kinsman were on
cf. Mt iv 18, 21 board the boat, with my father Peter and Andrew his brother,
cf. Jn xxi 3 mending our nets going about the lake to catch fish. 3 And
as for my father Peter, the boat and the nets were his, and
we also were under him as workmen: and Rufus also was
together[b] with us for the mending of the nets. 4 And our
Lord Jesus came walking by[a] the sea of Tiberias, and called
Mt iv 19 unto my father Peter and Andrew his brother, Come, follow
Me. 5 Now *as for* my father Peter, his name was formerly
cf. He iii 1 called[c] Simon. When the Lord called him unto the heavenly
cf. Jn i 43 calling He added two other names to him, Peter and Cephas,
so that his names became three, Simon, Peter, Cephas. 6 And
it came to pass when my father Peter and Andrew his
brother heard the gentle[d] voice of the Lord saying to them,
Follow Me; they did not stay at all, but bade farewell
cf. Mt iv 22; Lc v 11 to everything and to the boat, and came to the shore,
and followed Him. 7 And I also Evodius that am least of
cf. Mc xv 21 all[e] and Rufus and Alexander, we no longer departed any
more unto our fathers, but we also went and followed our
fathers *the* apostles, and we were ministering to Him in all
things that He might command us. 8 Those whom He
cf. Mc iii 14; Lc vi 13 called with my father Peter were twelve in number[f], whom
He called apostles. And there was also he whose very
cf. Lc vi 16 name is not worthy to be uttered, Judas the traitor; he
cf. Ac i 17, 26 also was numbered in the lot of the twelve apostles: but

[a] Or *on* [b] Lit. *one* [c] Or *his first name was called* [d] Or *sweet*
[e] Lit. *Evodius the least* [f] Lit. *in their number*

we also were seventy two. [9]Through this great matter cf. Lc x 1
therefore we remained hidden there, and were not able to go
out for a great while for fear of the Jews, lest they should cf. Jn xix
put us to death; until our Lord Jesus Christ came unto 38; xx 19
us, and shewed us the way wherein we should go[a]. [10]And cf. Ps cxlii 8
Mary the mother of our Lord Jesus Christ was with us in
the house, and the women also that followed her from
Jerusalem (for they were going with us until our Lord
Jesus was crucified), even Salome and Joanna and all the cf. Lc xxiv
rest of the virgins who went with her. [11]And my father 10
Peter sanctified an altar in the house in which we were,
even as the Lord taught us before He suffered; and again
after He rose from the dead, He taught us again.

VI. Now it came to pass on the twentieth of the month
Tobi, we were gathered together according to the command
of the Lord, in the place where the holy Virgin was, and were
still preparing the altar, to receive *a* blessing; and there
came unto us our Lord Jesus Christ, and stood in our midst, cf. Lc xxiv
and saith unto us, Peace *be* unto you all. [2]But we were in 36 f; Jn xx 19
great fear, and worshipped him in haste. [3]He answered and
said unto us, It is I; be not afraid. It is I, who was
crucified for the whole race of Adam. It is I, who died
and rose from the dead on the third day, and granted
resurrection of life to the sons of men. Peace *be* unto
you all, My honourable[b] apostles. Peace *be* unto My lesser[c]
disciples. Peace *be* unto Mary My virgin mother, who
brought Me forth on the earth. Peace *be* unto all the
women who follow you. The peace of My good Father I cf. Jn xiv
give unto you. [4]Be not afraid; for I am with you unto the 27
end[d] of the ages. [5]And our Saviour saluted His virgin cf. Mt xxviii 20
mother, and afterwards He saluted my father Peter, and
then again all the apostles and us the lesser[c] disciples; and
last of all He said to my father Peter, Make haste and
prepare the altar, that I may give *a* blessing unto you to-day;
for I must needs take a great offering from your midst on
the morrow, before that each one *of you* goes to the lot that

[a] Lit. *we will go* [b] Or *glorious* [c] Lit. *little*
[d] Or *consummation*

hath fallen to him to preach therein. [6]And the Lord gave
a blessing to us all on that day, and appointed my father
Peter archbishop, and we also the lesser[a] disciples, he made
some among us presbyters—I *being* one of them, Evodius the
least—and afterwards deacons for the perfecting[b] of the altar,
cf. Eph IV 12 and readers and psalmists and door-keepers for the perfecting[b]
of the Church: all these He made in our midst on the
twentieth of the month Tobi. [7]Afterwards He gave us the
cf. Ac I 9 *salutation of* peace, and went up to the heavens, as we were
all looking at Him. [8]And we spent all that day gathered
cf. Lc XXIV 53 together in one assembly, blessing[c] God because of the great
gift which had befallen us. [9]Again we sat and discussed[d]
with one another, *saying*, What then is this word which the
Lord spake to us, I must needs take a great offering from
your midst on the morrow?

VII. Now it came to pass at the hour of the light on the
twenty-first of the month Tobi, which was[e] the morrow, that
cf. Ps XVII 11 Christ the true Word came unto us riding on a chariot of
cf. Da VII 10 Cherubim, thousand thousands of angels following Him, the
powers of light surrounding Him and singing before Him:
David the holy singer riding on a chariot of light, having his
Ex XV 1 spiritual harp, crying out and saying, Let us sing unto the
cf. Jn XX 19, 26 Lord, for with glory hath He been glorified. [2]And our
Saviour stood in our midst, the doors being shut, and
cf. Mt XII 49 stretched forth His hand towards us all; the multitude of
the disciples being gathered together, and said unto us,
cf. Jn XX 19, 20 Peace be unto you all. [3]And we all arose together, and
worshipped His hands and His feet, and He blessed us
with the blessing of heaven; the angels answering Him,
Amen. [4]And He turned to my father Peter, and said to
him, Take care of the altar, that I may give *a* blessing to
you; for I must needs take a great offering from your midst
to-day. [5]But we fell down at His feet and worshipped Him,
cf. Jn XX 28 and besought Him, saying, Our Lord and our God, we beseech
Thee that Thou wouldest tell us this word which Thou hast
spoken to us, I must needs take a great offering from your

[a] Lit. *little* [b] Or *preparing* [c] Or *praising* [d] Or *arranged*
[e] Lit. *is*

midst to-day. 6 Our Saviour answered, and said to us, O my cf. Eph v
glorious[a] members, whom I chose out of all the world, this 30; Jn xv 19
is the day that the prophecy of My father David has been
fulfilled, The queen stood at thy right hand in garments Ps XLIV 10
worked with gold, arrayed and adorned in divers manners.
7 This is the day that I will receive My virgin mother, who
has been to me *a* dwelling-place on the earth for nine
months, and take her up with me to the heavenly places of
the heavens, and give her *as a* gift to My good Father, even
as David saith, There shall be brought in unto the king Ps XLIV 15
virgins behind her, there shall be brought in unto him all
her neighbours also. 8 He answered in His divine *and*
gentle[b] voice, and said, Arise and come unto Me, O my
beloved mother, in whom My soul was pleased to be; O thou
that art beautiful among the daughters of Kedar; O thou cf. Cant I
chosen[c] nest wherein *He that is* the beautiful Dove dwelt; 5
9 O thou chosen[c] garden that brought forth without seed and cf. Cant IV
without husbandry, bringing forth a goodly fruit; 10 O thou 12 cf. He IX
golden pot, wherein the manna is hidden, even I, the true 4; Ap II
manna; 11 O thou hidden treasure, wherein the true light 17 cf. Mt XIII
is hidden, which was manifested forth and bestowed wealth 44
on the sons of men. 12 Arise and come unto Me, O My cf. Cant V
beautiful dove, My holy bride, My pure field, and I will take 1, 2
thee into My garden with Me, and array thee with My
myrrh and My spice, and spread beneath thee the garments
of fine linen. 13 O Mary My mother, blessed art thou, because
thou didst bring Me forth upon the earth. Blessed are thy
breasts, because I received suck from them; *and* I am He
that nourisheth everyone. 14 I also will take thee to the
heavenly places of the height, and nourish thee with the
good things of My Father. 15 If then thou didst make me
sit upon thy knees, O Mary My virgin mother, I also will
place thee on[d] the chariots of Cherubim, and take thee to
the heavens with[e] Me and My good Father. 16 If thou didst cf. Lc II 7
wrap Me in swaddling clothes, O Mary My virgin mother, on
the day that thou didst bring Me forth, and *if* thou didst

[a] Or *honourable* [b] Or *sweet* [c] Or *choice* [d] For the Sahidic text and translation from c. VII 15[b] to c. VIII 13[a] see below, p. 66 ff [e] Or *unto*

place Me in a manger of cattle, and an ox and an ass
overshadowed Me: I also will wrap thy body to-day in
the garments of heaven, which I have brought from the
cf. Ge III 24 heavens with Me; and will place it under[a] the tree of life,
and make the[b] Cherubim watch it with the sword of fire.
And I will cover thy blessed soul with the coverings that
cf. He XII 22 cover the altar of the heavenly Jerusalem. 17 If thou didst
take Me down into[c] Egypt for fear of Herod the lawless, when
he was pursuing Me; I also will make My angels overshadow
thee with their wings, and ever keep singing thy praise.

VIII. Now when we heard these things, as our Saviour
was saying them to His virgin mother, we all knew that He
was wishing to take her from *the* body. 2 And we all turned
cf. Lc XXII 62 our face away[d] and wept bitterly; and she also wept with us,
the mother of us all, the holy Virgin Mary. 3 Our Saviour
said to us, Why weep ye? 4 Our father Peter said to Him,
cf. Jn XX 28 My Lord and my God, we weep over the great bereave-
ment that shall befall us. 5 At the time indeed that the
lawless Jews crucified Thee, we mourned for a few days;
cf. Jn XVI 20 afterwards our mourning was turned for us into joy by Thy
rising from the dead: *for* Thou didst appear to us and didst
comfort us, and didst entrust us to Thy virgin mother, even
Mary the mother of us all; and we remained as though Thou
wert yet in the body with us. 6 Now therefore if Thou wilt
take her from us, better is it for us that Thou shouldst take
us before her than the bereavement that shall befall us.
7 And our Saviour said to him, O My chosen Peter and all
My apostles whom I have chosen, said I not to you, I
Jn XIV 18 will not leave you desolate[e] but I come unto you again?
8 But weep not for the death[f] of My virgin mother. I will
not leave her without her appearing unto you soon. Even as
I have not hidden Myself from you, neither shall My virgin
mother also hide herself[g] from you. But every time that I
appear unto you, I will bring with Me My virgin mother, in
cf. Jn XVI 22 order that ye may see her and your soul may exult. 9 Now
my father Peter and the rest of the disciples said to our

[a] Or *by* [b] The article is in the singular number [c] Or *take Me into* [d] See note [e] Or *orphans* [f] Or *consummation* [g] Or *be hidden*

Saviour, Our Lord and our God, is it not possible that she
should never die[a]? 10 The Saviour said to them, I wonder at
you, O My holy apostles, for this word which ye have spoken
now. Can the word which I spake from *the* first prove *a* lie?
Nay, God forbid[b]. 11 But I pronounced[c] a sentence from *the* first
upon all flesh, that they must all needs taste death. 12 Because
of the flesh that I took, I also tasted death, I *who* am[a] the
Lord of all men, that I might loose the pangs of death. 13 My cf. Ac II 24
father Peter said to him, My Lord and my God, bid me speak cf. Ge
with Thee this time also. 14 The Lord said to him, Speak. XVIII 32
15 My father Peter said to Him, My Lord, we wish Thee
to have compassion upon us, and to leave Thy virgin
mother alive for us yet a few days, for she is our comfort
after Thee. 16 Our Saviour answered, saying, O my chosen
Peter, knowest thou not there is an appointed time laid
down for each man to accomplish in the world; and when
it is fulfilled, it is not possible for him to stay for a
single hour. Now therefore the appointed time of My
mother is fulfilled to-day. Therefore she must needs lay
down *her* body, and I will take her up to the heavens with
Me in glory. 17 Behold the orders of the heavens, that My
Father hath sent after the temple of His beloved Son, even
Me, are all waiting for her. 18 Arise and I will bless you
with her in the holy offering before I take her up unto
My Father.

IX. The women therefore that went with her, even
the virgins that followed her, turned their face away[d],
and all wept bitterly and with groaning; and she also
wept with them, the holy Virgin Mary. 2 Our good Saviour
answered and said to her, O Mary My virgin mother,
why weepest thou? 3 Thou shalt leave behind thee now cf. Jn XX 15
weeping, and depart into the joy that abideth for ever.
4 Thou shalt leave behind thee sorrow and groaning,
and dwell in splendour and gladness[e] for ever. 5 Thou cf. Lc XVI
shalt leave behind thee the things of the earth, and in- 19
herit the things of the heavens. 6 The Virgin Mary

[a] See note [b] Lit. *it shall not be* [c] Lit. *spake* [d] Lit. *backward*
[e] Or *mirth*

answered and said to our Saviour, My Lord and my God
and my Son, how shall I not weep and be in sorrow of
heart? I have heard Thee many times speaking with the
sons of men, *saying*, There are many shapes in Death,
terrifying and troubling those after whom he comes.
7 If these things be so, how shall I not weep, fearing in
what manner I shall be able to behold his fearful shape?
8 And our Lord Jesus said to her, O Mary My beautiful
1 Co xv 24, 26 mother, dost thou fear Death, when He that abolished
every power of Death is with thee? 9 How dost thou fear
his diverse shape, when the Life of all the world is with
thee? 10 And the Lord had compassion within Himself,
and drew Himself to His virgin mother, and wiped away
her tears, and kissed[a] her with His divine mouth. 11 And the
Lord Jesus stood at[b] the altar and gave us all *a* blessing,
and gave us the *salutation of* peace, and said to my father
Peter, Haste thee, look[c] upon the altar, and bring Me
these pure garments which My Father hath sent Me from
heaven, that I may shroud My blessed mother in them, for no
garment of this world can rest upon the body of My beloved
mother. 12 And my father Peter found garments of fine
cf. Jn xii 3 linen, pure, holy[d], very precious, giving forth a sweet odour.
13 And when we saw the garments sending forth rays of light,
we wondered exceedingly. 14 And the Saviour took the
garments from my father Peter, and spread them out with
His own hands; and called His virgin mother, and said
cf. Ps lxvii 14 to her, Arise and come unto Me, O My silver Dove, whose
cf. 1 Pe i 19 wings are overlaid with gold. 15 Come unto Me, My Lamb
guileless *and* without blemish.

X. And she arose, the queen of all women, Mary the
Virgin, the mother of the King of kings, to go unto her
beloved Son, our Lord Jesus Christ. 2 We all arose and
worshipped her hands and her feet, weeping. 3 And thus
our Lord Jesus, her beloved Son, saluted her; and said to
her, Go, get thee up into[e] the garments which I have spread,

[a] Lit. *saluted* [b] Lit. *to* [c] Lit. *see* [d] Or *pure*. This word is Coptic, the one before is Greek [e] Or *get thee upon*

and[a] turn thy face eastwards, and say[b] a prayer; and after-
wards lie down upon the garments, and fulfil thy dispensa-
tion as all men who are born on the earth. 4 And the queen
of all women, Mary the mother of our Lord Jesus Christ, the
King of kings, arose and went into the midst of the garments,
which the Saviour spread with His hands. She stood and
turned her face eastwards, and said[c] a prayer in the language
of the inhabitants of heaven. 5 When she had ended the
prayer, she said[c] the Amen; and we were standing, answering
her, Amen. 6 And afterward she lay down upon the gar-
ments, and put her hands at her side[d], her face being set
eastwards. 7 And our Saviour made us stand for the prayer,
that we might pray for her with the virgins also, who
used to minister formerly in the temple. They came and
followed her, when our Saviour was hanged on[e] the cross.
8 And we asked of them, Why have ye left the ministra-
tion of the temple? 9 They said to us, On the day that
Christ the Word of God the Father was crucified, we saw all
the places change[f]. 10 The sun was darkened, and the moon cf. Mt xxiv
became blood, and the stars fell down from heaven. 11 And 29; xxvii 45; Ac ii 20
we feared, and fled into the tabernacle, into the holy of
holies[g], and shut the door of the temple. 12 Straightway we cf. Ap x 1
saw a strong angel come down from heaven, being in great
anger, with a sword drawn in his hand, and he thrust it into cf. 1 Chr
the veil, and rent it in the midst, and divided it from the xxi 16 cf. Mt
top to the bottom. 13 And we heard a great voice saying, xxvii 51;
Woe to thee, woe to thee, Jerusalem, which killeth the Lc xxiii 45 f cf. Mt xxiii
prophets, and stoneth them that are sent unto her. 37 f; Lc
14 Often would I have gathered thy children, even as a xiii 34 f
bird gathereth its eggs together under[h] its wings, but ye
would not. 15 Behold your house, I have left it unto you.
16 We looked again, and saw the angel assigned to the
altar fly up in the canopy of the altar, and the angel
also[i] having the sword, *both* being in great mourning and
anger. 17 When we saw all these things come to pass, we

[a] For the Sahidic text and translation from c. x 3[b] to c. xviii 5[a] see below, p. 70 ff [b] Lit. *give* [c] Lit. *gave* [d] Lit. *sides* [e] Lit. *to* [f] Or *changed* [g] Lit. *the holy place of the holy* places [h] Lit. *unto* [i] Or *and the other angel*

knew that the Lord was angry with His people, and we
hasted, and came unto His Mother, and were with her, in
order that we might not come to be under the curse,
which we heard from the mouth of the angel of the Lord,
who rent the veil.

XI. The twelve virgins therefore and all the women
also who *were* with us, were all weeping with us together,
whilst we stood, encircling[a] the Virgin and singing her
praise with the songs of heaven, even as we were taught.
2 And Christ was sitting by His virgin mother honouring
her, and His hand was placed under her cheek. 3 And
when we had been a long while singing, He saluted His
mother, and He arose, and He brought us outside[b]. 4 And
the Virgin was saying to Him, I beseech thee, O Jesus,
cf. Mt XVI Thou Son of the living God and my beloved Son in truth,
16 without defilement of[c] sin, remember her who brought
Thee forth, O my Lord; for the forms of death have
drawn nigh unto me. 5 I beseech Thee, O my beloved Son,
cf. Lc XXII 53; Col I let the tyrannies of death and the powers of darkness flee
13; 2 Co XI 14 from me. 6 Let the angels of light draw nigh unto me.
cf. Mc IX 7 Let the worm that does not die[d] be still. 8 Let the outer
46; Mt VIII 12; XXII 13; darkness become light. 9 Let the accusers of Amenti shut
XXV 30 their mouths before me. 10 Let the dragon of the abyss
close his mouth as he sees me coming to Thee. 11 O my
beloved Son, command that the officers of the abyss flee
away from me, and terrify not my soul. 12 The stones of
cf. 1 Pe II stumbling which are in those paths[e], let them be destroyed[f]
8; Ro IX 32, 33 before me. 13 Let not the avengers with divers aspects see
me with their eyes. 14 The river of fire that tosseth *its*
waves before Thee as the waves of the sea, wherein are
proved the two portions, the righteous and the sinners—
when[g] I pass over it, let it not burn my soul. 15 Let me be
made worthy to worship Thee with a face wherein is no
cf. Mt VI shame. 16 For Thine is the power and the glory unto *the*
13 ages of all the ages. Amen.

[a] Lit. *being a crown* (or *garland*) *to* [b] Lit. *to the place outside*
[c] Lit. *in* [d] Or *sleep* [e] See note [f] Or *dissolved*
[g] Or *if*

XII. And our Lord Jesus Christ said to His mother
with His gentle[a] voice, Be of good cheer, O Mary my
mother. All these things I will cause to flee from thee, cf. Jn xiv 30
for they have nothing at all in thee; but the resting
places which *are* in the heavens and the good things cf. He xii 22
which *are* in the heavenly Jerusalem *are* prepared for thee,
that thou mayest rest in them for ever. 2 Behold the
heavenly garments of heaven and the flourishing branches
of palm are prepared that thy body may be shrouded
therein. 3 And thy blessed soul I will take up to the
heavens with Me, and give it *as a* gift to My good Father;
and thou art far better than all gifts, O thou who didst[b]
bring Me forth. 4 And our Lord Jesus said to the apostles,
Let us go outside for a little while; for this is the hour
wherein My beloved mother will go forth from *the* body, and
she cannot see Death face to face whilst I sit by her, for I
am the Life of all the world. Behold all the powers of the cf. Jn vi 51; xi 25; xiv 6
heavens are gathered together with us now, waiting for us.
5 And we the apostles all went with Him outside[c], and left
her lying down; all being gathered together to her, *even* the
virgins and Joanna and Salome and all the faithful women
also[d], comforting her. 6 And our Lord Jesus Christ was
sitting down on a stone outside the door of the gate, we all
being gathered together to Him, encircling[e] Him. 7 And
He looked up to heaven and groaned, and said, I have
overcome thee[f], O Death, that dwellest in the store-
houses of the south. Come, appear to My virgin mother,
that she may see thee; for thou art he whom I set *as*
king over all flesh. But let thy sting and thy victory be cf. 1 Co xv 55
crushed within thee, till Mary My mother see thee no more.
Afterwards devise thy fearful shape and thy sting and thy
victory wherewith thou art clothed for ever. 8 And moreover
in a moment and in the[g] twinkling of *an* eye, he appeared cf. 1 Co xv 52
whose name is bitter[h] with all men, *even* Death. 9 It came
to pass when she saw him with her eyes, her soul leaped

[a] Or *sweet* [b] Lit. *O she who did* [c] Lit. *unto the place outside*
[d] Or *and all the other faithful women* [e] Lit. *being a crown* (or *garland*) *to* [f] See note [g] Lit. *a* [h] Lit. *he of the bitter name*

from her body into the bosom of her beloved Son in the
place where He was sitting; for God the Word was sitting
with us in the place where we were[a], and He fills heaven
and earth. 10 And it came to pass, when He had hold of the
soul of His virgin mother—for it was white as snow—He
saluted it, and wrapped it in *garments of* fine linen, and gave
it to Michael the holy archangel, who bare it on his wings
of light, until He appointed the place for[a] her holy body.
11 All the women that were gathered to her, when they saw
cf. Jn xi 3, 14, 20, 32 that she was dead[b], they all wept and groaned[c]. And Salome
went out, and fell down at the feet of our Lord Jesus, and
worshipped Him, saying, My Lord and my God, behold, she
whom Thou lovest is dead. 12 Woe unto us and the great
bereavement and the dispersion which has befallen us to-day.
For if thou hadst not gone forth, she had not died. 13 Our
Lord Jesus answered and said to her, Mary My virgin
mother did not die, but lived. For the death of My mother
is not death, but it is life for ever. 14 And David the holy
Ps cxv 6 singer struck his spiritual harp, and cried out, saying, Precious
before the Lord is the death of His holy ones. 15 Be glad,
O Mary, thou mother of Christ, the King of kings. This is
the day that the prophecies are fulfilled which I spake
concerning thee, thou true Queen.

XIII. And our Saviour arose from the stone, and went
into the house, whilst we all went with Him. 2 And we saw
the face of the Virgin shining more than the sun, all her
body giving forth a sweet savour. 3 Now He stretched
Himself out on the body of His virgin mother and wept;
and was speaking such words as these over her, saying,
Blessed are thy lips, O Mary My mother, for thou didst kiss[d]
God with them. 4 Blessed are thine eyes, O thou who didst[e]
bring Me forth, for thou didst look into the face of Him,
cf. Ps ciii 32; Is xiii 13 who looketh upon the face of the earth, making it to be
disturbed unto its foundations. 5 Blessed are thine ears, O
thou[f] whom I desire, for thou didst hear Me speaking with
the angels many times in the language of the inhabitants of

[a] See note [b] Or *perfected* [c] Lit. *with groaning* [d] Lit. *salute* [e] Lit. *O she who did* [f] Lit. *she*

heaven. [6]Blessed are thine arms, O thou[a] in whom I dwelt,
for thou didst carry Him who beareth the universe by the He i 3
word of His power. [7]Blessed are thy breasts, O Mary My
virgin mother, for thou didst nourish Me from them, *and* I
am He that nourisheth all the creation. [8]Blessed are thy
knees, O thou[a] whom I loved, for I sat on them, I that sit
on the throne of His glory in the highest. [9]Blessed is thy cf. Mt xix
blessed[b] womb, for thou didst carry Me nine months. [10]Blessed 28; xxv 31
is all thy body and thy soul, for they were enlightened with
the light of My godhead.

XIV. Now when our good Saviour had said these things
over the body of His mother He wept: and we also were all
weeping with Him. [2]He arose and took hold of the heavenly
garments, and shrouded her holy body, He and Peter and
John; and the garments were fastened to her body. [3]And our
Saviour spake with the apostles, saying, Arise, take up the
body of My beloved mother, which was to Me a holy temple,
and bear it on your shoulders, for garments of the height are
wrapped upon it and palm branches of the heavenly *places*
of heaven. [4]And thou, O My chosen Peter, bear her head on
thy shoulder, and let John also carry her feet; for ye are My
brethren and My holy members. Let the rest of the apostles
sing before her. [5]Go ye all forth with her from the least to
the greatest to the east of Jerusalem, in the field of Jehosha-
phat. Ye shall find a new tomb, wherein no man has cf. Lc xxiii
yet been laid. Lay her holy body there, and keep watching 53; Jn xix 41
it three and a half days. Be not afraid. I am with you.
[6]Now when our Saviour had made an end of speaking with
the holy apostles, He prayed. David[c] the holy singer said
Allelujah[d], for there shall be brought in unto the king Ps xliv 15
virgins behind her, there shall be brought in unto him all
her neighbours also. [7]Afterwards our Lord Jesus gave us the
salutation of peace, and we all worshipped Him. Again cf. 2 Sa vi 16
David danced, saying, Allelujah. Arise, O Lord, into Thy Ps cxxxi
rest; Thou and the ark of Thy holy place, which is thou, 8
O Mary thou Virgin undefiled.

[a] Lit. *she* [b] Two different words are used for *blessed* in this sentence.
[c] See note [d] Lit. *the Allelujah*

cf. Ps xvii 11 XV. Straightway our Saviour rode upon His chariot of
Cherubim, all the orders of the heavens following Him and
singing His praise, [2]so that the air was covered by the
abundance of the sweet savour. Thus did He receive the
soul of His mother into His bosom, wrapped in napkins of
fine linen, sending forth flashes[a] of light; and went up
into the heavens, whilst we all looked at Him. [3]Straight-
way they took up the body of the Virgin. My father Peter
was carrying her head, my father John carrying her feet;
and the rest of the apostles, with censers of incense in their
hands going before us singing, and all the virgins going
behind her. [4]And it came to pass, when we came east of
Jerusalem to the place called the field of Jehoshaphat, the
cf. Mc xv 7 cursed Jewish people, that made insurrection, that put the
Lord to death[b], heard the gentle[c] voice of our holy fathers
the Apostles as they sang, and said one to another, Who is
this that died in this city to-day? [5]Some of them said to
them, It is the mother of Jesus the Nazarene, whom we
crucified. Behold she is taken out to the tomb. [6]And they
took counsel with one another, and came out to meet us in
anger of Satan, for he it is who filled their heart, being
minded[d] that they should kill us, and also take the body of
the holy Virgin and burn it with fire; even as they confessed
to us afterwards. [7]And it came to pass, when they drew
nigh to us, behold a wall of fire encompassed us and them,
and their eyes were darkened. For the Lord smote them
cf. Ex x 21 with a darkness which might be felt, even as He once did unto
the Egyptians. [8]But the body of the Virgin the apostles
bare, and put it into the tomb according to the word of our
Saviour, and they remained watching it three and a half
days.

XVI. Now the Jews, when they saw the great anger
which came upon them from the Lord, cried out, weeping
and saying, We beseech thee, O Mary the mother of Jesus
Christ, help us. We confess Jesus Christ, whom thou didst
bear, that He is the Son of God in truth. [2]We beseech thee,

[a] Lit. *lightnings* [b] Lit. *Lord-slayers* [c] Or *sweet*
[d] Or *wishing*

O Mary our sister, have mercy on us, for thou art of our
race. [3]We did many wrongs to Jesus thy Son, and He
never once did us wrong. [4]Do thou also, O our sister, have
mercy on us, and grant us the light of our eyes. [5]And
straightway their eyes were opened, they saw the light; and
they sought, and found not the body of the holy Virgin. And
they were in great amazement over the wonder which came
to pass; [6]so that they lifted up their voice, crying out and
saying, One is the God of Israel, who sent His beloved Son cf. Mc xii
into the world. In truth we have become guilty of a great 29, 32
sin.

XVII. Now when they had reached mid-day on the
fourth day, the apostles being gathered together with one
another and with virgins also by the tomb, wherein was the
body of the Virgin, singing and making melody; behold a
great voice came from heaven like the sound[a] of a trumpet,
saying, Go ye everyone to his place until the seventh month.
[2]For behold I have hardened[b] the heart of the chief priests cf. Jn xii
and of all the Jews, that they may not perceive nor know 40
this place any more, nor seek the body of My virgin mother
until I take it up to the heavens with[c] Me. [3]And ye all the
disciples, and the virgins also that have tarried with you,
come ye all hither on the sixteenth of the month Mesore,
that ye may see My virgin mother when I take her to the
heavens with[c] Me, her soul being in her body, living as it[d] was
on earth with you, that ye may believe with all your heart
the resurrection which shall be to all flesh. [4]And it came
to pass, when we heard this voice[e], we were glorifying God;
and we arose and prayed, and returned to the house wherein
we were dwelling, being in great mourning and weeping over
the separation from us of the holy Virgin Mary: and we
were praying God day and night, that He would comfort our
heart and shew us her again. [5]And it came to pass in the
seventh month from *the time* that the Virgin, the holy God-
bearer, Mary went forth from *the* body, which is the month
Mesore, we arose on the fifteenth of this month, and gathered

[a] Or *voice* [b] See note [c] Or *unto* [d] Or *she*
[e] Or *sound*

together to the tomb wherein was the body of the Virgin,
the virgins also being with us. We spent all the night
watching and singing, offering up incense, the virgins having
their lamps burning.

XVIII. Now at the hour of the light on this same night,
which is *the* morning of the sixteenth of the month Mesore,
there came unto us in the place where we were dwelling our
Lord Jesus Christ in great glory, and said unto us, Peace be
cf. Jn xiv 27 unto you all, My holy apostles. The peace of My Father I
give unto you. [2]And we fell down and worshipped Him,
and He blessed us all, and said to us, Wherefore are ye in
this great sadness and this grief of heart and this deep
mourning? [3]My father Peter said to Him, My Lord and
my God, we are grieved for the death[a] of Thy virgin
mother and the mother of us all, because Thou hast not
shewn us her again since the day that she went forth from
the body. [4]Our good Saviour answered and said to us, The
body of My beloved mother, behold it is with you, and My
angels watch it according to the command of My Father,
because it was a temple of His Son, even of Me; but her
soul is in the heavenly *places* of heaven, and the powers of
the height sing her praise. [5]And now I have sent for her
to be brought, that she may come and manifest to you the
cf. Mt xix 29 honours wherein she dwells, which I promised you in return
for those things which ye left behind you here. [6]Whilst
our Saviour was yet speaking with us, we heard hymns in
the height. [7]Straightway we looked, and saw a great chariot
of light. It came and stayed in our midst, Cherubim drawing
it[b], the holy Virgin Mary sitting upon it, and shining ten
thousand times more than the sun and the moon. [8]And we
were in fear, and fell on our face, and worshipped her; and
she stretched forth her hand towards us all, and blessed us,
and gave us the *salutation of* peace. [9]Again we worshipped
her, being in great joy and exultation; and she told us great
and hidden mysteries, which it is not lawful to manifest
because of the men that are unfaithful. [10]And the Lord

[a] Or *consummation* [b] Lit. *under it*

called into the tomb, and raised the body of His virgin
mother, and put her soul into her body again; and we saw
it[a] living in the body even as it[a] was with us formerly,
wearing the flesh. 11 And our Saviour stretched out His
hand, and set her on the chariot with Him. 12 And our
Saviour answered, and said to us in His gentle[b] voice,
Behold My beloved mother. This is she whose virgin
womb carried Me nine months, and I was three years also
receiving suck from her breasts which *were* sweeter than
honey. 13 Behold ye see her face to face, raised by Me from
the dead, and she has blessed you all. 14 Now therefore I
will not depart from you, saving you until ye complete your
struggle. 15 Arise therefore now, go ye forth in all the world cf. Mt
and preach the gospel everywhere, and baptize all the nations xxviii 19 f; Mc xvi 15,
in the name of the Father and of the Son and of the Holy 20
Ghost: teaching them to observe all things that I commanded
you. 16 And when our Saviour had said these things, He
spent all that day with us and with His virgin mother.
Afterwards He gave us the *salutation of* peace; and went up
to the heavens in glory, the angels singing before Him.

XIX. This is [the end of[c]] the life of the Lady of us all,
the holy God-bearer Mary, on the twenty-first of Tobi and
her assumption on the sixteenth of Mesore. 2 I Evodius, the
disciple of my father Peter, the apostle of our Lord Jesus
Christ, who speak with you now in this instruction, was
with the apostles, going with them; and I saw all these
things come to pass. 3 It is not another who spake them to
me, and I spake them to you; but those things which I have cf. 1 Jn i
seen with mine eyes, and those things which I have heard with 1
mine ears; they are *those* which I have spoken to your charity,
concerning the death[d] of the holy Virgin Mary, the undefiled,
the mother of Christ our God. 4 God, the righteous judge, cf. Ps vii
who shall judge the quick and the dead, He is witness to 12; 2 Ti iv 1, 8
me that I have not taken away from these words nor added cf. Ap xxii
unto them. 5 May it come to pass that the Lady of us all, 18 f

[a] Or *she* [b] Or *sweet* [c] These words are not in the text
[d] Or *consummation*

the holy God-bearer Mary, whose festival we keep to-day, may intercede for us with her beloved Son Jesus Christ, our God and the Son of God the Father in truth, in order that He may have compassion upon us, and have mercy on us. 6 Let us give an alms[a] into the hand of a poor man in the name of the holy God-bearer Mary; that she may not suffer us to be strangers in yonder place, but that she may make request for us to Christ our God, that He may shew His[b] mercy with us, and forgive us our sins. 7 Let us glorify Him always with

[a] Lit. an '*agape*' [b] Lit. *the*

SAHIDIC FRAGMENTS OF THE FALLING ASLEEP OF MARY.

FRAGMENT I.

Cod. Borg. CCLXXIII p. ⲕⲁ (c. VII)

15 ⲉϫⲙ ⲡϩⲁⲣⲙⲁ ⲛ̄ⲡⲉⲭⲁⲓⲣⲟⲩⲃⲓⲙ ⲧⲁϫⲓⲧⲉ ⲉⲙⲡⲏⲩⲉ ⲛ̇ⲙ̇ⲙⲁⲓ̈ · — 16 ⲕⲁⲛ ⲉϣϫⲉ ⲁⲣϭⲱⲱⲗⲉ ⲙ̄ⲙⲟⲓ̈ ⲛ̄ⲣⲉⲛⲧⲟⲉⲓⲥ ⲙ̇ⲡⲉϩⲟⲟⲩ ⲛ̄ⲧⲁⲣϫⲡⲟⲓ̈ ⲛ̇ϩⲏⲧϥ · ⲁⲣⲕⲱ ⲙ̇ⲙⲟⲓ̈ ϩⲛ̇ ⲟⲩⲟⲙϥ̇ ⲛ̇ⲧⲃⲛⲏ ⲁⲩⲉϩⲉ ⲙⲛ̄ ⲟⲩⲉⲱ̇ ⲣ̄ϩⲁⲓⲃⲉⲥ ⲉⲣⲟⲓ̈ · ⲁⲛⲟⲕ ϩⲱⲱⲧ ϯⲛⲁϭⲱⲱⲗⲉ ⲙ̇ⲡⲟⲩⲥⲱⲙⲁ ⲙⲛ̇ ⲧⲟⲩⲯⲩⲭⲏ ϩⲛ̇ ⲡⲉⲛⲧⲏⲙⲁ ⲛⲉⲡⲟⲩⲣⲁⲛⲓⲟⲛ ⲛⲁⲓ̈ ⲛ̇ⲧⲁⲓ̇ⲛ̇ⲧⲟⲩ[a] ⲉⲃⲟⲗ ϩⲛ ⲙ̇ⲡⲏⲩⲉ ⲛ̇ⲙ̇ⲙⲁⲓ̈ ⲁⲩⲱ ⲧⲁⲕⲱ ⲙ̇ⲡⲟⲩⲥⲱⲙⲁ ϩⲁ ⲡϣⲏⲛ ⲙ̄ⲡⲱⲛϩ ⲙ̇ⲡⲡⲁⲣⲁⲇⲓⲥⲟⲥ · ⲧⲁⲧⲣⲉ ⲡⲉⲭⲁⲓⲣⲟⲩⲃⲓⲙ ⲙⲛ̇ ⲧⲥⲏϥⲉ ⲛ̇ⲥⲁⲧⲉ ⲣ̇ϩⲁⲓⲃⲉⲥ ⲉⲣⲟ · ⲁⲩⲱ ϯⲛⲁⲥⲕⲉⲡⲁⲍⲉ ⲛ̇ⲧⲟⲩⲯⲩⲭⲏ ϩⲙ̄ ⲡⲉⲥⲕⲉⲡⲁⲥⲙⲁ ⲉⲧⲡⲟⲣϣ ⲉϫⲙ̇ ⲡⲉⲑⲩⲥⲓⲁⲥⲧⲏⲣⲓⲟⲛ ϩⲛ̇ ⲑⲓⲗ̄ⲏ̄ⲙ̄ ⲛ̄ⲧⲡⲉ · — 17 ⲕⲁⲛ ⲉϣϫⲉ ⲁⲣϥⲓⲧ ⲁⲣⲡⲱⲧ ⲛ̄ⲙ̄ⲙⲁⲓ̈ | ⲉⲕⲏⲙⲉ ⲉⲧⲃⲉ ⲑⲟⲧⲉ ⲛ̄ϩⲏⲣⲱⲇⲏⲥ ⲡⲡⲁⲣⲁⲛⲟⲙⲟⲥ ⲉϥⲇⲓⲱⲕⲉⲓ ⲛ̄ⲥⲱⲓ̈ · ⲁⲛⲟⲕ ϩⲱⲱⲧ ϯⲛⲁⲧⲣⲉ ⲛⲁⲅⲅⲉⲗⲟⲥ ϩⲁⲣⲡⲁⲍⲉ

[a] punct. sup. ⲓ ut vid.

ceaseless prayers day and night, crying out and saying, Let cf. 1 The v 17
Thy mercy be upon us, our Lord and our God and our Saviour Jesus Christ: through whom all glory and all honour is due to the Father and Him and the Holy Ghost, giver of life and of one essence with Him, now and always and unto *the* ages of all the ages. Amen.

Grant, O Lord, mercy to the sinner who wrote *this*, to Chael son *of* Matoi. Amen.

SAHIDIC FRAGMENTS OF THE FALLING ASLEEP OF MARY.

FRAGMENT I.[a]

VII. 15...on the chariot of the Cherubim, and take thee to
the heavens with Me. 16If thou didst wrap Me in swaddling cf. Lc II 7
clothes on the day wherein thou didst bring Me forth, and *if* thou didst place Me in a manger of cattle, and an ox and an ass overshadowed Me: I also will wrap thy body and thy soul in the garments of heaven, which I have brought from the heavens with Me; and will place thy body under the tree of cf. Ge III 24 life of Paradise[b], and make the[c] Cherubim with the sword of fire overshadow thee. And I will cover thy soul with the coverings that are spread upon the altar in the heavenly cf. He XII 22 Jerusalem.
17If thou didst take Me up and didst flee with
Me into Egypt for fear of Herod the lawless, when he was pursuing Me; I also will make the angels catch away thy

[a] For the translation of the Bohairic see p. 53 ff

[b] Lit. *the Paradise*

[c] The article is in the singular number

ⲛ̄ⲧⲟⲩⲯⲩⲭⲏ ⲙⲛ̄ ⲛⲟⲩⲥⲱⲙⲁ ⲙ̀ⲙⲟⲟⲩ ⲛ̄ⲥⲉϫⲓⲧⲉ ⲉⲛⲉⲛⲟⲩⲣⲁⲛⲓⲟⲛ
(c. VIII.) ⲛⲥⲉϭⲱ ⲉⲩϩⲩⲙⲛⲉⲩⲉ ⲉⲣⲟ ϣⲁ ⲉ̀ⲛⲉϩ:—[1]Ⲛⲁï ⲇⲉ ⲉⲣⲉ ⲡⲥⲱⲧⲏⲣ ϫⲱ
ⲙ̀ⲙⲟⲟⲩ ⲛ̀ⲧⲉϥⲙⲁⲁⲩ ⲙ̀ⲡⲁⲣⲑⲉⲛⲟⲥ · ⲁⲛⲉⲓⲙⲉ ϫⲉ ⲉϥⲕⲁⲗⲉⲓ ⲙ̄ⲙⲟⲥ
ⲉⲧⲣⲉⲥⲉⲓ ⲉⲃⲟⲗ ϩⲛ̄ ⲥⲱⲙⲁ·· [2]Ⲁⲛⲟⲛ ⲇⲉ ⲧⲏⲣⲛ ⲁⲛϥⲓ ϩⲣⲁⲛ ⲉⲃⲟⲗ
ⲁⲛⲣⲓⲙⲉ ϩⲛ̄ ⲟⲩⲥⲓϣⲉ ⲁⲩⲱ ⲁⲥⲣⲓⲙⲉ ϩⲱⲱⲥ ⲛ̄ⲙ̀ⲙⲁⲛ ·· [3]Ⲡⲉϫⲉ
ⲡⲥⲱⲧⲏⲣ ⲛⲁⲛ ϫⲉ ⲁϩⲣⲱⲧⲛ ⲧⲉⲧⲛ̄ⲣⲓⲙⲉ · [4]Ⲡⲉϫⲉ ⲡⲁⲉⲓⲱⲧ ⲡⲉⲧⲣⲟⲥ
ϫⲉ ⲡⲁϫⲟⲉⲓⲥ ⲁⲩⲱ ⲡⲁⲛⲟⲩⲧⲉ ⲉⲛⲣⲓⲙⲉ ⲉⲧⲃⲉ ⲧⲛⲟϭ ⲙ̀ⲙⲛ̄ⲧⲟⲣⲫⲁⲛⲟⲥ
p. ⲕⲃ ⲉⲧⲛⲁⲧⲁϩⲟⲛ · [5]Ⲛ̄ⲛⲉⲟⲩⲟⲉⲓϣ ⲅⲁⲣ ⲛⲧⲁ | ⲛⲓⲟⲩⲇⲁï ⲙ̀ⲡⲁⲣⲁⲛⲟⲙⲟⲥ
ⲥⲧⲁⲩⲣⲟⲩ ⲙ̀ⲙⲟⲕ ⲁⲛⲣ̄ϩⲛⲃⲉ ⲙⲉⲛ ⲡⲣⲟⲥ ϩⲉⲛⲕⲟⲩï ⲛ̀ϩⲟⲟⲩ·· Ⲙⲛ̄ⲛ̄ⲥⲱⲥ
ⲁ ⲡⲉⲛϩⲏⲃⲉ ⲕⲧⲟϥ ⲛⲁⲛ ⲉⲩⲣⲁϣⲉ ϩⲙ̄ ⲡⲧⲣⲉⲕⲧⲱⲟⲩⲛ ⲉⲃⲟⲗ ϩⲛ̄
ⲛⲉⲧⲙⲟⲟⲩⲧ ⲁⲕⲟⲩⲱⲛϩ ⲛⲁⲛ ⲉⲃⲟⲗ ⲁⲛⲥⲟⲗⲥⲗ̄ · Ⲁⲛⲧⲱϭⲉ ⲙ̄ⲙⲟⲛ
ⲉⲧⲉⲕⲙⲁⲁⲩ ⲁⲛϭⲱ ⲉⲛϭⲱϣⲧ ⲛ̀ⲥⲱⲥ ϩⲱⲥ ⲉⲕϣⲟⲟⲡ ⲛ̄ⲙ̀ⲙⲁⲛ ϩⲙ̀
ⲡⲥⲱⲙⲁ · [6]ⲧⲉⲛⲟⲩ ϭⲉ ⲉϣⲱⲡⲉ ⲕⲛⲁϥⲓⲧⲥ ⲛ̀ⲧⲟⲟⲧⲛ ⲛⲁⲛⲟⲩⲥ ⲉⲧⲣⲉⲕ-
ϥⲓⲧⲛ ⲛⲙⲙⲁⲥ ⲛ̀ϩⲟⲩⲟ ⲉⲧⲛⲟϭ ⲙⲙⲛ̄ⲧⲟⲣⲫⲁⲛⲟⲥ ⲉⲧⲛⲁⲧⲁϩⲟⲛ··
[7]Ⲡⲥⲱⲧⲏⲣ ⲇⲉ ⲡⲉϫⲁϥ ⲙ̄ⲡⲁⲉⲓⲱⲧ ⲡⲉⲧⲣⲟⲥ ϫⲉ ⲙⲏ ⲙ̄ⲡⲉⲓϫⲟⲟⲥ ⲛⲁⲕ
ϫⲉ ⲛ̄ϯⲛⲁⲕⲁⲧⲏⲩⲧⲛ ⲁⲛ ⲉⲧⲉⲧⲛ̄ⲟ ⲛ̄ⲟⲣⲫⲁⲛⲟⲥ ϯⲛⲏⲩ ϣⲁⲣⲱⲧⲛ ·
[8]Ⲙ̄ⲡⲣⲗⲩⲡⲉⲓ ⲉϫⲙ̀ ⲡⲥⲱⲕ ⲉⲃⲟⲗ ⲛ̄ⲧⲁⲙⲁⲁⲩ ⲛ̄ϯⲛⲁⲕⲁ|ⲁⲥ ⲉϩⲟⲩⲛ
ⲉⲣⲱⲧⲛ [ⲁ]ⲛ · Ⲛ̄ⲑⲉ ⲉⲧⲉ ⲙⲡⲉⲓ⌈ϩ⌉ⲱⲛ ⲉⲣⲱⲧⲛ ⌈ⲁ⌉ⲛ [9]Ⲡⲁⲉⲓⲱⲧ ⲇⲉ
ⲡⲉⲧⲣⲟⲥ ⲙⲛ ⲛⲕⲉⲥⲉⲉⲡⲉ ⲛⲛⲁⲡⲟⲥⲧⲟⲗⲟⲥ[a] ⲡⲉϫⲁⲩ ⲙ̄ⲡⲥⲱⲧⲏⲣ ϫⲉ ⲙⲏ
ⲡⲉⲛϫⲟⲉⲓⲥ ⲁⲩⲱ ⲡⲉⲛⲛⲟⲩⲧⲉ ⲙⲏ ⲙⲛ̄ ϣϭⲟⲙ ⲙ̄ⲙⲟⲕ ⲉⲧⲙ̀ⲧⲣⲉ ⲧⲁï
ⲙⲟⲩ ϣⲁ ⲉⲛⲉϩ·· [10]Ⲡⲉϫⲉ ⲡⲥⲱⲧⲏⲣ ϫⲉ ⲱ ⲡⲁⲙⲉⲗⲟⲥ ⲉⲧⲟⲩⲁⲁⲃ
ⲁïⲣ̀ϣⲡⲏⲣⲉ ⲙ̀ⲙⲱⲧⲛ ⲉⲧⲃⲉ ⲡⲉⲓϣⲁϫⲉ ⲛ̀ⲧⲁⲧⲉⲧⲛ̄ϫⲟⲟϥ Ⲙⲏ ⲟⲩⲛ̄
ϣϭⲟⲙ ⲉⲧⲣⲉ ⲡϣⲁϫⲉ ⲛ̀ⲧⲁ ⲡⲁⲓⲱⲧ ϫⲟⲟϥ ϣⲱⲡⲉ ⲛ̄ϭⲟⲗ · ⲙ̀ⲙⲟⲛ
[11]ⲁⲗⲗⲁ ⲛⲧⲁϥⲁ̀ⲡⲟⲫⲁⲛⲉ[b] ⲉϫⲛ ⲥⲁⲣⲝ ⲛⲓⲙ ϫⲉ ⲥⲉⲛⲁϫⲓϯⲡⲉ ⲙ̄ⲡⲙⲟⲩ·
[12]Ⲡⲉⲭⲣⲓ ⲡⲉϥϣⲏⲣⲉ ⲙ̄ⲙⲟⲛⲟⲅⲉⲛⲏⲥ ⲉⲧⲉ ⲁⲛⲟⲕ ⲡⲉ ⲁïϫⲓϯⲡⲉ ⲙ̄ⲡⲙⲟⲩ
ϩⲁⲣⲱⲧⲛ ϫⲉⲕⲁⲥ ⲉïⲉⲃⲱⲗ ⲉⲃⲟⲗ ⲛ̀ⲛⲛⲁⲁⲕⲉ ⲙ̀ⲡⲙⲟⲩ· [13]Ⲡⲁⲉⲓⲱⲧ ⲇⲉ
ⲡⲉⲧⲣⲟⲥ ⲡⲉ||[ϫⲁϥ]

[a] ⲡⲁⲡⲟⲥⲧⲟⲗⲟⲥ   [b] ⲛⲧⲁϥ· ⲁ̀ⲡⲟⲫⲁⲛⲉ

soul and thy body to-day, and take thee into the heavenly
places, and ever keep singing thy praise.

VIII. Now as the Saviour was saying these things to
His virgin mother, we knew that He was calling her to go
forth from *the* body. [2]And we all lifted up our voice and cf. Lc xxii 62
wept bitterly; and she also wept with us. [3]The Saviour said
to us, Why weep ye? [4]My father Peter said, My Lord and cf. Jn xx 28
my God, we weep for the great bereavement that shall befall
us. [5]For at the time that the lawless Jews crucified Thee,
we mourned indeed for a few days; afterwards our mourning cf. Jn xvi 20
was turned for us into joy by Thy rising from the dead: *for*
Thou didst appear to us and we were comforted. We clave
to Thy mother, and kept looking on her as though Thou
wert with us in the body. [6]Now therefore if Thou wilt take
her from us, better is it that Thou shouldest take us with her
than the great bereavement that shall befall us. [7]And the
Saviour said to my father Peter, Said I not to thee, I will not Jn xiv 18
leave you desolate[a], I come unto you? [8]Grieve not for the
death[b] of My mother. I will not suffer her to be hidden from
you, even as I have not been hidden from you. [9]Now my
father Peter and the rest of the apostles said to the Saviour,
Our Lord and our God, canst thou not cause her never to
die? [10]The Saviour said, O My holy members, I wonder at
you touching this word which ye have spoken. Can the
word which My Father spake prove false[c]? Nay. [11]But He
passed sentence on all flesh, that they shall taste death;
[12]even unto Me, His only begotten Son. I tasted death for
you, that I might loose the pangs of death. [13]And my father cf. Ac ii 24
Peter said...

[a] Or *orphans* [b] Or *departure* [c] Or *prove a lie*

FRAGMENT II.

Cod. Borg. CCLIX* p. ⲗⲉ (c. x)

3 ⲛ̄ⲧⲉⲕⲱ ⲧⲉ⌉ ⲙ̄ⲡⲟⲩϩⲟ ⲉⲡⲥⲁ ⲛ̄ⲧⲁⲛⲁⲧⲟⲗⲏ ⲧⲉϫⲱⲕ ⲉⲃⲟⲗ
ⲛ̄ⲧⲟⲩⲟⲓⲕⲟⲛⲟⲙⲓⲁ ⲛ̄ⲧⲁ ⲡⲁⲓⲱⲧ ⲧⲱϣⲥ ⲛⲏ ⲛ̄ⲑⲉ ⲉⲧϣⲟⲟⲡ ⲛ̄ⲣⲱⲙⲉ
ⲛⲓⲙ 4 ⲧⲣⲣⲟ ⲇⲉ ⲁⲩⲱ ⲧⲙⲁⲁⲩ ⲉⲙⲡⲣⲣⲟ ⲛ̄ⲛⲉⲣⲣⲟⲟⲩ ⲁⲥⲧⲟⲟⲩⲛ
ⲁⲥⲃⲱⲕ ⲉⲧⲙⲏⲧⲉ ⲛ̄ⲛⲉⲡⲉⲧⲉⲙⲁ ⲛ̄ⲧⲁ ⲡⲥⲱⲧⲏⲣ ⲡⲱⲣϣⲟⲩ ϩⲛ̄ ⲛⲉϥϭⲓϫ
ⲙ̄ⲙⲓⲛ̄ⲟⲩ ⲉⲙⲙⲟϥ ⲁⲥⲁϩⲉⲣⲁⲧⲥ ⲁⲥⲕⲱⲧⲉ ⲙ̄ⲡⲉⲥϩⲟ ⲉⲡⲓⲉⲃⲧ ⲉⲁⲥϣⲗⲏⲗ
ⲁⲥⲧⲁⲩⲟⲟ ⲛ̄ⲟⲩⲡⲣⲟⲥⲉⲩⲭⲏ ⲛ̄ⲧ⌈ⲉ⌉ ⲛⲁ ⲧⲡⲉ ⲕⲁⲧⲁ ⲑⲉ ⲛ̄ⲧⲁ ⲡⲉⲥ-
ϣⲏⲣⲉ ⲧⲥⲁⲃⲟⲥ ⲉⲣⲟⲥ 5 ⲛ̄ⲧⲉⲣⲉⲥϫⲱⲕ ⲉⲃⲟⲗ ⲙ̄ⲡⲉϣⲗⲏⲗ ⲁⲥϯ
ⲙ̄ⲡϩⲁⲙⲏⲛ | ⲁⲩⲱ ⲛⲉⲛⲟⲩ̄ⲱϩⲙ[a] ⲛ̄ⲥⲟⲥ ⲧⲏⲣⲛ̄ ϫⲉ ϩⲁⲙⲏⲛ 6 ⲙⲉⲛⲛ̄ⲥⲟⲥ
ⲁⲥⲉⲛⲕⲱⲧⲕ ϩⲛ̄ ⲧⲙⲏⲧⲉ ⲉⲛⲛⲉϩⲃⲟⲟⲥ ⲁⲥⲕⲉⲥⲕⲱⲥ ⲉⲃⲟⲗ ⲙⲁⲩⲁⲁⲥ
ⲁⲥⲉⲛ ⲛⲉⲥϭⲓϫ ⲉⲧⲟⲩⲏⲛ ⲉⲛⲉⲥⲥⲛⲓⲣⲟⲟⲩⲉ[b] 7 Ⲡⲥⲱⲧⲏⲣ ⲇⲉ ⲁϥⲟⲩⲛϩ-
ⲥⲁϩⲛⲉ ⲛ̄ⲁⲛ ⲁⲛⲧⲟⲟⲩⲛ ⲁⲛϣⲗ̄ⲗ̄§ **Ⲛⲉⲩⲉⲛ**[c] ⲙ̄ⲛ̄ⲧⲥⲛⲟⲟⲩⲥⲉ ⲇⲉ
ⲙ̄ⲡⲁⲣⲑⲉⲛⲟⲥ · ⲙⲟⲟϣⲉ ⲛ̄ⲙ̄ⲙⲁⲛ · ϫⲓⲛ ⲉⲡⲉϩⲟⲟⲩ ⲛ̄ⲧⲁⲩⲥⲧ̄ⲣ̄ⲟ̄ⲩ̄ ⲙ̄ⲡⲉⲭ̄ⲥ̄
ⲁⲩⲛⲁⲩ ⲉⲡⲉⲕϯⲥⲙⲁ ⲉⲁⲩϣⲓⲃⲉ ⲁ ⲡⲕⲁⲧⲁⲡⲉⲧⲁⲥⲙⲁ ⲙ̄ⲡⲣ̄ⲡⲉ ⲡⲱϩ ϩⲙ̄
ⲧⲉϥⲙⲏⲧⲉ ⲁϥⲉⲣⲥⲡⲁⲩ:—Ⲛ̄ⲧⲟⲟⲩ ⲇⲉ ⲁⲩⲁⲛⲁⲭⲱⲣⲉⲓ ⲛⲁⲩ ⲉⲃⲟⲗ ϩⲙ
ⲡⲣⲡⲉ · ⲁⲩⲉⲓ ⲁⲩⲙⲟⲟϣⲉ ⲛ̄ⲙ̄ⲙⲁⲛ—8 Ⲁⲛϣⲓⲛⲉ ⲉⲃⲟⲗ ϩⲓⲧⲟⲟⲧⲟⲩ ϫⲉ
ⲟⲩ ⲡⲉⲛⲧⲁϥϣⲱⲡⲉ ⲙ̄ⲙⲱⲧⲛ̄ ⲁⲧⲉⲧⲛ̄ⲕⲱ ⲛ̄ⲥⲱⲧⲛ̄ ⲛ̄ⲧⲇⲓⲁⲕⲟⲛⲓⲁ ⲙ̄ⲡⲣ̄ⲡⲉ
9 Ⲡⲉϫⲁⲩ ⲛⲁⲛ ϫⲉ ϩⲙ ⲡⲉϩⲟⲟⲩ | ⲛ̄ⲧⲁⲩⲥⲧ̄ⲣ̄ⲟ̄ⲩ̄ ⲙ̄ⲡ⌈ⲉ⌉ⲭ̄ⲥ̄ · ⲁⲛⲛⲁⲩ

Cod. Clarend. b 3 15 p. ?

Cod. Borg. CCLIX* (c. x)

7 ⲛⲉⲩⲉⲛ ⲙⲛ̄ⲧⲥⲛⲟⲟⲩⲥ ⲇⲉ ⲙ̄ⲡⲁⲣⲑⲉⲛⲟⲥ ⲙⲟⲟϣⲉ ⲛⲉⲙⲙⲁⲛ ϫⲓⲛ
ⲉⲡⲉϩⲟⲟⲩ ⲛ̄ⲧⲁⲩⲥⲧ̄ⲣ̄ⲟ̄ⲩ̄ ⲙ̄ⲡⲉⲭ̄ⲥ̄ ⲁ ⲡⲕⲁⲧⲁⲡⲉⲧⲓⲥⲙⲁ ⲙ̄ⲡⲣ̄ⲡⲉ ⲡⲱϩ
ϫⲓⲛ ⲉⲧⲡⲉ ⲉⲡⲉⲥⲏⲧ ⲁϥⲉⲣⲥⲡⲁⲩ ⲛ̄ⲧⲟⲟⲩ ⲇⲉ ⲁⲩⲁⲛⲁⲭⲱⲣⲓ ⲛⲁⲩ ⲉⲃⲟⲗ
ϩⲙ ⲡⲉⲣⲡⲉ ⲁⲩⲱ ⲁⲩⲙⲟⲟϣⲉ ⲛ̄ⲙⲙⲁⲛ 8 ⲁⲛϣⲓⲛⲉ ⲉⲃⲟⲗ | ϩⲓⲧⲟⲟⲧⲟⲩ
ϫⲉ ⲟⲩ ⲡⲛ̄ⲧⲁϥϣⲱⲡⲉ ⲉⲙⲙⲱⲧⲛ ⲁⲧⲉⲧⲉⲛⲁⲛⲁⲭⲱⲣⲓ ⲛⲏⲧⲛ ⲉⲃⲟⲗ ϩⲙ
ⲡⲉⲣⲡⲉ 9 ⲛ̄ⲧⲟⲟⲩ ⲇⲉ ⲡⲉϫⲁⲩ ⲛⲁⲛ ϫⲉ ⲙ̄ⲡⲉϩⲟⲟⲩ ⲛ̄ⲧⲁⲩⲥⲧ̄ⲣ̄ⲟ̄ⲩ̄

p. ⲗⲋ

[a] ⲛⲉⲛⲟⲩⲱϩ [b] ⲛⲉⲥⲛⲓⲣⲟⲟⲩⲉ [c] Cod. Clarend. b 3 15 sic incipit ϩⲓⲟⲩⲥⲟⲛ · — **Ⲛⲉⲩⲉⲛ**

FRAGMENT II.[a]

X. [3]...and turn thy face eastwards, and fulfil thy dispensation, which My Father hath appointed thee, as happens to all men. [4]And the queen and the mother of the King of kings arose and went into the midst of the garments, which the Saviour spread with His own hands. She stood and turned her face to the east praying, and uttered a prayer of the inhabitants of heaven, even as her Son taught her it. [5]When she had ended the prayer, she said[b] the Amen; and we all were answering her[c], Amen. [6]Afterward she lay down in the midst of the garments, and stretched herself out[d] of her own accord[e] and brought her open hands to her sides[f]. [7]And the Saviour commanded us, and we arose and prayed. Now there were twelve virgins going with us since the day that Christ was crucified, *when* they saw the things created change[g A], the veil of the temple was rent in the midst[B], and was divided. And they withdrew from the temple, and came[Γ] and went with us. [8]We asked of them, What has happened to you *that* ye have left the ministration of[Δ] the temple? [9]They[E] said to us, On the day that Christ[Z] was crucified, we

cf. Mt xxvii 51*; Lc xxiii 45

[a] For the translation of the Bohairic see p. 57 ff [b] Lit. *gave* [c] The MS has *were following her* [d] Or *was laid out* [e] Or *alone* [f] See note [g] Or *changed*

Variants in Codex Borgianus.

[A] om. *they saw the things created change* [B] *in the midst*] *from the top to the bottom* [Γ] om. *and came* [Δ] *ye have left the ministration of*] *ye have withdrawn from* [E] *They*] *And they* [Z] *that Christ*] *wherein Christ the Lord*

Cod. Clarend. b 3 15

ⲉⲡⲉⲕϯⲥⲙⲁ ⲉⲁⲩϣⲓⲃⲉ · [10]ⲁ ⲡⲣⲏ ⲉⲣⲕⲁⲕⲉ · ⲁ ⲡⲟⲟϩ ⲉⲣⲥⲛⲟϥ ·
[11]ⲁⲛⲡⲱⲧ ⲉϩⲟⲩⲛ ⲉⲡⲙⲁ ⲉⲧⲟⲩⲁⲁⲃ · ⲛ̄ⲧⲉ ⲡⲉⲧⲟⲩⲁⲁⲃ ⲁⲛⲱⲣϫ̄ ⲙ̄ⲡⲉⲣⲟ
ⲙ̄ⲡⲉⲣⲡⲉ Ⲉϯ ⲉⲡⲉⲣⲙⲟⲓϩⲉ ϩⲣⲁⲓ ⲛ̄ϩⲏⲧⲛ̄ ⲉϫⲙ̄ ⲡⲉⲛⲧⲁϥϣⲱⲡⲉ · —
[12]Ⲛⲧⲉⲩⲛⲟⲩ ⲉⲓⲥ ⲟⲩⲛⲟϭ ⲛⲁⲅⲅⲉⲗⲟⲥ ⲛ̄ϫⲱⲱⲣⲉ · ⲁϥⲉⲓ ⲉⲡⲉⲥⲏⲧ ⲉⲃⲟⲗ
ϩⲛ̄ ⲛ̄ⲙⲡⲏⲩⲉ ϩⲛ̄ ⲟⲩⲛⲟϭ ⲛ̄ϭⲱⲛⲧ ⲉⲣⲉ ⲟⲩⲥⲏϥⲉ ⲉⲥⲧⲏⲙ ϩⲛ̄ ⲧⲉϥϭⲓϫ
ⲛⲟⲩⲛⲁⲙ · — Ⲛⲧⲉⲣⲛ̄ⲛⲁⲩ ⲇⲉ ⲉⲣⲟϥ ⲁⲛⲣ̄ϩⲟⲧⲉ ⲁⲛϣⲧⲟⲣⲧⲣ̄ ⲙ̄ⲙⲁⲧⲉ ·
p. ? ⲁⲛⲡⲱⲧ ⲉϩⲟⲩⲛ ⲉⲧⲕⲛ̄ϩⲉ[a] ⲉⲛⲙⲉⲉⲩⲉ | ϫⲉ ⲉϥⲛⲁⲡⲁⲧⲁⲥⲥⲉ ⲙ̄ⲙⲟⲛ ϩⲛ̄
ⲧⲥⲏϥⲉ ⲉⲧϩⲛ̄ ⲧⲉϥϭⲓϫ Ⲛⲧⲟϥ ⲇⲉ ⲡⲁⲅⲅⲉⲗⲟⲥ ⲡⲉϫⲁϥ ⲛⲁⲛ ϫⲉ
ⲙ̄ⲡⲉⲣⲉⲣϩⲟⲧⲉ ⲛ̄ϯⲛⲁⲙⲉⲩⲉⲧⲧⲏⲩⲧⲛ̄ ⲁⲛ · ⲟⲩⲇⲉ ⲙⲛ̄ ⲡⲉⲑⲟⲟⲩ ⲛⲁⲧⲁ-
ϩⲱⲧⲛ̄ ⲁⲕⲙⲏⲛ ⲛ̄ⲕⲱⲟⲩⲉ ⲉⲧⲙⲟⲟⲩⲧ ⲥⲉⲛⲁⲧⲱⲟⲩⲛ · ⲛⲥⲉⲉⲓ ⲉⲃⲟⲗ ϩⲙ
ⲡⲧⲁⲫⲟⲥ Ⲛⲥⲉⲉⲓ ⲉϩⲟⲩⲛ ⲉⲧⲡⲟⲗⲓⲥ[b] ⲛ̄ⲥⲉⲟⲩⲟⲛϩⲟⲩ ⲉϩⲁϩ ⲛ̄ⲣⲱⲙⲉ
ⲉⲩϫⲡⲓⲟ · ⲁⲩⲱ ⲉⲩⲉⲗⲉⲓⲭⲉ · ⲛ̄ⲧⲙⲛ̄ⲧⲁⲧⲅⲛⲱⲙⲟⲛ ⲛ̄ⲛⲓⲟⲩⲇⲁⲓ ⲉⲧⲥϩⲟⲩ-
ⲟⲣⲉⲧ[c] · ⲙⲛ̄ ⲧⲉⲩⲙⲛ̄ⲧⲁⲧϣⲓⲡⲉ ⲛ̄ⲧⲁⲩⲧⲁⲁⲥ ⲉϩⲟⲩⲛ ⲉⲡϫⲟⲉⲓⲥ ⲛ̄ⲛⲁ ⲧⲡⲉ
ⲙⲛ̄ ⲛⲁ ⲡⲕⲁϩ Ⲛⲧⲉⲩⲛⲟⲩ ⲁϥⲥⲟⲟⲩⲧⲛ̄ ⲉⲃⲟⲗ ⲛ̄ⲧⲥⲏϥⲉ ⲉⲧϩⲛ̄ ⲧⲉϥϭⲓϫ

Cod. Borg. cclix*

ⲙⲡϫⲟⲉⲓⲥ ⲛϩⲏⲧϥ Ⲁⲛⲛⲁⲁⲩ ⲉⲡⲉⲥⲧⲓⲕⲙⲁ (sic) ⲉⲁⲩϣⲓⲃⲉ [11]Ⲁⲛⲛⲉⲣ-
ϩⲟⲧⲉ ⲁⲛⲡⲱⲧ ⲉϩⲟⲩⲛ ⲉⲡⲉⲣⲡⲉ ⲉⲡⲙⲁ ⲉⲧⲟⲩⲁⲁⲃ ⲁⲛⲛⲱϫⲣⲉϫ (sic)
ⲉⲣⲟⲛ ⲙⲡⲣⲟ ⸢ⲁⲓ⸣ϯ ⲉⲡⲉⲣ · ⲙⲟⲓϩⲉ (punct inter ⲣ et ⲙ ut vid) ⲉⲙ-
ⲡⲉⲛⲧⲁϥϣⲱⲡⲉ [12]Ϩⲛ ⲧⲉⲩⲛⲟⲩ ⲉⲓⲥ ⲟⲩⲛⲟϭ ⲛⲁⲅⲅⲉⲗⲟⲥ ⲛ̇ϫⲱⲱⲣⲉ (punct
sup ⲛ ut vid) ⲁϥⲉⲓ ⲉⲃⲟⲗ ϩⲛ ⲛⲉⲙⲡⲏⲩⲉ ⲉϥϣⲟⲟⲡ Ϩⲛⲛ ⲟⲩⲛⲟϭ
ⲉⲛϭⲱⲛⲧ ⲉⲣⲉ ⲟⲩⲥⲏⲃⲉ ⲧⲱⲕⲙ ϩⲛ ⲧⲉϥϭⲓϫ ⲉⲛⲟⲩⲛⲁⲙ̇ (punct sup ⲙ
ut vid) ⲛⲧⲉⲣⲉⲛ|ⲛⲁⲁⲩ ⲇⲉ ⲉⲣⲟϥ̇ (punct sup ϥ ut vid) ⲁⲛⲣϩⲟⲧⲉ
ⲙⲙⲁⲁⲧⲉ ϩⲛ ⲧⲉⲩⲛⲟⲩ ⲁⲛⲛⲟⲧ ⲉϩⲟⲩⲛ ⲉⲧⲕⲉⲛϩⲉ ⲉⲙⲙⲉⲩⲉ ϫⲉ ⲉϥⲛⲁ-
ⲙⲟⲟⲩⲧ ⲙⲙⲟⲛ ϩⲛ ⲧⲥⲏⲃⲉ ⲉⲧⲛⲧⲟⲟⲧϥ · (punct post ϥ ut vid) ⲡⲉϫⲁⲁϥ
ⲛⲁⲛ ⲛϭⲓ ⲡⲁⲛⲅⲉⲗⲟⲥ ϫⲉ ⲛⲧⲱⲧⲛ ⲙⲡⲉⲣⲉⲣϩⲟⲧⲉ ⲙⲉⲛ ⲡⲉⲑⲟⲟⲩ
ⲛⲁⲧⲁϩⲉⲧⲏⲩⲧⲛ ⲁⲕⲙⲉⲛ ⲛⲕⲟⲟⲩⲉ ⲉⲧϩⲛ ⲛⲧⲁⲫⲟⲥ ⲥⲉⲛⲁⲧⲟⲟⲩⲛ ⲛⲥⲉⲉⲓ
ⲉⲃⲟⲗ ⲛⲥⲉⲃⲱⲕ ⲉϩⲟⲩⲛ ⲉⲛⲉⲩⲡⲟⲗⲓⲥ ⲛⲥⲉⲟⲩⲟⲛϩⲟⲩ ⲉⲃⲟⲗ ⲛϩⲁϩ Ⲁⲩⲱ
ⲉⲩⲉⲗⲉⲗⲭⲉⲓ ⲉⲛⲧⲙⲛⲧⲁⲕⲛⲱⲙⲟⲛ ⲉⲛⲛⲓⲟⲩⲇⲁⲓ ⲙⲛ ⲧⲉⲩⲧⲱⲗⲙⲉⲣⲓⲁ
ⲛⲧⲁⲩⲧⲁⲁⲥ ⲉϩⲟⲩⲛ ⲉⲡϫⲟⲉⲓⲥ ⲛⲧⲡⲉ ⲙⲛ ⲡⲕⲁϩ ϩⲛ ⲧⲉ |

[a] ⲛ̄ⲕⲉϩⲉ [b] ⲗ sup. ras. ut vid. [c] ⲉⲧⲥϩⲟⲩⲟⲣⲉⲧ

saw the things created change[a]. 10 The sun was darkened, cf. Mt XXIV 29*; XXVII 45; Ac II 20
and the moon became blood[A]. 11 We fled[B] into the holy of
holies[b][Γ], and shut[c] the doors of the temple[Δ], still wondering
within ourselves[E] at that which happened. 12 Straightway
behold a great, strong angel came down[Z] from the heavens
in[H] great anger, with a sharp sword[Θ] in his right hand. And
when we saw him, we were afraid and were exceedingly
troubled[I]: and[K] we fled into the shrine[d], thinking that he
would smite[Λ] us with the sword which *was* in his hand. But
he[M] the angel said to us, Be not[N] afraid. I will not slay you:
neither shall evil[Ξ] befall you. Surely those also[e] who are cf. Mt XXVII 53 f*
dead[O] shall arise and come forth from the tomb[Π], and enter
into the city[P] and appear unto many men, reproving[Σ] and
convicting the folly of the cursed[T] Jews, and their shameless-
ness[Υ] which they wrought against the Lord of the inhabitants[Φ]
of heaven and of earth. Straightway[X] he stretched forth the
sword which *was* in his hand, and he brought it down upon

[a] Or *changed* [b] Lit. *into the holy place of the holy* places
[c] Or *made fast* [d] See note [e] Or *evil befall you at all. Those also.* See note

Variants in Codex Borgianus.

[A] om. *The sun was darkened, and the moon became blood* [B] *We fled*] *We feared, and fled* [Γ] *into the holy of holies*] *into the temple, to the holy place* [Δ] *the doors of the temple*] *the door* [E] om. *within ourselves* [Z] om. *down* [H] *in*] *being in* [Θ] *a sharp sword*] *a sword drawn* [I] *we were afraid and were exceedingly troubled*] *we were exceedingly afraid* [K] *and*] *and straightway* [Λ] *smite*] *slay* [M] om. *But he* [N] *not*] *not ye* [Ξ] *I will not slay you: neither shall evil*] *no evil shall* [O] *dead*] *in the tombs* [Π] om. *from the tomb* [P] *the city*] *their cities* [Σ] om. *men, reproving* [T] om. *cursed* [Υ] *shamelessness*] *audacity* [Φ] om. *of the inhabitants* [X] The MS breaks off in the middle of the word *straightway*. For another leaf of the same MS, see p. 82 ff

Cod. Clarend. b 3 15 ⲁϥⲏⲛⲧⲥ | ⲉⲡⲉⲥⲏⲧ ϩⲓ ⲡⲕⲁⲧⲁⲡⲉⲧⲁⲥⲙⲁ ⲙ̅ⲡⲣ̅ⲡⲉ ⲁϥⲡⲁϩϥ ⲁϥⲁⲁϥ
ⲛ̅ⲥⲛⲁⲩ 13 Ⲁⲛⲥⲱⲧⲙ̅ ⲉⲩⲥⲙⲏ ⲉⲃⲟⲗ ϩⲛ̅ ⲛ̅ⲧⲁⲡ ⲙⲡⲉⲑⲩⲥⲓⲁⲥⲧⲏⲣⲓⲟⲛ·
ⲉⲥϫⲱ ⲙⲙⲟⲥ ϫⲉ ⲟⲩⲟⲓ ⲟⲩⲟⲓ ⲛ̅ⲑ̅ⲓ̅ⲗ̅ⲏ̅ⲙ̅· ⲧⲉⲧϩⲱⲧⲃ̅ ⲛ̅ⲛⲉⲡⲣⲟⲫⲏⲧⲏⲥ·
ⲉⲧϩⲓⲱⲛ ⲉⲛⲉⲛⲧⲁⲩⲧⲛ̅ⲛⲟⲟⲩⲥⲟⲩ ϣⲁⲣⲟⲥ 14 Ϩⲁϩ ⲛ̅ⲥⲟⲡ[a] ⲁⲓⲟⲩⲱϣ ⲉⲥⲟⲟⲩϩ
ⲉϩⲟⲩⲛ ⲛ̅ⲛⲟⲩϣⲏⲣⲉ ⲛ̅ⲑⲉ ⲛⲟⲩϩⲁⲗⲏⲧ ⲉϣⲁϥⲥⲉⲩⲉϩ ⲛⲉϥⲙⲁⲥ ⲉϩⲟⲩⲛ[b]
ϩⲁ ⲛⲉϥⲧⲛ̅ϩ̅ ⲁⲩⲱ ⲙ̅ⲡⲉⲧⲛ̅ⲟⲩⲱϣ· 15 ⲉⲧⲃⲉ ⲡⲁⲓ ⲡⲉⲧⲛ̅ⲏⲓ ⲕⲏ ⲉⲣⲱⲧⲛ̅·—
p. ? 16 Ⲁⲩⲱ ⲁⲛϭⲱϣⲧ ⲁⲛⲛⲁⲩ ⲉⲡⲁⲅⲅⲉⲗⲟⲥ· ⲉⲧⲧⲏϣ | ⲉⲡⲣ̅ⲡⲉ· ⲁϥϩⲱⲗ
ⲉⲛϫⲓⲥⲉ ⲛⲧⲕⲟⲛⲭⲟⲥ ⲙ̅ⲡⲉⲑⲩⲥⲓⲁⲥⲧⲏⲣⲓⲟⲛ· ⲛ̅ⲧⲟϥ ⲙⲛ̅ ⲡⲉⲧⲉⲣⲉ ⲧⲥⲏϥⲉ
ⲛ̅ⲧⲟⲟⲧϥ· ⲉⲩϣⲟⲟⲡ ϩⲛ̅ ⲟⲩⲛⲟϭ ⲛ̅ϩⲏⲃⲉ:— 17 Ⲛⲧⲉⲣⲛ̅ⲛⲁⲩ ⲇⲉ ⲉⲡⲉ-
ⲛ̅ⲧⲁϥϣⲱⲡⲉ ⲁⲛⲙⲉ ⲛⲧⲉⲩⲛⲟⲩ ϫⲉ ϩⲛ̅ ⲟⲩⲙⲉ ⲁ ⲡϫⲟⲉⲓⲥ ⲕⲱ ⲛ̅ⲥⲱϥ
ⲙ̅ⲡⲉϥⲗⲁⲟⲥ Ⲁⲛϭⲉⲡⲏ ⲇⲉ ⲁⲛⲡⲱⲧ ⲉⲣⲁⲧϥ ⲙ̅ⲡⲉϥϣⲏⲣⲉ ⲓ̅ⲥ̅ ⲡⲉⲛ-
ⲧⲁⲩⲥⲧⲣ̊ⲟⲩ ⲙ̅ⲙⲟϥ· ϫⲉⲕⲁⲥ ⲛ̅ⲛⲉⲛϣⲱⲡⲉ ϩⲁ ⲡⲥⲁϩⲟⲩ· ⲛ̅ⲧⲁⲛⲥⲱⲧⲙ̅ϥ̅
ⲉⲃⲟⲗ ϩⲓⲧⲟⲟⲧϥ ⲙⲡⲁⲅⲅⲉⲗⲟⲥ. ⲙ̅ⲡⲣ̅ⲡⲉ ⲙⲛ̅ ⲡⲉⲛⲧⲁⲩⲡⲱϩ ⲙ̅ⲡⲕⲁⲧⲁ-
(c. xi) ⲡⲉⲧⲁⲥⲙⲁ 1 Ⲧⲉⲓⲙⲛ̅ⲧⲥⲛⲟⲟⲩⲥⲉ ⲇⲉ ⲙ̅ⲡⲁⲣⲑⲉⲛⲟⲥ | ⲉⲧⲙⲟⲟϣⲉ ⲛⲙⲙⲁ⸢ⲛ⸣
Ϫⲓ̈ⲛ ⲉϣⲟⲣⲡ̅ ⲁ ⲡⲥⲱⲧⲏⲣ ⲕⲉⲗⲉⲩⲉ ⲛⲁⲩ ⲉⲧⲣⲉⲩⲃⲱⲕ ⲉϩⲟⲩⲛ ⲉⲡⲉ-
ⲑⲩⲥⲓⲁⲥⲧⲏⲣⲓⲟⲛ ⲛⲧⲁϥⲥⲩⲛⲁⲅⲉ ⲙ̅ⲙⲟⲛ ϩⲓϫⲱϥ ⲁⲩⲉⲓⲛⲉ ⲛ̅ϩⲛ̅ⲃⲁϩ
ⲛ̅ⲛ̅ⲃⲛ̅ⲛⲉ[c]· ⲙⲛ̅ ϩⲛ̅ⲕⲗⲁⲧⲟⲥ ⲛⲥϯⲛⲟⲩⲃⲉ· ⲛⲁⲓ ⲛ̅ⲧⲁⲩⲉⲛ̅ⲧⲟⲩ ⲛⲁϥ ⲉⲃⲟⲗ
ϩⲛ̅ ⲛ̅ϣⲏⲛ ⲙ̅ⲡⲡⲁⲣⲁⲇⲓⲥⲟⲥ ⲁϥⲟⲩⲉϩⲥⲁϩⲛⲉ[d] ⲛⲁⲩ[e] ⲉⲧⲣⲉⲩⲉⲣ ⲟⲩⲕⲗⲟⲙ
ⲉⲣⲟⲥ ⲉⲛⲕⲟⲧⲉ ⲛ̅ⲥⲉϭⲟ ⲉⲩϩⲩⲙⲛⲉⲩⲉ ⲉⲣⲟⲥ ϩⲙ̅ ⲡϩⲩⲙⲛⲟⲥ ⲛ̅ⲛⲁ ⲧⲡⲉ·
ⲛⲁⲓ ⲛ̅ⲧⲁϥⲧⲥⲁⲃⲟⲟⲩ ⲉⲣⲟϥ:— 23 Ⲛⲧⲉⲣⲟⲩⲱⲥⲕ ⲇⲉ ⲉⲩⲉⲓⲣⲉ ϩⲓ ⲛⲁⲓ
ⲛⲟⲩⲛⲟϭ ⲛ̅ⲛⲁⲩ ⲉⲣⲉ ⲡⲥⲱⲧⲏⲣ ϩⲙⲟⲟⲥ ⲙⲡⲉⲙⲧⲟ ⲉⲃⲟⲗ ⲛⲧⲉϥⲙⲁⲁⲩ |
p. ? (c. xii) 4 ⸢Ⲡⲉϫ⸣ⲉ ⲡⲥⲱⲧⲏⲣ ⲛⲛⲁⲡⲟⲥⲧⲟⲗⲟⲥ ϫⲉ ⲱ ⲛⲁⲙⲉⲗⲟⲥ ⲉⲧⲧⲁⲓⲏⲩ·
ⲧⲱⲟⲩⲛ ⲛⲧⲛ̅ⲁⲛⲁⲭⲱⲣⲉⲓ ⲛⲁⲛ ⲉⲡⲥⲁⲛⲃⲟⲗ ⲛⲟⲩⲕⲟⲩⲓ· ⲇⲉ ⲙⲛ[f] ϣϭⲟⲙ
ⲉⲧⲣⲉ ⲡⲙⲟⲩ ⲉⲓ ⲉϩⲟⲩⲛ ⲉϫⲱⲥ· ⲉⲓϩⲙⲟⲟⲥ ϩⲁϩⲧⲏⲥ· ⲉⲁⲛⲟⲕ ⲡⲉ
ⲡⲱⲛϩ̅ ⲙ̅ⲡⲕⲟⲥⲙⲟⲥ ⲧⲏⲣϥ̅·— Ⲉⲓⲥ ⲛ̅ϭⲟⲙ ⲛ̅ⲛ̅ⲙⲡⲏⲩⲉ ⲛ̅ⲧⲁ ⲡⲁⲓⲱⲧ
ⲧⲛ̅ⲛⲟⲟⲩⲥⲟⲩ· ⲛ̅ⲥⲁ ⲡⲉⲣⲡⲉ ⲙⲡⲉϥϣⲏⲣⲉ ⲉⲧⲉ ⲁⲛⲟⲕ ⲡⲉ· ⲥⲉⲕⲁⲧⲉⲓⲭⲉ·—
5 Ⲛⲁⲓ ⲇⲉ ⲛ̅ⲧⲉⲣⲉϥϫⲟⲟⲩ ⲁⲛⲧⲱⲟⲩⲛ ⲁⲛⲉⲓ ⲉⲃⲟⲗ ⲉⲧⲁⲩⲗⲏ ⲉⲧϩⲛ̅
ⲧⲙⲏⲧⲉ ⲙ̅ⲡⲏⲓ· 6 ⲁⲩⲱ ⲁ ⲡⲥⲱⲧⲏⲣ ϩⲙⲟⲟⲥ ⲁⲛⲁϩⲉⲣⲁⲧⲛ̅ ⲉⲣⲟϥ ⲧⲏⲣⲛ̅:—|

[a] Ϩⲁϩⲛ̅ⲥⲟⲡ [b] ⲉϩⲟⲩⲛ script. sup. ⲙⲁⲥ eras. [c] ⲛ̅ϩⲛ̅ⲃⲁϩⲛ̅ⲛ̅ⲃⲛ̅ⲛⲉ
[d] ⲛ rescript., ⲉ 2° rescript. pro ⲁ [e] ⲛ rescript. ut vid. [f] ⲙⲉ

the veil of the temple and rent it, and divided it. 13 We
heard a voice from the horns of the altar saying, Woe, woe
to Jerusalem, which killeth the prophets, and stoneth them cf. Mt xxiii 37 f*; Lc
that are sent unto her. 14 Often would I have gathered thy xiii 34 f
children, even as a bird gathereth its young ones together
under its wings, and ye would not. 15 Therefore your house
is left unto you. 16 And we looked, and saw the angel assigned
to the temple: he flew to the top of the canopy of the altar,
he and *the* *angel* who had the sword; *both* being in great
mourning. 17 Now when we saw that which came to pass, we
knew straightway that in truth the Lord had left His people.
And we hasted, and fled to His Son Jesus who was crucified,
in order that we might not come to be under the curse, which
we heard from the angel of the temple and from those who
rent the veil.

XI. Now these twelve virgins who went with us from
the beginning, the Saviour commanded them to go in unto
the altar, by which He gathered us together: and they
brought branches of palms[a] and sweet smelling branches,
which they brought Him from the trees of Paradise[b]. He
commanded them to encircle[c] her about, and to keep singing
her praise with the hymn of the inhabitants of heaven,
which He taught them. 2, 3 Now when they had been a long
while doing so, whilst the Saviour was sitting before His
mother, (XII) 4 the Saviour said to the apostles, O My
glorious[d] members, arise and let us withdraw outside for a cf. Eph v
little while; for Death cannot enter in unto her, whilst I sit 30
with her, since I am the Life of all the world. Behold the cf. Jn vi
powers of the heavens which My Father hath sent after the 51*; xi 25; xiv 6
temple of His Son, even of Me, do stay. 5 Now when He had
said these things, we arose and went out to the court which
was in the midst of the house. 6 And the Saviour sat, and

[a] Lit. *the palms* [b] Lit. *the Paradise* [c] Or *be a crown* (or *garland*) *to* [d] Or *honourable*

Cod. Clarend. b 3 15 ⲁⲛⲣ̄ ⲟⲩⲕⲗⲟⲙ ⲉⲣⲟϥ ⲉⲛⲕⲱⲧⲉ · ⲁϥϭⲱ ⲉϥϣⲁϫⲉ ⲛ̄ⲙⲙⲁⲛ ϩⲛ̄
ⲛⲉⲙⲩⲥⲧⲏⲣⲓⲟⲛ ⲙ̄ⲡϫⲓⲥⲉ 9 Ⲁⲥϣⲱⲡⲉ ⲇⲉ ⲙⲛⲛⲁⲩ ⲛ̄ϫⲯⲓⲧⲉ ⲙ̄ⲡⲉϩⲟⲟⲩ
ⲛ̄ⲥⲟⲩ ϫⲟⲩⲧⲟⲩⲉ ⲙ̄ⲡⲉⲃⲟⲧ ⲧⲱⲃⲉ ⲁⲥϫⲱⲕ ⲉⲃⲟⲗ ⲛⲧⲉⲥⲟⲓⲕⲟⲛⲟⲙⲓⲁ
ⲛ̄ϭⲓ ⲧⲙ̄ⲙⲁⲁⲩ ⲧⲏⲣⲛ̄ ⲧⲉⲑⲉⲟⲇⲟⲕⲟⲥ · ⲉⲧⲟⲩⲁⲁⲃ ⲑⲁⲅⲓⲁ ⲙⲁⲣⲓⲁ ·
ⲧⲣⲉϥϫⲡⲉ ⲡⲛⲟⲩⲧⲉ ϩⲛ̄ ⲟⲩⲙⲉ :— 11 Ⲛⲉϩⲓⲟⲙⲉ ⲇⲉ ⲉⲧⲥⲟⲟⲩϩ ⲉⲣⲟⲥ
ⲉⲩϩⲩⲙ̄ⲛⲉⲩⲉ · ⲛ̄ⲧⲉⲣⲟⲩⲛⲁⲩ ϫⲉ ⲁⲥϫⲱⲕ ⲉⲃⲟⲗ · ⲁⲩϫⲓⲥⲉ ⲛ̄ⲧⲉⲩⲥⲙⲏ
ⲁⲩϫⲓϣⲕⲁⲕ ⲉⲃⲟⲗ ⲁⲩⲣⲓⲙⲉ · — Ⲥⲁⲗⲱⲙⲏ ⲇⲉ ⲁⲥⲉⲓ ⲉ⸢ⲥ⸣ⲛⲏⲧ ⲁⲥⲛⲁϩⲧⲥ |
p. ? ϩⲁ ⲛⲉⲟⲩⲉⲣⲏⲧⲉ ⲙ̄ⲡⲥⲱⲧⲏⲣ Ⲡⲉϫⲁⲥ ϫⲉ ⲡⲁϫⲟⲉⲓⲥ ⲁⲩⲱ ⲡⲁⲛⲟⲩⲧⲉ
ⲉⲓⲥ ϩⲏⲏⲧⲉ ⲁⲥⲙⲟⲩ ⲛ̄ϭⲓ ⲧⲉⲧⲉⲕⲙⲉ ⲙ̄ⲙⲟⲥ · 12 ⲟⲩⲟⲓ ⲛⲁⲛ ⲙⲛ̄ ϯⲛⲟϭ
ⲙ̄ⲙⲛ̄ⲧⲉⲃⲓⲏⲛ ⲛ̄ⲧⲁⲥⲧⲁϩⲟⲛ ⲙ̄ⲡⲟⲟⲩ · — Ⲉⲛⲉ ⲙ̄ⲡⲉⲕⲁⲛⲁⲭⲱⲣⲉⲓ ⲉⲛ-
ⲥⲁⲛⲃⲟⲗ · ⲛⲉⲥⲛⲁⲙⲟⲩ ⲁⲛ ⲡⲉ : — 13 Ⲡⲥⲱⲧⲏⲣ ⲇⲉ ⲡⲉϫⲁϥ ϫⲉ
ⲛ̄ⲧⲁⲥⲙⲟⲩ ⲁⲛ ⲁⲗⲗⲁ ⲛⲧⲁⲥⲱⲛⲉϩ Ⲡⲙⲟⲩ ⲅⲁⲣ ⲛ̄ⲧⲁⲙⲁⲁⲩ ⲛⲟⲩⲙⲟⲩ
(c. xiii) ⲁⲛ ⲡⲉ · ⲁⲗⲗⲁ ⲟⲩⲱⲛϩ̄ ⲡⲉ :— 1 Ⲁⲛⲧⲱⲟⲩⲛ ⲇⲉ ⲛ̄ⲧⲉⲩⲛⲟⲩ ⲁⲛⲡⲱⲧ
ⲉϩⲟⲩⲛ 2 ⲁⲛϭⲓⲛⲉ ⲙ̄ⲙⲟⲥ ⲉⲥⲛ̄ⲕⲟⲧⲕ ⲛ̄ⲑⲉ ⲛⲟⲩⲁ · ⲛ̄ⲧⲁϥ|ⲧⲱⲟⲩⲛ⸢...⸣
ⲣⲓⲥⲧⲱⲛ · ⸢ⲉϥⲛ⸣ⲕⲟⲧⲕ ⲉ⸢ϥ⸣ⲟⲃϣ̄ ⲉⲛⲉⲥⲣⲟⲟⲩⲧ ⲅⲁⲣ ⲙ̄ⲙⲁⲧⲉ · ⲉⲣⲉ ⲡⲉⲥϩⲟ
ⲡⲉϫ ⲁⲕⲧⲓⲛ ⲛⲟⲩⲟⲉⲓⲛ ⲉⲃⲟⲗ Ⲛⲧⲉⲣⲛ̄ⲛⲁⲩ ⲇⲉ ⲉⲣⲟⲥ ⲁⲛⲣ̄ϩⲟⲧⲉ ⲁⲩⲱ
ⲁⲛⲣ̄ϣⲡⲏⲣⲉ ⲙ̄ⲙⲁⲧⲉ · Ⲁⲩⲱ ⲁⲛⲛⲁϩⲧⲛ̄ ⲉⲛⲉⲥⲏⲧ ⲉϫⲱⲥ ⲁⲛⲣⲓⲙⲉ :—
3 Ⲡⲥⲱⲧⲏⲣ ⲇⲉ ⲁϥⲛⲟⲣϣ̄ϥ ⲉⲃⲟⲗ ⲉϫⲙ̄ ⲡⲥⲱⲙⲁ ⲛ̄ⲧⲉϥⲙⲁⲁⲩ ⲁϥⲣⲓⲙⲉ
ⲉⲛⲉⲥⲏⲧ ⲉϫⲱⲥ ⲛⲟⲩⲛⲟϭ ⲛ̄ⲛⲁⲩ · ⲁϥϯⲡⲓ ⲉⲣⲟⲥ ⲉϥϫⲱ ⲛ̄ⲛⲁⲓ ⲙⲛ̄
ⲛⲓⲕⲱⲟⲩⲉ ⲉⲛⲉⲥⲏⲧ ⲉϫⲱⲥ ⲉϥϫⲱ ⲙ̄ⲙⲟⲥ ⲛ̄ϯⲣⲉ ϫⲉ ⲛⲁⲓⲁⲧⲟⲩ ⲛⲛⲟⲩ-
p. ? ⲥⲛⲟⲧⲟⲩ ⲱ ⲙⲁⲣⲓⲁ ⲧⲁⲙⲁⲁⲩ ϫⲉ ⲁⲣⲙ̄ⲡϣⲁ | ⸢.....ⲛ⸣ϣⲁ ⲛⲁⲥ⸢ⲡⲁⲍⲉ⸣
ⲙ̄ⲡϣⲏⲣⲉ ⲙⲡⲛⲟⲩⲧⲉ ⲉⲃⲟⲗ ⲛ̄ϩⲏⲧⲟⲩ :— 4 Ⲛⲁⲓⲁⲧⲟⲩ ⲛ̄ⲛⲟⲩⲃⲁⲗ ⲱ
ⲧⲁⲙⲁⲁⲩ ϫⲉ ⲁⲣϭⲱϣⲧ ⲉϩⲟⲩⲛ ϩⲙ̄ ⲡϩⲟ ⲙ̄ⲡⲉⲧⲉ ϣⲁϥϭⲱϣⲧ ⲉϫⲙ̄
ⲡⲕⲁϩ ⲛ̄ϥⲥⲧⲱⲧ ϣⲁ ⲛⲉϥⲥⲛ̄ⲧⲉ · — 5 Ⲛⲁⲓⲁⲧⲟⲩ ⲛ̄ⲛⲟⲩⲙⲁⲁϫⲉ ⲱ
ⲧⲁⲙⲁⲁⲩ · ⲧⲛ̄ⲧⲁⲥϫⲡⲟⲓ ⲉⲓⲟ ⲛⲛⲟⲩⲧⲉ ⲉⲓⲟ ⲛⲣⲱⲙⲉ · Ϫⲉ ⲁⲣⲥⲱⲧⲙ̄
ⲉϩⲙ̄ⲙⲩⲥⲧⲏⲣⲓⲟⲛ ⲉⲩϩⲏⲡ ⲛⲁⲓ ⲉⲧⲛ̄ⲥⲧⲟ ⲁⲛ ⲉϫⲟⲟⲩ ⲉⲣⲱⲙⲉ 6 Ⲛⲁⲓⲁⲧⲟⲩ
ⲛ̄ⲛⲟⲩϭⲃⲟⲓ ϫⲉ ⲁⲣⲃⲓ ϩⲁ ⲡⲉⲧⲃⲓ ϩⲁ ⲡⲥⲱⲛⲧ ⲧⲏⲣϥ̄ :— 7 Ⲛⲁⲓⲁⲧⲟⲩ
ⲛ̄ⲛⲟⲩⲉⲕⲓⲃⲉ ⲱ ⲧⲁⲙⲁⲁⲩ ϫⲉ ⲁⲓⲥⲁⲁⲛϣ̄ ⲉⲃⲟⲗ ⲛ̄ϩⲏⲧⲟⲩ — | ⲉⲁⲛⲟⲕ
ⲡⲉⲧⲥⲁⲁⲛϣ̄ ⲙⲡⲥⲱⲛⲧ ⲧⲏⲣϥ̄ 8 Ⲛⲁⲓⲁⲧⲟⲩ ⲛ̄ⲛⲟⲩⲛⲁⲧ ⲱ ⲧⲛ̄ⲧⲁⲓⲙⲉⲣⲓⲧⲉ

we all stood by[a] Him, and we encircled[b] Him about: and
He kept speaking with us in the mysteries of the height.
[9]Now it came to pass at the ninth hour of the day on the
twenty-first of the month Tobi, she fulfilled her dispensation,
the mother of us all, the holy God-bearer, the holy[c] Mary,
the bearer of God in truth. [11]Now the women that were
gathered to her singing praise, when they saw that she was
dead[d], they lifted up their voice, cried out and wept. And cf. Jn xi
Salome came running, and fell down at the feet of the Saviour, 3, 14, 32
and said, My Lord and my God, behold, she whom Thou
lovest is dead[e]. [12]Woe unto us and the great misery which
has befallen us to-day. If Thou hadst not withdrawn outside,
she had not died. [13]But the Saviour said, She did not die,
but lived. For the death of My mother is not death, but it
is life.

XIII. And we arose straightway, and went in, [2]and
found her lying as one, who has... lying *and* sleeping, for
she was exceeding bright[f], her face sending forth rays of
light. Now when we saw her, we were afraid and wondered
exceedingly; and we fell upon[g] her and wept. [3]And the
Saviour stretched Himself out on the body of His mother
and wept upon[g] her for a long while. And He kissed
her, saying these and other[h] things over[g] her, speaking
thus, Blessed are thy lips, O Mary My mother, for thou
wast worthy......to kiss[i] the Son of God by them. [4]Blessed
are thine eyes, O My mother, for thou didst look into the cf. Ps ciii
face of Him, who looketh upon the earth, and it trembleth 32*; Is xiii 13
unto its foundations. [5]Blessed are thine ears, O My mother,
who bare Me being God *and* being Man; for thou didst hear cf. 2 Co
hidden mysteries which it is not lawful to tell to man. xii 4
[6]Blessed are thine arms, for thou didst bear Him who cf. He i 3
beareth all the creation. [7]Blessed are thy breasts, O My
mother, for I was nourished from them, even I who nourish
all the creation. [8]Blessed are thy knees, O thou[j] whom I

[a] Lit. *to* [b] Lit. *were a crown* (or *garland*) *to* [c] Two different words are used for *holy* in this verse [d] Or *perfected* [e] Lit. *died* [f] Or *cheerful* [g] Lit. *down upon* [h] Lit. *the other* [i] Lit. *salute* [j] Lit. *she*

Cod. Clarend. b 3 15 (c. xiv)

ϫⲉ ⲁⲣϥⲓ ϩⲁ ⲡⲉⲧϩⲙⲟⲟⲥ ϩⲓ ⲡⲉⲑⲣⲟⲛⲟⲥ ⲛ̄ⲧⲙ̄ⲛ̄ⲧⲛⲟϭ ϩⲛ̄ ⲛⲉⲧϫⲟⲥⲉ[a]
[9]ⲛⲁⲓⲁⲧⲥ ⲛ̄ⲧⲟⲩⲕⲁⲗⲁϩⲏ · ϫⲉ ⲁⲣϥⲓ ϩⲁⲣⲟⲓ ⲙ̄ⲯⲓⲥ ⲛⲉⲃⲟⲧ [1]ⲛⲁⲓ ⲇⲉ
ⲉϥϫⲱ ⲙ̄ⲙⲟⲟⲩ ⲛ̄ϭⲓ ⲡⲥⲱⲧⲏⲣ ⲁϥⲧⲱⲟⲩⲛ ⲉϥⲛⲁϩⲧ ⲉϫⲛ̄ ⲧⲉϥⲙⲁⲁⲩ
ⲙ̄ⲡⲁⲣⲑⲉⲛⲟⲥ · [2]ⲁϥⲁⲙⲁϩⲧⲉ ⲙ̄ⲡⲧⲱⲛ ⲥⲛⲁⲩ ⲛ̄ⲛⲉϩⲃⲟⲟⲥ · ⲉⲥⲛ̄ⲕⲟⲧⲕ
ϩⲓϫⲱⲟⲩ ⲁϥϭⲗ̄ⲙⲗⲱⲙⲟⲩ ⲉⲣⲟⲥ ϩⲛ̄ ⲛⲉϥϭⲓϫ ⲙ̄ⲙⲓⲛⲉ ⲙ̄ⲙⲟϥ[b] ⲁⲩⲱ
ⲁϥⲕⲟⲗⲗⲁ [ⲙ̄ⲙⲟⲟⲩ] ⲉϩⲟⲩⲛ[c] ⲉⲛⲉⲥⲥⲱⲙⲁ · ϩⲱⲥⲇⲉ ⲛⲧⲁⲩⲕⲟⲗⲗⲓⲍⲉ
p. ? ⲙ̄ⲙⲟⲟⲩ ϩⲛ̄ ⲟⲩ|ⲕⲉⲣⲱⲇⲏ · [3]ⲡⲉϫⲉ ⲡⲥⲱⲧⲏⲣ ⲛⲛⲁⲡⲟⲥⲧⲟⲗⲟⲥ ϫⲉ
ⲧⲁⲗⲟ ⲙ̄ⲡⲓⲥⲱⲙⲁ · ⲡⲁⲓ ⲛⲧⲁϥϣⲱⲡⲉ ⲛⲁⲓ ⲙⲙⲁⲛⲟⲩⲱϩ ϩⲓϫⲙ̄ ⲡⲕⲁϩ ·
ⲛ̄ⲧⲉⲧⲛ̄ⲕⲁⲁϥ ⲉϩⲣⲁⲓ ⲉϫⲱⲧⲛ̄ · ϫⲉ ⲙⲛ̄ ϭⲟⲙ ⲛ̄ⲧⲉ ⲛⲉⲛⲧⲏⲙⲁ ⲛ̄ⲧⲁϊ-
ⲧⲁⲁⲩ[d] ⲉⲣⲟⲥ ϫⲱϩ ⲉⲛⲉϭⲗⲟϭ ⲙ̄ⲡⲓⲕⲟⲥⲙⲟⲥ ϫⲉ ϩⲛ̄ⲛⲉⲛⲧⲏⲙⲁ ⲛⲉ ⲛ̄ⲧⲉ
ⲛⲟⲩⲟⲉⲓⲛ ⲛⲉⲡⲟⲩⲣⲁⲛⲓⲟⲛ : — [4]ⲁⲗⲗⲁ ϫⲉ ⲛⲧⲱⲧⲛ̄ ⲛⲁⲙⲉⲗⲟⲥ ⲉⲧ-
ⲧⲁⲓⲏⲩ · ⲁⲓⲧⲛ̄ⲧⲛ̄ⲧⲏⲩⲧⲛ̄ ⲉⲣⲟⲓ ⲧⲱⲟⲩⲛ ϩⲁ ⲧⲁⲙⲁⲁⲩ ϩⲙ̄ ⲡⲉⲧⲛ̄ⲥⲱⲙⲁ ·
ⲛ̄ⲧⲉⲧⲛ̄ⲯⲁⲗⲗⲉⲓ ϩⲁⲧⲉⲥϩⲏ [5]ⲛⲧⲉⲧⲛ̄ⲙⲟⲟϣⲉ ⲉⲃⲟⲗ ⲛ̄ⲙ̄ⲙⲁⲥ ϣⲁ
ⲡⲙⲁ · ⲉⲧⲉⲣⲉ ⲡⲁⲓⲱⲧ ⲛⲁⲟⲩⲉϩ|ⲥⲁϩⲛⲉ ⲉⲕⲱ ⲙ̄⸢ⲡⲉⲥ⸣ⲥⲱⲙⲁ ⲛ̄ϩⲏⲧϥ
ⲛ̄ⲛⲉⲣⲉϩⲟⲧⲉ ⲁⲛⲟⲕ ϯϣⲟⲟⲡ ⲛ̄ⲙⲙⲏⲧⲛ̄ [6]ⲛⲁⲓ ⲇⲉ ⲉⲣⲉ ⲡⲥⲱⲧⲏⲣ ϫⲱ
(c. xv) ⲙ̄ⲙⲟⲟⲩ [1]ⲁϥϩⲟⲛϥ ⲉⲣⲟⲛ [3]ⲁⲛⲟⲛ ⲇⲉ ⲁⲛⲧⲁⲗⲟ ⲙ̄ⲡⲥⲱⲙⲁ ⲛ̄ⲧⲡⲁⲣ-
ⲑⲉⲛⲟⲥ · ⲉⲣⲉ ⲡⲁⲓⲱⲧ ⲡⲉⲧⲣⲟⲥ ⲧⲱⲟⲩⲛ ϩⲁ ⲧⲉⲥⲁⲡⲉ[e] · ⲉⲣⲉ ⲡⲁⲓⲱⲧ
ⲓⲱϩⲁⲛⲛⲏⲥ ⲧⲱⲟⲩⲛ ϩⲁ ⲛⲉⲥⲟⲩⲉⲣⲏⲧⲉ · — ⲉⲣⲉ ⲡⲕⲉⲥⲉⲉⲡⲉ ⲛⲁⲡⲟ-
ⲥⲧⲟⲗⲟⲥ ⲙⲛ̄ ⲛ̄ⲕⲉϩⲓⲟⲙⲉ ⲙⲟⲟϣⲉ[f] ⲛ̄ⲙ̄ⲙⲁⲛ · ⲙⲛ̄ ⲙ̄ⲡⲁⲣⲑⲉⲛⲟⲥ ⲛ̄ⲧⲁⲩⲉⲓ
ⲉⲃⲟⲗ ϩⲙ̄ ⲡⲣ̄ⲡⲉ · ⲉⲣⲉ ⲛⲉϩⲓⲟⲙⲉ ⲙⲟⲟϣⲉ[g] ⲛ̄ⲙ̄ⲙⲁⲛ ϩⲓ ⲛⲁϩⲟⲩ ⲉⲣⲉ
p. ? ⲛⲉϩⲟⲟⲩⲧ ⲙⲟⲟϣⲉ ϩⲓⲑⲏ ⲉⲩϫⲱ ⲛⲟⲩϩⲩⲙⲛⲟⲥ ⲉϥⲏⲡ ⲉⲧⲡⲉ |[4]⸢ⲁⲥϣ⸣ⲱⲡⲉ
ⲇⲉ ⲛ̄ⲧⲉ⸢ⲣⲉⲛⲓ⸣ ⲉⲡⲓⲛⲉⲃⲧ[h] ⲛ̄ⲑ⸢ⲓⲗ⸣ⲏⲙ̄ · ⲁⲛⲓ ⲉⲡⲙⲁ ⲉⲧⲟⲩⲙⲟⲩⲧⲉ ⲉⲣⲟϥ
ϫⲉ ⲡⲓⲁ ⲛⲓⲱⲥⲁⲫⲁⲧ : ⲁ ⲡⲗⲁⲟⲥ ⲛ̄ⲥⲧⲁⲥⲓⲁⲥⲧⲏⲥ ⲛⲫⲟⲛⲉⲩⲥ ⲛ̄ⲣⲉϥϩⲉⲧⲃ̄
ⲛⲉⲩⲛⲟⲩⲧⲉ ⲛⲓⲟⲩⲇⲁⲓ ⲉⲧⲥϩⲟⲩⲟⲣⲧ : · — ⲛⲧⲉⲣⲟⲩⲥⲱⲧⲙ̄ ⲉⲛⲉϩⲣⲟⲟⲩ
ⲛ̄ⲛⲉϩⲩⲙⲛⲟⲥ · [6]ⲁⲩⲙⲟⲩϩ ϩⲙ̄ ⲡⲕⲱϩ ⲙ̄ⲡⲉⲩⲓⲱⲧ ⲡⲇⲓⲁⲃⲟⲗⲟⲥ ⲁⲩⲡⲱⲧ
ⲁⲩⲧⲁⲙⲉ ⲛⲁⲣⲭⲓⲉⲣⲉⲩⲥ ⲉⲛⲉⲛⲧⲁⲩϣⲱⲡⲉ · · — ⲁⲩⲧⲱⲟⲩⲛ ⲁⲩⲉⲓ
ⲉⲩⲛⲏⲩ · ϩⲛ̄ ⲟⲩⲛⲟϭ ⲛⲑⲩⲙⲟⲥ ⲉⲩⲟⲩⲱϣ ⲉϩⲁⲣⲡⲁⲍⲉ ⲙ̄ⲡⲥⲱⲙⲁ

[a] ⲡⲉϫⲟⲥⲉ [b] ϥ sup. ⲥ eras. [c] ⲁϥⲕⲟⲗⲗⲁ ⲉϩⲟⲩⲛ
[d] ⲓ sup. ⲩ eras. [e] ⲉ 2° e pr. man. rescript. pro ⲁ ut vid. [f] ⲉⲧⲙⲟⲟϣⲉ
[g] ϣ sup. ras. ut vid. [h] ⲡⲓⲛⲉⲃⲧ

loved, for thou didst carry Him who sitteth on the throne of cf. He i 3
the majesty on high[a]. [9]Blessed is thy womb, for thou didst
carry Me nine months.

XIV. Now as the Saviour said these things, He arose,
for He was fallen upon His virgin mother. [2]He took hold of
the two borders of the garments, as she lay upon them, and
wrapped them upon her with His own hands; and He fastened
them to her body, so that they were fastened with unguent.
[3]The Saviour said to the apostles, Take up this body which
was to Me *a* dwelling place upon earth, and place it upon
you, for the garments which I have given[b] her cannot
touch the bier of this world, for they are garments of
the heavenly light. [4]But ye, My glorious[c] members, I have
made you like to Me; carry My mother on your body, and
sing before her. [5]And go forth with her unto the place which
My Father shall command, to lay her body in it. Be not
afraid. I am with you. [6]Now as the Saviour said these
things, (XV) [1]He hid Himself from us. [3]And we took up the cf. Jn xii 36
body of the Virgin, my father Peter carrying her head, my
father John carrying her feet; the rest of the apostles also
and the women also going with us, and the virgins who
came forth from the temple; the women going with us
behind, the men going before, singing a heavenly hymn[d].
[4]And it came to pass when we came to the east of Jerusalem,
we came to the place called the valley of Jehoshaphat; and
the people that made insurrection, the murderers, slayers of
their God, the cursed Jews, when they heard the sound of
the hymns, [6]were filled with the jealousy of their father the cf. Jn viii 44
devil; and went and told the chief priests those things that cf. Mt
were come to pass. They arose and came running in great xxviii 11*
wrath, being minded[e] to catch away the body of the Virgin

[a] Lit. *in the high* places [b] Originally the MS had *which were given*
[c] Or *honourable* [d] Lit. *a hymn belonging to heaven* [e] Or *wishing*

Cod. Clarend. b 3 15 ⲛ̄ⲧⲡⲁⲣⲑⲉⲛⲟⲥ ⲛⲧⲟⲟⲧⲛ̄ ⲛ̄ⲥⲉⲣⲱⲕϩ ⲙ̄ⲙⲟϥ · ⲕⲁⲧⲁ ⲑⲉ ⲛ̄ⲧⲁⲩϩⲟⲙⲟ-
ⲗⲟⲅⲉⲓ ⲛⲁⲛ ⲙ̄ⲡϩⲁⲉ 7Ⲁⲥϣⲱⲡⲉ ⲇⲉ ⲛ̄ⲧⲉⲣⲟⲩϩⲱⲛ ⲉϩⲟⲩⲛ ⲉⲣⲟⲛ · ⲁ
ϩⲛ̄ⲛⲟϭ ⲛ̄ⲥⲟⲃ̄ⲧ̄ ⲛ̄ⲕⲱϩⲧ ϣⲱⲡⲉ ϩⲛ̄ ⲧⲙ̄ⲏⲧⲉ ⲛ̄ⲙ̄ⲙⲁⲩ ⲁⲩⲗⲟ ⲉⲩⲛⲁⲩ
ⲉⲛⲟⲩⲟⲉⲓⲛ ⲙ̄ⲡⲓⲕⲟⲥⲙⲟⲥ · ⲡϫⲟⲉⲓⲥ ⲅⲁⲣ ⲁϥⲡⲁⲧⲁⲥⲥⲉ ⲙ̄ⲙⲟⲟⲩ ϩⲛ̄
(c. xvi) ⲟⲩⲕⲁⲕⲉ ⲛ̄ϭⲟⲙϭⲙ ⲛ̄ⲑⲉ ⲛ̄ⲛⲉⲣⲉⲙⲛ̄ⲕⲏⲙⲉ ⲙⲡⲓⲟⲩⲟⲉⲓϣ :— 1Ⲁⲩϫⲓϣ-
ⲕⲁⲕ ⲉⲃⲟⲗ ⲉⲩϫⲱ ⲙ̄ⲙⲟⲥ ϫⲉ ⲙⲁⲣⲓⲁ ⲧⲙⲁⲁⲩ ⲛ̄ⲓ̅ⲥ̅ ⲃⲟⲏⲑⲓⲁ ⲉⲣⲟⲛ
Ⲧⲛ̄ϩⲟⲙⲟⲗⲟⲅⲉⲓ ϫⲉ ⲓ̅ⲥ̅ ⲡⲉ ⲡⲉⲭ̅ⲥ̅[a] ⲛ̄ⲧⲟϥ ⲡⲉ ⲡϣⲏⲣⲉ ⲙ̄ⲡⲛⲟⲩⲧⲉ
p. ? ⲉⲧⲟⲛϩ̄ · 2ⲛⲁ · ⲛⲁⲛ ⲧ̄ⲛ̄ⲥⲱⲡⲉ ⲙⲁⲣⲓⲁ | ϫⲉ ⲛⲧⲟ ⲟⲩⲉⲃⲟⲗ ϩⲙ̄ ⲡⲉⲛ-
ⲅⲉⲛⲟⲥ 3Ⲁⲛⲣ̄ ⲛⲁⲓ ⲧⲏⲣⲟⲩ ⲛ̄ⲓ̅ⲥ̅ ⲛⲟⲩϣⲏⲣⲉ ⲁⲩⲱ ⲙ̄ⲡⲉϥⲉⲓⲣⲉ ⲛⲁⲛ
ⲕⲁⲧⲁ ⲡⲉⲛⲧⲁⲛⲁⲁⲩ ⲛⲁϥ 4Ⲛ̄ⲧⲟ ϩⲱⲱⲧⲉ ⲛⲁ ⲛⲁⲛ ⲛ̄ⲧⲉⲭⲁⲣⲓⲍⲉ ⲛⲁⲛ
ⲙ̄ⲡⲟⲩⲟⲉⲓⲛ 5Ⲛ̄ⲧⲉⲩⲛⲟⲩ ⲁ ⲛⲉⲩⲃⲁⲗ ⲟⲩⲱⲛ ⲁⲩⲛⲁⲩ ⲉⲛⲉⲛⲧⲁⲩϣⲱⲡⲉ
ⲉⲩϫⲡⲓⲟ ⲁⲩⲱ ⲉⲩⲉⲗⲓⲭⲉ ⲉⲧⲉⲩⲙⲛ̄ⲧⲁⲧⲛⲁϩⲧⲉ Ⲛ̄ⲧⲉⲩⲛⲟⲩ ⲁⲩⲉⲓ ⲉⲃⲟⲗ
ϩⲛ̄ ⲧⲡⲉ ⲛ̄ϭⲓ ⲟⲩⲛⲟϭ ⲛ̄ⲭⲱⲣⲟⲥ ⲛⲁⲅⲅⲉⲗⲟⲥ ⲉⲙⲛ̄ ⲏⲡⲉ ⲉⲣⲟⲟⲩ ⲁⲩϯ

Cod. Borg. CCLVIII 6ⲉⲧⲟⲩⲁⲁⲃ ⲛ̄ⲧⲟⲟⲧⲛ ⲕⲁⲧⲁ ⲑⲉ ⲛ̇ⲧⲁⲩϩⲟⲙⲟⲗⲟⲅⲉⲓ ⲛⲁⲛ ⲉⲛϩⲁⲉ ·
p. ⲗ⌜ⲁ⌝ 7Ⲁⲥϣⲱⲡⲉ ⲇⲉ ⲛ̄ⲧⲉⲣⲟⲩϩⲱⲛ ⲉϩⲟⲩⲛ ⲉⲣⲟⲛ ⲁ ϩⲉⲛⲛⲟϭ ⲛ̄ⲥⲟⲃ̄ⲧ̄
ⲛ̄ⲕⲱϩⲧ ϣⲱⲡⲉ ϩⲛ̄ ⲧⲉⲙⲏⲧⲉ ⲛ̄ⲙ̄ⲙⲁⲩ ⲁⲩⲗⲟ ⲉⲩⲛⲁⲩ ⲉⲛⲟⲩⲟⲉⲓⲛ
ⲙ̇ⲡⲉⲓⲕⲟⲥⲙⲟⲥ · Ⲡϫⲟⲉⲓⲥ ⲅⲁⲣ ⲁϥⲡⲁⲧⲁⲥⲥⲉ ⲙ̄ⲙⲟⲟⲩ ϩⲛ̄ ⲟⲩⲕⲁⲕⲉ
(c. xvi) ⲛ̇ϭⲟⲙϭⲙ ⲛ̄ⲑⲉ ⲛ̄ⲣⲙ̄ⲛ̄ⲕⲏⲙⲉ ⲙ̄ⲡⲉⲓⲟⲩⲟⲉⲓϣ · 1Ⲁⲩϫⲓϣⲕⲁⲕ ⲉⲃⲟⲗ
ⲉⲩϫⲱ ⲙ̇ⲙⲟⲥ ϫⲉ ⲙⲁⲣⲓⲁ ⲧⲙⲁⲁⲩ ⲛ̄ⲓ̅ⲥ̅ ⲃⲟⲏⲑⲉⲓ ⲉⲣⲟⲛ — Ⲧⲛ̄ϩⲟⲙⲟ-
ⲗⲟⲅⲉⲓ ϫⲉ ⲓ̅ⲥ̅ ⲡⲉⲭ̅ⲥ̅ ⲡⲉⲛⲧⲁⲣϫⲡⲟϥ ⲛ̇ⲧⲟϥ ⲡⲉ ⲡϣⲏⲣⲉ ⲙ̇ⲡⲛⲟⲩⲧⲉ
ⲉⲧⲟⲛϩ 2ⲛⲁ ⲛⲁⲛ ⲱ ⲧⲉⲛⲥⲱⲡⲉ ⲙⲁⲣⲓⲁ ϫⲉ ⲛ̇ⲧⲟ ⲟⲩⲉⲃⲟⲗ ϩⲙ̄
ⲡⲉⲛⲅⲉⲛⲟⲥ · (punct post c rubro script) 3Ⲁⲛⲣ̄ ⲡⲉϩⲟⲩⲟ (cod
Ⲁⲛⲣ̄ⲡ̄ⲉϩⲟⲩⲟ) ⲉⲛⲁⲓ̈ ⲛ̄ⲓ̅ⲥ̅ ⲛⲟⲩϣⲏⲣⲉ ⲁⲩⲱ ⲙ̄ⲡⲉϥⲧⲱⲱⲃⲉ ⲛⲁⲛ ⲕⲁⲧⲁ
ⲡⲉⲛⲧⲁⲛⲁⲁⲩ ⲛⲁϥ · 4Ⲛ̇ⲧⲟ ϩⲱⲱⲧⲉ ⲛⲁ ⲛⲁⲛ ⲛ̄ⲧⲉⲭⲁⲣⲓⲍⲉ ⲛⲁⲛ
ⲙ̄ⲡⲟⲩⲟ|⌜ⲉⲓ⌝ⲛ 5Ⲛ̄ⲧⲉⲩⲛⲟⲩ ⲁ ⲛⲉⲩⲃⲁⲗ ⲟⲩⲱⲛ ⲁⲩⲛⲁⲩ ⲉⲛⲉⲛⲧⲁⲩϣⲱⲡⲉ
ⲧⲏⲣⲟⲩ ⲉⲩϫⲡ̄ⲓⲟ ⲛ̄ⲧⲉⲩⲙⲛ̄ⲧⲁⲧⲛⲁϩⲧⲉ: Ⲁⲩⲱ ⲁⲩⲉⲓ ⲉⲃⲟⲗ ϩⲛ̄ ⲧⲡⲉ ⲛ̄ϭⲓ
ϩⲉⲛⲛⲟϭ ⲛ̄ⲭⲟⲣⲟⲥ ⲉⲙⲛ ⲏⲡⲉ ⲉⲣⲟⲟⲩ ⲁⲩϯ ⲡⲉⲩⲟⲩⲟⲓ̈ ⲁⲩϩⲁⲣⲡⲁⲍⲉ

[a] ⲡⲉ eras. ut vid.

from us[A] and burn it[B], even as they confessed to us afterwards.
7 And it came to pass, when they drew nigh to us, great walls
of fire came between us and them, and they left seeing the
light of this world. For the Lord smote them with a dark- cf. Ex x 21*
ness which might be felt, as *He smote* the Egyptians once[a].

XVI. They cried out saying, Mary the mother of Jesus,
help us. We confess that Jesus is the Christ[b][Γ], He is the cf. Mt xvi 16*
Son of the living God. 2 Have mercy on us, our sister[Δ]
Mary, for thou art of our race. 3 We did all these things[E] to
Jesus thy Son, and He did not do to us[Z] according to those
things that we did to Him. 4 Do thou also have mercy on
us, and grant us the light. 5 Straightway their eyes were
opened, they saw the things[H] that were come to pass, their
unbelief being reproved and convicted[c][Θ]. Straightway[I] there
came from heaven a great choir[K] of angels[Λ] without number;

[a] Lit. *in the manner of the Egyptians once* [b] The scribe originally wrote *Jesus is the Christ*. The words appear to have been altered, perhaps by the scribe himself, into *Jesus the Christ* [c] Or *reproving and convicting their unbelief*

Variants in Codex Borgianus.

A The MS begins with the words *holy* [*Virgin*] *from us* B om. *and burn it* Γ *Jesus is the Christ*] *Jesus the Christ, whom thou didst bring forth* Δ *our sister*] *O our sister* E *all these things*] *more than these things* Z *do to us*] *recompense us* H *the things*] *all the things* Θ *their unbelief being reproved and convicted*] *their unbelief being reproved* (or *reproving their unbelief*) I *Straightway*] *And* K *a great choir*] *great choirs* Λ om. *of angels*

NOTE. The first leaf of Cod. Borg. CCLVIII. is a fragment of the same MS as is the leaf numbered Cod. Borg. CCLXXIII., which is given on p. 66 ff. The pages here are numbered 3⌜1⌝, ⌜32⌝: those of Cod. Borg. CCLXXIII. are 21, 22. The four intervening leaves are lost.

Cod. Clarend. b 3 15

ⲙ̄ⲡⲉⲩⲟⲩⲟⲓ ⲛ̄ⲧⲉⲩⲛⲟⲩ ⲁⲩϩⲁⲣⲡⲁⲍⲉ ⲙ̄ⲡⲥⲱⲙⲁ ⲛ̄ⲧⲡⲁⲣⲑⲉⲛⲟⲥ ⲉϥⲧⲁⲗⲏⲩ ⲉϫⲛ̄ ⲡⲥⲱⲙⲁ ⲛ̄ⲛⲉ|ⲛⲉⲓⲟⲧ⌈ⲉ ⲉⲧ⌉ⲟ⌈ⲩⲁⲁⲃ⌉ ⲛⲁⲡⲟⲥⲧⲟⲗⲟⲥ Ⲡⲁⲓⲱⲧ ⲇⲉ ⲡⲉⲧⲣⲟⲥ ⲙⲛ̄ ⲡⲁⲓⲱⲧ ⲓⲱϩⲁⲛⲛⲏⲥ · ⲁⲩϭⲱϣⲧ ⲛ̄ⲥⲱⲥ ⲉⲁⲩϩⲱⲗ ⲛ̄ⲙ̄ⲙⲁⲥ ⲙ̄ⲡⲏⲩⲉ · ⲉⲩϩⲩⲙⲛⲉⲩⲉ ϩⲁⲧⲉⲥϩⲏ ⲛ̄ϭⲓ ϩⲛ̄ϣⲟ ⲛ̄ϣⲟ[a] ⲙⲛ̄ ϩⲛ̄ⲧⲃⲁ ⲛ̄ⲧⲃⲁ ⲛⲁⲅⲅⲉⲗⲟⲥ ⲉⲙⲛ̄ ⲏⲡⲉ ⲉⲣⲟⲟⲩ Ⲁⲩⲱ ⲙⲡⲉⲛⲗⲟ ⲉⲛⲁϩⲉⲣⲁⲧⲛ̄ ⲉⲛϭⲱϣ⌈ⲧ⌉ ⲛ̄ⲥⲁ ⲡⲥⲱⲙⲁ ⲛ̄⌈ⲧ⌉ⲡⲁⲣⲑⲉⲛⲟⲥ · ϣ⌈ⲁⲛ⌉ⲧⲟⲩϩⲱⲛ ⲛ̄ⲙ̄ⲙ⌈ⲁϥ⌉ ϩⲙ̄ ⲡⲁⲏⲣ—Ⲁⲛⲟⲛ ⲇⲉ ⲙⲁⲩⲁⲁⲛ ⲁⲛ ⲡⲉⲛⲧⲁⲛⲛⲁⲩ ⲉⲛⲁⲓ · ⲁⲗⲗⲁ ⲛ̄ⲕⲉⲓⲟⲩⲇⲁⲓ ⲟⲛ ⲛ̄ⲧⲁⲩⲉⲓ ⲉⲃⲟⲗ ⲉⲉⲣⲡⲉⲑ⌈ⲟ⌉ⲟ⌈ⲩ⌉ ⲙ̄ⲡⲥⲱⲙⲁ ⲛ̄ⲧⲡⲁⲣⲑⲉⲛⲟⲥ · ⲉⲛⲉⲩⲑⲉⲱⲣⲉⲓ ⲛ̄ⲛⲁⲓ ⲧⲏⲣⲟⲩ
p. ? ⲛ̄ⲙ̄ⲙⲁⲛ | [6]⌈Ϩⲱⲥⲧⲉ ⲛ⌉ⲥ⌈ⲉ⌉ϫⲓⲥⲉ ⲛ̄ⲧⲉⲩⲥⲙⲏ ⲉⲩϫⲓϣⲕⲁⲕ ⲉⲃⲟⲗ ⲉⲩϫⲱ

Cod. Borg. CCLVIII

ⲙ̇ⲡⲥⲱⲙⲁ ⲛ̄ⲧⲡⲁⲣⲑⲉⲛⲟⲥ ⲉϥⲧⲁⲗⲏⲩ ⲉϫⲛ̄ ⲛ⌈ⲉ⌉ⲛ⌈ⲉⲓ⌉ⲟⲧ⌈ⲉ⌉ ⲛⲁⲡⲟⲥⲧⲟⲗ⌈ⲟⲥ⌉ ⲁ⌈ⲩ⌉ϩⲱⲗ ⲛ̄ⲙ̄ⲙⲁϥ ⲉϩⲣⲁϊ ⲉⲙⲡⲏⲩⲉ ⲉⲩϩⲩⲙⲛⲉⲩⲉ ϩⲁⲧⲉϥϩ⌈ⲏ⌉ ⲛ̄ϭⲓ ϩⲉⲛϣⲟ ⲛ̄ϣⲟ ⲙⲛ̄ ϩⲉⲛⲧⲃⲁ ⲛⲧⲃⲁ ⲛⲁⲅⲅⲉⲗⲟⲥ ⲉⲙⲛ̄ ⲏⲡⲉ ⲉⲣⲟⲟⲩ · — Ⲁⲩⲱ ⲙ̄ⲡⲉⲛⲗⲟ ⲉⲛⲁϩⲉⲣⲁⲧⲛ ⲉⲛϭⲱϣ̄ⲧ ⲛ̄ⲥⲱⲟⲩ · ϣⲁⲛⲧⲟⲩϩⲱⲛ ϩⲙ ⲡⲁⲏⲣ · Ⲁⲛⲟⲛ ⲇⲉ ⲙⲁⲩⲁⲁⲛ ⲁ̄ⲛ ⲁⲗⲗⲁ ⲛ̄ⲕⲉϊⲟⲩⲇⲁⲓ ⲟⲛ ⲛ̄ⲧⲁⲩⲉⲓ ⲉⲃⲟⲗ ⲉⲩⲟⲩⲱϣ ⲉⲣⲡ̄ⲉⲑⲟⲟⲩ ⲙ̄ⲡⲥⲱⲙⲁ ⲛ̄ⲧⲡⲁⲣ-
p. ⌈ⲗⲃ⌉ ⲑⲉⲛⲟⲥ ⲉⲛⲉⲩⲑⲉⲱⲣⲉⲓ ⲛ̄ⲛⲁϊ ϩⲱⲟⲩ | [6]ϩⲱⲥⲧⲉ ⲛ̄ⲥⲉϫⲓ⌈ⲥⲉ⌉ ⲛ⌈ⲧⲉⲩ⌉ⲥⲙⲏ ⲉⲩϫⲓϣⲕⲁⲕ ⲉⲃⲟⲗ ⲉⲩϫⲱ ⲙ̄ⲙⲟⲥ ϫⲉ ⲟⲩⲁ ⲡⲉ ⲡⲛⲟⲩⲧⲉ ⲙ̄ⲡⲓⲏ̄ⲗ ·

Cod. Borg. CCLIX*
p. ⲙⲉ

[6]ⲑⲉⲛⲟⲥ ⲉⲧⲟⲩⲁⲁⲃ ⲙⲁⲣⲓⲁ ⲉϥⲧⲁⲗⲏⲩ ⲉϫⲛ ⲡⲥⲱⲙⲁ ⲙⲡⲛⲓⲱⲧ ⲁⲡⲁ ⲡⲉⲧⲣⲟⲥ ⲙⲛ ⲓⲱϩⲁⲛⲛⲏⲥ ⲁⲩϩⲱⲗ ⲛⲙⲙⲁϥ ⲉϩⲣⲁⲓ ⲙⲡⲏⲩⲉ ⲉⲩϩⲩⲙⲛⲉⲩⲉ ϩⲁⲧⲉϥϩⲏ ⲛϭⲓ ϩⲛϣⲟ ⲉⲛϣⲟ ⲛⲁⲅⲅⲉⲗⲟⲥ Ⲁⲩⲱ ⲙⲡⲛⲗⲟ ⲉⲛⲁϩⲉⲣⲁⲧⲛ ⲉⲛϭⲱϣⲧ ⲛⲥⲱϥ Ⲁⲩⲱ ⲛϫⲓⲥⲙⲏ ⲉⲣⲟⲟⲩ ⲙⲛ ⲛⲉⲩϩⲩⲙⲛⲟⲥ ϣⲁ̄ⲛⲧⲟⲩϩⲱⲛ ϩⲙ ⲡⲁⲏⲣ · Ⲁⲛⲟⲛ ⲇⲉ ⲙⲁⲩⲁⲁⲛ ⲁⲛ ⲡⲉⲛⲧⲁⲛⲛⲁⲁⲩ ⲉⲣⲟⲟⲩ Ⲁⲗⲗⲁ ⲉⲛⲅⲉⲓⲟⲩⲇⲁⲓ ⲛⲧⲁⲩⲉⲓ ⲉⲃⲟⲗ ⲉⲉⲣⲡⲉⲑⲟⲟⲩ ⲉⲧⲡⲁⲣⲑⲉⲛⲟⲥ ⲉⲩⲑⲱⲣⲓ ⲛⲛⲁⲓ ⲧⲏⲣⲟⲩ ⲡⲉⲙⲙⲁⲛ [6]ϩⲱⲥⲇⲉ ⲉⲛⲥⲉ̇ϫⲓⲥⲉ ⲛⲧⲉⲩⲥⲙⲏ ⲉⲩϫⲓϣⲕⲁⲕ ⲉⲃⲟⲗ ⲉⲩ|ϫⲱ ⲙⲙⲟⲥ ϫⲉ ⲁⲟⲩⲁ

[a] ⲛ̄ϭⲓ ⲛ̄ϣⲟⲛ̄ϣⲟ

and they approached, and straightway[a] caught away the body of the Virgin[A], which was placed † on the body of[b] our holy[c] fathers *the* apostles*[B]. And my father Peter and my father John looked at her, when[dΓ] they flew with her[eΔ] to the heavens§; whilst there were singing before her[eΔ] thousand thousands and ten thousand ten thousands[E] of angels without number[Z]. And we did not leave standing and looking at the body of the Virgin[fH], until they were hidden with it[gΘ] in the air. And *it was* not we alone who saw these things[hI], but the Jews also, who came forth to do[i] harm to the body of[K] the Virgin, were beholding[Λ] all these things with us[j]; [6]so that they lifted

† Lit. *being placed* * Or *our holy fathers the apostles* § See note

Variants in Cod. Borg. CCLVIII.

[a] om. *straightway* [b] om. *the body of* [c] om. *holy* [d] om. *And my father Peter and my father John looked at her, when* [e] *her*] *it* [f] *at the body of the Virgin*] *at them* [g] om. *with it* [h] *And* it was *not we alone who saw these things*] *And not we alone* [i] *to do*] *wishing to do* [j] *all these things with us*] *these things also*

Variants in Cod. Borg. CCLIX*.

[A] *Virgin*] *holy Virgin Mary* [B] *our holy fathers* the *apostles*] *our father Apa Peter and John* [Γ] om. *And my father Peter and my father John looked at her, when* [Δ] *her*] *it* [E] om. *and ten thousand ten thousands* [Z] om. *without number* [H] *at the body of the Virgin*] *at it, and listening to them and their hymns* [Θ] om. *with it* [I] *these things*] *them* [K] om. *the body of* [Λ] *were beholding*] were *beholding*

NOTE. For another leaf of Cod. Borg. CCLIX* see p. 70 ff. The pages here are numbered 45, 46: the pages given before are 35, 36. The four intervening leaves are lost.

Cod. Clarend. b 3 15

ⲙ̄ⲙⲟⲥ ϫⲉ ⲟⲩⲁ ⲡⲉ ⲡⲛⲟⲩⲧⲉ ⲙ̄ⲡⲓⲏ̄ⲗ̄* ⲡⲉⲛ̄ⲧⲁϥⲧⲛ̄ⲛⲟⲟⲩ ⲙ̄ⲡⲉϥϣⲏⲣⲉ
ⲉⲡⲕⲟⲥⲙⲟⲥ · Ⲁⲩⲱ ⲁⲛϣⲱⲡⲉ ⲛⲉⲛⲟⲭⲟⲥ ⲛⲟⲩⲛⲟϭ ⲛ̄ⲛⲟⲃⲉ · ⲛⲁⲧⲕⲱ
(c. XVII) ⲉⲃⲟⲗ · [4]ⲁⲛⲟⲛ ⲇⲉ ⲁⲛⲕⲧⲟⲛ ⲉϩⲟⲩⲛ ⲉⲡⲏⲓ ⲉⲧⲛ̄ϣⲟⲟⲡ ⲛ̄ϩⲏⲧϥ —
Ⲁⲛⲃⲱⲕ ⲇⲉ ⲉϩⲟⲩⲛ ⲁⲛϩⲙⲟⲟⲥ ⲉϩⲣⲁⲓ ⲉⲛⲗⲩⲡⲉⲓ · ⲉϫⲉⲛ ⲧϭⲓⲙ̄ⲡⲱⲣϫ̄
ⲉⲣⲟⲛ ⲛ̄ⲧⲡⲁⲣⲑⲉⲛⲟⲥ ⲉⲧⲟⲩⲁⲁⲃ ⲙⲁⲣⲓⲁ Ⲁⲩⲱ ⲡⲉⲛⲥⲟⲛⲥ ⲙ̄ⲡⲛⲟⲩⲧⲉ
ⲙ̄ⲡⲉϩⲟⲟⲩ ⲙⲛ̄ ⲧⲉⲩϣⲏ ϫⲉⲕⲁⲥ ⲉϥⲉⲛⲓⲑⲉ ⲙ̄ⲙⲟⲛ · ⲛ̄ϥⲧⲣⲛ̄ⲛⲁⲩ ⲉⲣⲟⲥ
(c. XVIII) ⲛ̄ⲕⲉⲥⲟⲡ | ⲕⲁⲧⲁ ⲑⲉ ⲛ̄ⲧⲁϥⲉⲣⲏⲧ ⲛⲁⲛ [1]Ⲁⲥϣⲱⲡⲉ ⲇⲉ ⲙ̄ⲡⲛⲁⲩ
ⲙ̄ⲡⲟⲩⲟⲉⲓⲛ ⲙ̄ⲡⲙⲉϩϣⲙⲟⲩⲛ ⲛ̄ϩⲟⲟⲩ ϫⲓⲛⲧⲁⲥⲉⲓ ⲉⲃⲟⲗ ϩⲛ̄ ⲥⲱⲙⲁ

Cod. Borg. CCLVIII

Ⲡⲉⲛⲧⲁϥⲧⲛ̄ⲛⲟⲟⲩ ⲙ̄ⲡⲉϥϣⲏⲣⲉ ⲉⲡⲕⲟⲥⲙⲟⲥ ⲁⲩⲱ ⲛⲁⲙⲉ ⲁⲛϣⲱⲡⲉ
(c. XVII) ⲛⲉⲛⲟⲭⲟⲥ ⲛⲟⲩⲛⲟϭ ⲛⲛⲟⲃⲉ ⲛⲁⲧⲕⲱ ⲉⲃⲟⲗ · [4]Ⲁⲛⲟⲛ ⲇⲉ ⲁⲛⲕⲧⲟⲛ
ⲉϩⲟⲩⲛ ⲉⲡⲏï ⲉⲛⲉⲛϣⲟⲟⲡ ⌜ⲛϩⲏ⌝ⲧϥ ⲁⲛϩⲙⲟⲟⲥ ⌜ⲉϩ⌝ⲣⲁⲓ ⲉⲛⲗⲩⲡⲉⲓ
ⲁⲩⲱ ⌜ⲉ⌝ⲛ̄ⲣ̄ϩⲏⲃⲉ ⲉϫⲛ ⲧϭⲓⲛⲡⲱⲣϫ ⲉⲃⲟⲗ ⲙⲙⲟⲛ ⲛ̄ⲧⲡⲁⲣⲑⲉⲛⲟⲥ
ⲉⲧⲟⲩⲁⲁⲃ · Ⲁⲩⲱ ⲡⲉⲛⲥⲟⲛⲥ̄ⲛ̄ ⲙⲡⲛⲟⲩⲧⲉ ⲙ́ⲡⲉϩⲟⲟⲩ ⲙ̄ⲛ ⲧⲉⲩϣⲏ ϫⲉ
ⲉϥⲛⲁⲛⲓⲑⲉ ⲙ̄ⲙⲟⲛ ⲛϥⲧⲣⲉⲛⲛⲁⲩ ⲉⲣⲟⲥ ⲛⲕⲉⲥⲟⲡ ⲕⲁⲧⲁ ⲑⲉ ⲛ̇ⲧⲁϥⲉⲣⲏⲧ
(c. XVIII) ⲛⲁⲛ · (punct post ⲛ rubro script) [1]Ⲁⲥϣⲱⲡⲉ ⲇⲉ ⲙ̄ⲡⲙⲉϩϣⲙⲟⲩⲛ
(littera ut vid inter ⲙ tert et ⲟ erasa fortasse pr man) ⲛ̄ϩⲟⲟⲩ
ϫⲓⲛⲧⲁⲥⲉⲓ ⲉⲃⲟⲗ ϩⲛ̄ ⲥⲱⲙⲁ ⲙ̄ⲡⲛⲁⲩ ⲙ̄ⲡⲟⲩⲟⲉⲓⲛ ⲁϥⲟⲩⲱⲛϩ ⲛⲁⲛ

Cod. Borg. CCLIX*

ⲡⲉ ⲡⲛⲟⲩⲧⲉ ⲙⲡⲓ̄ⲏ̄ⲗ ⲛⲛⲧⲁϥⲧⲛⲛⲟⲟⲩ ⲙⲡⲉϥϣⲏⲣⲉ ⲉⲡⲕⲟⲥⲙⲟⲥ Ⲁⲩⲱ
(c. XVII) ⲛⲁⲙⲉ ⲁⲛϣⲟⲡⲉ ⲛⲉⲛⲟⲭⲟⲥ ⲉⲩⲛⲟϭ ⲛⲛⲟⲃⲉ ⲛⲁⲧⲕⲱ ⲉⲃⲟⲗ [4]ⲁⲛⲟⲛ
ⲇⲉ ⲁⲛⲕⲧⲟⲛ ⲉϩⲟⲩⲛ ⲉⲡⲡⲏⲓ ⲉⲛϣⲟⲟⲡ ⲉⲛϩⲏⲧϥ Ⲁⲛϩⲙⲟⲟⲥ ⲉϩⲣⲁⲓ
ⲉⲛⲣϩⲏⲃⲉ ⲉϫⲉⲛ ⲧϭⲓⲛⲡⲱⲣⲉϫ ⲉⲣⲟⲛ ⲉⲛⲧⲡⲁⲣⲑⲉⲛⲟⲥ ⲉⲧⲟⲩⲁⲁⲃ
ⲙⲁⲣⲓⲁ Ⲁⲩⲱ ⲡⲛⲥⲟⲛⲥ ⲉⲙⲡⲛⲟⲩⲧⲉ ⲙⲡⲉϩⲟⲟⲩ ⲙⲛ ⲧⲉⲩϣⲏ ⲉⲧⲣⲉϥ-
ⲛⲓⲑⲉ ⲉⲙⲙⲟⲛ ⲧⲛⲛⲁⲁⲩ ⲉⲣⲟⲥ ⲛⲅⲉⲥⲟⲛ ⲕⲁⲧⲁ ⲑⲉ ⲛⲧⲁϥⲉⲣⲏⲧ ⲛⲁⲛ
(c. XVIII) [1]Ⲁⲥϣⲱⲡⲉ ⲇⲉ ⲉⲙⲡⲛⲁⲩ ⲙⲡⲟⲩⲱⲉⲓⲛ ⲙⲡⲙⲉϩϣⲙⲟⲛ (sic) | ⲛϩⲟⲟⲩ
p. ⲙ̄ⲋ̄ ϫⲓⲛ ⲉⲛⲧⲁⲥⲉⲓ ⲉⲃⲟⲗ ϩⲛ ⲥⲱⲙⲁ Ⲁϥⲟⲩⲱⲛⲉϩ ⲛⲁⲛ ⲉⲃⲟⲗ ⲛϭⲓ ⲡⲛⲣⲣⲟ

* ⲡⲛⲟⲩⲧⲉⲙ̄ⲡⲓⲏ̄ⲗ̄

up their voice, crying out and saying, One is the God of cf. Mc XII 29*, 32*
Israel, who sent His Son into the world. And[a A] we have become guilty of a great *and* unpardonable sin.

XVII. [4]And we returned into the house[B] wherein we dwelt*[b], and we went in[c Γ], and we sat down, grieving[d Δ] for the separation from[e] us of the holy Virgin Mary[f]: and we were beseeching[g] God day and night that He would hearken to us§ and cause us to see her[E] again, even as He promised us.

XVIII. Now it came to pass at the hour of the light, on the eighth day after she went forth from *the* body[h], there

* Lit. *wherein we dwell* § Or perhaps, as the verb is followed by an accusative, *that He would assure us*. See note

Variants in Cod. Borg. CCLVIII.

[a] *And*] *And truly* [b] *we dwelt*] *we were dwelling* [c] om. *and we went in* [d] *grieving*] *grieving and mourning* [e] The preposition here translated *from* is the same as that found in the corresponding Bohairic, but it is a different one to that employed in the two other MSS [f] om. *Mary* [g] The verb here translated *beseeching* is a reduplicated form of the simple root employed in the two other MSS [h] *at the hour of the light, on the eighth day after she went forth from* the *body*] *on the eighth day after she went forth from* the *body, at the hour of the light*

Variants in Cod. Borg. CCLIX*.

[A] *And*] *And truly* [B] *into the house*] *into our house* [Γ] om. *and we went in* [Δ] *grieving*] *mourning* [E] *and cause us to see her*] *that we might see her*

Cod. Clarend. b 3 15 ⲁϥⲟⲩⲱⲛϩ̄ ⲛⲁⲛ ⲉⲃⲟⲗ ⲛ̄ϭⲓ ⲡⲉⲡ̄ⲣ̄ⲣⲟ ⲛ̄ϩⲟⲩⲛ ⲉⲡⲏⲓ ⲉⲛϣⲟⲟⲡ
ⲛ̄ϩⲏⲧϥ ⲡⲉϫⲁϥ ⲛⲁⲛ ϫⲉ ϯⲣⲏⲛⲏ ⲛⲏⲧⲛ̄ ⲁⲩⲱ ϯⲣⲏⲛⲏ ⲛⲧⲁ ⲡⲁⲓⲱⲧ
ⲧⲁⲁⲥ ⲛⲁⲓ ϯϯ ⲙ̄ⲙⲟⲥ ⲛⲏⲧⲛ̄ [2]ⲉⲧⲃⲉ ⲟⲩ ⲧⲉⲧⲛ̄ϣⲟⲟⲡ ϩⲙ̄ ⲡⲛⲟϭ
ⲛ̄ⲙ̄ⲕⲁϩ ⲛ̄ϩⲏⲧ [3]ⲡⲉϫⲉ ⲡⲁⲓⲱⲧ ⲡⲉⲧⲣⲟⲥ ⲛⲁϥ ·ϫⲉ ⲡⲁϫⲟⲉⲓⲥ ⲁⲩⲱ
ⲡⲁⲛⲟⲩⲧⲉ· ⲉⲛⲟⲩⲱⲗ̄ⲥ̄ ⲛ̄ϩⲏⲧ ⲉϫⲙ̄ ⲡⲥⲱⲕ ⲉⲃⲟⲗ ⲛ̄ⲧⲉⲕⲙⲁⲁⲩ[a] ⲙ̄ⲡⲁⲣ-
§ Cod. Borg. CCLVIII ⲑⲉⲛⲟⲥ· ⲙ̄ⲡⲉⲕⲁⲁⲛ ⲛⲁϩⲓⲟⲥ ⲉⲧⲣⲛ̄ⲛⲁⲩ ⲉⲣⲟⲥ· ⲛ̄ⲕⲉⲥⲟⲛ | §ϫⲓⲛⲧⲁⲥⲉⲓ
ⲉⲃⲟⲗ ϩⲛ̄ ⲥⲱⲙⲁ ·[b] ⲟⲩⲧⲉ ⲙ̄ⲡⲉⲕⲧⲁⲙⲟⲛ ϫⲉ ⲛ̄ⲧⲁⲕⲕⲁ ⲡⲉⲥⲥⲱⲙⲁ
ⲧⲱⲛ ϫⲉ ⲉⲛⲛⲁⲧⲁϣⲉⲟⲉⲓϣ ⲙⲡⲁï ⲛ̄ⲛ̄ϣⲏⲣⲉ ⲛ̄ⲛ̄ⲣⲱⲙⲉ [4]ⲁ ⲡⲥⲱⲧⲏⲣ
ⲟⲩⲱϣⲃ̄ ⲉϥϫⲱ ⲙ̄ⲙⲟⲥ ϫⲉ ⲡⲉⲥⲥⲱⲙⲁ ⲙⲉⲛ ⲁ ⲡⲁⲉⲓⲱⲧ ⲟⲩⲉϩⲥⲁϩⲛⲉ

Cod. Borg. CCLVIII ⲉⲃⲟⲗ ⲛ̄ϭⲓ ⲓ̄ⲥ̄ ⲡⲉⲡ̄ⲣ̄ⲣⲟ ⲛ̄ϩⲟⲩⲛ ⲙ̄ⲡⲏï ⲉⲛⲉⲛϣⲟⲟⲡ ⲛ̄ϩⲏⲧϥ· ⲁⲩⲱ |
ⲡⲉϫⲁϥ ⲛⲁⲛ ϫⲉ ϯⲣⲏⲛⲏ ⲛⲏⲧⲛ ⲛⲁⲁⲡⲟⲥⲧⲟⲗⲟⲥ ⲉⲧⲧⲁⲓⲏⲩ· ϯⲣⲏⲛⲏ
ⲛ̄ⲧⲁ ⲡⲁⲉⲓⲱⲧ ⲧⲁⲁⲥ ⲛⲁï ϯϯ ⲙ̄ⲙⲟⲥ ⲛⲏⲧⲛ· [2]ⲉⲧⲃⲉ ⲟⲩ ⲧⲉⲧⲛ̄ϣⲟⲟⲡ
ϩⲙ̄ ⲡⲉⲓⲛⲟϭ ⲛⲱⲕⲙ̄ ⲛ̄ⲧⲉⲓϩⲉ ⲧⲏⲣⲥ· [3]ⲡⲉϫⲉ ⲡⲉⲧⲣⲟⲥ ϫⲉ ⲱ ⲡⲁϫⲟⲉⲓⲥ
ⲉⲛⲟⲩⲟⲗ̄ⲥ̄ ⲛ̄ϩⲏⲧ ⲉϫⲙ̄ ⲡⲥⲱⲕ ⲉⲃⲟⲗ ⲛ̄ⲧⲉⲕⲙⲁⲁⲩ ϫⲉ ⲙⲡⲉⲕⲁⲁⲛ
ⲛ̄ⲙ̄ⲡϣⲁ ⲉⲧⲣⲉⲛⲛⲁⲩ ⲉⲣⲟⲥ ⲛ̄ⲕⲉⲥⲟⲛ-

Cod. Borg. CCLIX* ϩⲙ ⲡⲏⲓ ⲛϣⲟⲟⲛ ⲉⲛϩⲏⲧⲃ· (cod ⲉⲛ : ϩⲏⲧⲃ̄·) ⲡⲉϫⲁⲁϥ ⲛⲁⲛ ϫⲉ
ⲧⲓⲣⲏⲛⲏ ⲛⲏⲧⲛ ⲛⲁⲁⲡⲟⲥⲧⲟⲗⲟⲥ ⲉⲧⲁⲓⲏⲩ (sic) ⲧⲓⲣⲏ̈ⲛⲏ ⲛⲧⲁ ⲡⲁïⲱⲧ
ⲧⲁⲁⲥ ⲛⲁⲓ ⲧⲓⲧⲓ ⲙⲙⲟⲥ ⲛⲏⲧⲛ [2]ⲉⲧⲃⲉ ⲟⲩ ⲉⲧⲏⲧⲛϣⲟⲟⲛ ϩⲙ ⲡⲛⲟϭ
ⲡⲉⲙⲕⲁϩ ⲛϩⲏⲧ ⲙⲉⲛ ⲡⲛⲟϭ ⲛⲱⲕⲙ ⲛⲧⲓϩⲉ ⲧⲏⲣⲥ [3]ⲡⲉϫⲉ ⲡⲁⲓⲱⲧ
ⲡⲉⲧⲣⲟⲥ ⲙⲡⲥⲱⲧⲏⲣ ϫⲉ ⲡⲁϫⲟⲉⲓⲥ ⲁⲩⲱ ⲡⲁⲛⲟⲩⲧⲉ ⲛⲟⲩⲱⲗⲉⲥ ⲉⲛϩⲏⲧ
ⲉϫⲛ ⲡⲥⲟⲕ ⲉⲃⲟⲗ ⲛⲧⲉⲕⲙⲁⲁⲩ ⲙⲡⲁⲣⲑⲉⲛⲟⲥ ϫⲉ ⲙⲡⲉⲕⲁⲁⲛ ⲛⲁϩⲓⲟⲥ
ⲉⲧⲣⲛⲛⲁⲩ ⲉⲣⲟⲟⲥ (ⲣ in marg) ⲛⲕⲉⲥⲟⲛ ϫⲓⲛ ⲉⲛⲧⲁⲥⲃⲱⲕ ⲉⲃⲟⲗ
ϩⲓⲧⲟⲟⲧⲛ ⲟⲩⲇⲉ ⲙⲡⲉⲕ|ⲧⲁⲙⲟⲛ ϫⲉ ⲛⲧⲁⲕⲕⲁ ⲡⲉⲥⲥⲱⲙⲁ ⲧⲟⲛ ϫⲉ-
ⲕⲁⲁⲥ ⲉⲛⲉⲧⲁϣⲉⲟⲉⲓϣ ⲙⲙⲟϥ ⲛⲛϣⲏⲣⲉ ⲉⲛⲛⲣⲱⲙⲉ [4]ⲁϥⲟⲩⲱϣϥ ⲛ̄ϭⲓ
ⲡⲥⲱⲧⲏⲣ ϫⲉ ⲡⲉⲥⲥⲱⲙⲁ ⲙⲛ ⲁ ⲡⲁⲓⲱⲧ ⲟⲩⲛϩⲥⲁϩⲛⲉ ϫⲉⲉⲓⲁⲁⲥ

[a] ⲉⲃⲟⲗⲛ̄ⲧⲉⲕⲙⲁⲁⲩ [b] punct. rubro script.

appeared to us our King[a] within[A] the house wherein we
dwelt*[b], and said unto us, Peace be unto you[c][B], and[d][Γ] the peace cf. Jn xiv 27
which My Father gave unto Me, I give unto you. 2 Where-
fore are ye in this great grief of heart[e][Δ]? 3 My father[f] Peter
said to Him[g][E], My Lord and my God[h], we are distressed for
the death§ of Thy virgin mother. Thou[i][Z] hast not made us
worthy[j] to see her again since she went forth from *the* body[H],
neither hast Thou shewn us where her body is laid[Θ], that we
may proclaim this[I] to the sons of men. 4 The Saviour answered
saying[K], Her body My Father hath commanded to lay[Λ]

* Lit. *wherein we dwell* § Or *departure*

Variants in Cod. Borg. CCLVIII.

[a] *our King*] *Jesus our King* [b] *we dwelt*] *we were dwelling* [c] *you*] *you, My honourable* (or *glorious*) *apostles* [d] om. *and* [e] *in this great grief of heart*] *in this great sadness of* (or *in*) *all this wise* [f] om. *My father* [g] om. *to Him* [h] *My Lord and my God*] *O my Lord* [i] *Thy virgin mother. Thou*] *Thy mother; because Thou* [j] *worthy*] A Coptic word is here used, in the two other MSS a Greek word

Variants in Cod. Borg. CCLIX*.

[A] *within*] *in* [B] *you*] *you, My honourable* (or *glorious*) *apostles* [Γ] om. *and* [Δ] *in this great grief of heart*] *in this great grief of heart and this great sadness of* (or *in*) *all this wise* [E] *to Him*] *to the Saviour* [Z] *Thy virgin mother. Thou*] *Thy virgin mother; because Thou* [H] *from the body*] *from us* [Θ] *where her body is laid*] *where Thou hast laid her body* [I] *this*] *it* [K] om. *saying* [Λ] *to lay*] *that it be taken and laid*

NOTE. Cod. Clarend. b 3 15 breaks off in the middle of verse 3, after the words *Thou hast not made us worthy to see her again.* The rest of verse 3, together with verse 4, is found in Cod. Borg. CCLVIII and Cod. Borg. CCLIX*; the former MS breaks off in verse 5 after the words *But now behold I have sent for her.*

ⲉⲕⲗⲁⲁϥ ϩⲁ ⲡϣⲏⲛ ⲙ̀ⲡⲱⲛ̀ϩ ⲉⲧϩ̀ⲛ ⲧⲙⲏⲧⲉ ⲙ̀ⲡⲡⲁⲣⲁ̀ⲇⲓⲥⲟⲥ ϫⲉ
ⲁϥϣⲱⲡⲉ ⲙ̄ⲙⲁⲛⲟⲩⲱϩ ⲙ̄ⲡⲉϥϣⲏⲣⲉ ⲉⲧⲉ ⲁⲛⲟⲕ ⲡⲉ· [5]Ⲧⲉⲛⲟⲩ ⲇⲉ
§ Cod. Borg. CCLIX* ⲉⲓⲥ ϩⲏⲏⲧⲉ ⲁⲓⲧⲛⲛⲟⲟⲩ ⲛⲥⲱⲥ | §Ϫⲉⲕⲁⲥ ⲉⲥⲉⲟⲩⲱⲛⲉϩ ⲛⲏⲧⲛ ⲉⲃⲟⲗ
Ⲁⲩⲱ ⲛⲉⲥϫⲱ ⲉⲣⲟⲧⲛ ⲉⲛⲛⲧⲁⲓⲟ ⲛⲧⲁⲥⲛⲁⲁⲩ[a] ⲉⲣⲟⲟⲩ |

Cod. Borg. CCLIX* ⲉⲩⲉϫⲓⲧϥ ⲛⲥⲉⲩⲁⲁϥ ϩⲁ ⲡϣⲏⲛ ⲙⲡⲱⲛϩ ⲡⲁⲓ ⲉϥϩⲉⲛ ⲧⲙⲏⲧⲉ ⲙⲡⲁⲣⲁⲧⲓⲥⲟⲥ ⲉⲃⲟⲗ ϫⲉ ⲁϥϣⲟⲡⲉ ⲉⲙⲙⲁⲛⲟⲩⲱϩ ⲉⲙⲡⲉϥⲙⲉⲣⲓⲧ ⲉⲛϣⲏⲣⲉ· ⲉⲧⲉ ⲁⲛⲟⲕ ⲡⲉ Ⲧⲉⲛⲟⲩ ⲇⲉ ⲉⲓⲥ ϩⲏⲏⲧⲉ ⲁⲓⲧⲛⲟⲟⲩ ⲉⲛ̀ⲥⲟⲥ

[a] ⲛⲧⲁ⌜ϥ⌝ⲛⲁⲁⲩ

beneath the tree of life which *is* in the midst of Paradise[a][A], cf. Ge III 3*, 24
because it was *a* dwelling place of His Son[B], even of Me.
[5]But now behold I have sent for her, in order that she may
be manifested to you, and may tell you the honours which
she has seen...

[a] Lit. *the Paradise*

Variants in Cod. Borg. CCLIX*.

[A] The word *Paradise* is used without an article [B] *His Son*] *His beloved Son*

THE FALLING ASLEEP OF MARY.

Discourse of Theodosius.

Cod. Vat. LXI 4 p. [ⲁ] Ⲟⲩⲗⲟⲅⲟⲥ ⳾ ⲉⲁϥⲧⲁⲟⲩⲟϥ ⲛϫⲉ ⲡⲉⲛⲧⲣⲓⲙⲁⲕⲁⲣⲓⲟⲥ ⲛ̀ⲓⲱⲧ ⲁⲃⲃⲁ ⲑⲉⲟ̀ⲇⲟⲥⲓⲟⲥ[a] ⲡⲓⲁⲣⲭⲏⲉⲡⲓⲥⲕⲟⲡⲟⲥ ⲛ̀ⲧⲉ ⲣⲁⲕⲟϯ ⳾ Ⲟⲩⲟϩ ⲡⲓⲟⲙⲟⲗⲟⲅⲓⲧⲏⲥ ⳾ ⲉ̀ⲧⲉⲣⲫⲟⲣⲓⲛ ⲙ̀ⲡⲭ̅ⲥ̅ ⳾ ⲉⲁϥⲧⲁⲟⲩⲟϥ ⲇⲉ ⲉ̀ⲧⲁⲛⲁⲗⲩⲙⲯⲓⲥ ⲛ̀ⲧⲉⲛⲟ̅ⲥ̅ ⲧⲏⲣⲉⲛ ⳾ ϯⲑⲉⲟ̀ⲧⲟⲕⲟⲥ ⲉ̀ⲑⲟⲩⲁⲃ ⲙⲁⲣⲓⲁ̀ ⳾ ⲛ̀ⲥⲟⲩ ⲓ̅ⲉ̅ ⲙ̀ⲡⲓⲁ̀ⲃⲟⲧ ⲙⲉⲥⲟⲩⲣⲏ ⳾ Ⲉⲁϥⲉⲣϩⲏⲧⲥ ⲓⲥϫⲉⲛ ϯⲟ̀ⲓⲕⲟⲛⲟⲙⲓⲁ̀ ⲛ̀ⲧⲉ ⲡⲭ̅ⲥ̅ ⳾ ϣⲁ ⲡϫⲱⲕ ⲉ̀ⲃⲟⲗ ⲛ̀ⲧⲁⲓⲁ̀ⲅⲓⲁ̀ ⲙ̀ⲡⲁⲣⲑⲉⲛⲟⲥ ⳾ ⲛⲉⲙ ⲧⲉⲥⲁⲛⲁⲗⲩⲙⲯⲓⲥ ⲉ̀ⲑⲟⲩⲁⲃ ⳾ Ⲉⲧⲁϥⲧⲁⲟⲩⲟ̀ ⲇⲉ ⲙ̀ⲡⲁⲓⲗⲟⲅⲟⲥ ⳾ ϧⲉⲛ ϯϧⲁⲏ ⲛ̀ⲣⲟⲙⲡⲓ ⲉ̀ⲧⲉϥⲛⲁⲙ̀ⲧⲟⲛ ⲙ̀ⲙⲟϥ ⲛ̀ϧⲏⲧⲥ ⳾ ϧⲉⲛ ⲟⲩϩⲓⲣⲏⲛⲏ ⲛ̀ⲧⲉ ⲫ̅ϯ̅ ⲁ̀ⲙⲏⲛ :

. . . .

p. ⲓⲍ I. [1]Ⲁϥϫⲉⲕ ϩⲱⲃ ⲛⲓⲃⲉⲛ ⲉⲃⲟⲗ ⲛ̀ⲧⲉ ϯⲙⲉⲧⲣⲱⲙⲓ[b] × | ϣⲁⲧⲉⲛ
ⲫⲛⲟⲃⲓ ⲙ̀ⲙⲁⲩⲁⲧϥ × [2]Ⲁϥⲓ̀ ϩⲓϫⲉⲛ ⲡⲓ⳨ ⳾ ⲁϥϣⲉⲡⲙ̀ⲕⲁϩ ϧⲉⲛ ⲧⲉⲥⲁⲣⲝ
ⲉⲑⲃⲏⲧⲉⲛ ⳾ ⲁϥϫⲉⲙϯⲡⲓ ⲙ̀ⲫⲙⲟⲩ ⲉ̀ϩⲣⲏⲓ ⲉ̀ϫⲱⲛ ⳾ ϥⲟⲓ ⲇⲉ ⲛⲁⲧⲉⲙ-
ⲕⲁϩ ⳾ ⲟⲩⲟϩ ⲛ̀ⲁⲑⲙⲟⲩ ⳾ ϩⲱⲥ ⲛⲟⲩϯ ϣⲁ ⲉ̀ⲛⲉϩ × [3]Ⲁϥⲧⲱⲛϥ ⲉⲃⲟⲗ
ϧⲉⲛ ⲛⲏ ⲉⲑⲙⲱⲟⲩⲧ ⳾ ⲁϥϣⲉ ⲛⲁϥ ⲉ̀ϧⲟⲩⲛ ϣⲁ ⲛⲉϥⲙⲁⲑⲏⲧⲏⲥ ⳾
ⲉ̀ⲣⲉ ⲛⲓⲣⲱⲟⲩ ϣⲟⲧⲉⲙ ⳾ ⲁϥϯ ⲛⲱⲟⲩ ⲛ̀ⲧⲉϥϩⲓⲣⲏⲛⲏ ⳾ [4]Ⲡϫⲱⲕ ⲇⲉ
ⲛ̀ϩⲙ̅ ⲛⲉϩⲟⲟⲩ ⳾ ⲁⲥⲓ̀ ⲛ̀ϫⲉ ⲧⲉϥⲁⲛⲁⲗⲩⲙⲯⲓⲥ ⲉⲑⲟⲩⲁⲃ = ⳾ [5]ⲁϥϭⲓ
ⲛⲛⲉϥⲙⲁⲑⲏⲧⲏⲥ ⲉⲛϣⲱⲓ ⲉ̀ϫⲉⲛ ⲡⲓⲧⲱⲟⲩ ⲛ̀ⲧⲉ ⲛⲓϫⲱⲓⲧ ⳾ ⲁϥϥⲁⲓ
ⲛ̀ⲛⲉϥⲃⲁⲗ ⲉⲛϣⲱⲓ ⲉⲧⲫⲉ ⳾ ⲁϥⲥⲙⲟⲩ ⲉ̀ⲣⲱⲟⲩ ⳾ ⲁϥϯ ⲛⲱⲟⲩ ⲛ̀ϯⲙⲉⲧϩⲏⲧ

[a] ⲟⲇⲟⲥ sup. ras. [b] punct. sup. ⲧ ut vid.

THE FALLING ASLEEP OF MARY.

Discourse of Theodosius.

A discourse which our thrice blessed father Abba Theodosius, the archbishop of Alexandria and the confessor who bore Christ, delivered. Now he delivered it concerning the assumption of the Lady of us all, the holy God-bearer Mary, on the sixteenth of the month Mesoure; beginning from the incarnation[a] of Christ unto the death[b] of this holy Virgin and her holy assumption. And he delivered this discourse in the last year wherein he was about to die[c]; in the[d] peace of God, Amen.[e]

. . . .

I. He accomplished every work of mankind, sin only cf. He iv 15
excepted. [2]He went on to the cross: He suffered pain in
the flesh for our sakes: He tasted death on our behalf. But
He is painless and deathless as God for ever. [3]He rose from
the dead. He went in unto His disciples, the doors being cf. Jn xx 26
shut, and gave them His peace. [4]And *at* the end of forty cf. Ac i 2, 12
days came His holy assumption. [5]He took His disciples up
into the mount of Olives. He lifted up His eyes to heaven, cf. Lc xxiv 50; Jn xvii 1
and blessed them, and gave them oneness of heart and His

[a] Lit. *dispensation* [b] Or *consummation* [c] Lit. *rest*
[d] Lit. *a* [e] I have omitted here fifteen pages. See introduction

ⲛⲟⲩⲱⲧ ⳾ ⲛⲉⲙ ⲡⲉϥⲛⲟⲙⲟⲥ ⲉⲑⲟⲩⲁⲃ = – 6Ⲓⲧⲁ ⲡⲉϫⲁϥ ⲙ̀ⲡⲉⲧⲣⲟⲥ ⳾
ϫⲉ ⲡⲉⲧⲣⲟⲥ ⲡⲁⲉ̀ⲡⲓⲥⲕⲟⲡⲟⲥ ⳾ ⲕⲓⲣⲓ ⲁⲛ ⲙ̀ⲫⲙⲉⲩⲓ̀ ⳾ ϫⲉ̀[a] ⲁⲓⲙⲟⲩϯ
ⲉ̀ⲣⲟⲕ ⲙⲡⲓⲥⲛⲟⲩ ⳾ ϫⲉ ⲥⲓⲙⲱⲛ ⲃⲁⲣⲓⲱⲛⲁ ⳾ ⲉ̀ⲧⲉ ⲫⲁⲓ ⲡⲉ ϫⲉ ⲁⲓⲁ̀ⲓⲕ
ⲛ̀ϣⲏⲣⲓ ⲛ̀ϯϭⲣⲟⲙⲡⲓ ⳾ ⲉ̀ⲧⲉ ⲑⲁ̀ⲓ[b] ⲧⲉ ⲧⲁⲙⲁⲩ ⲉⲧⲥⲙⲁⲣⲱⲟⲩⲧ ⳾
7Ⲗⲟⲓⲡⲟⲛ ϣⲱⲡⲓ ⲉⲕⲙⲏⲛ ⲉ̅ⲣⲟⲥ ⳾ ϣⲁⲧⲉⲥϫⲱⲕ ⲉⲃⲟⲗ ⳾ ⲛ̀ⲧⲉⲥⲥⲙⲟⲩ
ⲉ̀ⲣⲱⲧⲉⲛ ⳾ 8Ⲓⲧⲁ ⲟⲛ ⲡⲉϫⲁϥ ⲛ̀ⲓⲱⲁⲛⲛⲏⲥ ⳾ ϫⲉ ⲓⲱⲁⲛⲛⲏⲥ ⲡⲁⲙⲉⲛ-
p. ιη ⲣⲓⲧ ⳾ ⲁ̀ⲣⲓⲫⲙⲉⲩⲓ̅ ϫⲉ ϯⲙⲉⲓ̈[c] ⲙ̀ⲙⲟⲕ ⳾ ⲉⲑⲃⲉ ⲫⲁⲓ ⲁⲓ|ⲧⲟ̀ⲩⲃⲟⲕ[d] ⳾
ⲁⲓⲱⲗⲓ ⲉ̀ⲃⲟⲗ ϩⲁⲣⲟⲕ ⲛ̀ⲑⲙⲁⲑⲟⲩⲓ ⲛ̅ⲧⲉ ⲡⲓϩⲟϥ ⳾ 9Ⲧⲟ ⲗⲟⲓⲡⲟⲛ ⲙⲟⲩⲛ
ⲉ̀ⲧⲁⲙⲁⲩ ⳾ ⲕⲁⲧⲁ ⲫⲣⲏϯ ⲉ̀ⲧⲉⲕⲙⲏⲛ ⲉ̀ⲣⲟⲓ ⳾ ϣⲁⲧⲉⲥϫⲱⲕ ⲉⲃⲟⲗ ⳾
ⲛⲧⲉⲕϣⲁϣⲛⲓ ⲉ̀ⲡⲉⲥⲥⲙⲟⲩ = × 10Ⲁⲣⲓⲫⲙⲉⲩⲓ̅ ϫⲉ ⲁⲓⲧⲏⲓⲥ ⲛ̀ⲁⲕ ⳾
ⲉⲓⲁ̀ϣⲓ ⲉⲡⲓⲥⲧⲁⲩⲣⲟⲥ ⳾ ⲉⲑⲣⲉⲕϣⲱⲡⲓ ⲛⲁⲥ ⲛ̀ϣⲏⲣⲓ ⲛ̀ⲧⲁϣⲉⲃⲓⲱ̅[e] ⳾
11Ⲛⲁⲓ ⲇⲉ ⲉ̀ⲧⲁϥϫⲟⲧⲟⲩ ⳾ ⲁϥϣⲉ ⲛⲁϥ ⲉⲛϣⲱⲓ ⲉ̅ⲛⲓⲫⲏⲟⲩⲓ̅ ϧⲉⲛ
ⲟⲩⲱ̀ⲟⲩ ⳾ Ⲟⲩϭⲏⲡⲓ ⳾ ⲁⲥϣⲟⲡϥ ⲉⲣⲟⲥ ⳾ ⲉⲃⲟⲗ ϩⲁ ⲛⲟⲩⲃⲁⲗ ⳾
12ⲁⲩⲕⲟⲧⲟⲩ ⲉ̀ⲓⲗ̅ⲏ̅ⲙ̅ ⳾ ⲉ̀ⲩϣⲉⲡϩⲙⲟⲧ[f] ϩⲓϫⲉⲛ ⲛⲏ ⲧⲏⲣⲟⲩ ⳾ ⲉ̀ⲧⲁϥϫⲟⲧⲟⲩ
II. ⲛⲱⲟⲩ ⳾ 1Ⲙⲁⲣⲓⲁ̅ ⲇⲉ ϯⲡⲁⲣⲑⲉⲛⲟⲥ ⲉ̀ⲑⲟⲩⲁⲃ ⳾ ⲛⲁⲥϣⲟⲡ ⲡⲉ ϧⲉⲛ
ⲟⲩⲙⲁ ⲉϥⲟⲣϥ ⳾ ϧⲉⲛ ⲓ̅ⲗ̅ⲏ̅ⲙ̅ ⳾ ⲉⲥϣⲟⲡ ϧⲉⲛ ⲧ̀ⲉⲥϩⲩⲡⲟⲧⲁⲅⲏ[g] ⳾ ⲛ̅ϫⲉ
ⲟⲩⲙⲏϣ ⲙⲡⲁⲣⲑⲉⲛⲟⲥ ⳾ ⲉⲥϯⲥⲃⲱ ⲛⲱⲟⲩ[h] ⲉ̀ⲡⲓⲧⲟⲩⲃⲟ ⳾ ⲛⲉⲙ ϯϩⲟϯ
ⲛ̀ⲧⲉ ⲡ̅ⲟ̅ⲥ̅ ⳾ 2Ⲁⲛⲟⲛ ϩⲱⲛ ϧⲁ ⲛⲓⲁ̀ⲡⲟⲥⲧⲟⲗⲟⲥ ⲡⲉⲧⲣⲟⲥ ⳾ ⲛⲉⲙ ⲓⲱ̀-
ⲁⲛⲛⲏⲥ ⳾ ⲛⲁⲛⲙⲏⲛ ⲉ̀ⲣⲟⲥ ⲡⲉ ⳾ ⲉⲛϫⲱⲕ ⲉⲃⲟⲗ ⲙ̀ⲡⲉⲥⲟⲩⲁϩⲥⲁϩⲛⲓ ⳾
ⲛⲉⲙ ⲡⲉⲥⲛⲟⲙⲟⲥ ⳾ ⲡⲉⲩⲁⲅⲅⲉⲗⲓⲕⲟⲛ ⳾ ⲉⲥϣⲟⲡ ⲛⲁⲛ ⲧⲏⲣⲟⲩ ⲛ̅ⲣⲉϥ-
p. [ιθ] ⲉⲣϩⲉⲙⲓ ⳾ ⲙ̀ⲫⲣⲏϯ ⲛⲟⲩⲛⲁⲩⲕⲗⲏⲣⲟⲥ ⲛ̅ⲥⲁⲃⲉ ⳾ | 3Ⲁⲥϣⲱⲡⲓ ⲇⲉ
ⲛ̀ⲟⲩⲉ̀ϩⲟⲟⲩ ⳾ ⲉ̅ⲧⲉ ⲥⲟ̀ⲩ[i] ⲕ̅ ⲛⲧⲱⲃⲓ ⲡⲉ ⳾ ⲁⲛϣⲉ ⲉ̀ϧⲟⲩⲛ ϣⲁⲣⲟⲥ̀ ⲟⲛ
ⲕⲁⲧⲁ ϯⲕⲁϩⲥ ⳾ ⲉⲛ̀ϭⲓⲥⲙⲟⲩ[j] ⲉⲃⲟⲗ ϩⲓⲧⲟⲧⲥ̀ × 4Ⲁⲛⲛⲁⲩ ⲉ̅ⲣⲟⲥ
ⲉⲥⲟⲛϣ ⲉⲃⲟⲗ ⳾ ⲡⲉϫⲁⲛ ⲛⲁⲥ ⳾ ϫⲉ ⲟⲩ ⲉⲧϣⲟⲡ ⲙ̀ⲙⲟ ⲙ̀ⲫⲟ̀ⲟⲩ[d] ⳾
ⲱ ⲑⲙⲁⲩ ⲙ̀ⲡⲱⲛϧ ⳾ ⲉ̀ⲣⲉ ⲡⲉϩⲟ ⲟ̀ⲕⲉⲙ ⲙⲡⲁⲓⲣⲏϯ · ⳾ 5Ⲁⲥⲉⲣⲟⲩⲱ̀ ⳾
ⲡⲉϫⲁⲥ ⲛⲁⲛ ⳾ ϫⲉ ⲁⲥϣⲱⲡⲓ ⲙⲙⲟⲓ ⲙ̀ⲡⲁⲓⲉ̅ϫⲱ̀ⲣϩ ⳾ ⲉ̀ⲧⲁⲓⲕⲏⲛ ⲉⲓⲣⲓ

[a] punct. sup. ⲉ ut vid. [b] punct. sup. ⲁ ut vid. [c] duo punct. sup. ⲓ ut vid. [d] punct. sup. ⲟ prim. ut vid. [e] punct. sup. ⲃ ut vid. [f] punct. sup. ⲩ ut vid. [g] punct. sup. ⲧ prim. ut vid. [h] pr. man. ⲉⲥϯⲥⲃⲱⲟⲩ (ⲱⲛ sup. recent. man.) [i] punct. sup. ⲥ ut vid. [j] punct. sup. ⲛ ut vid.

holy laws. [6]Then said He to Peter, Peter, My bishop, dost
thou not remember that I once called thee Simon Bar- cf. Mt xvi 17
Jona? which is, I made thee son of the Dove, which is My
blessed mother. [7]Now continue with her, until she die[a]
and bless you. [8]Then again He said to John, John, My
beloved, remember that I love thee. Therefore have I sanc-
tified thee, and I have taken from thee the poison of the cf. Ro iii 13
serpent. [9]Now continue with My mother, as thou dost con-
tinue with Me, until she die[a], and thou obtain her blessing.
[10]Remember that I gave her to thee, as I was hanging on
the cross, that thou shouldest be to her *a* son in My stead.
[11]Now when He had said these things, He ascended to cf. Ac i 9, 12
the heavens in glory; and a cloud received Him from their
eyes. [12]And they returned unto Jerusalem, giving thanks for
all those things that He spake to them.

II. Now Mary the holy Virgin was dwelling in a sepa-
rate[b] place in Jerusalem, having many virgins in subjection
to her, teaching them the purity and the fear of the Lord.
[2]We also, the apostles Peter and John, were continuing with
her, fulfilling her command and her evangelic laws, whilst
she was pilot to us all, like a wise captain. [3]And it came to
pass on a day, even the twentieth of Tobi, that we went in
unto her again according to custom, being blessed by her.
[4]We saw her amazed; and we said to her, What aileth cf. Ge xl 7
thee to-day, O thou mother of Life, seeing that thy face is
thus sad? [5]She answered and said to us, It happened to
me this night that when I had ceased making my little

[a] Or *be perfected* [b] Or *secluded*

ⲛ̀ⲧⲁⲕⲟⲩϫⲓ ⲡ̅ⲥⲩⲛⲁⲍⲓⲥ ⲁⲓϩⲓⲛⲓⲙ ⲛ̀ⲟⲩⲕⲟⲩϫⲓ ⁊ 6ⲁⲓⲛ̀ⲁⲩ ⲉ̀ⲟⲩⲁⲗⲟⲩ
ⲛ̀ⲥⲁⲓⲉ̀ ⁊ ⲉϥⲛⲁⲉⲣ ⲗ̅ ⲛ̀ⲣⲟⲙⲡⲓ ⲉϥⲟⲓ ⲛ̀ⲟⲩⲱⲓⲛⲓ ⁊ ⲉϩⲟⲧⲉ ⲫⲣⲏ
ⲛⲟⲩⲑⲃⲁ ⲛ̀ⲕⲱⲃ ⲛ̀ⲥⲟⲡ = ⁊ 7ⲁ̀ⲓⲛⲁⲩ ⲉ̀ⲣⲱⲧⲉⲛ ϩⲱ̀ⲧⲉⲛ[a] ⁊ ⲉ̀ⲣⲉⲧⲉⲛⲟ̀ϩⲓ
ⲉ̀ⲣⲁⲧⲉⲛⲑⲏⲛⲟⲩ ⁊ ⲥⲁⲟⲩⲓ̅ⲛⲁ̀ⲙ[b] ⲙ̀ⲙⲟϥ[c] ⁊ ⲉ̀ⲣⲉ ϩⲁⲛϩⲃⲱⲥ ϧⲉⲛ ⲛⲉ-
ⲧⲉⲛϫⲓϫ ⁊ ⲉ̀ⲣⲉⲧⲉⲛⲥⲱⲟⲩⲧⲉⲛ ⲙ̀ⲙⲱⲟⲩ ⲉ̀ⲣⲟⲓ ⁊ : — 8ⲁϥⲉⲣⲟⲩⲱ̀ ⲛ̀ϫⲉ
ⲡⲓϧⲉⲗϣⲓⲣⲓ ⲡⲉϫⲁϥ ⲛⲏⲓ ⁊ ϫⲉ ⲱ̀ ϯⲥϩⲓⲙⲓ ⲩ ⲁⲣⲉⲥⲟⲩⲱⲛⲧ ϫⲉ
ⲁ̀ⲛⲟⲕ ⲛⲓⲙ ⲭ 9ϧⲉⲛ ⲛ̀ϫⲓⲛⲑⲣⲓⲉⲣⲉⲥⲑⲁⲛⲉⲥⲑⲉ[d] ⁊ ϫⲉ ⲡⲁϣⲏⲣⲓ ⲡⲉ
ⲡⲉ̀ϫⲏⲓ ⲛⲁϥ ⁊ ϫⲉ ⲡⲁⲟ̅ⲥ̅ ⁊ ⲙⲏⲧⲓ ⲛ̀ⲑⲟⲕ ⲡⲉ ⲓ̅ⲏ̅ⲥ̅ ⲡⲁϣⲏⲣⲓ ⁊ ⲟⲩⲟϩ
ⲡϣⲏⲣⲓ ⲙ̀ⲫ̅ϯ̅ ϧⲉⲛ ⲟⲩⲙⲉⲑⲙⲏⲓ ⁊ 10ⲡⲉϫⲁϥ ⲛⲏⲓ ⁊ ϫⲉ ⲁ̀ⲛⲟⲕ ⲡⲉ ⁊
11ⲁ̀ⲓⲉⲣⲟⲩⲱ ⲡⲉϫⲏⲓ ⲛⲁϥ : ⁊ ϫⲉ ⲡⲁⲟ̅ⲥ̅ ⲟⲩ ⲡⲉ ⲡⲑⲱϣ ⲛ̀ⲛⲁⲓϩⲃⲱⲥ ⁊
p. κ ⲉⲧϧⲉⲛ ⲛⲉⲛϫⲓϫ ⲛ̀ⲛⲉⲕⲙⲁⲑⲏⲧⲏⲥ ✓ | ⲉⲩⲥⲱⲟⲩⲧⲉⲛ ⲙ̀ⲙⲱⲟⲩ ⲉ̀ⲣⲟⲓ ⁊
12ⲡⲉϫⲁϥ ⲛⲏⲓ ⁊ ϫⲉ ⲫⲁⲓ ⲡⲉ ⲡⲑⲱϣ ⲛ̀ⲧⲉ ⲧⲉⲕⲁⲓⲥⲓ ⁊ ⲁ̀ⲣⲉϣⲁⲛⲓ
ⲉⲃⲟⲗ ϧⲉⲛ ⲥⲱⲙⲁ ⁊ 13ⲡⲁⲓ ⲉ̀ⲧⲁϥϫⲟⲧⲟⲩ ⲛⲏⲓ ⁊ ⲁϥϩⲟⲡϥ ⲉ̀ⲃⲟⲗ
ϩⲁⲣⲟⲓ ⁊ 14ⲉⲑⲃⲉ ⲫⲁⲓ ϯⲉⲣϩⲟϯ ⲱ̀ ⲡⲁϣⲏⲣⲓ ⁊ ⲉⲑⲃⲉ ⲡⲓⲙⲁ ⲛ̀ⲙⲟϣⲓ
ⲉ̀ⲧⲉⲙⲙⲁⲩ ⁊ ϫⲉ ⲥⲉϫⲛⲟⲩ ⲉⲙⲁϣⲱ ⁊ 15ⲁ̀ⲓⲥⲱⲧⲉⲙ ⲉ̀ⲣⲟϥ ⲡ̅ⲟⲩⲙⲏϣ
ⲛ̀ⲥⲟⲡ ⁊ ⲉϥϯⲥⲃⲱ ⲛ̀ⲛⲓϣⲏⲣⲓ ⲛ̀ⲧⲉ ⲛⲓⲣⲱⲙⲓ ⁊ ⲉϥⲧⲁⲙⲟ ⲙ̅ⲙⲱⲟⲩ ⁊
ⲉ̀ⲉⲣⲙⲉⲧⲁⲛⲟⲓⲛ ⲉϥϫⲱ ⲙ̀ⲙⲟⲥ ⁊ 16ϫⲉ ⲟⲩⲟⲛ ⲟⲩⲓ̀ⲁⲣⲟ ⲛ̀ⲭⲣⲱⲙ[e] ⲭⲏ
ϧⲉⲛ ⲡⲓⲙⲁ ⲛ̀ⲙⲟϣⲓ ⁊ ⲉϥϩⲓϫⲟⲗ ⲉⲙⲁϣⲱ ⁊ ⲟⲩⲟϩ ⲥⲉϭⲟⲥⲓ ⲛ̀ϫⲉ
ⲛⲉϥϩ̀ⲱⲓⲙⲓ[f] ⁊ ⲉ̅ϩⲟⲧⲉ ⲧⲱⲟⲩ ⲛⲓⲃⲉⲛ ⁊ 17ϩⲱϯ ⲡⲉ ⲛ̀ⲧⲉ ⲥⲁⲣⲝ ⲛⲓⲃⲉⲛ ⁊
ⲉⲣϫⲓⲛⲓⲟⲣ ⲙ̀ⲙⲟϥ ⁊ ⲛ̀ⲧⲉ ⲑⲙⲏⲓ ⁊ ⲛ̀ⲧⲉ ⲣⲉϥⲉⲣⲛⲟⲃⲓ ⁊ ϩⲁⲣⲁ ⲡⲁϣⲏⲣⲓ ⁊
ϯⲛⲁϣⲛⲟϩⲉⲙ ⲛ̀ⲧⲟⲧϥ ⲙ̀ⲫⲁⲓ ⁊ 18ⲟⲩ ⲟⲩⲛ ⲡⲉϯⲛⲁϫⲟϥ ⲉ̀ⲑⲃⲉ[g]
ⲧ̀ϫⲓⲛⲫⲱⲣϫ[h] ⁊ ⲛ̀ϯⲯⲩⲭⲏ ⲉ̀ⲡⲓⲥⲱⲙⲁ ⁊ 19Ϣ ϯⲟⲩⲛⲟⲩ ⲉⲑⲙⲉϩ ⲛ̀ϩⲟϯ
ⲉ̀ⲧⲉⲙⲙⲁⲩ ⁊ ⲛⲉⲙ ⲥⲑⲉⲣⲧⲉⲣ ⁊ 20ⲡⲉϫⲱⲟⲩ ⁊ ϫⲉ ϣⲁⲣⲉ ⲉ̅ⲝⲟⲩⲥⲓⲁ̀
ⲃ̅ϯ ⲓ̀ ⲛ̀ⲥⲁ ϯⲯⲩⲭⲏ ⁊ ⲟⲩⲓ̅ ⲉⲥⲟⲓ ⲛ̀ⲟⲩⲱⲓⲛⲓ ⁊ ⲕⲉⲟⲩⲓ̅ ⲉ̀ⲥⲟⲓ ⲡ̅ⲭⲁⲕⲓ ⁊
ⲉⲥϫⲁⲓⲱ̀ⲟⲩ ⁊ ⲉⲥⲙⲉϩ ⲛⲉⲛϩⲟⲩⲣ ⁊ ⲛⲉⲙ ⲥⲑⲉⲣⲑⲉⲣ ⁊ 21ⲉϣⲱⲡ ⲟⲩ-
ⲯⲩⲭⲏ ⲡ̅ⲑⲙⲏⲓ ⲧⲉ ⁊ ϣⲁⲩⲉⲛⲥ ⲉⲃⲟⲗ ϧⲉⲛ ϩⲁⲛⲥⲟⲛⲥⲉⲛ ⁊[i] ⲉⲩⲟ̀ⲓ

[a] punct. sup. ⲱ ut vid. [b] punct. sup. ⲛ et ⲁ sec. ut vid. [c] punc. sup. ⲙ prim. ut vid. [d] punct. sup. ⲛ ut vid. [e] ⲙ̀ⲭⲣⲱⲙ'' ('' rubro script.), ⲭⲣⲱⲙ sup. ras. sed pr. man. [f] punct. sup. ϩ ut vid. [g] punct. sup. ⲉ prim. ut vid. [h] punct. inter ⲧ et ϫ prim. ut vid. [i] ⁊ script. sup. =

office, I slumbered for a little while; 6and I saw a beautiful
youth about thirty years *of age,* ten thousand times brighter
than the sun. 7I saw you also standing at his right hand,
with garments in your hands, stretching them out to me.
8The young man answered and said to me, O thou woman,
dost[a] thou know Me who I *am*? 9When I perceived that it
was[b] my Son, I said to Him, My Lord, art Thou Jesus, my
Son and the Son of God in truth? 10He said to me, I am.
11I answered and said to Him, My Lord, what is the appoint-
ment of these garments, which *are* in the hands of Thy
disciples, stretching them out to me? 12He said to me, This
is the appointment of thy shroud, when thou goest from
the body. 13When He had said these things to me, He hid cf. Jn XII 36
Himself from me.

14Therefore I fear, O my sons, because of those paths, for
they are very narrow. 15I heard Him many times teaching
the sons of men, telling them to repent, saying, 16There is
a river of fire set in the path, tossing *its* waves exceedingly,
and its waves are higher than any mountain. 17All flesh
must needs cross over it, whether righteous or sinners. Can
I, my sons, be delivered from this? 18What then shall I say
concerning the separation of the soul from the body? 19O
that hour full of fear and trembling! 20They say that two
powers come after the soul, one of light, another of darkness,
unseemly and full of shuddering[c] and trembling. 21If it be
a righteous soul, they bring it forth enticingly, being mild

9 [a] Or *didst* [b] Lit. *is* [c] Or *amazement*

ⲛ̀ⲣⲉⲙⲣⲁⲩϣ ⳼ ⲛⲉⲙ̀[a] ϩⲉⲗϫⲉ ⲉ̀ϧⲟⲩⲛ ⲉⲣⲟⲥ = ⳼ ϫⲉ ⲟⲩⲛⲓ ⲉⲩⲛⲁⲩ ⳼|
p. [ⲕⲁ] ⲉ̀ⲡⲉ̀ⲥⲣⲉϥⲑⲁⲙⲓⲟ̅[b] ⳼ ⲉϥⲟ̅ⲓ ⲛ̀ϩⲓⲣⲏⲛⲏ ⲉ̀ϧⲟⲩⲛ ⲉ̀ⲣⲟⲥ × · [22]Ⲉϣⲱⲡ ϩⲱϥ
ⲟⲩⲣⲉϥⲉⲣⲛⲟⲃⲓ ⲧⲉ ⳼ ϣⲁⲣⲉ ⲡⲁ ⲡⲓⲟⲩⲱⲓⲛⲓ ⲥⲟⲕⲟⲩ ⲛⲱⲟⲩ ⳼ ⲟⲩⲟϩ
ⲛ̀ⲧⲉ ⲡⲁ ⲡⲓⲭⲁⲕⲓ ϧⲱⲛⲧ̀ ⲉ̀ⲣⲟⲥ ϧⲉⲛ ⲟⲩϫⲱⲛⲧ ⳼ ⲉⲩϧⲟⲗϧⲉⲗ
ⲙ̅ⲙⲱⲟⲩ ⲟⲩⲟϩ ⲉⲩⲫⲱⲛⲕ ϧⲉⲛ ⲟⲩ ⲓ̅ⲏ̅ⲥ ⳼ ⲟⲩⲟϩ ⲉⲩⲉⲣⲙ̀ⲁⲥⲧⲓⲅⲅⲟⲓⲛ[c] :×
[23]Ⲉⲩϧⲣⲁϫⲣⲉϫ ⲛ̀ⲛⲟⲩⲛⲁϫϩⲓ ⳼ ⲟⲩⲟϩ ⲉⲩϩⲓ ϣⲁϩ ⲛ̀ⲭⲣⲱⲙ ⲉⲃⲟⲗ
ϧⲉⲛ ⲣⲱⲟⲩ ⳼ ⲉ̀ϧⲟⲩⲛ ϧⲉⲛ ⲡⲉⲥϩⲟ ⳼ ⲉⲩⲥⲱⲟⲩⲛ ϫⲉ ⲡⲉⲥϩⲃⲏⲟⲩ̅ⲓ̅
ϫⲁⲓⲱⲟⲩ ⳼ ⲟⲩⲟϩ ⲫ̅ϯ̅ ⳼ ⲟ̀ⲓ ⲛ̀ϩⲓⲣⲏⲛⲏ ⲛⲉⲙⲁⲥ ⲁⲛ ⳼ [24]Ⲟⲩⲟ̀ⲓ ⲛⲏⲓ
ⲡⲁϣⲏⲣⲓ ⳼ ⲛⲓⲙ ⲉⲑⲛⲁϣϯⲛⲟⲙϯ ⲛⲏⲓ ⳼ ϫⲉ ⲫ̅ϯ̅ ⲟ̀ⲓ ⲛ̀ϩⲓⲣⲏⲛⲏ
ⲛⲉⲙⲏⲓ ⳼ ϣⲁⲧⲁϣⲛⲟϩⲉⲙ ⳼ ⲉⲃⲟⲗ ϧⲉⲛ ⲧⲁⲓⲟⲩⲛⲟⲩ ⲑⲁⲓ ⳼ [25]Ⲁⲩ-
ⲧⲁⲙⲟⲓ[c] ⲟⲛ ⳼ ϫⲉ ⲟⲩⲟⲛ ⲟⲩⲭⲁⲕⲓ ⳼ ⲉϥⲧⲉⲙⲑⲱⲙ ϧⲉⲛ ⲡⲓⲙⲁ
ⲛⲙⲟϣⲓ ⳼ ⲟⲩⲟϩ ⲥⲉϣⲟⲡ ϧⲉⲛ ⲫⲁⲓ ⲛ̀ϫⲉ ϩⲁⲛⲁⲛⲏⲙⲱⲣⲓⲥⲧⲏⲥ ⲛ̀ⲁⲑ-
ⲛⲁⲓ ⳼ ⲉⲣⲉ ⲛⲟⲩϩⲟ ϣⲉⲃⲓⲏⲟⲩⲧ ⲉ̀ⲙⲁϣⲱ ⳼ ⲛⲁⲓ ⲉ̀ⲧⲁ ⲫ̅ϯ̅ ⲭⲁⲩ ⳼
ⲉⲑⲣⲟⲩϯⲥⲃⲱ ⲛ̀ⲛⲓⲁ̀ⲛⲟⲙⲟⲥ ϩⲓ ⲡⲓⲙⲱⲓⲧ ⳼ ⲕⲁⲧⲁ ⲫⲣⲏϯ ⲉⲧⲥϧⲏⲟⲩⲧ ⳼
ϩⲁⲣⲁ ϯⲛⲁⲟⲩϫⲁⲓ[d] ⲉⲃⲟⲗ ϧⲉⲛ ⲛⲁⲓⲟⲩⲟⲛ ⲙ̀ⲡⲁⲓⲣⲏϯ ⳼ [26]Ϥϣⲟⲡ[e] ⲟⲛ
ϧⲉⲛ ⲡⲓⲙⲁ ⲉ̅ⲧⲉⲙⲙⲁⲩ ⲛ̅ϫⲉ ⲡⲓϥⲉⲛⲧ ⲉ̅ⲛⲁⲧⲉⲛⲕⲟⲧ ⳼ ⲫⲁⲓ ⲉⲑⲟⲩⲱⲙ
p. ⲕⲃ ⲛ̅ⲥⲁ ⲛ̀ⲓⲁ̅ⲛⲟⲙⲟⲥ ⳼ ⲉ̀ϩⲟⲧⲉ ⲙⲁⲙⲉϯ ⲛⲓⲃⲉ̀ⲛ[a] · = × | Ⲁⲙⲟⲓ ⲱ̀ ⲡⲁϣⲏⲣⲓ
ⲙⲙⲉⲛⲣⲓⲧ ⳼ ⲛⲧⲁⲟⲩϫⲁⲓ ⳼ ⲉⲃⲟⲗ ϩⲓⲧⲟⲧϥ ⲙ̅ⲡⲁⲓⲭⲉⲧ ⲩ [27]Ⲁⲩⲧⲥⲁⲃⲟⲓ
ⲟⲛ ⲱ̅ ⲡⲁϣⲏⲣⲓ ⳼ ϫⲉ ⲟⲩⲟⲛ ⲟⲩⲭⲣⲱⲙ ϣ̇ⲟⲡ[f] ⲛⲁⲧϭⲉⲛⲟ ⳼ ⲫⲁⲓ
ⲉ̀ⲧⲉ ⲙ̀ⲙⲟⲛ ϣ̇ϫⲟⲙ[f] ⲛ̀ⲛⲓⲙⲱⲟⲩ ⲛ̀ⲧⲉ[g] ⲫⲓⲟⲙ ⳼ ⲟⲩⲇⲉ ⲛⲓⲁ̀ⲣⲱⲟⲩ ⳼
ⲟⲩⲇⲉ ⲛⲓⲙⲟⲩⲙ̀ⲓ ⳼ ⲟⲩⲇⲉ ⲛⲓⲙⲟⲩⲛϩⲱⲟⲩ ⳼ ⲛⲁϣϯ ⲛⲟⲩⲭⲃⲟⲃ[h]
ⲙ̀ⲡⲉϥϣⲁϩ ⳼ [28]Ⲁⲗⲗⲁ ⲡⲉϫⲱⲟⲩ ⳼ ϫⲉ ϣⲁⲣⲉ[i] ⲧ̅ⲅ̅ ⲛ̀ⲧⲉⲗⲧⲓⲗⲓ[d]
ⲛ̀ⲉⲣⲙⲏ ⳼ ⲱϣⲉⲙ ⲙ̀ⲡⲉϥϣⲁϩ[j] ⳼ [29]Ϣ̀ⲟⲩⲛⲓⲁⲧⲥ ⲛ̀ϯⲯⲩⲭⲏ ⲉ̀ⲧⲁⲥ-
ϯⲉⲣⲙⲏ ⳼ ϩⲓϫⲉⲛ ⲛⲉⲥⲛⲟⲃⲓ ⳼ ⲉ̀ⲧⲓ ⲉⲥϣⲟⲡ ϧⲉⲛ ⲡⲓⲕⲟⲥⲙⲟⲥ ⳼
ⲙ̀ⲡⲁⲧⲉⲥϯⲙⲁϯ ⲉⲡⲁⲓⲭⲣⲱⲙ ⲫⲁⲓ ⳼ [30]Ⲟⲩⲟ̀ⲓ ⲛⲏⲓ ⳼ ⲙ̀ⲡⲁⲛⲧⲁϥⲓⲣⲓ[k]
ⲣⲱ ⳼ ⲉⲑⲃⲉ ⲡⲁⲣⲭⲱⲛ ⲙ̅ⲡⲭⲁⲕⲓ ⳼ ⲫⲁⲓ ⲉ̀ⲧⲓⲣⲓ ⲛ̀ⲁⲩⲧⲟⲧϥ[l] ⲛ̀ⲥⲛⲟⲩ

[a] punct. sup. ⲉ ut vid. [b] punct. sup. ⲉ sec. ut vid. [c] punct. sup. ⲙ ut vid. [d] punct. sup. ⲛ ut vid. [e] Ⲥⲉϣⲟⲡ [f] punct. sup. ϣ ut vid. [g] punct. sup. ⲧ ut vid. [h] punct. sup. ⲩ ut vid. [i] punct. sup. ⲣ ut vid. [j] punct. sup. ⲙ rubro script. [k] duo punct. non eadem man. script. ut vid. [l] ′ sup. ⲛ rubro script.

and gentle towards it, because they see its Maker peaceful
towards it. 22 If indeed it be a sinner, the *powers* of
light withdraw themselves, and the *powers* of darkness
draw nigh to it in anger, slaying them and hastily cleaving
asunder and scourging *them*, 23 grinding their teeth and send-
ing forth flames of fire from their mouths into its face,
knowing that its deeds are unseemly, and that God is not at
peace with it. 24 Woe to me, my sons! Who can assure[a] me,
that God is at peace with me, that I may[b] be able to be cf. Jn XII 27
delivered from this hour? 25 They tell me also that there is
a gloomy darkness in the path; and there are therein mer-
ciless avengers, their faces being very diverse, whom God
hath set to teach the lawless in the way; even as it is cf. Ps XXIV 8, 9
written. Shall I be saved from such as these? 26 There is
also in that place the worm that does not die[c], which eats cf. Mc IX 46
the lawless more than any cancer. O my beloved sons, would cf. 2 Ti II 17
that I might be delivered from this also! 27 They inform me
also, O my sons, that there is an unquenchable fire, whose
flame cannot be cooled by the waters of the sea, or by the
rivers, or by the fountains, or by the rains[d]. 28 But they say
that three tear drops extinguish its flame. 29 Blessed is the
soul that has wept over its sins, whilst it is yet in the world,
or ever it reaches this fire. 30 Woe to me! I have not yet
told of the ruler of darkness, who always does what in him cf. Eph VI 12

[a] Or *comfort* [b] Or *until I may* [c] Or *sleep* [d] See note

ⲛⲓⲃⲉⲛ ⳾ ⲉⲥⲉⲕ ⲟⲩⲟⲛ ⲛⲓⲃⲉⲛ ⲥⲁⲛⲉⲥⲏⲧ ⲡ̄ⲛⲉϥϭⲁⲗⲁⲩϫ ⳾ ⲉⲃⲏⲗ ⲉ̀ⲛⲏ
ⲉⲑⲛⲁϩⲁⲗⲁⲓ ⲥⲁⲛϣⲱⲓ ⲙ̀ⲙⲟϥ ⳾ ϧⲉⲛ̀[a] ϩⲁⲛⲧⲉⲛϩ ⲛ̀ⲟⲩⲱⲓⲛⲓ ⳾ ⲉ̀ⲧⲉ
ⲛⲁⲓ ⲡⲉ ⲛⲟⲩⲡ̇ⲣⲁⲍⲓⲥ[b] ⲉⲑⲛⲁⲛⲉⲩ =– [31]Ⲓⲉ ⲛⲓⲙ ⲉⲑⲛⲁϣϯⲛⲟⲙϯ ⲛⲏⲓ ⳾
ϩⲓϫⲉⲛ ϯⲁⲡⲟⲫⲁⲥⲓⲥ ⲉⲑⲛⲏⲟⲩ ⲉⲃⲟⲗ ⳾ ϧⲉⲛ ⲣⲱϥ ⲙ̀ⲡⲓⲕⲣⲏⲧⲏⲥ
ⲙ̀ⲙⲏⲓ ⳾ ϫⲉ ϭⲓ ⲛ̀ⲧⲁⲓⲯⲩⲭⲏ[c] ⲙⲟⲓ ⲛⲁⲥ ⲕⲁⲧⲁ ⲛⲉⲥϩⲃⲏⲟⲩⲓ̈ ⲧⲏⲣⲟⲩ ⳾
[32]Ⲛⲁⲓ ⲧⲏⲣⲟⲩ ⲛ̀ⲁϣⲏⲣⲓ[a] ⳾ ⲥⲉϣⲟⲡ ⲛⲏⲓ ⲛ̄ϩⲟϯ ⲁ ⲥⲁ ⲥⲁ ⲛⲓⲃⲉⲛ ⳾
p. [ⲕⲅ] ⲁⲗⲗⲁ ⲫⲟⲩ|ⲱϣ ⲙ̀ⲡⲟ̄ⲥ̄ ⲙⲁⲣⲉϥϣⲱⲡⲓ ⲉ̀ϩⲣⲏⲓ ⲉ̀ϫⲱⲓ =× [33]Ⲛⲁⲓ ⲇⲉ
ⲉⲛⲥⲱⲧⲉⲙ ⲉ̀ⲣⲱⲟⲩ ⳾ ⲁⲛϥⲓ ⲉϩⲣⲁⲛ ⲉⲛϣⲱⲓ ⲁⲛⲣⲓⲙⲓ ⳾ ϧⲉⲛ ⲟⲩⲙ̀ⲕⲁϩ
ⲛ̀ϩⲏⲧ ⳾ ⲉⲛϫⲱ ⲙ̀ⲙⲟⲥ ⳾ [34]Ϫⲉ ⲡⲟ̄ⲥ̄ ⲙ̀ⲡⲁⲛⲧⲉⲛⲉⲣⲡⲱⲃϣ ⲣⲱ ⲙ̀ⲡⲓ-
ⲙ̀ⲕⲁϩ ⲛ̀ϩⲏⲧ ⲛ̀ⲧⲉ ϣⲟⲣⲡ ⳾ ⲉ̀ⲧⲉ ⲡⲉⲕⲙ̀ⲕⲁϩ ⲛ̀ⲣⲉϥⲧⲁⲛϧⲟ[d] ⳾ ⲉ̀ϥⲛⲁ-
ϫⲉⲙⲧⲉⲛ ⲇⲉ ⲟⲛ̀ ⳾ ⲛ̀ϫⲉ ⲡⲓⲙⲁϩⲃ̄ ⲩ [35]Ⲟⲩⲟⲓ ⲛⲁⲛ ⳾ ⲁⲥϣⲁⲛϫⲉⲙⲧⲉⲛ[e]
III. ⲛ̀ϫⲉ ⲧⲁⲓⲙⲉⲧⲟⲣⲫⲁⲛⲟⲥ ⲑⲁⲓ ⳾ :– [1]Ⲛⲁⲓ ⲇⲉ ⲉⲩϣⲟⲡ ⲙ̀ⲡⲁⲓⲣⲏϯ ⳾
ϩⲏⲡⲡⲉ ⲁⲩⲕⲱⲗϩ ⲉⲡⲓⲣⲟ ⳾ ⲛ̀ⲧⲉ ⲡⲓⲙⲁ ⲉ̀ⲛⲁⲓϣⲟⲡ ⲛ̀ϧⲏⲧϥ ⳾
[2]Ⲉⲧⲁⲛⲟⲩⲱⲛ ⲇⲉ ϩⲏⲡⲡⲉ ⳾ ⲁⲩⲓ̈ ⲉ̀ϧⲟⲩⲛ ⲛ̀ϫⲉ̀[f] ϩⲁⲛⲙⲏϣ ⲙ̀ⲡⲁⲣ-
ⲑⲉⲛⲟⲥ ⳾ ⲉⲃⲟⲗ ϧⲉⲛ ⲡⲧⲱⲟⲩ ⲛ́ⲛⲓϫⲱⲓⲧ[g] ⳾ ⲉⲩⲟⲛ ϩⲁⲛ̇ϣⲟⲩⲣⲏ[h]
ⲛ̀ⲧⲟⲧⲟⲩ ⳾ ⲉⲩⲥⲟⲧⲡ ⲛⲉⲙ ϩⲁⲛⲗⲁⲙⲡⲁⲥ ⳾ [3]Ⲉⲧⲁⲩⲓ̈ ⲇⲉ ⲉ̀ϧⲟⲩⲛ ⳾
ⲁⲩⲟⲩⲱϣⲧ ⲛ̀ϯⲡⲁⲣⲑⲉⲛⲟⲥ ⲉⲑⲟⲩⲁⲃ ⲙⲁⲣⲓⲁ̀ ⳾ [4]Ⲁⲥϣⲉⲛⲟⲩ ⲉⲥϫⲱ
ⲙ̀ⲙⲟⲥ ⳾ ϫⲉ ⲟⲩ ϩⲁⲣⲁ ⲡⲉ ⲡⲁⲓⲛⲓϣϯ ⲛ̀ⲥⲕⲩⲗⲙⲟⲥ ⳾ ⲉⲧⲁⲣⲉⲧⲉⲛⲁⲓϥ
ϣⲁⲣⲟⲓ ⲙ̀ⲫⲟⲟⲩ ⳾ ⲱ ⲛⲁϣⲉⲣⲓ ⲙ̀ⲙⲉⲛⲣⲓⲧ ⲩ [5]Ⲁⲩⲉⲣⲟⲩⲱ̀ ⳾ ⲉⲩϫⲱ
ⲙ̀ⲙⲟⲥ ⳾ :– Ϫⲉ ⲁⲥϣⲱⲡⲓ ⲙ̀ⲙⲟⲛ ⲧⲉⲛⲟ̄ⲥ̄ ⳾ ϧⲉⲛ ϯⲫⲁϣⲓ ⲙ̀ⲡⲁⲓⲉ̀-
ϫⲱⲣϩ ⲉ̀ⲧⲁⲛⲕⲏⲛ ⲉ̀ⲛⲓⲣⲓ ⲛ̀ⲧⲉⲛⲕⲟⲩϫⲓ ⲛ̀ⲥⲩⲛⲁⲍⲓⲥ ⳾ ⲁⲛⲥⲱⲧⲉⲙ ⲉ̀ⲟⲩⲥⲙⲏ
p. ⲕⲇ ⲉⲥϫⲱ ⲙ̀ⲙⲟⲥ ⳾ | [6]Ϫⲉ ⲁⲓϫⲉⲣⲱⲧⲉⲛ ⲛ̀ⲑⲱⲧⲉⲛ ⳾ ϧⲁ ⲛⲓⲡⲁⲣⲑⲉⲛⲟⲥ
ⲛ̀ⲧⲉ ⲡⲧⲱⲟⲩ ⲛ̀ⲛⲓϫⲱⲓⲧ ⳾ ⲧⲉⲛⲑⲏⲛⲟⲩ ⳾ ϩⲱⲗ ⲉ̄ⲓ̈ⲗⲏ̄ⲙ̄[i] ⳾ ϣⲁ ⲙⲁⲣⲓ̄ⲁ̄
ⲑⲙⲁⲩ ⲙ̄ⲡⲱⲛϧ ⳾ ϫⲉ ⲥⲛⲏⲟⲩ ⲉⲃⲟⲗ ϧⲉⲛ ⲥⲱⲙⲁ ⲛ̄ⲡⲁⲥϯ ⳾ [7]Ⲉⲑⲃⲉ
ⲫⲁⲓ ⲙ̀ⲡⲉⲛϣⲉⲣⲁⲧⲥⲱⲧⲉⲙ ⳾ ⲛ̈ⲥⲁ[j] ⲡⲓⲟⲩⲁϩⲥⲁϩⲛⲓ ⲛ̀ⲛⲟⲩϯ ⳾ ϩⲏⲡⲡⲉ
ⲁⲛⲑⲱⲟⲩϯ ⲉⲛⲁⲓⲙⲁ ⳾ × [8]ⲙⲁⲣⲓ̄ⲁ̄ ⲇⲉ ϯⲡⲁⲣⲑⲉⲛⲟⲥ ⲉⲑⲟⲩⲁⲃ ⳾ ⲉ̄ⲧⲁⲥ-

[a] punct. sup. ⲛ ut vid. [b] punct. sup. ⲣ ut vid. [c] ⲛⲧⲁⲯⲩⲭⲏ, (ⲓ sup. rubr. script.) [d] ⲣ sup. ras., sed pr. man. ut vid. [e] ⲁⲛϣⲁⲛϫⲉⲙⲧⲉⲛ [f] punct. sup. ⲉ ut vid. [g] ′ sup. ⲛ prim. rubr. script. [h] punct. sup. ϣ ut vid. [i] duo punct. perexig. sup. ⲓ [j] duo punct. aut lin. sup. ⲛ

lies to drag down every one under his feet, save those who
shall fly above him on wings of light, which are their good
deeds. [31]Who can comfort me over the sentence, which
cometh forth from the mouth of the righteous Judge, Take cf. 2 Ti 8
this soul, and give to it according to all its works. [32]All
these things, my sons, are fearful to me on every side. But
the will of the Lord be done upon me.

[33]And as we heard these things, we lifted up our voice
and wept in sorrow, saying, [34]Lord, we have not yet
forgotten the former sorrow, even Thy life-giving sorrows.
And shall the second also happen unto us? [35]Woe to us, if
this bereavement happen unto us!

III. Now whilst these things were so, behold there
was a knocking at the door of the place wherein we were
dwelling. [2]And when we had opened, behold there came in
many virgins from the mount of Olives, having choice
censers and lamps. [3]And when they were come in, they cf. Mt xxv 1
worshipped the holy Virgin Mary. [4]She asked them, saying,
What then is this great trouble which ye cause me to-day, O
my beloved daughters? [5]They answered, saying, It happened
to us, our Lady, in the middle of this night, that when we
had ceased making our little office, we heard a voice, saying,
[6]I say unto you, the virgins of the mount of Olives, arise, go to
Jerusalem unto Mary, the mother of the Life, for she is going
forth from *the* body to-morrow. [7]Therefore we could not be cf. Ac xxvi 19
disobedient to the divine command; and behold we are
assembled hither.

[8]And Mary, the holy Virgin, when she heard these things,

ⲥⲱⲧⲉⲙ ⲉ̀ⲛⲁⲓ ⁊ ⲁⲥϣⲉⲡϩⲙⲟⲧ ⲛ̀ⲧⲟⲧϥ ⲙ̄ⲫϯ ⁊ [9]Ⲡⲁⲗⲓⲛ ⲟⲛ ⁊ ⲡⲉϫⲁⲥ
ⲛⲁⲛ ⁊ ϫⲉ ⲥⲉⲕⲉⲑⲏⲛⲟⲩ ⲛ̀ⲟⲩⲕⲟⲩϫⲓ ⲡⲁϣⲏⲣⲓ ⁊ ϣⲁⲧⲁⲟⲩⲱⲛϩ ⲉ̀ⲃⲟⲗ
ⲙ̀ⲡⲟ̅ⲥ̅ ⁊ ⲫⲏ ⲉ̀ⲧⲁ ⲧⲁⲯⲩⲭⲏ ⲙⲉⲛⲣⲓⲧϥ ⁊ [10]ⲡⲑⲟⲥ ⲇⲉ ⲁⲥⲟⲩⲱⲛ
ⲛ̀ⲣⲱⲥ ⁊ ⲁⲥϯ ⲛ̀ⲧⲁⲓⲡⲣⲟⲥⲉⲩⲭⲏ ⁊ ⲉⲥϫⲱ ⲙ̄ⲙⲟⲥ ⁊ : — [11]Ϫⲉ ϯϣⲉⲡ-
ϩⲙⲟⲧ ⲛ̀ⲧⲟⲧⲕ ⲡⲁⲟ̅ⲥ̅ ⲓⲏ̅ⲥ̅ ⲡⲭ̅ⲥ̅ ⁊ ⲡⲓϣⲟⲣⲡ ⲙ̄ⲥⲁϫⲓ ⲉ̀ⲧⲁϥⲓ̀[a] ⲉ̀ⲃⲟⲗ
ϧⲉⲛ ⲣⲱϥ ⲙ̀ⲫⲓⲱⲧ ⁊ ⲁϥⲓ̅ ⲁϥϣⲱⲡⲓ ϧⲉⲛ ⲧⲁⲛⲉϫⲓ ⲙ̄ⲑ̄ ⲛ̄ⲁⲃⲟⲧ
ⲛⲉϩⲟⲟⲩ ⁊ [12]Ϯⲥⲙⲟⲩ ⲉ̀ⲣⲟⲕ ⲡⲓⲑⲩⲥⲁⲩⲣⲟⲥ ⁊ ⲛ̄ⲧⲉ ⲁ̄ⲅⲁⲑⲟⲛ ⲛⲓⲃⲉⲛ ⁊
ⲫⲏ ⲉⲧⲁⲓϯ ⲉ̀ⲣⲱϯ[b] ⲉ̀ⲣⲱϥ ⁊ ⲛ̀ⲑⲟϥ ⲉⲧϯϧⲣⲉ ⲛ̀ⲥⲁⲣⲝ ⲛⲓⲃⲉⲛ ⁊
[13]Ϯⲥⲙⲟⲩ ⲉ̀ⲣⲟⲕ ⲡⲓⲡⲁⲣⲁⲗⲓⲙⲡⲧⲟⲥ ⁊ ⲟⲩⲟϩ ⲛ̀ⲁⲱⲣⲁⲧⲟⲥ ⁊ ⲫⲏ ⲉⲧϥⲁⲓ
ϧⲁ ⲡⲧⲏⲣϥ ⁊ ϧⲉⲛ ⲛ̀ⲥⲁϫⲓ ⲛ̀ⲧⲉ ⲧⲉϥϫⲟⲙ[c] ⁊ ⲟⲩⲟϩ ⲉ̀ⲧⲁⲓϥⲁⲓ ϧⲁⲣⲟϥ
p. [κε] ϧⲉⲛ ⲛⲁϫⲓϫ × | [14]Ϯⲥⲙⲟⲩ ⲉ̀ⲣⲟⲕ ⲡⲱⲛϧ ⲛ̀ⲧⲉ ⲛⲓⲡⲁⲧⲣⲓⲁⲣⲭⲏⲥ ⁊
ⲫⲏ ⲉ̄ⲧⲁϥϣⲱⲡⲓ ⲛⲉⲙ ⲁⲃⲣⲁⲁⲙ ⁊ ⲁϥϯϫⲟⲙ ⲛ̀ⲓⲥⲁⲁⲕ ⁊ ⲁϥⲟⲩⲉⲥⲑⲉⲛ
ⲡⲓⲥ̅ⲗ̅ ⁊ [15]Ϯⲥⲙⲟⲩ ⲉ̀ⲣⲟⲕ ϯⲡⲣⲟⲫⲏⲧⲓⲁ̀ ⲛ̀ⲧⲉ ⲛⲓⲡⲣⲟⲫⲏⲧⲏⲥ ⁊ ⲁⲕⲓ̅
ⲁⲕϫⲟⲕⲟⲩ ⲉ̀ⲃⲟⲗ ɣ [16]Ϯⲥⲙⲟⲩ ⲉ̀ⲣⲟⲕ ⁊ ⲡⲑⲱϩⲉⲙ ⲛ̀ⲧⲉ ⲛⲓⲕⲣⲏⲧⲏⲥ ⁊
Ⲟⲩⲟϩ ⲡⲟⲩⲟⲩϫⲁⲓ ϧⲉⲛ ⲛⲓⲡⲟⲗⲉⲙⲟⲥ ⁊ [17]Ϯⲥⲙⲟⲩ ⲉ̀ⲣⲟⲕ ⲡⲓⲭⲗⲟⲙ
ⲛ̀ⲧⲉ ⲛⲓⲟⲩⲣⲱⲟⲩ ⲛ̀ⲑⲙⲏⲓ ⁊ Ⲟⲩⲟϩ ⲉⲧⲓⲛⲓ ⲙ̀ⲡⲟⲩϩⲁⲡ ⲉ̀ⲃⲟⲗ ϧⲉⲛ
ⲟⲩⲥⲱⲟⲩⲧⲉⲛ ⁊ [18]Ϯⲥⲙⲟⲩ ⲉ̀ⲣⲟⲕ ⁊ ⲡϩⲱⲥ ⲛ̀ⲧⲉ ⲛⲓⲁⲅⲅⲉⲗⲟⲥ ⁊ Ⲟⲩⲟϩ
ⲡϩⲩⲙⲛⲟⲥ ⲛ̀ⲧⲉ ⲛⲓⲁⲣⲭⲏⲁⲅⲅⲉⲗⲟⲥ ⁊ [19]Ϯⲥⲙⲟⲩ ⲉ̀ⲣⲟⲕ ⲧⲥⲁⲗⲡⲓⲅⲅⲟⲥ
ⲛ̀ⲧⲉ ⲛⲓⲭⲉⲣⲟⲩⲃⲓⲙ ⁊ ⲟⲩⲟϩ ⲧⲗⲁⲗⲓⲁ̄ ⲛ̄ⲧⲉ ⲛⲓⲥⲉⲣⲁⲫⲓⲙ ⋇ [20]ϯⲥⲙⲟⲩ
ⲉ̀ⲣⲟⲕ ⲧϩⲩⲡⲟⲙⲟⲛⲏ ⲛ̀ⲧⲉ ⲛⲓⲙⲁⲣⲧⲩⲣⲟⲥ ⁊ Ⲟⲩⲟϩ ⲡϣⲟⲩϣⲟⲩ ⲛ̀ⲧⲉ
ⲡⲟⲩⲭⲗⲟⲙ = ⁊ : [21]Ϯⲥⲙⲟⲩ ⲉ̀ⲣⲟⲕ ⲡⲁⲣⲏⲃ ⲛ̀ⲧⲉ ⲛⲓⲡⲁⲣⲑⲉⲛⲟⲥ ⁊ ⲟⲩⲟϩ
ⲫⲟⲩⲱⲓⲛⲓ ⲛ̀ⲧⲉ ⲛⲟⲩⲗⲁⲙⲡⲁⲥ ⋇ [22]ϯⲥⲙⲟⲩ ⲉ̀ⲣⲟⲕ ⲡⲓϩⲓⲱⲓϣ ⲛ̀ⲧⲉ ⲛⲓ-
ⲁ̀ⲡⲟⲥⲧⲟⲗⲟⲥ ⁊ Ⲟⲩⲟϩ ⲡⲓⲕⲏⲣⲓⲅⲙⲁ[d] ⲛ̀ⲧⲉ ⲛⲟⲩⲥⲑⲟⲓⲛⲟⲩϥⲓ = ⁊ Ϯⲥⲙⲟⲩ
ⲉ̀ⲣⲟⲕ ⲡⲁⲟ̅ⲥ̅ ⁊ ⲟⲩⲟϩ ⲡⲁϣⲏⲣⲓ ⲉⲩⲥⲟⲡ × [23]ϯϯϩⲟ ⁊ ⲟⲩⲟϩ ϯϧⲱⲛϫ
ⲉ̀ⲧⲉⲕⲙⲉⲧⲁ̀ⲅⲁⲑⲟⲥ ⁊ ϣⲱⲡⲓ ⲛⲏⲓ ⲙ̀ⲃⲟⲏ̀ⲑⲟⲥ ⁊ ⲟⲩⲟϩ ⲙ̀ⲡⲉⲣⲭⲁⲧ
p. κς ⲛ̄ⲥⲱⲕ × ⲇ· | [24]ⲁⲛⲓⲟⲩⲓ̀ ⲛ̀ⲧⲁⲯⲩⲭⲏ[e] ⲉ̀ⲃⲟⲗ ϧⲉⲛ ⲛⲁⲓϣⲧⲉⲕⲟ ⁊ ⲉⲛ-
ϫⲓⲛⲧⲁⲟⲩⲱⲛϩ ⲙ̀ⲡⲉⲕⲣⲁⲛ ⲉ̀ⲃⲟⲗ ⁊ [25]ⲙⲁⲣⲉϥϩⲉⲣⲓ ⲛ̀ϫⲉ ⲡⲓⲭⲣⲱⲙ ⁊
ⲙⲁⲣⲉϥⲉⲣϣⲟⲣⲡ ⲉ̀ⲣⲟⲓ ⲛ̀ϫⲉ ⲡⲉⲕⲛⲁⲓ ⁊ ⲙⲁⲣⲉϥⲥⲁϩⲱϥ ⲛ̀ϫⲉ ⲡⲓⲭⲁⲕⲓ ⁊

[a] ʹ sup. ⲓ rubr. script. [b] ⲣⲱϯ sup. ras. [c] ⲧ ex ⲡ mutat. ut vid. pr. man. [d] ⲡⲓⲣⲓⲅⲙⲁ [e] ⲛ̀ⲧⲁⲓⲯⲩⲭⲏ (ⲓ eras.)

gave thanks to God. 9 Again she said to us, Withdraw your-
selves for a little while, my sons, that I may give[a] thanks to
the Lord, whom my soul loveth. 10 And she opened her
mouth, and spake[b] this prayer, saying, 11 I thank Thee, my
Lord Jesus Christ, the first Word that came forth from the
mouth of the Father, and came and dwelt in my womb the
space of nine months[c]. 12 I praise Thee, the treasure-house
of all good things, to whom I gave suck, *even* Thee[d] who cf. Ps cxxxv 25
givest[e] food to all flesh. 13 I praise Thee, the Inheritor and cf. He i 2, 3
unseen, who bearest[f] the universe by the word of Thy[g] power,
and whom I bare in my hands. 14 I praise Thee, the Life of
the patriarchs, that dwelt with Abraham, strengthened Isaac,
and enlarged Israel. 15 I praise Thee, the prophecy of the
prophets. Thou didst come and fulfil them. 16 I praise Thee,
the calling of the judges, and their salvation in the battle.
17 I praise Thee, the crown of the righteous kings, who[h]
bringest forth their judgment aright. 18 I praise Thee, the cf. Is xlii 3
song of the angels, and the hymn of the archangels. 19 I
praise Thee, the trumpet of the Cherubim, and the speech of
the Seraphim. 20 I praise Thee, the patience of the martyrs,
and the glory of their crown. 21 I praise Thee, the espousals
of the virgins, and the light of their lamps. 22 I praise Thee, cf. Mt xxv 1
the proclamation of the apostles, and the preaching of their cf. 2 Co ii 15
sweet savour. I praise Thee, at once my Lord and my Son. 23 I cf. Mt xxii 45
beg and beseech Thy goodness, be to me *a* helper and forsake
me not. 24 Bring my soul out of this prison, that I may give Ps cxli 8
thanks unto Thy name. 25 Let the fire be still: let Thy
mercy prevent me: let the darkness depart: let Thy light cf. Ps lviii 11

[a] Or *until I give* [b] Lit. *gave* [c] Lit. *nine months of days*
[d] Lit. *Him* [e] Lit. *giveth* [f] Lit. *beareth* [g] Lit. *His*
[h] Lit. *and who*

ⲙⲁⲣⲉϥⲟⲩⲟⲛϩϥ ⲛ̀ϫⲉ ⲡⲉⲕⲟⲩⲱⲓⲛⲓ ⳹ 26Ⲙⲁⲣⲉϥϣⲑⲁⲙ ⲛ̀ⲣⲱϥ ⲛ̀ϫⲉ
ⲡⲓϫⲁϫⲓ ⳹ ⲉⲑⲟⲩⲱϣ ⲉ̀ϥⲓⲱⲡ ⲛⲉⲙⲏⲓ ⳹ 27Ⲙⲁⲣⲟⲩⲟⲩⲟⲛϩⲟⲩ ⲛ̀ϫⲉ ⲛⲏ
ⲉⲑⲟⲩⲱϣ ⲛⲧϩⲓⲣⲏⲛⲏ[a] ⲛ̀ⲧⲉⲕⲙⲁⲧ ⳹ 28Ⲙⲁⲣⲉϥⲙⲟⲩⲛⲕ ⲛ̀ⲭⲱⲗⲉⲙ ⲛ̀ϫⲉ
ⲡⲓϥⲉⲛⲧ ⲉ̀ⲛⲁⲧⲉⲛⲕⲟⲧ ⳹ ⲙⲁⲣⲉϥⲥⲟⲛⲥⲉⲛ ⳹ ⲉ̀ⲧⲁⲯⲩⲭⲏ ⲛ̀ϫⲉ ⲡⲉⲕⲛⲁⲓ
ⲉⲧⲟⲛϧ ⳹ 29Ⲁϩⲁ ⲡ̅ⲟ̅ⲥ̅ ⲡⲁⲛⲟⲩϯ ⳹ ⲟⲩⲟϩ ⲡⲁϣⲏⲣⲓ ⲉⲩⲥⲟⲛ × Ⲥⲟⲙⲥ
ⲉϧⲣⲏⲓ ⲉϫⲱⲓ ⳹ ϧⲉⲛ ⲧⲁⲓⲟⲩⲛⲟⲩ ⲉ̀ⲧⲟⲓ ⲛ̀ϩⲟϯ ⳹ ⲟⲩⲟϩ ⲉⲧⲙⲉϩ
ⲛ̀ⲥⲑⲉⲣⲧⲉⲣ ⳹ 30Ⲁⲙⲟⲩ ϣⲁⲣⲟⲓ ⳹ ⲫⲏ ⲉⲧⲁ ⲧⲁⲯⲩⲭⲏ ⲙⲉⲛⲣⲓⲧϥ ⳹
ⲙⲁⲣⲉ ⲡⲉⲕⲡ̅ⲛ̅ⲁ̅ ⲉⲑⲟⲩⲁⲃ ⳹ ϭⲓⲙⲱⲓⲧ ⲛⲏⲓ ϧⲉⲛ ⲛⲉⲧⲥⲟⲩⲧⲱⲛ = ⳹ : –
31Ⲙⲁⲣⲓⲟⲩⲱϣⲧ ⲙ̀ⲡⲉⲕⲙⲑⲟ ϧⲉⲛ ⲟⲩⲡⲁⲣⲣⲏⲥⲓⲁ̀ ⳹ ϩⲓⲛⲁ ⲛ̀ⲧⲁⲟⲩⲱⲛϩ
ⲛⲁⲕ ⲉ̀ⲃⲟⲗ ⳹ ⲡ̅ⲟ̅ⲥ̅ ⲡⲁⲛⲟⲩϯ ϧⲉⲛ ⲟⲩⲥⲕⲉⲩⲟⲥ ⲙ̀ⲯⲁⲗⲙⲟⲥ ⲛ̀ⲧⲉ
ⲧⲉⲕⲙⲉⲑⲙⲏⲓ × 32ϫⲉ ⲉ̀ⲣⲉ ⲡⲓⲱⲟⲩ ⲉⲣⲡⲣⲉⲡⲓ ⲛⲁⲕ ⳹ ⲛⲉⲙ ⲡⲉⲕⲓⲱⲧ
ⲛⲁⲅⲁⲑⲟⲥ ⳹ ⲛⲉⲙ ⲡⲓⲡ̅ⲛ̅ⲁ̅ ⲉⲑⲟⲩⲁⲃ ⳹ ϣⲁ ⲉ̀ⲛⲉϩ ⳹ ⲛ̀ⲧⲉ ⲡⲓⲉ̀ⲛⲉϩ
p. [κζ] IV. ⲁ̀ⲙⲏⲛ × | 1Ⲉⲧⲁⲥϫⲱⲕ ⲇⲉ ⲉ̀ⲃⲟⲗ ⲛ̀ⲧⲁⲓⲡⲣⲟⲥⲉⲩⲭⲏ ⳹ ⲁⲛϫⲱ ϩⲱⲛ
ⲙ̀ⲡⲓⲁ̀ⲙⲏⲛ ⳹ : – 2Ϩⲏⲡⲡⲉ ⲓⲥ ϩⲁⲛⲭⲁⲣⲁⲃⲁⲓ ⲁⲩϣⲱⲡⲓ ⳹ ⲛⲉⲙ ϩⲁⲛ-
ⲥⲉⲧⲉⲃⲣⲏϫ ⳹ ⲁ̀ ⲡⲓⲙⲁ ⲧⲏⲣϥ ⲕⲓⲙ ϣⲁ ⲡⲉϥⲥⲉⲛϯ = ⳹ 3Ⲁϥⲟⲩⲟⲛϩϥ
ϧⲉⲛ ⲧⲉⲛⲙⲏϯ ⲛ̀ϫⲉ ⲡ̅ⲟ̅ⲥ̅ ⲓ̅ⲏ̅ⲥ̅ ⳹ ⲉϥⲧⲁⲗⲏⲟⲩⲧ ϩⲓϫⲉⲛ ⲟⲩϩⲁⲣⲙⲁ
ⲛⲟⲩⲱⲓⲛⲓ ⳹ ⲉ̀ⲣⲉ ⲙⲱⲩ̈ⲥⲏⲥ ϩⲓⲧϩⲏ ⲙ̀ⲙⲟϥ ⳹ ⲛⲉⲙ ⲡⲥⲱϫⲡ ⲧⲏⲣϥ
ⲛ̀ⲛⲓⲡⲣⲟⲫⲏⲧⲏⲥ ⳹ Ⲇⲁⲩⲓⲇ ⲡⲟⲩⲣⲟ ⳹ ⲛⲉⲙ ⲛⲓⲟⲩⲣⲱⲟⲩ ⲛ̀ⲑⲙⲏⲓ ⳹ ⲁ
ⲡⲓⲙⲁ ⲧⲏⲣϥ ⲉⲣⲟⲩⲱⲓⲛⲓ ⲙ̀ⲫⲣⲏϯ ⲛⲟⲩⲭⲣⲱⲙ × 4Ⲉⲧⲉ ⲙ̀ⲡⲉⲛϣϥⲁⲓ
ϧⲁ ϯϩⲟϯ ⳹ ⲁⲛϩⲉⲓ ⲉ̀ⲛⲉⲥⲏⲧ ϧⲉⲛ ⲟⲩⲙⲏϯ ⳹ ⲁⲛⲉⲣ ⲙ̀ⲫⲣⲏϯ ⲛⲟⲩ-
ⲣⲉϥⲙⲱⲟⲩⲧ ⳹ 5Ⲛ̀ⲑⲟϥ ⲇⲉ ⲡⲉⲛⲟ̅ⲥ̅ ⲓ̅ⲏ̅ⲥ̅ ⳹ ⲁϥⲙⲟⲩϯ ϧⲉⲛ ⲧⲉϥⲥⲙⲏ
ⲉⲧϩⲟⲗϫ ⳹ ϫⲉ ⲭⲉⲣⲉ ⲧⲁⲙⲁⲩ ⲙ̀ⲡⲁⲣⲑⲉⲛⲟⲥ ⳹ ⲭⲉⲣⲉ ⲛⲁⲁ̀ⲡⲟⲥⲧⲟⲗⲟⲥ
ⲉⲑⲟⲩⲁⲃ ⳹ ⲭⲉⲣⲉ ⲛⲓⲡⲁⲣⲑⲉⲛⲟⲥ ⲉ̀ⲧⲁⲩⲑⲱⲟⲩϯ ⲉ̀ⲡⲁⲓⲙⲁ = 6Ⲟⲩⲟϩ
ⲥⲁⲧⲟ̀ⲧⲉⲛ ⲁⲥⲭⲁⲛ[b] ⲛ̀ϫⲉ ϯϩⲟϯ ⳹ ⲁⲛϩⲓⲧⲉⲛ ⲉⲛⲉⲥⲏⲧ ⲁⲛⲟⲩⲱϣⲧ
ⲙ̀ⲙⲟϥ ⳹ 7ⲛ̀ⲑⲟϥ ⲇⲉ ⲡⲉϫⲁϥ ⲛ̀ⲧⲉϥⲙⲁⲩ ⳹ ϫⲉ ⲁⲓⲥⲱⲧⲉⲙ ⲉⲛⲉⲧⲱⲃϩ
Ⲟⲩⲟϩ ⲧⲉⲡⲣⲟⲥⲉⲩⲭⲏ ⳹ ⲁⲥⲓ ⲉ̀ϧⲟⲩⲛ ⲙ̀ⲡⲁⲙⲑⲟ ⳹ ϩⲓϫⲉⲛ ⲡⲁⲑⲣⲟⲛⲟⲥ
ⲛ̀ⲧⲉ ⲡⲁⲱ̀ⲟⲩ × Ⲥⲁⲟⲩⲓ̀ⲛⲁⲙ ⲙ̀ⲡⲁⲓⲱⲧ ⳹ ⲛⲉⲙ ⲡⲓⲡ̅ⲛ̅ⲁ̅ ⲉⲑⲟⲩⲁⲃ = ⳹ · – |
p. κн 8Ⲗⲟⲓⲡⲟⲛ ⲱ̅ ⲧⲁⲙⲁⲩ ⲙ̅ⲡⲁⲣⲑⲉⲛⲟⲥ ⳹ ⲧⲱⲟⲩⲛⲓ ⲙⲁⲣⲟⲛ ⲉ̀ⲃⲟⲗ ⲧ̀ⲁⲓ ⳹
ⲉⲑⲃⲉ ⲟⲩ ⲧⲉⲟⲩⲱϣ ⲉ̀ϣⲱⲡⲓ ⳹ ϧⲉⲛ ⲛⲏⲓ ⲛ̀ⲧⲉ ⲛⲓⲣⲉϥⲉⲣⲛⲟⲃⲓ ⳹

[a] ⲛ 1° sup. rec. man. [b] ″ⲁⲥⲭⲁⲛ (″ rubr.)

appear. 26 Let the enemy who wisheth to reckon with me
shut his mouth. 27 Let those who wish the peace of Thy
mother appear. 28 Let the worm that doth not die[a] fail cf. Mc ix 46
quickly: let Thy living mercy comfort my soul. 29 Yea, Lord,
at once my God and my Son, look down upon me in this
hour, fearful and full of trembling. 30 Come unto me, Thou[b] cf. Cant i 7
whom my soul loveth. Let Thy Holy Ghost guide me aright.
31 Let me worship before Thee with boldness, that I may
give thanks to Thee, O Lord my God, with a psaltery[c] of cf. Ps lxx 22
Thy truth. 32 For the glory is due to Thee and Thy good
Father and the Holy Ghost unto *the* ages of the ages. Amen.

IV. Now when she had finished this prayer, we also
said the Amen. 2 Behold there were thunderings and light-
nings, and all the place was moved to its foundations. 3 And
there appeared in our midst the Lord Jesus, riding on a
chariot of light, Moses being before Him and all the rest of
the prophets, David the king and the righteous kings. And
all the place became[d] bright as fire. 4 When we could not
bear the fear, we fell down in the midst, and became as a
dead man. 5 But He, our Lord Jesus, called with His gentle[e]
voice, Hail, My virgin mother: hail, My holy apostles: hail,
ye virgins assembled hither. 6 And forthwith the fear left
us, and we fell down and worshipped Him. 7 And He said
to His mother, I have heard thy supplication; and thy
prayer has come in before Me unto My throne of My glory, cf. Mt xix 28; xxv 31
at the right hand of My Father and of the Holy Ghost.
8 Now, O My virgin mother, arise, let us go hence. Where- cf. Jn xiv 31
fore wouldest thou dwell in the house of the sinners, when cf. Ps lxxxiii 11

[a] Or *sleep* [b] Lit. *He* [c] Lit. *a psalm vessel* [d] Or *was*
[e] Or *sweet*

ευσεβτωτ μ̀πέεμθο ν̀ϫε πισκυνη ν̀τε πιθμηι ⳹ [9]Ερ ου ερο
πε ὠ ταμαυ ⳹ ἐρεϣοπ ϧεν νη εθναβωλ ἐβολ ⳹ μενενσα
κεκουϫι ν̀σνου ⳹ Ουοϩ ευϫουωϣτ εβολ ϧαϫω ν̀ϫε πιϣα
ἐνεϩ ὠ ταμαυ εθνεσως ⳹ τωουνι[a] εβολ ται ⳹ [10]Εθβε ου
ϯναχαϯ ϧεν ι̅λ̅η̅μ̅ ν̀τε πικαϩι ⳹ θη ἐτασϧωτεβ ν̀νιπρο-
φητης ⳹ ασϩιω̅πι ϩιϫεν νη ἐταυουορπου ϩαρος ⳹ Εσϭι-
ϣϣωου μμον ν̀ϫε ι̅λ̅η̅μ̅ ν̀τε[b] τφε ⳹ τπολις μ̀παιωτ νεμ
πιπ̅ν̅α̅ εθουαβ ⳹ ϫε τεσοτπ ἐϩοτερος ⳹ [11]Λοιπον ὠ
ταμεν̅ριτ μ̀μαυ ⳹ τωουνι μαρον εβολ ται ⳹ Επαϣ γαρ
ν̀ρηϯ ⳹ ϯνασοϫπι μ̅παιμα ϧεν παιηι ν̅καϩι ⳹ νεμ τωβι ⳹
ερε πιπυλων μ̀μαργαριτης ουνη μ̀πεμ̅θο ⳹· [12]Ειναώου
p. [κθ] ν̀ϩητ ν̀αϣ ν̀ρηϯ ὠ ταμ̀αυ εθνεσωσ̀ ⳹ θη ἐτας|ϣωπι νηι
ν̀ουμανουοϩ[c] ⳹ εθριχαϯ ϩιϫεν πικαϩι ⳹ ἐρε τφε ν̀τε
τφε ⳹ τασκυνη μ̀μηι ⳹ νεμ παιωτ ⳹ νεμ πιπ̅ν̅α̅ ἐθουαβ ⳹
ϭιϣϣ̅ωου μμο ⳹ [13]Λοιπον ὠ ταμένριτ μ̀μαυ ⳹ τωουνι ⳹
μαρον εβολ ταὶ ⳹ Παιωτ φη ἐτονϧ[d] ⳹ νεμ πιπ̅ν̅α̅ εθουαβ ⳹
φη εθνηου εβολ ϧεν πωνϧ ⳹ σομς εβολ ϧαϫωϥ ⳹ μ̀πε-
ϫινϣε ϣαρωου ⳹ ϫε αρεϥαι ϧα τουμετουαι ⳹ ἐτε θαι τε
ταμετνουϯ φυσι[e] ⳹ ἐτασϣωπι ν̀ϧηϯ ⳹ [14]Λοιπον ω̅ ταμενριτ
μ̀μαυ ⳹ τωουνι μαρον εβολ ται ⳹ εβολ ϧεν νηι μ̀φριμι ⳹
ἐϧουν ετπολις μ̀πουνοϥ ⳹ εβολ ϧεν τχωρα ν̅νιρεϥμωουτ ⳹
ἐϧουν ετχωρα ν̀νη ετονϧ ⳹ ϧεν φαι ὠ ταμενριτ μ̀μαυ
V. τωουνι μαρον εβολ ται ⳹ [1]Ναι δε εϥϫω μ̅μωου ⳹ μ̅πεν-
ϣϥαι ϧα πιμ̅καϩ ν̅ϩητ ⳹ εθναϣωπι μ̀μον ⳹ ανωϣ εβολ ⳹
ανριμι ϧεν ουενϣαϣι ενϫω μ̀μος ⳹ [2]Ϫε ω̅ πεν̅σ̅ς̅ ⳹ ισϫε
χναολς εβολ ϧεν τενμηϯ ⳹ ν̀τενϣωπι ν̀ορφανος ⳹ ιὲ
p. λ ϣοπτεν ἐροκ ν̀ϣορπ ἐρος ⳹ ϫε ν̀νενναυ ⳹ | ενεντακο μ̀μιν

[a] ϧαϫω usque ad εθνεσως ⳹ τωο sup. ras. pr. man. [b] τ sup. ras. [c] ʹ sup. ν prim. rubr. script. [d] punct. sup. ε ut vid. rec. man. ς add.

the tents of the righteous are prepared before thee? 9 What
reason hast thou, O My mother, for dwelling in those *things* cf. 2 Pe iii 11
which are to be dissolved after but a little while, when[a] the
eternal are awaiting thee? O My beautiful mother, arise,
let us go hence. 10 Wherefore shall I leave thee in the earthly
Jerusalem[b], which killeth the prophets, and stoneth them cf. Lc xiii 34
that are sent unto her; whilst the heavenly Jerusalem[c] cf. He xii 22
longeth for us, the city of My Father and of the Holy Ghost?
For thou art too good for[d] it. 11 Now, O My beloved mother,
arise, let us go hence. For how shall I leave thee here
in this house of earth and bricks, whilst the gates[e] of cf. 2 Co v 1; Ap xxi 21
pearl are opened before thee? 12 How shall I endure, O My
beautiful mother, who wast[f] to Me a dwelling place, to leave
thee on the earth; whilst heaven of heaven, My true taber-
nacle, and My Father and the Holy Ghost long[g] for thee?
13 Now, O My beloved mother, arise, let us go hence. My
Father who liveth and the Holy Ghost who proceedeth from cf. Jn vi 57; xv 26
the Life, wait for thy coming unto Them; for thou didst carry
Their unity, even My godhead by nature, which dwelt in
thee. 14 Now, O My beloved mother, arise, let us go hence,
from the house of weeping into the city of gladness, from
the land of the dead into the land of the living. Forthwith,
O My beloved mother, arise, let us go hence.

V. Now as He was saying these things, we could not
bear the grief which was about to come upon us; and we
cried out, and wept bitterly, saying, 2 O our Lord, if Thou
wilt take her away from our midst, and we become desolate;
receive us to Thyself before her, that we may not see our

[a] Lit. *and* [b] Lit. *Jerusalem of the earth* [c] Lit. *Jerusalem of heaven* [d] Lit. *thou art better than* [e] Or *portals* [f] Lit. *was* [g] See note

ⲙ̀ⲙⲟⲛ ⳾ [3]ⲟⲩⲟϩ ⲛⲓⲕⲉⲡⲁⲣⲑⲉⲛⲟⲥ ϩⲱⲟⲩ ⳾ ⲛⲁⲩⲣⲓⲙⲓ ⲡⲉ ϧⲉⲛ ⲟⲩϥⲓⲁ̀ϩⲟⲙ ⲧⲏⲣⲟⲩ ⳾ [4]Ⲛ̄ⲑⲟⲥ ⲇⲉ ⲁⲥⲕⲉⲧ ⲡⲉⲥϩⲟ ⲉ̀ϫⲱⲛ ⲡⲉϫⲁⲥ ⲛⲁⲛ ⳾ ϫⲉ ⲛⲁϣⲏⲣⲓ ⲉⲑⲃⲉ ⲟⲩ ⲧⲉⲧⲉⲛⲣⲓⲙⲓ ⳾ ⲛ̀ⲧⲉⲧⲉⲛϯ ⲉⲙⲕⲁϩ ⲙ̀ⲡⲁⲡ̄ⲡ̄ⲁ ⳾ [5]Ⲡⲏ ⲉⲥⲥϧⲏⲟⲩⲧ ⲁⲛ ⳾ ϫⲉ ϩⲱϯ ⲡⲉ ⲛ̀ⲧⲉ ⲥⲁⲣⲝ ⲛⲓⲃⲉⲛ ⳾ ϫⲉⲙϯⲡⲓ ⲙ̄ⲫⲙⲟⲩ ⳾ ϩⲱϯ ⲉ̀ⲣⲟⲓ ϩⲱ ⲡⲉ ⲉⲑⲣⲓⲧⲁⲥⲑⲟⲓ ⲉⲡⲓⲕⲁϩⲓ ⳾ ⲙ̄ⲫⲣⲏϯ ⲛ̀ⲛⲓⲣⲉⲙⲉⲛⲕⲁϩⲓ ⲧⲏⲣⲟⲩ ⳾ [6]Ⲗⲟⲓⲡⲟⲛ ϫⲉⲙⲛⲟⲙϯ ⳾ ϥⲛⲉⲙⲱⲧⲉⲛ ⲛ̀ⲥⲛⲟⲩ ⲛⲓⲃⲉⲛ[a] ⳾ Ⲟⲩⲟϩ ϥⲛⲁⲭⲁⲑⲏⲛⲟⲩ ⲁⲛ ⳾ ⲉ̀ⲣⲉⲧⲉⲛⲟ̀ⲓ ⲛ̀ⲟⲣⲫⲁⲛⲟⲥ ⳾ ⲕⲁⲧⲁ ⲫⲣⲏϯ ⲉ̀ⲧⲁϥϫⲟⲥ ⳾ [7]Ⲡⲁⲗⲓⲛ ⲡⲉϫⲁⲥ ⲛ̀ⲛⲓⲡⲁⲣⲑⲉⲛⲟⲥ ⳾ ϫⲉ ⲛⲁϣⲉⲣⲓ ⲉⲑⲛⲁⲛⲉⲩ ⳾ Ⲁⲣⲉϩ ⲉ̀ⲛⲓⲥⲩⲛⲑⲏⲕⲏ ⳾ ⲉⲧⲁⲣⲉⲧⲉⲛⲥⲉⲙⲛⲏⲧⲟⲩ ⳾ ⲛⲉⲙ ⲡⲉⲧⲉⲛⲛⲁⲧϣⲉⲗⲉⲧ ⲙⲙⲏⲓ ⲡ̄ⲭ̄ⲥ̄ ⳾ [8]Ⲟⲩⲟϩ ⲙⲁ ⲛⲉϩ ⳾ ⲛ̀ⲥⲁ ⲛⲉⲧⲉⲛⲗⲁⲙⲡⲁⲥ ⳾ ϩⲟⲧⲁⲛ ⲇⲉ ⲁϥϣⲁⲛⲧⲱⲛϥ ⲉ̀ⲓ̀ ⲉⲃⲟⲗ ⳾ ⲛ̀ⲧⲟⲩϫⲉⲙⲑⲏⲛⲟⲩ ⲉ̀ⲣⲉⲧⲉⲛⲣⲏⲥ ⳾ ⲛ̄ⲧⲉⲧⲉⲛϣⲉ ⲛⲱⲧⲉⲛ ⲉϧⲟⲩⲛ ⲉⲛⲓϩⲟⲛ ⲛⲉⲙⲁϥ ⳾ [9]Ⲓⲧⲁ ⲡⲉϫⲁⲥ ⲙ̀ⲡⲉⲛⲥⲱⲧⲏⲣ ⳾ ϫⲉ ⲱ̀
p. [λa] ⲛⲁϣⲏⲣⲓ ⲙ̀ⲙⲉⲛⲣⲓⲧ ⳾ ϯϯϩⲟ ⲉ̀ⲣⲟⲕ ϣⲱⲡⲓ ⲛⲱⲟⲩ ⲧⲏⲣⲟⲩ ⲛ̀|ⲣⲉϥϯⲛⲟⲙϯ ⳾ ⲙⲉⲛⲉⲛⲥⲁ ⲡⲁⲟⲩⲱⲧⲉⲃ ⲉⲃⲟⲗ ⳾ [10]ϫⲉ ⲟⲩⲏⲓ ϥϧⲉⲙϧⲱⲙ[b] ⲛ̀ϫⲉ ⲡⲟⲩϩⲏⲧ ⳾ ⲉ̀ϫⲉⲛ ⲛⲓⲡⲉⲧϩⲱⲟⲩ ⲉ̀ⲧⲁ ⲛⲟⲩⲃⲁⲗ ⲛⲁⲩ ⲉ̀ⲣⲱⲟⲩ ⳾ ⲉⲧⲁⲩⲁⲓⲧⲟⲩ ⲛⲁⲕ ⲛ̀ϫⲉ ⲛⲓⲓ̈ⲟⲩⲇⲁⲓ ⳾ [11]Ⲁ ⲛⲉⲛⲃⲁⲗ ⲛⲁⲩ ⲉ̀ⲣⲟⲕ ⲉ̀ⲣⲉ ⲡⲉⲕⲥⲱⲙⲁ ϫⲟⲕⲉⲙ ⳾ ϧⲉⲛ ⲟⲩⲥⲛⲟϥ ⳾ ϩⲓⲧⲉⲛ ⲡⲑⲟⲩⲝ ⲛ̀ⲛⲓⲛϥⲧ ⳾ ⲛⲉⲙ ϯϣⲉ ⲛ̀ⲗⲟⲭⲅⲏ ⳾ ⲉⲩⲥⲟⲛ ⳾ [12]Ⲁⲛⲛⲁⲩ ⲉ̀ⲣⲟⲕ ⲟⲛ ⳾ ⲉⲩⲧⲥⲓⲟ̀ ⲙ̀ⲙⲟⲛ ⲛ̀ⲟⲩⲉⲛϣⲁϣⲓ ⳾ ⲉⲩⲫⲙⲁ ⲛ̀ⲟⲩⲙⲱⲟⲩ ⳾ ⲛⲉⲙ ⲉⲩϯ[c] ⲛⲟⲩⲭⲗⲟⲙ ⲛ̀ⲥⲟⲩⲣⲓ ⲉ̀ϫⲱⲕ ⳾ ⲛⲉⲙ ⲉⲩϯ[c] ⲛⲟⲩϣⲉ ⲛ̀ⲗⲟⲅⲭⲏ ⲛⲁⲕ ⳾ ⲉⲑⲃⲉ ⲡⲉⲛⲟⲩϫⲁⲓ ⲧⲏⲣⲉⲛ = ⳾ [13]Ⲉⲃⲏⲗ ϫⲉ ⲁⲕⲧⲱⲛⲕ ⳾ ⲁⲕϯ ⲛⲱⲟⲩ ⲙ̀ⲡⲓⲣⲁϣⲓ ⳾ ⲙ̀ⲙⲟⲛ ⲛⲁⲩⲛⲁⲙⲟⲩ ⲧⲏⲣⲟⲩ ⲡⲉ ⳾ [14]Ⲁⲗⲗⲁ ϯϣⲟⲡ ⲛⲉⲙⲱⲟⲩ ⲛ̀ⲥⲟⲗⲥⲉⲗ ⳾ ϣⲁ ⲉϧⲟⲩⲛ ⲉⲛⲁⲓⲉ̀ϩⲟⲟⲩ ⳾ ⲉⲃⲟⲗ ϩⲓⲧⲉⲛ ⲧⲉⲕⲙⲉⲧⲁ̀ⲅⲁⲑⲟⲥ[d] ⳾ [15]Ⲁϥⲉⲣⲟⲩⲱ̀ ⲛ̀ϫⲉ ⲡⲉⲛⲟ̄ⲥ̄ ⳾ ⲟⲩⲟϩ ⲡⲉⲛⲛⲟⲩϯ ⳾ ⲡⲉϫⲁϥ ⲛ̀ⲧⲉϥⲙⲁⲩ ⳾ Ϫⲉ ⲱ̀ ⲧⲁⲙⲁⲩ ⲉⲑⲛⲉⲥⲱⲥ ϧⲉⲛ ⲡϫⲓⲛⲑⲣⲉ ⲁ̀ⲇⲁⲙ ⳾ ⲉⲣⲡⲁⲣⲁⲃⲉⲛⲓⲛ ⲛ̀ⲧⲁⲉⲛⲧⲟⲗⲏ ⳾ ⲁⲓϣⲱⲧ ⲉⲃⲟⲗ ⲉ̀ϫⲱϥ ⳾ ⲛⲟⲩⲁⲡⲟⲫⲁⲥⲓⲥ ⲉ̀ⲓϫⲱ ⲙ̀ⲙⲟⲥ ⳾ ϫⲉ ⲁ̀ⲇⲁⲙ ⲛ̀ⲑⲟⲕ ⲟⲩⲕⲁϩⲓ ⳾ ⲟⲩⲟϩ

[a] punct. sup. ⲛ prim. ut vid. [b] punct. sup. ⲙ prim. ut vid.
[c] ⲉ̀ϯ [d] ⲧⲉⲕⲙ sup. ras. pr. man. ut vid.

own destruction. [3]And the virgins also were all weeping
and[a] groaning. [4]But she turned her face to us, and said to
us, My sons, wherefore do ye weep and grieve my spirit? cf. Ac xxi 13
[5]Is it not written that all flesh must needs taste death? I cf. Job xxxiv 15
also must needs return to the earth, as all the inhabitants of
earth. [6]But be of good cheer, He is with you always, and cf. Mt xxviii 20;
He will not leave you desolate; even as He said. [7]Again Jn xiv 18
she said to the virgins, My good daughters, keep the cove-
nants that ye have made with your true Bridegroom Christ.
[8]And pour[b] oil into your lamps: and when He ariseth to cf. Mt xxv 4, 10; Lc
go forth, ye shall be found watching, and shall go in unto xii 37
the marriage feast with Him. [9]Then she said to our Saviour,
O my beloved Son, I beseech Thee, be to all of them *a* com-
forter after my translation[c]; [10]for their heart is broken over
the evils which their eyes saw, which the Jews did to Thee.
[11]Our eyes saw Thee, when Thy body was bathed with blood,
at once by the piercing of the nails and the spear wound. cf. Jn xix 34
[12]We saw Thee also given gall to drink instead of water, and cf. Mt xxvii 34
a crown of thorns put upon Thy head[d], and wounded by a cf. Mt xxvii 29;
spear for the salvation of us all. [13]Unless Thou hadst risen Mc xv 17;
and given them joy[e], surely[f] they all had died. [14]But I am Jn xix 2
with them for consolation until this day through Thy good-
ness.

[15]Our Lord and our God answered and said to His
mother, O My beautiful mother, when Adam transgressed cf. 4 Esd vii 11
My commandment, I passed[g] upon him a sentence, saying,
Adam, thou *art* earth and thou shalt return unto the earth cf. Ge iii 19

[a] Lit. *with* [b] Lit. *give* [c] Or *removal* [d] Or *upon Thee*
[e] Lit. *the joy* [f] Lit. *it not being so* [g] Lit. *cut*

p. ⲗⲃ ϫⲛⲁⲧⲁⲥⲑⲟⲕ ⲉⲛⲕⲁϩⲓ ⲟⲛ ⳾ | [16]Ⲕⲉ ⲅⲁⲣ ⲁⲛⲟⲕ ϩⲱ ⳾ ϧⲁ ⲡⲱⲛϧ
ⲛ̀ⲟⲩⲟⲛ ⲛⲓⲃⲉⲛ ⳾ ⲁⲓϫⲉⲙϯⲡⲓ ⲙ̀ⲫⲙⲟⲩ ϧⲉⲛ ϯⲥⲁⲣⲝ ⲉ̀ⲧⲁⲓϭⲓⲧⲥ ⳾
ⲉⲃⲟⲗ ⲛ̀ϧⲏϯ ⳾ ϧⲉⲛ ⲧⲥⲁⲣⲝ ⲛ̀ⲁ̀ⲇⲁⲙ ⳾ ⲡⲉϣⲟⲣⲡ ⲛⲓⲱⲧ ⳾ [17]Ⲕⲁⲛ ⳾
ⲉⲥⲟⲓ̈[a] ⲛⲟⲩⲁⲓ[b] ⳾[c] ⲛⲉⲙⲁⲥ ⲛ̀ϫⲉ ⲧⲁⲙⲉⲧⲛⲟⲩϯ ⳾ ⲉⲑⲃⲉ[d] ⲫⲁⲓ ⲁⲓⲧⲟⲩ-
ⲛⲟⲥⲥ ⲉⲃⲟⲗ ϧⲉⲛ ⲛⲏ ⲉⲑⲙⲱⲟⲩⲧ ⳾ [18]ⲛⲁⲓⲟⲩⲱϣ ⲁⲛ ⲡⲉ ⳾ ⲉ̀ϫⲁϯ
ⲉ̀ϫⲉⲙϯⲡⲓ ⲙ̀ⲫⲙⲟⲩ[e] ⳾ ⲁⲗⲗⲁ ⲉ̀ⲟⲩⲟⲑⲃⲓ ⲉⲛϣⲱⲓ ⲉⲛⲓⲫⲏⲟⲩⲓ̈ ⳾ ⲙ̀ⲫⲣⲏϯ
ⲛⲉⲛⲱⲭ ⳾ ⲛⲉⲙ ⲏ̀ⲗⲓⲁⲥ ⳾ [19]Ⲁⲗⲗⲁ ⲛⲁⲓⲕⲉⲭⲱⲟⲩⲛⲓ ⳾ ϩⲱϯ ⲉ̀ⲣⲱⲟⲩ
ϩⲱⲟⲩ ⲡⲉ ⳾ ⲉ̀ϫⲉⲙϯⲡⲓ ⲙ̀ⲫⲙⲟⲩ ⲉⲛϧⲁⲉ̄ × [20]Ⲟⲩⲟϩ ⲁⲣⲉϣⲁⲛ ⲫⲁⲓ
ϣⲱⲡⲓ ⲙ̀ⲙⲟ ⳾ Ⲥⲉⲛⲁⲙⲉⲩⲓ̀ ⲉ̀ⲣⲟ ⲡ̅ϫⲉ ϩⲁⲛⲣⲱⲙⲓ ⲙ̀ⲡⲟⲛⲏⲣⲟⲛ ⳾ ϫⲉ
ⲛ̀ⲑⲟ ⲟⲩⲇⲩⲛⲁⲙⲓⲥ ⳾ ⲉ̀ⲧⲁⲥⲓ̀ ⲉⲡⲉⲥⲏⲧ ⲉⲃⲟⲗ ⳾ ϧⲉⲛ ⲧⲫⲉ × [21]Ⲟⲩⲟϩ
ϫⲉ ⲧⲁⲓ̀ⲟⲓⲕⲟⲛⲟⲙⲓⲁ ⳾ ϫⲉ ⲉ̀ⲧⲁⲥϣⲱⲡⲓ ϧⲉⲛ ⲟⲩⲫⲁⲛⲧⲁⲥⲓⲁ̀ ⲩ ⲁ̀ⲛⲟⲕ
ⲉⲧⲥⲱⲟⲩⲛ ⲙ̀ⲡϩⲏⲧ ⲛ̀ⲟⲩⲟⲛ ⲛⲓⲃⲉⲛ ⳾ ⲟⲩⲟϩ ⲉ̀ⲧⲉⲙⲓ ⲉ̀ⲛⲟⲩⲙⲟⲕⲙⲉⲕ̄ ⳾
[22]Ⲛⲁⲓ ⲉ̀ⲧⲁϥϫⲟⲧⲟⲩ ⲛ̀ϫⲉ ⲡⲉⲛⲥⲱⲧⲏⲣ ⳾ ⲁϥⲕⲉⲧ[f] ⲡⲉϥϩⲟ ⲉ̀ϫⲱⲛ
ⲁⲛⲟⲕ ⲡⲉⲧⲣⲟⲥ ⳾ ⲛⲉⲙ ⲓⲱⲁⲛⲛⲏⲥ [23]ⲡⲉϫⲁϥ ⲛⲁⲛ ⳾ ϫⲉ ϫⲉⲙⲡⲟⲙϯ
p. [ⲗⲅ] ⲡⲁϣⲫⲉⲣ ⲛⲁⲡⲟⲥⲧⲟⲗⲟⲥ ⳾ [24]ϯⲡⲁ|ⲭⲁⲥ ⲁⲛ ⲉⲱⲥⲕ ⲥⲁⲃⲟⲗ ⲙ̀ⲙⲱ-
ⲧⲉⲛ ⲩ Ⲁⲗⲗⲁ ⲥⲛⲁⲟⲩⲟⲛϩⲥ ⲉ̄ⲣⲱⲧⲉⲛ ⲛ̀ⲭⲱⲗⲉⲙ ⳾ [25]Ⲅ̅ⲅ̅ ⲡ̅ⲉ̄ϩⲟⲟⲩ
ⲡⲉ ⳾ ⲓⲥϫⲉⲛ ⲡⲉⲥϫⲱⲕ ⳾ ϣⲁ ⲧⲉⲥⲁⲛⲁⲗⲩⲙⲯⲓⲥ ⲉ̀ⲑⲟⲩⲁⲃ ⳾ [26]ϯⲡⲁⲉⲛⲥ
ϩⲁⲣⲱⲧⲉⲛ ⳾ ⲉⲥϫⲟⲗϩ ⲙ̀ⲡⲁⲓⲥⲱⲙⲁ ⲟⲛ ⳾ ⲙ̀ⲫⲣⲏϯ ⲙ̀ⲡⲁⲓⲥⲱⲙⲁ ⲟⲛ ⳾
ⲉ̄ⲣⲉⲧⲉⲛⲛⲁⲩ ⲉ̀ⲣⲟⲥ[g] ⳾ ϯⲛⲟⲩ ⲉⲥϣⲟⲡ ⲛⲉⲙⲱⲧⲉⲛ ⳾ [27]Ⲏ̅ⲧⲁⲟⲩⲟⲑⲃⲉⲥ
ⲉⲛϣⲱⲓ ⲉⲛⲓⲫⲏⲟⲩⲓ̈ ϧⲁⲧⲉⲛ ⲡⲁⲓⲱⲧ ⳾ ⲛⲉⲙ ⲡⲓⲡ̅ⲛ̅ⲁ̅ ⲉⲑⲟⲩⲁⲃ ⳾
ⲉⲑⲣⲉⲥⲙⲟⲩⲛ ⲉⲃⲟⲗ ⳾ ⲉⲥⲧⲱⲃϩ ⲉ̀ϫⲉⲛⲑⲏⲛⲟⲩ ⲧⲏⲣⲟⲩ ⳾ [28]Ⲛⲁⲓ ⲇⲉ
ⲉ̀ⲧⲁϥϫⲟⲧⲟⲩ ⳾ ⲡⲁⲗⲓⲛ ⲟⲛ ⲡⲉϫⲁϥ ⲛⲁⲛ ⳾ Ϫⲉ ⲧⲉⲛⲑⲏⲛⲟⲩ ϩⲱⲗ
ⲉ̀ϧⲟⲩⲛ ⲉ̀ⲡⲓⲙⲁ ⲉⲑⲟⲩⲁⲃ ⳾ ⲧⲉⲧⲉⲛⲛⲁϫⲓⲙⲓ ϩⲓϫⲉⲛ ⲡⲓⲑⲩⲥⲓⲁⲥⲧⲏⲣⲓⲟⲛ ⳾
ⲛ̀ϩⲁⲛϩⲃⲱⲥ ⲛⲉⲡⲟⲩⲣⲁⲛⲓⲟⲛ ⳾ ⲛⲉⲙ ϩⲁⲛⲥⲑⲟⲓⲛⲟⲩϥⲓ ⲛ̀ⲧⲉ ⲛⲓⲫⲏⲟⲩⲓ̈ ⳾
Ⲉⲧⲁ ⲡⲁⲓⲱⲧ ⲛⲁⲅⲁⲑⲟⲥ ⲛⲉⲙ ⲡⲓⲡ̅ⲛ̅ⲁ̅ ⲉ̄ⲑⲟⲩⲁⲃ ⳾ ⲟⲩⲟⲣⲡⲟⲩ ⲛⲏⲓ ⳾
ⲉⲛⲧⲁⲓ̀ⲟ[h] ⲙ̀ⲡⲥⲱⲙⲁ ⳾ ⲛ̀ⲧⲁⲙⲉⲛⲣⲓ̀ⲧ ⲙ̀ⲙⲁⲩ × [29]Ⲉⲧⲁⲛϣⲉ ⲇⲉ ⲉ̀ϧⲟⲩⲛ
ⲁ̄ⲡⲉ̄ⲛⲟⲩ ⲉⲃⲟⲗ ϩⲁⲣⲟϥ ⳾ ⲡⲉϫⲁϥ ⲛⲁⲛ ⳾ Ϫⲉ ⲫⲟⲣϣⲟⲩ[i] ⳾ ϩⲓϫⲉⲛ

[a] ⲥⲉⲟⲓ̈ [b] ⲁ sup. ras. pr. man. [c] ⳾ sup. ras. pr. man. [d] punct. sup. ⲑ ut vid. [e] punct. sup. ⲙ prim. ut vid. [f] punct. sup. ⲧ ut vid. [g] punct. sup. ⲉ ut vid. [h] punct. sup. ⲟ ut vid. [i] ⲫⲟϣⲟⲩ (ⲣ sup. rec. man.)

again. 16 For also I, the Life of all men, tasted death in the
flesh which I took from thee, in the flesh of Adam, thy fore-
father. 17 Yet[a] since My godhead was one with it, therefore I
raised it from the dead. 18 I did not wish to suffer thee to
taste death, but to translate[b] thee up to the heavens as Enoch
and Elias. 19 But these also, even they must needs taste
death at last. 20 And if this happens to thee, wicked men
will think concerning thee, that thou *art* a power which came
down from heaven; 21 and that this dispensation took place
in appearance. I know the heart of all men, and under-
stand their thoughts.

22 When our Saviour had said these things, He turned His
face to us, *even* to me Peter and to John; 23 and said to us,
Be of good cheer, My friends *and* apostles. 24 I will not suffer
her to be long away from you, but she shall appear to you
quickly. 25 There are two hundred and six days from her
death[c] unto her holy assumption. 26 I will bring her unto
you arrayed in this body again, even as this body also, as ye
see[d] her now, whilst she is with you. 27 And I will translate[b]
her up to the heavens *to be* with My Father and the Holy
Ghost, that she may continue praying for you all. 28 Now
when He had said these things, again He said to us, Arise,
go into the holy place; and ye shall find on the altar
heavenly garments and perfumes of the heavens, which My
good Father and the Holy Ghost have sent Me for the
honour of the body of My beloved mother. 29 And when we
had gone in, we brought them out to Him; and He said to us,

[a] See note [b] Or *remove* [c] Or *consummation* [d] Lit. *whilst ye see*

ⲡⲁⲓⲙⲁ ⲛⲉⲛⲕⲟⲧ ⳹ [30]Ⲉⲧⲁⲛⲫⲟⲣϣⲟⲩ ⲇⲉ ⳹ ⲡⲉϫⲁϥ ⲛ̀ⲧⲉϥⲙⲁⲩ ⳹ ϫⲉ
ⲓ̅ⲱⲥ[a] ⲙ̀ⲙⲟ[b] ⲱ̀ ⲧⲟⲩⲣⲱ ⲛ̀ⲛⲓϩⲓⲟ̀ⲙⲓ ⲧⲏⲣⲟⲩ ⳹ ⲁⲙⲏ ⲉ̀ϫⲉⲛ ⲛⲁⲓ |
p. λⲁ ⲙ̅ⲧⲟⲛ[c] ⲙⲙⲟ ⳹ ⲉⲃⲟⲗ ϩⲁ ⲡⲓⲙ̀ⲕⲁϩ ⲛ̀ϩⲏⲧ ⳹ ⲛⲉⲙ ⲡⲓϧⲓⲥⲓ ⳹ ⲛⲉⲙ
ⲡⲓϥⲓⲁ̅ϩⲟⲙ ⳹ [31]ⲙⲁϣⲉ ⲛⲉ ⲉ̀ϧⲟⲩⲛ ⲉⲡⲓⲣⲁϣⲓ ⳹ ⲛⲉⲙ ⲟⲩⲛⲟϥ ⲉ̀ⲛⲉⲛⲉϩ ⲅ
[32]Ⲡ̅ⲑ̅ⲟ̅ⲥ ⲇⲉ ⳹ ⲁⲥⲧⲱⲛⲥ ⲁⲥⲫⲱⲣϣ ⲛ̀ⲛⲉⲥϫⲓϫ ⲉⲃⲟⲗ ⳹ ⲁⲥϯ ⲛ̀ⲧⲁⲓ-
ⲡⲣⲟⲥⲉⲩⲭⲏ ⳹ [33]ϫⲉ ⲁⲇⲱⲛⲁⲓ̈ ⳹ ⲉⲗⲱⲓ̈ ⳹ Ⲥⲁⲃⲁⲱⲧ ⲙⲉⲥⲓⲁⲥ ⳹
ⲣⲁⲃⲃⲁ · ⳹ Ⲉⲙⲁⲛⲟⲩⲏⲗ ⳹ ϣⲟⲡⲧ ⲉ̀ⲣⲟⲕ ⲡⲁϣⲏⲣⲓ ϧⲉⲛ ⲧⲁⲓⲟⲩⲛⲟⲩ
ⲑⲁⲓ ⳹ [34]Ⲡⲁⲣⲟⲩⲟⲩⲱⲛ ⲙ̀ⲡⲁⲙ̀ⲑⲟ ⲛ̀ϫⲉ ⲛⲓⲣⲱⲟⲩ ⲙ̀ⲃⲁⲥⲓⲗⲓⲕⲟⲛ ⳹ ⲛ̀ⲧⲉ
ⲡⲉⲕⲁⲩⲗⲏⲟⲩ ⲉⲑⲟⲩⲁⲃ ⳹ ϩⲓⲛⲁ ⲛ̀ⲧⲁⲓ̈ ⲉ̀ϧⲟⲩⲛ ⲛ̀ϧⲏⲧⲟⲩ ⳹ ⲛ̀ⲧⲁⲟⲩⲱϣⲧ
ⲙ̀ⲡⲉⲕⲙ̀ⲑⲟ ⲡⲁⲛⲏⲃ = ⳹ [35]Ϫⲉ ⲛ̀ⲑⲟⲕ[d] ⳹ ⲉ̀ⲣⲉ ⲡⲓⲱ̀ⲟⲩ ⲉⲣⲡⲣⲉⲡⲓ
ⲛⲁⲕ ⳹ ⲛⲉⲙ ⲡⲉⲕⲓⲱⲧ ⲛ̀ⲁ̀ⲅⲁⲑⲟⲥ ⳹ ⲛⲉⲙ ⲡⲓⲡ̅ⲛ̅ⲁ̅ ⲉⲑⲟⲩⲁⲃ ⲡⲣⲉϥ-
ⲧⲁⲛϧⲟ ⳹ Ⲟⲩⲟϩ ⲛⲟⲙⲟⲟⲩⲥⲓⲟⲥ ⲛⲉⲙⲁⲕ ⳹ ϣⲁ ⲉⲛⲉϩ · ⲁⲙⲏⲛ = ⳹ : –
VI. [1]Ⲛⲁⲓ ⲇⲉ ⲉ̀ⲧⲁⲥϫⲟⲧⲟⲩ ⳹ ⲁⲥⲉⲛⲕⲟⲧ ϩⲓϫⲉⲛ ⲡⲓϩⲗⲱⲥ ⳹ ⲁⲥⲕⲱϯ
ⲙ̀ⲡⲉⲥϩⲟ ⲉⲡⲉⲛⲥⲱⲧⲏⲣ ⳹ ⲟⲩⲟϩ ϧⲉⲛ ϯⲟⲩⲛⲟⲩ ⳹ ⲁⲥϯ ⲙ̀ⲡⲉⲥⲡ̅ⲛ̅ⲁ̅
ⲉ̀ϧⲣⲏⲓ ⲉ̀ⲛⲉϥϫⲓϫ ⳹ : [2]Ⲡⲉϫⲁϥ ⲛⲏⲓ ⳹ ⲁ̀ⲛⲟⲕ ⲡⲉⲧⲣⲟⲥ ⲛⲉⲙ ⲓⲱ-
ⲁⲛⲛⲏⲥ ⳹ ϫⲉ ϫⲱⲗⲉⲙ ⲙ̀ⲙⲱⲧⲉⲛ ⳹ ⲁⲩϫⲱⲗ ⲡⲥⲱⲙⲁ ⲛ̀ⲧⲁⲙⲁⲩ ⳹
p. [λε] ⲙ̀ⲡⲁⲛϯϣⲉ ⲛⲏⲓ ⲉ̀ⲃⲟⲗ ϩⲁⲣⲱⲧⲉⲛ ⳹ | [3]Ⲁⲛⲟⲛ ⲇⲉ ⲁⲛⲧⲱⲟⲩⲛⲟⲩ ⳹
ⲁⲛⲕⲟⲥⲥ ⳹ ⲛ̀ⲕⲁⲗⲱⲥ ⳹ ⲕⲁⲧⲁ ⲫⲣⲏϯ ⲉⲧⲁϥⲟⲩⲁϩⲥⲁϩⲛⲓ ⳹ [4]Ⲡ̅ⲑ̅ⲟ̅ϥ
ⲇⲉ ⲡ̅ⲟ̅ⲥ̅ ⳹ ⲁ̀ϥⲥⲟⲩⲧⲉⲛ[e] ⲛⲧⲉϥϫⲓϫ ⲉⲃⲟⲗ ⳹ ⲉⲛⲥⲁ ⲛ̀ϯⲁⲛⲁⲧⲟⲗⲏ ⳹
ⲁϥⲓⲛⲓ[f] ⲛⲁⲛ ⳹ ⲛ̅[g] ⲙ̀ⲃⲁⲓ ⳹ ⲃⲏⲧ ⳹ ⲉⲩⲣⲱⲟⲩⲧ ⳹ ⲛⲉⲙ ϩⲁⲛⲥⲑⲟⲓ-
ⲛⲟⲩϥⲓ[e] ⳹ ⲉⲃⲟⲗ ϧⲉⲛ ⲡⲓⲡⲁⲣⲁⲇⲓⲥⲟⲥ ⲛⲧⲉ ⲡⲟⲩⲛⲟϥ ⳹ [5]Ⲡⲁⲗⲓⲛ ⲟⲛ
ⲁϥⲕⲉⲧ ϩⲣⲁϥ ⳹ ⲁϥⲓⲛⲓ ⲛ̅ⲅ̅ ⲛ̅ϫⲁⲗ ⲛ̅ϫⲱⲓⲧ ⳹ ⲉⲃⲟⲗ ϧⲉⲛ ⲟⲩⲃⲱ
ⲛ̀ϫⲱⲓⲧ ⳹ ⲉⲧⲁ ϯϭⲣⲟⲙⲡⲓ : ⲓ̅ⲛⲓ ⲛ̀ⲛⲱⲉ ⳹ ⲉⲃⲟⲗ ⲛ̅ϧⲏⲧⲥ ⳹ ϣⲁⲧⲉϥ-
ⲉ̀ⲙⲓ ⳹ ϫⲉ ⲁ ⲡ̅ⲟ̅ⲥ̅ ⲛⲁⲓ ⲙⲡⲓⲕⲟⲥⲙⲟⲥ ⳹ [6]Ⲉⲧⲁⲛⲧⲏⲓⲧⲟⲩ ⲉⲛⲉⲥⲥⲱⲙⲁ
ⲉⲑⲟⲩⲁⲃ ⳹ ⲡⲉϫⲁϥ ⲛⲏⲓ ⳹ ϫⲉ ⲡⲉⲧⲣⲟⲥ ⲡⲁⲉ̀ⲡⲓⲥⲕⲟⲡⲟⲥ ⳹ ϥⲁⲓ
ⲛ̀ⲧⲉⲥⲁⲫⲉ[h] ϩⲓ ⲧⲉⲕⲡⲁϩⲟⲩⲃⲓ[i] ⳹ ϫⲉ ⲛ̀ⲑⲟⲕ ⲡⲉ ⲧⲁⲫⲉ ⲛ̀ϯⲉⲕⲕⲗⲏⲥⲓⲁ
ⲙⲉⲛⲉⲛⲥⲱⲓ ⳹ [7]Ⲓⲱ̀ⲁⲛⲛⲏⲥ ϩⲱϥ : ⲙⲁⲣⲉϥϥⲁⲓ ⲙ̅ⲡⲉⲥϭⲁⲗⲁⲩϫ ⳹ ϩⲓ

[a] lin. sup. ⲓ rubr. script. [b] punct. sup. ⲙ prim. ut vid. [c] lin. sup. ⲙ ut vid. [d] ⲛ̀ⲑⲟⲕ ⲡⲉ [e] punct. sup. ϥ ut vid. [f] punct. sup. ⲓ prim. rubr. script. [g] lin. sup. ⲛ ut vid. [h] pr. man. ⲛ̀ⲧⲉϥⲁⲫⲉ sed ⲥ ex ϥ mutat. [i] rec. man. del. ⲟⲩ

Spread them on this bed. 30 And when we had spread them,
He said to His mother, Haste thee, O thou queen of all
women, enter these; and rest thee from the grief and the
trouble and the groaning. 31 Enter thou into the joy and cf. Mt xxv 21, 23
eternal gladness.

32 And she arose, and spread forth her hands, and said[a]
this prayer, 33 Adonai, Eloi, Sabaoth, Messias, Rabba, Emmanuel,
receive me, my Son, in this very hour. 34 Let the royal doors
of Thy holy courts be opened before me, that I may enter in cf. Ps cxvii 19
by them, and worship before Thee, my Master. 35 For it is to
Thee that the glory is due[b], and to Thy good Father and the
Holy Ghost, giver of life and of one essence with Thee, for
ever. Amen.

VI. Now when she had said these things, she lay down
on the garments, and she turned her face to our Saviour,
and straightway she commended her spirit into His hands. cf. Lc xxiii 46
2 He said to me, *even* to me Peter and to John, Make haste,
shroud the body of My mother before I go away from you.
3 And we arose, and prepared her well for burial, even as He
commanded. 4 And He, the Lord stretched out His hand east-
wards, and brought us three flourishing[c] branches of palm, and
perfumes from the Paradise of delight[d]. 5 Again He turned cf. Ge iii 23
His face, and brought three branches of olive from an olive
tree, from which the dove brought to Noah, that he might cf. Ge viii 11
know[e] that the Lord had mercy on the world. 6 When we
had placed them on her holy body, He said to me, Peter,
My bishop, bear her head on thy shoulder; for thou art the
head of the Church after Me. 7 John also, let him bear her
feet on his shoulder; for I have sanctified him from *the time* cf. Je i 5

[a] Lit. *gave* [b] The MS has *For Thou art—the glory is due to Thee*
[c] Or *fresh* [d] Or *gladness* [e] Or *until he knew*

ⲧⲉϥⲡⲁϩⲟⲩⲃⲓ[a] ⳾ ϫⲉ ⲁⲓⲧⲟⲩⲃⲟϥ ⳾ ⲓⲥϫⲉⲛ ⲉϥⲭⲏ ϧⲉⲛ ⲑⲛⲉϫⲓ ⳾
[8]Ⲙⲁⲣⲉ ⲡⲓϩⲱⲟⲩⲧ ⲙⲟϣⲓ ⲉⲧϩⲏ ⳾ ⲟⲩⲟϩ ⲛⲓϩⲓⲟ̄ⲙⲓ ⲛ̄ⲧⲟⲩⲙⲟϣⲓ
ⲉ̀ⲫⲁϩⲟⲩ ⳾ ⲕⲁⲧⲁ ⲛⲉⲧⲥϣⲉ ⳾ [9]Ⲙⲟϣⲓ ϧⲉⲛ ⲟⲩⲥⲉⲙⲛⲓ ⳾ ⲛⲉⲙ
ⲟⲩⲕⲁⲧⲁⲥⲧⲁⲥⲓⲥ ⳾ ⲁⲧϭⲛⲉ ⲣⲓⲙⲓ ⳾ ϩⲓ ⲱϣ ⲉⲃⲟⲗ ⳾ ϫⲉ ⲓⲥ ⲡⲓⲁⲩ-
p. λϛ ⲡⲁⲙⲓⲥ[b] ⲛ̀ⲧⲉ ⲡⲓⲫⲛⲟⲩϯ ⳾ ⲥⲉⲉⲣϩⲩⲙⲛⲟⲥ ϧⲁϫⲱⲧⲉⲛ – | [10]Ⲕⲉ ⲅⲁⲣ
ⲧⲉⲧⲉⲛⲥ̀ⲱⲟⲩⲛ ϩⲱⲧⲉⲛ ⳾ ⲙ̄ⲡϫⲱⲛⲧ ⲛ̀ⲛⲓⲁⲣⲭⲏⲉⲣⲉⲩⲥ ⳾ ⲛⲉⲙ ⲧⲕⲁⲕⲓⲁ̄
ⲙ̄ⲡⲓϣⲗⲟⲗ ⲧⲏⲣϥ ⲙ̄ⲫⲉⲛⲉⲩⲥ ⲛ̄ⲧⲉ ⲛⲓⲓⲟⲩⲇⲁⲓ ⳾ ⲉ̀ϧⲟⲩⲛ ⲉ̀ⲣⲟⲓ ⳾ ⲛⲉⲙ
ⲧⲁⲙⲁⲩ – [11]Ⲁⲗⲗⲁ ⲛⲟⲩⲥⲟϭⲛⲓ ⲛⲁϭ̀ⲓ ⲉ̀ⲣⲁⲧϥ ⲁⲛ ⳾ ϯⲛⲁⲁⲓⲧⲟⲩ[c]
ⲙ̄ⲃⲉⲗⲗⲉ ⳾ ϣⲁⲧⲟⲩⲥⲟⲩⲉⲛ ⲡⲓⲱ̀ⲟⲩ ⲛ̀ⲧⲉ ⲧⲁⲙⲉⲑⲛⲟⲩϯ ⳾ ⲛ̀ⲥⲉϯⲱⲟⲩ
ⲡⲏⲓ ⳾ ⲛⲉⲙ ⲡⲁⲓⲱⲧ ⲛⲁⲅⲁⲑⲟⲥ ⳾ ⲛⲉⲙ ⲡⲓⲡ̄ⲛ̄ⲁ̄ ⲉⲑⲟⲩⲁⲃ = -
[12]Ⲁⲗⲓⲟⲩⲓ̈[d] ⲟⲩⲛ ⲙ̄ⲡⲥⲱⲙⲁ ⲛ̀ⲧⲉ ⲧⲁⲙⲁⲩ ⲉⲑⲟⲩⲁⲃ ⳾ ⲡⲗⲏⲛ ⲭⲁϥ
ϧⲉⲛ ϯⲥⲗⲏ ⲛ̀ⲱ̀ⲛⲓ ⳾ ϣⲑⲁⲙ ⲙ̀ⲙⲟⲥ ⳾ ⲟⲩⲟϩ ⲙⲟⲩⲛ ⲉⲣⲟⲥ ϧⲉⲛ
ϩⲁⲛⲡⲣⲟⲥⲉⲩⲭⲏ ⳾ ϣⲁ ϯⲛⲉⲓ̀[e] ⲛⲧⲉ ⲧⲉⲥⲁ̀ⲛⲁⲗⲩⲙⲯⲓⲥ[f] ⳾ [13]Ⲥ̄ⲉ̄[g]
ⲡⲉϩⲟⲟⲩ ⳾ ϯⲛⲏⲟⲩ ⳾ ⲛⲉⲙ ⲧⲉⲥⲙⲁⲕⲁⲣⲓⲁ̄ ⲙ̀ⲯⲩⲭⲏ[b] ⳾ ⲛ̀ⲧⲁⲁⲓⲥ
ⲛ̀ⲟⲩⲁⲓ : ⲛⲉⲙ ⲡⲉⲥⲥⲱⲙⲁ ⳾ ⲛ̀ⲧⲁⲟⲗⲥ ⲉⲛⲓⲫⲛⲟⲩϯ ϧⲉⲛ ⲟⲩⲱⲟⲩ ⳾
ϧⲁⲧⲉⲛ ⲡⲁⲓⲱⲧ ⲛⲁⲅⲁⲑⲟⲥ ⳾ ⲛⲉⲙ ⲡⲓⲡ̄ⲛ̄ⲁ̄ ⲉⲑⲟⲩⲁⲃ ⳾ [14]Ⲛⲁⲓ ⲇⲉ ⳾
ⲉⲧⲁϥϫⲟⲧⲟⲩ ⲁϥϯ ⲛⲁⲛ ⲛ̀ⲧⲉϥϩⲓⲣⲏⲛⲏ ⳾ ⲁϥϣⲉ ⲛⲁϥ ⲉⲛϣⲱⲓ
ⲉⲛⲓⲫⲛⲟⲩϯ ϧⲉⲛ ⲟⲩⲱⲟⲩ ⳾ ⲁϥⲧⲏⲓⲥ ⳾ ⲛ̀ⲇⲱⲣⲟⲛ ⲙ̄ⲡⲉϥⲓ̄ⲱⲧ ⳾ ⲛⲉⲙ
ⲡⲓⲡ̄ⲛ̄ⲁ̄ ⲉⲑⲟⲩⲁⲃ ⲉϥϫⲱ ⲙ̀ⲙⲟⲥ ⳾ [15]Ϫⲉ ⲱ̀ ⲡⲁⲓⲱⲧ ⲛ̄ⲁⲅⲁⲑⲟⲥ ⳾
p. [λζ] ϭⲓ ⲛ̀ⲧⲟⲩⲧ[h] ⲛ̀ⲧⲯⲩⲭⲏ ⲛ̀ⲧⲁⲙⲁⲕⲁⲣⲓⲁ̀ ⲙ̀ⲙⲁⲩ ⳾ | ⲑⲁⲓ ⲉ̀ⲧⲁⲥϣⲱⲡ[i]
ⲉ̀ⲣⲟⲥ ⲙ̄ⲡⲉⲕⲙⲟⲛⲟⲅⲉⲛⲏⲥ ⲛ̄ϣⲏⲣⲓ ϧⲉⲛ ⲡⲓⲕⲟⲥⲙⲟⲥ ⳾ [16]Ϭⲓ ⲛ̀ⲧⲟⲧ
ⲙ̀ⲡⲉⲕⲉⲣⲫⲉⲓ̄[j] ⲉⲑⲟⲩⲁⲃ ⲫⲁⲓ ⲉ̀ⲧⲁϥϣⲱⲡⲓ ⲙ̀ⲙⲁⲛⲟⲩⲟϩ ⲙ̀ⲡⲉⲕⲡ̄ⲛ̄ⲁ̄
ⲉⲑⲟⲩⲁⲃ ⳾ ⲉⲧⲉ ⲑⲁⲓ ⲧⲉ ⲑⲙⲉⲧⲟⲩⲁⲓ ⳾ ⲛ̀ⲧⲉ ϯⲙⲉⲑⲛⲟⲩϯ ⳾ [17]Ϭⲓ
ⲛ̀ⲧⲟⲧ ⳾ ⲱ̀ ⲡⲁⲓⲱⲧ ⲛⲁⲅⲁⲑⲟⲥ ⳾ ⲙ̄ⲡⲓⲃⲁⲧⲟⲥ ⳾ ⲫⲏ ⲉ̀ⲧⲁϥϣⲱⲡ ⲉ̀ⲣⲟϥ
ⲙ̀ⲡⲓⲭⲣⲱⲙ ⳾ ⲛ̄ⲧⲉ ϯⲙⲉⲑⲛⲟⲩϯ ⳾ ⲟⲩⲟϩ ⲙ̀ⲡⲉϥⲣⲱⲕϩ ⳾ [18]Ϯⲉⲣ-
ⲡⲣⲟⲥⲫⲉⲣⲓⲛ ⲛⲁⲕ ⲱ̀ ⲡⲁⲓⲱⲧ ⳾ ⲛⲟⲩⲇⲱⲣⲟⲛ ⲙ̄ⲃⲁⲥⲓⲗⲓⲕⲟⲛ ⲙ̄ⲫⲟⲟⲩ ⳾

[a] rec. man. del. ⲟⲩ [b] punct. sup. ⲙ ut vid. [c] ⲉ̀ⲣⲁⲧϥ ⲁⲛ ⳾ ϯ sup. ras. pr. man. [d] punct. sup. ⲓ prim. ut vid. [e] ʹ sup. ⲓ rubr. script. [f] ⲥ 1° sup. [g] Ⲥ̄ⲉ̄ ut vid., sed cf. supra v 25 [h] ⲛⲧⲟⲩⲧ fortasse pr. man., ⲧ 3° sup. ras. [i] ⲉ̀ⲧⲁⲥϣⲱⲡⲓ [j] ⲕ ex ⲣ mutat. pr. man. ut vid.

that he was in the womb. 8 Let the men go before, and the
women go behind, as is fitting[a]. 9 Go in order and in calmness
without weeping and crying out; for behold the powers of
the heavens sing hymns before you. 10 For also ye know the
anger of the chief priests and the malice of all the murderous
nation of the Jews against Me and My mother. 11 But their
counsel shall not stand. I will make them blind, that they
may know[b] the glory of My godhead, and glorify Me and My
good Father and the Holy Ghost. 12 Take up therefore the
body of My holy mother. Place it moreover in the stone
coffin. Shut it, and abide by it in prayers until the time
appointed for her assumption. 13 *In* two hundred and six
days I will come with her blessed soul, and make it one with
her body, and I will take her[c] to the heavens in glory *to be*
with My good Father and the Holy Ghost.

14 Now when He had said these things, He gave us His
peace, and went up to the heavens in glory, and gave her[c] *as*
a gift to His Father and the Holy Ghost, saying, 15 O My good
Father, receive from Me the soul of My blessed mother, who
received Thine only begotten Son in the world. 16 Receive
from Me Thy holy temple, which was *a* dwelling place of
Thy Holy Ghost, even the unity of the Godhead. 17 Receive
from Me, O My good Father, the bush which received the cf. Ex III 2
fire of the godhead and was not burnt. 18 I offer Thee, O My
Father, a royal gift to-day, even the soul of My virgin mother.

[a] Or *customary* [b] Or *until they know* [c] Or *it* (i.e. the soul)

ⲉ̀ⲧⲉ ⲑⲁⲓ ⲧⲉ ⲧⲯⲩⲭⲏ ⲛ̀ⲧⲁⲙⲁⲩ ⲙ̀ⲡⲁⲣⲑⲉⲛⲟⲥ ⳼ [19]Ϯⲓⲛⲓ ⲛⲁⲕ
ⲉ̀ϧⲟⲩⲛ ⲙ̀ⲫⲟⲟⲩ[a] ⳼ ⲱ ⲡⲁⲓⲱⲧ ⲡⲁⲅⲁⲑⲟⲥ ⳼ ⲛ̀ⲑⲏ ⲉⲧⲥⲟⲧⲡ ⲉ̀ϩⲟⲧⲉ
ϯⲕⲩⲃⲱⲧⲟⲥ ⲛ̄ⲧⲉ ϣⲟⲣⲡ ⳼ ⲑⲁⲓ ⲉ̀ⲧⲁⲕⲧⲟⲩϫⲟ ⲙ̀ⲡⲓⲕⲟⲥⲙⲟⲥ ⲧⲏⲣϥ ⳼
ϩⲓⲧⲉⲛ ⲡⲁϫⲓⲛϣⲱⲡⲓ ⲛ̀ϧⲏⲧⲥ ⳼ ⲡⲉⲕⲟ̀ⲙⲟⲟⲩⲥⲓⲟⲥ ⳼ [20]Ⲟⲩⲉ̀ϩⲟⲟⲩ ⲛ̀ⲣⲁϣⲓ
ⲡⲏⲓ ⲡⲉ ⲫⲟⲟⲩ ⳼ ⲱ ⲡⲁⲓⲱⲧ ⳼ ⲡⲓⲡⲁⲛⲧⲟⲕⲣⲁⲧⲱⲣ ⳼ ϫⲉ ⲁⲥⲓ̀ ϩⲁⲣⲟⲕ
ⲛ̄ϫⲉ ⲧⲁⲙⲁⲩ ⳼ ⲉⲥϫⲟⲗϩ ⳼ ⲉⲥⲥⲉⲗⲥⲱⲗ ⳼ ϧⲉⲛ ϩⲁⲛⲡⲣⲁⲝⲓⲥ ⲉⲑ-
ⲛⲁⲛⲉⲩ ⳼ [21]Ⲛⲓⲁⲅⲅⲉⲗⲟⲥ ⳼ ⲣⲁϣⲓ ⲛⲉⲙⲏⲓ ⲙ̀ⲫⲟⲟⲩ ⳼ ⲱ̀ ⲡⲁⲓⲱⲧ
ⲡⲁⲅⲁⲑⲟⲥ ⳼ ⲉⲩⲛⲁⲩ ⲉ̀ⲣⲟⲓ ⳼ ⲉ̀ⲓⲟⲩⲛⲟϥ ⳼ ⲛⲉⲙ ⲧⲁⲙⲁⲩ ⲙ̀ⲡⲁⲣⲑⲉ-
p. [λη] ⲛⲟⲥ ⳼ ⲉ̀ⲧⲁⲥⲓ̀ ϩⲁⲣⲱⲟⲩ ⳼ | ⲉⲥϫⲱⲗϩ ⳼ ⲛ̀ϩⲁⲛϩⲃⲱⲥ ⲛⲉⲡⲟⲩⲣⲁⲛⲓⲟⲛ × ⳼
[22]Ⲛⲓⲁⲣⲭⲏⲁⲅⲅⲉⲗⲟⲥ ϩⲱⲥ ⲉ̀ⲣⲟⲛ ⲙ̀ⲫⲟⲟⲩ ⳼ ⲱ ⲡⲁⲓⲱⲧ ⲡⲁⲅⲁⲑⲟⲥ ⳼
ⲉⲩϫⲱ ⲛ̀ϯϩⲱⲇⲏ ⲉⲧⲧⲟⲙⲓ ⳼ [23]ϫⲉ ⲟⲩⲱ̀ⲟⲩ ϧⲉⲛ ⲛⲏ ⲉⲧϭⲟⲥⲓ ⲙ̀ⲫϯ ⳼
ⲛⲉⲙ ⲟⲩϩⲓⲣⲏⲛⲏ ⲙ̀ⲡϫⲓⲛⲓ̄ ϣⲁⲣⲟⲛ ⲛ̀ⲑⲙⲁⲩ ⲙ̀ⲡⲉⲛⲟ̅ⲥ̅ ⳼ [24]Ⲛⲓⲭⲉ-
ⲣⲟⲩⲃⲓⲙ ⳼ ⲛⲉⲙ ⲛⲓⲥⲉⲣⲁⲫⲓⲙ ⲁⲩϯ[b] ⲛ̀ⲧⲟⲩⲇⲟⲝⲟⲗⲟⲅⲓⲁ̄ ⳼ ⲛ̀ⲥⲙⲟⲩ
ⲉⲑⲃⲉ ⲡⲁⲓⲣⲁϣⲓ ⲙ̀ⲫⲟⲟⲩ ⳼ ⲉⲩϫⲱ ⲙ̀ⲙⲟⲥ ⳼ × [25]ϫⲉ ⲭⲟⲩⲁⲃ ⳼
ⲭⲟⲩⲁⲃ ⲭⲟⲩⲁⲃ ⲡⲟ̅ⲥ̅ ⲥⲁⲃⲁⲱⲑ ⳼ ϥⲟⲩⲁⲃ ⲛ̀ϫⲉ ⲡⲉⲕⲉⲣⲫⲉⲓ̄ ⳼
ⲡⲉⲕⲑⲣⲟⲛⲟⲥ ⲛ̀ⲭⲉⲣⲟⲩⲃⲓⲕⲟⲛ ⳼ [26]Ⲛⲓⲙ ⲉⲑⲛⲁⲛⲁⲩ ⲉ̀ⲣⲟⲓ ⲙ̀ⲫⲟⲟⲩ ⳼
ⲉ̀ⲓⲣⲁϣⲓ ⲱ̀ ⲡⲁⲓⲱⲧ ⲡⲁⲅⲁⲑⲟⲥ ⳼ ⲟⲩⲟϩ ⲛ̀ⲧⲉϥϣⲧⲉⲙⲣⲁϣⲓ ⲛⲉⲙⲏⲓ ⳼
ϫⲉ ⲫⲁⲓ ⲡⲉ ⲡⲁⲉⲣⲫⲉⲓ ⳼ ⲟⲩⲟϩ ⲡⲁⲑⲣⲟⲛⲟⲥ ⲉⲩⲥⲟⲡ ⳼ [27]Ⲛⲁⲓ ⲇⲉ
ⲉ̀ⲧⲁϥϫⲟⲧⲟⲩ ⲛ̀ϫⲉ ⲡϣⲏⲣⲓ ⲡⲁⲅⲁⲑⲟⲥ ⳼ ⲟⲩⲃⲉ ⲡⲓⲓ̈ⲱⲧ ⲡⲁⲅⲁⲑⲟⲥ ⳼
ϧⲉⲛ ϯⲟⲩⲛⲟⲩ ⲁⲥⲥⲱⲧⲉⲙ ϩⲱⲥ ⳼ ⲛ̀ϫⲉ ⲧⲯⲩⲭⲏ ⲛ̀ϯⲡⲁⲣⲑⲉⲛⲟⲥ ⳼
ⲉ̀ϯⲥⲙⲏ ⲉⲧϩⲟⲗϫ ⲛ̀ⲧⲉ ϯⲧⲣⲓⲁⲥ ⳼ ⲉ̀ⲑⲟⲩⲁⲃ[c] ⲉⲥϫⲱ ⲙ̀ⲙⲟⲥ ⳼ [28]Ϫⲉ
ⲁⲙⲏ ϣⲁⲣⲟⲛ ⳼ ⲑⲏ ⲉⲧⲥⲙⲁⲣⲱⲟⲩⲧ ⲛ̀ⲧⲁⲛ ⳼ ⲁ̀ⲣⲓⲕⲗⲏⲣⲟⲛⲟⲙⲓⲛ
p. [λθ] ⲛⲉⲙⲁⲛ ⳼ ⲙ̀ⲡⲓⲣⲁϣⲓ[d] ⲛⲉⲛⲉϩ ⳼ ⲉ̀ⲛⲁⲧⲥⲁϫⲓ ⲙ̀ⲙⲟϥ ⳼ × | [29]Ⲧⲟⲧⲉ
ⲛ̀ⲑⲟⲥ ϩⲱⲥ ⳼ ⲧⲯⲩⲭⲏ ⲛ̀ϯⲡⲁⲣⲑⲉⲛⲟⲥ ⳼ ⲁⲥⲟⲩⲱϣⲧ ⲛ̀ϯⲧⲣⲓⲁⲥ ⳼
ⲉⲑⲟⲩⲁⲃ ⲉⲥϫⲱ ⲙ̄ⲙⲟⲥ ⳼ [30]Ϫⲉ ⲛⲁⲛⲉ ⲟⲩⲉ̀ϩⲟⲟⲩ ϧⲉⲛ ⲛⲉⲕⲁⲩ-
ⲗⲏⲟⲩ ⳼ ⲉ̀ϩⲟⲧⲉ ϩⲁⲛⲁⲛϣⲟ ⳼ ⲁⲓⲥⲟⲧⲡⲥ ⲛⲏⲓ ⳼ ⲉ̀ϣⲱⲡⲓ ϧⲉⲛ
ⲛⲉⲕⲁⲩⲗⲏⲟⲩ ⲛⲁⲛⲏⲃ ⳼ [31]Ⲟⲩⲟϩ ⲟⲛ ϫⲉ ⲡⲉⲕⲡ̅ⲛ̅ⲁ̅ ⲉⲑⲟⲩⲁⲃ ⳼
ⲡⲉⲧⲁϥⲉⲛⲧ ϩⲓϫⲉⲛ ⲡⲁⲓⲧⲱⲟⲩ ⲉⲑⲟⲩⲁⲃ ⳽ Ⲉⲑⲃⲉ ⲫⲁⲓ ϯⲛⲁⲓ̄ ⲉ̀ϧⲟⲩⲛ

[a] ⲫ sup. ras. [b] ⲛⲁⲩϯ [c] punct. sup. ⲉ ut vid. [d] punct. sup. ⲙ rubr. script.

19 I bring in unto Thee to-day, O My good Father, her who is
better than the ark of old; for Thou didst save the whole
world by My being in her, Thy coessential *Son*. 20 To-day is
a day of joy to Me, O My Father, the Almighty; for My
mother cometh to Thee, arrayed and adorned with good
deeds. 21 The angels rejoice with Me to-day, O My good
Father, as they see Me rejoicing[a] with My virgin mother,
who cometh to them arrayed in heavenly garments. 22 The
archangels sing Our praise to-day, O My good Father, singing
the befitting song, 23 Glory to God in the highest, and peace cf. Lc I 43; II 14;
at[b] the coming unto us of the mother of our Lord. 24 The XIX 38
Cherubim and the Seraphim give[c] their doxology of praise cf. Is VI 2, 3; Ap IV 8
for this joy to-day, saying, 25 Holy, holy, holy art Thou, Lord,
Sabaoth: holy is Thy temple, Thy cherubic throne. 26 Who cf. Ps XVII 11;
shall see Me to-day rejoicing, O My good Father, and not LXXIX 2
rejoice with Me? For this is at once My temple and My
throne.

27 Now when the good Son had said these things unto the
good Father, straightway the soul of the Virgin also heard
the gentle[d] voice of the Holy Trinity, saying, 28 Come unto Us, cf. Mt XXV 21, 23, 34
thou that art blessed of Us, inherit with Us the joy eternal,
unspeakable. 29 Then it also, *even* the soul of the Virgin,
worshipped the Holy Trinity, saying, 30 Better is a day in Thy cf. Ps LXXXIII 11
courts than thousands. I had rather dwell[e] in Thy courts, my
Master. 31 And again, Thy Holy Ghost hath brought me to cf. Ps V 8; XLII 3;
this holy mountain. Therefore I will go in unto Thy holy LXXVII 54; CXLII 10

[a] Or *being glad* [b] Or *to* [c] The MS has *were giving* [d] Or *sweet*
[e] Lit. *I chose me to dwell*

ⲛⲁϩⲣⲉⲛ ⲡⲉⲕⲙⲁ ⲉⲑⲟⲩⲁⲃ ⳾ ⲛ̄ⲧⲁⲟⲩⲱϣⲧ ⲙ̀ⲡⲉⲕⲉⲣⲫⲉⲓ̈ ⳾ ⲫⲏ ⲉ̀ⲧⲁ
ⲧⲁⲯⲩⲭⲏ ⲙⲉⲛⲣⲓⲧϥ ⳾ [32]Ⲛⲁⲓ ⲉ̀ⲧⲁⲥϫⲟⲧⲟⲩ ⲁⲥϣⲱⲡⲓ ϧⲉⲛ ⲟⲩⲣⲁϣⲓ
ⲛ̄ⲧⲁⲧⲥⲁϫⲓ ⲙ̀ⲙⲟϥ ⳾ ϧⲉⲛ ⲡⲓⲙⲁ ⲉ̀ⲧⲁϥⲫⲱⲧ ⲉⲃⲟⲗ ⲛ̀ϧⲏⲧϥ ⲛ̀ϫⲉ
VII. ⲡⲓⲙ̀ⲕⲁϩ ⲛ̀ϩⲏⲧ ⳾ ⲉⲥϧⲉⲛ ⲡⲱⲟⲩ ⲛ̀ϯⲧⲣⲓⲁⲥ = ⳾ – [1]Ⲁⲛⲟⲛ ⲇⲉ ϩⲱⲛ
ϧⲁ ⲛⲓⲁ̀ⲡⲟⲥⲧⲟⲗⲟⲥ ⳾ ⲁⲛϥⲁⲓ ⲙ̀ⲡⲉⲥⲥⲱⲙⲁ ⲉⲑⲟⲩⲁⲃ ⳾ ⲁⲛⲓ̀ ⲉⲃⲟⲗ
ⲛⲉⲙⲁϥ ⳾ ⲛⲉⲙ ⲛⲏ ⲉⲧⲑⲟⲩⲏⲟⲩⲧ ⲉ̀ⲣⲟⲛ ⳾ ϧⲉⲛ ⲟⲩⲥⲉⲙⲛⲏ ⳾ ⲛⲉⲙ
ⲟⲩⲕⲁⲧⲁⲥⲧⲁⲥⲓⲥ ⳾ ⲉⲛⲱⲗⲓ ⲙ̀ⲙⲟϥ ⳾ ⲉ̀ϯⲥⲉⲑⲓⲟ̀ϩⲓ[a] ⲛ̀ⲧⲉ ⲓ̄ⲱⲥⲁⲫⲁⲧ
[2]Ⲁⲛⲓ̀ ϩⲓϫⲉⲛ ⲟⲩⲑⲱⲟⲩⲧⲥ ⲛ̀ⲛⲓⲓ̈ⲟⲩⲇⲁⲓ[b] ⳾ ⲉⲩⲑⲟⲩⲏⲧ ⲉ̀ⲛⲟⲩⲉ̀ⲣⲏⲟⲩ[c] ⳾
[3]ⲉ̀ⲧⲁⲩⲛⲁⲩ[d] ⲉ̀ⲣⲟⲛ ⳾ ⲉⲛⲙⲟϣⲓ ⳾ ϧⲉⲛ ⲟⲩⲱⲣϥ ⳾ ⲛⲉⲙ ⲟⲩⲭⲁⲣⲱϥ ⳾
ⲁⲩⲥⲁϫⲓ ⲛⲉⲙ ⲛⲟⲩⲉ̀ⲣⲏⲟⲩ ⳾ [4]ϫⲉ ⲛⲓⲙ ⲡⲉ ⲡⲁⲓⲣⲉϥⲙⲱⲟⲩⲧ ⳾ ⲓⲉ̀
p. ⲙ ⲛⲓⲙ ⲡⲉ ⲛⲁⲓ ⲉⲧϥⲁⲓ ⲙ̀ⲙⲟϥ ⳾ ϫⲉ ⲥⲉⲙⲟϣⲓ ϧⲉⲛ ⲟⲩ|ⲕⲁⲧⲁⲥⲧⲁⲥⲓⲥ
ⲙ̄ⲡⲁⲓⲣⲏϯ ⳾ [5]Ⲟⲩⲕⲁϩⲥ ⲙ̄ⲃⲉⲣⲓ ⲧⲉ ⲑⲁⲓ ⳾ ⲑⲏ ⲉⲧⲉⲥϣⲟⲡ ⲁⲛ ϧⲉⲛ
ⲡⲓⲥ̄ⲗ̄ ⳾ [6]Ⲁϥⲉⲣⲟⲩⲱ ⲇⲉ ⳾ ⲛ̀ϫⲉ ⲟⲩⲁⲓ ⲉⲃⲟⲗ ⲛ̀ϧⲏⲧⲟⲩ[e] ⳾ ⲉ̀[f] ⲟⲩ-
ⲅⲁⲗⲓⲗⲉⲟⲥ ⲡⲉ ⳾ ⲉϥⲥⲱⲟⲩⲛ ⲛ̀ⲛⲓⲁⲡⲟⲥⲧⲟⲗⲟⲥ ⲛ̀ⲕⲁⲗⲱⲥ γ ⲁ ⲡⲓⲡ̄ⲛ̄ⲁ̄
ⲉⲑⲟⲩⲁⲃ ⲓ̀[g] ⲉ̄ϧⲣⲏⲓ ⲉ̀ϫⲱϥ ⲡⲉϫⲁϥ ⲛⲱⲟⲩ ⳾ [7]Ϫⲉ ⲡⲁⲓⲣⲉϥⲙⲱⲟⲩⲧ
ⲉ̀ⲧⲟⲩϥⲁⲓ ⲙ̀ⲙⲟϥ ⳾ ⲫⲁⲓ ⲡⲉ ⲡⲥⲱⲙⲁ ⲙⲙⲁⲣⲓⲁ̄ ⲧϣⲉⲣⲓ ⲛ̄ⲓⲱ̄ⲁ̄ⲕⲓⲙ[h] ⳾
ⲛⲉⲙ ⲁⲛⲛⲁ ⳾ ⲑⲏ ⲉ̀ⲧⲁⲥⲙⲓⲥⲓ : ⲙⲙⲉⲥⲓⲁⲥ ⳾ ⲉ̀ⲧⲉ ⲡ̄ⲭ̄ⲥ̄ ⲡⲉ = – [8]Ⲫⲁⲓ
ⲉ̀ⲧⲁϥⲧⲁⲗϭⲟ ⲛ̄ⲛⲏ ⲉⲧϣⲱⲛⲓ ⲛ̀ⲧⲱⲧⲉⲛ ⳾ ⲁϥϯ ⲙ̀ⲫⲟⲩⲱⲓⲛⲓ ⲛ̄ⲛⲉⲧⲉⲛ-
ⲃⲁⲗ ⳾ ⲟⲩⲟϩ ⲁϥⲧⲟⲩⲛⲟⲥ ⲛⲉⲧⲉⲛⲣⲉϥⲙⲱⲟⲩⲧ ⳾ [9]ⲧⲉⲛⲛⲁϩϯ ⳾ ϫⲉ
ⲙ̀ⲫⲣⲏϯ ⲉ̀ⲧⲁϥⲧⲟⲩⲛⲟⲥ ⲛⲉⲧⲉⲛⲣⲉϥⲙⲱⲟⲩⲧ ⳾ ϥⲛⲁⲧⲟⲩⲛⲟⲥ ⲧⲉϥⲙⲁⲩ
ⲟⲛ γ ⲛ̄ⲧⲉϥⲟⲗⲥ ⲉ̀ⲛⲓⲫⲏⲟⲩⲓ̈ ⲛⲉⲙⲁϥ ⳾ [10]Ⲛⲓⲓ̈ⲟⲩⲇⲁⲓ ⲇⲉ ⲉ̀ⲧⲁⲩⲥⲱⲧⲉⲙ
ⲡⲉ̀ϫⲱⲟⲩ ϧⲉⲛ ⲟⲩϣⲑⲟⲣⲧⲉⲣ ⳾ ϫⲉ ⲟⲩ ⲡⲉ ⲉ̀ⲧⲉⲛⲛⲁⲁⲓϥ ⳾ ϩⲏⲡⲡⲉ
ⲓⲥ ϯⲡⲗⲁⲛⲏ ϣⲟⲡ ⲛ̄ϧⲏⲧⲉⲛ ϣⲁ ϯⲛⲟⲩ ⳾ ⲕⲁⲧⲁ ⲫⲣⲏϯ ⲉ̄ⲧⲉⲛⲛⲁⲩ
ⲉ̄ⲣⲟⲥ ⳾ ⲛ̀ϧⲣⲏⲓ ϧⲉⲛ ⲫⲁⲓ : ⲉⲧⲥⲁϫⲓ ⲛⲉⲙⲁⲛ ϯⲛⲟⲩ ⳾ [11]Ⲁⲗⲗⲁ
ⲙⲁⲣⲉⲛⲓ̄ⲛⲥ[i] ⲙ̀ⲙⲟⲛ : ⲛ̄ⲧⲉⲛϭⲉⲣⲟ[j] ⲛ̀ⲟⲩⲭⲣⲱⲙ ⳾ ⲛ̀ⲧⲉⲛⲣⲱⲕϩ
p. [ⲙⲁ] ⲙ̀ⲡⲉⲥⲥⲱⲙⲁ ⳾ [12]ⲙ̀ⲙⲟⲛ ⲁⲛϣⲁⲛⲭⲁ ⲫⲁⲓ γ ⲇ | ⲛ̀ⲧⲟⲩⲑⲱⲙⲥ ⲙⲙⲟϥ
ϧⲉⲛ ⲛⲉⲛⲑⲟϣ γ ⲥⲉⲛⲁⲟⲩⲱⲛϩ ⲉⲃⲟⲗ ⲛ̀ϧⲏⲧϥ ⲛ̀ϫⲉ ϩⲁⲛⲙⲏⲛⲓⲛⲓ ⳾

[a] punct. sup. ⲉ pr. ut vid. [b] ⲛ̀ⲓⲓ̈ⲟⲩⲇⲁⲓ [c] ʹ sup. ⲉ rubr. script.
[d] pr. man. ⲉ̀ⲧⲁⲩ (ⲛⲁⲩ in marg. rubr. script.) [e] punct. sup. ⲛ ut vid.
[f] ʹ sup. ⲉ rubr. script. [g] punct. sup. ⲓ rubr. script. [h] ⲕ sup. ras. pr. man. [i] ⲁ sup. ras. pr. man. [j] ⲧ ex ϯ (?) mutat. pr. man.

place, and will worship at Thy temple, O Thou[a] whom my cf. Cant i 7
soul loveth. 32 When she had said these things, she was in
joy unspeakable, in the place whence grief has fled away, cf. Is xxxv 10; li 11
being in the glory of the Trinity.

VII. And we also, the apostles, bare her holy body; and
we went forth with it, with those who were assembled unto
us, in order and calmness, taking it to the field of Jehosha-
phat. 2 We came to an assembly of the Jews, assembled one
with another. 3 When they saw us going quietly and silently,
they spake one with another, *saying*, 4 What is this corpse, or
who are these that bear it? For they go in such calmness.
5 This is a new custom, which is not in Israel. 6 And one of cf. Mt ix 33
them, being a Galilean and knowing the apostles well, answered:
the Holy Ghost came down upon him, and he said to them,
7 This corpse that is borne, this is the body of Mary, the
daughter of Joakim and Anna, who bare Messias, which is
Christ. 8 He it was who healed your sick, and gave light to
your eyes, and raised your dead. 9 We believe that as He
raised your dead, He will raise His mother also, and will
take her to the heavens with Him. 10 And the Jews when
they heard, said in confusion, What shall we do? Behold cf. Jn xi 47
the error is among us still, as we see it in this *fellow* who
speaks with us now. 11 But let us make haste, and kindle a
fire, and burn her body. 12 Else, if we let this be buried in cf. Jn xi 47, 48
our borders, there will appear from it signs and wonders, and

[a] Lit. *He*

ⲛⲉⲙ ϩⲁⲛϣⲫⲏⲣⲓ ⳾ ⲥⲉⲛⲁⲑⲱⲟⲩϯ ⲉ̀ⲣⲟϥ ⲛ̀ϫⲉ ⲟⲩⲙⲏϣ ⲛ̀ⲥⲉⲛⲁϩϯ
ⲉ̀ⲣⲟϥ ⳾ 13 Ⲟⲩⲟϩ ⲥⲉⲛⲁⲱⲡ ⲉ̀ⲛⲓⲣⲱⲙⲉⲟⲥ ⳾ ⲥⲉⲛⲁⲉⲣⲡ̅ⲥ̅ ⲉ̀ⲡⲉⲛⲃⲁⲕⲓ ⳾
ⲟⲩⲟϩ ⲥⲉⲛⲁⲑⲉⲃⲓⲟ̅ ⲙ̀ⲡⲉⲛϣⲗⲟⲗ ⳾ 14 Ⲛⲁⲓ ⲇⲉ ⲉ̀ⲧⲁⲩϫⲟⲧⲟⲩ ϧⲉⲛ
ⲟⲩⲓ̈ⲏⲥ ⳾ ⲁⲩϭⲉⲣⲟ ⲛ̅ⲟⲩⲭⲣⲱⲙ ⳾ ⲛⲉⲙ ϩⲁⲛⲗⲁⲙⲡⲁⲥ ⳾ ⲁⲩⲓ̅ ⲉⲃⲟⲗ
ϩⲓⲫⲁϩⲟⲩ ⲙⲙⲱⲟⲩ ⳾ ⲉⲣⲱⲕϩ ⲙ̀ⲡⲓⲥⲱⲙⲁ ⲉ̀ⲑⲟⲩⲁⲃ ⳾ ⲛ̅ⲧⲉ ϯⲡⲁⲓⲁⲧⲥ
ⲙ̅ⲡⲁⲣⲑⲉⲛⲟⲥ ⳾ 15 Ⲛⲓⲁ̅ⲡⲟⲥⲧⲟⲗⲟⲥ ⲇⲉ ⳾ ⲉ̀ⲧⲁⲩⲛⲁⲩ ⲉ̀ⲫⲏ ⲉ̀ⲧⲁϥϣⲱⲡⲓ ⳾
Ⲁⲥϭⲓⲧⲟⲩ ⲛ̀ϫⲉ ⲟⲩϩⲟϯ ⲙ̅ⲙⲉⲑⲣⲱⲙⲓ ⳾ ⲁⲩⲭⲱ ⲙ̅ⲡⲓϭⲗⲟϫ ⲉϧⲣⲏⲓ ⳾
ⲟⲩⲟϩ ⲁⲩⲫⲱⲧ ⳾ 16 Ⲛⲓⲁⲛⲟⲙⲟⲥ ⲇⲉ ⲛ̀ⲓⲟⲩⲇⲁⲓ ⳾ ϧⲉⲛ ⲡϫⲓⲛⲑⲣⲟⲩⲫⲟϩ
ⲉⲡⲓϭⲗⲟϫ ⳾ ⲁϥⲓ̈ ⲉϩⲣⲏⲓ ⲉ̀ϫⲱⲟⲩ — ⲛ̀ϫⲉ ⲟⲩϩⲗⲟⲗ ⳾ ⲛⲉⲙ ⲟⲩⲭⲁⲕⲓ ⳾
ⲉⲁⲩϣⲱⲡⲓ ⲉⲩⲟ̅ⲓ ⲙ̀ⲃⲉⲗⲗⲉ ⳾ ⲙ̀ⲙⲟⲛ ⲫⲏ ⲉⲑⲛⲁϯⲧⲟⲧⲟⲩ ⳾ 17 Ⲡⲓⲕⲉ-
ⲭⲣⲱⲙ ⲉ̀ⲧⲁⲩⲥⲉⲃⲧⲱⲧϥ ⳾ ⲉⲛϫⲓⲛⲧⲟⲩⲣⲱⲕϩ[a] ⲙ̅ⲡⲥⲱⲙⲁ ⳾ ⲛ̀ϯⲁ̀ⲅⲓⲁ̅
ⲙ̀ⲡⲁⲣⲑⲉⲛⲟⲥ ⲛ̅ϧⲏⲧϥ ⳾ ⲁϥϯⲉⲣϧⲟⲧ ⳾ ⲛ̀ⲟⲩⲙⲏϣ ⲉⲃⲟⲗ ⲛϧⲏⲧⲟⲩ
18 Ⲕⲁⲧⲁ ⲫⲣⲏϯ ⲉ̀ⲧⲁϥϫⲟⲥ ⲛ̅ϫⲉ ⲡⲓⲡ̅ⲛ̅ⲁ̅ ⲉ̀ⲑⲟⲩⲁⲃ ⳾ ϧⲉⲛ ⲣⲱϥ
p. ⲙⲃ ⲛⲇⲁⲩⲓⲇ ⳾ ⲡⲓⲡⲣⲟⲫⲏⲧⲏⲥ ⳾ ϧⲉⲛ ⲡⲓⲙⲁϩⲡ̅ⲁ̅ | ⲙ̀ⲯⲁⲗⲙⲟⲥ[b] × 12 ϫⲉ
ⲙⲡⲟⲩⲉ̀ⲙⲓ ⳾ ⲟⲩⲇⲉ ⲙ̀ⲡⲟⲩⲕⲁϯ ⳾ Ⲥⲉⲙⲟϣⲓ ⲛϧⲣⲏⲓ ϧⲉⲛ ⲡⲓⲭⲁⲕⲓ ⳾
Ⲉⲩⲉ̅ⲓ ⲉ̀ϫⲱⲟⲩ ⲛ̀ϫⲉ ϩⲁⲛϫⲉⲃⲥ ⲛ̀ⲭⲣⲱⲙ ⳾ ϩⲓϫⲉⲛ ⲡⲕⲁϩⲓ :— 20 Ⲧⲟⲧⲉ
ⲁⲩⲱϣ ⲉⲃⲟⲗ ⲉⲩϫⲱ ⲙⲙⲟⲥ ⳾ ϫⲉ ⲟⲩⲟ̀ⲓ̅[c] ⲛⲁⲛ ⲱ̀[d] ⲡⲉⲛⲛⲏⲃ
ⲡ̅ⲭ̅ⲥ̅ ⳾ ϫ̇ⲉ[e] ⲁ̀ⲛⲉⲣⲛⲟⲃⲓ ⲉⲧϥⲉ ⳾ ⲛⲉⲙ ⲙⲡⲉⲕⲙⲑⲟ[f] ⳾ ⲭⲱ ⲛⲁⲛ
ⲉⲃⲟⲗ ⳾ ϫⲉ ⲁ̀ⲛⲟⲛ ϩⲁⲛϣⲏⲣⲓ ⲛ̀ⲧⲉ ⲁⲃⲣⲁⲁⲙ ⳾ × 21 Ⲁⲕϣⲁⲛϯ ⲛⲁⲛ
ⲙ̀ⲫⲟⲩⲱⲓⲛⲓ ⲛ̀ⲧⲉ ⲡⲉⲛⲃⲁⲗ ⳾ ⲧⲉⲛⲛⲁⲥⲟⲩⲉⲛ ⲡⲱⲟⲩ ⳾ ⲛ̀ⲧⲉ ⲧⲉⲕⲙⲉⲑ-
ⲛⲟⲩϯ ⳾ ⲟⲩⲟϩ ⲧⲉⲛⲛⲁⲛⲁϩϯ ⲉ̀ⲣⲟⲕ ⳾ ⲛⲉⲙ ⲧⲉⲕⲙⲁⲩ ⲙ̀ⲡⲁⲣⲑⲉⲛⲟⲥ ⳾
ϫⲉ ⲟⲩⲏⲓ ⲧⲉⲛⲥⲱⲛⲓ ⲧⲉ ⳾ 22 Ⲛⲁⲓ ⲇⲉ ⲉ̀ⲁⲩϫⲟⲧⲟⲩ ⲁϥϣⲉⲛϩⲏⲧ
ϧⲁⲣⲱⲟⲩ ⲛ̀ϫⲉ ⲡ̅ⲭ̅ⲥ̅ ⳾ ⲁ̀ϥⲭⲁⲩ ⲉⲃⲟⲗ ϧⲉⲛ ⲧⲟⲩⲙⲉⲧⲃⲉⲗⲗⲉ ⳾
ⲛⲉⲙ ⲧⲟⲩⲡⲗⲁⲛⲏ ⳾ 23 Ϩⲁⲛⲙⲏϣ ⲉⲃⲟⲗ ⲛϧⲏⲧⲟⲩ ⲁⲩⲱⲡ ⲉ̀ⲣⲟⲛ ⳾
ⲁⲩϯⲱⲟⲩ ⲛ̀ϯⲧⲣⲓⲁⲥ ⲉⲑⲟⲩⲁⲃ ⳾ 24 Ⲁⲛⲟⲛ ⲇⲉ ⲁⲛⲧⲁⲥⲑⲟⲛ ⲉ̀ⲓ̅ⲗ̅ⲏ̅ⲙ̅
ⲉⲛϯⲱⲟⲩ ⲙ̀ⲫ̅ϯ̅ ⳾ ⲉϩⲣⲏⲓ ⳾ ⲉ̀ϫⲉⲛ ⲡⲉϥϩⲙⲟⲧ ⲉⲑⲛⲁⲛⲉⲩ ⳾ :— 25 Ⲟⲩⲟϩ
ⲡⲉ ⲁⲛϣⲉ ⲛⲁⲛ ⲛ̀ⲟⲩⲙⲏϣ ⲛ̀ⲥⲟⲡ ⳾ ⲉ̀ⲡⲓⲙⲁ ⳾ ⲉ̀ⲧⲁⲛⲭⲱ ⲙ̀ⲡⲓϭⲗⲟϫ

[a] ⲉⲛϫⲓⲛⲧⲟⲩⲣⲱⲣϩ (ⲕ sup. rec. man.) [b] ʹ sup. ⲙ pr. rubr. script. [c] punct. sup. ⲟ sec. ut vid. [d] ʹ sup. ⲱ rubr. script. [e] punct. sup. ϫ ut vid. [f] ⲡⲉⲕⲙⲑⲟ

many will be assembled to it and believe on Him: [13]and
they will be numbered unto the Romans, and they will have
dominion over our cities, and will humble our nation. [14]Now
when they had hastily said these things, they kindled a fire
and torches, and went out behind them, to burn the holy
body of the blessed Virgin. [15]But the apostles, when they
saw that which was come to pass, a fear of man[a] took hold of
them; and they put down the bier, and fled.

[16]And the lawless Jews, when they approached the bier,
a mist and a darkness came upon them; they became cf. Ac xiii 11
blind, and there was no one to lead them by the hand.
[17]The fire also which they prepared, to burn the body of the
holy Virgin in it, smote many of them: [18]even as the Holy
Ghost said by the mouth of David the prophet in the eighty-
first Psalm, [19]They knew not, neither did they understand; Ps lxxxi 5
they go in darkness. There shall come upon them coals of cf. Ps cxxxix 11
fire on the earth. [20]Then they cried out, saying, Woe to us,
O our Master Christ; for we have sinned against heaven, cf. Lc xv 18, 21
and before Thee. Forgive us, for we are children[b] of Abra-
ham. [21]If Thou givest us the light of our eyes, we will know
the glory of Thy godhead, and we will believe on Thee and
on Thy virgin mother; for she is our sister. [22]Now when
they said these things, Christ was moved with compassion
for them, and set them free from their blindness and their
error. [23]Many of them were numbered unto us, and glorified
the Holy Trinity. [24]And we returned to Jerusalem, glorifying
God for His good favours. [25]And we went[c] many times to

[a] Lit. *mankind* [b] Or *sons* [c] Or *had gone*

ⲛ̀ϧⲏⲧϥ[a] ⳾ ⲉⲛϫⲱⲕ ⲉⲃⲟⲗ ⲛ̀ϩⲁⲛϩⲱⲥ ⳾ ⲛⲉⲙ ϩⲁⲛⲥⲙⲟⲩ ⳾ ⲉ̀ⲧⲉⲣ-
ⲡⲣⲉⲡⲓ ⲙ̀ⲫ̀ϯ ⳾ ϣⲁ ⲡⲓⲉ̀ϩⲟⲟⲩ ⳾ ⲛ̀ⲧⲉ ⲧⲉⲥⲁⲛⲁⲗⲩⲙⲯⲓⲥ ⲉⲧⲧⲁⲓⲏⲟⲩⲧ |
p. [ⲙⲅ̅] VIII. ¹Ⲁⲥϣⲱⲡⲓ ⲇⲉ ⲉⲧⲁⲩϫⲱⲕ ⲉⲃⲟⲗ ⳾ ⲛ̀ϫⲉ[a] ⲡⲓⲥ̅ⲅ̅[b] ⲛⲉϩⲟⲟⲩ ⳾ ⲁⲛⲧⲱ-
ⲟⲩⲛⲟⲩ ⲧⲏⲣⲟⲩ ⳾ ⲁⲛϣⲉ ⲛⲁⲛ ϩⲓϫⲉⲛ ⲡⲓⲗⲩⲙⲯⲁⲛⲟⲛ ⲉⲑⲟⲩⲁⲃ ⲩ
ⲛ̅ϩⲁⲛⲁⲣⲟⲩϩⲓ ⲛ̅ⲥⲟⲩ · ⲓ̅ⲉ̅ · ⲙ̀ⲙⲉⲥⲟⲣⲏ ⳾ ⲛ̀ⲧⲟⲟⲩⲓ ⲛ̀ⲥⲟⲩ ⲓ̅ⲅ̅ ⲡⲉ ⳾
²Ⲁⲛⲉⲣ ⲡⲓⲉ̀ϫⲱⲣϩ ⲧⲏⲣϥ ⲉ̀ⲛⲟⲓ ⲛ̀ϣⲣⲱⲓⲥ ⳾ ⲉⲛⲙⲏⲛ ⲉϯⲡⲣⲟⲥⲉⲩⲭⲏ ×
³Ϧⲉⲛ ⲁϫⲛ ⲓ̅ ⲇⲉ ⲛⲧⲉ ⲡⲓⲉϫⲱⲣϩ ⳾ ⲁⲛⲥⲱⲧⲉⲙ ⲉ̀ϩⲁⲛϧⲁⲣⲁⲃⲁⲓ ⳾
ⲛⲉⲙ ϩⲁⲛⲥⲙⲏ ⲛ̀ⲧⲉ ⲟⲩⲉϣⲗⲏⲗⲟⲩⲓ̅ ⳾ Ⲟⲩⲭⲱⲣⲟⲥ ⲛⲁⲅⲅⲉⲗⲟⲛ ⳾
ⲉⲩⲛⲏⲟⲩ ⲉ̀ⲡⲉⲥⲏⲧ ϩⲓϫⲉⲛ ⲡⲓⲧⲁⲫⲟⲥ ⳾ ⁴Ⲓⲧⲁ ⲟⲛ ⳾ ⲇⲁⲩⲓⲇ ⲡⲓϩⲩⲙ-
ⲛⲟⲇⲟⲥ ⳾ ⲉϥⲕⲉⲙⲕⲉⲙ ⲉ̀ⲧⲉϥ̀ⲕⲩⲑⲁⲣⲁ[c] ⳾ ⲉϥϫⲱ ⲙ̀ⲙⲟⲥ ⳾ ϫⲉ ⲧⲱⲛⲕ
ⲡ̅ⲟ̅ⲥ̅ ⲉ̀ⲡⲉⲕⲙ̀ⲧⲟⲛ ⳾ ⲛ̀ⲑⲟⲕ ⲛⲉⲙ ϯⲕⲩⲃⲱⲧⲟⲥ ⳾ ⲛ̀ⲧⲉ ⲡⲓⲙⲁ ⲉⲑⲟⲩⲁⲃ
ⲛ̀ⲧⲁⲕ ⳾ :– ⁵Ϧⲉⲛ ϯⲟⲩⲛⲟⲩ[d] ⳾ ⲁ̀ ⲡⲓⲙⲁ ⲧⲏⲣϥ ⲙⲟϩ ⲛ̀ⲭⲣⲱⲙ ⳾
⁶ⲁϥⲟⲩⲟⲛϩϥ ⲛ̀ϫⲉ ⲡ̅ⲟ̅ⲥ̅ ϩⲓϫⲉⲛ ⲡⲓϩⲁⲣⲙⲁ ⲛ̀ⲭⲉⲣⲟⲩⲃⲓⲙ ⳾ ⲉⲣⲉ
ⲧⲯⲩⲭⲏ ⲛ̀ϯⲡⲁⲣⲑⲉⲛⲟⲥ ϩⲉⲙⲥⲓ ϧⲉⲛ ⲕⲉⲛϥ ⳾ ⲉⲥⲥⲟⲩⲗⲱⲗ[e] ⳾ ϧⲉⲛ
ⲧⲉϥⲥⲧⲟⲗⲏ ⲛ̀ⲛⲟⲩϯ ⳾ ⁷Ⲁⲛⲟⲛ ⲇⲉ ⳾ ⲁⲛⲣⲱϧⲧ ⲉ̀ⲡⲉⲥⲏⲧ ⳾ ϩⲓⲧⲉⲛ
ϯϩⲟϯ ⳾ ⲁⲛⲉⲣ ⲙ̀ⲫⲣⲏϯ ⲛ̀ϩⲁⲛⲣⲉϥⲙⲱⲟⲩⲧ ⳾ ⁸ⲉ̀ⲧⲁϥⲧⲟⲩⲛⲟⲥⲧⲉⲛ ⳾
p. ⲙⲇ ⲁϥϣ̅ⲗⲓ ⲉⲃⲟⲗ ϩⲁⲣⲟⲛ ⲛ̀ϯϩⲟϯ ⳾ | ⁹Ⲉⲛⲁϥϫⲱ ⲙⲙⲟⲥ ⲛⲁⲛ ⲡⲉ ⳾ ϫⲉ
ⲭⲉⲣⲉ ⲛⲁⲥ̅ⲛⲏⲟⲩ[f] ⲙ̅ⲙⲉⲗⲟⲥ ⳾ ⲛⲉⲙ ⲛⲓⲡⲁⲣⲑⲉⲛⲟⲥ ⲉⲑⲛⲉⲙⲱⲧⲉⲛ ⳾
Ⲧⲉⲛⲑⲏⲛⲟⲩ ⲛ̅ⲧⲉⲧⲉⲛⲛⲁⲩ ⲉ̀ⲡⲱⲟⲩ ⲛ̅ⲧⲁⲙⲁⲩ ⳾ ¹⁰Ⲡⲁⲗⲓⲛ ⲁϥⲙⲟⲩϯ
ϩⲓϫⲉⲛ ϯⲥⲗⲏ ⳾ ⲉϥϫⲱ ⲙ̀ⲙⲟⲥ ⳾ ϫⲉ ⲧⲱⲛⲕ ϧⲉⲛ ⲡⲉⲕⲉⲛⲕⲟⲧ ⳾ ⲱ̀
ⲡⲓⲥⲱⲙⲁ ⲉⲑⲟⲩⲁⲃ ⲩ ⲉⲧⲁϥϣⲱⲡⲓ ⲛⲏⲓ ⲛ̅ⲟⲩⲉⲣⲫⲉⲓ̅ ⲩ Ⲁⲣⲓⲫⲟⲣⲓⲛ
ⲛ̅ⲧⲉⲕⲯⲩⲭⲏ[g] ⳾ ⲑⲁⲓ ⲉⲧⲁⲥϣⲱⲡⲓ ⲛⲏⲓ ⳾ ⲛ̅ⲟⲩⲥⲕⲩⲛⲏ ⲙ̅ⲙⲏⲓ ⳾
¹¹Ⲧⲱⲛⲕ × ⲱ̅ ⲡⲓⲥⲱⲙⲁ ⳾ ⲛ̅ⲣⲉϥⲙⲟⲩ ⲕⲁⲧⲁ ⲧⲉϥⲫⲩⲥⲓⲥ ⳾ Ⲁⲣⲓⲫⲟⲣⲓⲛ
ⲛ̅ⲧⲉⲕⲯⲩⲭⲏ ⲛⲁⲑⲙⲟⲩ ⳾ ϩⲓⲛⲁ ⲛ̅ⲧⲉⲕϣⲱⲡⲓ ⲛ̅ⲁⲑⲙⲟⲩ ⲧⲏⲣⲕ ⳾
ⲛ̅ⲧⲁϭⲓⲧⲕ ⲉ̅ⲧⲭⲱⲣⲁ ⲛ̀ⲛⲏ ⲉ̅ⲧⲟⲛϧ ⳾ ¹²Ⲧⲱⲛⲕ × ⲱ̅ ⲡⲓⲥⲱⲙⲁ ⳾ ⲉ̀ⲧⲉ
ϣⲁϥⲃⲱⲗ ⲉⲃⲟⲗ ⳾ ⲛ̅ⲧⲉϥⲧⲁⲕⲟ ⲕⲁⲧⲁ ϯⲫⲩⲥⲓⲥ ⳾ Ⲁⲣⲓⲫⲟⲣⲓⲛ ⲛ̅ⲧⲉⲕ-
ⲯⲩⲭⲏ ⲉ̀ⲛⲁⲧⲧⲁⲕⲟ ⳾ ϣⲱⲡⲓ ⲧⲏⲣⲕ ⲉⲛⲁⲧⲧⲁⲕⲟ ⳾ ⲟⲩⲟϩ ⲛⲁⲧⲃⲱⲗ

[a] punct. sup. ⲛ ut vid. [b] ⲡⲓ · ⲥ̅ⲅ̅ [c] punct. sup. ϥ ut vid. [d] ⲛⲟⲩ sup. post. man. rubr. script. [e] ⲕ sup. ⲥ sec. rec. man. [f] lin. parv. sup. ⲥ rubr. scr. ut vid. [g] punct. sup. ⲧ ut vid.

the place wherein we left the bier, accomplishing songs and praises befitting God, until the day of her glorious[a] assumption.

VIII. And it came to pass when the two hundred and
six days were fulfilled, we all arose and went to the holy
remains, on the evening of the fifteenth of Mesoure, which
is[b] on the morning of the sixteenth. [2]We spent the whole
night watching and continuing steadfastly in prayer. [3]Now cf. Col IV 2
at the tenth hour of the night we heard thunderings and
voices of shouting—a choir of angels coming down upon the
tomb. [4]Then also David the singer *was* striking his harp,
saying, Arise, O Lord, unto Thy rest; Thou and the ark of Ps CXXXI 8
Thy holy place. [5]Straightway the whole place burned with
fire. [6]And the Lord appeared on the chariots of Cherubim, cf. Ps XVII 11; Sir
the soul of the Virgin seated in His bosom, wrapped in His XLIX 8
divine robe. [7]And we fell down through fear, and became cf. Mt XXVIII 4
as dead men. [8]He raised us, and took away from us fear[c].
[9]And He said to us, Hail, My brethren *and* members and the
virgins who are with you: arise and see the glory of My
mother.

[10]Again He called over the coffin, saying, Arise from thy
sleep, O thou holy body, which was to Me a temple: wear
thy soul, which was to Me a true tent. [11]Arise, O thou body,
that dies according to its nature: wear thy deathless soul,
that thou mayest be altogether deathless, and that I may
take thee to the land of the living. [12]Arise, O thou body,
which dissolves and becomes corrupt according to nature:
wear thine incorruptible soul. Be altogether incorruptible

[a] Or *honourable* [b] Lit. *it is* [c] Or *the fear*

ⲉⲃⲟⲗ ⳼ ϣⲁ ⲉⲛⲉϩ ⲛ̀ⲧⲉ ⲡⲓⲉ̀ⲛⲉϩ[a] ⳼ [13]Ⲧⲱⲛⲕ × Ⲉⲑⲃⲉ ⲟⲩ ⲕⲉⲛⲕⲟⲧ
ϧⲉⲛ ⲡⲕⲁϩⲓ ϫⲉ ⳼ ϫⲟⲗϩⲕ ⲛ̀ⲧⲉⲕⲯⲩⲭⲏ ⲩ ⲛ̀ⲧⲉⲕⲓ̀ ⲉ̀ⲛⲓϥⲛⲟⲩⲓ̀
ⲛⲉⲙⲏⲓ ⳼ ϣⲁ ⲡⲁⲓⲱⲧ ⲛ̀ⲁ̀ⲅⲁⲑⲟⲥ ⳼ ⲛⲉⲙ ⲡⲓⲡ̅ⲛ̅ⲁ̅ ⲉⲑⲟⲩⲁⲃ ⳼ ϫⲉ
p. [ⲙⲉ] ⲥⲉϭⲓϣϣⲱⲟⲩ ⲙ̀ⲙⲟⲕ × :· | [14]Ⲧⲱⲛⲕ ⲱ ⲡⲓⲥⲱⲙⲁ ⲉ̀ⲑⲟⲩⲁⲃ ⳼ ⲉⲧⲁⲓ-
ⲕⲱⲧ ⲛⲏⲓ ⲛ̀ⲧⲁⲥⲁⲣⲝ ⲉ̀ⲃⲟⲗ ⲙ̀ⲙⲟϥ ⳼ ϧⲉⲛ ⲟⲩⲙⲉⲧⲁⲧϣⲕⲁϯ ⲉⲣⲟⲥ ⳼
Ⲁⲣⲓϥⲟⲣⲓⲛ ⲛ̀ⲧⲉⲕⲯⲩⲭⲏ ⲉ̄ⲧⲁⲥϣⲱⲡⲓ ⲛⲏⲓ ⲛ̀ⲟⲩⲙⲁⲛⲟⲩⲟϩ[b] ⳼
[15]Ⲧⲱⲛⲕ ⳼ ⲱ̀ ⲡⲓⲉ̀ⲗⲉⲩⲑⲉⲣⲟⲥ ⳼ ⲁ̀ⲣⲓϥⲟⲣⲓⲛ ⲛ̀ⲧⲉⲗⲉⲩⲑⲉⲣⲓⲁ̄ ⲙⲡⲓ-
ⲕⲟⲥⲙⲟⲥ ⲧⲏⲣϥ[c] ⳼ ⲑⲁⲓ ⲉ̀ⲧⲁⲓⲥⲱϯ ⲙ̀ⲡⲁⲑⲁⲙⲓⲟ ⲧⲏⲣϥ ⳼ ⲉⲃⲟⲗ
ϩⲓⲧⲟⲧⲥ[d] — [16]Ⲧⲱⲛⲕ ⳼ ⲱ̄ ⲡⲓⲥⲱⲙⲁ ⲉⲑⲟⲩⲁⲃ ⳼ ϩⲱⲧⲛ ⲉ̀ϯⲯⲩⲭⲏ[e]
ⲉⲧⲥⲙⲁⲣⲱⲟⲩⲧ ϭⲓ ⲡⲁⲕ ⲉⲃⲟⲗ ϩⲓⲧⲟⲧ ⳼ ⲛ̀ⲧⲉⲕⲁⲛⲁⲥⲧⲁⲥⲓⲥ ϧⲁϫⲉⲛ
ⲡⲓⲥⲱⲛⲧ ⲧⲏⲣϥ ⳼ [17]Ⲏⲣⲉⲙⲙ̀ϥⲉ[f] ⲡⲁⲧⲱⲙⲧ ⳼ ⲁⲩϣⲁⲛⲛⲁⲩ ⲉⲣⲟⲕ ⳼
ⲉⲕϫⲟⲗϩ ⲛ̀ⲧⲉⲕⲯⲩⲭⲏ ⲉ̀ⲧⲉ ϯⲙⲉⲧⲁⲑⲙⲟⲩ ⲧⲉ ⳼ [18]ⲥⲉⲛⲁϫⲟⲥ ⲛⲛⲟⲩ-
ⲉⲣⲏⲟⲩ ⳼ ϫⲉ ⲛⲓⲙ ⲡⲉ ϥⲁⲓ ⳼ ⲉ̀ⲧⲁϥϭⲓ ⲛ̀ⲧⲉϥⲁ̀ⲛⲁⲥⲧⲁⲥⲓⲥ ⳼ ϧⲁϫⲉⲛ
ⲡⲓⲥⲱⲛⲧ ⲧⲏⲣϥ ⳼ ⲉϥ̀ϫⲟⲗϩ[g] ⳼ ⲉϥⲥⲉⲗⲥⲱⲗ ⲙ̀ⲡⲁⲓⲣⲏϯ ⳼ [19]Ⲁⲣⲏⲟⲩ ⳼
ϥⲁⲓ ⲡⲉ ⲛⲏⲓ ⲙ̀ⲡ̅ⲟ̅ⲥ̅ ⳼ ⲑⲁⲓ ⲧⲉ ϯⲡⲩ̀ⲗⲏ ⲛ̀ⲧⲉ ⲧⲫⲉ ⳼ [20]ⲙⲁⲣⲉⲛϫⲱ
ⲛⲟⲩⲥⲙⲟⲩ ⳼ ⲉⲡⲉⲛⲛⲟⲩϯ ⲛ̀ϧⲏⲧⲥ ⳼ ϫⲉ ⲡ̅ⲟ̅ⲥ̅ ⲙⲉⲓ̀ ⲙ̀ⲙⲟⲥ ⳼ ⲉ̀ϩⲟⲧⲉ ⳼
ϥⲙⲁⲛϣⲱⲡⲓ ⲧⲏⲣϥ ⲛ̀ⲓⲁⲕⲱⲃ ⳼ Ⲉⲧⲉ ϥⲁⲓ ⲡⲉ ⲡⲓⲭⲱⲣⲟⲥ ⲛ̀ⲧⲉ
ⲛⲓⲁⲅⲓⲟⲥ ⳼ [21]Ⲡⲁⲓⲱⲧ · ⳼ ϥⲏ ⲉⲧⲟⲛϧ ⳼ ⲛⲉⲙ ⲡⲓⲡ̅ⲛ̅ⲁ̅ ⲉⲑⲟⲩⲁⲃ ⳼
p. [ⲙⲋ] ⲛ̀ⲁⲉⲣⲁⲙⲁⲗⲏϫ[h] ⲉ̀ⲣⲟⲕ | ⲛ̀ⲧⲟⲩⲉⲣⲁⲥⲡⲁⲍⲉⲥⲑⲉ ⲙ̀ⲙⲟⲕ ⳼ ϫⲉ ⲁⲕϣⲱⲡⲓ
ⲛⲟⲩⲙⲁⲛϣⲱⲡⲓ ⲛ̀ⲧⲟⲩⲙⲉⲧⲟⲩⲁⲓ ⳼ ϥⲩⲥⲓ ⳼ [22]Ⲡⲓⲇ̅ ⲛ̀ⲍⲱⲟⲛ : ⳼
ⲛⲁⲛⲓⲥ̅ ⳼ ⲛ̀ⲧⲉⲛϩ ⲉⲑⲙⲉϩ ⲙ̀ⲃⲁⲗ[i] ⳼ Ⲥⲁ ⳼ ⲥⲁ ⲛⲓⲃⲉⲛ ⲛⲁⲓ ⲉ̀ⲧⲟⲓ
ⲛ̀ϩⲁⲣⲙⲁ ⳼ ⲛ̀ⲑⲣⲟⲛⲟⲥ ⲛ̀ϯⲧⲣⲓⲁⲥ ⳼ Ⲥⲉⲛⲁⲧⲱⲙⲧ ⳼ ⲙ̄ⲡⲓⲛⲁⲩ ⲉⲧⲉⲙ-
ⲙⲁⲩ ⳼ ⲉⲩⲛⲁⲩ ⲉ̀ⲣⲟⲕ ⳼ ⲉⲕϫⲟⲗϩ ⳼ ⲉⲕⲥⲉⲗⲥⲱⲗ[j] ⳼ ϧⲉⲛ ⲡⲱⲟⲩ ⲛ̀ⲧⲉ
ⲧⲁⲙⲉⲑⲛⲟⲩϯ ⳼ [23]Ⲥⲉⲛⲁϫⲟⲥ ⳼ ϫⲉ ⲟⲩⲉⲃⲟⲗ ⲑⲱⲛ ⲡⲉ ⲡⲁⲓⲥⲱⲙⲁ ⳼
ⲉⲃⲟⲗ ϧⲉⲛ ⲡⲕⲁϩⲓ ⳼ ⲉϥⲉⲣϥⲟⲣⲓⲛ ⲛ̀ⲧⲁⲓⲯⲩⲭⲏ ⳼ ϧⲁϫⲉⲛ ⲡⲥⲛⲟⲩ
ⲙ̀ⲡϩⲁⲡ ⲉϥⲙⲟⲧⲉⲛ ⲙⲙⲟϥ ⳼ ϧⲁⲧⲉⲛ ⲧⲁⲓⲥⲕⲏⲛⲏ ⳼ ⲑⲁⲓ ⲉ̀ⲧⲟⲓ ⲛ̀ϩⲟⲩϯ

[a] ⲉⲃⲟⲗ ⳼ ⲛ̀ⲧⲉ ⲛⲓϣⲁⲓ (rec. man. 1 sec. del.) ⲉ̀ⲛⲉϩ ⳼ [b] ʹ sup. ⲛ pr. rubr. script. [c] punct. sup. ⲣ ut vid. [d] punct. inter ⲧ sec. et ⲥ ut vid. [e] ⲉ sup. ras. pr. man. ut vid. [f] punct. sup. ⲙ sec. rubr. script. [g] punct. sup. ϥ ut vid. [h] punct. sup. ⲁ pr. ut vid. [i] ⲃ sup. ras. pr. man. ut vid. [j] ⲥ 2° sup. ras. ut vid.

and indissoluble unto *the* ages of the ages. 13 Arise. Why cf. Mt xxvi 45,
sleepest thou yet in the earth? Array thyself with thy soul, 46; Mc xiv 41, 42;
and come to the heavens with Me, unto My good Father and Lc xxii 46
the Holy Ghost; for They long for thee. 14 Arise, O thou holy
body, from which I built Me My flesh in a manner incom-
prehensible[a]: wear thy soul which was to Me a dwelling
place. 15 Arise, O thou that art free: wear the freedom of
all the world, through which I have redeemed all that I have
made. 16 Arise, O thou holy body: be joined to the blessed
soul. Receive from[b] Me Thy resurrection before the whole
creation. 17 The inhabitants of heaven will be amazed, when
they see thee arrayed with thy soul, even *with* immortality.
18 They will say one to another, Who is this that hath received
his resurrection before the whole creation, arrayed and adorned
thus? 19 Peradventure this is the house of the Lord, this is cf. Ge xxviii 17
the gate of heaven. 20 Let us sing praise to our God herein,
for the Lord loveth it more than all the dwelling of Jacob; cf. Ps lxxxvi 2
which is the choir of the saints. 21 My Father Who liveth and cf. Jn vi 57
the Holy Ghost will embrace thee and salute thee; for thou
wast a dwelling place of Their unity by nature. 22 The four cf. Ap iv 6, 8
living creatures with the six wings, full of eyes on all sides,
which are chariots *and* thrones[c] of the Trinity, will be amazed
in that hour, as they see thee arrayed and adorned in the
glory of My godhead. 23 They will say, Whence is this
body from the earth, wearing this soul before the time of
the judgment; resting beneath[d] this tent, this that is

[a] Lit. *in an incomprehensibleness* [b] Or *through* [c] Or *chariot thrones* [d] Or *by*

ⲟⲩⲟϩ ⲉⲑⲙⲉϩ ⳾ ⲡⲉⲛϩⲟⲩⲣ ⲁⲛⲟⲛ ⳾ ⲧⲉⲛⲉⲙⲓ ⲁⲛ : ⳿ 24 Ⲧⲉⲛⲥⲱⲟⲩⲛ
ⲙ̀ⲙⲟⲛ : ⲙ̀ⲙⲓⲛ ⲙ̀ⲙⲟⲛ ⳾ ⲉⲁ ⲡ̅ⲟ̅ⲥ̅ ⲑⲁⲙⲓⲟ̀ⲛ ⳾ ⲙⲡ̅ⲛ̅ⲁ̅ ⲛ̀ϣⲁϩ ⳾
ⲛ̀ⲭⲣⲱⲙ ⳾ 25 ϩⲏⲡⲡⲉ ⲧⲉⲛϩⲱⲃⲥ ⳾ ⲛ̀ⲛⲉⲛϩⲟ ⳾ ⲙⲙⲓⲛ ⲙ̀ⲙⲟⲛ ⳾ ϧⲉⲛ
ⲛⲉⲛⲧⲉⲛϩ ⳾ ⲉⲑⲃⲉ ⲡⲱⲟⲩ ⳾ ⲛ̀ⲧⲉ ⲧⲉϥⲙⲉⲑⲛⲟⲩϯ ⳾ ⲛ̀ⲧⲉⲛϣϯⲛⲓⲁⲧⲉⲛ
ⲁⲛ ⳾ ⲉⲛⲧⲏⲣϥ ⲙ̀ⲡⲱⲟⲩ ⲛ̀ⲧⲉ ⲧⲉϥⲙⲉⲑⲛⲟⲩϯ ⳾ 26 Ϩⲏⲡⲡⲉ ⳾ ⲓⲥ ⲫⲁⲓ
p. [μζ] ⲟⲩⲥⲱⲙⲁ ⲡⲉ ⲉⲃⲟⲗ ϧⲉⲛ ⲡⲕⲁϩⲓ ⳾ ϥⲙⲏⲛ | ⲉ̀ⲛⲓⲁⲧϣⲙⲟⲩⲛ ⲉ̀ⲣⲟϥ ⳾
Ⲟⲩⲟϩ ϥϧⲱⲛⲧ ⲙ̀ⲙⲟϥ ⳾ ⲉⲛⲓⲁⲧϧⲱⲛⲧ ⲉⲣⲟϥ ⳾ 27 ϥϯⲙⲟⲩⲉ̅ ⳾ ϥⲥⲉⲗ-
ⲥⲱ̀ⲗ ϥϫⲟⲗϩ ϧⲉⲛ ⲡⲱⲟⲩ ⲛ̀ϯⲧⲣⲓⲁⲥ ⳾ 28 Ⲗⲟⲓⲡⲟⲛ ⲧⲱⲛⲕ ⳾ ⲛ̀ⲧⲉⲕ-
ϩⲱⲧⲡ ⳿ ⲉ̀ⲧⲉⲕⲙⲉⲧⲟⲩⲁⲓ ⲛ̀ⲧⲉ ϣⲟⲣⲡ ⳾ ϫⲉ ϯⲟ̀ϩⲓ ⲛⲁⲕ ⳾ ⲱ̀ ⲫⲏ
IX. ⲉⲧⲥⲙⲟⲛⲧ ⳾ ⲛⲉⲣⲫⲉⲓ[a] ⲛ̀ⲧⲏⲓ ⳾ × 1 Ⲛⲁⲓ ⲉ̅ⲧⲁϥϫⲟⲧⲟⲩ ⳾ ϩⲓϫⲉⲛ ϯⲥⲗⲏ
ⲛ̀ⲱⲛⲓ : ⲛ̀ϫⲉ ⲡ̅ⲟ̅ⲥ̅ · ϧⲉⲛ ϯⲟⲩⲛⲟⲩ ⳾ ⲁⲥⲟⲩⲱⲛ ⳾ ϫⲉ ⲟⲩⲏⲓ ⲛⲁⲥϣ-
ⲑⲁⲙⲛⲟⲩⲧ ⲡⲉ ⳾ ⲙ̀ⲫⲣⲏϯ ⲛ̀ϯⲕⲩⲃⲱⲧⲟⲥ ⲛ̀ⲧⲉ ⲛⲱⲉ̀ ⳾ ⲙ̀ⲡⲓⲥⲛⲟⲩ ⳾ ⲉ̀ⲧⲉ
ⲙ̀ⲡⲉ ϩⲗⲓ ϣⲟⲩⲱⲛ ⲙ̀ⲙⲟⲥ ⳾ ⲉⲃⲏⲗ ⲉⲫ̅ϯ̅ ⳾ ⲫⲏ ⲉ̀ⲧⲁϥϣⲑⲁⲙ ⲙ̅ⲙⲟⲥ
ⲙ̀ⲡⲓⲥⲛⲟⲩ ⳿ 2 Ⲥⲁⲧⲟⲧϥ ⳾ ⲁϥⲧⲱⲛϥ ⲛ̀ϫⲉ ⲡⲓⲥⲱⲙⲁ ⳾ ⲛ̀ⲧⲉ ϯⲡⲁⲣⲑⲉⲛⲟⲥ
ⲛ̀ⲥⲉⲙⲛⲏ ⳾ Ⲁϥⲉⲣⲁⲙⲁⲗⲏϫ ⳾ ⲉⲧⲉϥⲯⲩⲭⲏ[b] ⲙ̀ⲙⲓⲛ ⲙ̀ⲙⲟϥ ⳾
ⲙⲫⲣⲏϯ ·[c] ⲡ̅ⲥⲟⲛ ⲃ̅ ⳾ ⲉ̀ⲧⲁⲩⲓ̅ ⲉⲃⲟⲗ ϧⲉⲛ ⲡϣⲉⲙⲙⲟ ⳾ ⲟⲩⲟϩ
ⲁⲩⲉⲣⲟⲩⲁⲓ ⳾ ⲛⲉⲙ ⲛⲟⲩⲉ̀ⲣⲛⲟⲩ ⳾ 3 Ⲥⲁⲧⲟⲧϥ ⳾ ⲁϥⲓ̅ ⲉⲑⲙⲏϯ ⲛ̀ϫⲉ
ⲡⲓϩⲩⲙⲛⲟⲇⲟⲥ ⲇⲁⲩⲓⲇ ⳾ ϧⲉⲛ ϯⲟⲩⲛⲟⲩ[d] ⲉ̀ⲧⲉⲙⲙⲁⲩ ⳾ Ⲁϥⲕⲓⲙ
ⲉ̀ⲧⲉϥⲕⲩⲑⲁⲣⲁ ⲉϥϫⲱ ⲙⲙⲟⲥ ⳿ 4 Ϫⲉ ⲟⲩⲛⲁⲓ ⲛⲉⲙ ⲟⲩⲙⲉⲑⲙⲏⲓ ⲁⲩⲓ̅
p. μη ⲉⲃⲟⲗ ⲉ̀ϩⲣⲉⲛ ⲛⲟⲩⲉ̀ⲣⲛⲟⲩ · | Ⲟⲩⲇⲓⲕⲉⲟ̀ⲥⲩⲛⲏ ⳾ ⲛⲉⲙ ⲟⲩϩⲓⲣⲏⲛⲏ ⳿
ⲁⲩϣⲉⲛⲧⲟⲧⲟⲩ ⲛ̀ⲛⲟⲩⲉⲣⲛⲟⲩ ⳿ 5 Ⲛⲁⲓ ⲇⲉ ⲉ̀ⲧⲁⲩϣⲱⲡⲓ ⳾ ⲁϥϣⲉ
ⲛⲁϥ ⲉⲛϣⲱⲓ ⲉⲛⲓⲫⲏⲟⲩⲓ̅ ⳾ ⲉϥⲥⲙⲟⲩ ⲉ̀ⲣⲟⲛ ⳾ ⲛⲉⲙ ⲙⲏ ⲉⲑⲛⲁⲙⲟϣⲓ
ⲛ̀ⲥⲁ ⲛⲉϥⲛⲟⲙⲟⲥ ⲉϥϫⲱ ⲙ̀ⲙⲟⲥ ⳾ 6 Ϫⲉ ⲧϩⲓⲣⲏⲛⲏ ⲛⲱⲧⲉⲛ ⲛⲁϣⲫⲏⲣ
ⲙⲙⲉⲗⲟⲥ ⳾ 7 ⲧϩⲓⲣⲏⲛⲏ ⲙ̀ⲡⲓⲧⲁⲫⲟⲥ ⳾ ⲉ̀ⲧⲁϥϣⲱⲡⲓ ⲙ̅ⲙⲁⲛⲟⲩⲟϩ ⳾
ⲙ̀ⲡⲥⲱⲙⲁ ⲛ̀ⲧⲁⲙⲁⲩ ⳿ 8 Ⲟⲩⲟϩ ϯⲛⲁϫⲱ ⲙ̀ⲡⲁⲥⲙⲟⲩ ⲛⲉⲙ ⲡⲁϩⲙⲟⲧ ⳾
ⲛⲉⲙ ⲧⲁϫⲟⲙ ⲙ̀ⲙⲁⲩ ϣⲁ ⲉ̀ⲛⲉϩ ⳾ Ⲁⲩϣⲁⲛⲟ̀ϩⲓ ϧⲉⲛ ⲡⲓⲡⲁϩϯ
ⲉⲧⲥⲟⲩⲧⲱⲛ ⳾ ⲡ̅ⲥⲉϯⲱⲟⲩ ⲛⲏⲓ ϧⲉⲛ ⲟⲩⲙⲉⲧⲟⲩⲁⲓ ⳾ ⲛⲁⲧⲫⲱⲣϫ ⳾

[a] ρ sup. rubr. scr. [b] ⲉⲧⲉϥⲯⲩⲭⲏ ⲉⲧⲉϥⲯⲩⲭⲏ (corr. del. ⲉ̀ⲧⲉϥⲯⲩⲭⲏ) [c] punct. ut vid. [d] ϯⲟⲩⲛⲟⲩⲛⲟⲩ (rec. man. del. ⲛⲟⲩ sec.)

fearful and full of shuddering[a]? We know not. 24 As for
ourselves we know that we are made by the Lord spirit cf. Ps CIII 4; He I 7
and[b] flame of fire. 25 Behold we cover our faces with our cf. Is VI 2
wings for the glory of His godhead: we cannot look at all at
the glory of His godhead. 26 Behold this is a body from the
earth, and it abides by Him that none can abide by, and
approaches Him that none can approach unto. 27 It is cf. 1 Ti VI 16
bright[c], and is adorned and is arrayed in the glory of the
Trinity. 28 Now arise and be joined to thy former unity, for
I wait for thee, O thou that wast made *a* temple of Mine.

IX. When the Lord had said these things over the
coffin of stone, straightway it opened: for it was shut even
as the ark of Noah aforetime, which no one could open
save God, who shut it aforetime. 2 Forthwith the body cf. Ge VII 16
of the honourable Virgin arose, and embraced its own soul,
even as two brothers who are come from a strange country,
and they were united one with another. 3 Forthwith the
singer David came into the midst in that hour, and struck
his harp, saying, 4 Mercy and truth are come forth to meet Ps LXXXIV 11
one another; righteousness and peace have saluted one
another. 5 Now when these things had come to pass, He
went up to the heavens, blessing us and those who shall walk cf. Lc XXIV 51
after His law, saying, 6 Peace *be* unto you, My friends *and*
members. 7 Peace *be* unto the sepulchre, which was *a* dwelling
place of the body of My mother. 8 And I will set My
blessing and My grace and My power there for ever; if they
abide in the right faith, and glorify Me in an indivisible

[a] Or *amazement* [b] Or *of* [c] Or *It glitters*

[9]Ϯϩιρηνη ⲛ̀ⲛⲏ ⲉⲑⲛⲁϫⲱⲕ ⲉⲃⲟⲗ ⲛ̅ⲥⲛⲟⲩ ⲛⲓⲃⲉⲛ ⲙ̅ⲡⲉⲣⲫⲙⲉⲩⲓ̅
ⲛ̀ⲧⲁⲙⲁⲩ ⁊ ϧⲉⲛ ⲟⲩⲛⲁⲓ ⁊ ⲛⲉⲙ ⲟⲩϩⲁⲛ : ⁊ – [10]Ⲏ̅ⲑⲟⲥ ϩⲱⲥ
ⲧⲉⲛⲟ̅ⲥ̅ ⁊ ⲟⲩⲟϩ ⲧⲉⲛⲡⲣⲟⲥⲧⲁⲧⲏⲥ ⲉⲩⲥⲟⲛ ⁊ ⲁⲥⲥⲙⲟⲩ ⲉ̀ⲣⲟⲛ ⁊ ⲁⲛⲕⲏⲛ
ⲉⲛⲛⲁⲩ ⲉ̀ⲣⲱⲟⲩ ϒ [11]Ⲁⲗⲗⲁ ⲧⲥⲙⲏ ⲛ̅ⲛⲓⲇⲩⲛⲁⲙⲓⲥ ⲉⲧⲉⲣϩⲩⲙⲛⲟⲥ
ϧⲁϫⲱⲟⲩ ⁊ ⲛⲁⲥⲥⲉⲛⲥⲉⲛ ϧⲉⲛ ⲡⲉⲛⲙⲁϣϫ ⁊ ⲉⲥϫⲱ ⲙ̅ⲙⲟⲥ · [12]ϫⲉ
ⲁⲗⲗⲏⲗⲟⲩⲓ̅[a] ⁊ · · Ⲁⲛⲓⲟⲩⲓ̅ ⁊ ⲙ̀ⲡⲟ̅ⲥ̅ ⁊ ⲡⲟⲩⲱ̀ⲟⲩ ⁊ ⲛⲉⲙ ⲟⲩⲧⲁⲓⲟ̀ ⁊
Ⲁⲛⲓⲟⲩⲓ̅ ⲙ̀ⲡⲟ̅ⲥ̅ · ⲡⲟⲩⲱ̅ⲟⲩ ⲙ̅ⲡⲉϥⲣⲁⲛ ⲉⲑⲟⲩⲁⲃ[b] ⲁⲗⲗⲏⲗⲟⲩⲓ̅ⲁ̅ |
p. μθ [13]Ⲁⲛⲓⲟⲩⲓ̅ ⲙ̀ⲡⲟ̅ⲥ̅ ⁊ ⲛ̀ⲛⲓϣⲏⲣⲓ ⲛ̀ⲧⲉ ⲫ̅ϯ̅ ⁊ ⲟⲩⲟϩ ϩⲱⲥ̇[c] ⲡ̅ⲟⲩⲱⲟⲩ
ϧⲉⲛ ⲡⲉϥⲉⲣⲫⲉⲓ̅ ⲉⲑⲟⲩⲁⲃ ⁊ ⲁⲗⲗⲏⲗⲟⲩⲓ̀ⲁ ϒ [14]Ⲧⲟⲧⲉ ⲁ̀ⲛⲟⲛ ⲁⲛ-
ⲕⲁϯ ⁊ ϫⲉ ⲙ̀ⲫⲟⲟⲩ ⲁⲩⲓⲛⲓ ⲙ̀ⲡⲓⲟⲩⲣⲟ ⁊ ⲛ̅ϩⲁⲛⲡⲁⲣⲑⲉⲛⲟⲥ ⁊
Ϯⲯⲩⲭⲏ : ⲛⲉⲙ ⲡⲓⲥⲱⲙⲁ ⲉ̅ⲧⲁⲩⲉⲣⲟⲩⲁⲓ ⁊ [15]ⲁϥϫⲟⲥ ϫⲉ ϩⲓⲫⲁϩⲟⲩ
ⲙ̀ⲙⲟⲥ ⁊ ⲉ̀ⲩⲉ̀ⲓⲛⲓ[d] ⲛⲁϥ ⲉ̀ϧⲟⲩ̇ⲛ[e] ⲛ̀ⲛⲉⲥⲕⲉϣⲫⲉⲣⲓ ⲧⲏⲣⲟⲩ ⁊ ⲉⲧⲉ
ⲛⲉⲥⲡⲣⲁⲝⲓⲥ ⲉⲑⲟⲩⲁⲃ ⁊ [16]Ⲟⲩⲟϩ ⲛⲁⲓⲣⲏϯ ⁊ ⲁⲛⲕⲟⲧⲧⲉⲛ ⲉ̈ⲓ̈ⲗⲏ̅ⲙ̅ ⁊
X. ⲉⲛϯⲱ̀ⲟⲩ ⁊ ⲟⲩⲟϩ ⲉⲛϣⲉⲡϩⲙⲟⲧ ⲛ̅ⲧⲉ ⲡ̅ⲟ̅ⲥ̅ ⁊ [1]Ⲓⲥ ⲛⲁⲓ ⲙⲉⲛ ⲁⲛ-
ϫⲟⲧⲟⲩ ϣⲁ ⲡⲁⲓⲙⲁ ϒ ⲉⲛⲟⲩⲱⲛϩ ⲛⲱⲧⲉⲛ ⲉⲃⲟⲗ ⁊ ⲛ̀ⲛⲓⲇⲱⲣⲉⲁ̅ ⁊
ⲉⲑⲙⲉϩ ⲛ̀ϩⲙⲟⲧ ⁊ ⲛ̀ⲧⲉ ⲧⲁⲓⲁ̅ⲅⲓ̅ⲁ̅[f] ⲙ̅ⲡⲁⲣⲑⲉⲛⲟⲥ ⁊ ⲑⲁⲓ ⲉⲧϣⲟⲡ ⲛⲁⲛ
ⲛ̀ϣⲟⲩϣⲟⲩ ⁊ ϧⲁ ⲡⲅⲉⲛⲟⲥ ⲧⲏⲣϥ ⲛ̀ⲛⲓⲣⲱⲙⲓ[g] ⁊ [2]Ⲗⲟⲓⲡⲟⲛ[h] ⲥⲉⲙⲡϣⲁ
ⲛⲁⲛ ϩⲱⲛ ⁊ ⲁ̀ⲛⲟⲛ ϧⲁ ⲟⲩⲟⲛ ⲛⲓⲃⲉⲛ ⁊ ⲉ̀ⲧⲁⲩⲥⲟⲩⲉⲛ ⲡⲉⲥϩⲙⲟⲧ ⁊
ⲉⲑⲣⲉⲛⲓ̅ⲛⲓ ⲛⲁⲥ ⲉ̀ϧⲟⲩⲛ ⁊ ϧⲉⲛ ⲡⲁⲓⲉ̅ⲣⲟⲟⲩ ⲛ̅ϥⲁⲛⲟⲩⲧⲁϩ : ⲉⲩⲙ̅ⲡϣⲁ
ⲛ̅ϯⲙⲉⲧⲁⲛⲟⲓⲁ̅ ⁊ ⲡⲓⲟⲩⲁⲓ ⲡⲓⲟⲩⲁⲓ ⲕⲁⲧⲁ ⲧⲉϥϫⲟⲙ ⁊

[a] rec. man. add. ⲁ sup. [b] post hoc verb. rubr. lin. add. [c] punct. sup. ⲥ ut vid. [d] punct. sup. ⲉ pr. et sec. ut vid., ʹ sup. ⲓ pr. rubr. script. [e] punct. sup. ⲩ ut vid. [f] punct. sup. ⲓ sec. ut vid. [g] punct. sup. ⲛ prim. ut vid.

unity. 9 Peace *be* unto those who shall accomplish always the
memorial of My mother in mercy and judgment. 10 She also, cf. Ps c 1
at once our Lady and our succourer, blessed us: and we saw
them no more. 11 But the voice of the powers that sang
hymns before them was sounding in our ears, saying,
12 Alleluia. Bring to the Lord glory and honour; bring to cf. Ps xxviii 1,
the Lord honour to His holy name. Alleluia. 13 Bring to 2, 9
the Lord the sons of God, and sing glory in His holy temple.
Alleluia. 14 Then we understood that to-day there were
brought unto the King virgins, *even* the soul and the body cf. Ps xliv 15
which were united. 15 He said, Behind her there shall be
brought in unto Him all her neighbours also, which *are* her
holy deeds. 16 And so we returned to Jerusalem, glorifying
and thanking the Lord.

X. Behold these things we have said thus far, manifesting to you the gifts full of grace of this holy Virgin, who is our glorying unto[a] all the race of men. 2 Now it befits us also, even all that have known her grace, to bring in unto her on this day fruits worthy of repentance, each according cf. Mt iii 8; Lc iii 8
to his power[b].

[a] Or *against* [b] I have omitted here three pages. See introduction

BOHAIRIC ACCOUNT OF THE DEATH OF JOSEPH

WITH SAHIDIC FRAGMENTS

THE DEATH OF JOSEPH.

Bohairic Account[a].

cf. Mt XIII 55 This is the going forth from *the* body of our father Joseph
the carpenter, the father of Christ according to flesh, whose
life was one hundred and eleven years[b]. Our Saviour told
the apostles his whole life on the mount of Olives, and the
apostles also wrote these words, and left[c] them in the
Library at Jerusalem. And again[d] the day on which the
holy old man laid down *the* body is the twenty sixth of the
month Epep; in the[e] peace of God, Amen.

I. Now it came to pass on a day, as our good Saviour
cf. Mt XXIV 3 was sitting on the mount of Olives and His disciples were
assembled to Him, that He spake with them, saying, O My
brethren beloved and ye sons of My good Father, whom He
hath chosen from among the whole world. 2 Ye know that
many times now I have told you that I must needs be
cf. He II 9 crucified and taste death for the universe, and rise from the
cf. Mc XVI 15; Lc XXIV 47, 49; Ac I 8 dead, and give you the preaching of the gospel, that[d] ye may
preach it in all the world, and clothe you with power from on
high, and fill you with the[e] Holy Ghost, that ye may preach
to all the nations, saying to them, Repent; 3 for it is better
that a man find a cup of water in the age that is coming[f]
than all the riches of all the world. 4 And again, Better is a

[a] The Bohairic text is given by Lagarde: *Aegyptiaca*, pp. 1—37 [b] Lit. *who spent one hundred and eleven years in his life* [c] Or *placed* [d] See note [e] Lit. *a* [f] Lit. *better is a cup of water in the age that is coming, that the man find it*

single footstep in My Father's house than all the wealth of cf. Jn xiv 2
this world. 5 And again, Better is a single hour of the
righteous rejoicing than a thousand years of the sinners
weeping and mourning, whose tears shall not be wiped away,
neither shall they be heeded at all. 6 Now therefore, O My
glorious[a] members, when ye go, preach to them, *saying*, A Lev
just balance and a just measure are those wherewith My xix 36; Prov xvi
Father will take[b] account with you. And again, A single 11; Ez xlv 10
word of jest that ye shall speak shall be required of you. cf. Mt xii
7 Even as no one[c] can escape death, so no one can escape 36
those things which he hath done, whether *it be* good or cf. 2 Co v
evil. 8 But all these words have I told you now, *saying*, 10
No mighty one can be saved because of his strength, cf. Ps
neither can a man be saved because of the multitude of xxxii 16
his wealth. 9 Now therefore hear, and I will tell you the
life of My father Joseph, the blessed old man *who was a*
carpenter.

II. There was a man Joseph who was[d] from a city
called Bethlehem, which is the *city* of the Jews, and is the cf. Lc ii 4
city of king David. 2 And he learned well the wisdom and
the trade of carpentry. 3 And this man Joseph took to
himself a wife according to a union of a holy marriage. And
she bare him sons and daughters, four sons and two
daughters; whose names are these, Judas and Josetos, cf. Mc vi 3
James and Simon: and the names of his daughters are[e] Lysia
and Lydia. 4 And Joseph's wife died, even as it is appointed cf. He ix
for all men, and left James still little[f]. 5 And Joseph was a 27 cf. Mc xv
righteous man, glorifying God in all things. And he was 40
without[c], working at the trade of carpentry, he and his cf. Mt i 19
two sons, living by the work of their hands, according to the
law of Moses. 6 And this righteous man, of whom I speak,
this is Joseph My father according to flesh, to whom My cf. Mt i 18;
mother Mary was betrothed for a wife. Lc i 27

III. And whilst My father Joseph lived as a widower,
Mary also My mother, who was in every wise good and

[a] Or *honourable* [b] Lit. *draw* [c] See note [d] Lit. *he is*
[e] Lit. *the name...is* [f] Lit. *being little*

cf. Lc i 42 blessed[a], was dwelling in the temple, serving therein in purity, and she grew up until *she was* twelve years *old.* She spent three years in the house of her parents, and nine other years in the temple of the Lord. [2]Then the priests, when they saw the Virgin living austerely and dwelling in the[b] fear of the Lord, spake one with another, saying, Let us seek a good man and espouse her to him until the time of the marriage feast; lest by any means we let the custom of women happen to her in the temple, and we come to be under a great sin.

IV. And straightway[c] they called the tribe of Judah, and brought out therefrom twelve peoples[d], according to the name of the twelve tribes of Israel. [2]The lot fell[e] upon the good old man Joseph, My father according to flesh. [3]Then the priests answered and said to My blessed virgin mother, Go with Joseph, obey him, until the time comes that we make the marriage feast[d]. [4]My father Joseph received Mary My mother into his house. She found the little boy James in
cf. Mc xv 40; xvi 1; Lc xxiv 10 the sadness of bereavement, and was cherishing him. Therefore she was called Mary of James. [5]Now Joseph took her into his house: and he went to the place[f] wherein he worked[g] in carpentry. [6]Mary My mother spent two years in his house until[h] the good time.

V. Now in the fourteenth year of her life I came by My own will and dwelt in her, I *who* am Jesus your life. [2]Now when she was three months pregnant, the guileless Joseph came from the place[f] wherein he worked[g] in carpentry;
cf. Mt i 18, 19 and found[d] My virgin mother pregnant. He was troubled and feared, and purposed to put her away privily. [3]And from grief of heart he did not eat or drink.

cf. Mt i 20, 21 VI. But in the middle of the night, behold Gabriel, the archangel of joy, came unto him in a vision, according to the command of My good Father; and said to him, Joseph, thou son of David, fear not, take[d] Mary thy wife unto thee: for

[a] Lit. *she of all the good and blessed manners* [b] Lit. *a* [c] Lit. *in that hour* [d] See note [e] Lit. *came* [f] Lit. *way* [g] Lit. *works* [h] For the Sahidic text and translation from c. iv 6[b] to c. viii 1[a] see below, p. 140 ff

that which she will bear is of the[a] Holy Ghost. 2She shall
bear a Son; and thou shalt call His name Jesus; it is He cf. Ap XII 5
that will rule[b] all the nations with a rod of iron. 3And the cf. Lc I 38;
angel departed from him. And Joseph arose from his[c] sleep, Mt I 24
and did as the angel of the Lord commanded him, and took
Mary unto him.

VII. Now after these things there went out a decree cf. Lc II 1,
from Augustus the king, that all the world should give in its 3 ff
name, each one after his city. 2The good old man also arose,
and took Mary My virgin mother up to[d] his city Bethlehem,
for she was nigh to bear *a child*. And he wrote his name
through[e] the scribe: Joseph, the son of David, and Mary his
wife and Jesus his son are of the tribe of Judah. 3And
Mary My Mother bare Me in the way that turns[f] to cf. Ge
Bethlehem, by the tomb of Rachel, the wife of Jacob the XXXV 19, 20
patriarch, who is the mother of Joseph and Benjamin.

VIII. Satan gave counsel to Herod the great, the father cf. Mt II 22
of Archelaus, who beheaded John, My beloved and My kins-
man. 2Thus he sought after Me, to slay Me, thinking cf. Mt II 13,
that My kingdom was[g] of this world. 3And Joseph was told 16 cf. Jn XVIII
by My Father in a vision; and he arose, and took Me and 36
Mary My mother—I sitting on her arms and Salome follow- cf. Mt II 14
ing us. We went down to[h] Egypt, and dwelt there the
space of a year[i], until Herod's body bred worms, that he cf. Mt II
died, because of the blood of the sinless little children which 16, 20; Ac XII 23
he shed.

IX. Now when that lawless *man* Herod was dead, we
returned to the land of Israel, and we dwelt in a city of cf. Mt II
Galilee, whose name is Nazareth. 2And My father Joseph, 21 ff; Lc II 39
the blessed old man, was working at the trade of carpentry,
whilst we lived by the work of his hands. He never ate cf. 2 Th
bread for nought, doing according to the law of Moses. III 8

X. And after this long time his body was not without
power, nor were his eyes without light, nor was a single
tooth in his mouth destroyed. He was not without under-
standing in wisdom all this time, but he was as a youth.

[a] Lit. *a* [b] Lit. *feed* [c] Lit. *the* [d] Or *unto* [e] See note
[f] Lit. *the way of turning* [g] Lit. *is* [h] Or *into* [i] Lit. *a year of days*

And his life had come to one hundred and eleven years in a
good old age.

XI. Now his two elder sons Josetos and Symeon took
wives, and went to their house; and his two daughters also
took husbands: as it is laid down for all men. But Joseph
dwelt with James his youngest[a] son. ²When the Virgin bare
cf. Lc II Me, I was with them in all subjection of sonship: for I did
51; He IV 15; v 8; every work of mankind, sin only excepted. ³And I called Mary
1 Ti II 11 My mother, and Joseph My father; and I obeyed them in all
things that they told[b] Me. I did not answer a word unto
them, but I loved them exceedingly.

XII. Now it came to pass after these things that the
cf. He IX death of Joseph My father drew nigh, even as it is appointed
27 for all men. ²When his body was sick, his angel told him,
In this year shalt thou die. ³And when his soul was
troubled, he went up to Jerusalem, and he went into the
temple of the Lord, and he repented[c] before the altar, and
prayed thus, saying,

cf. 2 Co I XIII. God, the Father of all mercies[d] and the God of all
3; Jer flesh, the Lord of my soul and of my body and of my spirit:
XXXIX 27 ²if the days of my life which Thou hast given me in the
world, are ended; I beseech Thee, Lord God, that Thou
wouldest send me Michael the archangel, to stand by me,
until my wretched soul goes forth from my body without
trouble and confusion. ³For a great fear and grief is death
cf. Ge I 30; to all men, whether *it be* man or cattle or wild beast or
VI 17 creeping thing or bird: ⁴in short every creature which is
under heaven, wherein is *a* soul of life, there is trouble and
grief *to them*, until their soul is separated from their body.
⁵Now therefore, O my Lord, let Thine angel stand by my
soul and my body, until they are separated from one another
without trouble. ⁶Cause not the angel, appointed unto me
from the day that Thou didst form me until now, to burn in
his face with anger towards me in the path, as I come unto
Thee: but let him be at peace with me[e]. ⁷Let not those whose

[a] Lit. *little* [b] Lit. *will tell* [c] Lit. *gave repentance* [d] Or *mercy* [e] For the Sahidic text and translation from c. XIII 6[b] to c. XV 2[a] see below, p. 146 ff

face is diverse trouble me in the path, as I come unto Thee.
8 Let not those who *are* by[a] the gates restrain my soul;
neither put me to shame at Thy fearful judgment seat. 9 Let
not the waves of the river of fire be savage towards me, cf. Da VII
wherein all souls are purified, before they see the glory of 10
Thy godhead. 10 O God who judgest each one in truth and
righteousness. Now therefore, my Lord, let Thy mercy be
to me *a* consolation; for Thou art the Fountain of all good.
Thine is the glory unto *the* ages of the ages. Amen.

XIV.[b] Now it came to pass after these things, he went
unto[c] Nazareth, the city wherein he dwelt[d]. And he lay
down with the sickness wherewith[e] he should die, even as it is cf. He IX
appointed for all men. 2 And his sickness was very heavy, 27
beyond all the times that he was sick, from the day that he
was born into the world. 3 This is the manner of life of My
beloved father Joseph. 4 He was forty years *old, when* he
took *a* wife, and other forty nine years living in wedlock with
his wife. And she died: and he was a year alone. 5 My
mother was two other years in his house, when the priests
gave her to him, when he was told by the priests, *saying*,
Keep her until the time of your marriage[f]. 6 At the
beginning of the third year, whilst she was in his house,
which is the fifteenth year of her life, she bare Me on the
earth in a mystery: no one knoweth it in the whole creation,
save Me and My Father and the Holy Ghost, being as We
are in unity.

XV. Now all the days of the life of My father Joseph,
the blessed old man, are an hundred and eleven years, even
as My good Father commanded. 2 And the day wherein he
went forth from *the* body, is the twenty sixth of the month
Epep. 3 And the choice gold, even the flesh of My father
Joseph, began[g] to be altered; and the silver was changed,
even the mind and the wisdom. 4 He forgot to eat and to
drink[h]: the wisdom of the craft turned into error. 5 And it

[a] Or *on* [b] For the Sahidic translation from c. XIV to c. XXIV 1 see below, p. 152 ff [c] Or *up to* [d] Lit. *dwells* [e] Lit. *in the sickness wherein* [f] Lit. *the time of making the marriage feast for you* [g] See note [h] Lit. *the eating and the drinking*

came to pass when the light arose on that day, which is the
twenty sixth of the month Epep, My father Joseph was much
troubled on his bed; and he uttered a great groan, and smote
his hands together, and cried out in great trouble, speaking
thus:

XVI. Woe to me to-day. Woe to the day that my
mother brought me forth into the world. 2 Woe to the womb
wherein I received seed of life. Woe to the breasts which I
sucked. 3 Woe to the knees on which I sat. 4 Woe to the
hands which carried me, until I grew up and became sinful[a].
5 Woe to my tongue and my lips, for they have been en-
tangled often in violence and in backbiting and in false
slander and in idle words of jest, full of deceit. 6 Woe to my
eyes, for they have looked upon stumbling-blocks. 7 Woe to
my ears, for they have loved to hear vain words. 8 Woe to
my hands, for they have taken things which are not theirs.
9 Woe to my stomach and my bowels, for they have desired
foods which are not theirs: and if it found anything, it
cf. Da III 6 would consume it[b] more than a burning fiery furnace, and
make it[b] everywhere unprofitable. 10 Woe to my feet,
which served my body ill, taking it into no good ways.
11 Woe to my body, for it hath made my soul waste and
strange[c] to God Who made it. 12 What shall I do now? I
am shut in on every side. 13 Truly woe to every man who
shall sin. 14 Truly this is the great trouble, which I saw
cf. Mt I 16 upon Jacob my father, when he came forth from *the* body:
it also hath overtaken me the wretched one to-day. 15 But
Jesus[c], God, the mediator of my soul and of my body, doeth
His will in me.

XVII. Now as My beloved father Joseph was saying
these things, I arose and went in unto him as he lay down;
and I found him troubled in his soul and his spirit. I said
to him, Hail, My beloved father Joseph, whose old age is at
once good and blessed[d]. 2 He answered in great fear of
death, saying to Me, Hail many times, my beloved Son.

[a] Lit. *in sin* [b] Lit. *them* [c] See note [d] Lit. *he of the old age good and blessed at once*

Behold my soul rested within[a] me a little, when I heard Thy
voice. 3 Jesus my Lord, Jesus my true King, Jesus my
good and merciful Saviour, Jesus the Preserver, Jesus the
Pilot, Jesus the Shelterer, Jesus [who holdest fast[b]] the
universe in Thy[c] goodness, Jesus whose name is sweet in the
mouth of all and very rich[d], Jesus the Eye that sees, the Ear
that hears in truth, hear me to-day, even me Thy servant[e],
as I beseech Thee, pouring out my tears before Thee. 4 Thou
art God in truth, Thou art[e] the Lord in truth, even as the
angel said to me many times: especially *on* the day that my
heart doubted within[a] me, because of a human thought
against her, blessed *and* virgin, because she was pregnant;
when I said, I will put her away privily. 5 But as I thought cf. Mt i 19 ff
on these things, the angel appeared unto me in a vision,
saying unto me, Joseph, thou son of David, fear not, take[e]
Mary thy wife unto thee: for that which she will bear *is* of
the[f] Holy Ghost. 6 Do not doubt at all concerning her
pregnancy: for she will bear a Son; and thou shalt call His
name Jesus. 7 Thou art Jesus Christ, the Saviour of my
soul and of my body and of my spirit. Do not blame me,
Thy servant and the work of Thy hands. 8 I did not know, O cf. Job x 3; Ps cxxxvii 8
my Lord, neither do I understand the mystery of Thy
strange birth: neither did I ever hear that a woman was
pregnant without *a* man, or[e] *that* a virgin bare, sealed in
her virginity. 9 O my Lord, if *this* is not the ordinance of
this mystery, I will not believe on Thee and on Thy holy
birth, and glorify her who bare Thee, even Mary the holy
Virgin. 10 I remember also the day that the horned serpent
bit the boy, and he died. 11 His relations[g] surrounded Thee,
that they might deliver Thee to Herod. 12 Thy mercy laid hold
of him; and Thou didst raise him, concerning whom[h] they
slandered Thee, *saying* that Thou didst kill him. And there
was great joy in the house of him that died. 13 Straightway I
took hold of Thine ear, and spake with Thee, saying, Be
prudent, my Son. 14 Straightway Thou didst rebuke me,

[a] Lit. *to* [b] These words are not in the MS, but see note [c] Lit. *His*
[d] Lit. *fat* [e] See note [f] Lit. *a* [g] Lit. *men* [h] Or *because of whom*

saying, Unless Thou wert my father according to *the* flesh,
surely[a] I would have told thee what this *thing* is which Thou
cf. Jn xx 28 hast done to Me. 15 Now therefore, O my Lord and my God,
if Thou hast reckoned with me for that day, and hast caused
these fearful signs to come upon me; I beseech Thy goodness
cf. Ps cxv 7, 8 not to bring me in, to contend with me. 16 I am Thy servant
and the son of Thine handmaid. 17 If Thou breakest my bonds
asunder, I will sacrifice to Thee a sacrifice of praise, even the
confession of the glory of Thy godhead, that[b] Thou art Jesus
Christ, at once the Son of God in truth and the Son of man.

XVIII. Now as My father Joseph said these things, I
did not refrain from[c] shedding tears. And I wept as I
looked at him (for death had dominion over him), and as I
heard the words of misery which he spoke[d]. 2 And after
these things, O My brethren, remember[c] My death upon the
cross for the life of the whole world. 3 And My beloved
mother Mary arose, she whose name is sweet in the mouth of
all who love Me; and she said to Me in great grief, Woe to
me, my beloved Son; shall he die, he of the good and blessed
old age, Joseph Thy beloved father, honourable[e] according
to flesh? 4 I said to her, O My beloved mother, who is there
ever among men, who has worn flesh, that will not taste
death? 5 For death is the ruler of mankind, O My blessed
mother. 6 For thou also must needs die as all men. 7 Whether
it be Joseph My father or thou, My blessed mother, your
death is not death, but is life eternal *and* unceasing. 8 For I
also will die for the universe, because of the flesh that dies,
which I wore in thee. 9 Now therefore, O My beloved
mother, arise and go in unto the blessed old man Joseph,
until thou knowest[f] the ordinance which shall come to him
from on high.

XIX. And she arose, and went into the place[g] wherein
he lay[h], and she found him with the sign of death manifest
in him. 2 And I also, My beloved ones, was sitting at his
head, and Mary My mother was sitting by his feet. 3 And he

[a] Lit. *it not being so* [b] Or *for* [c] See note [d] Lit. *speaks*
[e] Or *glorious* [f] Or *that thou mayest know* [g] Lit. *way* See note
[h] Lit. *lies*

lifted up his eyes to My face, and was not able to speak, for the hour of death had dominion over him. [4]Moreover he lifted up his eyes, and he uttered a great groan. [5]And I held his hands and his feet for a great while; whilst he looked at Me and besought Me, *saying*, Suffer me not to be taken away. [6]And I put My hand in under his heart, and I found his soul brought to his throat, for it was about to be[a] brought up from his body. But the last hour had not yet been fulfilled for Death to come: otherwise he would not have held back; for Confusion was following him, and Weeping and Destruction go before him.

XX. When My beloved mother saw Me touching his body, she also touched his feet, and she found that the breath and the heat[b] had gone, and left them. [2]She said to Me in guilelessness, Thanks be to Thee, my beloved Son; for from the hour that Thou didst put Thy hand on his body, the heat[b] withdrew from[c] him. [3]Behold his feet and his legs are cold as crystal. [4]And I called his sons and his daughters, saying to them, Arise, and speak with your father; for this is the time to speak, before the mouth that speaks fails, and the wretched flesh is cold. [5]Then his sons and his daughters spake with Joseph. He was in danger because of the suffering of death, wishing to go forth from this world. [6]Lysia the daughter of Joseph answered and said to her brethren, Woe to me, my brethren; is not this[d] the sickness of our beloved mother, and until now we have not seen her? [7]This also is that which happens to[e] our father Joseph, that we should not see him for ever. [8]Then the children[f] of Joseph lifted up their voice, and wept. And I also and Mary My virgin mother wept with them, for the hour of death was come.

XXI. Now I looked towards the south, and I saw Death. He came unto[g] the house, Amenti following him, who is his instrument, and the devil, many attendants[h] following him, clothed with fire, without number, smoke and

[a] Or *that it might be* [b] Or *fever* [c] Lit. *for* [d] Lit. *if this is not* [e] Lit. *This also is in the manner of* [f] Or *sons* [g] Or *near* [h] Lit. '*decani*'

brimstone coming forth from their mouths. [2]And My father
Joseph looked, and he saw those who came after him, full of
anger towards him; even as they burn in their face with
anger towards every soul that comes forth from *the* body,
cf. Jn xiv 30 especially the sinners, in whom they will find a little of their
own. [3]When the good old man saw them, Death being with
them, he wept[a]. [4]In that hour the soul of My father Joseph
was distracted[b] with great groaning, seeking a way to be hid,
in order that it might be saved. [5]When I saw the groaning
of My father Joseph (for he saw powers which he had never
seen); I arose straightway, and rebuked the devil and all
those who *were* with him. [6]And they went in shame and
in great confusion. [7]And no man among those who sat
about My father Joseph knew, not even Mary My mother,
concerning all the fearful hosts that come after the soul of
cf. Lc xxii 53; Col i 13 men. [8]Now when Death saw that I rebuked the powers of
darkness, and put them forth, because they had[c] no power
over him, he was afraid. [9]And I arose straightway, and I
offered[d] up a prayer to My Father the exceeding merciful[e],
saying,

cf. 2 Co i 3 XXII. My Father and the Father of all mercies[f], the
Father of truth, the Eye that sees, the Ear that hears, hear
Thy beloved Son, even Me, as I beseech Thee for the work
of Thy hands, even My father Joseph; that Thou mayest
send Me a great choir of angels, and Michael, the steward
of goodness, and Gabriel, the evangelist of light; that they
may go with the soul of My father Joseph, until it pass by
the seven aeons of darkness: and also that it may not pass
through the narrow ways, wherein it is fearful[g] to go, and it
is very fearful[h] to see the powers which are upon them,
Da vii 10 the river of fire flowing there as the waves of the sea.
[2]And be merciful towards the soul of My father Joseph as he
cometh unto Thy holy hands: for this is the hour wherein he
has need of mercy. [3]I say unto you, O My honourable[i]
brethren and My blessed apostles, that every man, who is

[a] Lit. *his eyes wept* [b] Or *divided* [c] Lit. *have* [d] Lit. *said*
[e] Lit. *Him of the many mercies* [f] Or *mercy* [g] Lit. *a fear* [h] Lit. *a great fear* [i] Or *glorious*

born into the world, who has known good and evil, spending
all his time hanging from his eye-lids[a], has need of the mercy
of My good Father, when he comes to the hour of death, and
to the passing of the path, and to the fearful judgment seat,
and to the making of a defence. 4 But I will turn to the
going forth from *the* body of My father Joseph, the righteous
old man.

XXIII. Now when he gave *up* his spirit, I saluted him.
2 The angels took his soul, and put it into silken napkins of
fine texture[b]. 3 And when I went in, I sat by him: and no
man knew that he was dead, among those who sat about
him. 4 And I caused Michael and Gabriel to watch his soul
because of the powers which *were* in the way; and the angels
sang before it, until they gave it to My good Father.

XXIV. And I turned to the body of My father Joseph,
laid down like an empty vessel, and I sat and I drew down
his eyes, and I closed them and his mouth; and I stayed[c]
looking down upon[d] him. 2 I said to the Virgin, O Mary
My mother, where now are all works of trade which this
man hath wrought from his youth until now? They all have
passed away in this one hour, as though[a] he had not been
born into the world at all. 3 When his sons and his daughters
heard Me saying these things to Mary My virgin mother, they
said to Me with great weeping, Woe to us, O our Lord. Is
our father dead, and we knew it not? 4 I said to them, In truth
he is dead. But the death of Joseph My father is not death,
but life for ever. 5 Those *blessings* which My beloved father
Joseph will receive are great. For from the hour that his
soul went forth from *the* body, all trouble ceased for him. He
went into the kingdom for ever. He left behind him the cf. 2 Co v 4
burden of the body. He left behind him this world full of all
troubles and all vain cares. He went into the resting places
of My Father who *is* in the heavens, which are never des-
troyed. 6 Now when I had said these things to My brethren,
Your father Joseph, the blessed old man, is dead, they

[a] See note [b] Lit. *of 'byssus'* [c] Or *stood* [d] Or *looking upon*

arose; they rent their garments, and they wept for a great while.

XXV. Then the inhabitants of all the city *of* Nazareth and the inhabitants of Galilee, when they heard the mourning, they all were gathered to the place where we were, according to the law of the Jews; and they spent all the day mourning for him, until the ninth hour.
2 Now at the ninth
cf. Mc v 40 hour of the day I caused all to be put forth. I poured[a] water on the body of My beloved father Joseph, and I anointed him[b] with sweet smelling oil. I prayed to My good Father who *is* in the heavens with heavenly prayers, which I wrote
cf. Ex xxxi 18; Deut ix 10 with My own fingers on the tables of heaven, before I took flesh in the holy Virgin Mary.
3 And straightway when I
had said[c] the Amen of the prayer, there came a multitude of angels, and I commanded two of them to spread a robe, and I made them take up the blessed body of My father Joseph, and put it into the midst of the garments, and shroud it.

XXVI. And I placed My hands upon his body, saying, Let no evil smell of death have dominion over thee, neither let thine ears stink, and let corruption never flow forth from thy body, neither let thy shroud nor thy flesh, wherewith I have clothed thee, rot in[d] the earth, but let it remain on[e] thy body unto the day of the supper of the thousand years. Let not the hair of thy head waste away, of which I took hold with My hands many times, O My beloved father Joseph; and it shall be well with thee.
2 They who shall take thought
for an offering, and present it to thy shrine on the day of thy memorial, even the twenty sixth of the month Epep; I will bless each one of them[f] also in the heavenly offering which *is* in the heavens.
3 And also he who shall give bread into
the hand of a poor man in thy name; I will not suffer him to lack any good thing of this world in all the days of his life.
4 They who shall give a cup of wine into the hand of a
stranger or of a widow or of an orphan on the day of thy memorial; I will grant them to thee to take them to the supper

[a] Or *put* [b] Or *it* [c] Lit. *given* [d] See note [e] Lit. *in*
[f] Lit. *I will bless him*

of the thousand years. [5]They who shall write the book of thy going forth from *the* body, and all the words which have come forth from My mouth to-day, *I swear* by thy life[a], O My beloved father Joseph, that I will grant them to thee in this world; and also when they go forth from *the* body, I will tear the bond of their sins, that they may not receive any cf. Col II 14
torment, save the necessity of death and the river of fire which is before My Father, which cleanses all souls. [6]And if he is a poor man, and hath not *wherewith* to do those things which I have said, if he beget a son, and call his name Joseph, glorifying thy name; famine and pestilence shall not be in that house, because thy name is in it.

XXVII. After these things the great ones of the city came to the place, wherein the body of My father Joseph was laid: they who prepare for burial going with them, wishing to prepare his body according to the burying of the Jews. cf. Jn XIX 40
[2]And they found it already prepared, the shroud having been fastened to his body, as though it were fastened with iron clasps (?): and when they moved him[b], they found no entrance in the shroud. [3]And after these things they took him out to the tomb. [4]And when they had dug[c] at the door of the cave, that they might open its door, and lay him with his fathers; I remembered the day that he went down[d] with Me into Egypt, and the great troubles that he suffered because of Me: and I stretched Myself out on his body, and I wept for him for a great while, saying:

XXVIII. O death, that stirrest up many mournings and many[e] lamentations—but He Who is over all, He it is who has given thee this wonderful power. [2]But death is not to blame, like Adam and his wife: [3]and death does nothing without the command of My Father. [4]And there is *a* man who has lived nine hundred years before he died, and many others also have lived more than that[f]: [5]*yet* not one of them said, I have seen death, or that he comes from time to time troubling any one. [6]But he does not trouble them save one

[a] Lit. *health* [b] Or *it* [c] Or *hewn* [d] Or *went* [e] Two different words are used for *many* in this sentence [f] Lit. *these*

time: and that time also it is My good Father who sends him
after the man. 7 And at the hour that he comes after him,
he hears the sentence coming from heaven. 8 If the sentence
comes in confusion and is full of anger, death also comes in
confusion and in wrath, that he may fulfil the command of
My good Father, and receive the soul of the man, and give it
to his Lord. 9 Death is not able to cast him into the fire nor
to bring[a] him into the kingdom of the heavens. 10 As for
death, it is the command of God that he does, but Adam—
he did not do the will of My Father, but rather[b] wrought
transgression, until My Father was angry with him, in that
he[c] obeyed his wife, and was disobedient to My good Father,
cf. Ro v 12 until He brought death upon all flesh. 11 If Adam had not
been disobedient to My good Father, He would not have
brought death upon him. 12 What is there that hinders Me
from beseeching My good Father to send Me a great chariot
of light, that I may set My father Joseph thereon, that he
may not taste death at all; and that I may cause him to be
taken up in the flesh wherein he was born, to the places of
rest, and that he may dwell with My angels that have no
body? 13 But because of the transgression of Adam this great
trouble has come upon all mankind, and this great necessity
of death. 14 Inasmuch as I wear the flesh that suffers, I must
needs taste death in it, for the creature[d] which I have made,
in order that I may have mercy on them.

XXIX. As I was saying these things, and was embracing
My father Joseph, and weeping for him; 2 they opened the
cf. Mt i 16 door of the tomb, and laid his body in it by the body of Jacob
his father. 3 And his death[e] took place in his hundred and
eleventh year[f]. And not a single tooth in his mouth was
destroyed, nor were his eyes without light, but his seeing was
like that of a little child. 4 He never put away *his* strength,
but he was working at the trade of carpentry, until the day
that he lay down with the sickness wherewith[g] he should die.

[a] The word translated *bring* is the same as that translated *cast* before
[b] Lit. *also* [c] Or *when he* [d] Lit. *the thing formed* [e] Or *consummation* [f] Lit. *in an hundred and eleven years* [g] Lit. *in the sickness wherein*

XXX. But we the apostles, when we heard these things
from our Saviour, rejoiced; and we arose straightway, and[a]
saluted[b] His hands and His feet; rejoicing and saying, We
thank Thee, our good Saviour, that Thou hast made us
worthy to hear these words of life from Thee, our Lord. 2 But cf. Ac v 20
we wonder at Thee, O our good Saviour, why to Enoch and
to Elias Thou didst grant immortality: and until now they
are among the good *things*, dwelling in the flesh wherein
they were born, and until now their flesh has not seen cor- cf. Ac ii 31
ruption. 3 But the old man, he that is blessed, Joseph the
carpenter, to whom Thou hast given this great honour, having
called him Thy father—and Thou didst obey him in all cf. Lc ii 51
things; and Thou didst command us, saying to us, When I cf. Lc xxiv 49; Ac i 8
clothe you with power, and send upon you the promise of
My Father, even the Comforter, the Holy Ghost, and send cf. Jn xiv 26
you to preach the holy Gospel, *see* that ye[c] preach him also,
My beloved father Joseph. 4 And again, Speak these words cf. Ac v 20
of life in the testament of his going forth from *the* body.
5 And again, Read the words of this testament on the feast
days and on the honourable days. 6 And again, No man who
has not been taught to write well, shall[c] read this testament
on the feast days. 7 And again, He who shall take away cf. Ap xxii 18, 19
from these words, or shall add unto them, so that he account
Me *a* liar, I will take vengeance on him quickly—8 And we
wonder that, since the day that Thou wast born in Bethlehem,
Thou didst call him Thy father according to flesh; *and yet*
that Thou hast not promised even him immortality, and
given him life for ever.

XXXI. Our Saviour answered and said to us, The
sentence which My good Father passed against Adam, will
not be made of none effect, *which He passed* at the time[d] that
he was disobedient to His commandments. 2 If My Father
passes sentence upon the man that he shall be righteous,
he becomes His chosen one[e]. 3 If the man indeed loves the
works of the devil by his *own* will, and sins, and he is suffered[c]

[a] Or *arose, and straightway* [b] Lit. *worshipped upon* [c] See note [d] Lit. *hour* [e] Lit. *he becomes chosen to Him*

to spend a long life, does he not know that he is coming[a] into
his hands, if he repent not? 4If again one spends a long
life, his works being good, his deeds make him *an* old man.
cf. Ge vi 12 5But if again He sees one corrupting his way, He makes his
cf. Ps ci 25 life short. This is the manner *in* which He takes them away[b]
in the midst of their days. 6But all the prophecies which My
Father hath spoken, shall be fulfilled upon mankind, and all
things shall happen to them. 7And again ye have told Me
concerning Enoch and Elias, *saying,* They are living in the
flesh wherein they were born. But concerning Joseph
also, My father according to flesh, *ye have asked,* Where-
fore hast Thou not left him in the flesh until now? 8If he
had lived ten thousand years, *yet* must he needs die. 9I say
cf. Eph v 30 unto you, O My holy members, that every time Enoch and
Elias remember death, they would willingly have died
already, that they might escape this great necessity which is
laid down for them: especially as those *men* will die in a day
of confusion and of fear and of shouting and of threatening
cf. Ap xi 3, 6, 7 and of grief. 10For the antichrist shall kill these two men,

[a] Or *coming down* [b] Or *up*

SAHIDIC FRAGMENTS OF THE DEATH OF JOSEPH.

FRAGMENT I.

Cod. Borg. cxvi p. ⲡⲍ (c. iv, v)

6ⲉⲡⲕⲁⲓ̈ⲣⲟⲥ ⲉⲧⲛⲁⲛⲟⲩϥ · — 1ϩⲣⲁⲓ̈ ⲇⲉ ϩⲛ̄ ⲧⲙⲉϩⲙⲛ̄ⲧⲁϥⲧⲉ
ⲛ̄ⲣⲟⲙⲡⲉ ⲙ̄ⲡⲱⲛ̄ϩ ⲙ̄ⲙⲁⲣⲓⲁ̀ ⲧⲁⲙⲁⲁⲩ · ⲁⲓ̈ⲉⲓ̈[a] ϩⲙ̄ ⲡⲁⲟⲩⲱϣ ⲁⲓⲟⲩⲱϩ
ⲛ̄ϩⲏⲧⲥ̀ ⲕⲁⲧⲁ ⲡⲉⲧⲉϩⲛⲁⲓ̈ ⲉ̀ⲁⲛⲟⲕ ⲡⲉ ⲡⲉⲧⲛ̄ⲱ̀ⲛⲁϩ · — 2ⲁⲩⲱ
ⲛ̄ⲧⲉⲣⲉϥⲣ̀ ϣⲟⲙ̀ⲛ̄ⲧ ⲛⲉⲃⲟⲧ ⲡⲱ · ⲁ ⲡⲁⲧⲕⲣⲟϥ ⲓ̈ⲱⲥⲏⲫ ⲡⲁⲙⲉⲣⲓ̈ⲧ

[a] duo punct. sup. ı prim. ut vid.

and shed their blood upon the earth for[a] a pot of water, because of the rebukes which they shall give him, reproving him.

XXXII. We answered and said to Him, Our Lord and cf. Jn xx 28
our God, who *are* these two men concerning whom Thou
hast said, The son of perdition shall kill them for[a] a pot cf. Jn xvii 12; 2 Th ii 3
of water? [2]Our Saviour Jesus and our Life said to us,
They are Enoch and Elias. [3]Now it came to pass, when our good Saviour had said these things to us, we were glad and we rejoiced, and we gave thanks and we glorified Him[a], our Lord and our God, our Saviour Jesus Christ; through whom all glory and all honour is due to the Father and Him and the Holy Ghost, giver of life, now and always and unto *the* ages of all the ages. Amen.

Remember me, the least, the sinner, the wretched *one*, stinking in the pit of his sins, *even* Hapip[a]. Lord, have mercy upon him. Amen. I wrote *this on* the twenty eighth of the month Epep, *in the* year[b] of the martyrs seven hundred and eighty three.

[a] See note [b] Lit. *time*

SAHIDIC FRAGMENTS OF THE DEATH OF JOSEPH.

FRAGMENT I.[a]

IV. [6]...to the good time. (V.) [1]Now in the fourteenth year of the life of Mary My mother, I came by My *own* will and dwelt in her, I who am your life. [2]And when she had been three months pregnant[b], the guileless

[a] For the translation of the Bohairic see p. 132 f [b] Lit. *she had spent three months of pregnancy*

ⲛ̄ⲓ̈ⲱⲧ ⲉⲓ̈ ⲉ̀ϩⲟⲩⲛ ϩⲱⲱϥ ϩⲛ̄ ⲡⲉⲙⲁ ⲛ̄ⲕⲱⲧ · — Ⲁϥϭⲉⲛ ⲧⲁⲙⲁⲁⲩ
ⲛ̄ⲧⲁⲥⲟⲩⲱ̀ⲛ̄ϩ ⲉ̀ⲃⲟⲗ ϫⲉ ⲥⲉⲉⲧ · ⲁϥⲉⲣϩⲟⲧⲉ · ⲁⲩⲱ ⲁϥϣ̄ⲧⲟⲣⲧⲣ̄ · —
Ⲁϥⲟⲩⲱ̀ϣ ⲉ̀ⲛⲁϫⲉⲥ ⲉ̀ⲃⲟⲗ ⲛ̄ϫⲓ̈ⲟⲩⲉ̀ · ³ⲁⲩⲱ ⲉ̀ⲃⲟⲗ ϩⲉⲛ ⲧⲗⲩⲡⲏ ·
ⲁϥⲛ̄ⲕⲟⲧⲕ̀ ⲙ̀ⲡⲉϥⲟⲩⲉⲙ ⲗⲁⲁⲩ ⲉⲛⲧⲏⲣϥ̀ ϩⲛ̄ ⲧⲉⲣⲟⲩϩⲉ ⲉ̀ⲧⲙ̀ⲙⲟⲟⲩ · —
(c. vi) ¹Ϩⲛ̄ ⲧⲡⲁϣⲉ ⲇⲉ ⲛ̄ⲧⲉⲩϣⲏ · ⲉⲓ̈ⲥ ⲡⲁⲣⲭⲁⲅⲅⲉⲗⲟⲥ ⲅⲁⲃⲣⲓ̄ⲏⲗ ⲁϥⲃⲱⲕ
ϣⲁⲣⲟϥ ϩⲛ̄ ⲟⲩⲣⲁⲥⲟⲩ · ϩⲓ̄ⲧⲛ̄ ⲧⲉϩⲟⲩⲥⲓ̈ⲁ̀ ⲙ̀ⲡⲁⲓ̈ⲱⲧ ⲛ̄ⲁⲅⲁⲑⲟⲥ · —
Ⲡⲉϫⲁϥ ⲛⲁϥ ϫⲉ ⲓ̈ⲱⲥⲏⲫ ⲡ̄ϣⲏⲣⲉ ⲛ̄ⲇⲁⲩⲉⲓ̈ⲇ ⲙ̄ⲡⲣ̄ⲣ̄ϩⲟⲧⲉ · ϫⲓ̈
ⲙ̀ⲙⲁⲣⲓ̈ⲁ̀ ⲧⲉⲕⲥϩⲓ̄ⲙⲉ · ⲡⲉⲧⲉⲥⲛⲁϫⲡⲟϥ ⲅⲁⲣ ⲟⲩⲁ̀ⲁⲃ · ²ⲁⲩⲱ ⲉ̀ⲕⲉ-
ⲙⲟⲩⲧⲉ ⲉ̀ⲡⲉϥⲣⲁⲛ ϫⲉ ⲓ̅ⲥ̅ · ⲛ̄ⲧⲟϥ ⲡⲉⲧⲛⲁⲙⲟⲟ̀ⲛⲉ ⲙ̀ⲡⲉϥⲗⲁⲟⲥ ϩⲛ̄
p. ⲡⲏ ⲟⲩϭⲉⲣⲱⲃ ⲙ̀ⲡⲉⲛⲓ̈ⲛⲉ · — ³ⲁϥⲧⲱⲟⲩⲛ ⌜ⲇⲉ⌝ ⲛ̄ϭⲓ̈ ⲓ̈ⲱⲥⲏⲫ | ⲉ̀ⲃⲟⲗ ϩⲙ̀
ⲡ̄ϩⲓ̈ⲛⲏⲃ · ⲁϥⲉⲓ̈ⲣⲉ ⲕⲁⲧⲁ ⲑⲉ ⲛ̄ⲧⲁϥϩⲱⲛ ⲉ̀ⲧⲟⲟⲧϥ̀ ⲛ̄ϭⲓ̈ ⲡⲁⲅⲅⲉⲗⲟⲥ
ⲙ̀ⲡϫⲟⲉⲓ̈ⲥ · ⲁϥϩⲁⲣⲉϩ ⲉⲧⲡⲁⲣⲑⲉⲛⲟⲥ ⲉ̀ⲧⲟⲩⲁ̀ⲁⲃ ⲉ̀ϩⲟⲩⲛ ⲉ̀ⲡⲉϥⲏⲓ̄ · —
(c. vii) ¹Ⲙⲛ̄ⲛ̄ⲥⲁ ⲛⲁⲓ̈ ⲁⲩⲇⲟⲅⲙⲁ ⲉⲓ̄ ⲉ̀ⲃⲟⲗ ϩⲓ̄ⲧⲙ̀ ⲡ̄ⲣⲣⲟ ⲁⲩⲅⲟⲩⲥⲧⲟⲥ ·
ⲉⲧⲣⲉ ⲧⲟⲓ̈ⲕⲟⲩⲙⲉⲛⲏ ⲧⲏⲣⲥ̀ ⲥ̀ϩⲁⲓ̈ⲥ̀ ⲛ̄ⲥⲁ ⲡⲉⲥⲧⲙⲉ · — ²Ⲁϥⲧⲱⲟⲩⲛ
ⲇⲉ ⲛ̄ϭⲓ̈ ⲓ̈ⲱⲥⲏⲫ ⲡⲁ ⲧⲙⲛ̄ⲧϩⲗⲗⲟ ⲉⲧⲛⲁⲛⲟⲩⲥ · ⲁϥϫⲓ̄ ⲛ̄ⲧⲡ̀ⲁⲣⲑⲉⲛⲟⲥ
ⲛ̄ⲥⲉⲙⲛⲏ · ⲁϥⲉⲓ̈ⲛⲉ ⲙ̀ⲙⲟⲥ ⲉϩⲣⲁⲓ̈ ⲉⲡⲉϥⲏⲓ̄ ⲙ̀ⲙⲓ̈ⲛ ⲙ̀ⲙⲟϥ ⲉ̀ⲃⲏⲑⲗⲉⲉⲙ ·
ⲉ̀ⲁⲥϩⲱⲛ ⲉ̀ϩⲟⲩⲛ ⲉ̀ⲙⲓ̈ⲥⲉ · — ⌜Ⲁϥⲁ⌝ⲡⲟⲅⲣⲁⲫⲏ ⲙ̀ⲡⲉϥⲣⲁⲛ ϩⲁⲧⲛ̄
ⲡⲉⲅⲣⲁⲙⲁⲧⲉⲩⲥ̀ ⲡ̄ⲃ̄ⲏ̄ⲑⲗⲉⲉⲙ · ϫⲉ Ⲓ̈ⲱⲥⲏⲫ ⲡ̄ϣⲏⲣⲉ ⲛ̄ⲓ̈ⲁ̀ⲕⲱⲃ ⲙ̄ⲛ̄
ⲙⲁⲣⲓ̈ⲁ̀ ⲧⲉϥⲥ̀ϩⲓ̄ⲙⲉ · ⲙⲛ̄ ⲓ̅ⲥ̅ ⲡⲉⲩϣⲏⲣⲉ · ⲉ̀ⲡⲉⲉ̀ⲃⲟⲗ ⲡⲉ ϩⲙ̄ ⲡⲏⲓ̈
ⲛ̄ⲇⲁⲩⲉⲓ̈ⲇ ⲛ̄ⲧⲉ ⲧⲫⲩⲗⲏ[a] ⲛ̄ⲟⲓ̈ⲟⲧⲉ · ³Ⲁ ⲙⲁⲣⲓ̈ⲁ ⲧⲙⲁⲁⲩ [illegible]
ⲙⲓ̈ⲥⲉ ⲙ̀ⲙⲟⲓ̄ ⲛ̄ϩⲟⲩⲛ ⲉ̀ⲡⲙⲁ ⲛ̄ϭⲟⲓ̈ⲗⲉ ⲛ̄ⲃⲏⲑⲗⲉⲉⲙ · ϩⲓ̄ⲧⲟⲩⲱϥ ⲙ̀ⲡⲧⲁ-
ⲫⲟⲥ ⲛ̄ϩⲣⲁⲭⲏⲗ ⲧⲉⲥϩⲓ̄ⲙⲉ ⲛ̄ⲓ̈ⲁ̀ⲕⲱⲃ ⲛ̄ⲡⲁⲧⲣⲓ̄ⲁⲣⲭⲏⲥ · ⲡⲉⲓ̄ⲱⲧ
(c. viii) ⲛ̄ⲓ̈ⲱⲥⲏⲫ · ⲙⲛ̄ ⲃⲉⲛⲓ̈ⲁ̀ⲙⲓ̈ⲛ · — ¹Ⲁ ⲡⲥⲁⲧⲁⲛⲁⲥ ⲥⲩⲙⲃⲟⲩⲗⲉⲩⲉ̀ ϩⲙ̀
ⲡϩⲏⲧ ⲛ̄ϩⲏⲣⲱⲇⲏⲥ ⲛ̄ⲛⲟϭ ⲛ̄ⲓ̈ⲱⲧ ⲡⲁⲣⲭⲏ | [ⲗⲁⲟⲥ]

FRAGMENT II.

Cod. Br. M. Or. 3581 B p. ? (c. xiii) ⁶ⲣⲏⲛⲏ ⲛ̄ⲙⲙⲁⲓ̈ · Ⲙⲡⲣⲧⲣⲉ ⲡⲉϥϩⲟ ⲙⲟⲩϩ ⲛ̄ⲟⲣⲅⲏ ⲉϩⲟⲩⲛ ⲉⲣⲟⲓ̈
ϩⲓ ⲡⲉϩⲓⲟⲟⲩⲉ ⲉϥⲛⲏⲩ ⲉⲣⲁⲧⲕ̄ ⲡ̄ϩⲏⲧⲟⲩ · ⁷ⲟⲩⲧⲉ ⲙ̄ⲡⲣⲧⲣⲉϥⲕⲁⲁⲩ

[a] ⲛ̄ⲇⲁⲩⲉⲓ̈ⲇ · ⲧⲉⲛⲫⲩⲗⲏ

Joseph, My beloved father, came in also from the places
of building; and found My mother manifestly with child. cf. Mt I 18,
He feared and was troubled, and wished to put her away 19
privily. [3]And from sorrow he lay down, and he did not
eat anything at all in that evening.

VI. But in the middle of the night, behold the arch-
angel Gabriel went unto him in a dream, by the authority cf. Mt I 20,
of My good Father; and said to him, Joseph, thou son of 21
David, fear not, take Mary thy wife: for that which she
will bring forth is holy. [2]And thou shalt call His name cf. Lc I 35
Jesus; it is He that will rule[a] His people with a rod of cf. Mt II 6;
iron. [3]And Joseph arose from his[b] sleep, and did as the Ap XII 5* cf. Mt I 24
angel of the Lord commanded him, and kept the holy
Virgin in his house.

VII. After these things there went out a decree from cf. Lc II 1,
the king Augustus, that all the world should enrol[c] itself 4, 5
after its villages. [2]And Joseph, the good old man, arose,
and took the honourable Virgin; and brought her up to[d]
his own house to Bethlehem, since she was nigh to bear *a*
child. He enrolled his name with the scribes of Bethle-
hem: Joseph, the son of Jacob, and Mary his wife and cf. Mt I 16
Jesus their son, who are of the house of David, who *is*
of the tribe of Judah. [3]Mary My mother bare Me in the
inn of Bethlehem, near the tomb of Rachel, the wife of cf. Ge XXXV
Jacob the patriarch, the father of Joseph and Benjamin. 19*, 20*; Lc II 7

VIII. Satan gave counsel in the heart of Herod the
great, the father of Archelaus... cf. Mt II 22

FRAGMENT II.[e]

XIII. [6]...peace with me. Let not his face burn in[f]
anger towards me in the ways wherein I come to Thee.

[a] Lit. *feed* [b] Lit. *the* [c] Lit. *write* [d] Or *unto* [e] For the translation of the Bohairic see p. 134 f [f] Or *be full of*

ⲙⲁⲩⲁⲁⲧ ⲛ̄ⲧⲉ ⲛ̇ϣⲁⲃⲉϩⲟ ⲉⲧϩⲛ ⲛⲉϩⲓⲟⲟⲩⲉ ϫⲓⲧ ⲛ̄ϭⲟⲛⲥ̄ 8 Ⲙⲡⲣⲧⲣⲉ
ⲡⲉⲧϩⲓϫⲛ ⲙ̇ⲡⲩⲗⲏ ⲕⲁⲧⲏⲭⲉ ⲛ̄ⲧⲁⲯⲩⲭⲏ ϩⲛ ⲟⲩⲁⲡⲉⲓⲗⲏ :· —
Ⲙⲡⲣ̇ⲧⲣⲉϥϯϣⲓⲡⲉ ⲛⲁⲓ̈ ϩⲙ ⲡⲉⲕⲃⲏⲙⲁ ⲛ̇ϩⲟⲧⲉ ϩⲛ ⲡⲉϥⲕⲁⲧⲏ⸢ⲅ⸣ⲟⲣⲓⲁ
ϩⲁ ⲡⲉⲛⲧⲁⲓ̈ⲁⲁⲩ · 9 Ⲙ̇ⲡⲉⲣⲧⲣⲉⲩⲥⲟϣ⸢ϥ⸣ⲧ · ⲟⲩⲧⲉ ⲙ̇ⲡⲉⲣⲧⲣⲉⲩⲣ̇ⲁⲅⲣⲓⲟⲥ
ⲉϩⲟⲩⲛ ⲉⲣⲟⲓ̈ ⲛ̇ϭⲓ ⲛⲁⲡⲉⲓⲗⲏ ⲛ̄ⲛ̄ϩⲟⲉⲓⲙ ⲛ̄ⲣⲉϥϣⲁⲁⲣ · ⲛⲁⲓ̈ ⲉⲧⲉⲣⲉ
ⲯⲩⲭⲏ ⲛⲓⲙ ⲛⲁ|ϫⲱⲕⲣ̇ ⲛ̄⸢ϩⲏⲧⲟⲩ ⲙ⸣ⲡⲁⲧⲟⲩ⸢ⲛⲁⲩ ⲉⲡⲱⲟⲩ⸣ ⲛ̄ⲧⲉⲕ-
⸢ⲙⲉⲧⲛⲟⲩⲧⲉ⸣ 10 ⲱ ⲡⲛⲟⲩ⸢ⲧⲉ ⲡⲉⲧⲛⲁ⸣ⲕⲣⲓⲛⲉ ⲙ̄ ⸢........⸣ ϩⲛ
ⲟⲩϩⲁⲡ⸢.....⸣ ⲟⲩϣⲁϫⲉ ⲛ⸢.....⸣ Ⲧⲉⲛⲟⲩ ϭⲉ ⸢ⲡϫⲟⲉⲓⲥ ⲙⲁ⸣ⲣⲉ
ⲡⲉⲕⲡ⸢ⲁ ⲥⲉⲗ⸣ⲥⲱⲗ̇ⲧ ⸢ϩ.......... ⲟ.. ....ⲓ........
(c. xiv) ....⸣ ϣⲁ ⸢ⲉⲛⲉϩ ⲛⲛⲉⲛⲉϩ ϩⲁ⸣ⲙⲏⲛ 1 Ⲁⲥϣⲱ⸢ⲡⲉ⸣ ⲇⲉ ⸢ⲛⲧⲉⲣⲉϥ⸣ϫⲉ
ⲛⲁⲓ̈ ⲁϥⲧ⸢ⲱⲟⲩⲛ⸣ ⲁϥⲉⲓ ⲉϩⲣⲁⲓ̈ ⲉ⸢ⲡⲉϥⲏⲓ⸣ ⲛⲁⲍⲁⲣ⸢ⲉⲑ⸣ ⲧⲡ⸢ⲟⲗⲓⲥ
ⲉ⸣ⲡⲉϥⲟⲩ⸢ⲏϩ ⲛ̄ϩⲏⲧⲥ⸣ ⲁⲩⲱ ⲁϥϫ⸢ⲧⲟ ⲉⲛϣⲱ⸣ⲡⲉ ⲛⲁⲓ̈ ⸢ⲉⲧⲉϥⲛⲁ⸣ⲙ̇⸢ⲟⲩ
p. ? ⲛϩⲏⲧϥ⸣ ⲛ⸢ⲣⲟⲥ ⲡⲉⲧⲧⲏϣ ⲛⲣⲱⲙⲉ ⲛⲓⲙ⸣| 2 ⸢ⲁⲩⲱ ⲛⲉⲣⲉ ⲡⲉ⸣ϥϣⲱⲡⲉ
⸢ϩⲟⲣϣ ⲉⲙⲁⲧⲉ⸣ ⲛϩⲟⲩ̇ⲟ ⸢ⲉⲥⲟⲡ ⲛⲓⲙ ⲛⲧⲁ⸣ϥϣⲱ⸢ⲡⲉ ϫⲓⲛⲧ⸣ⲁⲩϫⲡⲟϥ
⸢ⲉⲡⲕⲟⲥⲙ⸣ⲟⲥ:·— 3 ⸢ⲧⲁⲓ ⲧⲉ ⲧⲁⲛⲁⲥⲧ⸣ⲣⲟⲫⲏ ⸢ⲙⲡⲁⲉⲓⲱⲧ⸣ ⲓ̈ⲱⲥⲏⲫ· 4 ⸢ⲁϥⲣ
ϩⲙⲉ ⲛ⸣ⲣⲟⲙⲡⲉ ⲁⲩ⸢ϫⲓ ⲥϩⲓⲙⲉ ⲛⲁ⸣ϥ ⲁⲩⲱ ⸢ⲕⲉⲯⲓⲧⲉ ⲛⲣ⸣ⲟⲙⲡⲉ
⸢ⲁϥⲁⲁⲩ ϩⲙ ⲡⲅ⸣ⲁⲙⲟⲥ ⸢..........................ⲧ.....
......⸣ ⲙⲁ⸢............⸣ ⲧⲉ⸢..........⸣ 5 ⲣⲟⲩ⸢ϣⲡⲧ⸣ⲟⲟⲧⲥ̄
ⲛⲁϥ ⲛ̄ⲥϩⲓ⸢ⲙⲉ⸣ ⲁⲩⲧ⸢ⲁ⸣ⲙⲟϥ ⸢ϩⲓⲧⲛ ⲛ⸣ⲟⲩⲏⲏⲃ ϫⲉ ϩⲁ⸢ⲣⲉϩ ⲉⲣⲟⲥ⸣
ϣ⸢ⲁ ⲡ⸣ⲉⲟⲩⲟ⸢ⲉⲓϣ ⲛ⸣ⲣⲧϣⲉⲗⲉⲉⲧ ⸢ⲉⲣⲱⲧⲛ·⸣ 6 ⲁⲩⲱ ⲁ ⸢ⲙⲁⲣⲓⲁ ⲧⲁ-
ⲙⲁⲁⲩ⸣ ϫⲡⲟⲓ̈ ⸢ϩⲛ ⲧⲁⲣⲭⲏ ⲛⲧⲙⲉ⸣ϩ⸢ϣⲟⲙⲧⲉ ⲛⲣⲟⲙⲡⲉ⸣ ⲉⲥ⸢ϩⲙ ⲡⲏⲓ
ⲙⲡⲁⲙⲉⲣⲓⲧ⸣| ⲛ̄ⲉⲓⲱⲧ ⲓ̈ⲱⲥⲏⲫ· ⲉⲥϩⲛ ⲧⲙⲉϩⲙⲛⲧⲏ ⲛ̄ⲣⲟⲙⲡⲉ ⲙ̇ⲡⲉⲥⲁϩⲉ
Ⲁⲩⲱ ⲕⲉⲙⲛ̄ⲧϣⲙⲏⲛⲉ ⲛⲣⲟⲙⲡⲉ ϫⲓⲛⲧⲁ ⲧⲁⲙⲁⲁⲩ ϫⲡⲟⲓ̈ ⲉϫⲙ ⲡⲕⲁϩ·
ϩⲛ ⲟⲩⲙⲩⲥⲧⲏⲣⲓⲟⲛ ⲛ̇ⲁⲧϩⲉⲧϩⲱⲧϥ̇ ⲟⲩⲧⲉ ⲛ̄ⲥⲉⲛⲁϣ̄ⲉⲓⲙⲉ ⲁⲛ ⲉⲣⲟϥ̄
ⲛ̄ϭⲓ ⲗⲁⲁⲩ ϩⲙ ⲛ̇ⲥⲱⲛ̄ⲧ ⲧⲏⲣϥ̇· ⲉⲓ ⲙⲏⲧⲉⲓ ⲁⲛⲟⲕ ⲙⲛ̄ ⲡⲁⲉⲓⲱⲧ ⲙⲛ̄
(c. xv) ⲡⲉⲡⲛ̄ⲁ̄ ⲉⲧⲟⲩⲁⲁⲃ ϩⲛ ⲟⲩⲙⲛ̇ⲧⲟⲩⲁ·:··— 1 Ⲛⲉϩⲟⲟⲩ ⲇⲉ ⲧⲏⲣⲟⲩ
ⲙ̇ⲡⲱⲛ̄ϩ ⸢ⲙ⸣ⲡⲁⲉⲓⲱⲧ ⲓ̈ⲱⲥⲏⲫ ⲉⲧⲥ̇ⲙⲁⲙⲁⲁⲧ · ⲁ ⲧⲉⲩⲏⲡⲉ ⲉⲓⲣⲉ ⲛ̇ϣⲉ
ⲙ̇ⲛⲧⲟⲩⲉ ⲛ̇ⲣⲟⲙⲡⲉ ⲕⲁⲧⲁ ⲡⲟⲩⲉϩⲥⲁϩⲛⲉ ⲙ̄ⲡⲁⲉⲓⲱⲧ ⲛ̇ⲁⲅⲁⲑⲟⲥ· —
2 Ϩⲣⲁⲓ̈ ⲇⲉ ϩⲙ ⲡϣⲱⲛⲉ ⲙ̇ⲡⲉϥⲙⲟⲩ·|

7 Neither let him leave me alone, that those with diverse
faces who *are* in the ways injure me. 8 Let not those
who *are* by[a] the gates restrain my soul with a threat.
Let him not put me to shame at Thy fearful judgment seat
with his accusations concerning the things which I have
done. 9 Let me not be shamefully entreated[b], neither let the
threatening[c] waves of demons be savage towards me; wherein
all souls will be purged, before they see the glory of Thy
godhead, 10 O God who wilt judge ...in judgment ...a word...
Now therefore, O Lord, let Thy mercy comfort me......unto
the ages of the ages. Amen.

XIV.[d] Now it came to pass, when he had said these
things, he arose and went unto[e] his house *to* Nazareth, the
city wherein he was dwelling. And he lay down of[f] the
sickness wherewith[g] he should die, according to that which cf. He IX 27
is appointed for all men. 2 And his sickness was very
heavy, more than all *the* times that he was sick, since he
was born into the world. 3 This is the manner of life of
My father Joseph. 4 He was forty years *old, when* he took
to him *a* wife[h], and other nine years he spent in wedlock
.... 5 was betrothed to him for wife, he was
told by the priests, *saying*, Keep her until the time of
your marriage[i]. 6 And Mary My mother brought Me forth
at the beginning of the third year, being in the house of
My beloved father Joseph, being in the fifteenth year of
her life. And *there are* other eighteen years since My
mother brought Me forth on the earth, in a mystery which
cannot be searched out, nor can any know it in the whole
creation, except Me and My Father and the Holy Ghost in
unity.

XV. Now all the days of the life of My father Joseph
who is blessed, their number is an hundred and eleven
years, according to the command of My good Father.
2 And in the sickness of his death...

[a] Or *on* [b] Or *set at nought* [c] Lit. *the threats of the*
[d] See the beginning of Fragment III p. 152 [e] Or *up to* [f] Lit. *to*
[g] Lit. *wherein* [h] Lit. *they took a wife to him* [i] Lit. *of making the marriage for you*

FRAGMENT III.[a]

XIV.[b] Now it came to pass, when he had said these things, he arose and went to his house *to* Nazareth, the city wherein he dwelt[c]. And thus he lay down of[d] the
cf. He IX 27 sickness wherewith[e] he should die, according to that which is laid down for all men. ²And behold his sickness was very heavy, more than all *the* times that he was sick, since he was born into the world. ³This is the manner of life of My beloved father[f] Joseph. ⁴He was forty years *old*, before he took to him *a* wife[g], and other nine years he spent in the world with his wife. And when she was dead, he was another year, remaining alone. ⁵My beloved mother was two other years in his house, from *the time* that she was betrothed to him for wife, when he was commanded by the priests, *saying*, Keep her until the time of the marriage. ⁶And Mary My mother brought Me forth at the beginning of the third year, being in the house of Joseph. In the fifteenth year[f] Mary My mother brought Me forth in a cave, which cannot be spoken of nor searched out, nor doth[h] any man in the whole creation know it, except Me and My Father and the Holy Ghost.

XV. Now all the days of My father Joseph, the blessed old man, are an hundred and eleven years, according to
cf. Is x 3*; 1 Pe II 12* the command of My Father[f]. ²The day of his visitation came to him, which is the twenty sixth of the month Epeph. ³The silver was changed[f], even the mind and the wisdom. ⁴It departed[i] into the other world. He forgot to eat and to drink[j]; and the wisdom and the craft turned into error and unreasonableness. ⁵And it came to pass when the light began to be shed abroad on that day, My beloved father Joseph began to be much troubled on his

[a] For the translation of the Bohairic see p. 135 ff. The Sahidic text is given by Lagarde: *Aegyptiaca*, pp. 9—29 [b] See above Fragment II p. 151 [c] Lit. *dwells* [d] Lit. *to* [e] Lit. *wherein* [f] See note [g] Lit. *before they took a wife to him* [h] Lit. *will* [i] Or *was changed* [j] Lit. *the eating and the drinking*

cause of Me, I arose and went outside the porch[a], and
I found him waiting[b] alone in great fear. 7 And straight-
way I said to him, O thou that hast[c] come from the
places of the south, get thee in quickly, and accomplish
that which My Father hath commanded thee. 8 But watch
him as the light of thine eyes; for he is My father
according to flesh, and he has suffered with Me in the days
of My youth, fleeing with Me from place to place be-
cause of the plot[d] of Herod. And I learned from him
as all sons[e], whom their fathers[f] teach for their profit. cf. He XII 9, 10
9 Then Abaddon[g] went in, and took the soul of My cf. Ap IX 11*
father Joseph, and brought it forth from *the* body at
the hour when the sun was about to rise on its course[d],
on the twenty sixth of the month Epep, in peace. 10 All
the days of the life of My beloved father Joseph are an
hundred and eleven years. 11 Michael took hold of the two
corners of a napkin, silken *and* precious; and Gabriel
took hold of the two other corners. They saluted the
soul of My beloved father Joseph, and put it down into
the napkin. 12 But none among those who sat with him
knew that he was dead; neither indeed did Mary My
mother know. 13 And I made Michael and Gabriel watch
the soul of My beloved father Joseph, because of the
plunderers that *are* in the ways. And I made the angels
that have no body keep singing before him, until they
took him to the heavens unto My good Father.

XXIV. And I turned to the body lying like a vessel.
I sat down, and drew down his eyes, and I looked down
upon him for a great while, weeping for him. 2 I said ...

[a] Lit. *the place of the door* [b] Or *remaining* [c] Lit. *O he that has* [d] See note [e] Or *children* [f] Or *parents* [g] The MS has *Abbaton*

VARIOUS SAHIDIC FRAGMENTS.

VARIOUS SAHIDIC FRAGMENTS.

FRAGMENT I.

Cod. Br. M. Or. 3581 B p. ⸢ϣ⸣ 1 ϣⲟⲟⲡ ⲛ̄ⲙ̄ⲙⲁϥ ⲡⲉ:ııııı— 2 Ⲁ ⲍⲁⲭⲁⲣⲓ̈ⲁⲥ ⲇⲉ ⲡⲉϥⲉⲓ̈ⲱⲧ
ⲙⲟⲩϩ̄ ⲉ̄ⲃⲟⲗ ϩ̄ⲙ̄ ⲡⲉⲡⲛ̄ⲁ̄ ⲉ̄ⲧⲟⲩⲁ̄ⲁ̄ⲃ· ⲁϥⲡ̄ⲣⲟⲫⲏⲧⲉⲩⲉ̄ ⲉϥϫⲱ ⲙ̄ⲙⲟⲥ·
3 ϫⲉ· ϥ̄ⲥ̄ⲙⲁⲙⲁⲁⲧ ⲛ̄ϭⲓ̈ ⲡ̄ⲛⲟⲩⲧⲉ ⲙ̄ⲡ̄ⲓ̈ⲏ̄ⲗ̄· ϫⲉ ⲁϥϭⲉⲛ ⲡⲉⲛϣⲓ̈ⲛⲉ·
ⲁϥⲉⲓ̈ⲣⲉ ⲛⲟⲩⲥⲱⲧⲉ ⲙ̇ⲡⲉϥⲗⲁⲟⲥ· 4 ⲁϥⲧⲟⲩⲛⲟⲥ ⲛⲁⲛ ⲛⲟⲩⲧⲁⲛ ⲛⲟⲩϫⲁⲓ̈·
ⲉ̄ⲃⲟⲗ ϩ̄ⲙ̄ ⲡⲏⲓ̈ ⲛ̄ⲇ̄ⲁ̄ⲇ̄ ⲡⲉϥϩ̄ⲙ̄ϩⲁⲗ:ııııı— 5 Ⲡϣⲏⲣⲉ ⲇⲉ ϣⲏⲙ
ⲉ̄ⲧⲟⲩⲁ̄ⲁ̄ⲃ ⲓ̄ⲱϩⲁⲛⲛⲏⲥ ⲡⲉⲧⲑⲁⲗⲡⲉⲓ̈ ⲙ̄ⲙⲟϥ ⲉ̄ⲙⲁⲧⲉ ϩ̄ⲙ̄ ⲡⲏⲓ̈ ⲛ̄ⲡⲉϥ-
ⲉⲓ̈ⲟ̄ⲧⲉ ⲛ̄ⲥⲟⲟⲩ ⲛⲉⲃⲟⲧ·· ⲉϥϫⲓ̈ ⲉ̄ⲃⲟⲗ ϩ̄ⲛ̄ ⲧⲉⲣⲱⲧⲉ ⲛ̄ⲧ̄ϩ̄ⲗ̄|ⲗⲱ
ⲛⲁϭⲣⲏⲛ· 6 ⲁⲩⲱ̄ ⲡⲉⲣⲉ ⲡⲉϥⲉⲓ̈ⲟ̄ⲧⲉ ϥⲓ̈ ⲙ̄ⲙⲟϥ ⲙ̄ⲙⲏⲛⲉ ϩⲓ̈ϫ̄ⲛ̄
ⲛⲉⲩϭⲓ̈ϫ ⲉ̄ⲡⲣ̄ⲡⲉ ⲙ̄ⲡ̄ϫⲟⲉⲓ̈ⲥ ⲉϥⲥ̇ⲙⲟⲩ ⲉ̇ⲣⲟϥ ⲛ̄ϭⲓ̈ ⲡⲉϥⲉⲓ̈ⲱⲧ:—
Ⲁⲩⲱ̄ ⲉϥⲥⲟⲟⲩⲧⲛ̄ ⲙ̄ⲙⲟϥ ϩⲓ̈ⲑⲏ ⲙ̄ⲡⲉⲑⲩⲥⲓ̈ⲁⲥⲧⲏⲣⲓ̈ⲟⲛ· ⲉⲛⲙⲁ ⲛ̄ⲧⲁ
ⲡⲁⲅ⸢ⲅ⸣ⲉ⸣ⲗⲟⲥ ⲟⲩⲱ̄ⲛ̄ϩ̄ ⲛⲁϥ ⲉ̄ⲃⲟⲗ ⲉϥϫⲱ ⲙ̄ⲙⲟⲥ· 7 ϫⲉ ⲡ̄ϫⲟⲉⲓ̈ⲥ̄
ⲡ̄ⲛⲟⲩⲧⲉ ⲙ̄ⲡ̄ⲓ̈ⲏ̄ⲗ· ϯϭⲟⲙ ⲙ̄ⲡⲁⲓ̈ ⲛ̄ⲧⲁⲕⲥ̇ⲃ̄ⲧⲱⲧϥ̄ ⲛⲁⲕ· 8 ⲁⲩⲱ̄ ⲡⲉⲣⲉ
ⲡ̄ϣⲏⲣⲉϣⲏⲙ ϯ ⲉ̄ⲡⲁⲛⲁⲓ̈ ⲙ̄ⲙⲏⲛⲉ:— 9 Ⲁⲥϣⲱⲡⲉ ⲇⲉ ⲙ̄ⲛ̄ⲛ̄ⲥⲁ ⲥⲟⲟⲩ
ⲛⲉⲃⲟⲧ· ϫⲓ̈ⲛⲧⲁⲩϫ̄ⲡⲟ ⲛ̄ⲓ̈ⲱ̄ϩⲁⲛⲛⲏⲥ ⲁⲩϫ̄ⲡⲟ ϩⲱⲱϥ ⲙ̄ⲡ̄ⲗⲟⲅⲟⲥ
p. ⸢ⲇ⸣ ⲙ̄ⲡⲉⲓ̈ⲱⲧ | ⲛ̄ⲁ̄ⲅⲁⲑⲟⲥ ⲉ̄ⲃⲟⲗ ϩ̄ⲛ̄ ⲧ̄ⲡⲁⲣⲑⲉⲛⲟⲥ ⲉ̄ⲧⲟⲩⲁ̄ⲁ̄ⲃ ⲙⲁⲣⲓ̈ⲁ̄· ϩ̄ⲛ̄
ⲧ̄ⲙⲛ̄ⲧ̄ⲣ̄ⲣⲟ ⲛⲁⲩⲅⲟⲩⲥⲧⲟⲥ ⲛ̄ⲣ̄ⲣⲟ ⲛ̄ⲛⲉϩⲣⲱⲙⲁⲓ̈ⲟⲥ· ⲙⲛ̄ ⲧ̄ⲙⲛ̄ⲧ̄ⲧⲉⲧⲣⲁ-
ⲁⲣⲭⲏⲥ ⲛ̄ϩⲏⲣⲱⲇⲏⲥ ϩ̄ⲛ̄ ϯⲟⲩⲇⲁⲓ̈ⲁ̄:ıııı— 10 ⸢Ⲁ⸣ⲩⲱ̄ ⲡ̄ⲧⲉⲩⲛⲟⲩ ⲁ̄
ⲡⲉϥⲥⲓ̈ⲟⲩ ϣⲁ ϩ̄ⲛ̄ ⲧⲁⲛⲁⲧⲟⲗⲏ· ⲁ ⲛϣⲟⲟⲥ ⲛⲁⲩ ⲉ̄ⲣⲟϥ ⲁⲩⲣ̄ϣⲡⲏⲣⲉ
ⲙ̄ⲙⲟϥ:ıııııı— 11 Ⲛⲟⲩⲥⲓ̈ⲟⲩ ⲅⲁⲣ ⲁⲛ ⲡⲉ ⲛ̄ⲑⲉ ⲛ̄ⲛⲉⲥⲓ̈ⲟⲩ ⲧⲏⲣⲟⲩ·

VARIOUS SAHIDIC FRAGMENTS.

FRAGMENT I.

...was with him. 2 And his father Zacharias was filled Lc I 66 ff
with the Holy Ghost, and prophesied, saying, 3 Blessed is the
God of Israel; for He hath visited us, and hath wrought
redemption for His people, 4 and hath raised up for us a
horn of salvation from the house of His servant David.

5 And the holy child John was cherished much in the cf. Lc I 80
house of his parents for six months, receiving suck from the cf. Lc I 7
barren old woman. 6 And his parents took him daily in[a] cf. 1 Sa I 24*
their hands to the temple of the Lord; his father blessing
him, and setting him before the altar at[b] the place where
the angel appeared to him, saying, 7 Lord God of Israel,
strengthen this *child*, whom Thou hast prepared for Thyself.
8 And the child was pleasing[c] daily.

9 Now it came to pass after six months from *the time that* cf. Lc I 26, 36
John was born, the Word of the good Father also was born
from the holy Virgin Mary, in the reign of Augustus the cf. Lc II 1; III 1*
king of the Romans, and when Herod was tetrarch in Judaea,
10 And straightway His star rose in the east, and the shep- cf. Nu XXIV 17; Mt II 2;
herds saw it, and wondered at it. 11 For it was[d] not a star Lc II 8, 18

[a] Lit. *on* [b] Lit. *to* [c] See note [d] Lit. *is*

ⲁⲗⲗⲁ ⲟⲩⲛⲟϭ ⲛ̄ⲥⲓ̈ⲟⲩ ⲡⲉ ⲙ̄ⲡⲉⲥⲙⲟⲧ ⲛⲟⲩⲧⲣⲟⲭⲟⲥ · ⲉ̄ⲣⲉ ⲡⲉϥⲧⲩⲡⲟⲥ
ⲟ ⲛⲑⲉ ⲛⲟⲩⲥ̄⳨ⲟⲥ̄ ⲉϥⲧⲉⲕ ⲉⲃⲣⲏϭⲉ ⲛⲟⲩⲟⲉⲓⲛ̄ ⲉ̄ⲃⲟⲗ · [12]ⲉ̄ⲣⲉ ϩⲉⲛⲥ̄ϩⲁⲓ̈ |
ⲥⲏϩ ⲉ̄ⲡⲉⲥ̄⳨ⲟⲥ̄ ϫⲉ ⲡⲁⲓ̈ ⲡⲉ ⲓ̄ⲥ̄ ⲡ̄ϣⲏⲣⲉ ⲙ̄ⲡⲛⲟⲩⲧⲉ : ।।। — [13]Ⲛ̄ⲙⲁⲅⲟⲥ
ⲇⲉ ⲛ̄ⲧⲉⲣⲟⲩⲛⲁⲩ ⲉⲛⲥⲓ̈ⲟⲩ ⲁⲩⲱ̄ ⲛ̄ⲥⲉⲱϣ ⲛ̄ⲛⲉⲥϩⲁⲓ̈ · ⲁⲩϭⲉⲛⲏ ⲁⲩⲉⲓ̈
ⲉϩⲣⲁⲓ̈ ⲉ̄ⲑⲓ̈ⲗⲏⲙ ϣⲁ ϩⲏⲣⲱⲇⲏⲥ ⲙⲛ̄ ⲛⲁⲣⲭⲓ̈ⲉⲣⲉⲩⲥ̄ · ⲉⲩϫⲱ ⲙ̄ⲙⲟⲥ
[14]ϫⲉ ⲉϥⲧⲱⲛ ⲡⲣⲣⲟ ⲛ̄ⲛ̄ⲓ̈ⲟⲩⲇⲁⲓ̈ ⲛ̄ⲧⲁⲩϫ̄ⲡⲟϥ · ⲁⲛⲛⲁⲩ ⲅⲁⲣ ⲉ̄ⲡⲉϥ-
ⲥⲓ̈ⲟⲩ ϩ̄ⲛ̄ ⲛⲉⲙⲁ ⲛϣⲁ ⲁⲛⲉⲓ̈ ⲉ̄ⲟⲩⲱϣⲧ̄ ⲛⲁϥ : ।।।।। — [15]Ⲁⲗⲗⲁ ⲟⲩⲛ̄
ⲟⲩⲁ̄ ⲡⲁϫⲟⲟⲥ ⲡⲁⲓ̈ · ϫⲉ ⲟⲩⲕⲟⲩⲛ̄ ⲉⲕⲟⲧⲉϩ ⲛ̄ⲡⲣⲟⲥⲑⲏⲕⲏ ⲉ̄ϫⲛ̄ ⲡⲉⲩ-
ⲁⲅⲅⲉⲗⲓ̈ⲟⲛ : ।।। — [16]Ⲙⲁⲣⲉ ⲡ̄ⲙⲉⲣⲓ̈ⲧ ⲉ̄ⲧⲙ̄ⲙⲁⲩ ⲥⲱⲧⲙ̄ ϩ̄ⲛ̄ ⲟⲩϯ̄ϩⲧⲏϥ ·
ⲁⲩⲱ̄ |

FRAGMENT II.

Cod. Br. M. Or. 3581 B p. ?

[1]⌈.......ⲛ.ϫⲉⲓ.ⲛ.⌉ⲟⲟⲛ ⲉⲃⲟⲗ ⌈Ⲛ⌉ⲉⲓⲟⲧⲉ ⲇⲉ ⲙ̄ⲡⲡⲁⲧϣⲉⲗⲉⲉⲧ
ⲁⲩϯ ⲡⲉⲧⲟⲩⲟⲓ ⲉⲙⲁⲣⲓⲁ · ϩⲱⲥ ⲉⲩⲑⲁⲣⲉⲓ ϫⲉ ⲧⲉⲩⲥⲱⲛ⌈ⲉ⌉ ⲧⲉ · —
[2]Ⲡⲉϫ⌈ⲁ⌉ⲩ ⲛⲁⲥ ϫⲉ ⲙⲁⲣⲓⲁ ⲧⲛ̄ⲥⲱⲛⲉ ⲟⲩ ⲡⲉⲧⲛ̄ⲛⲁⲁⲁϥ ⲁ ⲡⲏⲣⲡ̄
ⲱϫⲛ̄ [3]Ⲡⲏⲣⲡ̄ ⲅⲁⲣ ⲛⲧⲟϥ ⲡⲉⲛ̄ϣⲁϥⲧⲣⲉ ⲡⲉⲧⲟⲩⲱⲙ ⲉⲩⲫⲣⲁⲛⲉ · ⲁⲩⲱ
ⲉⲓⲥ ϩⲏⲏⲧⲉ ⲁϥⲱϫⲛ̄ [4]Ⲙ ⲡⲛⲟϭ ⲛ̄ϣⲡⲉ ⲛ̄ⲧⲁϥϣⲱⲡⲉ ⲛⲁⲛ ⲙ̄ⲡⲟⲟⲩ
ϩ̄ⲛ̄ ⲧⲙⲏⲧⲉ ⲛ̄ⲛⲉⲧⲧⲁϩⲙ̄ ⲧⲏⲣⲟⲩ ⲛ̄ϩⲟⲩⲟ ⌈ⲇ⌉ⲉ ⲉⲧⲃⲉ ⲛⲟⲩϣⲏⲣⲉ · ϫⲉ
ⲙ̄ⲡⲉⲛ̄ⲙ̄ⲡϣⲁ ⲉⲧⲣⲉϥⲉⲓ ⲉϩⲟⲩⲛ ⲉⲡⲉⲛⲏⲓ ϣⲁ ⲡⲟⲟⲩ | ⲁ..........
ⲧⲁϩⲟ⌈ⲛ [5]..ⲟⲩ⌉ⲉⲡⲉϩ ⲟⲩϣⲡⲏⲣⲉ ⲉⲃⲟⲗ ⲙⲡⲟⲟⲩ ϩ̄ⲛ̄ ⲧϭⲟⲙ ⲛ̄ⲧⲉϥ-
ⲙ̄ⲛⲧⲛⲟⲩⲧⲉ : — [6]Ⲧⲛ̄ⲡⲓⲥⲧⲉⲩⲉ ⲅⲁⲣ ϫⲉ ⲛⲧⲟϥ ⲡⲉ ⲡⲥⲱⲧⲏⲣ
ⲙ̄ⲡⲕⲟⲥⲙⲟⲥ[a] ⲁⲩⲱ ⲟⲩⲉⲛ ϭⲟⲙ ⲙ̄ⲙⲟϥ ⲉϩⲱⲃ ⲛⲓⲙ [7]Ⲙⲁⲣⲓⲁ ⲇⲉ
ϩⲱⲱⲥ ⲛⲉⲥⲑⲁⲣⲉⲓ ϫⲉ ⲛϥⲛⲁⲗⲩⲡⲉⲓ ⲙ̄ⲙⲟⲥ ⲁⲛ ϩ̄ⲛ̄ ⲗⲁⲁⲩ ⲛϩⲱⲃ
ⲉⲧⲉⲥⲛⲁⲁⲓⲧⲉⲓ ⲙ̄ⲙⲟϥ ⲛ̄ϩⲏⲧⲟⲩ [8]Ⲁⲥϯ ⲛⲉⲥⲟⲩⲟⲓ ⲉⲛⲙⲁ ⲉⲣⲉ ⲡⲉⲥϣⲏⲣⲉ

[a] ⲡⲥⲱⲧⲏⲣⲙ̄ⲡⲕⲟⲥⲙⲟⲥ

like all the stars, but it was[a] a great star in the form of a
wheel, its figure[b] being like a cross, sending forth flashes[c] of
light; 12letters being written on the cross, This is Jesus the
Son of God. 13And the wise men, when they saw the star cf. Mt II 1, 2, 4, 7
and read the letters, hastened and came to Jerusalem unto
Herod and the chief priests, saying, 14Where is the King of
the Jews that is born? for we saw His star in the east, and
are come to worship Him. 15But some one will say to me,
Art thou then adding *a* supplement to the gospels? 16Let
that beloved one listen attentively, and .....

FRAGMENT II.

...And the parents of the bridegroom approached to
Mary, as being of good courage because she was[a] their sister.
2And they said to her, Mary, our sister, what shall we do?
The wine has failed. 3For wine it is that maketh glad those cf. Jn II 3*; Ps CIII 15*
who eat. And behold it has failed. 4O the great shame
which has befallen us to-day in the midst of all those who
are bidden; and especially because of thy Son, for we were
not worthy that He should come into our house until to-day cf. Mt VIII 8; Lc VII 6*
..... 5manifest a wonder to-day in the power of His god-
head. 6For we believe that He is the Saviour of the world cf. Jn IV 41*, 42*
and that all things are possible to Him.

7And Mary also was assured[d] that He would[e] not grieve
her in any thing that[f] she should[e] ask Him. 8And she

[a] Lit. *is* [b] See note [c] Lit. *lightnings* [d] Lit. *was of good courage* [e] Lit. *will* [f] Lit. *in anything in* the things *which*

ⲡⲏϫ ⲛ̄ϩⲏⲧϥ ⲁⲥⲟⲩⲱϣⲧ ⲛⲁϥ [9]Ⲡⲉϫⲁⲥ ⲛⲁϥ · ϫⲉ ⲡⲁϣⲏⲣⲉ ⲡⲁⲙ⌈ⲉ⌉ⲣⲓⲧ · ⲡ⌈ⲉ⌉ⲛⲧⲁ ⲧ⌈ⲁ⌉ⲯⲩⲭ⌈ⲏ ⲟⲩ⌉ⲁϣϥ Ⲡⲁϫ⌈ⲟⲉⲓⲥ ⲁ⌉ⲩⲱ p. ? ⲡⲁⲛⲟⲩⲧⲉ | ⌈.........ⲡ⌉ⲁ⌈ⲅ⌉ⲁⲑⲟ⌈ⲥ ⲁⲩⲱ⌉ ⲛⲛⲁⲛⲧ [10]Ⲁⲩⲧⲁϩⲙⲉⲕ ϩⲱⲥ ϣⲏⲣⲉ ⲙ̄ⲙⲁⲣⲓⲁ ⲟⲩⲉⲛⲉϩ ⲧⲉⲕϭⲟⲙ ⲉⲃⲟⲗ . ϩⲱⲥ ϣⲏⲣⲉ ⲙ̄ⲡⲛⲟⲩⲧⲉ · — [11]Ⲡⲁⲣⲉ ⲛ̄ϩⲉⲑⲛⲟⲥ ⲧⲏⲣⲟⲩ ⲉⲓⲙⲉ ϫⲉ ⲛ̄ⲧⲟⲕ ⲡⲉ ⲡⲉⲭ̅ⲥ̅ ⲡϣⲏⲣⲉ ⲙⲡⲛⲟⲩⲧⲉ ⲉⲧⲟⲛϩ̄ ⲡⲁϣⲏⲣⲉ ⲙ̄ⲛ̄ⲧⲟⲩ ⲏⲣⲡ ⲙ̄ⲙⲁⲩ [12]Ⲡⲉϫⲁϥ ⲛ̄ⲧⲉϥⲙⲁⲁⲩ ϩⲛ̄ ⲟⲩⲥⲙⲏ ⲉⲥⲛⲟⲧⲙ̄ ϫⲉ ⲧⲉⲥϩⲓⲙⲉ · ⲉⲣⲟⲩⲉϣ ˙ⲟⲩ ⲛ̄ⲙ̄ⲙⲁⲓ ⲙ̄ⲡⲁⲧⲉ ⲧⲁⲟⲩⲛⲟⲩ ⲉⲓ · [13]ⲧⲉϥⲙⲁⲁⲩ ⲇⲉ ϩⲱⲱⲥ ⲉⲥⲑⲁⲣⲉⲓ ϫⲉ ⲛ̄ϥⲛⲁⲗⲩⲡⲉⲓ ⲙ̄ⲙⲟⲥ ⲁⲛ ϩⲛ̄ ⲗⲁⲁⲩ ⲛ̄ϩⲱⲃ ·[a] ⲁⲥϫⲟⲟⲥ ⲛ̄ⲛⲉⲧⲇ⌈ⲓⲁⲕ⌉ⲟⲛⲉⲓ Ⲁⲛⲟⲕ ⲟ⌈....⌉ⲗ ⲛ̄ϩⲏ⌈ⲧ... ⲛ⌉.⌈ⲕ⌉ | [14]Ⲛⲉⲩⲉⲛ ⌈ⲥⲱ ⲇⲉ ⲛϩⲏⲧ⌉ⲣⲓⲁ ⲛⲱⲛⲉ ⲕⲏ ⲉϩⲣⲁⲓ ϩⲙ̄ ⲡⲙⲁ ⲛ̄⌈ϣⲉ⌉ⲗⲉⲉⲧ · ⲉⲣⲉ ⲡⲉⲧⲛⲁⲛⲟϫⲟⲩ ⲧⲃ̄ⲃⲟ ⲉⲃⲟⲗ ⲛ̄ϩⲏⲧⲟⲩ · ϩⲁⲑⲏ ⌈ⲉ⌉ⲧⲣⲉⲩⲛⲟϫⲟⲩ ⲕⲁⲧⲁ ⲡⲛⲟ⌈ⲙⲟ⌉ⲥ ⲛ̄ⲛⲓⲟⲩⲇⲁ⌈ⲓ⌉ · ⲁⲩⲱ ⲛⲉⲣⲉ ⲧⲟⲩⲉⲓ ⲧⲟⲩⲉⲓ · ϣⲱⲡ ⲉⲣⲟⲥ ⲙ̄ⲙⲉⲧⲣⲉⲧⲏⲥ̣ ⲥⲛⲁⲩ ⲏ ϣⲟⲙⲛ̄ⲧ · — [15]Ⲡⲉϫⲁϥ ⲛⲁⲩ ϫⲉ ⲙⲉϩ ⲛ̄ϩⲏⲧⲣⲓⲁ ⲙ̄ⲙⲟⲟⲩ · [16]ⲁⲛⲓⲙⲉ ⲛ̄ⲧⲉⲩⲛⲟⲩ ϫⲉ ϥⲛⲁⲟⲩⲉⲛⲉϩ ⲟⲩϣⲡⲏⲣⲉ ⲉⲃⲟⲗ · ⲉⲣⲉ ⲡⲉⲧⲡⲏϫ ⲧⲏⲣⲟⲩ ⲑ⌈ⲉ⌉ⲱⲣⲉⲓ ⲙ̄ⲙⲟϥ — [17]Ⲁⲛϭⲉⲡⲏ ⲁⲛⲙⲉϩ ⲛ̄ϩⲏⲇⲣ⌈ⲓⲁ⌉ ⲙ̄ⲙⲟⲟⲩ ⲉⲛϣⲧⲣ̄ⲧⲱⲣ ⲉⲧⲃⲉ ϫⲉ ⲡϣⲟⲣⲡ ⲡⲉ ⲛ̄ⲡⲉⲧⲡⲏϫ |

[a] punct. ut vid.

approached to the place wherein her Son was reclining, and
she worshipped Him. 9 And she saith to Him, My Son, my
Beloved, Thou[a] whom my soul desireth[b], my Lord and my cf. Cant I 7*; Mt XII 18*
God . . . . . good and merciful. 10 Thou art bidden as Son of cf. Jn II 2*
Mary: manifest Thy power as Son of God. 11 Let all the
nations know that Thou art the Christ, the Son of the living cf. Mt XVI 16*
God. My Son, they have no wine. 12 He saith unto His cf. Jn II 3 ff*
mother in a kindly[c] voice, Woman, what wilt thou with
Me? Mine hour is not yet come. 13 But His mother, being
assured[d] that He would[e] not grieve her in anything, spake
unto those who served[f] . . . . . 14 Now there were six waterpots
of stone set down at the marriage, from which those who
would[e] recline were purified before they reclined, according
to the law of the Jews. And each one contained two or
three firkins. 15 He saith unto them, Fill the waterpots with
water. 16 We knew straightway that He would[e] manifest *a*
wonder, all those who reclined beholding it[g]. 17 We hasted
and filled the waterpots with water, being troubled because cf. Jn II 7*, 8*
he was[h] the chief[i] of those who reclined.

[a] Lit. *He* [b] Lit. *desired* [c] Or *sweet* [d] Lit. *being of good courage* [e] Lit. *will* [f] See note [g] Or *Him* [h] Lit. *is* [i] Lit. *first*

FRAGMENT III[a].

p. 21 . . . my friends. Ye have seen, O my brethren, the
cf. Lc xxii 21, 29, 30 Lord[b] always like this *one* loving His apostles, and promising
them His kingdom, that they should eat and drink with
Him at the table of His kingdom: whilst still on the earth,
eating with them at the table of the earth, *ye have seen Him*
reminding them of the table of His kingdom. For He took
no account at all of[c] the things of the world. [2]If thou wishest
to know, hear and I will tell thee. Doth not God earnestly
love[d] His apostles, *even* all of them? Hear John the
cf. Jn xvii 9, 11, 22 evangelist bearing witness that Christ makes request to His
Father for them, that they may be one, even as We *are* One.
cf. Jn vi 70* [3]Dost thou wish to know the truth, that[e] He chose[b] them, *even*
p. 22 the twelve that they should . . . . [f][to] them, saying, I have
cf. Mt xv 32*, 33* compassion on this multitude, for behold[b] three days they
continue with Me and have nothing to eat: and I would not
send them away fasting, lest haply they faint in the way.
cf. Jn vi 8* [4]Andrew saith unto Him, Master, where shall we find bread
cf. Mt xiv 18*; Mc vi 38*; Jn vi 8*, 9* in this desert place, that . . . . [g]Jesus saith unto Thomas, Go
to the[h] man, who hath the[i] five barley loaves, and the[i] two
fishes; and bring him hither to Me. [5]Andrew saith unto him,
Master, what will these five loaves be among[j] so great a multitude as this? Jesus said unto him, Bring them to Me, and the
matter will see *to it*. And they went, and brought the lad to
Jesus, and he worshipped Him straightway. Straightway he
p. 23 brought up the loaves and the two fishes. [6]The lad said to
cf. Lc v 5* Jesus, Master, I have toiled much for these. Jesus said to
to the lad, Give Me the five loaves which are entrusted to

[a] The Sahidic text is printed by Prof. Ignazio Guidi: *Rendiconti della R. Accademia dei Lincei* (1887), vol. iii, 2° semestre, pp. 373—380 (*Frammenti Copti*, Nota vi[a]). The numbers given in the margin of this and the following Fragment are those of the pages of the MSS [b] See note [c] Lit. *He did not reckon to Himself at all* [d] Lit. *desire with love* [e] Or *for* [f] There is a gap here in the MS of some six lines [g] There is a gap here in the MS of some five lines [h] Or *this* [i] Or *these* [j] Lit. *to*

thee. For it is not thou that hast saved this multitude from
affliction, but it is the dispensation which . . . [a] for a wonder-
ful work, and for a memorial[b] unfailing for ever, and for food
that they may be filled. 7 And Jesus took the loaves, and He cf. Mt xv
gave thanks over them, and He brake them, and He gave 36*; Mc vi 41*; viii
them to the apostles to set them before the multitudes. 6*; Lc ix 16; Jn vi
Now Judas was[c] the last who received of[a] the loaves. 8 Andrew 11*
saith unto Jesus, Master, Judas hath not received inheritance
in his loaves[a], that he should set them before these multitudes.
Dost Thou wish . . . . [a] Thy word, that he to whom I have not p. ⲕⲁ
given the breaking of the loaves from My hands is not worthy
of the breaking of My flesh. 9 Neither indeed does he care cf. Jn xii
for giving to the poor, but only for the bag[d]. A mystery 6
the breaking . . . flesh. 10 . . straightway He blessed them, say-
ing, My Father, My Father, all the Root of goodness[a], I pray
Thee to bless these five barley loaves, that they may fill all
this multitude; in order that Thy Son may be glorified in cf. Jn xi
Thee, and that those whom Thou hast drawn unto Him from 4; xiii 31, 32; xvii 6
the world may obey Him. 11 And straightway His word was Lc iv 32*
with authority. The blessing was in the loaves in the hands
of the apostles. And all the people did eat, and they were cf. Mt xiv
filled, and they blessed[e] God. 20*

12 Ye have seen, O my beloved, the love of Jesus towards p. 25
His apostles, because He did not hide anything from them
of[f] all the works of His godhead: now in the blessing of the cf. Mt xiv
five barley loaves, now in the giving of thanks to[a] His Father, 19*; Mc viii 6*
now in the giving of thanks for[g] the seven loaves. 13 Thomas
saith unto Jesus, My Lord, behold Thou hast shewn all
favours unto us in Thy goodness. There is one thing in
which we wish that Thou shouldest assure us. We wish, O
my Lord, to see dead men sleeping[h] in the tombs raised by
Thee, for a sign of Thy resurrection which shall take place.
14 For we know, O our Lord, that Thou didst raise the son of cf. Lc vii
the widow in Nain[i]. But the wonder at that time[j] was 11*, 12
different; for Thou didst find them going with him in the

[a] See note [b] Or *remembrance* [c] Lit. *For Judas is* [d] Or *box* [e] Or *praised* [f] Lit. *in* [g] Lit. *of* [h] Or *lying* [i] The MS has *Noein* [j] Lit. *hour*

way. We wish to see how bones in the[a] tomb which have
been dissolved are joined together and they speak (?) here.
p. ⌜κς⌝ 15 Jesus saith to Thomas, Thomas My friend, ask Me and
thy brethren[b] concerning everything that thou desirest; and
cf. Jn xx 27 I will hide nothing from you, that hardly (?) thou mayest see
and touch and thy heart be assured[c]. Didst thou desire to
see those who *are* in the tombs arise? Full well didst thou
seek after a sign of *the* resurrection. For I have told you
Jn xi 25 already[b], I am the resurrection, and the life: and if a[d] grain
cf. Jn xii 24 of wheat dieth not, it beareth not fruit. 16 If ye also do not
see with your eyes, your heart is not assured[c]. Did not I
cf. Jn xx 29 say to you, Blessed are they that have not seen, and have
believed, rather than they that have seen, and have not
believed? Ye see how many signs and wonders I have
wrought before the Jews, and they have not believed on Me.
p. κ⌜ζ⌝ 17 Now therefore, O brethren, ye know Lazarus the man of
cf. Jn xi 1, 3, 6, 11, 17, 39 Bethany, who is called My friend. Behold four days I abide
with you, and I have not gone to visit his sisters: for to-day
cf. Jn xi 15, 19 is the fourth day since Lazarus died[e]. Now therefore let us
go unto him, that ye may comfort them concerning their
cf. Jn xi 16 brother Lazarus. 18 Didymus, come with Me, that we may go
to Bethany, and that I may shew thee the figure of the
cf. Jn xi 24, 25 resurrection at the last day in his tomb; and your heart
shall be[f] assured[c] that I am the resurrection, and the life.
Come with Me, O Didymus, that I may shew thee the
bones which have been dissolved in the tomb gathered together again. Come with Me, O Didymus, that I may shew
thee the eyes of Lazarus which have been hollowed out[g]
sending forth[b] light. 19 Come with Me, O Didymus, unto the
mount of Bethany, that I may shew thee the tongue of
Lazarus, which has wasted away by reason of corrupt matter[b],
p. κη and that I may make it[b] speak with thee again. Come with
Me, O Didymus, unto the tomb of Lazarus, that thou mayest
see the corruption[h] of his bones and of his shroud, which the
worms have destroyed, that thou mayest see that which

[a] Or *this* [b] See note [c] Lit. *strengthened* [d] Lit. *the*
[e] Lit. *for to-day is the four of Lazarus since he died* [f] Or *and let your heart be* [g] Lit. *dug down* [h] Or *destruction*

befalls[a] him by[b] the voice wherewith[c] I call him. 20 Come cf. Jn xi
with Me[d], O Didymus, unto the tomb of Lazarus—to-day 43
is[e] the fourth day[f] since he died—that I may raise him up cf. Jn xi
alive again[g]. Thou hast sought after the sign of My resur- 11, 17, 39
rection[h], O Thomas. Come that I may shew it thee in the
tomb of Lazarus. 21 Thou hast sought to see how bones are
joined[i] together. Come with Me to the tomb of Lazarus,
that thou mayest see them[j] going and coming from the door
of his[k] tomb. 22 Thou hast sought for hands to be stretched
out[l]. Come, that I may shew thee the hands of Lazarus, cf. Jn xi
bound in grave-clothes, and wrapped in the linen cloths[m], set 44
upon them alone, coming forth from the tomb[n]. 23 Didymus,
My friend, come with Me to the tomb of Lazarus, for My
mouth hath desired that of which thou hast thought. For
to-day is the fourth day[o] of Lazarus, and Martha and Mary cf. Jn xi
are waiting for Me to go and enquire of them concerning 17, 39
their brother. 24 Now whilst Jesus was saying these things to
the apostles, Didymus approached, and said unto Him, My
Lord, how then shall we go thither, whilst the Jews are cf. Jn xi 8
seeking to stone Thee? He said this because he was grieved
concerning the words which Jesus spake concerning Lazarus,
in order that He might not go. 25 Jesus said to him, Didymus, p. ІН
he that walketh in the light stumbleth not. Jesus said this cf. Jn xi 9; 1 Jn i 7
word to Thomas that He might comfort him, because He
saw him grieving concerning the death of Lazarus.

26 Now after all these things He came not far from the tomb

[a] Lit. *which hath befallen* [b] Lit. *in* [c] Lit. *wherein* [d] A fragment preserved at the Bodleian Library in Oxford beginning with the words *with Me* and ending with the words *Thomas wept before Jesus, saying, If Thou hast* (verse 29) is given by Prof. Guidi (pp. 376, 377) [e] For *to-day is* the Oxford fragment has *it being* [f] Lit. *his four* [g] For *alive again* the Oxford fragment has *again alive* [h] For *the sign of My resurrection* the Oxford fragment has *a sign of resurrection* See note [i] Lit. *sought after the manner of seeing bones joined* The Oxford fragment omits *the manner of* [j] For *them* the Oxford fragment has *the* (or *these*) *multitudes of worms* [k] For *his* the Oxford fragment has *the* [l] For *Thou hast...out* the Oxford fragment has *Thou hast sought to see hands, that they may be stretched out* [m] For *in the linen cloths* the Oxford fragment has *in napkins* [n] The first MS breaks off at this point, and the Oxford fragment is given in the text [o] Lit. *the four*

cf. Jn xi 30 of Lazarus; and his sister met Him there. She said unto
Jn xi 21 Him, Lord, if Thou hadst been here[a], my brother had not died,
cf. Jn xi for[a] Thou art the resurrection, that raiseth the dead: for I
22, 25 ff know Thee from Thy youth and my brother Lazarus[a]. 27 Jesus
said unto her, Believest thou this, that I am the resurrection
that raiseth the dead, and the life of every one? Martha
Jn xi 23 saith unto Him, Yea, Lord, I believe. Jesus saith unto her,
Thy brother shall rise. 28 Then as they were saying these
things one with another, behold Martha and Mary and Jesus
cf. Jn xi 38, 39 came to the tomb of Lazarus, Jesus going before the apostles.
And He saith unto them, Take away the stone, that thou
mayest see the witness to the manner in which the dead are
raised[b]. 29 And straightway Thomas wept before Jesus, saying,
p. ιθ If Thou hast[c] suffered this trouble, and hast come to the
tomb of *the* dead, because of my unbelief, let Thy will be
done unto me, and let this tomb receive me unto the day of
Thy resurrection. 30 But Jesus knew that Thomas was grieved,
and He said unto him with a voice of joy and a word of life,
Jn xiii 7 Thomas, Grieve not. What I do thou knowest not. Is it a
cf. Jn xi 11 trouble to take away the stone of a friend enclosed in a
tomb, that he may arise and come forth? Grieve not, O
Thomas, because I said unto thee, Take away the stone, that
a witness to *the* resurrection may be manifested in a tomb of
the dead. Grieve not, O Thomas, because I said unto thee,
Take away the stone, to raise *the* dead. 31 Open the door of
the tomb, and I will bring forth him that is dead. Take
away the stone, O Thomas, that I may give life to him who
sleepeth[d] in the tomb. Drag far away the stone, O Thomas,
and he that is dead shall[e] find the way of coming forth from
the tomb. 32 I did not urge[f] thee, O Thomas, *saying*, Take
away the stone; because Lazarus cannot come forth, whilst
the door is shut: for[g] all things are possible to Me. But if
thou takest away the stone, O Thomas, the tomb is mani-
p. κ fested that all men may see it, and may see how he that is

[a] See note [b] Lit. *to the manner of raising* the *dead* [c] The Oxford fragment ends here. The rest of the MS is in Rome. See Introduction [d] Or *lieth* [e] Or *and let him that is dead* [f] Or *compel* [g] The MS has *whilst the stone is shut: yea,* But see note

dead sleepeth[a]. 33 Hast thou taken away the stone, O Thomas;
and the evil smell gone forth, and the corrupt matter, and
the worm, in the manner of all those who are dead? Nay,
God forbid[b].

34 Now after all these things Jesus said unto Mary, Believest cf. Jn xi
thou that thy brother shall rise? She saith unto Him, Yea, 23, 26, 27, 39
Lord, I believe. By this time he stinketh: for it is four
days[c] since he died. But I believe that all things are cf. Mc xiv
possible to Thee. 35 And Jesus turned to Thomas, and said 36*
unto him, Come, that thou mayest see the bones of *the* dead
lying in the tombs before I raise them. Come with Me, O
Thomas, that thou mayest see the eyes which have poured
themselves forth[d], before I give the light to them again.
36 Come, O Thomas, that thou mayest see how he who
sleepeth[a] is laid, before I raise him again. Come, O
Thomas, have faith in[e] Me; for all things are possible to
Me. 37 Martha and Mary, assure[f] your heart. Have more
faith than Martha and Mary, bearing witness to Me, *and
saying*, Yea, all things are possible to Thee. 38 And as Jesus cf. Mc xiv
said these things, He cried out, saying, My Father, My 36*; Jn xi 22, 27
Father, all the Root of goodness, I beseech Thee, for the p. 21
hour is come, that Thou wouldest glorify Thy Son, that all cf. Jn xvii 1
may know that Thou didst send Me for this end[g]. The cf. Jn
glory *be* to Thee unto *the* ages of *the* ages. Amen. xvii 23; xviii 37

39 And as Jesus was saying these things, He cried out, say- cf. Jn xi
ing, Lazarus, come forth. And straightway the mount went 43, 44
round as a wheel (?). They that were dead arose, and came
forth because of the voice of Jesus who called him, *saying*,
Lazarus, come forth. 40 And straightway Lazarus came
forth, wrapped in grave-clothes, his face bound with a
napkin, his head bound in grave-clothes. Jesus saith unto
them, Loose him, and let him go. 41 Now when Lazarus saw
Jesus standing at the door of the tomb, he fell down and
worshipped Him. And he cried out saying, Blessed art
Thou, Jesus, at whose voice Amente trembles, *even the voice*

[a] Or *lieth* [b] Lit. *it shall not be* [c] Lit. *it is his four* [d] See note [e] Lit. *into* [f] Lit. *strengthen* [g] Lit. *thing*

wherewith He called me: the glory of whose godhead those
who *are* in Amente desire to see. Blessed art Thou, Jesus,
to whom belongs this voice of resurrection; for Thou art He
cf. Ac xvii 31 who shall judge the whole world. 42 And as Lazarus was
cf. Jn xii 9 saying these things to Jesus, the multitudes followed after
cf. Mc v 31* him to see him. 43 Now when Jesus saw that the multi-
p. 22 tudes thronged Him and Lazarus also—[some[a]] of those
belonging to his family embracing him, some asking after
his welfare, his sisters kissing his mouth, in short there
being[b] a great clamour in the mount of Bethany: some
cf. Mt ix 33 shouting aloud, others confessing that there was never a
cf. Jn xi 25, 45 man like this in Israel, some *saying*, We believe on that
man, that He is the[c] resurrection, from[d] that which we
have seen in the tomb of Lazarus to-day: the[e] multitudes
cf. Ps cxvii 12* being gathered together to Lazarus, like bees to a honey-
comb, because of the wonder which was come to pass.

44 But Lazarus did not go away from the feet of Jesus,
kissing them, and bearing witness to the multitudes, *and
saying*, Jesus is the resurrection of the quick and of the
dead. What is[b] the sight of this place at all compared with
the sight of Amente at the hour that He called my name
cf. Jn xi 43 from the door of the tomb, *saying*, Lazarus[b], come forth? 45 I
say unto you, At that hour my father Adam knew His voice
cf. Job xxxviii 17; Ps ix 14; cvi 18 and His call[f], as though He were at the gates of death,
calling him. He spent a while with his ear inclined to His
call[f], thinking that He was calling him. 46 Adam bare witness
to the multitudes, *saying*, This call[f] that I have heard is the
call of my Creator: this voice that I have heard is the *voice* of
p. 23 my Surety, wherewith He calleth me in Paradise[g]. 47 Where
cf. He vii 22* is that hour when He cometh to Paradise[g] to call me? Who
is this good son whom my Creator calleth by this name,
cf. Jn xi 43 *saying*, Lazarus, come forth? 48 I pray thee, my son Lazarus,
upon whom the mercy of the Almighty has come, enquire of
my Creator concerning me, O my beloved son Lazarus,

[a] The word *some* is not in the MS, but see note [b] See note
[c] Lit. *a* [d] Lit. *in* [e] Or *these* [f] Lit. *voice or sound*
[g] Lit. *the Paradise*

saying, How long shall it be before I hear[a] this call[b] of
life?

49 Now as Lazarus was saying these things to the multi-
tude, lying prostrate at the feet of Jesus, the fame of Him[c]
reached unto the chiefs of the Jews[d], that Jesus did this cf. Jn v
work[e] on the sabbath. [And they came[f]] that they might 16*; viii
see Lazarus and stone Jesus. 50 Now it came to pass in those 59; x 31;
days, when Jesus raised Lazarus, there was a chief of Galilee xi 53; xii 9 cf. Mc vi
with Herod, for the care of the countries of Philip, over 21*; Lc iii
which he was[g] appointed, who was accused before the king 1*
that he was[g] laying them waste, for the sake of his wife,
because Herod took her from him. 51 And Carius, the chief cf. Mc vi
of the king, when he heard the mighty works[h] which Jesus 17*
was[g] doing, went unto Him that he might see Him. 52 Then
Carius brought the report of Jesus, and sent it to Herod,
saying, This man is worthy to be made king over all Judaea
and the countries of Philip. 53 When Herod heard these p. 24
things concerning Jesus, that He was[g] worthy to be made
king, he was greatly distressed, and brought[i] great accusa- cf. Mt ii 3
tions against Jesus. And so he gathered together all the
chiefs of the Jews, and spake to them that which Carius
thought concerning Jesus, that He would be made king.
54 And straightway Herod commanded them, saying, He who
is found consenting unto this matter shall come under the
destruction of the sword, and they that *are* in his house shall
be seized[j].

55 Now Annas and Caiaphas and the chiefs of the Jews
were gathered together unto Carius, the chief of Tiberius[e]
the king: and they agreed upon lying words and false cf. Mc xiv
testimonies, which did[k] not agree together, concerning Jesus, 56, 59
from His birth unto His death[l]: some *saying*, He is a
magician; others, He was born of fornication[m]; some, He
breaketh the sabbath; others, He hath abolished the cf. Jn v
18*

[a] Lit. *Until what time shall I hear* [b] Lit. *voice* or *sound* [c] Or *him* [d] The MS has *the chief Jews* But see note [e] See note [f] These words are not in the MS, but see note [g] Lit. *is* [h] Lit. *the powers* [i] Lit. *spake* [j] Or *those* things *which* are *in his house shall be spoiled* [k] Lit. *do* [l] Or *consummation* [m] Lit. *of a woman*

synagogue of the Jews. 56 And straightway they sent for
cf. Jn xix 38, 39 Joseph and Nicodemus, and brought them; who also were
cf. Lc xxiii 50, 51; Jn iii 1; vii 50*, 51* chiefs of the Jews; and they consented not with them unto
their lying accusations, but spake blessed words concerning
Jesus.

FRAGMENT IV[a].

p. 53 Nothing is impossible unto you in the removal of the
cf. Mt xvii 20 mountains. Now therefore have faith in the love of My
Father; for faith is the end of all things. 2 Now all these our
Saviour spake to His apostles comforting them on the
mount; knowing that which was spread abroad concerning
Him in Judaea, by the authorities that came after Him, to
cf. Jn vi 15 take Him by force, that they might make Him king. 3 And
the messengers of Theophilus came unto Jesus, and they
told Him, saying, They seek after Thee[b], wishing to make
Thee[b] king. The apostles said to Jesus, Our Lord, we are
glad[c] that they will make Thee king. 4 Jesus said to them,
cf. Jn xviii 36 Did I not say to you again, My kingdom is not of this world?
Do not have the joy of the kingdom of this world in your
p. 54 heart, O my brethren *and* apostles; for it is temporal. 5 Did
cf. Lc xxii 29, 30 I covenant with[d] you, O My holy members and My brethren,
to eat with you at the table of a kingdom of this world?
cf. Mt vi 10; Lc xi 2* But My kingdom continueth for ever in heaven and on earth.
6 Now as Jesus said these and other[e] things to His disciples,
cf. Jn vi 15 He was hidden[f] on the mount, because they sought[g] after
Him to make Him king. 7 And the authorities of Tiberius[d]
prevailed the second time concerning[d] Jesus, and indeed
Pilate also, that they might commend Jesus, to make Him
king. 8 And Pilate praised them exceedingly[h], saying, Truly

[a] The Sahidic text is printed by Prof. Ignazio Guidi: *Rendiconti della R. Accademia dei Lincei* (1887), vol. iii, 2° semestre, pp. 381—384 (*Frammenti Copti*, Nota vi[a]) [b] Lit. *Him* [c] Lit. *there is joy to us*
[d] See note [e] Lit. *these and these other* [f] Lit. *He being hidden*
[g] Lit. *seek* [h] Or *the more*

according to the signs and the wonders which that man
doeth, He is worthy. We will make (?) Him[a] king over
all Judaea, that He may rule over all the countries of
Judaea. And as for those things that I hear concerning
that man, He is a good man and He is fit to be made p. 55
king. 9 Now as Pilate was saying these things before the cf. Jn VII 12*
authorities of Tiberius[a] the king, Herod could not refrain from
setting Pilate at nought[b], saying, Thou art a Galilaean
foreign Egyptian Pontus (?). Thou dost not know any law
at all: and indeed thou hast not long been governor of this
city, that thou shouldest know the works of that man.
10 Herod said to him, Every one that opposeth the command cf. Jn XIX 12
of the king angereth the king: for[c] it is no care to me that
Jesus should reign over Judaea. And straightway there was
enmity between Herod and Pilate because of Jesus from cf. Lc XXIII 12
that day. 11 This saying[d] was spread abroad in all Judaea: p. 56
Jesus the king of the Jews. And Pilate wrote the report[e] cf. Mt XXVIII 15*;
of Jesus; and fastened it[f] to the cross, This is Jesus the king Jn XIX 19;
of the Jews. 12 Now when Herod heard these things, he still Lc XXIII 38
continued in his madness against Jesus, saying, My father
died at the occasion of this *man* in His youth; but I suffer
not myself to die, whilst this *man* lives. 13 And he gave
much money to the authorities; and he brought them on
their way to the king. And he spread abroad great guile
in all Judaea.

14 Now our Lord Jesus knew all things that were coming cf. Jn XVIII 4
upon Him, and He said to His disciples, My brethren, behold
the devil has mingled for himself a cup of guile, that I should
be crucified. 15 Now therefore let all My mysteries sink into cf. Lc IX 44*
your ears[g]. I have not left you lacking any of[h] all the p. ⲡⲍ
mysteries of My kingdom. I have given unto you all cf. Mt
authority in heaven and on earth. I have set the power of XIII 11*; XXVIII 18*;
serpents[i] and scorpions[j] under your authority. 16 Now there- Lc X 19*

[a] See note [b] Or *from insulting Pilate* [c] Or *otherwise*
[d] Or *because of Jesus. From that day this saying* [e] Lit. *the 'anaphora'*
[f] The MS has *Him* But see note [g] Lit. *set all My mysteries under your ears* [h] Lit. *in* [i] Lit. *the serpents* [j] Lit. *the scorpions*

cf. Lc xiii 31; Jn xiv 31 fore arise, let us go hence; for Herod seeketh Me to
kill Me.
[17]And our Lord Jesus came down from the mount with His
disciples. [18]And behold the devil met them: and he took the
form of a fisherman; many demons following him, carrying
many nets and drag-nets and hooks[a], and casting nets and
hooks on the mount. [19]Now the apostles when they saw
them casting nets hither and thither, and hooks, wondered
exceedingly. [20]And they said to Jesus, Our Lord, what man-
ner of one is this, doing these things in this desert? [21]Jesus
p. ⌜ⲛⲏ⌝ said to them, Peter, this is he of whom I spake to thee,
cf. Lc xxii 31, 32 *saying*, Behold Satan asked for you, that he might sift you
as wheat: but I made supplication for thee, that[b] thy faith
fail not. [22]John said to Him, What do these find in this
desert? [23]Jesus said to him, My beloved John, he who
seeketh him, behold he hath caught him already[c]. This is
cf. 2 Ti ii 26 the fisherman that catcheth every bad fish. This is the
snarer of every foul beast and of every one that is bad.
[24]Philip said to Him, My Lord, who shall be taken by the
hook of this one or by his nets? [25]Jesus said to him, Many
shall be taken by the hook of this one and by his nets[b].
[26]Andrew said to him, My Lord, what is the use of this
p. ⲛ⌜ⲑ⌝ one making men to transgress? [27]Jesus said to him, Did
I not come to take those who are Mine for My kingdom?
This one also seeketh those who are his for his punish-

FRAGMENT V.

Cod. Borg. CCLXVII [1]Ⲡⲉⲧⲉϣϣⲉ ⲟⲩⲛ̄ ⲡⲉ ⲉ̀ⲟⲩⲉⲛϩ̀ ⲛ̀ϩⲱⲃ ⲉⲃⲟⲗ ϫⲉ ⲉⲧⲃⲉ ⲁϣ
ⲛⲁïⲧïⲁ̀ ⲉⲩⲣ̄ϣⲁ ⲙ̄ⲡⲉⲥ⳨ⲟⲥ ⲙ̄ⲡⲟⲟⲩ : ׀׀׀ — [2]Ⲕⲁï ⲅⲁⲣ ⲛ̄ⲧⲁ
ⲛ̄ïⲟⲩⲇⲁï ϫïϭⲟⲗ ⲉ̄ⲧⲁⲛⲁⲥⲧⲁⲥïⲥ ⲉⲩϫⲱ ⲙ̄ⲙⲟⲥ ϫⲉ ⲙ̄ⲡⲉϥⲧⲱⲟⲩⲛ̄
ⲁⲗⲗⲁ ⲡⲉϥⲙⲁⲑⲏⲧⲏⲥ ⲡⲉⲛⲧⲁⲩⲉï ⲛ̀ⲧⲉⲩϣⲏ ⲁⲩϥïⲧϥ̄ ⲛ̀ϫïⲟⲩⲉ̀ ·

[a] Lit. *many nets and drag-nets and hooks being placed upon them* [b] See note [c] Or *that which he seeketh, behold he hath caught it already*

ment. [28]I suffered this great humiliation, and I came down
to the world, that I might pluck out this[a] talon of death,
even this one. [29]John said to Him, My Lord, command me
to go unto him, that I may know what he doth. [30]Jesus said
to him, Go, My beloved John, for I have sanctified thee from
the time that thou didst receive suck from thy mother[b]. [31]And
the holy John went to the devil. [32]He said to him, What dost
thou with[c] these nets? or what dost thou catch here? [33]The
devil said to him, I have heard concerning thee and thy
brethren, that ye *are* fishermen that catch fish. [34]I have
come hither to see your mastery to-day. Behold I and my
servants and my nets *are* here. Do thou also call thy p. 60
brethren; and let them come unto thee hither with their
nets, that we may cast them here. He who catcheth fish
here, he is the master. [35]It is not a wonder to catch fish in
the waters: the wonder is *in* this desert, to catch fish
therein. [36]John said to him, I have already heard of thy
mastery, before I came unto thee hither. But cast thy nets,
that we may see what thou wilt catch. [37]Straightway he
cast them. He caught every kind of foul fish which *was* in
the waters—some taken by their eyes, some caught by[d]
their entrails, others taken by their lips. [38]Jesus was afar
off with His apostles, beholding them. He said to them,
See how Satan catcheth the[d] sinners by their members.
[39]Jesus said to John, Say to him, Cast ...

FRAGMENT V[e].

[1]It is right therefore to manifest the matter, for what
cause the festival of the Cross is kept to-day. [2]For also the
Jews lied with regard to the resurrection, saying, He did cf. Mt
not rise, but His disciples came by night and took Him away xxviii 13*

[a] Or *the* [b] Lit. *thou wert in thy mother's milk* [c] Lit. *to*
[d] See note [e] I have omitted the beginning and end of this fragment.
See Introduction

p. ⲙⲃ 3 ⲉⲧⲟⲩⲱϣ ⲉ̀ϩⲟⲩⲛ | ⲙ̀ⲡⲉϥⲥ̄ⲣ̄ⲟ̄ⲥ ⲉⲧⲟⲩⲁ̄ⲁ̄ⲃ ⲛ̄ⲧⲙⲛⲧⲉ· ϫⲉ ⲛⲛⲉϥⲟⲩⲱ̄ⲛ̄ϩ̄
ⲉ̄ⲃⲟⲗ ⲉⲛⲧⲏⲣϥ̄ ⲕⲁⲧⲁ ⲛⲉⲛⲧⲁⲩϫⲟⲟⲩ ⲛ̀ϭⲓ ⲓ̈ⲱⲥⲏⲡⲡⲟⲥ· ⲙⲛ̄ ⲓ̈ⲉⲣⲏⲛ-
ⲛⲁⲓ̈ⲟⲥ· ⲛⲁⲛⲟ ϩⲉⲃⲣⲉⲟⲥ ϩ̄ⲛ̄ ⲛⲉⲩⲁⲣⲭⲏⲟ̀ⲗⲟⲅⲓ̈ⲁ̄:।।।— 4 Ⲉⲛⲉⲣⲉ
ⲟⲩⲛⲟϭ ⲙ̄ⲡⲟⲛⲏⲣⲓ̈ⲁ̀ ⲡⲉϫⲁⲩ ϩⲙ̄ ⲡ̄ϩⲏⲧ ⲛ̄ⲛ̄ⲓ̈ⲟⲩⲇⲁⲓ̈ ⲛ̄ⲧⲁⲩⲥ̄ⲣ̄ⲟ̄ⲟⲩ
ⲙ̄ⲡϫⲟⲉⲓ̈ⲥ· ⲉ̀ϩⲟⲩⲛ ⲉⲛⲕⲉϣⲉ ⲙ̀ⲡⲉⲥ̄ⲣ̄ⲟ̄ⲥ ⲉⲧⲟⲩⲱϣ ⲉ̀ϩⲟⲩⲛ ⲉ̀ϩⲟⲩⲛϥ:— 5 Ⲛ̄ⲛ̄ⲥⲁ
ⲉⲧⲣⲉ ⲡ̄ϫⲟⲉⲓ̈ⲥ̄ ⲇⲉ ⲧⲱⲟⲩⲛ̄· ⲛⲉⲣⲉ ⲡ̀ⲉⲥ̄ⲣ̄ⲟ̄ⲥ[a] ⲧⲟⲕⲥ̄ ϩⲙ̀ ⲡ̀ⲙⲁ
ⲛ̄ⲧⲁⲩⲟⲃⲧϥ ⲛ̄ϩⲏⲧϥ̄:।।।— | 6 Ⲛ̄ⲧⲉⲣⲉ ⲡⲉϣⲧⲟⲣⲧⲣ̄ ⲇⲉ ⲗⲟ ⲛⲟⲩⲕⲟⲩⲓ̈
ϫⲉ ⲛⲉⲣⲉ ⲙⲙⲁⲑⲏⲧⲏⲥ ϩⲏⲡ ⲡⲉ· ⲉⲧⲃⲉ ⲑⲟⲧⲉ ⲛ̄ⲛ̄ⲓ̈ⲟⲩⲇⲁⲓ̈:।।—
Ⲁϥⲧⲱⲟⲩⲛ̄ ⲛ̀ϭⲓ̈ ⲓ̈ⲱⲥⲏⲫ ⲡⲉⲃⲟⲗ ϩ̄ⲛ̄ ⲁ̄ⲣⲓ̈ⲙⲁⲑⲓ̈ⲁ̄· ⲁϥⲉⲓ̈ ϣⲁ
ⲛ̄ⲓ̈ⲕⲟⲇⲏⲙⲟⲥ ⲡⲉϫⲁϥ ⲛⲁϥ· 7 ϫⲉ Ⲉⲓ̈ⲥ ϩⲏⲛ̄ⲧⲉ ⲥⲉⲥⲩⲙⲃⲟⲩⲗⲉⲩⲉ̄ ⲛ̄ϭⲓ̈
ⲛⲁⲣⲭⲓ̈ⲉⲣⲉⲩⲥ̄· ⲙⲛ̄ ⲛ̄ⲥⲉⲉ̄ⲡⲉ ⸢ⲛ̄⸣ⲛ̄ⲓ̈ⲟⲩⲇⲁⲓ̈· ⸢ⲉⲩ⸣ϫⲱ ⲙ̄ⲙⲟⲥ ϫⲉ
ⲙⲁⲣⲉⲛⲣⲱⲕϩ̄ ⲙ̄ⲡϣⲉ ⲛ̄ⲧⲁⲩⲁϣⲧ̄ ⲓ̄ⲥ̄ ⲉ̄ⲣⲟϥ 8 Ⲁϥⲧⲱⲟⲩⲛ̄ ⲇⲉ ⲛ̄ϭⲓ̈

Cod. Borg. CCLVII ⲓ̈ⲱⲥⲏⲫ ⲙⲛ̄ ⲛ̄ⲓ̈ⲕⲟⲇⲏⲙⲟⲥ ⲛ̄ⲧⲉⲩϣⲏ· ⲁⲩⲃⲱⲕ ⲉ̀ϫ⸢ⲛ̄⸣ | ⲡ̄ⲙⲁ ⲙ̄ⲡⲉ-
p. ⲙⲅ ⲕⲣⲁⲛⲓ̈ⲟⲛ ⲙ̄ⲡⲉⲥⲛⲁⲩ· ⲡ̄ⲃⲟⲗ ⲛ̄ⲧ̄ⲡⲟⲗⲓ̈ⲥ ⲡ̄ⲙⲁ ⲛ̄ⲧⲁⲩⲥ̄ⲣ̄ⲟ̄ⲟⲩ ⲙ̄ⲙⲟϥ
ⲛ̄ϩⲏⲧϥ̄:।।।— 9 Ⲁⲩϩⲉⲓ̈ ⲙ̀ⲡⲉⲥ̄ⲣ̄ⲟ̄ⲥ ⲛ̄ⲓ̄ⲥ̄· ⲙⲛ̄ ⲛ̄ⲧⲓ̈ⲧⲗⲟⲥ ⲙ̄ⲡⲓ̈ⲗⲁⲧⲟⲥ
ⲉ̄ⲧⲟⲃⲧ̄ ⲉ̄ϩⲟⲩⲛ̄ ⲉ̄ⲣⲟϥ:— 10 Ⲁⲩϭⲓ̈ⲛⲉ ⲇⲉ ⲛ̄ⲛ̄ⲕⲉⲉⲓ̈ⲃⲧ̄ ⲛ̄ⲧⲁⲩⲟⲃⲧⲟⲩ
ⲉ̀ⲛⲉϥϭⲓ̈ϫ· ⲙⲛ̄ ⲛⲉϥⲟⲩⲉ̄ⲣⲏⲧⲉ ⲉⲩⲟϥⲧ̄ ⲉ̄ⲛⲉⲥ̄ⲣ̄ⲟ̄ⲥ:।।।।।— 11 Ⲁⲩⲱ̄ ⲧⲁⲓ̈
ⲧⲉ ⲑⲉ ⲛ̄ⲧⲁⲩϥⲓ̈ⲧⲟⲩ· ⲙⲛ̄ ⲛ̄ⲕⲟⲟⲩⲉ̄ ⲛⲛ̄ⲗⲓ̈ⲥⲧⲏⲥ· 12 Ⲙ̄ⲛⲟⲩϭⲛ̄ ⲑⲉ ⲛ̄ⲃⲱⲕ
ⲛ̄ⲙⲙⲁⲩ ⲉ̄ϩⲟⲩⲛ̄ ⲉⲧⲡⲟⲗⲓ̈ⲥ ⲉⲧⲃⲉ ⲑⲟⲧⲉ ⲛ̄ⲛ̄ⲓ̈ⲟⲩⲇⲁⲓ̈:।।— 13 Ⲡⲉϫⲉ
ⲓ̈ⲱⲥⲏⲫ ⲛ̀ⲛ̄ⲓ̈ⲕⲟⲩⲇⲏ|ⲙⲟⲥ· ϫⲉ ⲙⲁⲣⲉⲛϫⲓ̈ⲧⲟⲩ ⲉ̄ϩⲟⲩⲛ̄ ⲉⲛⲧⲁⲫⲟⲥ
ⲛ̄ⲧⲁⲩⲕⲁ ⲓ̄ⲥ̄ ⲛ̄ϩⲏⲧϥ̄· ⲕⲁⲓ̈ ⲅⲁⲣ ⲛⲱⲓ̈ ⲡⲉ· ⲁⲩⲱ̀ ⲙ̀ⲡⲓ̈ⲕⲁ ⲗⲁⲁⲩ
ⲛ̀ⲥⲱⲙⲁ ⲛ̀ϩⲏⲧϥ̄ ⲉ̀ⲛⲉϩ:···— 14 Ⲁⲩⲧⲱⲟⲩⲛ̄ ⲇⲉ ⲙ̀ⲙⲁⲩ ⲁⲩϫⲓ̈ⲧⲟⲩ
ⲉ̀ϩⲟⲩⲛ̄ ⲉⲛⲧⲁⲫⲟⲥ· ϫⲉ ⲛⲉϥϩⲏⲛ ⲉ̀ϩⲟⲩⲛ̄ ⲉⲡⲙⲁ ⲛ̄ⲧⲁⲩⲥ̄ⲣ̄ⲟ̄ⲟⲩ ⲛ̀ⲓ̄ⲥ̄
ⲛ̀ϩⲏⲧϥ̄:— 15 Ⲁⲩⲱ̀ ⲁⲩϫⲓ̈ⲧⲟⲩ ⲉ̀ϩⲟⲩⲛ̄ ⲉ̄ⲛⲉⲙϩⲁⲁⲩ· ⲁⲩⲥ̄ⲕⲉⲣⲕⲱⲣ
ⲛⲱⲛⲉ ⲉ̄ⲣⲱϥ ⲙⲡⲣⲟ ⲁⲩⲃⲱⲕ ⲛⲁⲩ:।।।।— 16 Ⲁⲩⲱ̀ ⲙ̀ⲡⲉ ⲗⲁⲁⲩ
ⲉⲓ̈ⲙⲉ ⲛⲟⲩⲛⲟϭ ⲛⲟⲩⲟⲉⲓϣ ⲉ̄ⲛⲉⲛⲧⲁⲩⲁ̄ⲁϥ:।।।।— 17 Ⲛⲉⲣⲉ ⲙⲙⲁ-
p. ⲙⲇ ⲑⲏ|ⲧⲏⲥ ⲇⲉ ⲙⲛ̄ ⲛ̄ⲙⲏⲛ̄ϣⲉ ⲛⲙ̄ⲡⲓ̈ⲥⲧⲟⲥ ⲃⲏⲕ ⲉⲃⲟⲗ ⲉⲛⲧⲁⲫⲟⲥ
ⲛ̄ϫⲓ̈ⲟⲩⲉ̀ ⲛ̄ⲓ̈ⲉⲩϣⲏ ⲉⲩϣ̄ⲗⲏⲗ· 18 ϩⲱⲥⲧⲉ ⲛ̄ⲧⲉ ⲟⲩⲙⲏⲛ̄ϣⲉ[b] ⲉⲩϯϩⲓ̈ⲥⲉ
ⲛⲁⲩ ϩⲓ̈ⲧ̄ⲛ̄ ⲛⲉⲡⲛ̄ⲁ̄ ⲛⲁⲕⲁⲑⲁⲣⲧⲟⲛ ⲉⲓ̈ ⲛ̀ⲥⲉϫⲱϩ ⲙ̄ⲙⲁⲧⲉ ⲉ̄ⲛⲱⲛⲉ

[a] punct. sup. ⲡ ut vid. [b] duo punct. sup. ϣ ut vid.

secretly: [3]wishing to hide His holy cross from[a] the midst,
that it might not be made manifest at all; according to those
things which Josephus and Irenaeus who *were* of *the* Hebrews
said in their Antiquities. [4]There was, they say, great malice
in the heart of the Jews who crucified the Lord against the
wood also of the cross, wishing to hide it. [5]Now after the
Lord was risen, the cross was fixed in the place in which it
was nailed. [6]And when the tumult was a little abated, for
the disciples were hidden for fear of the Jews; Joseph who cf. Jn xix 38, 39; xx
was from Arimathaea arose, and came unto Nicodemus, and 19
said unto him, [7]Behold the chief priests and the rest of the
Jews take counsel, saying, Let us burn the wood on which
Jesus was crucified. [8]And Joseph arose and Nicodemus by
night; and they both went to the Place of the skull without cf. Mt
the city, where they crucified Him. [9]And they took away xxvii 33; Mc xv 22;
the cross of Jesus and the title of Pilate which was nailed to Jn xix 18, 19; He xiii
it. [10]And they found the nails also which were nailed to 12
His hands and His feet nailed to the cross. [11]And thus they
took them away and those also of the robbers. [12]They could
not go[b] with them into the city for fear of the Jews. [13]Joseph
said to Nicodemus, Let us take them into the tomb in which
Jesus was laid: for also it is mine, and a body I never laid cf. Mt
in it. [14]And they arose thence and took them into the xxvii 60*; Lc xxiii
tomb, for it was nigh to the place where Jesus was crucified. 53; Jn xix 41, 42
[15]And they took them into the tomb; and they rolled the cf. Mt
stone to the door of the tomb, and they went their way. xxvii 60*; Mc xv 46*
[16]And no one knew for a great while that which they did.

[17]Now the disciples and the multitude of the faithful were
going forth to the tomb secretly by night, praying: [18]so that
many who were troubled by unclean spirits[c] came, that they

[a] Lit. *in* [b] Lit. *They found not the manner of going* [c] Lit. *the unclean spirits*

ⲉⲧϩⲓ̈ ⲣⲱϥ ⲙ̅ⲡ̅ⲧⲁⲫⲟⲥ 19ϣⲁⲩⲱϣ ⲉ̀ⲃⲟⲗ ⲛ̅ⲧⲉⲩⲛⲟⲩ · ϫⲉ Ⲱ ⲓ̅ⲥ̅ ⲡⲉⲕⲉ̀-
ⲡⲓ̈ⲧⲓⲙⲁ ⲛⲁⲛ ⲉⲕϩⲛ̅ ⲧ̅ⲥⲁⲣⲝ̅ · 20Ⲁⲩⲱ̅ ⲛⲧⲉⲣⲟⲩⲥ̅ⲧ̅ⲣⲟⲩ ⲙ̀ⲙⲟⲕ ⲟⲛ ·
ⲉⲓ̈ⲥ ⲛ̀ϣⲉ ⲛ̅ⲧⲁⲩⲁϣⲧ̅ⲕ̅ ⲉⲣⲟϥ · ⲙⲛ̅ ⲛ̅ⲧⲁⲫⲟⲥ ⲛ̅ⲧⲁⲩⲕⲁⲁⲕ ⲛ̅ϩⲏⲧϥ̅
ⲁⲩⲟⲩⲱ̅ⲛ̅ϩ̅ ⲉ̀ⲃⲟⲗ ⲉⲩϯϩⲓ̈|ⲥⲉ ⲛⲁⲛ : ⲁⲩⲱ̅ ⲉⲩⲛⲟⲩϫ ⲙ̅ⲙⲟⲛ ⲉ̀ⲃⲟⲗ ϩⲛ̅
ⲛ̅ⲥⲱⲙⲁ · ⲛ̅ⲧⲁⲩⲥⲩⲛⲭⲱⲣⲉⲓ̅ ⲙ̅ⲙⲟⲟⲩ ⲛⲁⲛ : — 21Ⲁⲩⲉⲓ̈ⲥ ϭⲉ ⲟⲩⲛ̅
ⲱ̅ ⲛ̅ⲗⲁⲟⲥ ⲙ̅ⲙⲁⲓ̈ⲛⲟⲩⲧⲉ ⲛ̅ⲧⲛ̅ⲥⲩⲙⲁⲛⲉ ⲛⲏⲧⲛ̅ ⲛ̅ⲧⲉⲓ̈ⲛⲟϭ ⲛ̅ϣⲡⲏⲣⲉ · ⲉ̅ⲁ̅
ⲛⲉⲛⲉⲓ̈ⲟ̅ⲧⲉ ⲛⲁⲣⲭⲁⲓ̈ⲟⲥ ϫⲟⲟⲥ ⲉ̀ⲛⲉⲩϣⲏⲣⲉ · ⲁ̅ ⲛⲉⲩϣⲏⲣⲉ ϩⲱⲟⲩ ϫⲟⲟⲥ
ⲉ̅ⲛⲉⲛⲧⲁⲩⲉⲓ̈ ⲙⲛ̅ⲛ̅ⲥⲱⲟⲩ · ϣ̈ⲁⲛⲧⲉ[a] ⲛ̅ϩⲱⲃ ⲕⲁⲧⲁⲛⲧⲁ ⲉ̅ⲣⲟⲛ ϩⲱⲱⲛ
ⲛ̅ⲥⲉϫⲟⲟϥ ⲉ̀ⲣⲟⲛ : — 22Ϩⲙ̅ ⲛⲉⲟⲩⲟ̀ⲉⲓ̈ϣ̈ ⲟⲩⲛ̀ ⲉ̀ⲧⲙ̅ⲙⲁⲩ ⲡⲉϫⲁⲩ · ⲡⲉ
p. ⲙⲉ ⲟⲩⲛ̅ ⲟⲩⲛⲟϭ ⲛ̀ⲓ̈ⲟⲩⲇⲁⲓ̈ ϩⲛ̅ ⲑⲓ̈ⲗⲏ̅ⲙ̅ · ⲉϥ|ⲟⲩⲟ̅ⲗⲉ ⲉ̅ⲙⲁⲧⲉ ϩⲛ̅ ⲟⲩⲛⲟϭ
ⲙ̅ⲙⲛ̅ⲧ̅ⲣ̅ⲙ̅ⲙⲁⲟ̅ · ⲉ̀ⲛⲉϥⲣⲁⲛ ⲡⲉ ⲕⲗⲉⲟ̅ⲡⲁ · 23ⲉ̀ⲛⲉ ⲟⲩⲛⲟⲧⲁⲕⲣⲟⲥ ⲡⲉ
ⲙ̀ⲡⲉϥⲙⲟⲟ̅ϣⲉ ⲛⲟⲩⲛⲟϭ ⲛⲟⲩⲟ̀ⲉⲓ̈ϣ̈ · 24ⲟⲩⲇⲉ ⲙⲉϥⲉϣⲧⲁⲗⲉ ⲉ̀ⲧⲃ̅ⲛ̅ⲏ ·
ⲁⲗⲗⲁ ⲡⲉ ϣⲁⲩⲧⲁⲗⲟϥ ⲉⲩⲗⲏⲕⲧⲓⲕⲏ · ⲛ̀ⲥⲉϫⲓ̈ⲧϥ̀ ⲛ̀ⲥⲉϫⲟⲕⲙⲉϥ : · · · · —
25Ⲡⲉⲧⲙ̅ⲙⲁⲩ ⲇⲉ ⲟⲩⲛ̅ ⲉ̀ⲧⲉ ⲕⲗⲉⲱ̀ⲡⲁ ⲡⲉ · ⲧⲁⲭⲁ ⲙ̀ⲡⲉϥⲃⲱⲕ ϩⲙ̅
ⲛ̀ϣⲟϫⲛⲉ ⲛ̅ⲙ̅ⲡⲁⲣⲁⲛⲟⲙⲟⲥ ⲛ̅ⲓ̈ⲟⲩⲇⲁⲓ̈ · ⲙ̅ⲛ̀ⲛⲁⲩ ⲛ̀ⲧⲁⲩⲥ̅ⲧ̅ⲣⲟⲩ ⲙ̀ⲡ-
ϫⲟⲉⲓ̈ⲥ · 26ⲁⲗⲗⲁ ⲁϥⲣ̅ ⲛ̅ⲕⲉϩⲱⲛ ⲉ̅ⲧⲟⲟ̅ⲧⲟⲩ ⲛ̅ⲛⲉϥⲥⲩⲅⲅⲉ|ⲛⲏⲥ · ⲙⲛ̅
ⲛⲉϥϩ̅ⲙ̅ϩⲁⲗ · ϫⲉ ⲙ̅ⲡⲣ̅ⲥⲩⲛⲉⲩⲇⲟⲕⲉⲓ̈ ⲙ̅ⲛ̅ ⲛ̅ⲓ̈ⲟⲩⲇⲁⲓ̈ ⲉⲧⲛⲁϩⲱⲧ̅ⲃ̅
ⲙ̅ⲡⲉⲓ̈ⲣⲱⲙⲉ ⲛ̅ⲇⲓ̈ⲕⲁⲓ̈ⲟⲥ · ϫⲉ ⲉⲩⲛⲁϩⲱⲧ̅ⲃ̅ ⲙ̅ⲙⲟϥ ⲉⲧⲃⲉ ⲟⲩⲕⲱϩ : ı ı —
27Ⲕⲁⲓ̈ ⲅⲁⲣ ⲛ̅ⲧⲟϥ ⲡⲉ ⲡϣⲏⲣⲉ̀ ⲙⲙⲁⲣⲓ̈ⲁ̅ · ⲧ̅ϣⲉⲉ̅ⲣⲉ ⲛ̅ⲕ̅ⲗⲉⲱ̅ⲡⲁ ·
ⲛ̅ⲥⲟⲛ ⲙ̅ⲡⲁⲉⲓ̈ⲱⲧ : · — Ⲁⲩⲱ̅ ⲕⲁⲧⲁ ⲛⲉⲡⲣⲟⲫⲏⲧⲓ̈ⲁ̀ ⲛ̀ⲧⲁ ⲛⲉⲡⲣⲟ-
ⲫⲏⲧⲏⲥ ϫⲟⲟⲩ · ⲛ̅ⲧⲟϥ ⲡⲉ ⲡϣⲏⲣⲉ ⲙ̅ⲡ̅ⲛⲟⲩⲧⲉ : — 28Ⲗⲟⲓ̈ⲡⲟⲛ
ⲁϥϣⲱⲡⲉ ⲛ̅ϭⲓ̈ ϩ̅ⲣⲟⲩⲫⲟⲥ ⲡ̅ϣⲏⲣⲉ ⲛ̅ⲕ̅ⲗⲉⲱ̅ⲡⲁ · ⲉⲩⲙⲟⲛⲟⲅⲉⲛⲏⲥ ⲛⲁϥ
p. ⲙϛ ⲡⲉ : ı ı ı — | 29Ⲁϥϫⲟⲟⲥ ⲇⲉ ⲛ̅ⲛⲉϥϩ̅ⲙ̅ϩⲁⲗ[b] ϫⲉ ⲃⲱⲕ ϫⲓ̈ ⲛⲟⲩⲗⲁⲍⲟⲥ
ϣⲓ̈ⲕⲉ ⲙ̅ⲡⲙ̅ϩⲁⲁⲩ[c] ⲙ̅ⲡⲁϣⲏⲣⲉ · ϩ̅ⲙ̅ ⲡ̅ⲕⲱⲧⲉ ⲙ̅ⲡ̅ⲙϩⲁⲁⲩ[d] ⲙ̅ⲡϣⲏⲣⲉ
ⲙ̅ⲡ̅ⲛⲟⲩⲧⲉ · ⲁⲩⲱ̀ ⲉⲓ̈ϣⲁⲛⲙⲟⲩ ϩⲱⲱⲧ ⲟⲛ ⲟⲩⲁϩⲧ̅ ⲛ̅ϩⲏⲧϥ̅ : ı ı ı ı —
30Ⲙⲛ̅ⲛ̅ⲥⲁ ϩⲟⲟⲩ ⲇⲉ ⲥ̅ⲛⲁⲩ ⲁϥⲙⲟⲩ ⲛ̅ϭⲓ̈ ϩ̅ⲣⲟⲩⲫⲟⲥ ⲡ̅ϣⲏⲣⲉ ⲛ̅ⲕ̅ⲗⲉ-
ⲱ̀ⲡⲁ · 31ⲉ̀ⲛⲉ ⲡⲥⲁⲃⲃⲁⲧⲟⲛ ⲇⲉ ⲡⲉ ⲡⲉϩⲟⲟⲩ ⲉ̀ⲧⲙ̅ⲙⲁⲩ · ⲁⲩⲱ̀
ⲙ̀ⲡⲟⲩⲉϣϥⲓ̈ⲧϥ̀ ⲉ̀ⲃⲟⲗ ⲉ̅ⲧⲟⲙⲥ̅ϥ̅ : ı ı — 32Ϩⲧⲟⲟⲩⲉ̀ ⲇⲉ ⲙ̅ⲡⲟⲩⲁ̅

[a] duo punct. sup. ϣ ut vid. [b] lin. sup. ⲙ ut vid. [c] lin. sup. ⲙ sec. ut vid. [d] man. post. ut vid. ⲙ̅ⲡⲉⲙϩⲁⲁⲩ

might but touch the stone that *was* at the door of the tomb.
19 And they would cry out straightway, *saying*, O Jesus, Thou
didst rebuke us when Thou wert in the flesh. 20 And also
when Thou wast crucified, behold the wood on which Thou
wast crucified, and the tomb wherein Thou wast laid, were
made manifest; troubling us and casting us out of the bodies,
which were yielded to us. 21 Come then, O people that love
God, let us declare to you this great wonder, which our
fathers of old told their sons, and their sons also told those
who came after them; until the matter reached to us also,
and they told it us. 22 At that time then, they say, there was
a great Jew in Jerusalem, abounding much in great wealth,
whose name was[a] Cleopas. 23 He was diseased in the feet,
and had not walked for a great while; 24 neither could he
ride on *an* animal, but he used to be placed on a litter and
taken to be bathed. 25 Now that *man*, even Cleopas, did not
indeed[b] go in the counsel of the lawless Jews, at the time[c] cf. Lc xxiii 51
that they crucified the Lord; 26 but he gave commandment
also to his kinsmen and to his servants, *saying*, Consent not cf. Mt xxvii 18, 19
with the Jews who will kill this righteous Man, for they will
kill Him for jealousy. 27 For also He is the Son of Mary,
the daughter of Cleopas, the brother of my father: and according
to the prophecies which the prophets spake, He is
the Son of God. 28 Moreover Rufus the son of Cleopas was
sick, who was[a] his only[d] *son*. 29 And he said to his servants,
Go, take a pick, and hew the tomb of my son near the tomb
of the Son of God: and when I also die, place me in it. cf. 1 Ki xiii 31*
30 Now after two days Rufus the son of Cleopas died. 31 Now
it was the sabbath *on* that day, and they could not take him cf. Jn v 9
out to bury him. 32 But in the morning on the first day[e] of

[a] Lit. *is* [b] See note [c] Lit. *hour* [d] Lit. *only begotten* [e] Lit. *the one*

ⲙ̇ⲡ̄ⲥⲁⲃⲃⲁⲧⲟⲛ ⲁⲩ̇ⲥⲡⲟⲩⲇⲁⲍⲉ ⲉ̇ϥⲓ̈ⲧϥ̇ ⲉ̇ⲃⲟⲗ ϫⲉ ⲛ̇ⲛⲉϥ|ⲕ̄ⲛⲟⲥ : ıııı —
33 Ⲁⲩⲧⲁⲗⲟϥ ⲇⲉ ⲙⲛ̄ ⲡ̄ⲕⲉⲕⲗⲉⲱ̄ⲡⲁ ⲡⲉϥⲉⲓ̈ⲱⲧ ⲁⲩⲡⲱⲧ ⲛ̄ⲙ̄ⲙⲁϥ : ııı —
34 Ⲛ̇ⲧⲉⲣⲟⲩⲛⲱϩ ⲇⲉ ⲉ̇ⲡⲙ̄ϩⲁⲁⲩ ⲁⲩⲟⲩⲁϩϥ̄ ⲉ̇ⲡⲉⲥⲏⲧ ϩⲓ̈ⲧⲟⲩⲱϥ ⲙ̇ⲡ̄-
ⲧⲁⲫⲟⲥ ⲛ̇ⲓ̄ⲥ̄ · ϫⲉ ϣⲁⲛⲧⲟⲩⲱⲛ ⲙ̇ⲡ̄ⲣⲟ ⲙ̇ⲡⲙ̇ϩⲁⲁⲩ : ıııı — 35 Ⲁⲩⲱ̇
ⲁⲩⲑ̄ⲙ̄ⲥⲟ ⲙ̇ⲡⲉϥⲉⲓ̈ⲱⲧ ϩⲓ̈ⲧⲟⲩⲱϥ · ⲉ̇ⲣⲉ ⲡⲉϥⲥⲟⲓ̈ ⲧⲏⲕ ⲉ̇ⲡⲱⲛⲉ · ⲉⲧϩⲓ̈ⲣⲙ̇
ⲛ̇ⲣⲟ ⲙ̇ⲡ̄ⲧⲁⲫⲟⲥ ⲡ̄ⲓ̄ⲥ̄ : ıı — 36 Ⲁⲩⲱ̇ ⲡⲉϥⲣⲓ̄ⲙⲉ ⲉϥϫⲱ ⲙⲙⲟⲥ · ϫⲉ
Cod. Borg. Ϩⲁⲙⲟⲓ̈ ⲱ̇ ⲡⲁϣ̈ⲏⲣⲉ ⲙ̄ⲙⲉⲣⲓ̈ⲧ · ⲉ̇ⲛⲉ ⲡⲉ | ⌜. . . . . ⲉ . . . .⌝ⲱ
CCLXVII
p. ⲙⲍ ⌜. . . . . .⌝ϫⲙ̄ⲡ⌜. . . .⌝ 37 ⲡⲉⲓ̈⌜ⲛⲁⲃ⌝ⲱⲕ ϣⲁⲣⲟϥ ⲡⲉ ⲡ̄ⲧⲁⲡⲁⲣⲁⲕⲁⲗⲉⲓ̈
ⲙ̄ⲙⲟϥ · ⲛ̄ϥⲉⲓ̈ ⲛ̄ϥⲧⲟⲩⲛⲟⲥⲕ̄ :[a] 38 ⲕⲁⲓ̈ ⲅⲁⲣ ⲁϥⲕ̄ⲧⲉ ⲟⲩⲙⲏⲛ̄ϣⲉ ⲛ̄ⲧⲁⲩ-
ⲙⲟⲩ : ıı — 39 Ⲁϥⲧⲟⲩⲛⲉⲥ ⲟⲩⲁ̄ ϫⲉ ⲗⲁⲍⲁⲣⲟⲥ ⲡ̄ⲧⲁϥⲟⲩⲱ̄ ⲉϥⲣ̄
ⲕⲉϥ̄ⲧⲟⲟⲩ ⲛ̄ϩⲟⲟⲩ ⲉϥϩ̄ⲙ̄ ⲡ̄ⲧⲁⲫⲟⲥ · ⲁⲩⲱ̇ ⲉⲓ̈ⲥ ϩⲏⲛ̇ⲧⲉ ϥ̄ϩⲙ ⲡⲥⲱⲙⲁ
ⲙ̇ⲡⲟⲟⲩ : ı — 40 ⌜Ⲁⲩ⌝ⲱ̄ ⲁϥⲧⲟⲩ⌜ⲛ⌝ⲉⲥ ⲧϣⲉⲉ̇ⲣⲉ⌜. .⌝ⲁⲛⲛⲁ · ⲧ̇⌜ϣⲉⲉⲣ⌝ⲉ
ⲛ̄ⲓ̈ⲁ̄ⲉⲓ̈⌜ⲣⲟⲥ ⲡⲁⲣⲭⲏⲥ⌝ⲩ⌜ⲛⲁⲅⲱⲅⲟⲥ . . . .
. . . .⌝| 41 ⲡⲉ ⲡⲁⲓ̈ · ⲉ̇ⲣⲉ ⲓ̄ⲥ̄ ϣⲟⲡⲕ ⲉ̇ⲣⲟϥ : — 42 Ⲉⲧⲉⲓ̈
ⲇⲉ ⲉϥϫⲱ ⲛ̇ⲛⲁⲓ̈ · ⲁⲩⲛ̇ⲟϭ ⲛ̄ⲥϯⲛⲟⲩⲃⲉ ϣⲱϣ ⲉ̄ⲃⲟⲗ ϩⲙ̄ ⲡ̄ⲧⲁⲫⲟⲥ
ⲛ̇ⲓ̄ⲥ̄ : ı — 43 Ⲁϥⲛⲁⲩ ϩⲛ̄ ⲡⲉϥⲃⲁⲗ ⲉⲩⲧⲩⲡⲟⲥ ⲛ̇ⲥ̄⳨ⲟ̄ⲥ̄ · ⲉ̇ⲁϥⲉⲓ̄ ⲉ̇ⲃⲟⲗ
ϩⲙ̄ ⲡ̄ⲧⲁⲫⲟⲥ ⲛ̇ⲓ̄ⲥ̄ · 44 ⲁϥⲟⲩⲱϩ ⲉϩⲣⲁⲓ̈ ⲉϫⲙ̄ ⲡⲉⲧⲙⲟⲟⲩⲧ̄ ⲛ̄ⲧⲉⲩⲛⲟⲩ
ⲁϥⲧⲱⲟⲩⲛ̄ ⲁϥϩⲙⲟⲟⲥ : — 45 Ⲛ̄ⲧⲉⲣⲉ ⲕ̄ⲗⲉⲱⲡⲁ ⲇⲉ ⲛⲁⲩ ⲉ̇ⲡⲉϥϣⲏⲣⲉ
ⲉϥϩ̄ⲙⲟⲟⲥ · ⲁϥⲃⲟϭϥ̄ ⲉϩⲣⲁⲓ̈ ⲛ̇ⲧⲉⲩⲛⲟⲩ · ⲁϥⲁ̄ϩⲉⲣⲁⲧϥ̇ · ⲉϣϫⲉ ⲙ̇ⲡⲉ
ⲡⲉϥⲟⲩⲉ̇ⲣⲏⲧⲉ ϣⲱⲡⲉ ⲉⲛ⌜ⲧⲏ⌝ⲣ̄ϥ̄ : ııı —

[a] punct. inf. incert.

the week, they gave diligence to take him out, that he might
not stink[a]. 33 And they took him up and Cleopas his father,
and they went with him. 34 And when they came to the
tomb, they set him down by the tomb of Jesus, until they
opened the door of the tomb. 35 And they placed his father
by him, his back being stayed up by the stone, which *was* at
the door of the tomb of Jesus. 36 And he was weeping, saying,
Would, O my beloved son, that . . . 37 I would have gone unto
Him and besought Him to come and raise thee. 38 For also
He brought back many that were dead. 39 He raised one,
even Lazarus, who had been four days already in the tomb, cf. Jn xi 17
and behold he is in the body to-day. 40 And He raised the . . .
daughter of Jairus the ruler of the synagogue[b] . . . . cf. Mc v 22*, 23*
41 is this. Jesus will receive thee. 42 Now as he was yet
saying these things, a great *and* sweet savour was given forth
from the tomb of Jesus. 43 He saw with his eyes a figure of
the cross come forth from the tomb of Jesus. 44 It rested
upon him that was dead; and straightway he arose and sat.
45 Now when Cleopas saw his son sitting, he leaped up cf. Ac iii 8
straightway and stood, as though his feet were not at all
diseased.

[a] Or *become corrupt* [b] See note

NOTES ON SAHIDIC FRAGMENTS OF THE LIFE OF THE VIRGIN.

Fragment I.

1. *a strange land*] This fragment is part of a sermon delivered on the festival of the Nativity of the Virgin (*v.* 62). The preacher is combating heretical teaching which affirmed that our Lord was born in a strange land. He maintains that the Virgin was of Davidic descent (*v.* 16 ff), and 'bare her Son in the land of her fathers' (*v.* 15).

2. *our fathers the apostles*] The sermon claims to have been delivered by a follower of the apostles. For a similar claim see Rossi, *Pap. Cop.* vol. II fasc. IV p. 87, 'Even as our fathers the apostles taught us.' Nicephorus Callistus (II 3 ed. Paris. 1630 tom. I p. 134) says that Evodius, the successor of the holy apostles, in his writings and especially in a letter called 'Light,' gave chronological details as to (1) the ministry of Christ, (2) the early history of the Acts, (3) the life of the Virgin. He related that Mary was three years old when brought to the temple, that she spent eleven years in the Holy of holies, was delivered to Joseph to keep, and was four months in his house before the Annunciation. The passage is as follows: ὁ δὲ πολὺς τὰ θεῖα Εὐώδιος, τῶν ἱερῶν δ' ἀποστόλων καὶ οὗτος διάδοχος, ἐν τοῖς αὐτοῦ συγγράμμασι, μάλιστα δὲ ἐν τῇ ἐπιστολῇ ἣν Φῶς ἐπέγραψε, καὶ ταῦτα προστίθησιν· Ὁ Χριστὸς, λέγων, ἰδίαις χερσὶ τὸν Πέτρον μόνον ἐβάπτισε· Πέτρος δὲ Ἀνδρέαν καὶ τοὺς Ζεβεδαίου υἱούς· Ἀνδρέας δὲ καὶ οἱ τοῦ Ζεβεδαίου τοὺς λοιποὺς ἀποστόλων. Τοὺς δὲ ἑβδομήκοντα Πέτρος καὶ Ἰωάννης ὁ θεολόγος βαπτίζουσι· προσεπιλέγων καὶ ταῦτα· Ἀπὸ τοῦ βαπτίσματος ἕως τοῦ πάθους Χριστοῦ ἔτη διελθεῖν τρία· ἀπὸ δὲ τοῦ πάθους καὶ τῆς ἀναστάσεως καὶ ἀναλήψεως εἰς οὐρανοὺς μέχρι τῆς λιθοβολίας Στεφάνου ἔτη εἶναι ἑπτά· ἀπὸ δὲ τῆς μαρτυρίας Στεφάνου μέχρι τοῦ φανέντος τῷ Παύλῳ φωτὸς μῆνες ἕξ· ἀπὸ τοῦ φανέντος τῷ Παύλῳ φωτὸς μέχρι τῆς τελειώσεως τῆς ἁγίας θεοτόκου ἔτη γʹ. Τὰ δὲ πάντα ἀπὸ τῆς γεννήσεως τοῦ Χριστοῦ ἄχρι τῆς μεταστάσεως τῆς ἁγίας θεοτόκου ἔτη λέγει εἶναι μδʹ. Τὸν δὲ ὅλον τῆς ζωῆς αὐτῆς χρόνον ἔτη εἶναι νθʹ.

Τριετὴς γὰρ γενομένη τῷ ἱερῷ προσήχθη, καὶ ἐν τοῖς ἁγίοις τῶν ἁγίων ἔτη ἕνδεκα διεβίβασε, καὶ εὐθὺς διὰ χειρὸς τῶν ἱερέων τῷ Ἰωσὴφ πρὸς φυλακὴν παρεδόθη. Τέσσαρας δὲ μῆνας ἐν τῇ οἰκίᾳ τοῦ Ἰωσὴφ διετέλεσε· καὶ ὑπὸ τοῦ ἀρχαγγέλου εὐαγγελίζεται Γαβριήλ· καὶ τίκτει τὸ φῶς τοῦ κόσμου, χρόνων ὑπάρχουσα ιε´, τῇ εἰκοστῇ πέμπτῃ τοῦ δεκεμβρίου μηνός. Εἶτα ἕτερα λγ´ ἔτη ζῇ· ἃ καὶ ὁ προαιώνιος λόγος καὶ υἱὸς αὐτῆς ἐπὶ τῆς γῆς διεβίβασε· καὶ μετὰ τὴν σταύρωσιν ἐν τῇ τοῦ Ἰωάννου οἰκίᾳ ἔτη διετέλεσεν ια´· ὡς ὁμοῦ τὰ ἔτη ταύτης ν´ καὶ θ´ συνάγεσθαι (Migne, *P. G.* CXLV 757). From this we see that in one of the works ascribed to Evodius there were details of the early life of the Virgin. There are two sermons extant in Coptic, one describing her Assumption (see p. 44 ff), and another delivered on the festival of the Resurrection, published from a papyrus now at Turin by Prof. Rossi. This latter, as far as it is preserved to us, does not describe the early life of the Virgin, but only states that she was fifteen years old when she bore Christ (Rossi, *Pap. Cop.* vol. II fasc. IV p. 7 ff). May not this fragment be part of one of the lost writings ascribed to Evodius?

4. The quotation may be based on Job XLII 5.

6. *the godless Jews*] The abuse of the Jews is a favourite theme in Coptic apocryphal sermons. In Evodius' sermon on the Assumption he abuses the Jews before he enters on his main topic (see p. 47 ff, c. IV 2—23). In his sermon given on the day of the Resurrection he says, 'The time then will fail me telling of thy reproach, O ignorant nation. Let us turn now to the dispensation (ⲟⲓⲕⲟⲛⲟⲙⲓⲁ) of the Son of God' (Rossi, *Pap. Cop.* vol. II fasc. IV p. 14).

with their tongue...] Similar denunciations of heretics are not uncommon in Coptic sermons. See e.g. Ephraim, *on Transfig.* p. ⲣⲙⲇ, *Proc. Soc. Bib. Arch.* 1887, vol. IX p. 323.

7. *to burn her holy body*] An allusion to the day of her burial. See pp. 62, 81, 117.

8. *a power*] δύναμις. In one of the most remarkable speeches in the Pistis Sophia the Virgin speaks of 'the power (ⲧϭⲟⲙ) which sojourned with me, that came forth from Barbelo, and became to Thee (i.e. Christ) *a* hylic body' (*PS.* p. 121; cf. also p. 13). See p. 109 *v.* 20 f.

or say as...that] The whole of the first page of this MS is indistinct, and here the vellum is badly torn. I am unable to emend the text. The opposition to a bodily assumption is remarkable. In the Greek, the two Latin, the three Syriac and the Arabic accounts of the Assumption, the Virgin's body is taken up.

10. There is an allusion in a Sahidic fragment of a sermon among the Turin papyri to a definite sect, that held Joseph to be the father of Christ. 'Let the evil heretical wolves, that are hidden from us (?), and that hear us to-day, be ashamed. Let the abominable service of the Platonites (ⲛⲉⲡⲗⲁⲧⲱⲛⲓⲧⲏ⸢ⲥ⸣) be destroyed *and go* into the abyss, who say with their mouth that ought to be closed and their tongue that

ought...she had carnal intercourse (reading ⲁⲥ⸢ⲕ⸣ⲟ⸢ⲓⲛⲱ⸣ⲛⲉⲓ ⲉⲩⲥⲩⲛⲟⲩⲥⲓⲁ) with Joseph' (Rossi, *Pap. Cop.* vol. II fasc. IV p. 57).

13. *the works of...the apostles*] Here an appeal is made to writings of the apostles; in verses 2—4 the appeal is to their actual words. In the same manner Evodius in his sermon given on the day of the Resurrection sometimes claims to be an eyewitness: 'We also were three and a half years following Him with the apostles' (Rossi, *Pap. Cop.* vol. II fasc. IV p. 15): 'For it is not a stranger that hath declared to me these things, but I was there myself' (p. 8 f); whilst in another part of the same sermon he appeals to a written Gospel 'The Evangelist saith, Pilate commanded the Jews; and they went with the soldiers, and sealed the tomb as they wished' (p. 34).

14. Joakim and Anna (*v.* 18) are said to be both of the royal tribe of Judah. Stress is probably laid on the fact here, because the preacher is combating false teaching (see *v.* 1). In Pseudo-Matthew (I 1, 2) a similar statement is made. In De Nat. Mar. Joakim is of Nazareth, Anna only of Judah (I 1). The Syriac *History of the Virgin* makes Joakim 'the seed of Nathan the son of David, of the tribe of Judah,' but does not give the descent of Anna (Wright, *Eng. trans.* p. 19).

15. *The matter is manifest*] This expression introduces a comment of the preacher's. Cf. the use of a similar expression 'The matter is manifest through this word' in Athanasius' sermon on the Virgin (Rossi, *Pap. Cop.* vol. II fasc. I p. 33).

17. As for *such a man*] Lit. 'this man of this kind.' The phrase is used in 2 Cor. XII 3 to translate ὁ τοιοῦτος ἄνθρωπος. It is a common form of expression in legal documents. Cf. Ciasca, *I Papiri Copti del Museo Borgiano* ⲡⲉⲓⲏⲓ ⲟⲩⲛ ⲛⲧⲉⲓⲙⲉⲓⲛⲉ ϯⲇⲓⲟⲣⲣⲓⲍⲉ ⲙⲙⲟϥ ⲉϩⲟⲩⲛ ⲉⲧϩⲉⲛⲉⲉⲧⲉ ⲉⲧⲟⲩⲁⲁⲃ 'The afore-mentioned house therefore I assign to the holy monastery' (*Testo Copto* I p. ⲋ l. 2; cf. also l. 8 and p. ⲍ l. 16).

The identification of Joakim and Cleopas is noteworthy. It evidently arises from Jn XIX 25, where the Sahidic reads, 'His mother and His mother's sister, Mary the daughter of Clopas (ⲧϣⲉⲉⲣⲉ ⲛⲕⲗⲱⲡⲁ) and Mary Magdalene.' Mary is taken to be the sister of the Virgin, and Clopas is changed to Cleopas. See p. 183, where we find the same identification, and we read also of another Cleopas, who was cousin to the Virgin. See also Ludolf, *Ad Hist. Aeth. Com.* (Francov. 1691) p. 397 not. (a) 'Maritus ejus fuit...*Joachimus Calliops*, vel *Calliopaeus* vel *Cleophas* secundum Aethiopes *in vita B. Mariae Virginis.*' According to the mediaeval tradition, 'Anna tribus nupsit, Joachim, Cleophae, Salomaeque.' Evodius in his sermon on the Assumption (V 5) discusses in a similar manner the name of Peter (see p. 50).

20. Joakim is said to be πλούσιος σφόδρα in the Protevangelium (I 1). The tradition of his wealth probably arose from the story

which makes Joachim, the husband of Susanna, πλούσιος σφόδρα (Sus I 4).

22. In De Nat. Mar. (II 1) and in one MS (B) of Ps-Mt (II 1) the feast is said to be that of the dedication. Here the passover is strangely identified with the feast of tabernacles. The mistake may have its origin in a misunderstanding of Jn VI 4. For a full discussion of the difficulty in that verse see Westcott and Hort, *The New Testament in the Original Greek*, *Appendix* p. 77 ff.

32. The construction of this sentence is like that of Ga IV 27 **naϣe nϣhpe ntete mntc ϩai nϩoto tete ountac nϩai** 'More are the children of her that hath no husband than of her that hath the husband.' Cf. also *PS.* p. 26 l. 23 f. The form **nwn = noun**, and is made on the analogy of **nwn**. For the use of **para** cf. *PS.* p. 4 l. 14; p. 11 l. 8; p. 231 l. 15. The thought expressed in the verse may be compared with that of Lc XIII 2: 'Think ye that these Galilaeans sinned above all the Galilaeans (**ntaurnobe para ngalilaioc throu**), because they have suffered these things?'

35. *distress*] Or 'shame.' The root of this word is **ouwlc**. Thus in Ps LXVIII 20 **paouwlc** = τὴν ἐντροπήν μου, and in Col III 21 **ϫe nneuouwlc nϩht** = ἵνα μὴ ἀθυμῶσιν. See also p. 86 l. 5. Here **ouwlc** may stand for **ououwlc**. It is unnecessary to suppose a root **wlc** (see Peyron *Lex.* p. 274). **ou** is not infrequently written for **ouou**. See *v.* 73; Lc I 5; II 7; and 2 Ti II 17 (Boh.), where **oumeϯ** almost certainly = **ououmeϯ**. Cf. also the two forms **ϣououaϣϥ** and **ϣouaϣϥ** given by Peyron (*Lex.* p. 157). Even if **ou** does not here stand for **ouou**, it is quite possible to omit the indefinite article with the second of two substantives connected by **mn**. Cf. *Death of Joseph* c. XIII 3 (Vat. MS). The phrase 'sorrow and shame of heart' is found again p. 155 (*Death of Joseph* c. XVIII 3).

37. *forty days*] In the Protevangelium the same period is mentioned in connection with Joakim's fasting (I 4).

38 ff. There is no exact parallel to this and the following dream in Latin and Greek accounts. But the incident of the dove flying and sitting on Joakim's head may be compared with Prot. IX 1 καὶ ἰδοὺ περιστερὰ ἐξῆλθεν ἐκ τῆς ῥάβδου καὶ ἐπετάσθη ἐπὶ τὴν κεφαλὴν Ἰωσήφ. Cf. Ps-Mt VIII 3 ('columba nive candidior'); De Nat. Mar. VIII 1. The Protevangelium also gives a description of Anna sitting under a tree and seeing a sparrow's nest (III 1): cf. Ps-Mt II 2. The meaning of these dreams is given in verse 61, where the dove is seen to be the Virgin. See also p. 15 *vv.* 4, 10; p. 93 *v.* 6.

41. *When she herself fell asleep*] The phrase is perhaps derived from Ac XX 9 **ere ounoϭ nϩinhϥ cwk mmoϥ**, where the Greek is καταφερόμενος (V. L. κατεχόμενος) ὕπνῳ βαθεῖ.

42. *in the midst of the tree*] cf. 2 Sa XVIII 14 ἐν τῇ καρδίᾳ τῆς δρυός; Mt XII 40, where in the Bohairic version **ϧen nϩht mpkaϩi** = ἐν τῇ καρδίᾳ τῆς γῆς.

45. *Parmoute*] This is probably a transcriptional error for Paremhat. See verse 59.

49. *as though she had brought*] The construction is the same as ϩⲱⲥ ⲛⲧⲁⲛⲉⲣ ⲡⲁⲓ 'as though we had done this' (Ac III 12).

54. *she spake*] As the text stands it can only be translated 'she spake.' A slight alteration, reading ⲁⲥϫⲟⲟϥ for ⲁⲥϫⲟⲟⲥ, would give the sense 'she told it (i.e. the vision).'

58. *nine months were*] If we emend the MS and read ⲡⲙⲉϩⲯⲓⲥ for ⲯⲓⲥ, we may translate 'the ninth month was.'

58 f. *of that* month. *But*] ⲙⲡⲏ may here mean not 'of that' but 'nay.' Translate in that case 'Nay; but if.' Paremhat, Parmoute, Pashons and Hathor correspond *roughly* to March, April, May and November. The date of the birth of the Virgin given here does not agree with that found in S. C. Malan's translation 'from a manuscript calendar in Arabic which,' he says, 'until quite lately, was used in a Jacobite church at Cairo.' The date there given is Bashnash (viz. Pashons) 1st (*Calendar of the Coptic Church* 1873, p. 29). This represents the tradition of the Coptic Church. But in older calendars we find a second date given. Thus in Ludolf's Calendar the festival of her birth is mentioned on Tot x (Sep VII) as well as Bashnash 1st. In a note to the latter date he says: 'Aethiopes cum Coptitis diem nativitatis beatissimae Virginis *Calendas Maji* esse firmiter persuasum sibi habent. Sic enim notatum in Calendariis eorum reperitur. Idem tradit Rex Aethiopiae *Zera-Jacobus* in epistula sua; suprà Lib. 3 c. 3 n. 30 § 10. Idem bis extat *in vita S. Mariae*, quam Aethiopicè manuscriptam possideo. Ne tamen traditionem Ecclesiae Latinae et Graecae negligerent, etiam x *die Septembr.* secundum computum suum, eam commemoraverunt; et ne S. Virgo bis nata videretur, encomiastes meus ad illum diem addit: *prout Macarius scripsit.* Id est, *secundùm Macarii traditionem*' (Ludolf, *Ad Hist. Aeth. Com.* p. 431 f, Annot. ad Cal. XIX). See also Selden, *De Synedris Vet. Ebraeorum* (Amstel. ed. ult. 1679) lib. III c. XV pp. 221, 238; Wüstenfeld, *Synax. der Copt. Christ.* (Gotha 1879) I pp. 19, 20.

59. The form ⲉϭⲉⲛ, which occurs twice in this verse, is, as far as I know, unparalleled. It clearly has the same meaning as the Boh. ⲓⲥϫⲉⲛ and the Sah. ϫⲓⲛ.

62. *faces*] ϩⲁ here = ϩⲟ of verses 29, 86. The same scribe could use the two forms side by side. Thus on three pages of the Pistis Sophia (pp. 255—257) the form ϩⲟ occurs four, and the form ϩⲁ nine times.

67. *These and other*] ⲛⲉⲓ is here used in a weak sense. Cf. Z. p. 377 l. 15 ⲁϥⲕⲟⲥⲙⲉⲓ ⲙⲙⲟⲛ ϩⲛ ⲡⲁⲓ ⲙⲛ ⲛⲉⲓⲕⲟⲟⲩⲉ. See also p. 76 l. 19 f; *Various Sahidic Fragments* IV *v.* 6 (translated p. 176).

69. *seven days*] Cf. Prot. V 2 (MS A).

73. *he was old*] The word ⲛⲟϭ, which usually means 'great,' is also used in the sense of 'old.' Cf. Z. p. 395 l. 21, 22 'Who are not only

youths and maidens, but who are also old (ⲛⲟϭ) men and old (ⲛⲟϭ) women.'

74. The Coptic idiom makes it impossible to translate 'An angel of the Lord said to him.' Some word or words must have fallen out. I have supplied ⲁϥⲟⲩⲱⲛϩ ⲛⲁϥ ⲉⲃⲟⲗ from what I conjecture to have been the original reading in the MS published by M. Amélineau of Lc I 11.

75. *Malachias*] Zacharias is here as elsewhere (see e.g. Prot. XXIII and Wüstenfeld *Syn. Cop. Chr.* I p. 15 ff) identified with the Zacharias mentioned in Mt XXIII 35, whose father is there said to be Barachias. For the interchange of 'm' and 'b' cf. ϩⲓⲛⲏⲃ (Sah.), ϩⲓⲛⲓⲙ (Boh.); and of 'l' and 'r' cf. ⲕⲗⲩⲥⲧⲁⲗⲗⲟⲥ in the Sahidic and ⲭⲣⲏⲥⲧⲁⲗⲟⲥ in the Bohairic account of the Death of Joseph (c. XX 3).

shalt thou say] If we retain the reading of the MS, we may perhaps translate it by a future. Cf. Mt IV 10, where for the Greek futures *προσκυνήσεις* and *λατρεύσεις* we have present forms in the Bohairic. (See also the Bohairic of Lc IV 8. In the parallel in Deut. *ap.* Lagarde the future is used.) An easy emendation of the text, reading ⲡⲉⲧⲉⲕⲉϫⲟⲟⲩ for ⲡⲉⲧⲉⲕϫⲟⲟⲩ, would give us the ordinary future form.

Keep...for] The preposition which follows ϩⲁⲣⲉϩ ('keep') in the sense of 'for' is either (1) ⲉ, as in Jn XII 7; Ac XXV 21; or (2) ⲛ, as in 1 Pe I 4 (Boh.); 2 Pe III 7 (v. L. ⲉ). Here ⲛ is more natural; for the passage is a reminiscence of 2 Co XI 2, where ⲛ represents the Greek Dative.

76. *after three years*] Cf. Prot. VII 1, 2; Ps-Mt IV; De Nat. Mar. VI 1; Nic. Call. II 3 (quoted in note on *v.* 2).

77. *wean...from*] For the construction cf. Z. p. 538 l. 7.

85. *Torine*] Here and in Frag. IV *v.* 4 (see p. 24 f), ⲧⲟⲣⲓⲛⲏ is closely connected with ⲡⲟⲗⲓⲥ, and there is no preposition between. ⲧⲟⲣⲓⲛⲏ might be the name of the ⲡⲟⲗⲓⲥ. In that case the mistake has probably arisen from a misinterpretation of Lc I 39 (Sah.). As given by Amélineau, the text there is ⲁⲥⲃⲱⲕ ⲉⲧⲟⲣⲓⲛⲏ ϩⲛ ⲟⲩϭⲉⲡⲏ ⲧⲡⲟⲗⲓⲥ ⲛϯⲟⲩⲇⲁⲓⲁ 'she went to ⲧⲟⲣⲓⲛⲏ in haste, the (=*to* the ?) city of Judæa.' On the other hand this rendering can by no means be considered certain; for (1) elsewhere *ἡ ὀρινή* is taken as meaning 'the hill country.' Thus in a papyrus fragment at Turin we read, 'She arose therefore in haste, and went to ⲧⲟⲣⲓⲛⲏ, to the city of Judæa' (Rossi, *Pap. Cop.* vol. II fasc. I p. 7). Cf. also Lc I 39 (Boh.), 65 (Sah. and Boh.): (2) though as a rule in such a clause the preposition is repeated before each noun (cf. Lc II 39 'they returned unto—ⲉϩⲣⲁⲓ ⲉ—Galilee, to—ⲉ—their city Nazareth.' See also the Sahidic and Bohairic of Mt VIII 28; Jn XI 54; and the Bohairic of Mt XXVIII 16; Mc V 1; IX 43; Lc II 4), yet sometimes the second preposition is omitted. This seems to be the case in M. Amélineau's MS of Lc II 4, written presumably by the same scribe as Lc I 39. It is certainly the

case in *The Death of Joseph* XIV 1 (Sah. see Lagarde, *Aegyptiaca* p. 10).

86. *arms*] The word thus translated is used to denote the bosom or the bent arms. For this latter sense see Lc II 28, where ⲉⲡⲉϥϩⲁⲙⲏⲣ = εἰς τὰς ἀγκάλας αὐτοῦ: and Z. p. 537 l. 19.

87. *answered her*] The MS here reads ⲟⲩⲱϩ. If we retain the MS reading, we must take ⲟⲩⲱϩ in the sense of ⲟⲩⲱϩⲙ. The same word recurs in Cod. Borg. CCLIX* p. ⲗⲉ (see p. 70). In both cases I have ventured to emend the text into the more usual form, which occurs e.g. in Lagarde, *Aegyptiaca* p. 27 (Sah.).

89. In the Protevangelium Anna composes a song when her child is a year old (VI 2 f). In Ps-Mt IV f she is three years old. The substance of this song is not at all similar. It bears some resemblance to the first part of the song which Isaac of Tiphre sang before his execution: 'Ye angels of light, stand by me (ⲛⲉⲙⲏⲓ) to-day. Ye archangels of light, stand by me (ⲛⲉⲙⲏⲓ) to-day. Ye Seraphim of light, stand by me (ⲛⲉⲙⲏⲓ) to-day.' (*The Martyrdom of Isaac of Tiphre*, MS p. 191, published by Dr E. A. Budge, *Trans. Soc. Bibl. Arch.* vol. IX p. 106.)

92. *I have learned*] The verb thus translated has usually an active signification in Sahidic (cf. p. 14 l. 14). In Bohairic it is occasionally passive: cf. *The Death of Joseph* II 2. The use of it here may be due to Bohairic influence, which can be traced elsewhere in this MS. Cf. ⲉⲛⲧⲟⲩϯ (=Boh. ⲛⲧⲟⲩϯ) *v.* 21, ⲛⲧⲉϩⲏ *v.* 27.

FRAGMENT II. A.

This fragment is not written by the same hand as the MS immediately preceding, but it is probably part of the same story. The fact that the last MS breaks off at p. 14 and that this one begins at p. 17, the pages in each case containing about the same amount of writing, suggests that the two were copied from a common original. If this be so, the present incident would not be far separated from Anna's song. This order agrees with that of the Protevangelium, where a similar scene is recorded in the chapter immediately following Anna's song (c. VII). Ps-Mt on the contrary places the song last (c. IV f).

1. *altar*] The word ⲑⲩⲥⲓⲁⲥⲧⲏⲣⲓⲟⲛ is here used. This might indicate the court of the altar (cf. *Ign. Eph.* V, Lightfoot *in loc.*). In Prot. VII 3 she is placed ἐπὶ τρίτου βαθμοῦ τοῦ θυσιαστηρίου, where

θυσιαστήριον probably means 'altar.' There is, however, another reading (MS K), ἐν τῷ θυσιαστηρίῳ ('court of the altar'?). In Ps-Mt IV she is placed 'ante templum domini' or 'ante foras templi': in De Nat. Mar. VI 1 the reason why the altar was approached by steps is given (cf. reading of B in Ps-Mt).

2. *shine upon her*] For the phrase cf. Ac XXII 6. This participial form is sometimes used to express the Greek Aorist. Cf. Lc X 18 (Boh.) **ⲁⲓⲛⲁⲩ ⲉⲛⲥⲁⲧⲁⲛⲁⲥ ⲉⲁϥⲉⲓ ⲉⲃⲟⲗ ϧⲉⲛ ⲧⲫⲉ** 'I saw Satan fall (πεσόντα) from heaven.'

3. The glory of Mary's face is not alluded to in the Protevangelium or De Nat. Mar., but cf. Ps-Mt VI 1 'Et resplendebat facies ejus sicut nix, ita ut vix possent in ejus vultum intendere' (MSS C, D).

4. Cf. *v.* 10. A similar statement is made in the Protevangelium (VIII 1) ἦν δὲ Μαρία ἐν τῷ ναῷ κυρίου ὡς περιστερὰ νεμομένη, καὶ ἐλάμβανεν τροφὴν ἐκ χειρὸς ἀγγέλου.

5. *Anna the prophetess*] I have restored the text here, but some such restoration is almost certain. I have used the form **ⲡⲣⲟⲫⲏⲧⲏⲥ** as it is found in M. Amélineau's text in Lc II 36, upon which this statement is probably grounded.

virgins] Cf. Prot. X 1; Ps-Mt IV; De Nat. Mar. VI 3.

handiwork] Cf. Ps-Mt VI 1. In the Protevangelium the Virgin works in 'purple and scarlet' after she has left the temple (c. X).

7. *was pleasing*] The phrase **ϯ ⲉⲡⲁⲛⲁⲓ** is used of John the Baptist (*Various Sah. fragments*, I *v.* 8). The word is apparently connected with the root **ⲁⲛⲁⲓ**. The verb **ⲉⲣⲁⲛⲁⲓ**=to be pleasing. Cf. Z. p. 417 l. 8 **ⲁⲣⲓⲁⲛⲁⲓ ⲙⲡⲁⲙⲡⲧⲟ** (MS **ⲙⲡⲁⲙⲡⲁⲧⲟ**) **ⲉⲃⲟⲗ** (εὐαρέστει ἐναντίον ἐμοῦ). Kabis (A. Z. 1874, p. 126) suggests 'placere' as the meaning of **ϯ ⲉⲡⲁⲛⲁⲓ** also. I am not satisfied with this suggestion, as the word literally means 'give to beauty,' but I am unable to propose a better.

8. *intercourse*] **ϩⲟⲙⲉⲗⲓⲁ**. Cf. *PS.* p. 270, l. 1 f. **ⲁϥⲁⲡⲟⲧⲁⲥⲥⲉ ⲙⲡⲕⲟⲥⲙⲟⲥ ⲧⲏⲣϥ ⲙⲛ ⲛⲉϥⲣⲟⲟⲩϣ ⲧⲏⲣⲟⲩ ⲙⲛ ⲛⲉϥϩⲟⲙⲓⲗⲓⲁ ⲧⲏⲣⲟⲩ.**

9. *thought...come up*] Cf. Frag. I *v.* 5.

13. *raiment*] The word **ϣⲧⲏⲛ** (cf. preceding fragment, *v.* 29) is used for χίτων (Mt X 10) or ἱμάτιον (Mt IX 16; Lc VIII 44). It appears to have been used somewhat loosely. For in Ac IX 39, where the Greek has χιτῶνας καὶ ἱμάτια, the MSS published by Woide vary between **ⲉϩⲉⲛϩⲟⲓⲧⲉ ⲙⲛ ϩⲉⲛϣⲧⲏⲛ** and **ⲉϩⲛϣⲧⲏⲛ ⲙⲛ ϩⲛϩⲟⲓⲧⲉ.**

foul] The same root is used in *The Death of Joseph* (Boh.) XXVI 1, of Joseph's hair, where I have translated it 'waste away.' (See p. 142.) The root idea is that of wasting or becoming foul. Thus the root is used in Ja I 11 (Boh.) for μαραίνεσθαι and Ja II 2 (Sah.) for ῥυπαρός.

14. *daily*] After the last part of the word 'Mary' has been supplied, there is still a gap in the MS of five or six letters. Possibly

some word such as ⲁⲩϩⲁⲡⲉ is gone; in that case translate '*As regards* that which the Virgin Mary increased daily.'

16. *painted*] Lit. 'put στίμμι (ⲥⲧⲏⲙ) upon.' Different kinds of eye-paint (ⲥⲧⲏⲙ) were used by the ancient Egyptians at different seasons of the year. See Budge, *The Mummy*, p. 228 f, where the composition of ⲥⲧⲏⲙ is discussed, and copies of inscriptions printed. 'These inscriptions show that one kind of eye-paint was to be used from the first to the fourth month of the inundation season; a second from the first to the fourth month of the season of coming forth; a third from the first to the fourth month of the period of growing; and also that a fourth was to be used every day.' Christian women still continued the use of eye-paint (Z p. 422 l. 13 f), though the practice was condemned (Rossi, *Pap. Cop.* vol. I fasc. II p. 39).

17. *She never washed in a bath*] Cf. Hegesippus's account of St James, ἔλαιον οὐκ ἠλείψατο, καὶ βαλανείῳ οὐκ ἐχρήσατο. Τούτῳ μόνῳ ἐξῆν εἰς τὰ ἅγια εἰσιέναι (Eus. *H. E.* II 23). The form of asceticism here ascribed to the Virgin was commonly indulged in by Egyptian monks and nuns. Thus in Z p. 567 l. 7 ff. we read: 'Cursed is a man or a woman among us who shall bathe their feet amiss in lustfulness (ⲉⲡⲓⲑⲩⲙⲓⲁ), or who shall wash secretly in water, or who shall anoint themselves secretly with oil, before they have first asked the old man among us, or without *the permission of* the aged woman among you.' Baths were only necessary for those who were ill. 'But if it be necessary for thee to go to a bath to wash in sickness, only *go* once or twice (ϣⲁ ⲟⲩⲥⲟⲡ ⲏ ⲥⲛⲁⲩ). For when thou art in good health thou hast no need of baths, O thou monk and thou priest.' (Z p. 575 l. 10 ff.)

Among the papyri preserved at Turin, there is an interesting passage in which the duty of ascetic life for virgins is based upon the example set by the Virgin. M. Revillout[1] first published the text in 1873 (see *Le Concile de Nicée d'après les textes Coptes*, p. 32 ff). More recently Prof. Rossi has republished the same (*Pap. Cop.* vol. I fasc. II p. 40 ff). I give selections from Prof. Rossi's text. 'And who can speak of the beauty of the Mother of our (? Z's MS has 'the,' Z p. 576 l. 5) Lord, whom God loved because of her works?' 'Mary never saw the face of *a* strange man. Therefore indeed she was troubled when she heard the voice of Gabriel the angel. And she did not eat as though she were nourishing (ⲉⲥⲥⲁⲁⲛϣ) a body, but she used to eat

[1] On p. 28, note 4, M. Revillout says: 'C'est ici que se termine le fragment de manuscrit correspondant que possédait Zoega. Depuis cet endroit, tout ce que nous donnons est donc complètement inédit.' No more of the MS is given in that place (p. 248) in the catalogue, nor does Pitra (*Sp. Sol.* tom. I p. 525) speak of more; yet if I am not mistaken, selections from the same MS are given by Zoega later in his catalogue. Cf. Z p. 575, line 27—end, and Z p. 576 with M. Revillout's work, p. 29 ff.

because of the necessity of her nature, lest she should die before (reading ϩ⌈ⲁ⌉ⲑⲏ) her time.' 'For she withdrew in her house alone, being ministered to by her own mother.' 'And she was always sitting, her face looking eastwards; because she was praying without ceasing (ⲉϫⲛ ⲱϫⲛ). For her brethren were desiring to see her and speak with her. And she would not suffer *them* (ⲁⲛⲉⲭⲉ). For the angels were coming unto her often, looking at the manner of her conversation (ⲡⲉⲭⲁⲣⲁⲕⲧⲏⲣ ⲛⲧⲉⲥⲡⲟⲗⲓⲧⲉⲓⲁ), and wondering at it.' For neither did she ever see the nakedness of her body; but when she was about to wear a garment, she would shut (reading ⲛⲉ ϣⲁⲥϣⲧⲁⲙ) her eyes.'

19. I am unable to make any certain emendation. Probably ⲛⲉⲥⲁ or ⲉⲥⲁ must be supplied between ⲙ and ⲛ. ⲱⲣⲉⲓ appears to be the ending of ⲑⲉⲱⲣⲉⲓ. The two words ⲁⲛⲉⲭⲉ and ⲑⲉⲱⲣⲉⲓ occur together in the account of the Virgin in the Turin Papyrus (cf. Rossi, *Pap. Cop.* vol. I fasc. II p. 41 ll. 25, 27).

Fragment II. B.

The numbers of the remaining pages of this fragment are lost. On the first page however, the no. ⲕⲅ has been written in by a modern hand. This may be a copy of a number now lost, and I have therefore given it in square brackets. If this enumeration be correct, four pages are gone. The accounts of the Virgin's turning to the east in prayer and of her never seeing a stranger are not so far separated in the Turin Papyrus.

1. *Spouse...Bridegroom*] In the first case a Coptic, in the second case a Greek word is used.

3. *two years*] Cf. *The Death of Joseph* XIV 6 (Boh. Sah. and Arabic). Nicephorus Callistus (II 3) gives the period as four months. See note on Frag. I 2.

7. *But*] Or 'Moreover' (ⲗⲟⲓⲡⲟⲛ).

9—11. The account is based upon St Luke, but one of the words spoken by the angel to Joseph is inserted from St Matthew. Contrast this with *The Death of Joseph* VI (Sah.), where the account of Joseph's dream is based on St Matthew, but is influenced by words addressed to the Virgin in St Luke.

9. *the doors...being shut*] Cf. Ephr. *Diat.* Moes. p. 24 'Sed sicut Dominus intravit portis clausis, eodem modo ex utero virginali exiit, quia haec virgo sine partus doloribus realiter et vere peperit.' See also Ez XLIV 2 where Sah. is not, as far as I know, extant.

13. *that which*] The Coptic has no Neuter, and therefore must use the Masculine to translate the Neuter Participle.

15. *the hearing of her ears*] Cf. Eph. *Diat.* Moes. p. 49 'Vide quod reipsa angelus, qui venit, ut eam in auribus Mariae quasi semen demitteret, clara voce ita semen spargere coepit: *Salus tecum*, ait, *benedicta in mulieribus*': and p. 249 'Quia mors per aurem Evae intraverat, per aurem Mariae vita intravit.' See also the Syriac Acts of John (Wright, *Eng. trans.* p. 14) and Jacob Sarug. *Carm.* I *de B. V.M.* 293 ff.

16. *put...away*] The same Sahidic word is used in Lc XVI 18 to translate ἀπολύειν.

18. *allowed such a thing to happen*] The general sense of the passage is evident, but the text appears to be corrupt. If the emendation that I have suggested, reading ⲁⲩ for ⲁ, be right, then the literal translation would be 'I have suffered *it and* such a thing has happened.' But the emendation is uncertain. Ciasca in Job VI 26 gives the form ⲁⲛⲉⲓϫⲉⲁ, but in that passage the final ⲁ probably goes with the following ⲛ, and the text must be emended.

23. In a Sahidic fragment in the possession of Lord Crawford (MS 36) there is an account of the birth of our Lord, which differs from the account in the text, and resembles more closely that of the Protevangelium (cc. XVII—XX).

'Moreover the days were fulfilled that she should bear. There went out a decree from the king Augustus that all the world should be enrolled (*lit.* be written ⲥϩⲁⲓ) after its villages (ⲧⲙⲉ). Joseph arose, and took Mary his wife, and set her on his ass, and went with her in (ϩⲓ) the way. And he went up to be enrolled (*lit.* be written ⲥϩⲁⲓ) after his city (ⲡⲟⲗⲓⲥ), because he was (ϫⲛ . . ⲡⲉ) of the house and the family of David. They went in (ϩⲛ) the way at (ϩⲛ) the borders of Bethlehem. And seeing the face of the Virgin exceedingly bright (ⲉϥⲣⲟⲟⲩⲧ ⲉⲙⲁⲧⲉ) as lightning, he wondered exceedingly. The Virgin said to him, Let me down from the ass (ⲕⲁⲁⲧ ⲉⲡⲉⲥⲏⲧ ϩⲓϫⲙ ⲡⲉⲓⲱ), for that which is in my womb (ⲡⲉⲧϩⲛ ϩⲏⲧ) moves (ⲕⲓⲙ) me, that I should bring it forth (ⲉⲧⲣⲁϫⲡⲟϥ). And Joseph lifted up his eyes hither and thither, †him (*or* it ⲙⲙⲟϥ) in the way† (*text corrupt*) and saw no place into which to go; and he knew not the end of the dispensation (ⲡϫⲱⲕ ⲛⲧⲟⲓⲕⲟⲛⲟⲙⲓⲁ) of God. And that place was a desert, there being a tomb (ⲟⲩⲙϩⲁⲁⲩ) therein in the way. And Joseph brought the Virgin, and left her therein (ⲁϥⲕⲁⲁⲥ ⲛϩⲏⲧϥ). It was the hour of evening. Joseph went forth among all the borders of Bethlehem, seeking a woman, that he might leave her with her (ⲉⲧⲣⲉϥⲕⲁⲁⲥ ϩⲁϩⲧⲏⲥ). Now whilst Joseph was without, the Virgin brought forth her Son; and she took swaddling clothes, and wrapped Him in them, and laid Him in a manger of cattle (ϩⲛ ⲟⲩⲟⲙϥ ⲛⲧⲃⲛⲏ), out of which cattle eat; for there was no room for them in the inn. And Joseph found a woman at the hour of dawn, whose name was (*lit.* is) Salomé. Now she was a midwife. He brought her unto the Virgin, and he saw the babe wrapped in the swaddling clothes: and she saw the Virgin, her face bright from the Holy Ghost. She ran (ⲁⲥⲡⲱⲧ) and came outside, and cried out with a loud (*lit.* great) voice to all the borders of Bethlehem, Come ye, and see this great wonder. A virgin has born *a child*, and has not known *a* man, being *a* virgin like her (? The MS has ⲉⲥⲟ ⲙⲡⲁⲣⲑⲉⲛⲟⲥ ⲛⲧⲉⲥϩⲉ ⲧⲉⲥϩⲉ). And through the great wonder she believed on Him, that He was (*lit.* is) the Son of God. And she did not cease following the Virgin and the Saviour, until He was crucified, and rose from the dead and went up to the heavens.' Though the above account resembles that of the Protevangelium, it differs from it and also from the shortened form of it found in Syriac in the following main points: (1) It omits the remarkable passage in the Protevangelium, where Joseph speaks in the first person, and which as it stands there appears an interpolation. (2) Our Lord is said to be born in a tomb. The tomb would undoubtedly be a cave; but the word for 'tomb' and 'cave' are not the same. (3) Salome, instead of being the unbeliever whose hand drops off, is here the midwife herself. In Ps-Mt XIII 3, 4 Salome is represented as an unbelieving midwife, who comes into the cave after Zelomi. With regard to the contents of the MS, see further the Introduction.

enrol itself] This reading is found in Amélineau's edition in Lc II 1, but ⲥϩⲁⲓ 'be enrolled' is the reading of Lord Crawford's fragment, which also occurs in Rossi, *Pap. Cop.* vol. II fasc. I p. 26.

villages] ⲧⲙⲉ is said by Peyron (*Lex.* p. 243) to mean 'homo qui alitur, altus,' and in his Appendix (*Gram.* p. 186) 'filius, filia.' But I have little doubt that it is only another form of ϯⲙⲉ (= κώμη as e.g. in Mt IX 35), and that ⲛⲥⲁ ⲛⲉⲥⲧⲙⲉ has much the same meaning as ⲛⲥⲁ ⲧⲉϥⲡⲟⲗⲓⲥ (Lc II 3). Thus ⲧⲙⲉ is used to translate κῶμαι in Nu XXXII 42; Josh XV 44, 47; XVI 7, 9. It is true that it is used for θυγατέρες in Jud I 27, but θυγατέρες there represents בנות 'daughter towns.' The form ⲧⲙⲉ for ϯⲙⲉ was apparently preferred in semi-legal enumerations. It is found in Amélineau's edition of Lc II 1, and also in Rossi, *Pap. Cop.* vol. II fasc. I p. 26, where the text is quoted, and in Lord Crawford's MS (36) given above.

27. *thy face sad*] According to the Protevangelium the Virgin's face was alternately laughing and sorrowful; and the reason is given (*Prot.* XVII 2). Here the narrative is so condensed as to be obscure. In Ephraem's Commentary Joseph is said to have seen her face joyful (Ephr. *Diat.* Moes. p. 22).

30. *inn*] ⲡⲁⲛⲧⲟⲕⲓⲟⲛ. In Lc II 7 and in Lord Crawford's MS (36) ⲙⲁ ⲛϭⲟ(ⲉ)ⲓⲗⲉ (= κατάλυμα) is used. I know no parallel to the statement that our Lord was born in an inn, found here and on p. 149 c. VII *v.* 3

which they had] See note on *Sah. Frag. Falling asleep of Mary* II c. X 12.

31. *Do* me *the kindness*] This form of expression is found in Bohairic (e.g. Z p. 42 l. 20; p. 90 l. 40) and Sahidic (e.g. Rossi, *Pap. Cop.* vol. II fasc. IV p. 70).

33. *virginity*] The word ⲙⲛⲧⲁⲧⲥⲟⲟⲩⲛ is commonly used to translate ἄγνοια: cf. Wisd XIV 22; Ac III 17; XVII 30; Eph IV 18; 1 Pe I 14). In the last four cases the Bohairic uses ⲙⲉⲧⲁⲧⲉⲙⲓ (cf. also Boh. of Ge XXVI 10; XLIII 12). Here the form ⲙⲛⲧⲁⲧⲉⲓⲙⲉ is found, and ⲉⲣⲟⲥ is added to the abstract word, as on p. 122 l. 5. If we translate the word *ignorance*, the meaning is probably 'virginity.' But ⲙⲛⲧⲁⲧⲉⲓⲙⲉ may be used in the sense of 'unknowableness.' In that case translate it 'in an unknowable manner.' Cf. *The Death of Joseph* c. XIV 6.

FRAGMENT III.

In the Gospel of Pseudo-Matthew several miracles are wrought by Jesus on the way to Egypt, and one is wrought by the Virgin and her Child in a city of Egypt (see c. XVIII ff.). An allusion to the muleteer (*v.* 6) makes it probable that these belong to the same cycle of miracles. A 'Hegemon' is referred to in this and the following miracle. In Ps-Mt XXIV mention is made of 'dux civitatis,' and in Wright's Syriac Apocrypha, *Eng. trans.* p. 35, an account is given of the cure of the son of a 'Hegemon.' Cf. also Wright, *Journal Sac. Lit.* vol. VII p. 146 f.

2. *took wings*] Cf. Z p. 316 l. 18 ⲁⲩϫⲓⲧⲉⲛϩ ⲁⲩϩⲱⲗ ⲉⲃⲟⲗ.

5. *cooks*] This may refer to those who prepare sacrifices. In Boh. of Ez XLVI 24 ⲙⲁⲅⲓⲣⲟⲥ occurs in this sense.

tasted] Cf. Z p. 576 l. 15 f. ⲧⲉⲛ ⲛⲉⲕϣⲏⲣⲉ ⲉⲧⲉⲕⲕⲗⲏⲥⲓⲁ ⲁⲩⲱ ⲉϩⲉⲛⲙⲁ ⲛⲥⲱ ⲁⲛ 'Make thy sons taste'—give them a taste for—'the church and not taverns.'

7. *image*] Cf. Ps-Mt c. XXII ff. In the Arabic Gospel of the Infancy (c. X) the Virgin, Joseph and the Holy Child enter a city on their way to Memphis, in which is an idol, from which Satan used to speak. The idol speaks, and falls down. It is not unlikely that the account of this miracle exists in Ethiopic MSS not yet translated. See e.g. *Cat. Cod. Or. Br. Mus.* III XLI f. (Add. MSS 16192, 16193); Paris Bibl. Nat. 60 ff. (Zotenberg's *Catalogue*).

9. *What do ye*] Lit. *What is your work?* Cf. Z p. 344 l. 17. ⲁⲣⲁ ⲁϣ ⲡⲉ ⲡϩⲱⲃ ⲛⲛⲁⲓ.

14. *wilt thou not*] Lit. 'dost thou not.' The gnomic aorist in Coptic sometimes practically corresponds to our English future. See Stern, *Kop. Gram.* § 396.

20. *witness against*] For this use of ⲉ cf. Mt XXVII 13; Mc XIV 60; XV. 4.

21. *standards*] In the Acta Pilati (c. I) when Jesus is brought before the judgment seat (ⲃⲏⲙⲁ) of Pilate the busts (ⲛⲉⲡⲣⲟⲧⲟⲙⲏ) of the standards worship Him. He is taken out, and brought in again, when the standards again worship Him (ⲛⲧⲉⲣⲉϥⲉⲓ ⲇⲉ ⲉϩⲟⲩⲛ ⲁⲩⲣⲁⲕⲧⲟⲩ ⲉⲃⲟⲗ ⲟⲛ ⲛϭⲓ ⲛⲥⲓⲅⲛⲟⲛ ⲁⲩⲟⲩⲱϣⲧ ⲛⲓⲥ). See Rossi, *Pap. Cop.* vol. I fasc. I pp. 13, 15, 17.

prepared] Cf. Lc XXII 12 ⲉⲩⲙⲁ ⲛⲧⲡⲉ ⲉϥⲡⲟⲣϣ (ἐστρωμένον).

22. *will worship...will sit*] The future in ⲛⲁ sometimes has, as here, practically a present meaning. See note on *v.* 54 of next Fragment.

23. *Magrinus*]=Macrinus. The change of ⲕ and ⲅ is not unusual: cf. ϯⲡⲁⲁⲅⲉ for ϯⲡⲁⲁⲕⲉ (*Death of Joseph*, Sah. XXIII 4). The name does not occur elsewhere in this kind of literature.

25. *Straightway*] There is space in the MS after ⲛⲧ for one or more letters. I have supplied ⲁ, and read ⲛⲧⲁ, a form which occurs after ⲛⲧⲉⲩⲛⲟⲩ in the next Fragment (*v.* 125).

27. *storehouses*] Or treasuries (ⲧⲁⲙⲓⲟⲛ). In the Pistis Sophia the treasuries of punishment are said to be twelve in number. 'And Jesus answered and said to Mary, The outer darkness is a great dragon, whose tail is in his mouth, who is outside the whole world and surrounding the whole world: and there are many places of judgment therein, which are (ⲉϥⲟ ⲙ) twelve grievous treasuries (ⲧⲁⲙⲓⲟⲛ) of punishment.' Then there follows a list of the Archons of the treasuries (*PS* p. 319 ff.).

FRAGMENT IV.

1. The words with which the Fragment opens are evidently spoken by Elisabeth. Elisabeth and Mary (cf. *v.* 7) seem both to be represented as belonging to Judah. Ephraem cites as a quotation (apparently from Diat. I 28 or II 12, 13) concerning Joseph and Mary: 'they were both of the house of David' (Ephr. *Diat.* Moes. p. 16). See also his Commentary on 2 Ti II 8.

2. *from my mother's womb*] The exact Sahidic phrase (ϫⲓⲛ ⲉⲓⲛϩⲏⲧⲥ ⲛⲧⲁⲙⲁⲁⲩ) found here occurs in Ps XXI 11 and Ga I 15, where it represents in both cases ἐκ κοιλίας μητρός μου: ϫⲓⲛ with the Present Participle meaning: 'from the time that I was (in my mother's womb).' See also Ac III 2. A clear parallel is 2 Ti III 15, where ϫⲓⲛ ⲉⲕⲥⲟⲃⲕ represents ἀπὸ βρέφους. The same use is found with ⲓⲥϫⲉⲛ in Bohairic. Thus in Lc XIII 7 ⲓⲥϫⲉⲛ ⲉⲓⲛⲏⲟⲩ=ἀφ' οὗ ἔρχομαι. Stern

(*Kop. Gram.* § 621) translates ϫⲓⲛ with the Present Participle by 'während.' Steindorff (*Kop. Gram* § 471) translates Ac III 2 by 'seit'; but—like Peyron (*Lex.* p. 388)—does not mention the other use in the sense of 'whilst'; which is however undoubtedly found: cf. Lc XXIV 44 ϫⲓⲛ ⲉⲓϣⲟⲟⲡ ⲛⲙⲙⲏⲧⲛ (ἔτι ὢν σὺν ὑμῖν v. L. ἐν ᾧ ἤμην).

to serve Him all the days of my life] These words appear to be based on Lc I 74 f. But it is noteworthy that the Sahidic (*ap.* Amélineau) and the Bohairic (*ap.* Schwartze and Wilkins) both omit any mention of 'life' in *v.* 75. They follow the five principal uncials in rejecting τῆς ζωῆς before ἡμῶν.

3. *the scriptures inspired of God*] Cf. Z p. 563 l. 23 f. The ⲛ of ⲛⲓϥⲉ might (see note *b* on p. 25) grammatically='the.' But it is better taken as the ⲛ prefixed to a qualifying adjective. In that case ⲛⲓϥⲉ, as in corresponding Boh., is used as an adjective: 'that which is inspired.' Cf. the use of ϫⲡⲟ in *v.* 80 of this Fragment, where ⲣⲱⲙⲉ ⲛϫⲡⲟ ⲛⲥϩⲓⲙⲉ ='man born of woman.' See *Corrigenda* p. 246.

4. *Torine*] See note on the first of these Fragments (*v.* 85).

6. *kinswoman*] Cf. p. 13 *v.* 81.

9. *trouble*] Cf. Phil III 1 ⲛⲟⲩϩⲓⲥⲉ ⲛⲁⲓ ⲁⲛ ⲡⲉ (ἐμοὶ μὲν οὐκ ὀκνηρόν).

10. *or drawing forth*] There is room for one capital letter between ⲉϥⲟϣ and ⲉϥⲡⲟⲛⲕ. The letter appears to have been either **H** or **Π**. Probably the text is corrupt. If we read ⲉϥⲟⲩⲱϣ ⲉⲡⲟⲛⲕ for ⲉϥⲟϣ **H** ⲉϥⲡⲟⲛⲕ, the sense is somewhat improved. Translate in that case: 'For as one wishing to dig for water, wishing to draw forth *the water of* a fountain.' For the metaphor see Z p. 272 l. 7 ff. 'And Athanasius sat on the throne of the bishopric, all the people drinking from the fountain of water of life of his teachings'; Z p. 315 f. 'He found Ephrem teaching, and he heard (*lit.* and hearing) him as a fountain welling up in his mouth.'

11. *the falling asleep*] ⲉⲛⲕⲟⲧⲕ here=κοίμησις. It is found in Sah. as the translation of κοίμησις in Jn XI 13 (Boh. ⲉⲛⲕⲟⲧ).

12. *lift up our voice*] I have had to emend the MS twice in this verse. ⲛⲧⲛϫⲓⲥⲙⲏ is hardly possible here. ⲡⲉⲛⲛⲁ requires some preposition before it.

15. *the other disciple*] The rule that ⲕⲉ with the definite article means 'also' (see Stern, *Kop. Gram.* § 271; Steindorff, *Kop. Gram.* § 155) admits of many exceptions. Here ⲡⲕⲉ means 'the other,' as we see from Jn XX 2, 3, where ⲡⲕⲉⲙⲁⲑⲏⲧⲏⲥ is found in Sahidic for ὁ ἄλλος μαθητής (cf. also Boh.). This is the meaning in many other places: e.g. Z p. 15 l. 45 f. (Boh.) ⲁⲓⲁⲓϥ ⲛⲃ̄ ⲁⲓϯ ⲧⲉϥⲫⲁϣⲓ ⲉⲣⲟϥ ⲙⲡⲥⲙⲟⲛⲧ ⲛⲟⲩⲕⲁⲓⲥⲓ ϯⲕⲉⲫⲁϣⲓ ⲁⲓϫⲟⲗϩⲧ ⲙⲙⲟⲥ (I divided it. I put half upon him...and *as for* the other half, I wrapped myself in it); Z p. 346 l. 28; *The Death of Joseph* (Sah.) XXIII 11. Besides this use, ⲧⲕⲉ is found with ⲣⲟⲙⲡⲉ 'year' in the sense of 'the next.' Cf. Ge

XVIII 10, 14; Lc XIII 9. This may be the meaning on p. 6 l. 15 (see Trans. p. 7 *v.* 37).

16. *Man, behold, thy mother!*] The Sahidic version in Jn XIX 27 has the common reading 'Behold, thy mother!' Here the addition of 'Man' is remarkable. From the Armenian version of Ephraem's commentary we see that Tatian's reading here was 'Thou young man, behold, thy mother!' (See Ephr. *Diat.* Moes. p. 54 where the rendering should be 'Juvenis, ecce mater tua.')

In the Greek account of the Assumption, when John came from Ephesus, 'the holy God-bearer glorified God, because I John came unto her, remembering the voice of the Lord which said, Behold, thy mother! and, Behold, thy son!' (*Joh. Lib. Dor. Mar. v.* 7. Cf. also *Trans. Mar.* A *v.* 6; B III 1.)

17. *death*] I have here and elsewhere translated **ϫωκ ⲉⲃⲟⲗ** by the word 'death,' giving below in the note 'Or *consummation.*' It means 'end' or 'consummation.' Thus it is the translation of *τέλος* in 1 Pe III 8 and of *τελείωσις* in He VII 11. Hence it came to be used of death. Cf. the use of the verb in Z p. 343 l. 19 f. 'And when we came in, we found him dead (**ⲁⲛϩⲉ ⲉⲣⲟϥ ⲉⲁϥϫⲱⲕ ⲉⲃⲟⲗ**).'

19. *she also*] **ⲟⲛ** strengthens **ϩⲱⲱⲥ.** Cf. Mt XXVI 69 **ⲛⲧⲟⲕ ϩⲱⲱⲕ ⲟⲛ ⲛⲉⲕϣⲟⲟⲡ** 'Thou also wast' (*καὶ σὺ ἦσθα*).

20. *like those of...Jesus Christ*] Cf. Z p. 266 l. 9 f. **ⲛⲉϥⲥⲁⲛϣ ⲛⲛⲉⲧϣⲱⲛⲉ ⲉϥⲉⲓⲣⲉ ⲛϩⲛⲛⲟϭ ⲛϭⲟⲙ ⲉⲧⲟϣ ⲛⲑⲉ ⲛⲉⲛⲧⲁ ⲡⲥⲱⲧⲏⲣ ⲁⲁⲩ ⲉϥϣⲟⲟⲡ ϩⲁϩⲧⲏⲛ.**

21. *to write*] I have ventured to alter the MS **ⲧⲙ** into **ⲉⲧⲙ.** The construction is then the same as in Ac XVI 6.

23. *making them eager for*] Cf. Ming. p. 203 **ⲛⲅϯⲟⲩⲣⲟⲧ ⲛⲁⲩ ⲉϩⲟⲩⲛ ⲉⲣⲟϥ** 'that thou mayest make them eager for him' i.e. make them readily accept Horsiesius as the new head of the community. For a similar use of **ⲁⲅⲱⲛ** see Lagarde, *Aegyptiaca* p. 278 l. 6.

25. *without stumbling*] The mention of 'the straight way' in this verse, and of 'stones of stumbling' in *v.* 111, makes this translation the most natural. Otherwise it might be 'void of offence,' as in Ac XXIV 16.

26. *after fifteen years*] The Syriac *Transitus B. Virginis* gives the period as sixteen years (see Wright, *Eng. Trans.* p. 32): the two Latin accounts make the Assumption take place in the second year after the Ascension (*Trans. Mar.* A *v.* 4; B II 1), in the latter account there being a v. l. 'twenty second.' The Syriac *Departure of my Lady Mary* gives the date 345 'of the Seleucian or Greek era, A.D. 33 or 34' (see Wright *Journal Sac. Lit.* April 1865 p. 133, and cf. Enger's Arabic *Trans. Mar.* p. 15).

Josephus and Irenaeus who were *of* the *Hebrews*] Cf. p. 180 l. 2 f. (see Trans. p. 181 *v.* 3). **ⲛⲁⲛⲟ** in both cases = Greek *οἱ ἀπὸ*. Zoega translates the phrase 'Hebraeorum' (p. 223) and 'ex Hebraeis oriundi' (p. 621).

27. *the holy virgins and the apostles*] Read '*he who is* the holy virgin and the apostle' (see *Corrigenda* p. 246). So Dulaurier, 'l'apôtre qui conserva toujours sa virginité.' This refers to John, who is constantly called 'the virgin'. See e.g. *PS* p. 67 l. 8; p. 231 l. 21; *Trans. Mar.* B x. Cf. Wright, *Syr. Apoc.*, *Eng. Trans.* p. 44, where Paul asks John of his doctrine, and 'John says to him, I, if I go forth to teach and preach, will say, that no one who is not a virgin all his days, is able to see God.'

29. *and called them*] This and the other Coptic accounts of the Assumption represent the Apostles as remaining near the Virgin. The Greek (*Joh. Lib. Dor. Mar. v.* 15), Latin (*Trans. Mar.* A *v.* 7; B IV) Syriac (Wright, *Trans. B. Virg.*, *Eng. Trans.* p. 32; *Journal Sac. Lit.* April 1865 p. 138 ff.) and Arabic (Enger, *Trans. Mar.* p. 41) accounts tell how the apostles were brought to the Virgin on clouds.

30. *they three*] **ⲙⲡⲱⲟⲙⲛⲧ**. Cf. the frequent use of **ⲙⲡⲉⲥⲛⲁⲩ** ('both'). See e.g. Mt IX 17.

33. *a portion of*] Cf. Lc XV 12, where **ϩⲛ** after **ⲙⲉⲣⲟⲥ** is used for the Greek genitive; **ϩⲛ ⲧⲟⲩⲥⲓⲁ** standing for τῆς οὐσίας. **ⲙⲉⲣⲟⲥ** is found again in this Fragment, *v.* 116.

41. *eating and drinking*] This is based on Ac I 4 **ⲁⲩⲱ ⲉϥⲟⲩⲱⲙ ⲛⲙⲙⲁⲩ** ('and eating with them').

54. *as He went up*] Here the future in **ⲛⲁ** may be rendered by our present. The Sahidic version translates πορευομένου αὐτοῦ in Ac I 10 by **ⲉϥⲃⲏⲕ**, but αὐτὸν πορευόμενον in I 11 by this future **ⲉϥⲛⲁⲃⲱⲕ**.

55. *Ye men*] The omission of 'of Galilee,' which is found in the Sahidic of Ac I 11, is noteworthy. In Woide's edition the clause 'This is Jesus who was received up from you into heaven' is not found.

56. *fifty days*] The MS has **ⲛϩⲟⲟⲩ ⲛϩⲟⲟⲩ**. If the reading is retained, translate 'the space of fifty days' (*lit.* 'the fifty days of days'). This would be an unusual expression modelled on such a phrase as occurs on p. 101 *v.* 11 'nine months of days.' The fact that the scribe in the next verse reads **ϯϯ** for **ϯ** makes it probable that the second **ⲛϩⲟⲟⲩ** is due to carelessness.

58. *those things which*] I have left the reading of the MS **ⲛⲉⲛⲧⲁϥⲧⲥⲁⲃⲱⲧⲛ**. Probably an **ⲛ** has fallen out at the beginning of the word.

59. The first part of this verse reads like a reminiscence of Ac IV 26, 29. The Sahidic in this Fragment uses the Greek word (**ⲁⲡⲓⲗⲏ**) for 'threat.' But the Sahidic and Bohairic versions give a Coptic word in Ac IV 29.

73. *to meet thee*] Lit. 'to thy meeting' (**ⲉⲧⲟⲩⲁⲡⲁⲛⲧⲏ**). In *v.* 76 a Sahidic word (**ϩⲁⲧⲟⲩϩⲏ**) is used in the same sense.

85. *A lordly shrine*] **ⲟⲩⲁⲩⲑⲉⲛⲧⲓⲕⲟⲛ ⲛⲧⲟⲡⲟⲥ**. The word **ⲧⲟⲡⲟⲥ**

is often used in Martyrdoms of a 'shrine.' See Hyvernat, *Act. Mart.* vol. I pp. 76, 91, 93, 94, 313. It is found in *Boh. Acc. of the Death of Joseph* XXVI 2. The epithet ⲁⲩⲑⲉⲛⲧⲓⲕⲟⲛ is remarkable. It occurs in the Pistis Sophia in the list of the Archons of the treasuries, where it is used in close connection with ⲧⲟⲡⲟⲥ of the names and faces of the Archons. Thus the description of the first Archon ends with these words: 'whose ⲁⲩⲑⲉⲛⲧⲓⲕⲟⲛ name is called in his ⲧⲟⲡⲟⲥ, Enchthonin.' Sometimes the form ⲁⲩⲑⲉⲛⲧⲏⲥ is used. See *PS* p. 320 ff.

palaces] There is room for four letters in the MS between ⲉⲙ and ⲁⲧⲓⲟⲛ. I have read ⲉⲙⲡⲁⲗⲗⲁⲧⲓⲟⲛ. The word occurs in Coptic either with a single (Z p. 34 l. 40) or a double ⲗ (Z p. 284 l. 37; Hyvernat, *Act. Mart.* vol. I p. 4).

86. *give the order*] ϯ ⲡⲧⲱϣ may mean 'give the arrangement' of the shrine. Cf. use of ⲑⲱϣ in Z p. 42 l. 30. ϯ ⲙⲡⲑⲱϣ is found in *First Boh. Acc. Falling Asleep of Mary* I c. XII 10, where see note.

87. *take away*] This word is used of taking away a corpse to bury it. Cf. Z p. 343 l. 20 f. 'Come, my brother, let us take away his body' (ⲛⲧⲛⲱⲗ ⲙⲡⲉϥⲥⲱⲙⲁ).

91. *for*] The word ⲙⲙⲟⲛ or ⲉⲙⲙⲟⲛ has primarily a negative force. Cf. Lc XII 51 'I say unto you, Nay' (ⲙⲙⲟⲛ). From the meaning 'it not being so' is derived (1) its use in the apodosis of a conditional sentence: cf. p. 106 l. 23 (Boh., see Trans. p. 107 *v.* 13); *The Death of Joseph* (Boh. XVII 14); Z p. 481 l. 17; see Stern, *Kop. Gram.* § 631: (2) its use in the sense of 'else' or 'otherwise.' I have noted four passages (Ro XI 6; 1 Co XIV 16; XV 29; He IX 26) in the Sahidic N.T., where ⲙⲙⲟⲛ or ⲉⲙⲙⲟⲛ is found for the Greek ἐπεὶ in this signification. As ἐπεὶ is used in the sense of 'since,' so ⲙⲙⲟⲛ comes to be used in this sense; and may often be translated, as here, by the English 'for': cf. *PS* p. 216 l. 22 ⲛⲁ ϩⲁⲣⲟⲓ ⲡⲁϫⲟⲉⲓⲥ ⲉⲙⲙⲟⲛ ⲁ ⲛⲁⲥⲛⲏⲩ ⲥⲱⲧⲙ ('Have mercy upon me, my Lord; for my brethren have heard'); p. 280 l. 14 f. ⲉⲙⲙⲟⲛ ⲟⲩⲛ ⲟⲩⲙⲏⲏϣⲉ ⲛⲏⲩ ϩⲙ ⲡⲁⲣⲁⲛ ('For many shall come in My name'); p. 390 l. 15 ff. ⲛⲁ ⲛⲁⲛ ⲛⲁ ⲛⲁⲛ ⲡϣⲏⲣⲉ ⲙⲡⲉⲧⲟⲩⲁⲁⲃ ⲛⲅϣⲛϩⲧⲏⲕ ϩⲁⲣⲟⲛ ϫⲉ ⲉⲛⲉⲟⲩϫⲁⲓ ⲉⲛⲉⲓⲕⲟⲗⲁⲥⲓⲥ ⲙⲛ ⲛⲉⲓⲕⲣⲓⲥⲓⲥ ⲉⲩⲥⲃⲧⲱⲧ ⲛⲣⲣⲉϥⲣⲛⲟⲃⲉ ⲉⲙⲙⲟⲛ ⲁⲛⲣⲛⲟⲃⲉ ϩⲱⲱⲛ ⲡⲉⲛϫⲟⲉⲓⲥ ⲁⲩⲱ ⲡⲉⲛⲟⲩⲟⲉⲓⲛ ('Have mercy upon us, have mercy upon us, Thou Son of the Holy One, and have compassion upon us, that we may be saved from these punishments and these judgments prepared for the sinners; for we also have sinned, our Lord and our Light'). See also *PS* p. 122 l. 13; p. 250 l. 11. In all five instances the sense is obscured in Petermann's edition by the translation 'alioquin' (4 times) or 'saltem' (once). In Woide's edition of the N.T. (see Mt XXIV 5) the second passage is wrongly translated. Neither Stern nor Steindorff notice this use in their grammars. Yet it is not confined to the Pistis Sophia. Cf. Z p. 368 l. 19 f. 'Come to me to the desert; for (ⲙⲙⲟⲛ) the robbers have stripped me, and have bound me,

wishing to kill me.' See also *Various Sah. Frag.* III 14; IV 4 (and perhaps also IV 10); Hyvernat, *Act. Mar.* vol. I p. 57 l. 5.

93. *Mary Magdalene*] Cf. p. 47 *v.* 6. A possible reference to Mc XVI 9: but it may be a Sahidic reading in Lc VIII 2, found in Boh[wi] et[dz], and Syr[cu]. Mary Magdalene is a prominent figure in the Pistis Sophia. In describing His kingdom Jesus gives a special preeminence to her and John. 'But Mary Magdalene and John the virgin shall be greater than all My disciples' (p. 231 l. 20 ff.). She distinguishes herself by her pious curiosity, until at last Peter complains, and 'Jesus said to Mary and the women, Give place to your brothers that they also may ask' (p. 383 l. 1 ff.). See Schmidt, *Gnost. Schrift.* p. 452 f.

95. *covenants*] See p. 107 *v.* 7. Cf. Chrys. *ad Illum. Catech.* II ἀποτάσσομαί σοι Σατανᾶ...καὶ συντάσσομαί σοι Χριστέ (Migne, *P. G.* XLIX col. 240): also *Const. Ap.* VII 41.

98. *keep*] Lit. 'keep your Catholicon holy.' For the construction cf. Z p. 277 l. 22 f. ⲉⲣⲉ ⲡⲛⲟⲩⲧⲉ ⲣⲟⲉⲓⲥ ⲉⲣⲟⲕ ⲉⲕⲟⲩⲟϫ ⲡⲥⲟⲛ ⲉⲧⲧⲁⲉⲓⲏⲩ 'God keep thee in good health, honoured brother.' See *Addenda* p. 246.

103. *departure*] There is a gap in the MS between ⲁⲛⲁ and ⲥⲓⲥ. Zoega (p. 224) reads ⲁⲛⲁⲡⲁⲩⲥⲓⲥ. If we read ⲁⲛⲁⲗⲩⲥⲓⲥ cf. *v.* 61, where the Sahidic word corresponding to ⲁⲛⲁⲗⲩⲥⲓⲥ is used. See also *Joh. Lib. Dor. Mar. vv.* 17, 19.

109. *without intercourse*] Cf. Rossi, *Pap. Cop.* vol. I. fasc. II p. 27, l. 13 ff, where the Virgin is confessed to have conceived without intercourse with man (ⲛⲟⲩⲉϣ ⲛⲥⲩⲛⲟⲩⲥⲓⲁ ⲛϩⲟⲟⲩⲧ), to have brought forth without defilement (ⲛⲟⲩⲉϣ ⲛϫⲱϩⲙ), and to have given nourishment without trouble (ⲛⲟⲩⲉϣ ⲛϩⲓⲥⲉ).

111. *all these divers faces*] Cf. pp. 56 *v.* 6; 58 *v.* 13, where see notes.

113. *they have found nothing*] The Sahidic in Jn XIV 30 (*ap.* Amélineau) has ⲁⲩⲱ ⲙⲛⲛⲧϥ ⲗⲁⲁⲩ ϩⲣⲁⲓ ⲛϩⲏⲧ ('and he hath nothing in Me'), but εὑρήσει οὐδέν is read by some Greek MSS. Cf. Epiph. *Adv. Haer.* II 2 66 διὰ τὸ εἰρηκέναι τὸν Σωτῆρα, ὅτι Ἔρχεται ὁ ἄρχων τοῦ κόσμου τούτου, καὶ ἐν ἐμοὶ οὐδὲν τῶν αὐτοῦ εὑρίσκει (Migne, *P. G.* XLII col. 132). Dulaurier (*Frag. Rév. Apoc.* p. 21) wrongly translates: 'car elles n'ont trouvé aucune *tache* en moi.' See James, *Test. Abr.* p. 19 f.

114. *be manifested to*] Apparently a confusion between Ps CXVII 19 and Ps XLI 3. ⲉⲧⲣⲁⲟⲩⲱⲛϩ ⲉⲃⲟⲗ is a natural rendering of ἐξομολογήσομαι, but followed by ⲙⲡϩⲟ ⲙ ('the face of'), it is best taken as representing ὀφθήσομαι. Thus Ciasca has in the latter passage ⲧⲁⲟⲩⲱⲛϩ ⲉⲃⲟⲗ ⲙⲡϩⲟ ⲙⲡⲁⲛⲟⲩⲧⲉ.

115. In the Pistis Sophia, after Jesus has explained that the outer darkness is a dragon, with its tail in its mouth, surrounding the world, in which are the twelve treasuries of punishment (*PS* p. 319 f, see note on *v.* 27 of last Fragment), He explains how there are one or more Archons in each treasury, each Archon having a different face.

The first has the face of a crocodile with its tail in its mouth. After describing the faces of the other Archons, He says 'These Archons then of these twelve treasuries are inside the dragon of the outer darkness, and each of them has a name hour by hour, and each of them changes his face hour by hour.' When He has further described how an angel of the height watches each of the mouths of the treasuries; 'Mary Magdalene answered and said, My Lord, are the souls then which are taken into that place, taken through these twelve mouths of the treasuries, each *man* according to the judgment which he deserves? The Saviour answered and said to Mary, No souls are taken into the dragon through these mouths, but the souls of the blasphemers' and of those who commit different sins which are named in detail. 'They shall be taken through the entrance (*lit.* mouth **ⲧⲁⲡⲣⲟ**) of the tail of the dragon into the treasuries of the outer darkness: and when they have ceased taking the souls into the outer darkness in the entrance (*lit.* mouth **ⲧⲁⲡⲣⲟ**) of his tail, he turns again his tail into his own mouth that he may shut their mouths. This is the manner in which souls will be cast into the outer darkness' (*PS* p. 320 ff.). See also note on *The Falling Asleep of Mary*, *First Boh. Account*, c. XI 13.

116. *the river of fire*] Allusions to a fiery lake in Amenta are found in the Egyptian Book of the Dead. There is a picture of the lake in the British Museum Papyrus 9913 c. 126. In the Papyrus of Ani we read: 'Deliver thou [me] from the god whose face is like unto that of a dog, whose brows are as those of a man, and who feedeth upon the dead, who watcheth at the Bight of the Fiery Lake, and who devoureth the bodies of the dead and swalloweth hearts, and who shooteth forth filth, but he himself remaineth unseen....As concerning the Fiery Lake, it is that which is in Anrutf, hard by the *Shenit* chamber' (Budge, *Book of the Dead*, *Pap. of Ani* p. 288 f.). In the Pistis Sophia Jesus bids the apostles preach to the whole world thus: 'Say to them, Renounce plunderings, that ye may be worthy of the mysteries of the light, and be delivered from the rivers of smoke of Ariel. Say to them, Renounce evil words that ye may be worthy of the mysteries of the light, and be delivered from the punishments of *the* river of smoke. Say to them, Renounce villainies, that ye may be worthy of the mysteries of the light, and be delivered from the seas of fire of Ariel. Say to them, Renounce acts of unmercifulness (**ⲛⲓⲙⲛⲧⲁⲧⲛⲁ**), that ye may be worthy of the mysteries of the light, and be delivered from the judgments of the faces of the dragons. Say to them, Renounce acts of anger (**ⲛⲓϭⲱⲛⲧ**), that ye may be worthy of the mysteries of the light, and be delivered from the rivers of smoke of the faces of the dragons. Say to them, Renounce cursing, that ye may be worthy of the mysteries of light, and be delivered from the fire of the seas of the faces of the dragons.' The apostles are to tell men to renounce various other sins, that they may be worthy of the mysteries of light, and delivered from

various punishments, e.g. 'the rivers of fire of the face of *a* lion' and 'the archon of *the* face of *a* crocodile' (see *PS* p. 256 ff.). Descriptions of the river of fire are by no means confined to the Gnostics. See e.g. Z p. 124 f., where Abba Macarius as he walked on the mountain 'saw a head of a corpse...and he moved the head, and it answered him. The old man said to it,...Of what kind is the punishment? The skull said, As the heaven is higher than the earth, so also is *the* river of fire above our head, bubbling up (*or* boiling ⲉϥⲃⲉⲣⲃⲉⲣ); and it is beneath us, tossing *its* waves under our feet, and we stand in its midst.' Indeed this river is a common feature of visions of Hell in all apocryphal literature. See *Testament of Abraham, Appendix* pp. 147, 159 f.

121. *the chariots of the Cherubin*] Cf. Sir XLIX 9 (8) ϩⲓϫⲙ ⲫⲁⲣⲙⲁ ⲛⲛⲉⲭⲉⲣⲟⲩⲃⲉⲓⲛ (ἐπὶ ἅρματος χερουβείμ). I have omitted in the text this reference to Sirach here and on p. 52 c. VII 1. See also *Testament of Abraham, Appendix* p. 150.

122. *all the Life*] So MS. Possibly ⲙⲡⲧⲏⲣϥ should be read for ⲧⲏⲣϥ. Translate in that case: 'the Life of all (*or* of the universe).'

124. *the King*] About five letters appear to be gone after ⲡⲣⲣⲟ ('the King'). There is room for some such word as ⲙⲡⲏⲩⲉ ('of the heavens') or ⲙⲡⲱⲛϩ ('of life').

the south] The allusion to the south as the place of death is remarkable, and is not, as far as I can find, derived from ancient Egyptian sources. Cf. p. 59 *v.* 7 and *Death of Joseph* c. XXI 1.

the hidden place] i.e. the underworld. The word 'Amenta' which is used in ancient Egyptian of the underworld appears to have meant originally 'the hidden place.' Cf. also use of 'Shetait' in the Book of the Dead.

127. The day on which the Virgin fell asleep was the twenty-first of Tobe. Cf. pp. 44, 52, 65, 77. Thus in Malan's *Coptic Calendar* (p. 10) the commemoration on Tubeh XXI is: 'Rest in the Lord of the Virgin Mother of God, the pure Lady Mary.' See also Wüstenfeld, *Synax. Cop. Chr.* II p. 251 f. Zoega (p. 225) wished to emend the text, and read ⲛⲥⲟⲩϫⲟⲩⲧⲏ (or as he writes it ⲛⲥⲟⲩϫⲟⲩⲧϯⲟⲩ) for ⲛⲥⲟⲩϫⲟⲩⲧⲣⲉ, i.e. 'twenty-fifth' for 'twenty-first,' in order to bring the Roman and the Coptic dates into harmony. But any such emendation is quite unnecessary. January and Tobe are taken by the writer as practically synonymous, and the night of Jan. XX is the beginning of the next day, Jan. XXI. See Rossi, *Pap. Cop.* vol. I fasc. III p. 67, where September I is made to correspond to Thoout I. 'On the first of the month September, which is Thoout according to the language of the Egyptians.'

early in the morning] ⲉϩⲧⲟⲟⲩⲉ is used for πρωί (Sir XXXIV 21; Jn XX 1) and ἅμα πρωί (Mt XX 1). The passage is an interesting illustration of the Greek of Mt XXVIII 1. Cf. p. 121 c. VIII *v.* 1.

128. *Prepare her body well for burial*] Cf. Z p. 90 l. 32 ⲁⲩⲕⲟⲥϥ

ⲡⲕⲁⲗⲱⲥ. The word ⲕⲱⲱⲥ is derived from the hieroglyphic *qes*, to 'wrap up in bandages,' i.e. make a dead man into a mummy (see Budge, *The Mummy* p. 175). The root is found in the Bohairic of Ge L 2 ⲁⲩⲕⲱⲥ ⲙⲡⲓⲥⲣⲁⲏⲗ ⲛϫⲉ ⲛⲓⲣⲉϥⲕⲱⲥ (ἐνεταφίασαν οἱ ἐνταφιασταὶ τὸν Ἰσραήλ). When embalming was no longer practised, the word was still used: (1) of preparing the body with ointments and spices. Thus in Mt XXVI 12, when the woman put ointment on our Lord's body, 'she did it' He said 'to prepare Me for burial' (ⲉⲡⲕⲟⲟⲥⲧ πρὸς τὸ ἐνταφιάσαι με); (2) of wrapping the corpse round with cloths. Cf. Ac V 6 ⲁⲩⲕⲟⲟⲥϥ ⲁⲩⲱ ⲁⲩϫⲓⲧϥ ⲉⲃⲟⲗ ⲁⲩⲧⲟⲙⲥϥ (συνέστειλαν αὐτὸν καὶ ἐξενέγκαντες ἔθαψαν). So ⲕⲁⲓⲥⲓ or ⲕⲁⲓⲥⲉ is the cloth in which the corpse is wrapped (cf. last line of Z p. 15): (3) of the whole preparation for burial. Cf. Jn XIX 40 ⲁⲩⲙⲟⲣϥ ⲛϩⲉⲛϩⲃⲱⲱⲥ ⲙⲛ ϩⲉⲛϩⲏⲛⲉ ⲕⲁⲧⲁ ⲡⲥⲱⲛⲧ ⲛⲛⲓⲟⲩⲇⲁⲓ ⲉⲕⲟⲟⲥⲟⲩ (καὶ ἔδησαν αὐτὸ ὀθονίοις μετὰ τῶν ἀρωμάτων, καθὼς ἔθος ἐστὶν τοῖς Ἰουδαίοις ἐνταφιάζειν): (4) of actual burial. Cf. Lc XVI 22 (Boh.) ⲁⲩⲕⲟⲥϥ (ἐτάφη).

the valley of Jehoshaphat] The body of the Virgin is buried in this valley according to the two Latin accounts (*Trans. Mar.* A 14, 16; B XV 1). See also the Syriac narratives (Wright, *Trans. Mar.*, *Eng. Trans.* p. 37 ff.; *Journ. Sac. Lit.* April 1865 p. 148). In the Greek the MSS differ. One MS makes her buried ἐν Γεθσημανῇ ἐν μνημείῳ καινῷ. Cf. Enger's Arabic *Trans. Mar.*, *Lat. Trans.* p. 71. The rest say that the body was taken up to Paradise, whilst it was being taken out of Jerusalem to burial (*Joh. Lib. Dor. Mar.* 48). In the two Bohairic accounts the apostles go towards the field of Jehoshaphat, and either bury it there in a tomb (p. 62 c. XV 4, 8), or leave it suddenly on their way (p. 119 *v.* 15). Here the narrative suddenly breaks off; but in the other Sahidic fragment the body is caught away when the apostles reach the valley of Jehoshaphat (see p. 79 c. XV 4; p. 83).

FIRST BOHAIRIC ACCOUNT OF THE FALLING ASLEEP OF MARY.

Evodius is here represented not as first bishop of Antioch (see Eus. *H. E.* III 22), but as archbishop of Rome. In the heading of the sermon attributed to him among the papyri of Turin, he is spoken of as 'Evodius the patriarch and the archbishop of the great city Rome,' and as the second 'after Peter the great apostle[1]' (Rossi, *Pap. Cop.* vol. II fasc. IV p. 7).

[1] The papyrus containing the heading of the sermon is badly torn on the left-hand side, and the name of the author has perished. But on another

I 1. This Sermon commences, as e.g. Theodosius' Sermon on the Archangel Michael (see Budge, *Michael the Archangel* p. 2 f.), with an elaborate simile. The description of the marriage is Eastern throughout, but an unusual number of Greek and Latin words are found. Thus (1) the names of dignitaries and officers are Greek or Latin. See *v.* 2 'orders' (ⲧⲁⲝ̀ⲓⲥ), *v.* 3 'courtiers' (ⲥⲭⲟⲗⲁⲥⲧⲓⲕⲟⲥ), *v.* 4 'tribunes' (ⲧⲣⲓⲃⲟⲩⲛⲟⲥ), *v.* 5 'counts' (ⲕⲟⲙⲏⲥ), *v.* 6 'governors' (ⲉⲡⲁⲣⲭⲟⲥ), *v.* 7 'generals' (ⲇⲟⲩⲝ̀), 'commanders' (ⲥⲧⲣⲁⲧⲩⲗⲁⲧⲏⲥ), *v.* 8 'standard-bearers' (ⲥⲩⲅⲛⲟⲫⲟⲣⲟⲥ), *v.* 9 'trumpeters' (ⲃⲟⲩⲕⲓⲛⲁⲧⲱⲣ). Again (2) the names of actors, musicians and the common people are not Egyptian. See *v.* 11 'actors' (ⲑⲉⲁⲧⲣⲓⲕⲟⲥ), *v.* 12 'keepers' (ⲕⲏⲛⲏⲕⲓⲟⲛ), *v.* 13 'harpers' (ⲕⲩⲑⲁⲣⲓⲱⲧⲏⲥ), *v.* 14 'players' (ⲟⲣⲅⲁⲛⲓⲧⲏⲥ), *v.* 15 'the people of the market' (ⲁⲅⲟⲣⲉⲟⲥ).

3. *courtiers*] The word thus translated comes in Evodius' Sermon among the Turin Papyri, where it is connected with rulers (ⲁⲣⲭⲱⲛ) who are round about the emperor's (?) throne (⌜ⲛ⌝ⲉⲥⲭⲟⲗⲁⲥⲧⲓⲕⲟⲥ ⲙⲛ ⲛⲁⲣⲭⲱⲛ ⲉⲧⲙⲛⲕⲱⲧⲉ ⲙⲡⲉϥⲑⲣⲟⲛⲟⲥ). See Rossi, *Pap. Cop.* vol. II fasc. IV p. 29.

16. *branches of palm and branches of olive*] Cf. Z p. 90 l. 30 ff., where palm and olive branches are a sign of joyful victory in preparing a corpse for burial. ⲛⲁⲓⲣⲏϯ ⲁⲩⲓ ⲉⲛϣⲱⲓ ⲛϫⲉ ⲛⲓϧⲉⲗⲗⲟⲓ ⲛⲧⲉ ⲡⲓⲉⲛⲁⲧⲟⲛ ϧⲉⲛ ⲟⲩⲛⲓϣϯ ⲛⲣⲁϣⲓ ⲛⲉⲙ ϩⲁⲛⲃⲁⲓ ⲛⲉⲙ ϩⲁⲛϫⲁⲗ ⲛϫⲱⲓⲧ ⲟⲩⲟϩ ⲁⲩⲕⲟⲥϥ ⲛⲕⲁⲗⲱⲥ.

II 1. *which shall pass away*] Cf. Hyvernat, *Act. Mar.* vol. I p. 20 'God forbid (ⲛⲛⲉⲥϣⲱⲡⲓ ⲛⲏⲓ) that I should seek after a kingdom of this world which shall soon pass away' (ⲉⲑⲛⲁⲥⲓⲛⲓ ⲛⲭⲱⲗⲉⲙ).

and *its*] Lagarde has here unnecessarily rejected the MS reading. Instead of his ⲉⲑⲛⲁⲥⲓⲛⲓ, ⲫⲁⲓ ⲉ ϩⲱϯ ⲡⲉ, I have read with the MS ⲉⲑⲛⲁⲥⲓⲛⲓ ⲫⲁⲓ ϩⲱϯ ⲡⲉ. ⲫⲁⲓ emphasizes the previous phrase. See Stern, *Kop. Gram.* § 244. Coptic sometimes uses a coordinate where we might use a dependent sentence. Cf. c. IV 8.

set against] ⲭⲏ ⲉϩⲣⲏⲓ ⲉϫⲉⲛ. If we retain the MS reading, ⲉϩⲣⲏⲓ ⲉϫⲉⲛ may be rendered 'against.' Cf. Ps III 2 ⲁⲩⲧⲱⲟⲩⲛⲟⲩ ⲉϩⲣⲏⲓ ⲉϫⲱⲓ. Perhaps however we should translate it: 'which is laid down for': either (1) reading ⲉϧⲣⲏⲓ for ⲉϩⲣⲏⲓ: cf. *The Death of Joseph* XI 1 ⲙⲫⲣⲏϯ ⲉⲧⲉⲥⲭⲏ ⲉϧⲣⲏⲓ ⲛⲣⲱⲙⲓ ⲛⲓⲃⲉⲛ 'as it is laid down for all men'; or (2) taking ⲉϩⲣⲏⲓ in the sense of ⲉϧⲣⲏⲓ. In c. IV 9 ϭⲁϩⲉⲙ = ϭⲁϧⲉⲙ.

piece of papyrus, which is apparently the close of the sermon, the name ⲉⲩϩⲟⲇⲓⲟⲥ (Euhodios) can be clearly read. I examined the two pieces at Turin, and have no doubt that M. Revillout (*Études Égyptologiques* fasc. I p. XI f.) and Prof. Rossi (*Pap. Cop.* vol. II fasc. IV) are right in attributing this sermon to Evodius. In the passage given above I have had to fill in gaps in the papyrus, but the emendation is practically certain.

IV 8. *rather remember that He*] Lagarde reads and punctuates thus ⲁⲗⲗⲁ ⲙⲡⲉⲕⲉⲣ ⲫⲙⲉⲩⲓ, ⲛⲑⲟϥ ⲇⲉ ('but thou didst not remember, and He'). This reading cannot be right. The sense is weak, and ⲛⲑⲟϥ ⲇⲉ ⲛⲑⲟϥ ⲡⲉ ⲉⲧ is an unnatural expression. If we read ϫⲉ for ⲇⲉ, and take ⲛⲑⲟϥ in the sense of 'rather' (as in the preceding verse: cf. also use of ⲛⲧⲟϥ in Sah., for which see Stern, *Kop. Gram.* § 598), the sense is plain.

9. *pierce*] Lagarde emends the MS ⲁⲕⲧⲟⲥ into ⲁⲕⲧⲟⲕⲥ. I prefer to keep the form in the MS, as it is found elsewhere. See Kabis, *Auct. Lex. Cop.* (A. Z. 1876 p. 12).

12. *custom*] ⲇⲏⲙⲟⲥⲓⲟⲛ. In Lc XXIII 2 the words used for φόρους are ϩⲱϯ (Boh.) and ϣⲱⲙ (Sah.).

13. *give toll*] ⲧⲉⲗⲟⲥ. The word ϩⲱϯ is used in the Bohairic of Lc XX 22 for φόρον, and of Mt XXII 17; Mc XII 14 for κῆνσον. Here the MS reads ⲛⲧⲉ ⲛⲓⲧⲉⲗⲟⲥ. Lagarde emends, and reads ⲛⲧⲉⲛⲉⲛ ⲧⲉⲗⲟⲥ ('that we bring toll'). I prefer ⲛⲧⲉⲛϯ ⲧⲉⲗⲟⲥ ('that we give toll'), because (1) ϯ not ⲉⲛ is used in the Synoptic accounts, (2) the form ⲛⲧⲉⲛϯ occurs in the latter part of Mc XII 14, (3) the mistake (ⲓ for ϯ) is here easily accounted for by the similarity of sound.

He...blotted out the letters...and wrote on it] This addition to the Gospel narrative is not, as far as I know, found elsewhere.

25.] Cf. p. 3 *v.* 4.

V 3. *my father Peter*] Peter occupies an important place in this narrative of the Assumption, for it is told by Evodius his disciple (XIX 2), successor (p. 44) and spiritual son. Cf. V 11; VI 5, 6; VII 4; VIII 4, 7, 9, 13 ff.; IX 11 ff.; XIV 4; XVIII 3. The Greek account purports to be told by John, though Peter has a special dignity assigned to him. In the second Latin account Peter refuses to take the precedence. 'Dixeruntque ad invicem apostoli, Quis palmam hanc ante feretrum ejus portabit? Tunc Iohannes ait ad Petrum, Tu [qui] praecedis nos in apostolatu, debes palmam hanc ante lectum ipsius [ferre]. Cui Petrus respondit, Tu solus ex nobis virgo es electus a domino....Tu igitur portare debes hanc palmam' (*Trans. Mar.* B X 1).

7. *Rufus and Alexander*] They were the sons of Simon of Cyrene (Mc XV 21). They are mentioned in connection with Peter and Andrew in *Acta Petri et Andreae* (Tisch. *Apocal. Apoc.* p. 162). See also Malan, *Conflicts of the holy Apostles* p. 99.

our fathers the *apostles*] The apostles are here regarded as the spiritual fathers, who take the place of earthly fathers. It is in this sense that Evodius calls Peter his father.

8. *seventy-two*] ⲟⲃ. In Lc X 1, 17 (Boh. *ap.* Schwartze and Wilkins) the reading is ⲟ ('seventy').

10. *Salome*] Cf. p. 59 *v.* 5; 60 *v.* 11; 77 *v.* 11. Salome is one of the speakers in the Pistis Sophia. See *PS* pp. 102 ff., 114, 342 f., 381; Schmidt, *Gnost. Schr.* p. 454. Cf. also p. 133 c. VIII 3 (where see note).

VI 1. *receive a blessing*] The first meaning of ϭιϲⲙⲟⲩ is 'receive *a* blessing' or 'be blessed'. Cf. Ge XII 3, where ⲛⲥⲉϭιϲⲙⲟⲩ = εὐλογηθήσονται. Thence it came to be used of 'receiving the eucharist'. Cf. Z p. 23 l. 25. ⲛιϲⲕⲉⲩⲟϲ ⲉⲧⲟⲩϭιϲⲙⲟⲩ ⲛⲁⲛ ⲛϧⲏⲧⲟⲩ 'Our vessels wherewith we receive the eucharist (*lit.* the vessels wherewith a blessing is received for us)'. See also Z p. 35 ll. 10, 11; p. 47 l. 10.

5. *lot*] ⲕⲗⲏⲣⲟϲ. An allusion to the common tradition that each apostle had a separate lot in which to preach. Cf. Tisch. *Act. Apost. Apoc.* p. 190. In a Sahidic Fragment in the British Museum (Or. 3581 B) there is a statement of the lots which fell to Peter, Andrew, James, John, Philip, Bartholomew, Thomas and Matthew. In another (Or. 3581 B), describing the preaching of Bartholomew, allusion is made to the apostles dividing the countries among themselves, by casting lots (ⲁϲϣⲱⲡⲉ ⲇⲉ ⲛⲧⲉⲣⲉ ⲛⲁⲡⲟϲⲧⲟⲗⲟϲ ⲡⲱϣ ⲉϫⲱⲟⲩ ⲛⲛⲉⲭⲱⲣⲁ ⲉⲁⲩⲛⲉϫ ⲕⲗⲏⲣⲟϲ ⲙⲛ ⲛⲉⲩⲉⲣⲏⲩ).

6. *appointed*] The word thus translated is ⲁϥⲉⲣⲭιⲣⲟⲇⲟⲛιⲛ (χειροτονεῖν). For a Sahidic account of the appointment of Peter as archbishop, see Clarendon Press MS b 3 16 (second leaf); the text of which has been printed by Prof. Guidi in *Rendiconti della R. Accademia dei Lincei* (1887) vol. III, 2° sem. p. 34 f. At the beginning of the Sahidic *Canones Ecclesiastici* (Lagarde, *Aegypt.* p. 239) our Lord commands His apostles to assign the functions of presbyters, deacons and readers before they divide the countries among themselves. Presbyters and deacons were to be ordained, but not readers (pp. 250; 277). The office of a ⲯⲁⲗⲧⲏⲥ is also spoken of (p. 280). For the corresponding Bohairic account see Tattam, *Apostolical Constitutions* pp. ⲁ, ⲗⲍ, ⲣⲕⲉ, ⲣⲗⲍ.

7. *gave us the salutation of peace*] ϯ ⲛϯϩιⲣⲏⲛⲏ 'give the peace' = 'dare pacem'. For the various occasions on which the kiss was given see *Dictionary of Christian Antiquities* vol. II p. 902 ff. Cf. also Tattam, *Apost. Const.* p. ⲡⲁ 'And when he is made a bishop, let every one give peace (ϯ ⲛⲟⲩϩιⲣⲏⲛⲏ) to him with their mouth'; p. ⲙⲑ 'And let the faithful salute one another alone'—not the catechumens—'the men with the men, and the women with the women: and let not *a* man salute *a* woman'. See also pp. ⲣιⲍ, ⲣιⲑ.

VII 6. *My glorious members*] The word 'member' (ⲙⲉⲗⲟϲ) is found in a mystical sense in Sahidic Gnostic writings. Thus in the First Book of Jeû the following expression is repeated several times, ⲥⲱⲧⲉ ⲙⲙⲉⲗⲟⲥ ⲛιⲙ ⲛⲧⲁι (ⲛⲁι) ⲉⲧϫⲟⲟⲣⲉ ⲉⲃⲟⲗ ϫιⲛ ⲧⲕⲁⲧⲁⲃⲟⲗⲏ ⲙⲡⲕⲟⲥⲙⲟⲥ 'Redeem all my members scattered from the foundation of the world' (Schmidt, *Gnost. Schrift.* p. 79 ff.). See also *PS* p. 252 ff.

7. *behind her*] On p. 127 *v.* 15 these words are connected with what follows. Here they appear to go with the preceding clause.

16. *wrap*] In the first case ϫⲟⲗϩ, in the second case ⲁⲩϫⲱⲗ is used. I have taken ⲁⲩϫⲱⲗ as connected with the root ϫⲱⲗ, and as

having the same meaning as ϫⲟⲗϩ. Cf. Z p 47 l. 26 f. 'And when our holy father Abba Antonius had finished his course, we shrouded (ⲁⲩϫⲱⲗ) his holy body.' There ⲁⲩϫⲱⲗ has the same sense as ϫⲱⲗ in Z p. 134 l. 17 'And when it was evening, the brethren of the saint came and shrouded his holy body.' See also Z p. 13 l. 31.

17. *and...keep singing*] ⲛⲧⲟⲩϣⲱⲡⲓ ⲉⲩⲉⲣϩⲩⲙⲛⲟⲥ. The distinction noticed by Stern (*Kop. Gram.* § 448) between the forms ⲛⲧⲟⲩ and ⲛⲥⲉ cannot, I believe, be maintained. 'ⲛⲧⲟⲩ' he says 'drückt die wirkliche folge, ⲛⲥⲉ die beabsichtigte folge (den griech. conjunctivus futuri) aus.' His examples are not convincing. Amongst others he refers to Lc XVI 4 for ϩⲓⲛⲁ ⲛⲥⲉ and Lc XVI 9 for ϩⲓⲛⲁ ⲛⲧⲟⲩ. But the Greek (ἵνα...δέξωνται) is the same in both cases.

VIII 2. *turned our face away*] ϯ ϩⲣⲁⲛ ⲉⲃⲟⲗ. In Bohairic the usual meaning of ϩⲣⲁ is 'face'. If this rendering be adopted here, the phrase literally is: 'we gave our face from'. Zoega (p. 636 not. 2) translates it 'prospicere'. But perhaps it is best to take ϩⲣⲁ in the sense (found in Sahidic) of 'voice': for (1) ϩⲣⲁ can be used in that sense in Bohairic; see p. 98 l. 8 (trans. p. 99 *v.* 33): (2) in the Sahidic corresponding to the text (p. 69) we have the phrase 'lifted up our voice (ϩⲣⲁⲛ)'. Translate in that case: 'we lifted up (*lit.* gave forth) our voice'. For the use of a form which resembles a Sahidic form, but which is not unknown in Bohairic, see ϭⲁⲗⲟ (=ϫⲁⲗⲟ) *v.* 5. I have noted it again in Hyvernat, *Act. Mart.* vol. I p. 66. See Z p. 634 not. 19.

9. *is it not possible...*] ⲙⲏ ⲙⲙⲟⲛ ϣϫⲟⲙ ⲉⲑⲣⲉ ⲑⲁⲓ ⲙⲟⲩ ϣⲁ ⲉⲛⲉϩ Lit. 'is it not possible that she should ever die?' The sense is evidently that given in the translation in the text. See corresponding Sahidic (p. 69). The negative question has caused the confusion.

12. *I* who *am the Lord*] Lagarde has ⲁⲛⲟⲕ ⲡⲉ, ⲡϭⲟⲓⲥ. I have omitted the stop, and connected ⲡⲉ with the words which follow.

13. *bid me speak*] Or 'suffer me to speak'. For ⲟⲩⲁϩⲥⲁϩⲛⲓ in the sense of 'suffer' see Mt XIX 8; Mc V 13; Lc IX 59, 61.

IX 6. *There are many shapes in Death*] For a description of the faces which Death assumes see James, *Testament of Abraham* p. 101 f. See also notes on c. XI 13, and on *Sah. Frag. Life Virg.* IV *v.* 115.

X 12. See *Addenda* p. 246.

16. *canopy*] Or *apse* (κόγχη, in corresponding Sah. κόγχος). In Eastern Churches κόγχη was the apse in the middle of the east end of the Church (Soph. *Lex.* p. 671). In Syriac ܩܘܢܟܐ was used for the apse. Mr N. McLean has given me the following references: Payne Smith, *Syr. Lex.* col. 3666; Hoffmann in Z. D. M. G. XXXII p. 752; Budge, *Hist. Mon. of Thomas of Margâ* p. L ff; Wright, *Chronicle of Joshua the Stylite* p. 29 l. 6 (*Eng. trans.* p. 24). For a description of the arrangement of the altars in a Coptic Church, see Butler, *Ancient Coptic Churches of Egypt* vol. II c. I.

XI 6. *angels of light*] Cf. the expression 'rulers of light' in *Sah. Frag. Life Virg.* I *v.* 94.

12. *those paths*] Lagarde gives MS reading as **ⲙⲁⲛⲙⲟϣⲓ ⲉⲧⲉⲙⲙⲁⲩ**. Perhaps we should read **ⲛⲓⲙⲁⲛⲙⲟϣⲓ ⲉⲧⲉⲙⲙⲁⲩ**.

13. *the avengers with divers aspects*] Or 'faces'. In the Book of the Dead reference is made to several monsters in Amenta, who attack the dead man. Thus there is a description in a papyrus at the British Museum (9901) of a devourer whose fore part is that of a crocodile; her hind-quarters those of a hippopotamus; her middle part that of a lion. In the Papyrus of Ani prayer is offered for deliverance from the 'Tchatcha,' i.e. the four gods of the cardinal points: 'May there be nothing to resist me at [my] judgment; may there be no opposition to me from the *Tchatcha*; may there be no parting of thee from me in the presence of him who keepeth the scales!' (Budge, *Book of the Dead*, *Pap. of Ani* p. 257 f.) Cf. also c. XXXI Book of the Dead, where there is a representation in the Turin Papyrus of the dead man repelling four crocodiles with his spear (see Lepsius, *Todtenbuch* XVI).

XII 6. *the door of the gate*] The words thus translated are used in Ac XII 13 for ἡ θύρα τοῦ πυλῶνος.

7. *overcome thee*] Lagarde puts a comma between **ⲁⲓϭⲉⲣⲟⲕ** and **ⲛⲑⲟⲕ**, which appears to me unnecessary. **ⲛⲑⲟⲕ** makes the pronominal ending more emphatic.

9. *where we were*] I have retained the MS reading. Lagarde reads **ⲛⲁϥ** for **ⲛⲁⲛ**. Translate in that case: 'For He was sitting with us in the place where God the Word was.'

10. *fine linen*] Here the soul is regarded as something material which can be wrapped in linen. Cf. James, *Test. of Abraham* p. 103; *Death of Joseph* XXIII 2 (Boh.). In the Papyrus of Ani (c. XCI) the soul is represented as a bird with a human head. The word translated 'fine linen' is **ϣⲉⲛⲥ**, and is used in Lc XVI 19 for βύσσος. It has been conclusively proved that the mummy cloths of the ancient Egyptians were made of linen. 'The marvellous skill which the Egyptians displayed in making linen did not die out with the fall of the native sovereigns of Egypt, and the Copts, or native Christians of that country, carried on the industry with splendid success until the twelfth century of our era. Although they ceased to mummify their dead, for the hope of the resurrection of the body given by Christianity practically killed the art of embalming, they continued to dress them in garments which are remarkable for the beauty of the embroidery and tapestries with which they are decorated' (Budge, *The Mummy* p. 191 f.).

appointed the place for] **ϯ ⲙⲡⲑⲱϣ ⲙ**. The word **ⲑⲱϣ** (Sah. **ⲧⲱϣ**) was technically used of the place assigned to a corpse. Cf. Z p. 619 l. 1 ff. 'I hope to go unto Egypt...and see the place assigned (**ⲡⲧⲱϣ**) for (**ⲙ**) his body and his holy shrine (**ⲙⲁⲣⲧⲏⲣⲓⲟⲛ**).'

Cf. p. 36 l. 2; Hyvernat, *Act. Mart.* vol. I p. 76 l. 9. See also p. 94 l. 12 (trans. p. 95 *v.* 12, where see note).

XIV 2. Cf. corresponding Sahidic (p. 79), and *Death of Joseph* XXVII 2. The garments here referred to are probably the final covering laid over all the bandages, which in the best time of Egypt was made of purple linen. In 1884 a Christian cemetery was discovered at Akhmîm. The bodies in it were dressed, it would appear, in their best clothes. 'The head was provided with a band or cap, and was sometimes supported on a pillow. The body wore a tunic, and the feet had stockings, sandals or shoes upon them; the head, breast, arms, and fingers were decorated with ornaments... The body was entirely covered over with linen and laid upon a board, and thus dressed was then deposited in the earth' (Budge, *The Mummy* p. 192). A. J. Butler (*Ancient Coptic Churches of Egypt* vol. I c. III p. 91 f.) gives a description of a curious painting of the Resurrection of Lazarus on the choir screen of the Church of Abu-'s-Sifain; where Lazarus is represented as 'standing upright swathed from head to foot in bands of linen like a mummy, while over his head and falling behind is a dark heavy robe which forms a head-dress or hood, precisely like the arrangement seen on mummy-cases. Two men are represented as unwinding the strips of fine linen.'

6. *David*] I have retained the MS reading. Lagarde has changed **ⲛϫⲉ** into **ⲛⲧⲉ**. Translate in that case: 'He prayed: He said the Allelujah of David the holy singer.' But the change is unnecessary.

XVII 2. *I have hardened*] **ⲁⲓⲑⲱⲙ**. The root idea of **ⲑⲱⲙ** is 'to close.' It is used for πωρόω (2 Co III 14; cf. Mc III 5; VI 52; VIII 17; Ro XI 25), or τυφλόω (2 Co IV 4; 1 Jn II 11). See Jn XII 40 **ⲁϥⲑⲱⲙ** (τετύφλωκεν) **ⲛⲛⲟⲩⲃⲁⲗ ⲟⲩⲟϩ ⲁϥⲑⲱⲙ** (ἐπώρωσεν) **ⲙⲡⲟⲩϩⲏⲧ**.

5. *lamps*] Cf. Mt XXV 1. See p. 101 *v.* 21.

XIX 1. *the sixteenth of Mesore*] Cf. pp. 91, 121. Mesore *roughly* corresponds to August. This date represents the ordinary Coptic tradition. Thus Malan (*Cal. of Cop. Church* p. 38) gives Mesre XVI (Aug. IX) as the day on which 'the body of Our Lady' was 'taken up to heaven.' See also Wüstenfeld, *Synax. Cop. Chr.* II p. 252.

5. *intercede*] **ⲡⲣⲉⲥⲃⲉⲩⲓⲛ**. Cf. Budge, *Michael the Arch.*, *Theod. Dicourse* p. 60 l. 11, where Michael is asked to intercede (**ⲉⲑⲣⲉⲕⲉⲣⲡⲣⲉⲥⲃⲉⲩⲓⲛ ϧⲁⲣⲟⲛ ϧⲁⲧⲉⲛ ⲡϭⲥ ⲫϯ ⲛⲟⲩ**). The plea for intercession of the saint is commonly found at the end of the discourse delivered in his honour.

6. *alms*] Cf. Budge, *St George of Cappadocia* p. 82 l. 3 f. 'He was a man that loved God, that loved alms (**ⲁⲅⲁⲡⲏ**), that loved men'; l. 8 'giving great alms (**ⲁⲅⲁⲡⲏ**).' The same word (**ⲁⲅⲁⲡⲏ**) is used in *v.* 3, where I have translated it 'charity.'

SAHIDIC FRAGMENTS OF THE FALLING ASLEEP OF MARY.

Fragment I.

VII 16. *manger*] ⲟⲩⲟⲙϥ=ⲟⲩⲟⲩⲟⲙϥ Cf. Lc II 7 (*ap.* Amélineau); Rossi, *Pap. Cop.* vol. II fasc. I p. 28. See note on *Sah. Frag. Life Virg.* I *v.* 35.

the Cherubim] Cf. p. 157 c. XXII 1, where see note.

VIII 8. I have read ⲁⲛ twice in this verse. In the first case the MS has ⲛ, and the scribe seems accidentally to have omitted the ⲁ. In the second case there is room for a letter before ⲛ, and very doubtful traces of an ⲁ.

9. *the rest of the apostles*] I have ventured to correct the MS, and have read ⲛⲛⲁⲡⲟⲥⲧⲟⲗⲟⲥ for ⲛⲁⲡⲟⲥⲧⲟⲗⲟⲥ. Cf. Ac II 37, where the phrase ⲡⲕⲉⲥⲉⲉⲡⲉ ⲛⲛⲁⲡⲟⲥⲧⲟⲗⲟⲥ is found.

Fragment II.

X 6. *stretched herself out*] Kabis is undoubtedly right in taking the verb ⲕⲉⲥⲕⲱⲥ ⲉⲃⲟⲗ in a wider signification than that given in Peyron's Lexicon (see A Z 1875 p. 59).

her open hands to her sides] The MS appears corrupt; I have therefore emended the text.

12. *shrine*] ⲕⲛϩⲉ here probably=ναός. See Bsciai, *Nov. Auct. Lex.* (A. Z. 1886 p. 91).

which was *in his hand*] Cod. Borg. has ⲉⲧⲛⲧⲟⲟⲧϥ, which might= 'which he had': cf. Jn IV 11 ⲙⲛ ⲕⲁⲗⲟⲥ ⲛⲧⲟⲟⲧⲕ (*οὔτε ἄντλημα ἔχεις*); XV 13 (Boh.). But perhaps ⲧⲟⲟⲧ here retains its original signification of 'hand,' and ⲉⲧⲛⲧⲟⲟⲧϥ=ⲉⲧϩⲛ ⲧⲉϥϭⲓϫ of Cod. Clar., 'which *was* in his hand.' In *Sah. Frag. Life Virg.* II B *v.* 30 ⲉⲧⲛⲧⲟⲟⲧⲟⲩ probably='which they had.' But it may='which *was* in their hand.'

Surely those also] The word translated 'surely' is ⲁⲕⲙⲏⲛ or ⲁⲕⲙⲉⲛ (ἀκμήν). There is no indication in the MSS as to whether it is to be taken with the preceding or following words. Greek particles were sometimes used in a somewhat loose manner, as e.g. ⲧⲁⲭⲁ p. 182 l. 14. For the use of ⲛⲕⲱⲟⲩⲉ (ⲛⲕⲟⲟⲩⲉ) in the sense of 'those also,' see note on the words 'this also' on p. 97 *v.* 26.

13. *We heard a voice*] See note on *Second Boh. Acc. Falling Asleep of Mary* c. III 5.

16. *canopy*] Or *apse* (ⲕⲟⲛⲭⲟⲥ). See note on corresponding Bohairic.

XIII 1. *who has...lying*] After ⲛⲧⲁϥⲧⲱⲟⲩⲛ (which may mean 'who has risen') some three or four letters are lost in the MS.

3. *worthy...to kiss*] Probably the scribe wrote 'for thou wast worthy' (ϫⲉ ⲁⲣⲙⲡϣⲁ) twice by mistake, at the end of one page and the beginning of the next. But, owing to a defect in the MS, only ϣⲁ and perhaps ⲡ of the second ϫⲉ ⲁⲣⲙⲡϣⲁ are left.

5. *to tell to man*] So Sah. Version in 2 Co xii 4 (*ap.* Amélineau).

xiv 2. *unguent*] ⲕⲉⲣⲱⲗⲏ = κηρωτή = κήρωμα.

xv 4. *Jews*] In the Coptic accounts of the Assumption (see pp. 3 *v.* 7; 62 f.; 119) the Jews attempt to burn the Virgin's body, but are smitten with blindness. Other narratives mention one person as specially prominent in offering an insult to the corpse. According to the Greek account his name is Jephonias (*Joh. Lib. Dor. Mar. v.* 46): according to the Latin, Ruben (*Trans. Mar.* A 14) or 'a chief of the priests of the Jews' (*Trans. Mar.* B c. xi 3): according to the Syriac, Yuphanya (Wright, *Syr. Apoc.* p. 37; *Journal Sac. Lit.* April 1865 p. 149); according to the Arabic Juphia (Enger, *Trans. Mar.* p. 71). In each case his punishment is graphically described.

xvi 5. *to the heavens*] ⲙⲡⲏⲩⲉ = ⲉⲙⲡⲏⲩⲉ. Cf. Z p. 553 l. 18 ⲁⲩϫⲓⲧ ⲙⲡⲏⲩⲉ.

xvii 4. *that He would hearken to us*] ⲡⲓⲑⲉ (ⲡⲓⲑⲏ, ⲡⲉⲓⲑⲉ) is used in Sahidic with various shades of meaning. (1) It = *persuade.* See Mt xxvii 20 (with ⲛ). Cf. Guidi, *Rendiconti d. R. Accad. d. Lincei* ser. v vol. ii p. 526 l. 11 (with ⲙⲙⲟϥ). Hence (*a*) *comfort, assure.* See 1 Jn iii 19 (with ⲙ). Cf. Guidi, *op. cit.* p. 523 l. 20 (with ⲙⲙⲟⲕ). On p. 169 *v.* 13, where it is followed by ⲙⲙⲟⲛ, I have translated it 'assure': (*b*) *convince.* Cf. Revillout, *Le Concile de Nicée* p. 45. 'But it is easier to raise *the* dead than to convince (ⲡⲉⲓⲑⲉ ⲛ) an heretic.' (2) It = *be persuaded.* See Ac xvii 4; xxi 14. Hence (*a*) *agree to.* See Ac v 40 (with ⲛⲁϥ). Cf. Rossi, *Pap. Cop.* vol. ii fasc. iv p. 17 'He hearkened to (ⲡⲓⲑⲉ ⲙ) the multitude, and released Barabbas unto them': (*b*) *allow.* Cf. Z p. 263 l. 24 f. 'They besought him to allow them (ⲡⲉⲓⲑⲉ ⲛⲁⲩ) to take away the bones of the saints.'

SECOND BOHAIRIC ACCOUNT OF THE FALLING ASLEEP OF MARY.

Dr Budge has lately published a sermon by Theodosius on St Michael the Archangel. He thinks that the Theodosius in both cases was probably the Jacobite Patriarch of Alexandria (elected 536 AD, died 567 or 568. See *Dict. of Chr. Biog.* vol. iv p. 969). In his sermon on

St Michael allusion is made to discourses by him on the new year and on St John the Baptist. (See Budge's *St Michael the Archangel* p. xv f. See note 2 on p. xv f. for references to discourses by Theodosius in Syriac. Cf. also p. 5 of the Coptic text.)

The phrase **ετερφοριн мпχc** ('who bore Christ') is a translation of χριστοφόρος (cf. Ign. *Ep. Eph.* IX 2). Cf. Lightfoot, *Apost. Fathers* part II vol. II sect. II p. 865, where **θεοφοροc** is used of Ignatius and thus explained: **πιαгιος ιгнатιος фн етеγмоγ+** (sic) **ероq же θеофорос ете фн петерфорін мф+.**

I 6. *son of the Dove*] In St John the Bohairic version makes Peter the son of John (I 43; XXI 15 ff.). In St Matthew he is spoken of as **вαριωнα** i.e. son of Jona or a Dove (בר יונה). See p. 9 *v.* 61.

II 2. *in Jerusalem*] In the first Bohairic account Mary is in the house, with women who followed her from Jerusalem (p. 51 *v.* 10). The house seems to have been in or near the city. Here she lives in Jerusalem. Cf. *Trans. Mar.* A 9. In the Greek account she is in Bethlehem (*Joh. Lib. Mar. Dor. v.* 4). Cf. Wright's Syriac *Transitus Virginis, Eng. Trans.* p. 32.

4. *amazed...sad*] **ониш евол . . . окем.** Cf. Rossi, *Pap. Cop.* vol. I fasc. IV p. 33 **аγωкм тнроγ аγωнш нса петерну.**

5. *office*] **cγнаζic.** This word is not uncommon in Coptic literature. Cf. e.g. Z. p. 77 l. 11; p. 320 l. 17; Budge, *Michael the Archangel*, where it is found four times (see index p. 233). For the various uses of Synaxis (σύναξις) see *Dict. Chr. Ant.* vol. II p. 1947.

6. *about thirty years*] **еqнаер λ нромпι.** Cf. Ac I 15 **еγнаер рк нран** (ὡς ἑκατὸν εἴκοσι).

12. *appointment*] **θωш** here = 'appointment' or 'ordinance,' as e.g. on p. 137 *v.* 9, where 'ordinance' is in Coptic **θωш.** Cf. Z p. 553 l. 22 f. **пажоеіс матамоі ентωш мпеішнн енесωш нтеіϩе тнрс.** In *First Boh. Acc. Falling Asleep of Mary* c. XII 10 **θωш** has a technical meaning, where see note.

22. *slaying them*] The root **ϫολϫελ**, which I have translated 'slay,' is used either (1) of butting with the horns; cf. Ex XXI 28, where it = κερατίζειν: or (2) of slaying; cf. Lc XIX 27, where it = κατασφάττειν.

26. *cancer*] **маме+ = оγаме+.** This form is noticed by Zoega (*Cat.* p. 337 not. 371) as found in his MS copied from ours; and Kabis (A. Z. 1875 p. 111) speaks of **оγмаме+** (and **оγоγмаме+**?) as 'often read in Vatican MSS for the more usual **оγаме+**' (**оγаме+** in these cases evidently = **оγоγаме+**, see note on *Sah. Frag. Life Virg.* I 35). **оγаме+** is connected with the root **оγωм** ('to eat'). Cf. Z p. 68 l. 14 f. 'the disease which is called the cancer (**+оγаме+**), it having eaten (**еасоγем**) all his face.' For the interchange of **м** and **оγ**, cf. forms **жωм** (Sah.) and **жωоγ** (Boh.). See Stern, *Kop. Gram.* § 46.

this also] For this use of ⲡⲁⲓϫⲉⲧ see Ge XXIX 33 ⲁϥϯ ⲙⲡⲁⲓϫⲉⲧ ⲛⲏⲓ (καὶ προσέδωκέν μοι καὶ τοῦτον); Lc XIX 19 ⲡⲉϫⲁϥ ⲇⲉ ⲟⲛ ⲙⲡⲁⲓϫⲉⲧ (εἶπεν δὲ καὶ τούτῳ). So ⲛⲁⲓⲕⲉϫⲱⲟⲩⲛⲓ in V 19 = 'these also', and on p. 180 l. 18 ⲛⲕⲟⲟⲩⲉ = 'those also'. Cf. p. 72 ll. 10, 25. Stern does not notice these uses in his discussion on ⲕⲉ (*Kop. Gram.* § 270 f.).

27. There is a confusion of constructions in this verse. After ⲙⲙⲟⲛ ϣϫⲟⲙ ⲛ we should have expected an infinitive ⲉϯ. Cf. Mt III 9; VII 18. But the scribe when he reached the end of the sentence had forgotten how he began, and wrote a future (ⲛⲁϣϯ) instead.

30. *the ruler of darkness*] According to the Pistis Sophia there are one or more rulers (ⲁⲣϫⲱⲛ) in each treasury inside the dragon, which is the outer darkness (*PS* p. 319 ff.). Mention is also made of 'the ruler of the outer darkness', ⲡⲁⲣϫⲱⲛ ⲙⲡⲕⲁⲕⲉ ⲉⲧϩⲓⲃⲟⲗ (cf. *PS* p. 105 l. 21).

III 5. *we heard a voice*] Here the voice directs the virgins to go to Mary. In the other account (see pp. 57, 75), the voice pronounces the doom of Jerusalem, and the incident may be compared with Josephus' narrative of the fall of the city (*De Bello Jud.* VI 299—309 Ed. Niese vol. VI p. 552 ff.).

13. *the Inheritor*] ⲡⲓⲡⲁⲣⲁⲗⲓⲙⲡⲧⲟⲥ. The word may be derived from Gnostic sources. In the Pistis Sophia we read of 'the παραλήμπτορες (ⲙⲡⲁⲣⲁⲗⲏⲙⲡⲧⲱⲣ) of the sun and the παραλήμπτορες (ⲙⲡⲁⲣⲁⲗⲏⲙⲡⲧⲱⲣ) of the moon,' and Melchizedek is called 'the ⲡⲁⲣⲁⲗⲏⲙⲡⲧⲱⲣ of light' (*PS* p. 35). Cf. also *PS* p. 106 l. 9 (ⲡⲁⲣⲁⲗⲏⲙⲧⲏⲥ); p. 349 l. 4 (ⲡⲁⲣⲁⲗⲏⲙⲡⲧⲏⲥ); and Schmidt, *Gnost. Schrift.* p. 99, where ⲡⲁⲣⲁⲗⲏⲙⲡⲧⲏⲥ occurs in close connection with ⲑⲏⲥⲁⲩⲣⲟⲥ and ⲁϩⲟⲣⲁⲧⲟⲥ. 'Unter den Genien', says Dr Schmidt, 'welche jeden Äon bevölkern und das Pleroma durch ihre Gesammtheit ausmachen, giebt es eine Hierarchie der παραλῆμπται oder παραλήμπτορες, deren Aufgabe darin besteht, die Seelen nach dem Tode aus dem Körper zu holen und durch alle Äonen bis zum Topos des Gottes der Wahrheit zu führen. Diese vergleicht Amélineau mit Anubis, dem ψυχοπόμπος der ägyptischen Religion, welcher die Seelen in den Saal des Osiris und seiner 42 Beisitzer führte und ihnen "den Weg öffnete." Auch ähnelt die Reise einer gnostischen Seele durch die Äonen ganz derjenigen einer ägyptischen zum Amente. Jene bedarf der Siegel und Losungsworte, um die Ungeheuer zu bekämpfen, diese muss auf ihrer Reise zum Osiris viele Ungeheuer, die sich ihr entgegenstellen, überwinden, muss bei der Überfahrt über den grossen Fluss der Unterwelt ein Verhör bestehen, um sich in betreff der Kenntnis der Mysterien zu rechtfertigen' (Schmidt, *Gnost. Schrift.* p. 553 f.).

21. *espousals*] The word thus translated is ⲁⲣⲏⲃ (ἀρραβών) 'an earnest'. Peyron (*Lex.* p. 11) gives a secondary meaning 'sponsalia'. Cf. the use of ἀρραβωνίζεσθαι in *Euchol.* p. 240 f. (as cited by Soph.

Lex. p. 251). For the history of the word see Lightfoot, *Notes on Epistles of St Paul* p. 323 f.

IV 12. *My true tabernacle, and My Father and the Holy Ghost long*] Possibly the words may mean, 'My true tabernacle, and *the tabernacle of* My Father and *of* the Holy Ghost, longs.' In that case **ⲡⲁⲓⲱⲧ = ⲑⲁ ⲡⲁⲓⲱⲧ.**

13. *proceedeth*] The same verb (**ⲡⲏⲟⲩ ⲉⲃⲟⲗ**) is used of the procession of the Spirit in the Creed (as given in Tuki, *Missale, Anaph. Bas.* p. **ⲡⲋ**), 'the Holy Ghost, the Lord, giver of life, who proceedeth from the Father and the Son' (**ⲡⲣⲉϥϯ ⲙⲡⲱⲛϧ ⲫⲏ ⲉⲑⲛⲏⲟⲩ ⲉⲃⲟⲗ ϧⲉⲛ ⲫⲓⲱⲧ ⲛⲉⲙ ⲡϣⲏⲣⲓ**).

14. *the land of the living*] M. Renouf in speaking of Egyptian tombs and inscriptions says, 'The word *ānchiu*, which literally signifies the "living," is in innumerable places used emphatically for the "departed," who are enjoying everlasting life. The notion of everlasting life, *ānch t'eta*, is among the few words written upon the wooden coffin, now in the British Museum, of king Mykerinos, of the third pyramid. *Neb ānch*, "Lord of life," is one of the names given to the sarcophagus. In the very ancient inscription of Una, the coffin is called *hen en ānchiu*, "the chest of the living." It is only evil spirits who are spoken of in the sacred writings of the Egyptians as "the dead".' (Renouf, *Hibbert Lectures* 1879, second edition p. 127 f.).

Forthwith] **ϧⲉⲛ ⲫⲁⲓ.** The phrase is used in Jn IV 27, where ℵ*D have ἐν τούτῳ, and most of the other Greek uncials ἐπὶ τούτῳ. The Sahidic has in that place **ⲛⲧⲉⲩⲛⲟⲩ** ('straightway').

V 8. *pour...into*] **ⲙⲁ ⲛⲉϩ ⲛⲥⲁ.** Cf. Lc X 34 **ⲉⲁϥϯ ⲛⲉϩ ϩⲓ ⲏⲣⲡ ⲛⲥⲱⲟⲩ** (*ἐπιχέων ἔλαιον καὶ οἶνον*).

9. *translation*] **ⲟⲩⲱⲧⲉⲃ ⲉⲃⲟⲗ.** The same word is found in He XI 5 for the *μετάθεσις* of Enoch.

10. *heart is broken*] Cf. Is LXI 1 **ⲛⲏ ⲉⲧϧⲉⲙϧⲱⲙ ϧⲉⲛ ⲛⲟⲩϩⲏⲧ.**

12. *for the salvation of us all*] Cf. words of the Creed (as given in Tuki, *Missale, Anaph. Bas.* pp. **ⲡⲉ, ⲡⲋ**) **ⲫⲁⲓ ⲉⲧⲉ ⲉⲑⲃⲉⲧⲉⲛ ⲁⲛⲟⲛ ϧⲁ ⲛⲓⲣⲱⲙⲓ ⲛⲉⲙ ⲉⲑⲃⲉ ⲡⲉⲛⲟⲩϫⲁⲓ ⲁϥⲓ ⲉⲡⲉⲥⲏⲧ ⲉⲃⲟⲗ ϧⲉⲛ ⲧⲫⲉ** ('Who for us men, and for our salvation came down from heaven').

15. *sentence*] Cf. p. 145 c. XXXI 1. The whole passage may be compared with James, *Test. Abraham* p. 85 l. 25 ff.; p. 86.

17. *Yet*] The word thus rendered is **ⲕⲁⲛ.** I do not know what it means here. The text is corrupt. I have had to emend the next word **ⲥⲉⲟⲓ**, and the **ⲁ** of **ⲛⲟⲩⲁⲓ** has been written by the first hand over an erasure.

20. *power*] *δύναμις.* See note on *Sah. Frag. Life Virg.* I 8.

21. *that this dispensation took place*] Lit. 'that this dispensation, that it took place,' or perhaps 'that this dispensation moreover (*or* further) took place.'

25. *two hundred and six days*]. The length of time between the

Falling Asleep and the Assumption of Mary, which is found in the two Bohairic accounts, is remarkable. The Sahidic (p. 85) has a much shorter period. In the two Latin accounts there is no such interval. The body is taken up immediately (*Trans. Mar.* A *v.* 16) or almost immediately (*Trans. Mar.* B cc. XV, XVI) after the apostles have laid it in the tomb. In the Greek narrative some MSS state that as the apostles were carrying her forth, twelve clouds of light caught them away with the body, and translated them to Paradise. One MS (C) says that when they had buried her body in Gethsemane in a new tomb ἕως τριῶν ἡμερῶν ἀοράτων ἀγγέλων φωναὶ ἠκούοντο δοξαζόντων τὸν ἐξ αὐτῆς τεχθέντα Χριστὸν τὸν θεὸν ἡμῶν. καὶ πληρουμένης τῆς τρίτης ἡμέρας οὐκέτι ἠκούοντο αἱ φωναί, καὶ λοιπὸν ἐκεῖθεν πάντες ἔγνωσαν ὅτι μετετέθη τὸ ἄμωμον καὶ τίμιον αὐτῆς σῶμα ἐν παραδείσῳ. (*Joh. Lib. Dor. Mar. v.* 48.) For the Syriac accounts see Wright, *Syr. Apoc.* p. 37 ff.; *Journ. Sac. Lit.* April 1865 p. 148 ff.; and for the Arabic see Enger, *Trans. Virg.* p. 71 ff.

VI 1. *she lay down*] A Bohairic MS (46) in the possession of Lord Crawford contains two fragments of this sermon. The first begins with **κοτ ϩιϫεη ηιϩϐωc** (VI 1) and ends with **ceepϩⲩⲙnoc ϧaϫωτεn** (VI 9). The second begins with **ωⲑ ϥoⲩaϐ** (VI 25) and ends with **epoη** (VII 1). I refer to the MS as C_1: for a description of it see Introduction.

to our Saviour] C_1 has 'to our good Saviour' (**επεncωτηp ηaгa-ⲑoc**).

2. *the body*] **ⲙπcωⲙa** C_1.

3. *commanded*] + 'us' (**ηaη**) C_1.

4. *stretched out His hand*] **aϥcoⲩτωη τεϥϫιϫ εϐoλ** C_1.

6. *her head*] **ητεcaφε** C_1.

shoulder] **ηaϩϐι** C_1 (so in *v.* 7).

of the Church] C_1 has these words in the margin.

7. *let him bear her feet*] **ⲙapεϥϥaι ϧa ηεcϭaλaⲩϫ** C_1.

8. *behind*] **ϩι φaϩoⲩ** C_1.

9. *without*] **aϭηε** C_1.

the heavens] 'the height' (**ηϭιcι**) C_1.

13. *six*] The Vatican MS appears to have 'three.' I have read 'six.' Cf. V 25; VIII 1.

28. *unspeakable*] **ηaτcaϫι ⲙⲙoϥ** C_1.

31. *hath brought me*] C_1 omits, as it seems, the **η** of **ηετaϥ-εητ**.

to] **εϫε⌜η⌝** C_1.

VII 1. *who were assembled*] **ετⲑoⲩηт** C_1.

19. *come upon them*] **εⲩει εϫωoⲩ.** The Boh. Version in Ps CXXXIX 11 (*ap.* Schwartze) has **εⲩεϩει εϧpηι** (v.l. **εϩpηι**) **εϫωoⲩ** (πεσοῦνται ἐπ' αὐτούς).

20. *and before Thee*] MS **ηεⲙ ηεκⲙⲑo.** Cf. reading of Dz., P. IV

in Lc xv 18, 21. I have read ⲛⲉⲙ ⲙⲡⲉⲕⲙⲑⲟ, as the second ⲙ was probably omitted through carelessness.

25. *we went*] Here ⲡⲉ followed by ⲁⲛ may have the same force as the Greek aorist. Cf. Ge xviii 15 ⲡⲉ ⲁⲥⲉⲣϩⲟϯ ⲅⲁⲣ ⲡⲉ (ἐφοβήθη γάρ).

ix 2. *the body...embraced its own soul*] See the picture in the British Museum Papyrus of Ani (c. xci), where the soul, represented as a bird with a human head, is being united to the body of the dead man. (Renouf, *Facsimile of Pap. of Ani* 1894, plate 17.)

10. *succourer*] Cf. Budge, *Encom. on Elijah* (*Trans. Soc. Bibl. Arch.* vol. ix pt. 2, 1893), where St Chrysostom towards the end of his discourse on Elijah (p. ⲣⲕⲇ) speaks of him as ⲡⲣⲟⲥⲧⲁⲧⲏⲥ ⲙⲡⲅⲉⲛⲟⲥ ⲧⲏⲣϥ ⲛⲛⲓⲣⲱⲙⲓ ('succourer of the whole race of men'), and adds ⲙⲁⲣⲉⲛϫⲁϥ ⲛⲁⲛ ϩⲱⲛ ⲙⲡⲣⲟⲥⲧⲁⲧⲏⲥ ('Let us also have him *as our* succourer'). See p. 28 l. 5.

13. *the sons of God*] Here, as in the Boh. version of Ps xxviii 1 (*ap.* Schwartze), 'the sons of God' is the object of the verb. The Sah. version takes it as subject. The Greek has υἱοὶ θεοῦ.

BOHAIRIC ACCOUNT OF THE DEATH OF JOSEPH.

L. Stern has published (*Z. f. w. Theol.*, 1883, p. 270 ff.) a German translation of the Bohairic narrative, and has noticed variations in the Sahidic. In each case he has used Revillout's edition of the Coptic text. Dulaurier has made a somewhat free translation into French (see *Fragment des Révelations Apocr. de S. Barthelemy* p. 24 ff.) of the Sahidic text of cc. xiv 3—xv 2 and of cc. xxi—xxiii. His translation of cc. xxi—xxiii has been reprinted with modifications of details by Revillout (*Rev. Égypt.*, vol. ii, p. 65 f.). Dulaurier used Zoega's text (*Cat.* 225 ff.).

The commemoration of Joseph's 'rest in the Lord' on Epep xxvi or July xx is mentioned in Malan's *Calendar of the Coptic Church* (p. 36). See also Selden, *De Syn. Vet. Ebr.* (ed. ult.) lib. iii c. xv p. 245; Ludolf, *Ad Hist. Aeth. Com.* p. 423; Mai, *Script. Vet. Col.* iv, *Cod. Arab.* xv p. 32.

the Library at Jerusalem] Theodosius in his account of the Falling Asleep of Mary (see Introduction to *Second Boh. Account*) claims to have derived his information from records in Jerusalem. ⲕⲁⲧⲁ ⲫⲣⲏϯ ⲉⲧⲁⲓϫⲉⲙⲥ ⲓⲥⲧⲟⲣⲓⲕⲱⲥ ϧⲉⲛ ϩⲁⲛⲥⲩⲛⲧⲁⲅⲙⲁ ⲛⲁⲣⲭⲉⲟⲥ ϧⲉⲛ ⲓⲗⲏⲙ ⲛⲁⲓ ⲉⲧⲁⲩⲓ ⲉⲧⲟⲧ ϧⲉⲛ ϯⲃⲓⲃⲗⲓⲟⲑⲏⲕⲏ ⲛⲧⲉ ⲡⲓⲁⲅⲓⲟⲥ ⲙⲁⲣⲕⲟⲥ ϧⲉⲛ ⲣⲁⲕⲟϯ ('Even as I found it in detail in ancient records in Jerusalem, which came into my hand in the Library of the holy Mark at Alexandria').

And again] ⲟⲩⲟϩ ⲟⲛ ϫⲉ. This phrase is probably used here as in cc. I 4 f.; XXX 4 ff. to introduce further words of the Saviour. Stern has 'Der Tag aber.'

I 1. *sitting on the mount of Olives*] Almost at the beginning of the first book of the Pistis Sophia we read of 'the disciples sitting one with another on the mount of Olives...and saying one with another, We are more blessed than all the men that *are* on the earth, because the Saviour has revealed these things to us, and we have received the fulness and the whole consummation' (*PS* p. 4; cf. also p. 169 ff). See Schmidt, *Gnost. Schrift.* pp. 440, 596 f.

2. *many times now*] ⲓⲥ is probably not here used in the sense of 'behold'. See Ac XXIV 10, where ⲓⲥ ⲟⲩⲙⲏϣ ⲛ̀ⲣⲟⲙⲡⲓ = ἐκ πολλῶν ἐτῶν.

for the universe] ϧⲁ ⲡⲓⲉⲛⲧⲏⲣϥ. Stern translates this 'vollends' here, but in XVIII 8 he has a better rendering 'für die Gesammtheit.'

that ye may] ϫⲉ, ϩⲓⲛⲁ Lagarde. There is no need of a stop after ϫⲉ. For the use of ϫⲉ ϩⲓⲛⲁ see Stern, *Kop. Gram.* § 613.

preach it in all the world] In the Pistis Sophia Jesus tells His disciples at some length the message which they are to 'preach to the whole world'. Cf. *PS* p. 254 ff.

7. *no one*] After the first ⲙ̀ⲙⲟⲛ Lagarde has omitted ϩⲗⲓ, which is however found in the MS.

II 1. *the* city *of the Jews*] ⲑⲁ ⲛⲓⲓⲟⲩⲇⲁⲓ. Cf. Lc XXIII 51, where Arimathaea is called ⲟⲩⲃⲁⲕⲓ ⲛ̀ⲧⲉ ⲛⲓⲓⲟⲩⲇⲁⲓ ('a city of the Jews').

3. *four sons*] According to the Syriac *Letter of Pilate* Joseph had 'five sons by a former wife' (Wright, *Syriac Apoc.* p. 16).

Josetos] Ἰωσῆτος. This use of the Greek genitive is also found in Syriac. See *Apology of Aristides* ܝܢ l. 11, where ܡܢ ܕܙܘܣ = 'from Zeus'.

4. *and left*] A Bohairic MS (39) in the possession of Lord Crawford contains two fragments of *The Death of Joseph.* The first begins with ⌜ⲟⲩⲟϩ ⲁ⌝ⲥ⌜ⲭⲱ⌝ (only ⲥ can now be read) in II 4 and ends with ⲉϧⲟⲩⲛ ⲉⲡⲉϥⲏⲓ (IV 4). The second begins with ϧⲉⲗⲗⲟ ⲉⲛⲁⲛⲉⲥ (end of X) and ends with ⲉⲧⲉ ⲟⲩⲟ⌜ⲛ⌝ (XIII 4). I refer to the MS as C_2: for a description of it see Introduction.

5. *was without*] Lagarde has emended the text, reading ⲛⲁϥⲓ ⲙ̀ⲃⲟⲗ ('went without') for ⲛⲁϥⲙ̀ⲃⲟⲗ ('was without'). I have followed the MSS (C_2 also has ⲛⲁϥⲙ̀ⲃⲟⲗ). So Stern 'er war auswärts.'

carpentry] ϯⲙⲉⲧⲁⲙϣⲉ C_2 (ut vid.).

living by] ⲉⲩⲟⲛϧ ⲉ. For construction see Deut VIII 3.

of their hands] ⲛ̀ⲛⲟⲩϫⲓϫ C_2.

III 1. *And*] C_2 seems to omit 'And' (ⲟⲩⲟϩ).

lived as a widower] ϩⲉⲙⲥⲓ ⲉϥⲟⲓ ⲛⲭⲏⲣⲁ. Contrast such a phrase as that found in Deut XXII 22 ⲟⲩⲥϩⲓⲙⲓ ⲉⲥϩⲉⲙⲥⲓ ⲛⲉⲙ ϩⲁⲓ (γυναικὸς συνοικισμένης ἀνδρί). ⲭⲏⲣⲁ here seems to mean 'widower'.

twelve years old] This statement agrees with the reading of most MSS in Prot. VIII 2 and with that of two MSS (BD) in Ps-Mt VIII 1.

She spent] C_2 seems to have read 'Now she spent' (reading ⲁⲥϯ ⲇⲉ for ⲁⲥϯ. There is room for ⲁⲥϯ, but it can no longer be read, and ⲉ of ⲇⲉ is doubtful).

three years] Cf. Prot. VII 1; Ps-Mt IV; De Nat. Mar. VI 1; Nic. Call. II 3 (quoted in note on *Sah. Frag. Life Virg.* I *v.* 2).

2. *living austerely*] ⲉⲥⲉⲣⲁⲥⲕⲓⲛ. Stern has wrongly translated 'wie sie wohlgefällig...war.'

IV 1. *twelve peoples*] The text must be corrupt. The Arabic has 'twelve old men.' C_2 seems to have an ⲛ for ⲙ in ⲙⲓⲃ. The letter ⲃ can still be read, but the middle letter is no longer legible.

In Prot. VIII 3 an angel appears to Zacharias and says, Ζαχαρία Ζαχαρία, ἔξελθε καὶ ἐκκλησίασον τοὺς χηρεύοντας τοῦ λαοῦ.

2. *lot*] Cf. Prot. IX 1; Ps-Mt VIII 2.

upon] ⲉϩⲣⲏⲓ ⲉϫⲉⲛ C_2.

3. *answered*] C_2 omits this word (ⲁⲩⲉⲣⲟⲩⲱ).

the marriage feast] Lagarde has emended the text, reading ⲡⲉϩⲟⲡ ('thy marriage feast') for ⲡⲓϩⲟⲡ ('the marriage feast'). I have followed the MSS (C_2 also has ⲡⲓϩⲟⲡ).

4. *Mary of James*] There is a tendency in Apocryphal narratives to identify persons of the same name. But Mary of James is not always regarded as the same as the Virgin. In a Sahidic fragment of a discourse on the Virgin by 'Cyril the archbishop' in the British Museum (Or. 3581 A) I find her regarded as a separate person. 'And Anna arose, and called all the virgins that *were* in Jerusalem. And they sought in Israel, and found also (*or* other) seven Maries. The first is Mary of James (ⲙⲁⲣⲓⲁ ⲧⲁ ⲓⲁⲕⲱⲃⲟⲥ). The second is Mary of John who is called Mark. The third is Mary the sister of Lazarus. The fourth is Mary of Judaea. The fifth is Mary of the mount of Olives. The sixth is Mary Magdalene. The seventh is Mary the mother of the Lord. These seven Maries therefore...' The fragment ends here.

V 1. *in the fourteenth year*] See Prot. XII 3 ἦν δὲ ἐτῶν δέκα ἓξ ὅτε ταῦτα ἐγένετο τὰ μυστήρια (where note various readings). Cf. c. XIV 6; Nic. Call. II 3 (quoted in note on *Sah. Frag. Life Virg.* I *v.* 2).

2. *three months*] Cf. De Nat. Mar. X 1. According to Prot. XIII 1 Joseph found her pregnant in the sixth month. See also Ps-Mt X 1.

found] ⲁϥϫⲓⲙⲓ MS. Lagarde has wrongly transcribed 'she found' (ⲁⲥϫⲓⲙⲓ, cf. also Revillout, *Apoc. Copt.* p. 47 l. 11).

VI 1. *Gabriel*] Cf. Lc I 26 f., where Gabriel is the angel sent to Mary.

take] Lagarde has emended the Bohairic MS here and in XVII 5, and has read the Infinitive 'to take' (ⲉϣⲉⲛ for ϣⲉⲛ). I prefer with Stern to keep to the MS. In each case the Sahidic has the Imperative. The mistake has doubtless originated in Sahidic by an ⲉ falling out (reading ⲙⲡⲣⲣϩⲟⲧⲉ ϫⲓ for ⲙⲡⲣⲣϩⲟⲧⲉ ⲉϫⲓ), and been adopted into the Bohairic. The Sahidic version in Mt I 20 has the Infinitive.

VII 1. *decree*] ⲇⲟⲅⲙⲁ. The Bohairic version in Lc II 1 uses a Coptic word (ϩⲱⲛ) for 'decree.' The Sahidic version has ⲇⲟⲅⲙⲁ.

each one after his city] ⲡⲓⲟⲩⲁⲓ ⲡⲓⲟⲩⲁⲓ ⲛⲥⲁ ⲧⲉϥⲃⲁⲕⲓ. These words in the Boh. Version do not occur until the end of Lc II 3. In the Sahidic similar words are found in Lc II 3, but ⲛⲥⲁ ⲛⲉⲥⲧⲙⲉ ('after their villages') comes at the end of Lc II 1. Here the Bohairic may be a translation of the Sahidic (see p. 148); the translator having rendered ⲛⲥⲁ ⲛⲉⲥⲧⲙⲉ by a familiar phrase in his own Bible, which occurs in the immediate context.

2. *through*] So MS ϩⲓⲧⲉⲛ. Lagarde emends the text to ϩⲁⲧⲉⲛ, which in Sadidic (cf. corresponding Sah.) means 'with.'

Joseph...and Mary...are] Another way of taking these words is 'for Joseph...and Mary...were (*lit.* are).' So Stern 'denn Joseph...und Maria...waren.'

3. *by the tomb*] Cf. Lord Crawford's Sah. MS 36, which says that our Lord was born in a tomb (quoted in note on *Sah. Frag. Life Virg.* II B *v.* 23).

VIII 2. *My kingdom*] Cf. p. 176 *v.* 4 f.

3. *Salome*] Cf. p. 51 *v.* 10 (where see note). Salome is mentioned in citations of Clement of Alexandria from the Gospel according to the Egyptians. See the citations collected by Zahn, *NT. Kan.* II p. 632 ff.

down to] These prepositions (ⲉϧⲣⲏⲓ ⲉ), which are not used in Mt II 14 (Boh.), may be a translation of Sah. ⲉϩⲣⲁⲓ ⲉ (found in Sah. of Mt II 14).

IX 2. *whilst we lived*] MS has ⲛⲟⲛϧ. Lagarde reads ⲉⲛⲟⲛϧ. Stern wishes to read ⲉϥⲟⲛϧ ('whilst he lived'). If the text must be emended, Lagarde's suggestion is the simplest.

X. Cf. XXIX 3 f.

XI 1. *Symeon*] C_2 seems to have 'Symon' (ⲥⲩⲙⲱⲛ).

also] C_2 omits this word (ϩⲱⲟⲩ).

2. *subjection*] ϩⲩⲡⲟⲇⲁⲕⲏ C_2. Both Bohairic MSS have a Greek word (ὑποταγή) for subjection. The Greek word is not found in the Boh. Vers. in 1 Ti II 11, but it is found in the Sahidic.

3. *obeyed them*] After ⲛⲥⲱⲟⲩ C_2 has, as it seems, the word ⲡⲉ.

they told Me] Lit. 'they will tell Me.' C_2 has the past tense 'they told Me' (ⲁⲩϫⲟⲧⲟⲩ).

exceedingly] For **ⲡⲉ ⲉⲙⲁϣⲱ** C_2 has **ⲉⲙⲁϣⲱ ⲡⲉ.**

XII 2. *his angel*] Cf. James, *Test. Abr.* pp. 84 f.; 111 f. There the angel who warns Abraham is Michael. Here Joseph prays that Michael may stand by him (XIII 2). For the expression 'his angel' see Ac XII 15. See note on *Sah. Frag. Death Joseph.* III c. XXII 1.

In] **ⲛϧⲣⲏⲓ ϧⲉⲛ.** For the first **ϧ** C_2 seems to have **ϩ**, but the MS is here difficult to read. The letter before **ϩ** (?) is illegible.

3. *prayed thus*] The prayer which follows may be compared with prayers offered by the Apostles before death in the Greek accounts. See Tisch. *Apocal. Apoc.* p. 150; *Acta Apost. Apoc.* pp. 92 f.; 127 f.; 239.

XIII 2. *without*] **ⲁϭⲛⲉ** C_2.

3. *a great fear...is death*] The fear of death played an important part in the religious life of Ancient Egyptians and of Coptic Christians. M. Revillout has collected interesting information on the subject in his articles on 'Les Affres de la Mort' in *Rev. Égypt.* (vol. I p. 139 ff.; vol. II pp. 18 ff.; 64 ff.). The attitude of Joseph towards death may be compared with that of Abraham in the Testament of Abraham, *Recension A.* There Abraham actually refuses to follow Michael, when he tells him that he has come for his soul; and Michael goes up to heaven, and tells God of Abraham's refusal (cc. VII, VIII). For 'Abraham's unwillingness to die' see James, *Test. Abr.* p. 64 ff.

grief] C_2 has 'a grief' (**ⲟⲩⲙⲕⲁϩ**).

8. *those who* are *by the gates*] Cf. the picture of the door-keepers at the gateways of Osiris given by Renouf, *Facsimile of Pap. of Ani* plate 11.

XIV 4. Joseph is here represented as being ninety years old, when the Virgin was entrusted to him. The tradition of his old age is very general. Cf. Prot. IX 2 καὶ ἀντεῖπεν Ἰωσὴφ λέγων· υἱοὺς ἔχω καὶ πρέσβύτης εἰμί, αὕτη δὲ νεᾶνις.

6. *mystery*] See corresponding Sahidic p. 151 f.

XV 3. *began*] **ⲁϥϩⲓ ⲁⲣⲭⲏ**=lit. 'put (*or* cast) *a* beginning. Perhaps we should read **ⲁϥϭⲓ ⲁⲣⲭⲏ** which='received (*or* took) *a* beginning.' Cf. He II 3 **ⲉⲧⲁϥϭⲓ ⲁⲣⲭⲏ ⲛⲥⲁϫⲓ ϧⲁⲣⲟϥ** (ἀρχὴν λαβοῦσα λαλεῖσθαι).

XVI. This Chapter forms a striking contrast to the 'Negative Confessions' in c. 125 of the Book of the Dead, where the deceased asserts the purity of various acts during his life on earth as the ground of his hope for admission into the Hall of the Two-fold Maat.

9. *my stomach and my bowels*] For the conception of the intestines as the cause of offences in this life see Porphyry, *De Abstinentia* lib. IV 10 and other passages cited by Budge, *The Mummy*, p. 181 f. (notes 1 and 2).

11. *waste and strange*] Or '*a* waste and *a* stranger.' Substantives are frequently used in Coptic in an adjectival sense. Cf. Steindorff,

Kop. Gram. § 146 'Es giebt im Koptischen verhältnismässig wenig Adjektiva...Die Form der Adjektiva is die der Substantiva.'

13. In the Pistis Sophia, when the Saviour describes the torments of the wicked, Mary Magdalene answers 'Woe to the sinners, for very grievous are their judgments' (*PS* p. 325 l. 9 f.; cf. also p. 324 l. 14 f.). In a passage which is quoted by M. Revillout from a Bohairic MS (*Rev. Égypt.* vol. II p. 68; see also Z p. 43), a mummy speaks and describes his torments in the other world. Pisentius asks him whether he had never heard of Christ during his life. 'Didst thou not hear before thou didst die that Christ came into the world?' He said, 'Nay, my father; but my parents were (*lit.* are) Greeks. And I also followed their life (ⲃⲓⲟⲥ). Woe, woe, woe to me that I was born into the world. Wherefore did not the womb of my mother become my grave (ϣⲱⲡⲓ ⲛⲏⲓ ⲛⲧⲁⲫⲟⲥ)? Now it happened to me when I came to the necessity of death (ⲧⲁⲛⲁⲅⲕⲏ ⲙⲫⲙⲟⲩ), that the world-rulers (ⲕⲟⲥⲙⲟⲕⲣⲁⲧⲱⲣ) were (*lit.* are) the first that came about me (ⲉⲧⲁⲩⲓ ⲙⲡⲁⲕⲱϯ). They spake to me all the evil things that I had done, and they said to me, Let them come now and deliver thee from the punishments into which thou wilt be cast....After a little while my eyes were opened; and I saw Death hanging in the air in many forms (ⲉϥⲁϣⲓ ϧⲉⲛ ⲡⲓⲁⲏⲣ ⲛⲟⲩⲙⲏϣ ⲛⲥⲙⲟⲧ). And straightway the merciless angels brought my wretched soul from my body...O woe to all sinners like me who are born into the world.' He then speaks of his merciless punishers, the outer darkness, the reptiles and the worms. Cf. also Hyvernat, *Act. Mart.* vol. I p. 56 f., where a man who had been dead six hours, and was raised to life again by Macarius, gives a description of the torments he had suffered.

15. *Jesus*] Lagarde has printed ⲓⲏⲥ ('make haste'). But the MS has here its usual contraction (ⲓⲏ̅ⲥ̅) of the name Jesus, which elsewhere Lagarde has written in full (ⲓⲏⲥⲟⲩⲥ).

XVII 3. *Jesus* [*who holdest fast*] *the universe*] 'Jesus is the universe' (ⲓⲏⲥⲟⲩⲥ ⲡⲉ ⲡⲓⲉⲛⲧⲏⲣϥ) can scarcely be right as it stands. We may read for ⲡⲉ either ⲡⲉⲧⲁⲙⲁϩⲓ or ⲡⲉⲧⲁⲙⲟⲛⲓ, reading ⲙ before ⲡⲓⲉⲛⲧⲏⲣϥ. The corresponding Sahidic has ⲡⲉⲧⲁⲙⲁϩⲧⲉ. Stern suggests ⲓⲏⲥⲟⲩⲥ ⲡⲉⲧⲁⲙⲁϩⲓ ⲉⲡⲧⲏⲣϥ ('der Alles mit seiner Güte erfasst').

Thy servant] Lagarde has wrongly transcribed ⲡⲉϥⲃⲱⲕ. The MS has ⲡⲉⲕⲃⲱⲕ.

4. *Thou art the Lord*] ⲛⲑⲟⲕ ⲛⲉ ⲡϭⲟⲓⲥ Lagarde. ⲛⲉ seems to be a printer's error for ⲡⲉ.

put...away] ϩⲓ ⲉⲃⲟⲗ. This is not the phrase used in the Boh. of Mt I 19; but appears to be a translation of Sah. ⲛⲟϫ ⲉⲃⲟⲗ, used in Sah. version and found in Sah. *Death of Joseph* in this place.

5. *thought*] ⲙⲉⲩⲓ. This verb is not used in the Boh. of Mt I 20; but ⲙⲉⲉⲩⲉ is used in the Sah. version, and is found in the Sah. *Death of Joseph* in this place.

take] See note on VI 1.

8. *or*] Lagarde has wrongly transcribed ⲓⲥϫⲉ. The MS has ⲓⲉ.

10. *serpent*] Cf. Ev. Th. Gr. A c. XVI 1; Lat. c. XIV; Ps-Mt XLI 1.

12. *they slandered Thee*, saying *that Thou didst kill him*] Cf. Ev. Th. Gr. A c. IX 2; B c. VIII 2; Lat. c. VII 2; Syr. c. IX (see Wright, *Syr. Apoc.* p. 9); Ps-Mt XXXII.

13. *I took hold of Thine ear*] Cf. Ev. Th. Gr. A c. V 2 ἐγερθεὶς ὁ Ἰωσὴφ ἐπέλαβεν αὐτοῦ τὸ ὠτίον καὶ ἔτιλεν σφόδρα.

XVIII 1. *refrain from*] ⲙⲡⲓⲙⲟⲛⲓ ⲁϭⲛⲉ. The word ⲙⲟⲛⲓ is probably a translation of Sah. ϭⲱ ('remain'). In that case the literal translation is 'I did not remain without.' So Stern, 'da bleib ich nicht ohne Thränen.'

2. *remember*] A simple emendation, reading ⲁⲓⲉⲣ ⲫⲙⲉⲩⲓ for ⲁⲣⲓ ⲫⲙⲉⲩⲓ, gives a better sense, 'I remembered' (see corresponding Sah. p. 155).

XIX 1. *place*] Lagarde emends the text, and reads ⲙⲁ for ⲙⲱⲓⲧ. But ⲙⲱⲓⲧ ('way') is practically used in the sense of ⲙⲁ ('place') in c. IV 5, where Lagarde has left the text unchanged. It is not necessary to emend the text in either place.

6. In the Apocalypse of Esdras a graphic account is given of the difficulty that the angels had in trying to take away the soul of Esdras. They cannot bring it through his mouth, his nostrils, his eyes, his head, or the ends of his nails; and they return to God in despair. καὶ ἀπῆλθον οἱ ἄγγελοι ἄπρακτοι, λέγοντες· κύριε, οὐ δυνάμεθα παραλαβεῖν τὴν ψυχὴν αὐτοῦ (Tisch. *Apocal. Apocr.* p. 31). Cf. also the Apocalypse of Sedrach X (James, *Apoc. Anecd.* p. 133 f.). In the *De Morte Mosis* the soul of Moses is taken away by God with a kiss (Gfrörer, *Prophetae veteres Pseudepigraphi* p. 333).

XXI 1. *I saw Death*] Cf. the personification of Death in the Testament of Abraham. See James, *Test. Abr.* p. 55 ff.

attendants] ⲇⲏⲕⲁⲛⲟⲥ. For their presence at the hour of death see Hyvernat, *Act. Mart.* vol. I p. 56. Attendants (ⲇⲉⲕⲁⲛⲟⲥ) are mentioned in conjunction with rulers (ⲁⲣⲭⲱⲛ) and ministers (ⲗⲓⲧⲟⲩⲣⲅⲟⲥ) in the first book of Jeû (Schmidt, *Gnost. Schrift.* p. 79 ff.). Cf. also *PS* p. 14 l. 6 f. 'the attendants (ⲇⲉⲕⲁⲛⲟⲥ) of the rulers (ⲁⲣⲭⲱⲛ) and their ministers (ⲗⲓⲧⲟⲩⲣⲅⲟⲥ).'

2. *a little of their own*] Cf. p. 39 *v.* 113, where see note.

4. *was distracted*] ⲫⲱϣ ⲉⲃⲟⲗ. Revillout has ⲱϣ ⲉⲃⲟⲗ ('cried out'). The verb ⲫⲱϣ usually='divide' (e.g. Mc III 24 ff. μερίζειν) or 'break' (e.g. Ac XX 7 κλάζειν). I have taken this to be the primary meaning of ⲫⲱϣ ⲉⲃⲟⲗ here. But in Ez XIII 18 ⲉⲑⲣⲟⲩⲫⲱϣ ⲉⲃⲟⲗ ⲛϩⲁⲛⲯⲩⲭⲏ=τοῦ διαστρέφειν ψυχάς. ⲫⲱϣ ⲉⲃⲟⲗ may therefore represent the Passive of διαστρέφειν. Perhaps the translator misunderstood the Sahidic (ⲟⲩⲱϣ ⲉⲓ ⲉⲃⲟⲗ), and used an expression which he found in his own Bible.

8. *he was afraid*] Cf. p. 158 c. XXIII 5, where see note.

XXII 1. *the seven aeons of darkness*] See James, *Test. Abr.* p. 101 καὶ ὁ θάνατος εἶπεν· Ἄκουσον, δίκαιε Ἀβραάμ, τοὺς ἑπτὰ αἰῶνας ἐγὼ λυμαίνω τὸν κόσμον (where the seven aeons refer to time). Cf. also the Egyptian conception of the seven *Arits* through which the dead man was supposed to pass (Budge, *Book of the Dead*, *Papyrus of Ani* p. 291, note 2). See Renouf, *Facsimile of Pap. of Ani*, plates 11, 12.

3. *hanging from his eye-lids*] If my interpretation of the corresponding Sahidic (where see note) is correct, the phrase may be due to a mistake on the part of the Bohairic translator.

XXIII 2. *silken napkins of fine texture*] Lit. 'napkins of byssus (**ϣενс**) all of silk (**ολοсιριкоп**).' For the use of silk amongst the Copts see Budge, *The Mummy* pp. 187 f.; 193. In a note to p. 187 Dr Budge says: 'The custom in Italy of wrapping dead bodies in silk is probably not earlier than the end of the third century, and in Egypt we may place it about one hundred years later.'

XXIV 1. *vessel*] The word used here and in the Sah. is **κονφоп**. Cf. Crum, *Copt. manuscripts from the Fayyum*, Papyr. 51, 54.

2. *as though*] I take **ιсϫεк** here in the same sense as **ⲙⲫⲣⲏϯ ιсϫεк** in Ge XXXVII 9 and as **ϩωс ιсϫεк** in c. XXVII 2. This may be the meaning of the word in Ge XXXVII 7; XL 16; XLI 1. Cf. use of **εϣϫε** in Sahidic. See p. 184 l. 19; Ac XVI 9. Stern translates: 'siehe, er ist wie überhaupt nicht zur Welt geboren.'

XXV 2. *poured...on*] **ϩιουι . . . εϫεп** (*lit.* 'put...on'). Cf. the use of the verb in Mt XXVI 12.

on the tables of heaven] **ϧεп пιпλαξ пτε τφε** (ἐν ταῖς πλαξὶ τοῦ οὐρανοῦ). Cf. *Test. Aser* VII. For a discussion of the subject see Fabricius, *Cod. Pseud. Vet. Test.* I p. 551 ff.

XXVI 1. *Let no evil smell of death have dominion over thee*] The wish which finds expression in these words is the same as that which led the ancient Egyptians to spend extraordinary pains in embalming their dead. It was necessary that the dead man should have his body as well preserved as possible when he went to the underworld. Cf. the Book of the Dead c. 154: 'Chapter of not allowing to pass away the body of king Ra-men-kheper in the underworld...Let not this my body pass away...Do not give me over to that slaughterer...making the members dead, making [them] helpless, hidden; inflicting harm on many bodies...Do not gain the mastery over me...Homage to thee, O my father Osiris! Thy members exist. Thou didst not decay. Thou didst not become worms. Thou didst not rot away. Thou didst not suffer corruption. Thou didst not moulder away. Thou didst not turn into worms. I am Khepera; my members shall exist for ever. I shall not decay; I shall not suffer corruption; I shall not moulder away' (see Budge's *First Steps in Egyptian* p. 168 ff.).

thy shroud nor thy flesh] The text as it stands is difficult. Perhaps 'nor thy flesh' is a later addition; or the original reading may have been ϯⲕⲁⲓⲥⲓ ⲛ̀ⲧⲉ ⲧⲉⲕⲥⲁⲣⲝ ('the shroud of thy flesh').

in] Lagarde has ⲉⲃⲟⲗϧⲉⲛ. I have taken ⲉⲃⲟⲗ with the verb, and ϧⲉⲛ with the word which follows.

hair] ϥⲱ here=ϥⲱⲓ.

2 ff. Cf. the Testament of Isaac (James, *Test. Abr.* p. 148 f.), where the Lord says to Abraham, 'Every man who shall name his son by the name of Isaac My beloved, or shall write his testament, shall have a blessing which shall not come to an end, and My blessing in his house shall not cease; or if he shall give a poor man to eat on the day of the feast of My beloved Isaac, verily I will give him to you in My Kingdom.' In case he is not able to write; 'the Lord said to Abraham, Let him give the hungry bread to eat, and I will give him a place in My Kingdom, and he shall be present with you at the first hour of the banquet of the thousand years.' If he is too poor to give bread, he is to keep a night's vigil in memory of Isaac.

XXVII 2. *the shroud...fastened*] Cf. p. 61 c. XIV *v.* 2 (where see note).

clasps (?)] ⲫⲉⲣⲟⲛⲓ. Stern has 'mit eisernen Spangen (?).' Dr James has pointed out to me that the word is no doubt a corruption of περόνη. The correct translation therefore is 'pins.' See *Corrigenda* p. 246.

XXVIII 1. *O death*] Cf. Budge, *First Steps in Egyptian*, p. 175 f. 'Death cometh: it seizeth the babe which is on the breast of his mother, as well as him that hath become an old man.' There is true pathos in some of the Coptic lamentations over death. See Revillout's article 'Les prières pour les Morts, etc.' in *Rev. Égypt.* vol. IV p. 1 ff., and the inscriptions that he quotes, especially *Br. Mus.* 900 'O Death, the name that is bitter in the mouth of all, that cuttest off, that separatest fathers from their children and children from their fathers' (ⲱ ⲡⲙⲟⲩ ⲡⲣⲁⲛ ⲉⲧⲥⲁϣⲉ ϩⲛ ⲧⲧⲁⲡⲣⲟ ⲛⲟⲩⲟⲛ ⲛⲓⲙ ⲡⲉⲧϣⲱⲱⲧ ⲉⲃⲟⲗ ⲡⲉⲧⲡⲱⲣϫ ⲉϩⲉⲛⲉⲓⲟⲧⲉ ⲉⲛⲉⲩϣⲏⲣⲉ ⲁⲩⲱ ϩⲉⲛϣⲏⲣⲉ ⲉⲛⲉⲩⲉⲓⲟⲧⲉ); *Bibl. Nat.* 44 'The necessity of death hath come upon me: they that knew me have all forgotten me' (ⲁⲥⲉⲓ ⲉϩⲣⲁⲓ ⲉϫⲱⲓ ⲛϭⲓ ⲧⲁⲛⲁⲅⲕⲏ ⲙⲡⲙⲟⲩ ⲁ ⲛⲉⲧⲥⲟⲟⲩⲛ ⲙⲙⲟⲓ ⲧⲏⲣⲟⲩ ⲉⲣⲡⲁⲱⲃϣ).

12. *that have no body*] ⲛⲁⲥⲱⲙⲁⲧⲟⲥ. Cf. p. 159 *v.* 13. The word ἀσώματος sometimes=ἄγγελος. See e.g. James, *Test. Abr.* p. 95 l. 20.

XXIX 3 f. Cf. c. X.

XXX 1. *saluted His hands*] Cf. Z p. 122 l. 12 f. ⲁⲓⲥⲟϭⲛⲓ ϧⲉⲛ ⲡⲁϩⲏⲧ ⲉⲟⲩⲱϣⲧ ⲉϫⲉⲛ ⲛⲉⲛϫⲓϫ ⲡⲁⲃⲃⲁ ⲙⲁⲕⲁⲣⲓ.

3. see *that ye*] Compare a somewhat parallel use of the conjunctive in Tuki, *Missale*, *Anaph. Cyr.* (p. ⲥⲟⲃ) ⲛ̀ⲧⲉϥⲥⲙⲟⲩ ⲉⲣⲟⲛ ⲧⲏⲣⲉⲛ ⲛ̀ⲧⲉϥⲧⲟⲩⲃⲟ ⲛ̀ⲛⲉⲛϩⲏⲧ ⲛ̀ⲧⲉϥⲧⲁⲗϭⲟ ⲛ̀ⲛⲓϣⲱⲛⲓ ⲛ̀ⲧⲉ ⲛⲉⲛⲯⲩⲭⲏ ⲛⲉⲙ ⲛⲉⲛⲥⲱⲙⲁ.

6. *shall*] I have followed the MS. Lagarde would read ⲉⲛⲉ for

ⲛⲛⲉ. Some corruption in the text is probable, but this emendation appears to me unsatisfactory.

XXXI 3. *he is suffered*] Lit. 'and He (*or* he) suffers him.' In Coptic the Passive is often expressed by using the third person plural of the active; but sometimes the third person singular is used in a practically passive sense. Cf. the use of ⲫⲏ ⲉⲧⲁϥϫⲟϥ in Mt II 17, 23; IV 14, where the Greek has τὸ ῥηθέν.

10. *for*] ⲉⲑⲃⲉ. The preposition translated 'for' usually = 'because of' or 'concerning'. I do not understand the allusion. I am indebted to Mr W. E. Barnes for the following translation of the Arabic version, as published by Lagarde, of *vv.* 9, 10: 'And I say to you, O My brethren, that those [men] must come to Earth in the end of the times, on the day of anxiety and fear and oppression and trouble, and die. For Messiah the Deceiver will slay the four—in the body—and will pour out their blood like a measure of water, because of the blaming wherewith they blamed and exposed him while they lived.' The literal translation of the Arabic phrase rendered 'like a measure of water' is 'like a portion (a *measured* portion) of water.'

XXXII 1. *for*] ⲉⲑⲃⲉ. The Arabic here has no allusion to water. It runs thus: 'Who are those four, those of whom Thou hast said that the Antichrist shall slay them because of their reproaching? The Saviour answered, They are Henoch, Elias, Schila and Tabitha.'

3. *glorified Him*] Lagarde has ⲛⲁϥ, ⲛⲑⲟϥ. I would omit the stop, and take ⲛⲑⲟϥ closely with ⲛⲁϥ, which it emphasizes.

stinking] Lagarde has ⲉⲧϩϫⲟⲛⲉ, but the MS has, as it seems, ⲉⲧϩϫⲟⲛⲥ.

Hapip] This must be the name of the scribe. The copy of this MS which is in the Propaganda (*Cod. Borg. Boh.* XXV) has according to Zoega (p. 33) ϩⲓⲛⲁ for ϩⲁⲡⲓⲡ.

seven hundred and eighty three] i.e. 1065 A.D.

SAHIDIC FRAGMENTS OF THE DEATH OF JOSEPH.

FRAGMENT I.

V 2. *the places of building*] Cf. Prot. XIII 1 καὶ ἰδοὺ ἦλθεν Ἰωσὴφ ἀπὸ τῶν οἰκοδομῶν αὐτοῦ (D om. αὐτοῦ), καὶ εἰσελθὼν ἐν τῷ οἴκῳ αὐτοῦ (AEH om. εἰσ. ἐ. τ. οἴκ. αὐτοῦ) εὗρεν αὐτὴν ὀγκωμένην.

VII 2. *And*] ϫⲉ. The Sah. Version in Lc II 4 has ϩⲱⲱϥ (*ap.* Amélineau. See also Rossi, *Pap. Cop.* vol. II fasc. I p. 27), whilst the

Bohairic has ⲇⲉ followed by ⲡⲕⲉ (cf. Greek δὲ καὶ). Here the Sahidic has ⲇⲉ and in the corresponding Bohairic we find ϩⲱϥ.

enrolled] Cf. Rossi, *Pap. Cop.* vol. II fasc. I p. 27 ⲁⲩϭⲛ ⲧⲁⲡⲟⲅⲣⲁⲫⲏ ⲙⲛ ⲛⲉⲧⲟⲩⲁⲡⲟⲅⲣⲁⲫⲏ ⲙⲙⲟⲟⲩ ('they found the enrolment and those who enrolled them').

3. *inn*] The Sahidic word found here is that used in Lc II 7. Cf. p. 21 *v.* 30, where see note.

Fragment II.

XIV 4. *other nine*] The MS is badly torn, and these letters are entirely lost. I have supplied the words from the other Sahidic MS (see p. 152). We might however supply ϩⲙⲉ ⲯⲓⲧⲉ ('forty nine'). Such an emendation would give a better sense. For as our Lord was 18 years old (*v.* 6) when Joseph was 111, and He was born four years after the death of Joseph's wife; the reading 'other nine' must be corrupt. Cf. corresponding Bohairic.

Fragment III.

XIV 1. *lay down*] I have not met with another instance of the intransitive use of ϫⲧⲟ.

3. *father*] This word is in the margin, but may have been written by the first hand (ⲡⲉⲓⲱⲧ in mg. ⲧ parv. sup. ras.).

4. *forty years*] ϩⲙⲉ ⲛⲣⲟⲙⲡⲉ. Three(?) letters are erased in the MS between ⲙ 2° and ⲡ.

6. *the fifteenth year*] Lagarde emends the text, reading ⲛⲧⲁⲥ ⲁ for ⲛⲧⲁ. Translate in that case 'her fifteenth year.' I prefer the MS reading.

cave] The description which follows is more suitably applied to a mystery (cf. Boh. and the other Sah. MS) than to a cave; which may be a later interpolation in this place. The common tradition of the birth in a cave appears in another form in Lord Crawford's Sah. MS 36, quoted in note on *Sah. Frag. Life Virg.* II B *v.* 23. It is found in Justin Martyr (*Dial. c. Tryph.* 78 13) and elsewhere.

XV 1. *according to the command of My Father*] These words are connected by Lagarde with the verse which follows.

3. *The silver was changed*] Lagarde thinks that something has fallen out before these words. The root rendered 'changed' is often used of the translation of good men (e.g. Sap IV 10; Sir XLIV 15; He XI 5); and it is found in Jn XIII 1, where ἵνα μεταβῇ ἐκ τοῦ κόσμου τούτου is rendered ϫⲉⲕⲁⲥ ⲉϥⲉⲛⲱⲱⲛⲉ ⲉⲃⲟⲗ ϩⲙ ⲡⲉⲓⲕⲟⲥⲙⲟⲥ ⲛϥⲃⲱⲕ.

This is its meaning in the next verse, where I have translated it 'departed'. For the sense of 'change' cf. Ming. p. 315 'So that their nature should change (ⲡⲱⲱⲛⲉ) and cease being man's, and become gold.' For the metaphor here and in the corresponding Bohairic cf. Eccl. XII 6 ⲙⲡⲁⲧⲉϥϣⲓⲃⲓ ⲛϭⲓ ⲡⲉⲓⲛⲉ ⲙⲫⲁⲧ ⲁⲩⲱ ⲛϥⲧⲁⲕⲟ ⲛϭⲓ ⲡⲥⲁ ⲛⲡⲛⲟⲩⲃ 'Or ever the likeness of the silver be altered, and the beauty of the gold perish.'

4. *the other world*] ⲡⲕⲉⲁⲓⲱⲛ. Cf. Z p. 284 l. 20.

XVI 4. *that I might grow up*] ϣⲁⲛⲧⲉⲓⲉⲓ ⲉⲛⲧⲉ. A difficult expression. Perhaps ⲧⲉ is the same root as that found in Jn IX 21 (*ap.* Ming. p. 32), where ⲁϥⲣⲧⲉ = ἡλικίαν ἔχει (translated ⲁϥⲣⲛⲟϭ in *v.* 23).

7. *the words of swearing*] Zoega (*Cat.* p. 491 note 43) translates the expression 'nugae,' 'scurrilia,' and says that it is used in *Cod. Borg. Sah.* CC in contrast to ⲡϣⲁϫⲉ ⲙⲡⲱⲣϫ. Stern has 'und allerlei ränkevolle Worte.' I have suggested the meaning 'swearing,' as ⲱⲙⲥ is used for ὁρκωμοσία in the Fayyum Version in He VII 28 (see Z p. 160). The Bohairic translator may either have misunderstood, or thought it desirable to weaken the expression.

8. *which are not mine*] There is no need to correct the MS ⲛⲛⲟⲩⲓ, as in Lagarde's edition. In the next verse ⲛⲛⲉⲧⲉ is omitted before ⲛⲛⲟⲩⲓ; see a similar construction in 1 Ti V 22.

14. *upon*] The MS has ϩⲓⲧⲙ. Perhaps we should read ϩⲓϫⲙ. Peyron (*Lex.* p. 337) gives 'super' as one of the meanings of ϩⲓⲧⲛ, but his example is not convincing.

15. *mediator*] Cf. Z p. 400 l. 21 f ⲓⲥ ⲡⲙⲉⲥⲓⲧⲏⲥ ⲛⲧⲁⲥⲩⲛⲓⲇⲏⲥⲓⲥ ('Jesus the mediator of my conscience').

XVII 2. *He returned answer*] ⲧⲁϣⲉ ⲟⲩⲱϣⲃ would naturally mean 'to make much reply.' But ⲧⲁϣⲉ may be used in a weakened sense, as in ⲧⲁϣⲉⲟⲉⲓϣ ('to preach').

7. *Did not I trouble myself, O my Lord?*] The same verb (ⲡⲉⲣⲉⲓⲉⲣⲕⲁⳉⲉ) is used here as in *v.* 4. If the text is not corrupt, it must probably be translated as a question. Stern translates in *v.* 4 'Ich war ängstlich' and here 'Ich war nicht kleinlich.' The Bohairic has omitted the clause here.

9. *I will not*] ⲛⲧⲉⲓⲛⲁⲛⲓⲥⲧⲉⲩⲉ is used for the common ⲛϯⲛⲁⲡⲓⲥⲧⲉⲩⲉ, and should be written as one word.

lamb] MS form ⲧⲉⲓⲉϩⲁⲓⲃⲉ = ⲧⲉϩⲉⲓⲁⲓⲃⲉ.

10. *foot*] Cf. Ev. Th. Gr. A c. x 2. Cf. this verse in the corresponding Bohairic, where see note.

11. *relations*] Lit. 'men.' Cf. Z p. 294 l. 18 f., where ⲛⲉϥⲣⲱⲙⲉ ⲧⲏⲣⲟⲩ means 'all those belonging to him.'

12. *Thee*] Read ⲉⲣⲟⲕ for the MS ⲉⲣⲟⲥ.

laid hold of him] ⲧⲁϩⲟϥ (ⲧ written—by first hand?—over an ϩ which has been erased). A possible emendation of the text is ⲧⲁⲛϩⲟϥ ('restored him to life'). ⲁⲛ might have been written ⲁ̄ at the end of a line, and hence the reading ⲧⲁϩⲟϥ. If this be so, the mistake must have originated in Sahidic.

13. *But*] The MS has ⲇⲉ not ϫⲉ, as in Lagarde's edition.

I requested Thee] ϫⲛⲟⲩ here='request.' Cf. use of Boh. ϭⲛⲟⲩ.

14. *surely I...because*] The literal translation is 'since (*or* else ⲉⲡⲉⲓ) I will warn thee, because (*or* will tell thee that).' The passage is probably corrupt. For ⲉⲡⲉⲓ ϯⲛⲁⲧⲁⲙⲟⲕ ϫⲉ read either (1) ⲛⲉⲓⲛⲁⲧⲁⲙⲟⲕ ϫⲉ 'I would have warned thee, because (*or* would have told thee that)'; or (2) ⲛⲉⲓⲛⲁⲙⲟⲟⲩⲧⲕ ϫⲉ 'I would have killed thee, because.' The Boh. translator has put ⲙⲙⲟⲛ for ⲉⲡⲉⲓ, and taken ⲧⲁⲙⲟ in the sense of 'tell,' and then changed the end of the sentence.

XVIII 1. *saw him already caught in* (?)] For the construction of the sentence see Jn XIX 33. ⲉϥϫⲓ ϩⲉⲛ is difficult. If the text is correct, ϫⲓ must be used passively in the sense of ϫⲏⲩ. See Z p. 473 l. 5 f ϩⲉⲛϩⲁⲗⲁⲧⲉ ⲉⲩϫⲏⲩ ⲛϩⲏⲧⲕ.

XIX 1. *in him*] Two (?) letters have been erased before ⲛϩⲏⲧϥ ('in him'). Perhaps the original reading was ⲉⲧⲛϩⲏⲧϥ ('which *was* in him').

3. *to*] ϩⲁ. The root meaning of ϩⲁ in Sahidic is 'under.' In Bohairic it is commonly used of direction towards.

6. *for*] ϫⲉⲕⲁⲥ. The passage is difficult. I have taken ϫⲉⲕⲁⲥ in the sense of ϫⲉ. Stern translates, 'denn wenn der Tod kommt, so zögert er nicht.'

go before] The scribe originally wrote 'follow him' (ⲟⲩⲏϩ ⲛⲥⲱϥ). This writing has been almost erased, and the word 'go' (ⲙⲟⲟϣⲉ) has been written instead, perhaps by the same hand.

XX 2. *on*] ⲉⲃⲟⲗϩⲙ. The ⲉⲃⲟⲗ goes with the verb, and ϩⲙ with the noun. I prefer to write ⲉⲃⲟⲗ ϩⲙ.

3. *feet*] ϭⲟⲧ=ϭⲟⲛ. Cf. Z p. 46 l. 9, where ϩⲟⲧ probably =ϩⲟⲛ.

4. *I moved My head*] ⲁⲓⲕⲓⲙ ⲉⲧⲁⲁⲡⲉ. Here the movement is a signal to the children to approach. Cf. the end of the papyrus fragment of Evodius' sermon now preserved at Turin, where the preacher explains why our Lord bowed His head (⸢ⲉⲧ⸣ⲃⲉ ⲟⲩ ⲁϥⲣⲓⲕⲉ ⲛ⸢ⲧⲉ⸣ϥⲁⲡⲉ) on the cross. 'Moreover when the elements (ⲥⲧⲟⲭⲓⲟⲛ) reverenced their Maker (ⲇⲏⲙⲓⲟⲩⲣⲅⲟⲥ), *even* Christ, and Death feared to approach Him; straightway the Lord moved His head (ⲕⲓⲙ ⲛⲧⲉϥⲁⲡⲉ), *saying*, Come, be not afraid, it is I that command thee' (Rossi, *Pap. Cop.* vol. II fasc. IV p. 38 f.).

7. *remove*] Lagarde has wrongly divided the words. Read ⲡⲉⲧⲛⲁϣⲉⲉⲛⲉ ⲛⲉⲛⲉⲓⲱⲧ ⲉⲣⲟⲛ. For the construction see Z p. 284 l. 25 ⲛϥϣⲟⲟⲛⲟⲩ ⲉⲡⲉϥⲑⲩⲥⲓⲁⲥⲧⲏⲣⲓⲟⲛ.

XXI 2. *a sinful one*] The Bohairic translator has taken ⲛ of ⲛⲣⲉϥⲣⲛⲟⲃⲉ as the definite article.

4. *wished to go forth*] ⲟⲩⲱϣ is here used as ⲟⲩⲉϣ in He XII 17. Cf. Z p. 335 ll. 1, 2 ⲛⲥⲟⲩⲱϣ ⲁⲛ ⲉⲓ ⲉⲃⲟⲗ.

and found not a place] ⲙⲡⲉⲥϩⲉ ⲙⲁ. Either an ⲉ has been elided, or the original meaning of ϩⲉ is lost sight of, and the preposition has been omitted.

5. *I arose straightway*] The MS has ⲁⲓⲧⲱⲟⲩⲛ ⲧⲉⲩⲛⲟⲩ (sic).

8. *and that*] Divide the words thus, ⲁⲩⲱ ϫⲉ ⲙⲛⲧⲁⲩ.

XXII 1. *all the Root of goodness*] See p. 169 *v.* 10; p. 173 *v.* 38. Cf. Zahn, *Acta Joannis* p. 243 ἡ ῥίζα τῆς ἀθανασίας.

the Eye...the Ear] Or 'this Eye...this Ear'; as in c. XVII *v.* 3. ⲡⲉⲓ or ⲡⲓ are often used in Sahidic in a weak sense, and practically are equivalent to our definite article.

Cherubin] For this use cf. Ge III 24, where the singular ⲡⲉⲭⲉⲣⲟⲩⲃⲓⲛ (Sah.) and ⲡⲓⲭⲉⲣⲟⲩⲃⲓⲙ (Boh.)=הכרבים (τὰ χερουβίν). Cf. also Ex XXV 19 (Boh.) ⲟⲩⲭⲉⲣⲟⲩⲃⲓⲙ, and Ez XXVIII 14, 16 (Sah. and Boh.). See also p. 67, where 'Cherubim' occurs twice, in the first case with the plural, in the second with the singular article.

Michael...and Gabriel] The duty of Michael and Gabriel is to watch the soul of Joseph and to place it in a napkin. Abaddon actually takes it away. In the Testament of Abraham (Recension A) Michael is first sent to take the soul; and later on Death appears. Abraham kisses Death's hand, and his soul cleaves to it, and he dies. Then Michael and a multitude of angels appear, καὶ εὐθέως παρέστη Μιχαὴλ ὁ ἀρχάγγελος μετὰ πλήθους ἀγγέλων, καὶ ἦραν τὴν τιμίαν αὐτοῦ ψυχὴν ἐν ταῖς χερσὶν αὐτῶν ἐν σινδόνι θεοϋφαντῷ (James' *Test. Abr.* pp. 85, 103). Zoega in his Catalogue (p. 334 f.) gives in Sahidic an account of a certain monk who once wished 'to see the soul of a righteous man, and of a sinner coming forth from *the* body.' God would not disappoint him in his wish. The monk first saw the soul of a man esteemed righteous in this world coming forth from his body in torments. 'After these things the brother went into the city; and found a stranger (ⲟⲩⲣⲱⲙⲉ ⲛϣⲙⲙⲟ) lying sick, no man watching him: and the brother sat by him for a day. Straightway, when he was about to fall on sleep (reading ⲉϥⲛⲁⲛⲕⲟⲧⲕ ⲙⲙⲟϥ), the brother saw Michael and Gabriel come, wishing to take his soul. The one sat on his right hand, and the other on his left. They kept beseeching the soul to come forth from *the* body. But it would not come forth. Michael said to Gabriel, Bring this soul forth; and let us go. Gabriel said to him, God said, Do not trouble it, to bring it forth violently (ⲛϭⲟⲛⲥ): now therefore I cannot bring it forth forcibly (ⲛϫⲛⲁϩ). Michael cried out, saying, God, what wilt Thou do to this soul? It will not come forth. And a voice came unto him, Behold I will send David with (ⲙⲛ) his harp and (ⲙⲛ) all the singers of Jerusalem, that it may hear their beautiful voice (*or* sound), and come forth (reading ⲛⲥⲉⲓ ⲉⲃⲟⲗ). And straightway they all came down, and surrounded it, and sang to (ⲁⲩϩⲩⲙⲛⲉⲩⲉ ⲉ) the soul; and it came forth, and sat (ⲁⲥϩⲙⲟⲟⲥ) in the hand of Michael; and they took it up with joy.' In the Pistis Sophia (p. 138 l. 4f.) we read of Gabriel and Michael being commanded to take Pistis Sophia on their hands. See Schmidt, *Gnost. Schrift.* p. 430.

the aeons] Cf. *PS* p. 12 l. 3, where Gabriel is called 'the angel of the aeons' (ⲡⲁⲅⲅⲉⲗⲟⲥ ⲛⲧⲉ ⲛⲁⲓⲱⲛ).

of light] ⲉⲛⲟⲩⲟⲉⲓⲛ probably=ⲙⲡⲟⲩⲟⲉⲓⲛ. Cf. *Various Sah. Frag.* III *v.* 18 'the eyes of (ⲉ) Lazarus.' Stern translates 'für das Licht,' adding, 'vielleicht ⲙⲡⲟⲩⲟⲉⲓⲛ "des Lichts" zu lesen.'

the powers] The MS has ⲛⲇⲩⲙⲓⲟⲥ ('the executioners'). I have read ⲛⲇⲩⲛⲁⲙⲓⲥ. Stern also emends, and reads ⲉⲛⲇⲩⲛⲁⲙⲓⲥ. But ⲛ (en) can be written for ⲉⲛ. Cf. Z p. 553 l. 18 ⲁⲩϫⲓⲧ ⲙⲡⲏⲩⲉ (where ⲙ (em)=ⲉⲙ). I am not sure whether any emendation of the MS is necessary.

cease] The MS reading ⲟⲩⲱ makes good sense. Lagarde's emendation (ⲁⲩⲱ) must be rejected.

3. *craving after*] The phrase ⲁⲥϣⲉ ⲉϩⲣⲁⲓ ⲛⲥⲁ is here used to express eager desire. The nearest parallels which I have found are in the Bohairic of Deut XXVIII 32; Lc XIX 48, where ⲁϣⲓ and ⲉⲓϣⲓ are used with ⲛⲥⲁ. See also Ge XLIV 30 (Boh.).

the lusts] Zoega (*Cat.* p. 291 not. 29) regards ⲗⲟⲟⲩⲉ as another form of ⲗⲟⲃⲉ, which he connects with the root ⲗⲁⲃ found in ⲗⲁⲃⲥϩⲓⲙⲉ ('lusting after a woman'), and translates the phrase (*Cat.* p. 639 not. 6) 'concupiscentiae oculorum suorum.' He has been rightly followed by Peyron (*Lex.* p. 78) and Tattam (*Lex.* p. 185). Stern however renders it 'Wimpern.'

when he comes to die] Cf. Z p. 326 l. 1 ⲛⲧⲉⲣⲉϥⲉⲓ ⲉϥⲛⲁⲙⲟⲩ.

4. *of goodly memory*] Lit. 'him of the (*or* this) good remembrance.' Cf. Z p. 605 l. 18f. ⲡⲁ ⲡⲉⲓⲣⲡⲙⲉⲉⲩⲉ ⲛⲉⲩⲥⲉⲃⲏⲥ, which Zoega translates 'piae memoriae.'

XXIII 2. *stood by*] ⲁⲩϩⲉⲣⲁⲧⲟⲩ ⲉϫⲙ. Zoega and Stern are probably right in emending ⲁⲩϩⲉⲣⲁⲧⲟⲩ into ⲁⲩⲁϩⲉⲣⲁⲧⲟⲩ. Stern translates 'standen über.' But ⲉϫⲙ may mean 'by.' Cf. Ac XVI 13, where ⲉϫⲙ ⲡⲉⲓⲉⲣⲟ = παρὰ τὸν ποταμόν.

3. *numbness* (?)] ϩⲉⲗϩⲓⲗⲉ may be connected with the Boh. ϩⲉⲗⲓ ('fear'). Zoega (*Cat.* p. 548 not. 1) renders it 'angor,' Stern 'die Starrheit.'

4. *affliction*] ϩⲁϫ. Kabis rightly connects this with the root ϩⲟϫϩⲉϫ (see A. Z. 1876 p. 81).

5. *fear did not suffer him to enter*] Cf. p. 140 *v.* 8. See James, *Test. Abr.* (Recension A) p. 96 l. 20ff. ἀκούσας δὲ ὁ θάνατος ἔφριξεν καὶ ἐτρόμαξεν δειλίᾳ πολλῇ συνεχόμενος, καὶ ἐλθὼν μετὰ φόβου πολλοῦ ἔστη ἔμπροσθεν τοῦ ἀοράτου πατρὸς, φρίττων στένων καὶ τρέμων, ἀπεκδεχόμενος τὴν κέλευσιν τοῦ δεσπότου. Cf. also Rossi, *Pap. Cop.* vol. II fasc. IV p. 39 (the passage is quoted in note on c. XX 4 of this fragment).

8. *the plot*] The MS has ⲡⲉⲓⲃⲟⲩⲗⲏ. I have read with Lagarde ⲧⲉⲡⲉⲓⲃⲟⲩⲗⲏ. Zoega suggests ⲡⲉⲡⲉⲓⲃⲟⲩⲗⲏ.

9 *on its course*] ϩⲛ ⲧⲉϥⲃⲁⲥⲓⲥ. A similar phrase is found in the Pistis Sophia (p. 4 l. 19 f.): 'When the sun had come forth on its course (ⲃⲁⲥⲓⲥ).' The passage in which it occurs is discussed by Usener, *Das Weihnachtsfest* I p. 20 f.

XXIV 1 *weeping for him*] For the construction cf. Z p. 231 l. 34.

VARIOUS SAHIDIC FRAGMENTS.

FRAGMENT I.

This Fragment is part of a sermon, the main theme of which was probably the life of John the Baptist. I have seen two other fragments in the British Museum, one of which certainly belongs to the same MS; but I have selected this leaf for publication as it contains the most interesting apocryphal matter.

The life of John the Baptist and the visit of the Magi were not uncommon themes for Coptic sermons. There are fragments of a long discourse on the former among the Turin papyri (Rossi, *Pap. Cop.* vol. I fasc. III pp. 53—82); and the latter is naturally discussed in sermons on the Nativity (see e.g. Rossi, *Pap. Cop.* vol. II fasc. I p. 28 ff.; fasc. II p. 71), and an allusion is made to it in the Coptic Acta Pilati (Rossi, *Pap. Cop.* vol. I fasc. I p. 32). In Z p. 596 f. there is a discussion as to whether the Magi found mercy with God, in spite of the fact that they were not baptized. The belief is expressed that they did find mercy. Lord Crawford's Sahidic MS 36 contains an account of the Magi and of Zacharias, which follows two pages after the story of the Birth of our Lord (which I have already quoted in my note on *Sah. Frag. Life Virg.* II B 23), and which should be compared throughout with the account in the Protevangelium (c. XXI ff.). As it is of considerable interest, I quote it at length. 'It was His star that the Magi saw in the east (ϩⲛ ⲙⲙⲁ ⲛϣⲁ), and left their magic arts (ⲛⲛⲉⲩⲙⲁⲅⲓⲁ), which their fathers served (*lit.* serve). And seeking in the host of heaven, they knew that the star which appeared was (*lit.* is) that of which Balaam the diviner (ⲙⲁⲛⲧⲓⲥ) prophesied (ⲡⲣⲟⲫⲏⲧⲉⲩⲉ). They hasted and brought their gifts to (ⲙ) the Son of God. They came as (*lit.* being) Magi; they renounced the service (ϣⲙϣⲉ) of the demons (ⲇⲁⲓⲙⲱⲛ); they worshipped the Son of God. The angel of the Lord appeared to them, and warned them that they should go another way, which he shewed them. They came as (*lit.* being) Magi; they went as (*lit.* being) confessors (**ϩομολογητης**). And when the Magi went, according to that which is written, they did not return unto Herod. Fear took *hold of* him; and Herod thought concerning John the son of Zacharias the priest, that it was (*lit.* is) for his sake that the Magi came. He sent to the temple unto Zacharias the priest, thinking that perchance he would find the little child John; and he found him not. Those who were sent by Herod after the little child asked him, Where is thy son? Zacharias told them, *saying*, His mother has taken him, and has fled into the wilderness, and has hidden him. Herod was angry and sent murderers; and they murdered Zacharias whilst he was in prayer to God (**εϥϣοοπ ϩμ πεϣληλ μπνουτε**). And his body was taken, and hidden in the night; and no man saw his blood [contrast Prot. XXIV 3]. Herod also, through the anger which he had (*lit.* which *was* with him), sent to all the borders of Bethlehem and round about it; and they snatched away the young children (**ϣηρεϣημ**) from two years old *and* under; and they brought them unto Herod, and he commanded to slay them before him. And John also was hidden; and Herod found him not, that he might put him to death with the little children whom he slew. And the bodies also of the young children, and the body of Zacharias the priest were hidden.' Mr F. C. Burkitt has also called my attention to a remarkable Sahidic fragment published by M. Bouriant (*Mém. Miss. Arch. Franç. au Caire* tome I p. 402), in which the Magi are mentioned. The fragment is very short, and is, says M. Bouriant, 'composé de deux feuilles simples provenant d'un manuscrit très petit, et très mutilées.' I have attempted a translation, giving in square brackets words entirely omitted in the MS. In the second line of the first leaf I have read **ϣωι** for **ϣοι**, and in the first line of the second leaf **ϭc** for **ϭο**. As I have not seen the MS, and do not know the size of the gaps in it, my translation is very uncertain. (*First leaf, recto* ?) '...Bethlehem...in the way...and it came and stood above the inn...I say unto you my...my brethren,... went to Bethlehem first (?); others went...to Herod, *saying*, [Magi have] come from the east...gifts, and have given them to a new king...(*verso* ?)...Jesus Christ; but...we first [saw] that star...and...was first...of the power of Christ...the star left Bethlehem, [and came] and stood above...the power of Christ blinded...Herod and his mind, that he might not seek after anything... (*Second leaf* ?) he came into the temple of the Lord, and found the young child Jesus and Mary His mother and the old man Joseph, the righteous man. And Simeon received Him into his arms, and worshipped Him, and blessed Him, and gave [Him to] His mother, saying, Behold this *child* is set for [the falling and] rising of many [of] Israel; and every one...And thou (?) also, a...thy soul; [that the thoughts of many] hearts may be revealed...child...they returned from (?)...Jerusalem, and were hidden in the house of Misael, until the day that the Magi went to Bethlehem. And Herod was troubled, and was at a loss concerning the Magi and the words which they spake concerning Jesus. And he said to them, If ye were not told (?) where...Christ...[was] born, then tell [me], that I may not...Him, that (?) Thou...art the king who...king, as...the earth...The king grew (?) ...Lord, they...all the earth.' If the phrase 'the power of Christ,' which occurs in this Fragment, be used of the star, we may compare Rossi, *Pap. Cop.* vol. II fasc. I p. 30, where the star is said not to be a star 'like all the stars,' but 'a power of the height, which took the likeness of a star.'

8. *was pleasing*] The same phrase occurs in *Sah. Frag. Life Virg.* II A *v.* 7, where see note.

10. *rose in the east*] Cf. Nu XXIV 17 ἀνατελεῖ ἄστρον (**ⲟⲩⲛ ⲟⲩⲥⲓⲟⲩ ⲛⲁϣⲁ**). Balaam's prophecy of a star is alluded to in connection with the visit of the magi in Rossi, *Pap. Cop.* vol. II fasc. I p. 29.

11. *a great star*] Cf. Prot. XXI 2; Ps-Mt XIII 7.

figure] **ⲧⲩⲡⲟⲥ.** The same word is used on p. 184 l. 16 of a 'figure' of the cross coming forth from the tomb of Jesus (trans. p. 185 *v.* 43). The statement that the star was in the form of a wheel, its figure being like a cross, with letters on it, is not found elsewhere.

15. *But some one will say*] The answer to the objector is lost. Evodius, in his sermon published by Prof. Rossi, deals with this not unnatural difficulty. He thinks that the man who adds adornments (**ϩⲉⲛⲕⲟⲥⲙⲏⲥⲓⲥ**) to the Gospel is worthy of praise and blessing. 'Many things the Gospels have passed by (**ⲡⲁⲣⲟⲩⲉⲗⲑⲟⲩ**), and have not written; and the ordinances (**ⲑⲉⲥⲙⲟⲥ**) of the Church commend (**ⲥⲩⲛϩⲓⲥⲧⲁ**) them.' He then proceeds to show the value of these additions (Rossi, *Pap. Cop.* vol. II fasc. IV p. 11).

FRAGMENT II.

The Miracle of turning water into wine is here recorded by one who purports to have been an eye-witness, and to have helped to fill the water-pots with water. He may have been Evodius. There is no other extant apocryphal account which resembles it. Unfortunately the MS is torn at the top, and I have reason to believe (see note on *v.* 13) that some lines are lost at the beginning of each column. I cannot therefore say how many words must be supplied between *vv.* 4 and 5, between the words 'my God' and 'good' in *v.* 9, or between *vv.* 13 and 14; for in each of these cases a fresh column begins.

12. *Woman, what wilt thou with Me?*] This is the translation of τί ἐμοὶ καὶ σοί, γύναι; in the Sah. version of Jn II 4 as given by Dr Oscar von Lemm in his *Bruchstücke der Sahidischen Bibelübersetzung* p. 19.

13. *spake unto those who served*] The word ⲁⲛⲟⲕ ('I') follows in the MS. This word cannot be part of the Virgin's speech, because there is no ϫⲉ (=ὅτι) to introduce it. It must therefore be part of a parenthesis; and the speech of the Virgin must follow later. I would suggest the following emendation ⲁⲛⲟⲕ ⲟⲩⲉⲃⲟⲗ ⲛϩⲏⲧⲟⲩ ⲁⲛⲟⲕ | ⲉⲥϫⲱ ⲙⲙⲟⲥ ϫⲉ ⲡⲉⲧⲉϥⲛⲁϫⲟⲟϥ ⲛⲏⲧⲛ ⲁⲣⲓϥ. The translation will then run: 'spake unto those that served (I *being* one of them), saying, That which He shall say unto you, do it.' If this suggestion be correct, some three lines are lost at the head of this—and therefore probably at the head of each—column.

Fragment III.

1. *the Lord*] For ⲉϫⲟⲉⲓⲥ we must probably read ⲉⲡϫⲟⲉⲓⲥ.

at the table of His kingdom] Cf. p. 176 *v.* 5. In the Pistis Sophia Mary Magdalene, after listening to one of the mystical sayings of Jesus, 'came forward and said, Lord, concerning this Thou didst speak to us aforetime in a parable,' and the 'parable' that she quotes is Lc XXII 28—30 (*PS* p. 89 l. 10 ff.).

For] ⲉⲃⲟⲗ ⲅⲁⲣ ϫ⌜ⲉ⌝. Cf. *PS* p. 148 l. 13.

3. *chose*] The MS has ⲁϥⲥⲱⲡⲧ and not, as Guidi, ⲁϥⲥⲱⲧⲡ. It resembles forms found in the Fayyum Version. Cf. e.g. 1 Thess I 4 (*ap.* Zoega, *Cat.* p. 167).

behold] ⲉⲓⲥ. The word ⲓⲥ (=Sah. ⲉⲓⲥ) is found in the Bohairic of Mt XV 32; Mc VIII 2, where the Greek text has ἤδη. It may simply have the force of the English 'now'. Cf. p. 130 *v.* 2, where see note.

5. *the matter will see to it*] For this use of ⲣⲱϣⲉ see Mt XXVII 4, 24.

6. *hast saved*] See note on the words 'that which befalls' in *v.* 19.

from] For the construction cf. Ps VII 1.

but it is the dispensation which...for] The MS has ⌜ⲁⲗ⌝ⲗⲁ ⲧⲟⲓⲕⲟ-⌜ⲛⲟⲙ⌝ⲓⲁ ⲧⲉ ⲉⲧ⌜ⲉ . . .⌝ⲛⲁⲩ ⲉϩⲣⲁⲓ ⲉ.

7. *the multitudes*] The MS has ⲛⲛⲉⲙⲙⲏⲏϣⲉ and not, as Guidi, ⲛⲛⲉⲙⲏⲏϣⲉ.

received of] Lit. 'received in.' If the MS reading be retained, ϩⲉⲛ (for the form cf. *v.* 12) may be taken to mean 'of' or 'from'. Perhaps we should read ϫⲓ ⲛⲛⲟⲉⲓⲕ ('received the loaves') or ϫⲓ ⲛϩⲉⲛⲟⲉⲓⲕ ('received loaves').

8. *his loaves*] Guidi reads ⲛⲧⲁϥⲓ; but I am convinced that there is no final ⲓ, but only a dark stroke which is seen through the vellum from the opposite side of the leaf. I have therefore read ⲛⲧⲁϥ.

these multitudes] There is space for two letters between the first ⲉ and the ⲙ of this word. I therefore read ⲛⲛⲉ⌞ⲓⲙ⌟ⲙⲏⲏϣⲉ, and not, as Guidi, ⲛⲛⲉ[ⲓ]ⲙⲏⲏϣⲉ. For the form ⲙⲙⲏⲏϣⲉ we may compare the MS reading in *v.* 7.

Dost Thou wish...] The MS, as far as I can read it, has Ⲕⲟ⸢ⲩ . . . . ⲣ⸣ⲅⲁ⸢ϥ⸣ⲇⲟⲩ . . . ⲁⲣⲉⲛ⸢ϯ⸣ⲛ⸢ⲁϥ⸣ⲧ . . . . . ϣ⸢ⲏ . . . .⸣ ⲟⲩ⸢ⲁ⸣ϥⲓ⸢ . . . . . .⸣ϩ⸢ⲁ⸣ϫ . . . . . . ⲏϣ⸢. . . . . . . ⸣Ⲡ⸢ϫ . . . . ⲁ . . ϩⲉ . . . .⸣ |

9. *bag*] The MS has ⲕⲗⲱⲥⲱⲅⲱⲙⲱⲛ (not, as Guidi, -ⲙⲟⲛ).

9 f. *A mystery...goodness*] The MS, as far as I can read it, has Ⲟⲩⲙⲩⲥ . ⲏⲣⲓⲟⲛ ⲅ . . . . . ⲓⲱ . ⲁ . . . . . ⲉϥⲕ⸢. . . . .⸣ ⲉⲛⲛⲱϣ ⸢. . .⸣ ⲥⲁⲣⲝ ⸢ⲗ . . . .⸣ ⲉⲩⲛⲟⲩ . . . . ⲟⲩⲉⲣⲟⲟⲩ ⸢. . . . .⸣ ⲙⲙⲟⲥ . . . . . ⲓⲱⲧ . . . . . ⲧⲧⲛⲟⲩ ⸢. . . .⸣ⲏⲣⲥⲛⲧ | ⲙⲉⲛⲧⲁⲅⲁⲑⲟⲥ. The latter part I have emended thus: ⲛⲧⲉⲩⲛⲟⲩ ⲁϥⲥⲙⲟⲩ ⲉⲣⲟⲟⲩ ⲉϥϫⲱ ⲙⲙⲟⲥ ϫⲉ ⲡⲁⲉⲓⲱⲧ ⲡⲁⲉⲓⲱⲧ ⲧⲛⲟⲩⲛⲉ ⲧⲏⲣⲥ ⲛⲧⲙⲉⲛⲧⲁⲅⲁⲑⲟⲥ. Possibly we should read in *v.* 9 ⲛⲧⲁⲥⲁⲣⲝ (translate 'the breaking of My flesh').

12. *giving of thanks to*] Guidi has omitted after ϩⲉⲙ ⲡϣⲉⲡϩⲙⲟⲧ the words ⲙⲡⲉϥⲉⲓⲱⲧ ⲟⲩⲥⲟⲡ ϩⲉⲙ ⲡϣⲉⲡϩⲙⲟⲧ; but they are found in the MS. Possibly they are due to a mistake of the scribe, and we should omit the clause 'now in the giving of thanks to His Father.' The construction with ⲙ is remarkable. 'To give thanks to' is usually ϣⲉⲡϩⲙⲟⲧ ⲛⲧⲛ (ⲛⲧⲟⲟⲧ): cf. e.g. Lc XVIII 11; Jn XI 41; I Co I 4.

13. *Thou hast shewn...unto us*] ⲁⲕⲁⲁⲩ ⲛⲙⲙⲁⲛ. Cf. 2 Sa IX 3 ϯⲛⲁⲉⲓⲣⲉ ⲛⲙⲙⲁϥ ⲛⲟⲩⲛⲁ ποιήσω μετ' αὐτοῦ ἔλεος.

14. *and they speak* (?)] ⲛⲥⲉϣ⸢ⲁ⸣ϫⲉ. Lit. 'so that they (i.e. the dead men?) speak.' There is room in the MS for one letter between ϣ and ϫ, but the letter is gone.

15. *ask Me and thy brethren*] The word for 'and' is ⲙⲛ. This word also = 'with.' I am not sure whether the phrase could be rendered 'ask Me with thy brethren' (i.e. 'do thou with thy brethren ask Me'). See note on the phrase 'and my brother Lazarus' in *v.* 26.

hardly (?)] The word thus rendered is ⲙⲱⲅⲓⲥ (μόγις).

Didst thou] ⲉϣϫⲉ is probably interrogative. Cf. the use of ⲉϣⲱⲛ in *The Death of Joseph* XX 6 (Boh.). See also Stern, *Kop. Gram.* § 523.

I have told you already] The MS has ⲉⲓϫⲱ, and not, as Guidi, ⲉϫⲱ.

16. *rather than they*] Lit. 'rather than it, *even* they.' For the construction see Ming. p. 159 ⲁⲩⲡⲁⲣⲁⲇⲓⲇⲟⲩ ⲙⲡⲉⲩⲥⲱⲙⲁ ⲉⲛⲕⲱϩⲧ ⲉϩⲟⲩⲉ ⲉⲣⲟⲥ ⲉⲧⲣⲉⲩⲁⲣⲛⲁ ⲙⲡⲛⲟⲩⲧⲉ ⲛⲛⲉⲩⲉⲓⲟⲧⲉ.

17. *sisters*] ⲥⲛⲏⲩ. Cf. Z p. 91 l. 17 f., where ⲥⲛⲏⲟⲩ = 'sisters.'

the fourth day] Cf. Jn XI 39 (Boh.) ⲡⲉϥⲇ ⲅⲁⲣ ⲡⲉ ⲫⲟⲟⲩ 'For today is his four' (τεταρταῖος γάρ ἐστιν). There the Sahidic Version has 'for it is his four'; whilst in Jn XI 17 the literal translation of the Sahidic is: 'So when Jesus came, He found him, it being his four, being in the tomb.'

18 ff. The statements as to the probable state of Lazarus' body

are grounded on the words of Martha, 'Lord, by this time he stinketh' (Jn XI 39). When Lazarus actually is raised, we might have expected a realistic description of his appearance. But there is none. In simple and almost Biblical language we read that he came forth dressed as a corpse (*v.* 40). Indeed we have been already prepared to find him unlike others who have been dead for any length of time (*v.* 33). The whole account should be compared with that given in the Anaphora of Pilate: νεκρόν τινα Λάζαρον τετραήμερον ἐκ νεκρῶν ἀνέστησεν, λόγῳ μόνῳ κελεύσας ἐγερθῆναι τὸν τεθνεῶτα, διεφθαρμένον ἤδη ἔχοντα τὸ σῶμα ὑπὸ τῶν ἑλκογενήτων σκωλήκων· καὶ τὸ δυσῶδες ἐκεῖνο σῶμα τὸ κείμενον ἐν τῷ τάφῳ ἐκέλευσεν τρέχειν, καὶ ὡς ἐκ παστοῦ νυμφίος οὕτως ἐκ τοῦ τάφου ἐξῆλθεν εὐωδίας πλείστης πεπληρωμένος (*Anaph. Pil.* B 1, Tisch. p. 444).

18. *of Lazarus*] **ⲉⲗⲁⲍⲁⲣⲟⲥ.** Cf. *The Death of Joseph* XXII 1 (Sah.) 'the aeons of (ⲉ) light' (where see note).

hollowed out] Cf. Prov XXIV 52 **ⲉⲣⲉ ⲛⲁⲃⲟⲟⲕⲉ ϣⲕϣⲱⲕϥ ⲉⲃⲟⲗ ϩⲛ ⲛⲉⲓⲁ.**

sending forth] The text is difficult and perhaps corrupt. As it stands, it seems to mean either (1) 'and they have let go (*or* released) the light': **ⲕⲉ ⲉⲃⲟⲗ** is found in the Fayyum Version in the sense of **ⲕⲁ ⲉⲃⲟⲗ**; or (2) 'and they have put forth': **ⲕⲉ** must then be taken in the sense of **ϫⲉ.**

19. *wasted away*] See Zech XIV 12 (Peyron, *Lex.* p. 154).

by reason of corrupt matter] Reading **ⲉⲧ⸢ⲃⲉ⸣ ϯⲁⲓⲃⲉ.** Here **ⲓⲁⲓⲃⲉ** =**ⲉⲓⲁⲁⲃⲉ**, which is found in Job II 8; VII 5 for the Greek ἰχώρ. Cf. *The Death of Joseph* (Boh.) XXVI 1 **ϯⲓⲁⲃⲓ** ('corruption').

and that I may make it speak] There is room in the MS for one letter between **ⲁ** and **ⲣ**. I am not sure that this must be **ϥ**, as Guidi suggests. I have therefore read **ⲧⲁ⸢ⲧ⸣ⲣⲉϥϣⲁϫⲉ.**

that which befalls] The perfect tense is used four times in this Fragment, where we might in English use a future: here and in *v.* 6 'that hast saved,' and twice in *v.* 33.

20. *to-day is*] See note on the words 'the fourth day' in *v.* 17. The word 'to-day,' which is omitted in the Oxford MS, is found in the Boh. Version of Jn XI 39. It comes in the Oxford MS in *v.* 23.

The Borgian MS has **ⲡⲉϥϥⲧⲟⲟⲩ** and not, as Guidi, **ⲉⲡⲉϥϥⲧⲟⲟⲩ.** It also reads in this verse **ⲡϫⲓⲛⲧⲁϥⲙⲟⲩ** not **ϫⲓⲛⲧⲁϥⲙⲟⲩ** (Guidi), **ⲛⲧⲁⲁⲛⲁⲥⲧⲁⲥⲓⲥ** ('of My resurrection') not **ⲛⲧⲁⲛⲁⲥⲧⲁⲥⲓⲥ** (Guidi), **ϩⲉⲙ** not **ϩⲙ** (Guidi). Between **ⲛⲧⲁⲁⲛⲁⲥⲧⲁⲥⲓⲥ** and ⲱ there seem to have been two letters, but the MS here is hard to decipher.

21. *coming*] The Borgian MS has here **ⲉⲩⲛⲁⲩ** and not, as Guidi, **ⲉⲩⲛⲏⲩ**; and the Oxford MS in this verse reads **ⲉⲛⲉⲓⲙⲏⲏϣⲉ** not **ⲉⲛⲉⲓⲙⲏϣⲉ.**

22. *bound*] The Borgian MS has **ⲉⲩⲥⲟⲛⲁϩ** not **ⲉⲩⲥⲟⲛϩ** (Guidi); and **ⲉⲩⲧⲁⲗⲁ** not **ⲉⲩⲧⲁⲗⲟ** (Guidi).

25. *in the light*] Tischendorf gives εν τω φωτει as the reading of the uncial X in Jn XI 9.

26. *here*] The MS has ⲙⲡⲉⲓⲙⲁ not ⲙⲡⲉ ⲙⲁ.

for] Read ⲡⲉ ϫⲉ not ⲡⲉϫⲉ.

and my brother Lazarus] Here ⲙⲛ is used for 'and'. It can also ='with'. The sense would be improved if we could translate 'with my brother L.' (i.e. 'I and my brother L. know Thee from Thy youth'). See note on the phrase 'ask Me and thy brethren' in *v.* 15.

30. *What I do thou knowest not*] The Sahidic Version of Jn XIII 7 (*ap.* Amélineau) omits ἄρτι after οἶδας.

32. *whilst the door is shut: for*] The MS has ⲉⲣⲉ ⲡⲱⲛⲉ ϣⲟⲧⲙ ⲥⲉ. If ⲡⲱⲛⲉ be right, ϣⲟⲧⲙ ('shut') must be taken transitively. But no object is expressed. ⲡⲱⲛⲉ may have come in from the immediate context. I have read ⲡⲣⲟ for ⲡⲱⲛⲉ, and ϫⲉ for ⲥⲉ.

33. *Hast thou taken...gone forth*] Here the perfect tenses are used practically in a future sense. Cf. note on the words 'that which befalls' in *v.* 19.

34. *Believest thou*] The form ⲧⲉⲣⲡⲓⲥⲧⲉⲩⲉ is remarkable. In Jn XI 26 the ordinary form ⲧⲉⲡⲓⲥⲧⲉⲩⲉ is found.

35. *which have poured themselves forth*] I take ϩⲁⲁⲧⲉ ⲙⲙⲟⲟⲩ in the sense of ϩⲁⲁⲧⲟⲩ. Zoega in his note on ϩⲁⲁⲧⲟⲩ (*Cat.* p. 646 note 26) compares the use of ϩⲓϯ in Bohairic of the eye, which he renders 'lippire.' Peyron however (*Lex.* p. 370) gives a different signification to ϩⲓϯ.

39. *a wheel* (?)] ⲟⲩϣⲁⲗⲟⲟⲩ. I have not met with ϣⲁⲗⲟⲟⲩ elsewhere. Peyron (*Lex.* p. 408) gives a word ϭⲁⲗⲓⲗ meaning a waterwheel, which also occurs in Crum's *Coptic MSS brought from the Fayyum*, p. 53. The verb ⲕⲱⲧⲉ might well be used of a wheel 'going round'. Cf. the use of ⲕⲱϯ in Is XXVIII 27 (Boh.).

They that were dead] The statement may be founded on Mt XXVII 52 f. This was amplified in the Anaphora of Pilate. See Tisch. *Evang. Apoc.* pp. 440 f., 447 f.

43. [*some*] *of those*] I have followed Guidi's emendation, and read ϩⲟⲓⲛⲉ before ⌜ⲉⲃⲟ⌝ⲗ, which is the first word of a new page. The scribe probably forgot that he had not written ϩⲟⲓⲛⲉ on the last page.

there being] The MS has ⲉⲣⲉ and not, as Guidi, ⲉⲧⲉ.

44. *What is*] Reading ⲟⲩ ⲧⲉ instead of ⲟⲩⲧⲉ.

compared with] ⲛⲛⲁϩⲣⲛ. Cf. Wisd VII 9 ⲡⲛⲟⲩⲃ ⲧⲏⲣϥ ⲛⲛⲁϩⲣⲁⲥ ⲉϥⲟ ⲛⲑⲉ ⲛⲟⲩϣⲏⲙ ⲛϣⲱ (ὁ πᾶς χρυσὸς ἐν ὄψει αὐτῆς ὡς ψάμμος ὀλίγη).

Lazarus] The MS has here ⲗⲁⲍⲁⲣⲉ and not, as Guidi, ⲗⲁⲍⲁⲣⲟⲥ.

45. *the gates of death*] Cf. p. 135 *v.* 8.

49. *the chiefs of the Jews*] Reading ⲛⲛⲟϭ ⲛⲛⲓⲟⲩⲇⲁⲓ for ⲛⲛⲟϭ ⲛⲓⲟⲩⲇⲁⲓ. Cf. *v.* 53.

did this work] There is room for five or six letters after **ρπ.** I have read **ρ πειϩωβ.**

on the sabbath] The raising of Lazarus is said to have taken place on the sabbath in the Anaphora of Pilate. Cf. *Anaph. Pil.* B 5 *κατεμήνυον δὲ οἱ Ἰουδαῖοι ἐκτελεῖν ταῦτα ἐν σαββάτῳ τὸν Ἰησοῦν* (Tisch. p. 446).

[*And they came*] *that*] The MS is corrupt. I have supplied **αυει** before ⌜**πc**⌝**εναυ.**

50. *the king*] i.e. the emperor.

51. *Carius*] **καριος.** He is evidently the same as Quirinius (**κυρινος**) of Lc II 2.

52. *it*] Or perhaps 'Him'. Cf. Lc XXIII 7. For the construction with **π** cf. Rossi, *Pap. Cop.* vol. I fasc. I p. 18 **αcϫοου ναι πϭι τacϩιμε.**

53. *thought concerning*] **μεευε εϩουπ ε.** Cf. Wisd XIV 30 *κακῶς ἐφρόνησαν* (**μεευε**) *περὶ θεοῦ* (**εϩουπ εππουτε**).

55. *Annas and Caiaphas*] Cf. Coptic *Acta Pilati* I 1, 'Viri cognominati Annas et Caiaphas...et ceteri etiam Judaeorum, hi omnes adierunt Pilatum accusantes dominum nostrum Jesum Christum dicentes: Scimus Jesum esse filium Josephi fabri natum ex Maria; hic porro dicit se esse filium dei et regem, violat sabbata legis patrum nostrorum, volens solvere legem nostram'; II 1 'Responderunt Judaei Pilato: Nonne diximus tibi eum esse magum? (**ϫε ουμαroc πε**)'; II 3 'Presbyteri Judaeorum responderunt dicentes: Quid dispiciemus? Primo scimus te ex fornicatione (**ϩπ ουπορπια**) genitum esse.' (See Peyron's Translation of the Sahidic in Tisch. *Evang. Apoc.* pp. 216, 224 f.) In the Anaphora of Pilate Herod and Annas and Caiaphas are mentioned among those who delivered Jesus to Pilate (*Anaph. Pil.* A 6, Tisch. p. 439).

Tiberius] The MS has 'Tiberias'. In the Coptic *Acta Pilati* we have the form **τεβελιοc** (see Peyron's translation in Tisch. *Evang. Apoc.* p. 213; Rossi, *Pap. Cop.* vol. I fasc. I p. 11).

the synagogue of the Jews] Cf. *Anaph. Pilati* A 10 *εἰ μὴ μία τις συναγωγὴ τῶν Ἰουδαίων οὐχ ὑπελείφθη ἐν αὐτῇ τῇ Ἰερουσαλήμ, ἐπεὶ πᾶσαι ἀφανεῖς τῇ πτώσει ἐκείνῃ ἀπῆλθον* (Tisch. p. 441).

56. *Joseph and Nicodemus*] Cf. p. 181 *v.* 6 ff. The attitude of these two men towards Annas and Caiaphas should be compared with the statements on the subject in the Acta Pilati. (For the Sahidic text see Rossi, *Pap. Cop.* vol. I fasc. I p. 10 ff.; for Peyron's translation see Tisch. *Evang. Apoc.* p. 210 ff.) There Annas and Caiaphas reject the testimony of those who said that Jesus was not born of fornication (II 5); but Nicodemus takes the opposite side (IX 1). The Jews seek him and Joseph to put them to death. Nicodemus does not hide himself (XII 1); Joseph however is hidden and only found with difficulty (XV 1). But when he is found, Annas and Caiaphas actually become the guests of Nicodemus, and they eat and drink with Joseph (XV 4).

FRAGMENT IV.

This fragment is closely connected with the preceding one, and seems to be a later continuation of the same narrative (see Introduction).

3. *Theophilus*] Cf. Lc I 3; Ac I 1. The name is not found elsewhere in Apocryphal literature, except in the account of the Chair of Peter at Antioch, which is found e.g. in the Golden Legend.

5. *covenant with*] The same Sahidic verb is used as a translation of *διατίθεμαι* in Lc XXII 29, one of the verses upon which this passage is based. The verb is used with ⲇⲓⲁⲑⲏⲕⲏ of making a covenant. Cf. Ge IX 9; Ac III 25. For the construction see Z p. 308 l. 4 f. ⲁⲩⲥⲙⲛⲧⲥ ⲙⲛ ⲛⲉⲩⲉⲣⲏⲩ ⲉⲉⲓ ⲉⲃⲟⲗ. The MS has ϩⲓϫⲉⲛ and not, as Guidi, ϩⲓϫⲉⲙ before ⲧⲉⲧⲣⲁⲡⲏⲍⲁ.

7. *Tiberius*] MS 'Diberias.' See note on preceding Fragment *v.* 55.

prevailed...concerning] ⲁⲙⲁϩⲧⲉ . . . ⲉⲧⲃⲉ. A difficult phrase. Perhaps we should read ⲙⲛ for ⲉⲧⲃⲉ, and translate 'took the side of Jesus the second time.'

8. *He is worthy. We will make* (?) *Him*] I cannot translate the MS reading ϥⲙⲁⲧⲉ ⲛⲛⲁⲁⲁϥ. I have tried to keep as near the MS as possible, and have read ϥⲙⲡϣⲁ ⲧⲉⲛⲛⲁⲁⲁϥ; but probably the text requires a more thorough emendation.

9. *the authorities*] The MS has ⲛⲛⲉⲉⲝⲟⲩⲥⲓⲁ and not, as Guidi, ⲛⲛⲉⲝⲟⲩⲥⲓⲁ.

Tiberius] MS 'Tiberias.' See note on preceding Fragment *v.* 55.

Thou art...Pontus (?)] The Sahidic of this clause is ⲛⲧⲕ ⲟⲩⲡⲱⲛⲧⲟⲥ ⲛⲅⲁⲗⲓⲗⲁⲓⲟⲥ ⲛⲁⲗⲗⲱⲫⲱⲗⲱⲥ ⲛⲣⲉⲙⲛⲕⲏⲙⲉ. There is apparently a play on the name 'Pontius.' I do not understand the allusions.

11. *report*] ⲁⲛⲁⲫⲟⲣⲁ. For the use of the word in Coptic cf. Hyvernat, *Act. Mart.* vol. I p. 44. It is used of the apocryphal report sent by Pilate to the Roman emperor concerning Jesus (see Tisch. *Evang. Apoc.* pp. 435—449). Here the report (*ἀναφορά*) is confused with the inscription (*τίτλος*) on the cross.

it] The MS must here be corrupt. I have read ⲁϥⲧⲁϭⲥ for ⲁϥⲧⲁϭϥ.

12. *suffer*] For the form ⲁⲛⲓⲭⲉ cf. Lc IX 41; Ac XVIII 14.

13. ⲑⲫⲟ=ⲑⲡⲟ. Cf. Boh. ⲧⲫⲟ.

14. *mingled*] For the form ⲕⲩⲣⲁ (ⲕⲉⲣⲁ) cf. Prov IX 5; Is V 22.

15. The root ⲕⲱ (ⲕⲁ) is thrice repeated in this verse; twice it is used with ϩⲁ. The repetition may be an intentional play on the word

18. *took the form of*] Cf. Z p. 369 l. 10 f. ⲁ ⲡⲇⲓⲁⲃⲟⲗⲟⲥ ⲡⲱⲱⲛ ⲛⲧⲉⲩⲛⲟⲩ ⲁϥⲉⲣ ⲡⲉⲥⲙⲟⲧ ⲛⲟⲩⲙⲟⲛⲟⲭⲟⲥ ('the devil changed straight way, and took the form of a monk').

nets] ϣⲛⲏ is found in this Fragment in the sense of ϣⲛⲏⲩ.

casting] ⲛⲏϫ = ⲛⲉϫ. Cf. ⲑⲏ for ⲑⲉ in *v.* 21.

21. *but*] ⲇⲉ. Cf. Lc XXII 32 (Boh.), where the Greek text has δὲ. The Sah. version (*ap.* Woide) has ϩⲱ. He gives another reading omitting ϩⲱ.

that] Reading ϫⲉ for ⲇⲉ. I have made no note of the MS reading here, but probably Guidi's reading ⲇⲉ is simply a misprint.

22. *find*] Or, reading ϭⲉⲡ for ϭⲉⲛ, 'catch.' Cf *v.* 32.

23. *caught*] ϭⲱⲡⲉⲓ = ϭⲱⲡⲉ. Cf. Boh. ϭⲱⲡⲓ.

beast] ⲍⲱⲟⲛⲧ = ⲍⲱⲟⲛ.

24. *taken*] ϭⲱⲗϭ (in *vv.* 24, 25) or ϭⲁⲗϭ (in *v.* 37) is another form of the root ϭⲱⲣϭ ('to snare'). Cf. the forms ϫⲱⲗϫ (see Z p. 416 note, ⲛⲉⲥⲁⲗⲟⲟⲩⲉ ⲙⲛ ⲛⲉϣⲛⲏⲩ ⲛⲧⲁⲩϫⲱⲗϫ ⲛϩⲏⲧⲟⲩ) and ϭⲱⲗϫ.

25. The scribe has accidentally repeated this verse twice, reading ϩⲉⲛ for ϩⲛ the second time.

26. *making...to transgress*] ⲡⲁⲣⲁⲃⲁ is here used transitively.

35. *the waters*] ⲛⲉⲙⲙⲟⲟⲩ here = ⲙⲙⲟⲟⲩ. Cf. *v.* 37.

36. *before I came*] ⲙⲡⲁⲧⲁⲉⲓ. Here ⲙⲡⲁⲧⲁ = ⲙⲡⲁϯ.

37. *caught by*] ⲉⲩⲧⲟⲛⲁϩ ⲉ. I have not found ⲧⲟⲛⲁϩ elsewhere; but some such meaning as 'catch' is required by the context.

38. *beholding*] The MS has ⲉϥⲑⲉⲱⲣⲉⲓ.

the sinners] The MS has ⲛⲛⲉⲣⲉϥⲣⲛⲟⲃⲉ and not, as Guidi, ⲛⲉⲛⲣⲉϥⲣⲛⲟⲃⲉ.

their members] Cf. *The Death of Joseph* c. XVI *v.* 5 ff.

FRAGMENT V.

This is part of a sermon on the Festival of the Cross, apparently ascribed to Cyril (see Introduction). Among the Turin papyri there is 'an exposition (ⲉⲝⲏⲅⲏⲥⲓⲥ) of the holy Theophilus the Archbishop which he delivered concerning the cross and the robber (ⲡⲗⲏⲥⲧⲏⲥ)'; in which he discusses our Lord's words to the penitent robber, and afterwards speaks of 'the holy greatness of the glorious cross' (ⲡⲙⲉⲅⲉⲑⲟⲥ ⲉⲧⲟⲩⲁⲁⲃ ⲙⲡⲉⲥⲧⲟⲥ ⲉⲧⲧⲁⲉⲓⲏⲩ) (Rossi, *Pap. Cop.* vol. I fasc. I p. 64 ff.). Among the same papyri there is an account of the finding of the title of the cross in the time of Constantine (Rossi, *Pap. Cop.* vol. I fasc. III p. 48). I have examined such Sahidic fragments relating to the crucifixion, as I could find in the British Museum; but I have not met with any of special interest.

3. *Josephus and Irenaeus*] Cf. p. 29 *v.* 26, where see note.

6. *were hidden*] In Evodius' sermon published by Rossi the disciples are said to have spent the day before the resurrection in

hiding. 'And we spent the whole sabbath hidden, when we heard that Joseph was taken (ϭⲱⲡⲉ), who took (ϫⲓ) the body of Jesus, for fear of the Jews' (Rossi, *Pap. Cop.* vol. II fasc. IV p. 30). See also the *Gospel according to Peter* VII.

8. *Joseph...and Nicodemus*] They are mentioned together on p. 176 *v.* 56.

14. *thence*] ⲙⲙⲁⲩ. Cf. the use of ⲙⲙⲁⲩ after ϥⲓ.

18. *might but touch*] Cf. Mt IX 21 ⲉⲓϣⲁⲛϫⲱϩ ⲙⲙⲁⲧⲉ (ἐὰν μόνον ἅψωμαι).

22. *Cleopas*] Evodius in the sermon published by Rossi makes mention of Cleopas, and claims to have been his brother. The Cleopas of whom he speaks is the one mentioned in Lc XXIV 18 (Rossi, *Pap. Cop.* vol. II fasc. IV p. 32 f.). Guidi has published and translated a short Sahidic account of the martyrdom of Simon the son of Cleopas, who succeeded James as bishop of Jerusalem (*Rendiconti della R. Accad. dei Lincei* ser. V vol. II p. 513 ff.). There is a fragment of this account in the British Museum (Or. 3581 B). He has also published (*Rendiconti della R. Accad. dei Lincei* ser. IV vol. III sem. 1 p. 62) and translated (*Giornale della Soc. Asiatica Italiana* vol. II p. 20 f.) a fragment of the preaching of the same Simon. See also Malan, *Conflicts of the Holy Apostles* p. 24 ff.; Lipsius, *Apostelg.* III 148 ff. The Cleopas of our Fragment claims to have been the cousin of the Virgin.

25. *indeed*] ⲧⲁⲭⲁ is here used in a loose sense. See note on the words 'Surely those also' (p. 73 *v.* 12).

27. *the daughter of Cleopas*] Cf. p. 5 *v.* 17, where see note.

36. *Would, O my beloved son, that*] After these words a new leaf begins, and the MS is badly torn on the left-hand side. I have left space for the number of letters which are omitted; but I am not sure how many have been lost.

40. I cannot be certain of the translation of this verse. At the close of it some five lines are gone.

43 *figure*] ⲧⲩⲡⲟⲥ. The word is used in *Various Sah. Frag.* I 11; III 18. Cf. the account of the cross coming forth from the tomb in the *Gospel according to Peter* X. πάλιν ὁρῶσιν ἐξελθόντας ἀπὸ τοῦ τάφου τρεῖς ἄνδρας, καὶ τοὺς δύο τὸν ἕνα ὑπορθοῦντας, καὶ σταυρὸν ἀκολουθοῦντα αὐτοῖς. For a representation of the combination of the cross and the sepulchre Dr James refers me to the engraving given by Schultze, *Archäol. d. altchr. Kunst* (Munich 1895) p. 333.

Addenda et Corrigenda.

p. 16 l. 20. For ⸢ϭⲟ⸣ⲧ̅ⲡ̅ read ⸢ϭⲟ⸣ⲧ̅ⲡ̅.

p. 25. For 'Mt XXVII 51 ff' read 'Mt XXVII 51 ff*'. Strike out note b.

p. 28 l. 13. For ⲡⲁⲡⲟⲥⲧⲟⲗⲟⲥ read ⲡⲁⲡⲟⲥⲧⲟⲗⲟⲥ. Strike out note b.

p. 29 *v.* 27. For 'the holy virgins and the apostles' read '*he who is* the holy virgin and the apostle'. Strike out note b.

p. 37 *v.* 98. *Catholic*] Perhaps we may compare *Pass. Perpet.* XIII, where in the vision the angels say to the bishop Optatus, 'Corrige plebem tuam'. In an Egyptian statement of accounts (*Berl. Pap. Graec.*) the word seems to be used in some technical sense in the phrase τ[ῷ] ἑκατοντάρχῳ τοῦ καθολικοῦ (*Aegyptische Urkunden* 1892 no. 21 col. 3 l. 10).

p. 40 l. 18. I have made no note as to whether the MS reads here ⲉϩⲧⲟⲟⲩⲉ (Zoega's reading) or ⲉϩⲧⲟⲟⲟⲩⲉ (Revillout's reading).

p. 41 *v.* 121. For 'cf. Ps XVII 11' read 'cf. Ps XVII 11; Sir XLIX 8 (9)'. So also on p. 52 c. VII *v.* 1.

p. 53 *v.* 6. *My glorious members*] Cf. the later recension of *Acta Thomae* § 1 (James, *Apocrypha Anecdota*, 2nd series), where our Lord addresses the apostles as τὰ μέλη μου τὰ ἰσχυρὰ καὶ ἅγια.

v. 7. For 'heavenly places' read 'heavenly *places*'.

p. 57 *v.* 12. Cf. the translation from the Slavonic given by Vassilieu, *Anecdota Graeco-Byzantina* (Moscow 1893) p. IX; where Jesus explains to Bartholomew why a certain angel refused to ascend to heaven. 'Et dixit Jesus...Iste erat unus angelorum ultorum, Patris mei thronum circumstantium, quem mihi Pater misit; ea de causa in coelum intrare noluit quod mundi potestatem perdere in animo habebat, cum autem eum ascendere jussissem flamma exibat e manu ejus et templi velum divisit disciditque in duas partes in documentum passionis filiis Israel, quia me crucifixerunt.'

p. 64 c. XVIII *v.* 1. For 'Peace be unto' read 'Peace *be* unto'.

p. 77 *v.* 9. For 'Tobi' read 'Tobe'. In note h, for 'Lit. *the other*' read 'Lit. *these and these other*.'

p. 90. For 'Cod. Vat. LXI 4' read 'Cod. Vat. LXI 3'.

p. 92 l. 15. For ⲡⲁϣⲟⲡ read ⲡⲁⲥϣⲟⲡ.

p. 139 c. XX *v.* 3. For 'crystal' read 'ice'.

p. 143 c. XXVII *v.* 2. For 'clasps (?)' read 'pins'.

INDEX OF SCRIPTURE PASSAGES.

SAHIDIC.

The numbers refer to the pages: those in thicker type indicate direct citations. Where a number is bracketed, the Sahidic text has not been printed in this edition. The use of the asterisk is the same as in the margin of the text.

GENESIS

iii	3*	89
	19	35
	23	35
	24	67, 89
xiii	2	5
xv	3	5
xxxv	19*	149
	20*	149
xl	6	21
	7	21

NUMBERS

xxiv	17	163

DEUTERONOMY

xxxiv	6*	35

JUDGES

xiii	4*	9, 11
	7*	9, 11

1 SAMUEL

i	6*	5
	24*	163

2 KINGS

ix	30*	17

JOB

x	3	(154)
xxxviii	17	(174)
xli	23	23

PSALMS

ix	14	(174)
xiii	2	13
xvii	8	25
	9	25
	10	25
	11	13, 41
	16	25
	20	11
	28	13
xviii	5	3
xxvi	11	29
xxxii	13	13
xli	3	39
xlvii	7	(158)
	8	(158)
lx	3	11
lxv	12	11
lxxix	2	13
lxxxviii	18	35

lxxxix 14 11
15 11
xcviii 1* 23
ciii 15* 165
32* 77
cvi 18 (174)
cxv 7* (155)
8* (155)
cxvii 12* (174)
19* 39
cxviii 98* 27
99* 27
130* 27
cxxxvii 8* (154)

CANTICLES

i 7* 167

ISAIAH

vi 2* 13
x 3* (152)
xi 10* 5
xiii 13 77

EZEKIEL

i 6* 13
iii 14* 13
x 12* 13
21* 13, 81

DANIEL

vii 10 33, 39, (158)

S. MATTHEW

i 6 5
16 149, (153)
18 149
19 19, 21, 149, (154)
20 19, 149, (154)
21 19, 149, (154)
23 17
24 149
ii 1 165
2 163, 165
3 (175)
4 165
6 149
7 165
16 21
22 9, 149
iv 11 15
vi 10 (176)
viii 8 165
ix 33 (174)
xii 18* 167
40* 35
xiii 11* (177)
xiv 18* (168)
19* (169)
20* (169)
xv 31* 9
32* (168)
33* (168)
36* (169)
xvi 16* 19, 29, 81, 167
19* 37
xvii 5 29
20 (176)
xxiii 37* 75
38* 75
xxiv 14* 29
29* 73
xxv 9* 37
xxvii 18 183
19 183
33 181
45 73
51* 25, 71
52* 25
53* 25, 73
54* 73
60* 181 *bis*
63* 23
xxviii 10* 31
11* 79
13* 179
15* (177)
18* 31, (177)
19* 31
20* 31

S. MARK

i 13* 15
iii 17* 37
v 22* 185
23* 185
31* (174)
vi 17* (175)
21* (175)
38* (168)
41* (169)
viii 6* (169 *bis*)
ix 2 29
22* 23
xii 29* 85
32* 85
xiv 36* (173 *bis*)
56 (175)
59 (175)

xv 22	181
46*	181
xvi 9*	37
15*	31

S. LUKE

2	3
5	11
7	11, 163
8	11
11	11
19	17
23	9
26	17, 163
28	**17**
29	17
31	9, 17
34	**17**
35	**19**, 39, 149
36	27, 163
38	**19**
39	25
56	25
58	11
66	**163**
67	**163**
68	**163**
69	**163**
74	25
75	25
80	163
ii 1	19, 149, 163
2	19
3	19
4	19, 149
5	19, 149
7	3, 9, 21, 67, 149
8	163
18	163
22	5
52*	15
iii 1*	163, (175)
iv 32*	(169)
v 5*	(168)
vi 36	37
vii 6*	165
11*	(169)
12	(169)
viii 2*	37
ix 16	(169)
44*	(177)
x 19*	(177)
xi 2*	(176)
xiii 31	(178)
34	75
35	75
xxii 21	(168)
29	(168, 176)
30	(168, 176)
31	(178)
32	(178)
53	39, (157)
62	69
xxiii 12	(177)
38	(177)
45	71
50	(176)
51	(176), 183
53	181

S. JOHN

ii 2*	167
3*	165, 167
4*	167
5*	167
6*	167
7*	167
8*	167
13*	5, 9
iii 1	(176)
iv 41*	165
42*	165
v 9	183
16*	(175)
18*	(175)
32*	29
vi 4*	5
8*	(168 *bis*)
9*	(168)
11*	(169)
15	(176 *bis*)
51*	75
70*	(168)
vii 2*	5
12*	(177)
50*	(176)
51*	(176)
viii 44	79
59	(175)
x 31	(175)
xi 1	(170)
3	77, (170)
4	(169)
6	(170)
8	(171)
9	(171)
11	(170, 171, 172)
14	77
15	(170)
16	(170)
17	(170, 171 *bis*), 185
19	(170)
21	(**172**)

xi 22 (172, 173)
23 (172, 173)
24 (170)
25 75, (170, 170, 172, 174)
26 (172, 173)
27 (172, 173 *bis*)
30 (172)
32 77
38 (172)
39 (170, 171 *bis*, 172, 173)
43 (171, 173, 174 *bis*)
44 (171, 173)
45 (174)
53 (175)
55 9
xii 6 (169)
9 (174, 175)
24 (170)
36 79
xiii 7 (172)
31 (169)
32 (169)
xiv 6 75
18 31, 69
27 87
30 39
31 (178)
xvi 7 31
20 69
xvii 1 (173)
3 39
4 31
6 (169)
9 (168)
11 (168)
22 (168)
23 (173)
xviii 0 00
4 (177)
36 (176)
37 (173)
xix 12 (177)
18 181
19 (177), 181
26 27
27 27, 37
38 (176), 181
39 (176), 181
41 181
42 181
xx 2 27
17 31
19 17, 31, 181
21 31
22 31
26 31
27 (170)
28 33, 69, (155)
29 (170)

ACTS

i 3 31
4 31
5 31
6 31
8 27
10 33
11 33
12 29, 31
13 29
14 29
ii 20 73
23 29
24 29, 69
iii 8 185
iv 26 33
29 33
viii 36 19
xvi 14 (156)
xvii 31 (174)

ROMANS

x 18 3
xv 19* 5

1 CORINTHIANS

ii 9 33
xii 27 (158)
28 (158)
xv 52* 35

2 CORINTHIANS

v 10* 25
xi 2 11
xii 4 77

GALATIANS

i 15 25

EPHESIANS

v 30 75

COLOSSIANS

i 13 39, (157)
16 15

2 THESSALONIANS

i	11	(154)
ii	26	(178)

2 TIMOTHY

iii	16*	25
iv	6*	33

HEBREWS

i	3	77, 79
ii	9*	(155)
	14*	35
vii	22*	(174)
ix	27	151, (152)
xii	9	(159)
	10	(159)
	22	35, 67
xiii	12	181

1 PETER

ii	12*	(152)

2 PETER

i	17	29
	18	29

1 JOHN

i	7	(171)
iii	8	(157)

APOCALYPSE

ii	16*	37
iv	4	13
	8	13
ix	11*	(159)
xii	5*	149
xiv	4	35
xxi	6*	29
xxii	2*	15
	7*	37
	12*	37
	16*	5

INDEX OF SCRIPTURE PASSAGES.

BOHAIRIC.

The numbers refer to the pages: those in thicker type indicate direct citations. Where a number is bracketed, the Bohairic text has not been printed in this edition.

GENESIS

i 30	(134)
iii 13	(46)
19	107
23	111
24	(54)
vi 12	(146)
17	(134)
vii 16	125
viii 11	111
xviii 32	(55)
xxviii 17	123
xxxv 19	(133)
20	(133)
xl 7	93

EXODUS

iii 2	113
x 21	(62)
xv 1	(**52**)
xxiii 7	(49)
xxxi 18	(142)

LEVITICUS

xix 36	(131)

DEUTERONOMY

ix 10	(142)

2 SAMUEL

vi 16	(61)

1 CHRONICLES

xxi 16	(57)

JOB

x 3	(137)
xxxiv 15	107

PSALMS

v 7	(48)
8	115
vii 12	(65)
xvii 11	(52, 62), 115, 121
xxiv 8	97
9	97
xxviii 1	127
2	127
9	127
xxxii 16	(131)
xlii 3	115
xliv 10	(**53**)
15	(**53**, **61**), 127
lviii 11	101
lxvii 14	(56)
lxx 22	103
lxxvii 54	115
lxxix 2	115

lxxxi 5	**119**
lxxxiii 11	103, 115
lxxxiv 11	**125**
lxxxvi 2	123
c 1	127
ci 25	(146)
ciii 4	125
32	(60)
cxv 6	**(60)**
7	(138)
8	(138)
cxvii 19	111
cxxxi 8	**(61)**, **121**
cxxxv 25	101
cxxxvii 8	(137)
cxxxix 11	**119**
cxli 8	101
cxlii 8	(51)
10	115

PROVERBS

xvi 11	(131)

CANTICLES

i 5	(53)
7	103, 117
iv 12	(53)
v 1	(53)
2	(53)

ISAIAH

vi 2	115, 125
3	115
xiii 13	(60)
xxxv 10	117
xlii 3	101
li 11	117

JEREMIAH

i 5	111
xxxix 27	(134)

EZEKIEL

xlv 10	(131)

DANIEL.

iii 6	(136)
vii 10	(52, 135, 140)

4 ESDRAS

vii 11	107

SIRACH

xlix 8	121

SUSANNA

52	(49)
53	(49)

S. MATTHEW

i 16	(136, 144)
18	(131, 132)
19	(131, 132, 137)
20	(132, 137)
21	(132, 137)
24	(133)
ii 13	(133)
14	(133)
16	(133 *bis*)
20	(133)
21	(133)
22	(133 *bis*)
23	(133)
iii 8	127
iv 18	(50)
19	(50)
21	(50)
22	(50)
vi 13	(58)
viii 12	(58)
ix 6	(48)
20	(48)
33	117
xii 10	(48)
13	(48)
24	(47)
36	(131)
49	(52)
xiii 44	(53)
55	(130)
xvi 16	(58)
17	93
xix 28	(61), 103
29	(64)
xxii 13	(49, 58)
18	(48)
21	(48)
45	101
xxiii 32	(49)
37	(57)
38	(57)

xxiv	3	(130)
	29	(57)
xxv	1	99, 101
	4	107
	10	107
	21	111, 115
	23	111, 115
	30	(58)
	31	(61), 103
	34	115
	41	(49)
xxvi	45	123
	46	123
	67	(47)
xxvii	25	(48)
	29	107
	30	(47)
	34	(48), 107
	45	(57)
	48	(48)
	51	(57)
xxviii	4	121
	19	(65)
	20	(51, 65), 107

S. MARK

iii	14	(50)
v	9	(47)
	13	(47)
	22	(47)
	23	(47)
	40	(142)
vi	3	(131)
ix	46	(58), 97, 103
xii	15	(48)
	16	(48)
	29	(63)
	32	(63)
xiv	41	123
	42	123
xv	7	(62)
	17	107
	21	(50)
	40	(131, 132)
xvi	1	(132)
	15	(65, 130)
	20	(65)

S. LUKE

i	27	(131)
	38	(133)
	42	(132)
	43	115
ii	1	(133)
	9	(133)
ii	4	(131, 133)
	5	(133)
	7	(53)
	14	115
	39	(133)
	51	(134, 145)
iii	8	127
v	11	(50)
vi	13	(50)
	16	(50)
vii	11	(47)
	12	(47)
viii	2	(47)
x	1	(51)
xi	15	(47)
	54	(48)
xii	37	107
xiii	34	(57), 105
	35	(57)
xv	18	119
	21	119
xvi	19	(55)
xix	27	(49)
	38	115
xx	20	(48)
	21	(48)
	22	(48)
xxii	46	123
	53	(58, 140)
	62	(54)
xxiii	2	(48)
	18	(48, 49)
	21	(47)
	45	(57)
	46	(57), 111
	53	(61)
xxiv	10	(51, 132)
	36	(51)
	37	(51)
	47	(130)
	49	(130, 145)
	50	91
	51	125
	53	(52)

S. JOHN

i	43	(50)
vi	51	(59)
	57	105, 123
viii	44	(48)
ix	6	(47)
xi	3	(60)
	14	(60)
	17	(47)
	20	(60)
	25	(59)

xi	32	(60)
	39	(47)
	47	117 *bis*
	48	117
xii	3	(56)
	27	97
	36	95
	40	(63)
xiv	2	(131)
	6	(59)
	18	(54), 107
	26	(145)
	27	(51, 64)
	30	(59, 140)
	31	103
xv	19	(53)
	26	105
xvi	20	(54)
	22	(54)
xvii	1	91
	12	(147)
xviii	36	(133)
xix	2	107
	6	(47)
	28	(48)
	29	(48)
	34	107
	38	(51)
	40	(143)
	41	(61)
xx	15	(55)
	19	(51 *bis*, 52 *bis*)
	20	(52)
	26	(52), 91
	28	(52, 54, 138, 147)
xxi	1	(50)
	2	(50)
	3	(50)

ACTS

i	2	91
	8	(130, 145)
	9	(52), 93
	12	91, 93
	17	(50)
	26	(50)
ii	20	(57)
	24	(55)
	31	(145)
v	20	(145 *bis*)
xii	23	(133)
xiii	11	119
xvii	31	(49)
xxi	13	107
xxvi	19	99

ROMANS

ii	6	(49)
iii	13	93
v	12	(144)
vi	17	(46)
	18	(46)
ix	32	(58)
	33	(58)

1 CORINTHIANS

xv	24	(56)
	26	(56)
	52	(59)
	55	(59)

2 CORINTHIANS

i	3	(134, 140)
ii	15	101
v	1	105
	4	(141)
	10	(131)
x	4	(48)
	5	(48)
xi	14	(58)
xii	2	(46)

EPHESIANS

iv	12	(52)
v	30	(53, 146)
vi	12	97

COLOSSIANS

i	13	(58, 140)
	16	(46)
ii	14	(143)
iv	2	121

1 THESSALONIANS

v	17	(67)

2 THESSALONIANS

ii	3	(147)
	8	(48)
iii	8	(133)

1 TIMOTHY

ii 11 (134)
vi 16 125

2 TIMOTHY

ii 17 97
iv 1 (65)
8 (65), 99

HEBREWS

i 2 101
3 (61), 101
7 125
ii 9 (130)
iii 1 (50)
iv 12 (49)
15 91, (134)
v 8 (134)
ix 4 (53)
27 (131, 134, 135)
xii 22 (54, 59), 105

1 PETER

i 19 (56)
ii 8 (58)

2 PETER

iii 11 105

1 JOHN

i 1 (50, 65)

APOCALYPSE

ii 17 (53)
iv 6 123
8 115, 123
x 1 (57)
xi 3 (146)
6 (146)
7 (146)
xii 5 (133)
xxi 21 105
xxii 18 (65, 145)
19 (65, 145)

INDEX OF COPTIC WORDS.

The words marked with an asterisk are those of the Bohairic text.

ⲁⲡⲏ 6, 20
*ⲁⲣⲏⲃ (ערבון) 100, 21
ⲁⲟⲩⲁ 82, 26
*ⲁⲩϫⲱⲗ 110, 16

ⲃⲱϣ 20, 11

*ⲉⲛϩⲟⲩⲣ 94, 25; 124, 1
ⲉϭⲉⲛ 8, 23, 24

*ⲓⲣⲓ ⲛⲁⲩⲧⲟⲧϥ 96, 26

ⲕⲛϩⲉ, ⲕⲉⲛϩⲉ *shrine* 72, 7, 22
ⲕⲉⲥⲕⲱⲥ 70, 9
ⲕⲱⲟⲩⲉ 72, 10; 76, 20

ⲙⲙⲟⲛ *for* 36, 9
ⲙⲙⲓⲛⲉ 78, 5
ⲙⲙⲓⲛⲟⲩ 70, 5
*ⲙⲁⲙⲉϯ 96, 17
ⲙⲙⲁⲩ *thence* 180, 22
ⲙⲙⲟⲟⲩ (=ⲙⲙⲁⲩ) 148, 4
ⲙⲛⲧⲥⲛⲟⲟⲩⲥ 70, 18

ⲛⲱⲛ (=ⲛⲟⲩⲛ) 6, 7
*ⲛⲁϩⲟⲩⲃⲓ 110, 26; 112, 1
ⲛⲁϫ 148, 3
ⲛϫⲓⲛ 2, 11

ⲡⲟⲛⲅ 26, 8

ⲣⲙⲙⲏⲧ 8, 5
*ⲣⲱϧⲧ *fall down* 120, 15

*ⲥⲑⲉⲣⲑⲉⲣ 94, 25
ⲥⲁⲕ 16, 5
ⲥⲉⲕⲟⲩⲉⲗⲗⲓ 12, 25
ⲥⲁⲙⲟⲟⲩ 6, 19
*ⲥⲟⲩⲗⲱⲗ 120, 14

ϯ ⲉⲡⲁⲛⲁⲓ 14, 16; 162, 13
ϯ ⲡⲧⲱϣ 36, 2, 6
ⲧⲉⲕ 164, 2
ⲧⲙⲉ 18, 26; 148, 14
ⲧⲁⲣⲡ 2, 14
ⲧⲥⲁⲃⲟ *learn* 12, 25

ⲟⲩⲏ 4, 28
ⲟⲩⲛⲧⲏ (=ⲟⲩⲛⲧⲉ) 32, 29
*ⲟⲩⲉⲥⲑⲉⲛ 100, 12

*ⲫⲱⲛⲕ 96, 5

*ⲭⲁⲣⲁⲃⲁⲓ 102, 14

ⲱϫⲣⲉϫ 72, 16

ϣⲙⲟⲛ 84, 24
ϣⲟⲣⲡⲉ 18, 27

ϩⲁ (=ϩⲟ) 10, 1
ϩⲏ *manner* 2, 17; 4, 4; 6, 1
ϩⲃⲁⲣⲃⲉⲣ 4, 27
*ϩⲣⲁ *voice* 98, 8

ϫⲧⲟ *lie down* 150, 12

ϭⲁⲛ 8, 28

INDEX OF GREEK WORDS.

Only the more important words are here given.

ⲁⲕⲙⲏⲛ 72, 10; -ⲙⲉⲛ 72, 25
ⲁⲛϩⲟⲗⲱⲙⲁ 20, 8
ⲁⲥⲱⲙⲁⲧⲟⲥ 12, 27
ⲁⲩⲑⲉⲛⲧⲓⲕⲟⲛ 34, 29

ⲇⲏⲙⲱⲣⲓⲥⲧⲏⲥ 96, 12
ⲇⲩⲛⲁⲙⲓⲥ 2, 14; 108, 10; 112, 4; 126, 4

ⲉⲓⲕⲟⲛⲟⲙⲟⲥ 14, 2
ⲉⲗⲁⲭⲓⲥⲧⲏⲥ nom. propr. 20, 25

ⲑⲩⲥⲁⲩⲣⲟⲥ 100, 7

ⲕⲁⲑⲟⲗⲓⲕⲟⲛ 36, 21
ⲕⲁⲧⲁⲥⲧⲁⲥⲓⲥ 112, 4; 116, 7, 11
ⲕⲁⲧⲉⲓⲭⲉ intrans. 74, 26
ⲕⲉⲣⲱⲇⲏ 78, 7
ⲕⲟⲛϩⲭⲟⲥ 74, 8

ⲗⲁⲝⲟⲥ 182, 23
ⲗⲏⲕⲧⲓⲕⲏ (lectica) 182, 13
ⲗⲓⲯⲁⲛⲟⲛ 36, 3; ⲗⲩⲙⲯ- 120, 4

ⲙⲉⲗⲟⲥ metaph. 68, 21; 74, 22; 78, 11; 120, 18; 124, 24
ⲙⲟⲣⲫⲏ 22, 26
ⲙⲟⲩⲗⲗⲓⲁⲣⲏⲥ 20, 23

ⲟⲓⲕⲟⲛⲟⲙⲓⲁ 30, 17; 70, 2; 76, 3; 90, 5; 108, 11
ⲟⲓⲕⲟⲛⲟⲙⲟⲥ vide ⲉⲓⲕⲟⲛⲟⲙⲟⲥ
ⲟⲙⲟⲗⲟⲅⲓⲧⲏⲥ 90, 2
ⲟⲙⲟⲟⲩⲥⲓⲟⲥ 110, 12; 114, 4; ϩⲟⲙⲟⲟⲩⲥⲓⲟⲛ 38, 29

ⲡⲁⲛⲧⲟⲕⲓⲟⲛ 20, 8
ⲡⲁⲣⲁⲑⲏⲕⲏ 10, 26
ⲡⲁⲣⲁⲕⲗⲏⲧⲟⲥ 30, 23
ⲡⲁⲣⲁⲗⲓⲙⲡⲧⲟⲥ 100, 9
ⲡⲏⲅⲏ 6, 17; ⲡⲓ- 26, 8 f; ⲡⲩ- 6, 18, 24; 26, 12; (of the Virgin) 28, 19
ⲡⲣⲟⲥⲧⲁⲧⲏⲥ 126, 3

ⲥⲕⲩⲗⲙⲟⲥ 98, 18
ⲥⲕⲩⲛⲏⲡⲱⲅⲓⲁ 4, 22
ⲥⲩⲛⲁⲝⲓⲥ 94, 1; 98, 21
ⲥⲩⲛⲑⲏⲕⲏ 36, 15; 106, 9
ⲥⲫⲣⲁⲅⲓⲍⲉ 40, 4

ⲧⲁⲙⲓⲟⲛ 24, 4, 6; 40, 13
ⲧⲁⲣⲧⲁⲣⲟⲥ 24, 4
ⲧⲁⲭⲁ 182, 14
ⲧⲉⲱⲥ 4, 9
ⲧⲓⲙⲱⲣⲓⲥⲧⲏⲥ vide ⲇⲏⲙⲱⲣⲓⲥⲧⲏⲥ
ⲧⲟⲡⲟⲥ *shrine* 34, 29
ⲧⲣⲓⲁⲥ 114, 21, 24; 116, 4; 118, 25; 122, 22; 124, 8
ⲧⲩⲡⲟⲥ 164, 1; 184, 16

ⲫⲁⲛⲧⲁⲥⲓⲁ 108, 11
ⲫⲩⲥⲓ 104, 19; 122, 20

ϩⲟⲙⲉⲗⲓⲁ 14, 17
ϩⲩⲙⲡⲉⲩⲧⲏⲣⲓⲟⲛ 14, 3

INDEX OF SUBJECTS.

Abaddon, 159, 233
Abraham, warned by Michael, 224; see *Testament*
Acta Pilati, xiii, xvii, 199, 235, 242
Adam, 51, 107, 109, 143, 144, 145, 174
Aeons of darkness, the seven, 140, 158, 227; of light, 158
Akhmîm, cemetery at, 213
Alexander, 50, 209
Alexandria, Library at, xxvi, 221
Altar in Temple, canopy of; see *Temple*
Amenta, monsters in, 212
Amenti, following Death, 139, 157
Anaphora Pilati, xvii, 240, 241, 242
Andrew, 168, 169, 178
Anna, 5, 7, 9, 47, 117, 188, 189, 222; song of, 13, 192
Anna, the prophetess, 15, 193
Annas, 175, 242
Anthropophagi, *pref.*, 23
Antichrist, 146, 147, 229
Antioch, chair of Peter at, 243
Apocalypse of Esdras, 226
Apocrypha, Coptic, form of, xi; importance of, xi
Archbishop, Peter appointed; see *Peter*
Archelaus, 133, 149
Archons of storehouses of punishment, 204, 205
Arimathaea, 221; see *Joseph of Arimathaea*
Arits of death, the seven, 227
Assumption of Mary; see *Mary* (D)
Athanasius, sermon on the Virgin, 188
Augustus, 163, 196; decree of, 19, 133, 149

Balaam, prophecy of, 235, 237
Barabbas, 49
Barbelo, 187
Bar-Jona, explanation of name, 93
Bashnash, or Pashons, 190
Belzeboul, 47
Benjamin, son of Rachel and Jacob, 133, 149
Bethany, home of Lazarus, 170, 174; Mount of, goes round as a wheel, 173
Birrus, disciple of Peter, 37
Book of the Dead, xiii, 205, 212, 224, 227
Burning bush, Mary the, 113

Caiaphas, 175, 242
Canopy of altar in Temple; see *Temple*
Carius (Quirinius), 175, 242
Cave, Jesus born in a, 152, 230
Chael, son of Matoi, 67
Chelkias, father of Susanna, 49
Christ; see *Jesus*
Cleopas (1), identified with Joakim, 5, 183, 188
Cleopas (2), cousin of Mary, 183, 188, 245; father of Rufus, 183, 185
Cleopas (3), use of name elsewhere, 245
Clopas, 188

Constantine, 244
Coptic, Apocrypha; see *Apocrypha*; Christians, popular religion of, xiii; expressions for passive voice, 229; tenses; see *Tenses*; signs above letters, xviii; substantives in adjectival sense, 224; words, division of, xvii
Covenants of virgins; see *Virgins*
Cross, festival of, 179, 244; figure of, xvii, 185, 237, 245
Cyril, xxxii, 222, 244

Darkness, the seven aeons of; see *Aeons*
Dead, bandaging of, 213; Book of the; see *Book*; embalming of, 227
Death, fear felt by, 56, 95, 134; fear of, 224; of Joseph; see *Joseph*; place of; see *South*; shapes assumed by, 211; terrors of, 58, 95; torments after, mummy describes, 225
Demons, sea of, 151, 158
De Nativitate Mariae, xv
Devil, fishing of, xi, 178, 179; rebuked by Jesus, at Joseph's death, 140, 157; weeps, 23
Didymus, 170, 171
Dove, Mary the, 9, 53, 56, 93
Dragon, the, 39, 58, 199, 204, 217

Ears, Mary conceives by her, 19, 196
Egypt, flight of Joseph to, 133, 143
Egyptian Pontus, term of reproach, 177, 243
Egyptians, Gospel according to, 223
Elachistes, image called, 21
Elias, 109, 145, 146, 147, 229
Elisabeth, Mary visits, 25
Enoch (Henoch), 109, 145, 146, 147, 229
Esdras, manner of death of, 226; see *Apocalypse*
Evodius, 188, 237, 244, 245; a lesser disciple, 51; appointed presbyter, 52; archbishop of Rome, 44, 207; disciple of Peter, 209; instruction by, 44—67; kinsman of Alexander, 50; witness of death of Mary, 50, 65; works of, xiv, 186, 187, 232
Eye-paint, use of, 194

Falling asleep of Mary; see *Mary* (D)
Fear felt by Death, 56, 95, 134; of death, 224
Feeding of the multitudes; see *Miracles*
Festival, of cross, 179, 244; of nativity of Virgin, 46, 66, 186
Figure of the cross; see *Cross*
Fire, after death, 101; quenched by three tear-drops, 97; river of, 39, 58, 95, 135, 140, 143, 145, 151, 158, 205; see *Demons*
Fountain, Mary the, 29

Gabriel, 140, 141, 158, 159, 194, 233, 234; appears to Joseph, 19, 132, 137, 149; sent to Mary, 17
Garments, heavenly, 41, 54, 56, 59, 61, 67, 79, 95, 109, 115
God-bearer, Mary the; see *Mary* (F)
Golden Legend, 243
Gospel, according to the Egyptians, 223; of Nicodemus, 199; of Peter, xvii, 245

Hapip, 147
Hathor, 190
Heaven, tables of; see *Tables*; garments of; see *Garments*; language of; see *Language*
Henoch; see *Enoch*
Herod, 133, 137, 149, 154, 159, 163, 165, 175, 177, 178, 236, 237, 242

Inn, Jesus born in an, 21, 149, 197
Irenaeus, 29, 181
Isaac of Tiphre, 192
Isaac, Testament of, 228

Jacob (the patriarch), 5, 133, 149
Jacob, father of Joseph, 144, 153

Jairus, 47, 185
James (1), son of Joseph, 131, 134; 'the little,' 131; Mary of, 132
James (2), Bishop of Jerusalem, 245
Jehoshaphat, valley *or* field of, 41, 61, 62, 79, 117, 207
Jerusalem, Library at, 130, 220
Jesus, ascension of, 31; birth of, 135, 151, 163; in a cave, 152, 230; in an inn, 21, 149, 197; in a tomb, 196, 223; near Rachel's tomb, 133, 149; discourse of, on Mount of Olives, 130; laments over Mary's body, 60, 77; miracles of the Child, 198; prays for Joseph, 140, 157; prays over Joseph's body, 142; raises a boy bitten by a serpent, 137, 154; rebukes the devil and his hosts, 140, 157; seized by the ear by Joseph, 137, 154, 226
Jews, abuse of, 187; attempt to burn Mary's body; see *Mary* (D); confess Christ's Godhead, 62, 81, 119; smitten with blindness, 62, 81, 119, 215
Joakim (Joachim), husband of Susanna, 49, 189
Joakim, 188, 189; brother of Zacharias, 13; father of Mary, 47, 117; vision of, 7; see *Cleopas* (1)
Joanna, 51, 59
John, the 'virgin,' 29, 202, 204; watches the Devil fishing, 179
John the Baptist, life of, 163, 235; see *Zacharias*
Joseph, 236; blessing on sons named after, 143; burial of, 143; chronology of life of, 135, 151, 152; death of, accounts of, xvi; in Bohairic, 130—147; in Sahidic, 147—159; dies at Nazareth, 135; flight into Egypt of, 133, 143; former marriage of, 131; four sons and two daughters of, 131, 156; five sons of, 221; intercourse of, with Mary denied, 3, 188; lament of, 136, 153; Mary in house of, 17, 132; natural power not abated, 133, 144; prayer of, before death, 134; receives Mary by lot, 132; shrine of, 142; son of Jacob, 144, 153; soul placed in napkin, 141, 159; see *Gabriel*, *Jesus*
Joseph of Arimathaea, 176, 181, 242, 245
Joseph (the patriarch), 133, 149
Josephus, 29, 181
Josetos, 131, 134, 221
Judah, third son of Jacob, 5
Judas, son of Joseph, 131
Judas (the traitor), 169

Kiss of peace, 210

Language, heavenly, 57, 60, 71, 75, 158
Lazarus, 47, 170—5, 239, 240; Martha, sister of, 171—173; Mary, sister of, 171—3, 222; painting of resurrection of, 213; raising of, xi, 170—5, 185; on the sabbath, 175, 242
Library at Alexandria, xxvi, 221; at Jerusalem, 130, 220
'Light,' letter of Evodius called, 186
Light, aeons of, 158
Loaves, five barley, miracle of, 168, 169
Lot, assigned to Apostles for preaching, 210; Mary assigned to Joseph by, 132
Lydia, daughter of Joseph, 131, 134
Lysia, daughter of Joseph, 131, 134, 139, 156

Macrinus, *pref.*, 199
Magdalene, Mary, 37, 204, 222
Magdalia, 37
Magi, visit of, 165, 235
Magrinus (=Macrinus), 23, 199
Malachias, father of Zacharias, 11, 191
Manuscripts, description of, xx
  Life of the Virgin, MSS of: Borg. CXVII, xxi; Borg. CXVIII, xxi;

Borg. cxix, xxii; Borg. cxx, xxii; Clarend. B 3 14, xxi; Crawford, Coptic MS 36, xxii; Pap. xi Sams, xxiii
Falling asleep of Mary, MSS of: Borg. ccLix*, xxv; Cant. Add. 1876 8, xxvi; Clarend. B 3 15, xxv; Crawford, Coptic MS 46, xxvi; Vat. LXI 3, xxv; Vat. LXII 5, xxiv
Death of Joseph, MSS of: Borg. cxvi, xxviii; Borg. cxxi, xxix; Br. Mus. Or. 3581 B, xxviii; Crawford, Coptic MS 39, xxviii; Vat. LXVI 11, xxvii
Sahidic fragments, MSS of: Brit. Mus. Or. 3581 B, xxix; Borg. cxi, xxx; Borg. cxii, xxx; Borg. cxiii, xxxi; Borg. cxiv, xxxi; Borg. cxv, xxxi; Borg. ccLvii, xxxii; Borg. ccLxvii, xxxii; Clarend. B 3 16, xxx
Mariae, de Nativitate, xv
Marriage festival, description of, 44, 208
Martha, sister of Lazarus, 171—3
Mary, life of, fragments on, xv, 2—41
A. *Birth*, date of, 9, 190; Davidic descent of, 186, 199; daughter of Joakim and Anna, 47, 117; daughter of Cleopas, 183; sister of parents of bridegroom at Cana, 165
B. *Early Life*, 15, 132, 194; asceticism, 17, 132, 194; fed from tree of life, 15; assigned by lot to Joseph, 132
C. *Later Life*; in Joseph's house, 17, 132; intercourse with Joseph denied, 3, 188; annunciation, 17; visit to Elisabeth, 25; conceives by the ears, 19, 196; flight into Egypt, 133; asks a miracle of Jesus, 167; at the tomb of Jesus, 31; at the Ascension, 31; rules over many virgins, 29, 93
D. *Falling asleep*, accounts of, 43—127; vision of Mary, 33, 95; farewell address of, 29—37; prayer before death, 39, 58, 101, 111; blessed by Jesus, 60, 67, 77; presented by Jesus to the Father, 113; laid by tree of life, 89; date of death, 41, 44, 65, 206; death witnessed by Evodius, 50, 65; burial, 61, 79; Jews attempt to burn body, 3, 62, 81, 117, 215; body caught up to heaven, 83; soul restored to body, 65, 125; assumption of body of, 121; date of assumption, 65, 201; interval between death and assumption, 109, 113, 218; appears in glory, 64; teaches hidden mysteries, 64
E. *Doctrinal*; Mary was born and died as all men, 3, 5, 47; not a 'power' from heaven, 109; doctrine in the *Pistis Sophia*, 187
F. *Titles of Mary*; Our Lady and our succourer, 127; the burning bush, 113; dove, 9, 53, 56, 93; fountain, 29; God-bearer, 39, 44, 65, 66, 67, 91; Mary of James, 132; queen, 3, 9, 27, 46, 56, 57, 60, 71, 111
G. *Miscellaneous*; accounts of assumption, Greek and Latin, xv, discourse of Cyril on, 222; festival of nativity of, 46, 66, 186; miracles of, 21, 27, 198; sermon on assumption of, 187, 188; shrine of, 35, 202; standards worship the throne of, *pref.*, 23
Mary, the sister of the Virgin, 188
Mary Magdalene; see *Magdalene*
Mary of James, 132, 222
Mary of John (Mark), 222
Mary of Judaea, 222
Mary of Mount of Olives, 222
Mary, sister of Lazarus, 171—3, 222
Matoi, father of Chael, 67

Michael, 25, 60, 134, 140, 141, 158, 159, 224, 233, 234; sermon of Theodosius on, 208, 215
Miracles: feeding of the multitudes, xi, 168, 169; raising of Lazarus, xi, 170—5, 185; water turned into wine, xi, 165—7, 237; worked by the cross, 185; worked by Mary; see *Mary* (G)
Misael, 237
Mount, Jesus hidden on the, 176
Mount of Olives; see *Olives*
Mummy describes torments after death, 225

Nain, widow of, 47, 169
Napkin, Joseph's soul placed in, 141, 159
Nativity of Mary; see *Festival*
Nazareth, death of Joseph at, 135
Nicephorus Callistus, quoted, 186
Nicodemus, 176, 181, 242, 245

Olives, Mount of, 31, 91, 130, 221; Mary of, 222; virgins from, 99
Orphic religion of Greece, xiii

Painting of resurrection of Lazarus, 213
Parallel literature, xv—xvii
Paremhat, 190
Parmoute, 190
Pashons, or Bashnash, 190
Passive voice in Coptic, expressions for, 229
Passover = Feast of Tabernacles, 5, 189
Peace, kiss of, 210
Peter, addressed as bishop by Jesus, 93, 111; appointed archbishop, xxxi, 52, 210; chair of, at Antioch, 243; Gospel of, xvii, 245; sanctifies an altar, 51; teacher of Birrus, 37; teacher of Evodius, 209
Philip, the countries of, 175
Pilate, 47, 48, 176, 177, 243
Pilati, Acta; see *Acta*
Pilati, Anaphora; see *Anaphora*
Pistis Sophia, references in, to archons of treasuries, 203, 205; dragon, 199, 204, 217; the Virgin Mary, 187; Mary Magdalene, 204, 225, 238; Salome, 209
Place of the skull, 181
Platonites, sect of the, 187
Pontus, Egyptian, term of reproach, 177, 243
Protevangelium, xv; description of birth of Jesus in, 197
Pseudo-Matthaei Evangelium, xv

Queen, Mary the; see *Mary* (F)
Quirinius; see *Carius*

Rachel, Jesus born near tomb of, 133, 149
Resurrection of Lazarus, painting of, 213
River of Fire; see *Fire*
Rufus (1), 209; fishing with Evodius and Alexander, 50
Rufus (2), son of Cleopas, 183, 185

Sabbath, Lazarus raised on the, 175, 242
Salome, 51, 59, 60, 77, 133, 196, 209, 223
Schila, 229
Shrine, of Joseph, 142; of Mary, 35, 202
Signs above letters in Coptic, xviii
Silk, dead bodies wrapped in, 227
Simeon, 236
Simon of Cyrene, 209
Simon, son of Cleopas, 245
Simon, son of Joseph; see *Symeon*
Skull, place of the, 181
Soul leaving body, account of a, 233; position of, at approach of death, 139, 156; placed in a napkin, 141, 159, 233; wrapped in linen, 60, 62, 212
South, place of death, 41, 59, 139, 157, 159, 206; storehouses of, 59
Standards, worship by, *pref.*, 23, 199

Star, seen by shepherds and Magi, 163
Storehouses of punishment, 25, 41, 199; archons of, 204—5; of the south, 59
Substantives, Coptic, in adjectival sense, 224
Supper of the thousand years, 142, 143
Susanna, wife of Joakim, 49, 189
Symeon (Symon, Simon), 131, 134, 223
Symon; see *Symeon*

Tabernacles, feast of (=Passover), 5, 189
Tabitha, 229
Tables of Heaven, 142, 227
Tatian, 201
Temple, canopy of altar in, 57, 75, 211; veil of, rent, 57, 71, 75; virgins of, xvi, 15, 57, 75, 79; visit of Joakim and Anna to, 5
Tenses (Coptic), gnomic aorist used for future, 198; perfect used for future, 240, 241; present used for future, 191
Testament of Abraham, xvii, 211, 212, 218, 224, 226, 227, 228, 233, 234; of Isaac, 228
Text, previous editions of, xx
Theodosius, 200; archbishop of Alexandria, 91; discourse of, 91—127; sermon on Michael, 208, 215; other sermons of, 216
Theophilus, 176, 243, 244
Thomas, 168, 169, 170, 171, 172, 173; grief of, 172
Tiberius, 175, 176, 177, 242, 243; Carius the chief of, 175
Tiphre, Isaac of, 192
Titles of Mary; see *Mary* (F)
Tomb, Jesus born in a, 196, 223; of Rachel, Jesus born near, 133, 149
Torine, city of Elisabeth, 25; city of Zacharias, 13; meaning of, 191
Torments after death, mummy describes, 225
Tot, 190
Tree of life, Mary fed from, 15; Mary laid by, 89
Tribute money, blotting out inscription on, 48
Trinity, the Holy, 115, 117, 119, 123, 125

Veil of Temple; see *Temple*
Virgin; see *Mary*
Virgins, covenants of, with Christ, 37, 107, 204; from Mount of Olives, 99; Mary rules over many, 29, 93; of the Temple; see *Temple*

Water turned into wine; see *Miracles*
Words, division of Coptic, xvii

Zacharias, 163, 235; brother of Joakim, 13; father of John, 200, son of Malachias, 11, 191; =Z. son of Barachias, 191; vision of, 11
Zelomi, 197